This book is, to my knowledge, the most comprehensive and reliable guide to organisational theory currently available. What is needed is a text that will give a good idea of the breadth and complexity of this important subject, and this is precisely what McAuley, Duberley and Johnson have provided. They have done some sterling service in bringing together the very diverse strands of work that today qualify as cons_____ subject of organisational theory. Whilst their writing is accessible and engagin_____larly and serious. It is so easy for students (and indeed others who _____ very problematic and challenging subject. This is no_____ is a book that deserves to achieve a wide readershi_____

Professor S_____rsity, UK

This new textbook usefully situates organization theory within the sc_____s on modernism and postmodernism, and provides an advanced introduction to the heterogeneous study of organizations, including chapters on phenomenology, critical theory and psychoanalysis. Like all good textbooks, the book is accessible, well researched and readers are encouraged to view chapters as a starting point for getting to grips with the field of organization theory.

Dr Martin Brigham, Lancaster University, UK

McAuley *et al.* provide a highly readable account of ideas, perspectives and practices of organization. By thoroughly explaining, analyzing and exploring organization theory the book increases the understanding of a field that in recent years has become ever more fragmented. Organization theory is central to managing, organizing and reflecting on both formal and informal structures, and in this respect you will find this book timely, interesting and valuable.

Peter Holdt Christensen, Associate Professor,
Copenhagen Business School, Denmark

McAuley *et al.*'s book is thought-provoking, witty and highly relevant for understanding contemporary organizational dilemmas. The book engages in an imaginative way with a wealth of organizational concepts and theories as well as provides insightful examples from the practical world of organizations. The authors' sound scholarship and transparent style of writing set the book apart, making it an ingenious read which invites reflexivity, criticalness and plurality of opinion from the audience. This is a book that will become a classic in organization studies.

Mihaela L. Kelemen, Professor of Management Studies,
Keele University, UK

An unusually rich and deep philosophical book on organization theory with several new thinkers and ideas. Pedagogically a well-structured book with many clear learning objectives, cases, examples and good summaries for every chapter.

Professor Martin Lindell, Hanken Business School, Swedish
School of Economics and Business Administration, Finland

This book makes it easier to understand the current stand of organization theory. I strongly recommend it to anyone seriously interested in the different intellectual traditions that contribute to our understanding of organizations.

Professor Tomas Müllern, Jönköping International Business School, Sweden

McAuley, Duberley and Johnson's *Organizational Theory* takes you on a joyful ride through the developments of one of the great enigmas of our time – How should we understand the organization?

*Jan Ole Similä, Assistant Professor, Nord-Trøndelag University College, Norway*

I really enjoyed this new text and I am sure my students will enjoy it, too. It combines rigorous theoretical argument with application and consideration of how managment practice is formed and shaped by ideas and concepts. The authors have brought their wealth of experience and understanding and provided the field with an imaginative resource to address the dynamics between theory and practice.

*Dr Susanne Tietze, Bradford University, UK*

The key to success for managers is not only to be result oriented but also to be wise in their decision making. This requires that they have a deeper than superficial understanding of management and organization issues. McAuley *et al.* helps student and managers understand organizational performance without having to go through extensive reading. It deepens their understanding of issues with which they are confronted in practice, by putting them into a larger context. This book really helps students and managers to become wiser.

*Professor René Tissen, Nyenrode Business University, The Netherlands*

This book will appeal to the student who seeks a thorough and critical understanding of organization theory. It is both rigorous and accessible, clearly and unashamedly pitched for readers who wish to engage with theoretical issues whilst also maintaining a practical focus on why organization theory matters. I felt in good hands here, confident that I was being offered a deeply informed, reliable and intelligently constructed account. The opening chapter carefully and helpfully explains terms, including 'theory' and 'epistemology' that can form an unexplored bedrock to texts in the field. It then offers thoughtful, scholarly and well-illustrated discussions of prominent theoretical perspective, including managerialism and postmodernity, supported by specified learning outcomes and guides to further reading.

*Dr Paul Tosey, University of Surrey, UK*

The field of organization theory is extremely fragmented and there is no agreement concerning the underlying theoretical dimensions nor methodological approach to be employed. With the recognition of different approaches to organization theory, there is a widely perceived need to bring some order to the field. This textbook offers a well-integrated synthesis of approaches to organization theory. It will be welcomed by organization theory scholars and reflective practitioners and is a valuable companion for scholars and students of organization theory.

*Henk W. Volberda, Chair of the Department of Strategic Management & Business Environment and Vice-Dean of the RSM Erasmus University, Netherlands*

At last, a text that brings organization theory into the 21st century! This is the first organization theory textbook to provide full and informed coverage of a range of contemporary developments in the field. Notably, it includes diverse contributions to organization theory made by critical management studies. It really is pathbreaking in terms of its inclusion of material that does not appear in other texts.

*Professor Hugh Willmott, Cardiff Business School, UK*

This is one of the most up-to-date and comprehensive texts in the field of organization studies. It takes the reader through different perspectives and various topics on management and organizing, discussing these in some depth and detail. It offers a historically grounded, critical-reflexive approach to studying organizations that will prove to be extremely helpful guidance to students.

*Dr Sierk Ybema, Vrije Universiteit Amsterdam, The Netherlands*

# Organization Theory

## Challenges and Perspectives

**John McAuley**
Faculty of Organization and Management, Sheffield Hallam University

**Joanne Duberley**
Birmingham Business School, The University of Birmingham

**Phil Johnson**
The Management School, The University of Sheffield

**FT** Prentice Hall
FINANCIAL TIMES

*An imprint of* **Pearson Education**
Harlow, England • London • New York • Boston • San Francisco • Toronto • Sydney • Singapore • Hong Kong
Tokyo • Seoul • Taipei • New Delhi • Cape Town • Madrid • Mexico City • Amsterdam • Munich • Paris • Milan

**Pearson Education Limited**
Edinburgh Gate
Harlow
Essex CM20 2JE
England

and Associated Companies throughout the world

*Visit us on the World Wide Web at:*
www.pearsoned.co.uk

First published 2007

ISBN-13: 978-0-273-68774-0
ISBN-10: 0-273-68774-3

**British Library Cataloguing-in-Publication Data**
A catalogue record for this book is available from the British Library

**Library of Congress Cataloging-in-Publication Data**
McAuley, John, FIPD.
   Organization theory : challenges and perspectives / John McAuley, Joanne Duberley, Phil Johnson.
      p.   cm.
   Includes bibliographical references and index.
   ISBN-13: 978-0-273-68774-0
   ISBN-10: 0-273-68774-3
1. Organizational sociology.   I. Duberley, Joanne.   II. Johnson, Phil, 1955-
III. Title.

HM786.M33 2007
302.3'5—dc22
2006022347

10 9 8 7 6 5 4 3 2 1
10 09 08 07 06

Typeset in 10/12.5 pt sabon by 72
Printed by Ashford Colour Press Ltd., Gosport

*The publisher's policy is to use paper manufactured from sustainable forests.*

# Brief Contents

# Contents

Supporting resources
Visit **www.pearsoned.co.uk/mcauley** to find valuable online resources

**For Instructors**
- PowerPoint slides that can be downloaded and used for presentations
- Additional exercises

For more information please contact your local Pearson Education sales representative or visit **www.pearsoned.co.uk/mcauley**

# Preface

## Introduction

Over the past hundred years or so, Organization Theory has developed into a distinctive social science discipline. It is a body of thinking and writing that describes, explains and influences what goes on in organizations. It provides an underpinning body of knowledge that enables us to explore and develop management and leadership theory. In recent decades Organization Theory has become increasingly diverse in terms of the perspectives that writers use to study and understand organizations. These perspectives provide, in their different ways, profound challenges to the ways in which we live in and design organizations. They pose important challenges to organization members about issues such as:

- The relationship between organization control and freedom.
- The nature of power and authority in organizations.
- The relationship between individualism and collectivism in modern organizations.
- The relationship between organizations and society.
- The ways in which organizations are designed.
- The relationship between organizations and leadership and management.
- The development of understanding of organization culture as means of control or vehicle for development.

The book explores approaches to Organization Theory from its origins through to the most recent debates. We show how the different traditions of organizational theory are intertwined, sometimes in sympathy, sometimes with profound disagreement. Chapter One provides an extended introduction to the nature and complexity of Organization Theory. This provides a springboard to the exploration, in each of the following chapters, of a distinctive 'epoch' of organization theory. In these chapters we look at the fundamental issues that each of these theories of organization poses. In this spirit we examine the challenges of:

- Modernist theories of organization that form the controversial and challenging foundations of organization theory.
- The development of neo-modernist theories of organization that claim to 'put people first' and then the ways that these theories have been transformed into

'new wave' approaches in which there is an emphasis on the control of organization members.

- We then explore the ways in which postmodern philosophies and theories of organization pose radical challenges for modernism and neo-modernism.

- We then explore theories and concepts which develop the idea that organization theory is a means by which members can gain deep understanding of their organizations. This is achieved through exploration of organizations as symbols, through critical theory and through psychoanalysis.

- In many respects the study of organizations is linked with the study of management, and in Chapter 9 we explore the ways in which theories of management have achieved such an important place in organization theory.

- The concluding chapter synthesizes many of the issues in the earlier chapters and then looks at some of the emergent trends in organization theory.

We explore the strengths and limitations of these theories and perspectives and show how they continue to exert challenges to organizations.

The three authors come from somewhat different standpoints in relation to their understandings about organization theory so there is a sense of dialogue between different perspectives, rather than the uniformity of view found in many books. This will enable the reader to see the issues as living, controversial and challenging.

## The aim of this book

Our vision is that the book covers the core issues in organization theory in a manner which shows how various forms of organizational theory both underpin and challenge common sense ways of viewing (and managing) organizations.

The aim of this book is to provide a clearly structured and interesting exploration of the ways in which the variety of theories and perspectives that constitute Organization Theory provide profound challenges for organizations in the twenty-first century.

The book develops understanding of the increasing pressures created by heightened competition and processes of globalization by analysing their impact upon organizations with specific reference to the ways in which organization theory can help develop understanding and appropriate action.

## Who should use this book?

The target audience is anticipated to be postgraduate students and undergraduate students for whom Organizational Analysis or Organizational Theory represents a core module, or is a significant part of a core module. Typically the audience would be students in Business Schools but could also be students in Departments of Sociology, Schools of Education and so on. The learning needs of these students is for a book that reflects the best of Anglo-American, European and other thinking on organization theory in a manner that shows that different sorts of theory are relevant and can be made interesting for an understanding of the organizational world.

## Distinctive features

### The structure of the book

The 'historical' epoch based approach enables students to see the relevance and challenge of all the different perspectives and theories that constitute organization theory. Because of the way the book was developed by its three authors, readers can see that there are differences in the way that its theories and challenges can be understood, that organization theory is not a monolithic subject but rather a rich resource for developing understanding of organizations.

Each chapter begins with an **Introduction** which outlines the content and direction of the chapter, provides a clear guide to the structure of the chapter and then outlines the **Learning outcomes**. These learning outcomes provide a guide to the different sections of the chapter.

### Stop and think

Each of the chapters contains 'stop and think' boxes. These are designed to form the basis for brief discussion amongst group members or for personal reflection on some key issue raised in the text.

### Case studies

These are designed to enable the reader to relate theoretical issues to organization practice, or to give a practical organizational example.

### Ideas and perspectives

These are designed to provide an outline of a perspective, theory or key idea in organization theory. They provide the reader with an introduction to ideas that are developed within the chapter.

### The chapter so far

These are provided at key points in the chapter. They provide the reader with a summary of the issues that have been covered in the chapter and a link with the next part.

### Biography

These are designed to provide a brief intellectual history of key figures in organization theory. They provide an indication of the ways in which different theorists developed their understanding of organization and social science theory as part of the background in which the different periods of organization theory developed.

## Concluding grid

Most of the chapters conclude with a grid in which we return to the learning outcomes and then summarize the way in which these learning outcomes provide challenges to the organization in the twenty-first century.

## Annotated further reading

Each chapter concludes with an indication of further reading. We have also included, wherever possible, indications of films and other media that provide insights into the issues covered in the chapter.

## Discussion questions

Finally, each chapter concludes with a number of questions that have been developed for use in seminar discussions or would be suitable as the basis for assessments.

# List of figures

# List of tables

# Acknowledgements

## Author's acknowledgements

The creation of this text was a challenging adventure, and we would like to acknowledge the contribution of many others to its development. We would like to express our thanks to Jacqueline Senior, who was our original commissioning editor, and to Matthew Walker, who took over that role. We also would wish to thank David Cox and Stuart Hay, who have been our development editors. Their contribution to the pedagogic shaping of the text challenged many of our initial assumptions about the nature of a 'textbook' on organization theory and have enabled us to produce what we hope is an accessible text that preserves intellectual integrity.

We also owe a debt of gratitude to our academic reviewers. Although during the process of the development of the book they were anonymous, we now know that they included the following distinguished academics:

Dr Martin Brigham, Lancaster University, United Kingdom

Professor Tor Busch, Trondheim Business School, Norway

Professor Su Mi Dahlgaard-Park, Lunds University, Sweden

Peter Holdt Christensen, Associate Professor, Copenhagen Business School, Denmark

Dr Philip Hancock, Warwick University, United Kingdom

Dr Anders Hytter, Vaxjo University, Vaxjo, Sweden

Ad van Iterson, Associate Professor, Maastricht University, The Netherlands

Professor Markus Kallifatides, Stockholm School of Economics, Sweden

Professor Martin Lindell, Hanken Business School, Swedish School of Economics and Business Administration, Finland

Professor Tomas Müllern, Jönköping International Business School, Sweden

Professor Rolland Munro, Keele University, United Kingdom

Jan Ole Similä, Assistant Professor, Nord-Trøndelag University College, Norway

Dr Karin Svedberg Nilsson, Stockholm School of Economics and Score, Sweden

Dr Susanne Tietze, Bradford University, United Kingdom

Professor René Tissen, Nyenrode Business University, The Netherlands

These reviewers always challenged us, sometimes praised us, sometimes criticized us, and sometimes pointed out the error of our ways. They provided us with advice and issues to consider and consistently made a real contribution to the academic development of the book, although responsibility for it lies with us.

We would also like to thank the following people for their interest in the book: Fulnahar Begum, Catherine Cassell, Murray Clark, Laurie Cohen, John Darwin, Keith Duberley, Yvonne Hill, Lynda Hinxman, Claire McAuley, T.F. McAuley, Gill Musson, Michelle Odendaal and Jane Whitmarsh. Finally, Phil would like to thank Carole for her forbearance, Jo would like to thank Ross for his support and Tom for being there, and John would like to thank Maria for her uncurbed enthusiasm.

This book was a collaborative endeavour, although we have, as we developed the text, been aware of differences between us of interpretation and understanding of different aspects of organization theory. This is in the spirit that organization theory, as with any significant body of knowledge, is not a 'settled' uniform discipline. Jo Duberley was primarily responsible for Chapters 5, 6 and 10; Phil Johnson was primarily responsible for Chapters 1, 4 and 9; and John McAuley was primarily responsible for Chapters 2, 3, 7 and 8.

## Publisher's acknowledgements

We are grateful to the following for permission to reproduce copyright material.

Figure 2.1 (top left) © Hulton-Deutsch Collection/CORBIS, (top right) © Edifice/ CORBIS, (bottom left) © Michael Nicholson/CORBIS, (bottom right) © Mikael Andersson/Nordic Photos/Getty Images; Figure 2.3 © Sean Justice/The Image Bank/ Getty Images; Figure 2.4 © Bruce Hands/Stone/Getty Images; 3.1, 3.2, 3.3, 3.4, and 3.5 based on Human relations: rare, medium, or well-done? in *Harvard Business Review* Vol. 26 No. 1 Harvard Business School Publishing (Roethlisberger, F. J. 1948); Figure 3.6 Courtesy of AT&T Archives and History Center, Warren, NJ; Figure 4.1 The Trustees of the Imperial War Museum, London; Figure 4.2 adapted from Performance evaluation and control: supporting organizational change in *Management Decision* Vol. 39 No. 10 MCB University Press (Johnson, P., et al. 2001); Figure 5.1 Pete Saloutos/CORBIS; Table 5.1 © *Managerial Leadership in the Post Industrial Society*, P. Sadler, 1988, Ashgate; Figure 5.2 J Gross/Getty Images/Sport; Figure 5.3 after Manpower strategies for flexible organizations, *Personnel Management* August, Chartered Institute of Personnel and Development (Atkinson, J. 1984); Figure 5.4 from Kalleberg, A., Flexible firms and labour market segmentation: effects of workplace restructuring on jobs and workers, *Work and Occupations* (Vol. 30 Issue 2) pp. 154–175, copyright 2003 by Sage Publications, reprinted by permission of Sage Publications Inc.; Figure 5.5 reprinted by permission of Sage Publications Ltd from Clegg, S., *Modern Organizations: Organization Studies in a Postmodern World*, Copyright © Sage Publications 1990; Figure 6.1 © Tate, London 2006; Table 6.1 adapted from The postmodern turn in educational administration: apostrophic or catastrophic development? in *Journal of School Leadership* Vol 8, originally published in Postmodern Theory, The Guilford Press (Best, S. and Kellner, D. 1991); Table 6.2 from *Postmodernism and Social Sciences: Insights, Inroads and Intrusions*, Princeton University Press (Rosenall, P.M. 1992); Figure 6.2 © Bettmann/CORBIS; Figure 7.2 from *The Theory and Practice of Change Management*, Palgrave Macmillan (Hayes, J. 2002) reproduced with permission of Palgrave Macmillan; Figure 8.1 ©

Bettmann/CORBIS; Figure 8.2 © London Aerial Photo Library/CORBIS; Figure 9.1 The Arkwright Society and The Bodleian Library, University of Oxford, *The Mirror*. Vol. 28, page 257 Illustration of Cromford Mill (Shelfmark) Per. 2705 d.407 October 22nd 1836; Table 9.1 with permission of PricewaterhouseCoopers; Figure 10.1 reprinted by permission of Sage Publications Ltd from Johnson, P. and Duberley, J., *Understanding Management Research*, Copyright © Sage Publications 2000, originally published in Burrell and Morgan © *Sociological Paradigms and Organizational Analysis*, Burrell, G. and Morgan, G. (1979) Ashgate; Figure 10.2 from Phillips, N. and Hardy, C., *Discourse Analysis*, copyright 2002 by Sage Publications, Inc, reprinted by permission of Sage Publications, Inc; Figure 10.3 © Photodisc/PunchStock; Table 10.1 reprinted by permission of Sage Publications Ltd adapted from Gibbons, M. et al., The New Production of Knowledge: The Dynamics of Science and Research in *Contemporary Societies*, Copyright © Sage Publications 1994; Table 10.2 from *Organization Theory and Design*, 8th edition by Daft. 2004 reprinted with permission of South-Western, a division of Thomson Learning (www.thomsonrights.com), fax 800-730-2215.

Alan Brodie Representation Ltd. for an extract from *YES MINISTER* © Jonathan Lynn and Antony Jay Copyright agent: Alan Brodie Representation Ltd, 6th floor, Fairgate House, 78 New Oxford Street, London WC1A 1HB, info@alanbrodie.com; Guardian Newspapers Limited for extracts from 'AA to log call centre staff's trips to loo in pay deal' by David Hencke published in *The Guardian* 31st October 2005, 'Fall of the arrogant' by Madeline Bunting' published in *The Guardian* 28th January 2002, 'Volkswagen targets Euros 10bn savings as director' by David Gow published in *The Guardian* 14th July 2005, 'VW Starter' by Dr. George Menz published in *The Guardian* 16th July 2005, and 'Fat cats pay is the result of greed, not competition' by Polly Toynbee published in *The Guardian* 24th December 2003 © Guardian Newspapers Limited; The Scotsman Publications Ltd. for an extract from 'Great programmes and he made people happy' by Jason Beattie published in *The Scotsman* 30th January 2004; 'Microsoft's Mission and Values' used by permission from Microsoft Corporation, is Copyright © 2004 Microsoft Corporation, One Microsoft Way, Redmond, Washington 98052-6399 U.S.A. All rights reserved; NI Syndication for extracts from 'Society of the future?' by Alan Hamilton published in *The Times* 1st October 2005 and 'Intelligence chiefs appoint businessmen to bring management expertise' published in *The Times* 12th January 2005; The Washington Post Writers Group for an extract from 'McDonald's Goes for Gold With Olympic Sponsorships' published in *The Washington Post* 14th August 2004 © 2004, The Washington Post. Reprinted with Permission; Mr. Andrew Bibby for an extract from his article 'Home Start' published in *People Management* 10th January 2002; SAGE Publications Inc. for an extract from *The Post Bureaucratic Organisation: New Perspectives on Organisational Change* by C. Hecksher and A. Donnellon, Reprinted by Permission of Sage Publications Inc; Kendal Hunt Publishing Company for an extract from *Managing in the Postmodern World: America's Revolution against Exploitation* by D.M. Boje and R. Dennehy; SAGE Publications Ltd. for the use of the table 'It's Good to Talk' from *Understanding Organizations Through Language* by Stephen Tietze, 2003; The Essex Chronicle for an extract published in *The Essex Chronicle* 25th February 2005; Swann-Morton Limited for an extract from www. swann-morton.com/history.html; Pearson Education Limited for an extract from *The Town Labourer* by J. Hammond & L. Hammond; and The

New York Times Agency for an extract from 'Guatemala: supermarket giants crush farmers' by Celia W. Dugger published in The *New York Times* 28th December 2004.

We are grateful to the Financial Times Limited for permission to reprint the following material:

Chapter 5 Example, Insurer plans to save £10m in Indian job shift, © *Financial Times*, 12 October 2004.

We are grateful to the following for permission to use copyright material:

Chapter 5 Case study, Adapted from Creating Sustainable Competitive Advantage: the Toyota Philosophy and its Effects from *FT.com*, 5 September 2002, © M Reza Vaghefi.

In some instances we have been unable to trace the owners of copyright material, and we would appreciate any information that would enable us to do so.

# Chapter 1

# Introducing organization theory: what is it, and why does it matter?

## Introduction

Over the past 100 years or so, organization theory has developed into a distinctive social science discipline, a body of thinking and writing that tries to describe, explain and sometimes influence what goes on in organizations. Nevertheless, during the past two decades, organization theory has also become increasingly diverse in terms of the perspectives that organization theorists use to study these important social phenomena which affect so many aspects of our lives. This chapter introduces the reader to organization theory by initially considering what organization theory is and how it relates to human practices, including management. Then the chapter explains some aspects of the diverse perspectives encountered when studying organization theory. The chapter concludes with an overview of the different perspectives covered in this book. Above all, the chapter shows how and why organization theory affects all of us through its often unnoticed influence on how organizations operate.

## Learning outcomes

- Explore what might be meant by the term *theory* by identifying what theories are and what they do.

- Consider how the phenomenon 'organization' has been defined in different ways.

- Identify why organization theory is important, especially in terms of how it impacts upon people through influencing their behaviour and practices.

- Explore the relationship between organization theory and management practice and discuss some of the debates around this issue.

- Describe and explain the apparent diversity of organization theories in terms of competing philosophical assumptions.

- An overview of the structure of, and rationale for, the rest of this book is also presented.

## Structure of the chapter

- This chapter begins by considering what organization theory is. It continues by considering the nature of theory in the social sciences. This important issue is developed by using examples of theory to illustrate the different components and uses of theory, especially with regard to how we undertake practical activities. The chapter then considers how organizations have been defined in the literature and discusses some of the pitfalls encountered in developing a definition. Having come to a working definition of organizations, the chapter then explores how organization theories operate to both explain and influence human behaviour in organizational contexts. Aspects of these issues are considered with reference to the problematic relationship between organization theory and management practice and to forms of theory that do not adopt a managerialist perspective. The chapter concludes by putting forward an explanation of the apparent diversity we find in organization theory and relates this diversity to the structure and rationale of the rest of the book.

## What is organization theory?

Since time immemorial, people have socially come together to undertake various activities, often out of sheer necessity because there are so many things we cannot do alone without the help of other people. We are, if we are anything, social beings who are usually reliant on other members of our species for survival. To put it bluntly, we are mutually interdependent because we rely on one another and this may be both a strength and a weakness. Imagine if you had to survive alone for a long period of time without the support of the various organizations that provide you with everything from food and clothing to water, fuel, shelter, health care, education, transport and so on. Could you cope, either physically or psychologically? Probably not! Certainly, your life would change drastically. Indeed, many activities in any society usually require people to socially interact in various ways and, to a degree, cooperate and coordinate their efforts with some sense of purpose. This seems to be the case whether we are referring to hunter–gatherer communities that use a relatively simple technology or to today's vast, technologically complex, industrial and post-industrial communities. In other words, organizing ourselves is at the heart of much of what we are and what we do as human beings. Our organizations are largely the outcomes of this collective behaviour as well as being significant influences on that behaviour.

However, although these human creations may well be crucial to enabling so many aspects of our lives, through their development they might come to dominate our lives and remove much of what we do from our own control. For instance, when we go to work or attend school or university as students, we inevitably give up some of our freedom of choice over what we can do and how we do it. We lose some of our autonomy, and our behaviour becomes channelled in particular directions by the requirements and expectations of the other people involved in those organizations. The result is that in our contemporary world, organizations are a central and all-pervasive phenomena that impact upon all of us, all our lives, from maternity hospital to funeral parlour. Indeed, there may be no escape from living in an organized manner and the discipline or control over our behaviour that comes with it that often remains unnoticed because it is so mundane and appears normal. Just think about queuing for a bus to arrive. In many, but not all, countries, this is such ordinary organizational behaviour that we barely notice doing it; we often just automatically form an orderly queue and wait our turn. It is often when the subtle and fairly informal self-organizing rules that we routinely follow and expect to be obeyed by others are broken by a 'queue jumper' or when they do not apply in a country we are visiting that we become aware of, and get rather concerned about, what is going on.

Just about everything we do is tacitly organized in some respects. Moreover, organizations themselves, in a formal manner, do so many different things for us – and to us – by enabling, transforming, yet also constraining the things we can do in numerous different ways. Although it is obvious to say that organizations organize most aspects of what we do and how we do it, this also raises issues around who decides what should be done and how it should be done, as well as raising questions about the effects of some of these social processes upon people. Therefore, studying organizations is also about trying to grapple with what sort of world we have created and what alternatives we might desire. Indeed, these complex social institutions have come to epitomise and constitute many aspects of our lives by influencing how we see ourselves and others. In other words, these institutions influence our sense of identity, whether we are students, university lecturers, managers, coal miners and so on. Through these processes, organizations are and will remain a pervasive influence on most kinds of human activity. Therefore, studying organizations entails investigating many aspects of our own lives, which is why organization theory is so interesting and will remain important for the foreseeable future.

Because organizations impact on so many aspects of our lives, organization theory is important in two key respects. Firstly, organization theory helps us to reflect upon and understand who we are and why we are who we are. Secondly, organization theory is about us and how we interact with others during our encounters in a vast array of different, often deceptively ordinary and mundane, social contexts that we take for granted because we cannot see or imagine any alternative to how things appear to be. As one leading contemporary organization theorist puts it:

> Today, no one can pretend to understand the human condition that does not understand the organizations in which it is constituted, constrained and transformed. Organization studies should be at the core of the study of the human condition, because without such subject matter – how in what ways, we collectively organize, dispute, do and change the things that we do – we would have nothing of any consequence to discuss (Clegg, 2002, p. xxvii).

Of course, this begs the question, 'What is organization theory?' Or in Clegg's terminology, 'What is organization studies?' Unfortunately, this is not a question that is easily answered because it in turn begs questions such as: 'What is a theory?' and 'What are these social phenomena we call organizations that are so important to us?' Below we deal with each of these questions in turn.

## Defining theory

There is often a great deal of confusion around what the term *theory* means because it is a rather abstract term that is often ill defined. Only too often one hears the lament from students that something they have been taught is 'too theoretical' or 'it's just a theory', only to then hear in reply to the question 'Well, what do you mean by *theory*?' the response 'I don't know . . . it's so academic!' It is as if theory is something that does not directly concern them in their lives outside their university courses, something also to be rather wary of, or even frightened about, and something that does not have any practical use. However, nothing could be further from the truth. Rather, theories influence all aspects of our everyday lives and how we understand and act upon what is going on around us. Indeed, theories are inherently practical devices; we often just do not realize it because we deploy and apply our theories so tacitly that we often remain unaware of their subtle influence upon how we understand and do things. It is often as if theories have only a ghostly presence in our everyday lives. Partly because of this, the famous British economist John Maynard Keynes (1936) warned us that:

> . . . the ideas of economists and political philosophers . . . are more powerful than is commonly understood. . . . Practical men [sic],who believe themselves quite

exempt from any intellectual influences, are usually the slaves of some defunct economist. Madmen in authority, who hear voices in the air, are distilling their frenzy from some academic scribbler of a few years back (p. 383).

Although he wrote specifically about economic and political theory, Keynes' insights are equally relevant to organization theory. Here Keynes alludes to the pivotal role any theory generally plays in how we make sense of and act in the world. He also suggests that hidden dangers lurk when we are unaware of the sources of the theories we inevitably apply in practically undertaking whatever it is that we do. Therefore, we must be cautious about what it is that influences our behaviour and be able to reflect upon and assess the implications of the theories we are using to guide our activities. So what are these theories that are so important in influencing how we practically engage with, make sense of and act in the world?

Any theory entails the deployment of an explanation of some apparent aspect of our worlds. Moreover, it is a short step from explaining why something has happened to thinking about what we might be able to do about it in order to change things. Theories help us describe and understand what has happened as well as predict what will happen in different circumstances. In part, therefore, a theory entails describing and conceptualizing the phenomenon in which we are interested. This aspect of theory involves our identifying particular phenomena in terms of their evidently common features. Our invention and use of concepts such as management, organization, control, hierarchy, authority and so on allow us to give order to our experiences and convey a sense of meaning when communicating with other people. In doing so, we simplify the world by putting these phenomena together, thereby abstractly classifying them as being either similar phenomena, being the same phenomenon or being somehow different. We often do this automatically and without really thinking about it, yet it is a key part of how we make sense of our surroundings. Indeed, if for some reason, we were unable to undertake this classification and instead treated all the mundane phenomena we regularly encounter as being unique and different, we could end up in a situation of continual distraction, with our attention becoming absorbed by trying to make sense of each distinct phenomenon we encounter. The result could be a form of sensory overload, which would play havoc with our ability to function effectively or indeed 'normally'. We might then become classified as being 'odd' or even clinically ill by other people because our ability to communicate would be diminished.

Now the important point here is that any theory, including those about organizations, uses our common sense ability to lump together phenomena in terms of their perceived similarities and differences to make sense of the world. It is just that when organization theorists do this, how they define phenomena as of the same type is more closely interrogated and debated than is usually the case in everyday life. For instance, we could conceptualize all the apparently very different organizations that provide paid employment to their members as 'work organizations' as something distinct, because of these common features, from other categories of organization that do not provide their members with a source of income in return for their time. Simultaneously, we are defining 'work' as paid employment, something that could be debated because one could argue that there is much 'work' that we do that does not earn financial returns (just ask any parent). The point is that coming to a precise definition of something is quite difficult, but there is always the danger that a concept can mean very different things to different people if it is not precisely defined. Despite these problems, when we define or conceptualize some phenomena, we eliminate some of the complexity that confronts us. This simplification enables us to define what we might be trying to investigate.

---

**Stop and think**

Try to identify organizations that do not provide any members with paid employment. You will find this actually quite difficult because most organizations, even, for instance, churches or sports teams, provide someone involved with their running some form of financial remuneration. Hence, what is a work organization for some members is nothing to do with work for other members. So perhaps our definition of work organization needs a more precise revision.

---

Although it is an important part of theory, this act of conceptualizing, classifying or categorizing aspects of our world does not make a theory in its own right. So although the concepts and definitions are the basic materials that all theories use, of great importance is how theories also entail our trying to explain *why* what we think we have observed has happened. Often we then try to apply that explanation to other identifiable occurrences of what we consider to be the same phenomenon of interest. At the heart of such explanations is the possibility of taking action to change or maintain situations when we come across what we take to be the same or similar phenomenon of interest. In other words, explanations provide us with reasons as to why something might have happened, but they also provide us with a rationale for doing things. The question that now arises is *how* such explanation is provided by a theory.

All theories link abstract concepts together in order to explain the occurrence, variation in or non-occurrence of some phenomenon. Central to this process of theoretical explanation is the notion of cause and effect: theories stipulate *why* things happen in terms of putting forward a causal relationship between different phenomena. Here the behaviour of something is seen as causing the behaviour of something else to happen. Simultaneously, theories specify *when* and *where* this effect may (or may not) happen, thereby limiting the scope or applicability of the theory to particular circumstances.

For instance, the recent relatively poor performance of the Scottish international football team in various competitions might be explained by there being too many foreign players in the top teams that play in the Scottish Premiership League. The *hypothesized* causal link or reason presented by this theory suggests that Scottish players (as defined by the appropriate regulations regarding ancestry) are underrepresented in premiership teams and therefore the pool of experienced indigenous players who participate at a high level of competition and who are available for international selection has shrunk. The result is a relative failure in international competitions, much to the despair of Scottish football supporters. Of course, other theoretical explanations of this organizational problem might be possible, including poor management, bad tactics, poor organization on the field of play, bad luck, fate and so on. But the point is that if our first theory is correct, it also indicates possible remedies that might be used to practically change the situation. We might also wish to try to generalize our analysis to other countries because our theory might also predict future problems for English and Welsh international football teams given the increasing numbers of foreign players also evident in those countries' top-flight football leagues. Moreover, we might want to explore the possibility of an alternative but related theory to explain the perceived situation by focusing instead upon the declining number of British managers or coaches in the top flight of all British and European football. If you think that this is an important cause of, or reason for, the relatively poor performance of these teams, you would have to explain how these appointments actually might cause a relative decline in competitive performance compared with how these teams performed when indigenous coaches or managers were employed. This is a very complex organizational issue that might not withstand critical scrutiny of the evidence. If the evidence did not support the theory, it would then be necessary to search for an alternative explanation because the theory would have been disproved.

Nevertheless, such theories not only allow us to explain what might be going on but also allow us to predict what should happen if we were to intervene and change things. This is because if we think that something is causing a particular problem or issue to arise, it follows that acting to change that causal factor should simultaneously impact upon the problem that has arisen. Therefore, theory is at the heart of how we attempt to understand and change aspects of our lives. In other words, theories help us to intervene and try to assert control over the events that affect us.

The point of the above quick departure into the hotly debated issue of Scottish international football is that even arguments you might witness or get involved in during various everyday social gatherings entail the deployment of theory. For instance, in our above football examples, the behaviour or phenomenon of interest (poor performance) is caused by the behaviour or action of another phenomenon (insufficient indigenous players in the Scottish Premiership). Let us take another example: one commonly accepted idea, if recent management practise in Europe and North America is anything to go by, is illustrated by Figure 1.1.

Here the phenomenon that is being explained is economic performance. In formal theoretical language, this is often called the *explanandum* or *dependent variable*. This is because its own variation is being explained in terms of being an effect of (i.e., it is dependent upon) the behaviour or action of another organizational phenomenon – downsizing that reduces costs. In this case, downsizing would be called the *explans* or *independent variable* because the theory proposes that its variation explains or causes particular changes in the dependent variable, changes

. . . in specific organizational conditions or contexts

*If the above relationship holds, we could use this theory to change things in organizations in the hope of improving organizational performance*

Figure 1.1: Relating cause and effect.

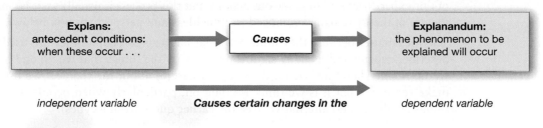

Figure 1.2: How theory provides explanation.

that the theory predicts. For example, we could argue that organizational downsizing reduces costs by reducing the number of people employed. This in turn should cause an improvement in organizational performance if we measure such performance in terms of profits. Here we are more precisely defining what we mean by abstract concepts such as downsizing and organizational performance. Of course, we could define and measure these concepts in different ways; much might depend on how we do this. Nevertheless, if what the theory predicts is actually the case, we could then use this theory to promote particular changes in organizations that should improve their performance. Theories also usually specify the particular sets of conditions in which the proposed cause-and-effect relationship should actually operate. For instance, much might depend upon the effects of the experience of downsizing upon the attitudes of the organization members who continue to be employed. In other words, in some situations this relationship might not hold. Another way of presenting this theoretical relationship is illustrated in Figure 1.2.

In sum, as we can see from our examples, theories do the following:

1. Theories are linguistic, conceptual devices that try to tell us things about the world by representing it in a causal manner. In the case of any social science theory, including organization theory, this is to do with the behaviour of people in various social contexts.

2. Theories define, classify or categorize aspects of the world – the *what* of that which we are studying.

3. Theories propose reasons in the form of cause-and-effect relationships that explain the variation of a particular phenomenon in terms of the effects of the action of, or the variation in, another phenomenon – the *why* and the *how*.

4. Theories identify the situation(s) or contexts *when* these causal relationships will or will not operate, and thereby set the boundaries to *where* they are applicable.

5. Based upon this *what, why, how, when* and *where* analysis, theories then can guide our actions because they enable predictions and hence potentially enable us to anticipate and try to influence or even control events. By intervening and changing the explans (or independent variable), the explanadum (or dependent variable) should also change in a manner predicted by the theory, provided that the theory holds.

6. Theories are not divorced from our everyday lives and behaviours. Indeed, we regularly deploy theory often in the form of 'common sense' in order to make sense

of our experiences and to guide our actions, but this process is usually tacit because the use of theory remains unnoticed (see the Ideas and perspectives box below).

7. Theories matter because they influence what happens to people; they are used to describe, explain and, equally significantly, justify the things that we do and how we do them. Therefore, we need to be very careful about the theories we use to make sense of what it is we think is going on, particularly when people present things as 'there is no alternative' (see the earlier quote from Keynes).

The differences between the theories that we informally use to make common sense of our worlds and those formally presented by social scientists to causally explain and predict phenomena are subtle and complex, something we shall further explore later in this chapter when we return to the relationship between social science theory and practice. Nevertheless, for the time being, one way of understanding these differences relates to the extent to which social scientists rigorously try to look for mistakes in the processes used to develop and test their theories. This process of quality control usually entails the submission of their theories to the scrutiny of other social scientists who, through what is called peer review, attempt to identify weaknesses that may have been overlooked. For instance, publication in

## Ideas and perspectives

## Theories and everyday life

In trying to understand and explain the social and natural phenomena that surround us and in our attempts at making decisions about what to do in particular circumstances, nobody escapes making or assuming . . . theoretical linkages. Every intentional act can be seen as an attempt to produce some desired state of affairs. This implies the belief on the part of the actor that a causal relationship exists between his or her decision, or act, and the state of affairs he or she desires. In this sense much of our everyday social lives and our work activities are in essence theory-dependent activities. Now this clearly illustrates the conjectural and practical aspects of theory, since people act in accordance with their expectations, or prejudices, as to what will happen in particular circumstances – conjectures often derived from impressions regarding what has previously happened in similar circumstances. Thus, even the most mundane activity, such as walking down a street, might be considered in terms of an actor applying theoretical assertions, virtually without thinking about them in a conscious fashion, that are borne out by being able to accomplish that activity. Often it is only when we become aware that our expectations, that are grounded in such tacit or taken-for-granted knowledge, have not been met (perhaps due to the intervention of some capricious circumstances) that we begin consciously to re-evaluate the webs of causal relationships that have previously been used to orientate our action. Out of this re-evaluation we begin to generate a new theory to account for the previously unconsidered anomalies. . . . such tacit knowledge is ordered and reordered according to the ebb and flow of situations.

So it is evident that theories are a means by which we generate expectations about the world; often they are derived from what we have perceived to have happened before and thus they influence (tacitly or otherwise) how we set about future interactions with our world(s). Moreover, it is also evident that if we have the expectation that by doing A, B will happen, then by manipulating the occurrence of A we can begin to predict and influence the occurrence of B. In other words, theory is clearly enmeshed in practice since explanation enables prediction which in turn enables control (Gill and Johnson, 2002, pp. 32–33).

peer-refereed journal publications is usually seen as the 'gold standard' for judging the credibility of theoretical claims. As Bedeian (2004, p. 198) observes, they provide the stamp of scientific authority despite the inevitably complex and problematic social processes that underpin how these judgements are made during the peer-reviewing process before publication. Notionally, theories that have survived this process have a superior provenance to ones that have not. However, as we shall see throughout this book, many organization theories are around that have been highly influential upon what happens in organizations, and these theories have not been through a peer-review process. This raises some interesting issues around how organization theories are often disseminated, particularly to managers. We shall return to this later.

In contrast, the theories we informally use to make sense of our everyday lives are not usually precisely written down and then submitted to such extensive review, debate and the critical scrutiny of our peers. Usually we do not have to worry about the problems inherent in the ways in which we acquire or formulate, use, evaluate, test and disseminate these 'common sense' theories. But perhaps, as we shall illustrate, we should be concerned: social scientists must concern themselves with such problems. As we shall see, they do this in different ways because their attitudes toward these issues actually do vary considerably. This is because the underlying philosophical stances of organization theorists, which influence how they engage with and make sense of their areas of interest, also vary. This is a very important point that we shall return to later in this chapter. All theories do not just represent for inspection the way the world is. Rather, theories themselves have encoded into them all kinds of philosophical assumptions that influence the form that a specific theory takes. As we shall see, just the idea that there is a world 'out there' awaiting our unbiased inspection is, in itself, a major philosophical assumption that influences how we operate. Perhaps our acts of perceiving and observing create much what we assume to be 'out there' rather than report what 'is' – a very different philosophical stance. This issue becomes evident when we turn to what is meant by the term *organization* below.

In sum, theories are highly influential upon what we do and why we do it. Theories allow us to see the world in particular ways. In doing so, they guide our reasoning and our actions. These actions potentially provide a source of feedback upon the viability of the theory. For instance, did whatever was practically undertaken (e.g., downsizing) actually achieve what we predicted by the theory (e.g., improved organizational performance)? Did it result in what we intended? If it did not, why not? Moreover, the emergence of a body of theory regarding, for instance, organizations, provides the possibility of intervening and controlling, or at least influencing, what is going on so as to achieve particular purposes. One question that might haunt us here is do we agree with or value the purposes that have been encoded into how and why the theory has been developed? Think about how organizational performance might be defined in our downsizing example: how we define things might inadvertently exclude the interests or needs of the vast majority of those who have a stake in an organization's operation (e.g., employees, especially those who have been made redundant by downsizing).

However, we still have not fully dealt with the question: what is *organization* theory? Indeed, what are these human creations we call organizations that organization theorists seek to describe, understand and explain? What are these social phenomena that are so important to us and in which we should be so interested in and concerned about?

---

**The chapter so far**

Up to this point, we have considered why organization theory is important in our everyday lives, which are, in so many respects, 'organized'. We have then moved on to providing an overview of what theories are, what they enable us to do and how they are related to our everyday lives and behaviour.

---

## What are organizations?

It is extremely difficult to define what we mean by the concept *organization* because in doing so, one inevitably deploys particular sets of assumptions that lead us to perceive these phenomena in a particular, often very partial, manner. Indeed, much of this book is about the different ways theorists have defined and engaged with these important phenomena.

---

**Stop and think**

Spend a few minutes writing down a formal definition of what you think an organization is.

Now compare your definition with the one that is initially presented below.

---

Here we will use one fairly common way of defining organizations to illustrate how problematic this whole process is. In order to conceptually differentiate organizations from other forms of social institution, such as the family, theorists have traditionally centred their definitions on the issue of 'goals'. For instance, more than 45 years ago, Talcott Parsons (1960), a highly influential social scientist, argued that:

> As a formal analytical point of reference, primacy of orientation to the attainment of a specific goal or purpose is used as the defining characteristic of an organization which distinguishes it from other types of social system (p. 17).

Whilst admitting that it is surprisingly difficult to give a simple definition of an organization, Schein (1970) provides a similar but somewhat more expanded working definition:

> An organization is the rational coordination of the activities of a number of people for the achievement of some common explicit purpose or goal, through division of labor or function, and through a hierarchy of authority and responsibility (p. 9).

One aspect both of the above slightly different definitions shares is that organizations are defined as collectivities of people whose activities are consciously designed, coordinated and directed by their members in order to pursue explicit purposes and attain particular *common objectives* or *goals*. If our organizations and the process of organizing are about goal attainment, it could follow that organization theory is about conceptualizing, explaining and ultimately guiding action regarding the different ways in which people act in unison together to achieve particular, desirable shared ends or 'common' organizational goals.

Here we might infer that because these goals are shared, it is important that organization theory should aim to improve organizational efficacy and efficiency in relation to those goals. That is, organization theory can and should contribute to enabling organizations to successfully achieve those goals (efficacy) with as little use of its resources as currently feasible (efficiency). Moreover, organization theory should also enable people to deal with issues that might prevent or hinder such purposeful goal attainment. Now such a view of both organizations and organization theory might seem benign because surely that is what organizations are all about, and it is only right for theorists to try to understand, explain, advise upon and improve upon such important social processes. Indeed, much – but by no means all – of organization theory has adopted this perspective.

However, conceptual dangers might lurk here, depending upon your point of view. It is possible to see a link between a managerial orientation to the study of organizations that prioritizes the concerns and interests of senior managers and how organization and organization theory is being defined and used by people. These possible dangers have to do with a conceptual process that we have deployed in our very definition of *organizations*.

In this context, the famous organization theorist and methodologist David Silverman has pointed to the problems created by the common view that organizations have specific goals or definite purposes. For Silverman (1970), such a definition entails attributing:

> the power of thought and action, to social constructs. We can ask an individual about his goals or purposes but it is difficult to approach an organization in the same way. It seems doubtful whether it is legitimate to conceive of an organization as having a goal except where there is an ongoing consensus between members of the organization about the purposes of their interaction (p. 9).

Here Silverman is raising several important issues. Firstly, to talk of social collectivities such as organizations as having goals, as if they were an individual person, can be misleading because it creates an image of agreement amongst members regarding the purposes of an organization that might not exist. Surely, we cannot talk of a collectivity having a goal unless everyone who makes up that collectivity agrees to that goal. Secondly, there may be a danger that by according to organizations a goal, we may inadvertently be prioritizing the particular goals of certain individuals or groups at the expense of the goals and aspirations of others who are involved with the same organization as members. If we are then concerned with helping the organization to achieve 'its' goals, the ideological implications are only too obvious because we might be taking sides on a contested terrain – whose goals are we prioritizing?

In most of the organizations with which we interact, it is not possible to presume the existence of the consensus to which Silverman refers. Indeed, different members might have an array of different goals regarding their involvement with a particular organization. These different goals reflect different people's particular interests and needs, goals that might conflict with one another.

So perhaps notions such as 'organizational goal' create a modern myth that obscures a threatening possibility, that organizations are not consensual or at least they should not be presumed to be always consensual. However, conceiving an organization in such terms might also serve to reinforce power structures and legitimizes the status quo by creating a deceptive aura of objectivity and neutrality around what is a very partisan conception of organization. This is because we may be inadvertently giving conceptual priority to the concerns and activities of particular organization members at the cost of those of other groups, both 'inside' and 'outside' the organization, by according their particular preferences the status of 'organizational' goals – a status that accords an impression of neutrality.

So with regard to the notion of organizational goal, Gouldner (1959) warns that:

> . . . an organization as such cannot be said to be orientated towards a goal. A statement an organization is orientated towards certain goals often means no more than these are the goals of its top administrators (p. 420).

Hence, defining organization theory as being concerned with understanding and explaining how organizations operate so as to enhance our ability to design more effective and efficient organizations in terms of 'their' goals might end up incorporating, prioritizing and legitimizing, by default, the perspectives and problematics of Gouldner's 'senior' managers. Of course, such a prioritization is not a problem if one assumes that those senior managers are there on merit and, moreover, that they rightly act as guardians of the overall purposes of the organization, purposes that all members have a vested interest in pursuing, even if they do not realize it. However, by conceptualizing organizations in this way, we might accidentally exclude and subjugate the priorities of the vast majority of organization members and those in the wider community who are not members but who are simultaneously affected by the organization's operation. More efficient and effective *for whom* becomes a question that is unasked and sublimated. This is because the ways that the concepts 'organization' and 'goal' have been devised and used lead us to perceive organizational phenomena as if they are always consensual or *unitary* entities in which members' interests and aspirations are always shared. These unitary tendencies are evident in much of our everyday language; take the concept 'corporation'.

> Corporation (noun): body corporate authorized to act as a single individual; artificial person created by royal charter, prescription, or act of the legislature, with authority to preserve certain rights in perpetual succession (*The Oxford English Dictionary*).

Here, for instance, the very word *corporation* metaphorically invokes an image of the body corporate in which the leaders of the organization are similar to the brains of the human body. This entails what is called *anthropomorphization*, literally meaning the ascription of human form, qualities and attributes. As we shall see in this book, a great deal of organization theory deploys concepts that anthropomorphize aspects of organizations, thereby treating them as if they were human individuals with individual qualities, rather than seeing them as social collectivities. We have already dealt with one form of anthropomorphization: organizational goal. However, here in this example of the body corporate, leaders have the right to direct and control what goes on in the organization, just like our brains do. Other members of the organization are thus relegated to performing the function of various subordinate body parts at the behest of messages and commands originating in the brain. Any resistance to the directions of the brain thereby becomes, metaphorically, rendered to be similar to an illness that needs to be treated because it is unhealthy and therefore puts the organization at some risk. Rationality is thus automatically accorded to the decision making of the leadership (and, for instance, their goals), and the behaviour of subordinates who might be recalcitrant or even resistant to such direction becomes deemed to be irrational, if not pathological. For how can the parts of the body corporate not automatically respond to the commands of the brain, or even conflict with one another, unless there is some illness present? The ideological significance of such a way of conceiving organizations becomes only too evident. For a very different view of the corporation, see the Ideas and perspectives box, overleaf.

As noted earlier, organizations have come to dominate human society. Hence, theories of organization are about a significant aspect of human life and can potentially have important practical consequences for how we lead our lives. Although some people might be advantaged by how organizations operate, others might be disadvantaged or even harmed. Indeed, this importance might explain the emergence of organization theory as a distinct academic discipline. However, this also raises questions about the form and content of organization theory itself.

1. Where do organization theories come from?
2. Who gets to read and write organization theory?
3. Who benefits from organization theories and the particular taken-for-granted assumptions and concepts that theorists might deploy with regard to how they (re)present organizations for analysis?
4. How might organization theories both express and simultaneously impact upon existing power relations in organizations?

## Ideas and perspectives

### *The Corporation* (2004) by Joel Bakan (a book and a film)

Bakan, who is a professor of law in Canada, argues in his film and book that the corporation is now threatening the very society that created it. Whilst the corporation has come to dominate economic activity, it has simultaneously created through its operation a dangerously narrow and materialist view of human nature that is impacting upon how people generally behave in wider society. If the corporation actually was an individual person, he or she might qualify in the United Kingdom as a psychopath, or in North America as a sociopath – immoral, antisocial, self-serving, self-interested, self-aggrandizing, incapable of accepting responsibility for his or her own actions and a considerable danger to other members of society.

Talking primarily about North America, Bakan argues that the seeds of this dangerous malaise were set legally by granting limited liability and awarding the corporation a legal personality with its managers and directors having a legal duty to put shareholders first above all other interests. The result was that the 'corporate person' legally took the place of the real people who actually owned the corporation and acquired the status of a 'natural entity' with the same rights to exist as an individual person but which had an exclusive emphasis upon profit making. For Balkan, this particular form of *anthropomorphization* has resulted in several significant consequences:

- The corporation has no interest in serving the interests of wider society, indeed the corporation is obliged, in a self-interested manner, to export onto others as many of the social, environmental and economic costs of making profits in order to preserve profit margins.

- Backed up by a wide range of evidence concerning how corporations regularly transgress the wider public interest in the immoral pursuit of competitive advantage and profits, Bakan shows how the whole notion of the corporation being socially responsible to a wider set of interests beyond those of shareholders is a logical and practical impossibility. For Bakan, the concept corporate social responsibility is an oxymoron.

For Bakan, the corporation is not a natural individual entity. It only has a right to exist because society gave it one, and it is time for us to remake legally the corporation so that this pervasive phenomenon begins to serve wider society's needs rather than continue a relentless pursuit of competitive advantage regardless of the social and environmental costs. Similar dangers may lie in defining organizations in terms of having a goal unless all members freely agree to that goal.

5. Why is so much organization theory primarily based upon research and theorizing produced in the United States, where the intellectual establishment has been accused (e.g., Clegg and Hardy, 1996) of actively constraining the form and content of organization theory and of being hostile to new ideas, especially when they originate from outside the United States?

6. Whose interests are included in such analyses, and whose are inadvertently – or perhaps purposely – excluded?

These questions about organizations are best considered by turning to the purposes of organization theory and its relationship with human activities, especially management practice.

## The chapter so far

At this point, it is important to summarize the debate so far regarding organizations. As we have argued, organizations are social entities created and sustained by collective human interaction. In this, organizations enable people to achieve objectives and satisfy needs that could not be attained or satisfied through the efforts of individuals alone. However, despite this mutual dependency and consequent synergy, this does mean that every member of an organization shares or is even aware of the objectives and needs of others. To talk of organizations as having goals, as if they exist independently of the people who make up the collectivity, can be misleading because it creates an aura of consensus regarding those matters that might not exist. Moreover, whose goals are being accorded priority in such a definition? However, organizations do involve some groups attempting to ensure that their particular purposes for the organization are imposed upon, or influence, the organizational behaviour of others. The pursuit of these particular purposes usually entails the exercise of power and control by some members as they try to influence what other members do and how they do it. This, of course, can lead to covert and overt forms of conflict: people might resist these attempts at controlling, coordinating, and influencing their behaviour in particular directions whilst simultaneously trying to pursue their own purposes with regard to their involvement with the collectivity.

## The relationship between organization theory and human activities

Theory . . . becomes a material force once it has gripped the masses
(Karl Marx, [1844] 1975, p. 251).

There is nothing so practical as a good theory
(Kurt Lewin, 1951, p. 169).

The relationship of any type of social science theory, such as organization theory, and its subject matter is always problematic. This is because its subject matter consists of knowledgeable beings who are self-aware, aware of others' behaviour and who have the power of sensory perception and are capable of feeling. In other words, social science theory is concerned with the behaviour of sentient human beings. Because social science theory attempts to understand and explain all aspects of human behaviour, including organizational phenomena, a key issue is that those theories can impact upon and change the very behaviour that constitutes the social scientist's focus precisely because those theories are irrevocably part and parcel of that human domain: they are created by it, they are investigated in it, they are disseminated in it and they can change it!

In contrast, for natural scientists who investigate the behaviour of physical, nonsentient phenomena, their relationship with those phenomena is not problematic in these respects. For example, physicists and chemists who conduct experiments investigating the behaviour of water do not have to worry whether or not the results of their experiments will affect the subsequent behaviour of that water; they seem to deal with a world that does not answer back. As far as we know, water does not have a self-conscious understanding of its own behaviour and the contexts in which that behaviour takes place. Hence, water cannot intentionally decide not to boil at 100°C at sea level. But people evidently do have such subjective capacities, and they have the ability to attempt to purposively and self-consciously change their behaviours in the light of knowledge that has been disseminated to them by social scientists or other people. To put it bluntly, social science's theoretical analyses and interpretation of human behaviour are constantly fed back into that which they are about, the social world.

As illustrated earlier in this chapter, the social world is a domain in which the same process of theoretical analysis and interpretation also take place, albeit usually in a less rigorous manner, through the action of what we often refer to as common sense. Hence, the social world can – and does – answer back in unpredictable ways as people make use of theory to conceptualize and explain their experiences. Of course, such processes might undermine, enhance or indeed remain indifferent to the explanatory power of the social science theory.

Social scientists (e.g., Giddens, 1982, 1984, 1993) and philosophers of science (e.g., Bhaskar, 1989) have called this process the *double hermeneutic* – that is, the social sciences are themselves aspects of the social world in that they are affected by it, but they are also causal forces that can act upon and shape that which they are trying to explain. People can and do read social science theory and in the light of that knowledge, change what they do. Hence, the double hermeneutic is a notion that has at its heart the relationship between social science theory and the everyday practices of human agents. So as Giddens puts it (1984, pp. xxxii–xxxiii), social science theories can have the property of 'self-fulfilling prophecies' in the sense that they 'cannot be kept wholly separate from the universes of meaning and action which they are about'. But for Giddens, because social science produces theoretical explanations of social phenomena, social scientists inevitably produce judgements regarding the rationality of social actors' practices. Therefore, as Giddens claims, social science must have an inherently evaluative (how appropriate is what is going on?) and normative (what ought to be going on?) relationship to social change and development through its criticism of the taken-for-granted beliefs of actors that are encoded into and expressed in their everyday social practices.

As we have argued, social scientists' analysis of actors' social practices is constantly fed back, or disseminated, into what it is about. Their analyses can therefore change their subject matter if actors subsequently decide to incorporate those criticisms within their own understanding and practices. For instance, people might begin to use social scientists' analyses to understand their own behaviour and that of other people. In doing so, they might change their own behaviours and attempt to influence the behaviour of others in particular directions. These possibilities raise the issue of dissemination and how social science theories are actually translated into the very practices that then become the focus for subsequent social science investigation. This issue has important consequences for a subject such as organization theory. Not only does organization theory try to describe and explain the institutional forms that organizations take, it might also have the effect of being an active agent that participates in changing and creating those organizational forms through its own dissemination in, and impact upon, the social world. This paradox is illustrated by Figure 1.3.

Hence, the double hermeneutic raises two sets of issues.

1. The ways in which social science-derived organization theories, through their social dissemination, can influence: the creation, maintenance and development of organizations and the routine practices of their participants; the nature of that membership; the relations between those members (e.g., the various types of managers and their hierarchical relations with different types of subordinates).

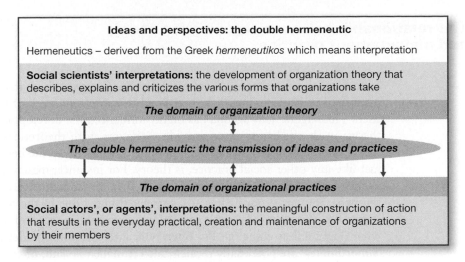

Figure 1.3: The double hermeneutic.

2. The ways in which organizational members deploy theory from various sources in understanding and practically developing, maintaining and changing their organizations; the ways in which these everyday social processes and practices exert influence upon the development of social scientists' theories about organizations.

Undoubtedly, it is difficult to separate these two sets of issues because of the reciprocal relationship between social science theory and the social practice processes those theories are about, as illustrated in Figure 1.3. Nevertheless, for our purpose here, the two issues raise significant questions about how organization theory is developed and how it is communicated to, disseminated to and used by various organizational audiences. Moreover, it also raises questions about how what is going on in organizations is made available to organization theorists and for wider public consumption.

## The chapter so far

In the last section, we looked at how we might define the phenomenon 'organization'. We have shown that organizations are often defined in terms of being purposeful goal-seeking entities. However, there is a danger here that we inadvertently incorporate the goals of particular powerful organizational groups in our definition, which can be misleading because it confers an aura of consensus that may not exist. It can also give us a very slanted view of organizations because the goals of the powerful are accorded a privileged status over those of other members. Perhaps if we want to incorporate the notion goal into our definition of organization, it is better to be very cautious by seeing that organizations may entail certain social groups trying to impose their particular goals for the organization upon others during organizational activities, a process that might be understandably resisted and therefore lead to some form of conflict. As the double hermeneutic suggests, we need to be very careful how we use definitions in our theories and how we formulate those theories because we can influence actual practice through their dissemination to organizational audiences. The ideological ramifications of even how organizations are sometimes defined as entities that pursue common goals are only too evident.

## The relationship between organization theory and management practice

Even a cursory inspection of organization theory would show that much (but by no means all) of it seeks to meet the presumed concerns and needs of particular potential users – managers. This agenda has highly influenced the development of organization theory in that it has tried to provide managers with theoretical frameworks that they can deploy to best achieve competitive advantage. At the heart of management, just like any other social practice, is theory. For instance, managers have a role that usually entails their active intervention in their organizations in order to influence the behaviour of subordinates so as to get things done in the manner they desire. Inevitably, this is based upon some prior theoretical description and explanation of what they think is going on. But often built into this point of view is the notion that 'subordinates' are potentially recalcitrant yet malleable and, of course, their management 'superiors' have a more valid understanding of what is needed in the organization and what priorities should be attended to. Hopefully, from the managers' point of view, their subsequent interventions into organizational processes produce the intended change in subordinates' behaviour. Hence, many organization theorists are overtly concerned with helping managers improve how these analyses and practices are undertaken. In doing so, they align organization theory with the presumed problems and preoccupations of managers. So, for some commentators (e.g., Donaldson, 1996), organization theory is about enabling the description, explanation and prediction of members' behaviour in organizational settings. But organization theory must also promise to improve the effectiveness of managers by conferring the power of control through better analysis and explanation of what is going on. Organization theory should provide something to help managers use more incisive interventions that get to the heart of the organizational 'problems' that concern them.

Hence, it seems that there is often no clear distinction between the presumed theoretical needs of managers and the focus of what is often called *mainstream* organization theory. This is because the practical utility of organization theory is only too often presented in terms of specific relevance to practising managers. For instance, in a widely read text, Pugh (1977) defines organization theory as being:

> . . . the study of the structure, functioning and performance of organizations and the behaviour of groups and individuals within them . . . [in order] . . . to distil theories of how organizations function and *how they should be managed* [our emphasis] (p. 9).

Such a definition raises four questions for which mainstream organization theory attempts to provide answers:

1. How and why do organizational forms vary and change at particular points in time?
2. How do these different organizational forms impact upon the behaviour of their members?
3. What are the practical implications of questions 1 and 2 for the effective and efficient management of organizations?

4. How can organization theorists design their research and communicate their findings so that it is perceived as relevant to the problems faced by practising managers and is accessible to them?

For example, the observation of management practices in what have been categorized as exemplary or 'excellent' organizations has been presented in a populist form of mainstream organization theory through its dissemination as various recipes and tool kits (e.g., Peters and Waterman, 1982). If followed, these theorists claim, these guides to practice will enable the more efficient and effective management of members and thereby ensure organizational success by securing competitive advantage in the changing social and economic circumstances that confront so many contemporary organizations. Usually these changed circumstances are presented as having made the previously accepted tenets of good management practice and effective organization no longer appropriate (see also Kanter, 1989; Peters, 1992). Of course, this type of organization theory, with its careful packaging for its targeted audience, raises numerous questions, not just about its practical impact upon organizations and how, if at all, organization theory is actually disseminated to management practitioners, but also with regard to how those managers might appropriate, consume and apply this type of organization theory to their organizations. For instance, do managers actually read these writings and then try and implement their prescriptions in the hope of securing the holy grail of competitive advantage? Or is communication more by word of mouth?

It is evident that despite the many spectacular successes of the populist mainstream genre in terms of the number of books sold to management practitioners (e.g., Peters and Waterman, 1982), a great deal of management-orientated theory and research is not successfully disseminated to practitioner audiences, who seem to remain blind to the fruits of this research. This creates an irony: it might be managerially orientated, but it is not read by managers. In part, this situation happens because despite its overriding orientation, much of this mainstream organization theory is concerned with narrow theoretical preoccupations. Although these narrow concerns are easier to research and meet the dominant standards of methodological rigour they often result in apparently trivial findings from the point of view of practising managers. Moreover, the findings are usually only published in peer-reviewed academic journals that are unread by practising managers.

Therefore, it has been argued that the channels by which this theory is usually disseminated and, crucially, the technical language that has to be used to meet the requirements of peer-reviewed journals all tend to reflect the intellectual interests and elitist disciplinary concerns of academia rather than directly addressing the pragmatic concerns and business needs of management practitioners (see Keleman and Bansal, 2002; Tranfield and Starkey, 1998). These issues were noted some time ago by Weick (1989) when he suggested that one possible reason for this situation was that such theoretical endeavours were 'hemmed in by methodological strictures that favour validation rather than usefulness' (p. 516). In other words, to meet the academic requirements of peer-reviewed journals and meet their 'gold standard', the rigorous testing of theory takes precedence over making research understandable and useable by practising managers despite its managerialist orientation. Unlike the more populist managerialist genre, a result of this continuing emphasis upon methodological rigour, at the expense of relevance to the conceptually and morally favoured managerial community, is that:

> . . . a great deal of research is simply being 'wasted', because academics may not be skilled at translating their theories in a language that appeals to practitioners, or indeed, because there are no institutional incentives to do so (Keleman and Bansal, 2002, p. 104).

Also, organization theorists would probably encounter major difficulties if they try to publish research, especially in the prestigious refereed journals mentioned earlier that used language that appeals to management practitioners.

Nevertheless, despite these institutional barriers to ensuring relevance, some management-orientated organization theory does get disseminated to practitioner audiences from an array of sources, in various forms, and through different media. However, when this does happen, a further set of significant questions arises:

1. Do the innovations that are prescribed to practitioners actually achieve what they claim to do when implemented?

2. Do managers creatively improvise, selectively modify and elaborate the received wisdoms of organization theorists to tactically deal with their own preoccupations rather than slavishly following their recipes for success?

3. How, when these new practices are implemented, are their effects upon the organization systematically evaluated and assessed, if at all?

4. Are managers forced to actually implement organizational changes deriving from the more fashionable theory, regardless of the content and efficacy of such practices, but because not to do so would make them appear to be behind the times, out of touch with the 'latest' thinking and therefore incompetent?

5. Alternatively, are these theories merely rhetorical tools that are used by managers just to 'talk the talk' and thereby earn status and prestige without really changing anything of significance because such a presentation of themselves enables them to appear to be competent in their own eyes and, perhaps more importantly, in the eyes of significant others inside and outside their organizations?

## Social engineering and organization theory

The implicit and explicit requirement that organization theory must be relevant to the problems and concerns of managers has been both supported and criticized by various commentators. Indeed, organization theory has often been developed precisely to enable managers to manage more efficiently and effectively by enhancing their capacity to deal with a range of problems ranging from how to design organizations through how to motivate recalcitrant employees. Here the prevailing perspective is that organization theory can provide a solution to what are identified as managerial problems, through the improvement of the technical content of managerial practice based upon the use of social science, rather than common sense, theory as well as more rigorous analysis. This orientation to the purposes of organization theory articulates aspects of an argument put forward by the highly influential philosopher, Karl Popper.

Popper thought that any social scientific knowledge can form the basis of and be developed by what he called 'social engineering':

> . . . the planning and construction of institutions with the aim, perhaps, of arresting or of controlling or quickening social developments (1967, pp. 44–45).

This involves the use of what Popper called 'technological predictions', which through experimental testing and 'piecemeal tinkering. . . combined with critical analysis', would enable human intervention to manipulate social processes in accordance with their intentions in order to solve the 'practical questions of the day' (ibid, pp. 58–59). At first thought, such aims might seem harmless – surely, social progress can be achieved by deploying social scientific knowledge in such a manner, and is this not the whole purpose of social theory anyway? Popper, however, remains silent regarding the institutional processes by which social engineering might be done. For instance, he ignores the issue of whose perceived urgent 'question' or 'problem' is the social scientist to apply himself or herself to in the development of viable theoretical solutions. In other words, there could be the danger that the problems and questions of the powerful are pursued at the expense of the less powerful, especially in hierarchical organizations.

Although talking generally about sociology, rather than specifically about organization theory (which, of course, draws heavily upon sociology), Benton's (1977) warnings about social engineering are relevant here. He argues that for social engineering to be possible:

> . . . there must be an identity between, on the one hand, the political problems of those who have the power to implement reforms as a means of solving these problems and, on the other hand, the theoretical problems of the sociological theorist. To advocate that sociological theory be, in this respect, an articulation of the political problems of a ruling group is to accede to a conception of sociology as a ruling ideology or as a variant of such a ruling ideology (pp. 40–41).

Therefore, it is hardly surprising that organization theorists who adopt, intentionally or inadvertently, a managerialist perspective have long been criticized regarding their uncritical acceptance of the status quo and for being 'servants of power' who manipulate the human side of the enterprise through colluding with those elites (i.e., senior managers) in organizations to whom they feel they need to make themselves pragmatically accountable (Baritz, 1960; Ramos, 1981; Reed, 1985). The danger is that the kinds of questions that are then asked about organizations become severely restricted because organizational researchers and theorists feel the need to present their work in a manner that appeals to possible sponsors and particular consumers of that work. As Rose (1978) has noted, this 'creates the constant risk that only that work which excites rich or powerful groups will prosper' (p. 270).

However, in their discussion of developments primarily in North America, Stern and Barley (1996) vigorously argue that a managerialist frame of reference was not always quite so dominant in organizational research. Rather, they associate its rise at the expense of a more critical sociological tradition with the migration of organizational researchers from sociological departments to business schools during the

1980s and the subsequent institutionalization of organization theory as a separate discipline. Business schools' agenda for organization theory was not one that values critique of how organizations operate and how they impact upon society in terms of distribution of power, rewards and status. Rather, the business school agenda was one of demonstrating professional relevance to managers. As Stern and Barley (1996) observe, the political and intellectual climate in business schools 'discouraged examination of broad social questions, promoted a particular approach to science and created specific career incentives' (p. 146). As they go on to note, many sociologists were willing victims in all this because being previously tied to departments that had the reputation of being 'anti-business' hampered their ability to disseminate their ideas about organizations outside academia. Moreover, migrating to business schools not only gave them a larger share of departmental resources but also provided better access to corporations, which became significant subsidizers, sponsors and consumers of their research, provided that the sociologists spoke about issues of concern to managers. Hence, the long-established 'administrative' stream in organization theory that focused upon enhancing efficiency and effectiveness in managerial terms steadily advanced at the expense of a more sociologically informed orientation. Indeed, two of the authors of this book, who were once sociologists in a British business school that is no more, can attest to having experienced these pressures and have often during our private conversations referred to our disciplinary background as 'the subject that dare not speak its name'.

Despite the developments noted above, it is important not to simply generalize the North American experience to the rest of the world. This is especially the case when it comes to European organization theory. It has long been argued (e.g., Kassem, 1976; Lammers, 1990; Usdiken and Pasadeos, 1995) that there are significant differences between North America and Europe. Although these differences are complex and are evolving, it seems that mainstream North American organization theory remains largely wedded to a managerialist orientation that has little concern with how power differences affect organizations and society. In contrast, organization theory, especially in the United Kingdom, has retained a critical tradition often inspired by German philosophers and, moreover, in the past 15 years or so, postmodernist thinking that was originally inspired by French philosophers has become much more evident.

These recent developments, together with the history of organization theory in the United States, imply that although management practice always depends upon the application of organization theory in some form, not all organization theory adopts a management orientation.

---

### Stop and think

Why are you reading this book? For instance, is it because you hope to know more about management as a distinct organizational function done by a particular social group in organizations? Or is it because you wish to know more about how organizations operate and impact upon the individual? Or is it both? Or is it because of some other reason? What assumptions are you bringing to bear in thinking about these issues about 'organizations', 'management' and 'knowing more'?

## Critical alternatives to managerialism in organization theory

Despite the dominance of managerialist approaches to organization theory, some organization theorists overtly refuse to align their work, either practically or ideologically, with the presumed perspective and concerns of management. For instance, one of these alternatives, which originated in Frankfurt and which is discussed in Chapter 8, is called critical theory. This approach overtly rejects management-orientated organization theory as both misconceived and unethical because it is only concerned with the problems of a small minority of people in organizations and therefore is inherently undemocratic. Instead, critical theorists aim to reveal the structures of oppression and injustice that are taken to be part of organizing in capitalist society, whose main beneficiaries, in terms of financial reward and social status, are the higher echelons of management themselves.

Hence, critical theorists start from the premise that it is unethical to tie organization theory to the presumed interests of those who constitute a powerful minority in organizations. They ask whose problems should organization theory attend to, and why do their problems become significant questions? Organization theorists who do not raise such questions end up becoming servants of the powerful in organizations by helping to maintain the status quo. Instead, organization theory must be more concerned with the relatively disempowered majority of organization members to enhance their democratic rights and responsibilities. Of course, this raises an important point: many of us live in long-established liberal democracies where democratic rights are taken for granted in civic life. Yet there seems to be a stark contrast between the democratic values that infuse civic life outside the workplace and our everyday experience of hierarchy and authority within the organizations where we work, where democractic rights are usually left at the entrance.

According to critical theory's stance, a task is to undermine the technically neutral imagery used by both management practitioners and organization theorists who align their theoretical endeavours with management. This is important because management-orientated organization theory is seen as being concerned with identifying and implementing the most efficient *means* for instrumentally achieving *given ends*. From the point of view of critical theory, crucial questions are not asked regarding:

- What is the nature of those ends?
- Whose ends are they?
- Whose interests do they serve?
- How have they been developed?
- Why help with their achievement?

Not asking such questions reduces the organization theorist to the status of a social engineer who merely tries to improve management practice without questioning those practices and the ends that they incorporate. Here we can see the utility of notions such as 'organizational goal', which provides a veneer of neutrality that masks the partisan nature of these issues. So, for critical theorists, all this creates an ideological facade.

By failing to reflect upon the nature and desirability of those ends, an 'instrumental rationality' is created that by default *accepts* those inevitably partisan ends as natural, as normal, as unchallengeable and as given. By then limiting the focus of organization theory to understanding the structure and functioning of organizations so as to advise upon how to better manage and lead them, those ends become unquestioned and hidden in the apparently neutral technical 'fixes' that managers claim to deploy. Debate and critique are thereby stifled with regard to the nature of those ends, and the unequal status quo is subtly reinforced. Moreover, we may be unable to imagine any alternative to the status quo.

In response to these perceived problems, the task of the critical theorist is directly concerned with the double hermeneutic. As one critical theorist puts it, here the aims are:

> . . . first to understand the ideologically distorted subjective situation of some individual or group, second to explore the forces that have caused that situation, and third to show that these forces can be overcome through awareness of them on the part of the oppressed individual or group in question (Dryzek, 1995, p. 99).

Hence, a key practical aim of this form of organization theory is through such a critique of the ideologies articulated by mainstream managerialist organization theory and practice, the empowerment and emancipation of the disadvantaged and disenfranchised in organizations will be encouraged. So, through the development of what critical theorists call a critical consciousness, alternative ways of organizing become conceivable, knowable and hence possible to formally disempowered people. Alvesson and Willmott (1996), two leading critical theorists, embed such notions in how they define a critical organization theory. This approach:

> . . . seeks to open up radically new understandings of organizational life that have a potential to promote new modes of work that give voice to, and promote, critical reflection and autonomy' (p. 114).

> . . . its purpose is to stimulate and contribute to a . . . process of challenging and removing . . . practices which are incompatible with the development of greater autonomy and responsibility (ibid, p. 119).

In other words, critical theorists always seek alternatives to the status quo. However, most people usually accept the status quo as normal, as given and as unchangeable because they cannot see or imagine any alternative. In a sense, they are trapped by the way they see things. Critical theorists want to free people from these ideological constraints. So, through critique, reflection, debate and the development of democratic relations, the status quo might be challenged and alternative forms of organization developed that express the perceived interests of those currently excluded from a say in how organizations are organized.

It would seem, therefore, that despite the general dominance of management-orientated approaches, organization theory is a much more diverse disciplinary area than it would appear at first glance. As illustrated with the case of critical theory, some of these alternative approaches do not attempt to service what are presumed to be management concerns by providing more accurate theories and accounts of organizing that practically aid the design of organizations so as to improve efficiency and effectiveness in the pursuit of competitive advantage. Indeed, the whole notion that organization theory can be more accurate and objective than 'lay' actors' theories has become a contested terrain. This philosophical dispute about the possibility of an objective organization science has a direct bearing on the recent proliferation of different approaches to undertaking organization theory (to which we shall soon turn). This proliferation reflects considerable disagreement over the nature of the phenomena of interest being studied and how to study them. In other words, what constitutes organization, organization theory and the theorist's role are highly controversial issues.

## The chapter so far

As we have tried to show in the last two sections, organization theory is a highly contested disciplinary area, especially with regard to whether or not it should adopt a managerialist perspective. Similar to any body of social science theory, organization theory matters because it can influence how we understand our experiences and how we might then behave in our organizations. Hence, the form that organization theory takes, the perspective that is adopted and its assumptions about social science itself are important and should be always interrogated and subjected to critical scrutiny rather than just being taken to be self-evident and incontestable. Inevitably, any organization theorist makes choices about how he or she engages with the subject of interest. These choices often might remain unnoticed and uninterrogated. Surely, it is important that we should notice how these choices have been made to see if we are happy with them because they affect how we understand organizations and can affect what people do in organizations through the action of the double hermeneutic.

We now wish to turn to further explaining some important philosophical disputes and debates that underlie the creation of this diverse range of organization theories. In doing so, we will introduce the reader to the structure of this book and its underlying rationale. A key aim here is to try to model the nature of these competing philosophical positions by creating a framework that can aid our understanding of organization theory itself.

## Philosophical disputes and debates: explaining and understanding the diverse nature of organization theory

When one first comes to the area of organization theory, one is immediately struck by the vast array of different perspectives that people adopt and use to understand organizations. It seems to be a contested terrain often hotly disputed by theorists who wave different flags to signify their allegiances: positivism, modernism, interpretivism, critical theory, postmodernism and so on. This immediately poses the question: Why? What is it that makes these people see and analyse what is going on so differently? This is a very difficult question to answer, and this book is concerned with mapping out these different schools of thought. The book also explains some

## Some key philosophical issues

**Stop and think**  **What is truth?**

Undertake the following tasks:

1. Identify and list the different ways by which you might decide whether or not some claim about what is happening in the world is either true or false.
2. Which of these ways of establishing truth and falsity do you prefer, and why?
3. Which of these ways of establishing truth and falsity are primarily used in the social sciences?
4. Now compare your preferences with those expressed below.

of their differences and what they mean for understanding organizations and the behaviour of the people who make them up. Here, however, we need to introduce one key dimension of this diversity that explains some of the differences between these different theorists.

This dimension is concerned with philosophy and how philosophical issues are inevitably embedded in how we engage with, understand and study organizations. In doing so, we aim to introduce the reader to certain key philosophical questions, to which there is no single correct answer or solution, and around which some of these disputes rage. There are just different answers, and these different answers lead to different approaches to doing organization theory and therefore explain some of the apparent diversity mentioned earlier at a very basic level. Moreover, in order to fully understand any approach to organization theory, one has to be able to understand the philosophical orientation of those using the approach because this is what justifies how they engage with organizations in the ways that they do.

It is important to realize that *any* scientific endeavour is underpinned by philosophical assumptions about ontology and epistemology. No one is immune from their influence; it is just that we do not often reflect upon how our tacit answers to these philosophical issues influence how we understand the world. Often, just as we noted with regard to theory earlier in this chapter, as soon as one mentions such issues to many students, they are received with a look of abject horror. 'What on earth do these words mean, and what on earth do they have to do with us?' seem to be the questions that form in the students' minds. Well again, just like with theory, the glib response to these questions is that people inevitably have to deal with these philosophical issues *all the time*. Perhaps people usually just do not realize that they do this and almost certainly do not call them epistemological and ontological questions!

You have just engaged with the issue of epistemology – the study of the criteria we deploy and by which *we know* and decide what does and does not constitute a warranted claim about the world or what might constitute warranted knowledge. Epistemology has to do with how we know when some claim about the world is justified. This is illustrated by the Greek derivation of the word 'epistemology' (Figure 1.4).

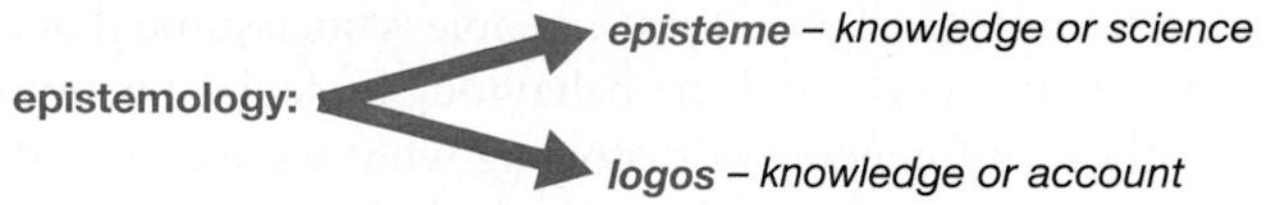

epistemology:

episteme – knowledge or science

logos – knowledge or account

**Figure 1.4:** The derivation of 'epistemology'.

## Example: Sir Humphrey's view

In an episode of the famous BBC comedy *Yes Minister*, the following exchange occurred between Sir Humphrey, a senior officer in the British Civil Service and Jim Hacker, the minister for administrative affairs.

HACKER: Was there one question today to which I could give a clear, simple, straightforward, honest answer?

SIR HUMPHREY: Yes, unfortunately although it was clear, simple and straightforward, there is some difficulty in justifiably assigning to it the fourth of the epithets you apply to the statement, in as much as the precise correlation between the information you communicated and the facts, in as far as they may be determined and demonstrated, is such to cause epistemological problems of sufficient magnitude as to lay upon the logical and semantic resources of the English language a heavier burden than they can be reasonably expected to bear.

HACKER: Epistemological! What are you talking about?

SIR HUMPHREY: You told a lie.

*Source: Yes Minister © Jonathon Lynn and Anthony Jay*

Although epistemology is also about our everyday assumptions about *how* we know whether or not a claim presented to us about the world is true or false, epistemological issues are also at the heart of what we take to be science (after all, the term *science* means 'systematic and formulated knowledge', *Oxford English Dictionary*). Thus, it begs the question how do we know if and when the knowledge claims of (social) scientists are warranted? Indeed, we might tacitly undertake these judgmental tasks in different ways in different social contexts by deploying different epistemological conventions. How we epistemologically judge the claims of social scientists might be quite different from how we judge those of friends, relatives or politicians such Jim Hacker. In the case of social science, we might look for evidence that could confirm, contest or even refute any claim (e.g., those made by organization theorists). However, epistemology raises the issue of whether or not we can objectively or neutrally know what there is out there in the world and thereby collect the necessary evidence. In other words, is it possible to neutrally observe the social world – in our case, organizations – without influencing what we see during that very act of observation? If we cannot, then the idea that what is true is something that corresponds with the facts becomes very difficult to defend. Now usually we assume that what we see is what there is, that perception is a passive process whereby what is out there can be accessed through our senses, provided that we give it sufficient attention. Although many organization theorists accept this epistemological idea, others see it as woefully naïve because they think that in observing the world, we influence what we see through how we perceive phenomena.

At this point, we can see the first major philosophical dispute arising that affects organization theory and how it is undertaken. Here we can identify what we shall call *epistemological objectivists*, people who assume that it is possible to neutrally observe the social world and the behaviour of social phenomena such as organizations (i.e., without influencing or distorting what we see by and through that act of observation or perception). For epistemological objectivists, what we see is what there is. Provided that we have been suitably trained to observe in a rigorous manner, we can, for instance, collect objective evidence to test the truthfulness of our theories.

For epistemological objectivists, the facts 'out there' can and must be the ultimate arbiter of whether or not our theories are true and hence can be used to guide practice. If we cannot use empirical evidence from reality to judge the adequacy of our theories, we are in danger of being held in thrall by a mixture of guesswork, dogma, superstition, prejudice and so on. It is interesting to note that the television series *The X Files*, which was about the paranormal and supernatural, actually used a rather objectivist epistemological stance in all its opening sequences – 'the truth is out there'. The problem for one of the key protagonists in the series, Agent Scully, seemed to be getting the necessary evidence to convince her that the supernatural actually existed.

At first sight, epistemological objectivism seems eminently sensible and coincides with ideas that we routinely use to differentiate between, for instance, truth and falsity. Surely, the facts speak for themselves. However, it raises the question of whether or not we can actually observe and collect 'the facts out there' in order to test our theories without influencing what we see. Now undertake the exercise below.

## Exercise

What you see is what there is.

Describe in as few words as possible what you see in Figure 1.5 and refer to Figure 1.5 for the rest of the exercise.

Almost certainly, most of you will have described the below object in three-dimensional terms such as a cube.

If you have done so, which face of the cube is facing toward you?

Strange isn't it, that the face toward us keeps changing!

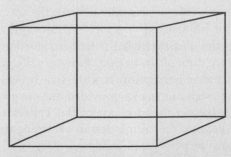

**Figure 1.5:** What is this?

Why should this happen?

What is even stranger is that you have automatically assumed that this is a three-dimensional object. Why?

Surely, it is just as possible to see this as flat, as a mixture of oblongs, parallelograms and triangles. Is there something that we bring with us to observing what is, after all, a very simple set of data (12 lines drawn on some paper), which makes us *interpret* these data in a particular way, as three dimensional?

Does what has happened above cast any doubt upon the epistemological objectivist claim that we can observe what is 'out there' in a passive manner so that we do not contaminate what we see during that act of observation?

If, for instance, you think we cannot do this, what does this mean for social scientific knowledge, especially when that knowledge concerns complex social phenomena, such as organizations, rather than just a few lines drawn on a book page?

If you assume that it is impossible to neutrally observe what is 'out there' without inevitably influencing what you perceive, because of the action of a perceptual process that processes sensory inputs in variable ways according to, for instance, their variable cultural backgrounds, then you are adopting what might be called an *epistemologically subjectivist* philosophical stance. Such a stance assumes that what we perceive is, at least in part, an outcome of us and the conceptual baggage that we bring to bear in order to make sense of what we experience. The origins of this baggage are usually assumed to be social in origin. So, for instance, most people from industrialized and urbanized countries would see the diagram in the exercise above as being three dimensional – but people from hunter–gatherer communities would most likely see it in two dimensions. Such variance is probably caused by different cultural and physical environments. In Western society, most of us are surrounded by lots of cube-like objects (just look around; you are probably sitting in one), but hunter–gatherer communities do not have the same cultural and experiential resources available to them in making sense of the world. They just see things differently from us and neither way is right or wrong.

Whether we think we can be objective in how we perceive the world has major implications for whether we think we can objectively test our theories about organizations and then use those theories to make changes to organizations with some confidence. In *X Files* terminology, the truth may be 'out there', but how can we ever know it? However, this epistemological debate about *how* we can know and if we can ever be neutral and objective in that knowing must also entail reference to the nature of *what* we are trying to know things about. In *X Files* terms, is there an 'out there'? In our case, this is to do with the social world, or more specifically, a particular aspect of the social world – organizations. The word *ontology* is used to refer to this philosophical area and this, too, has a Greek derivation (Figure 1.6).

Ontology is concerned with the nature of phenomena and their existence – the 'out there' we have talked about so far. For our purposes, ontology raises questions regarding whether or not a phenomenon we are interested in actually exists independently of our knowing and perceiving it. Or is what we see and usually take to be real, instead,

**Figure 1.6:** The derivation of ontology.

**Stop and think**

If you do not believe that these philosophical assumptions and choices are always at play, just try operating without them!

an outcome or creation of these acts of knowing and perceiving? Here we are primarily concerned with the ontological status of social reality and the phenomena (e.g., organizations) we take to constitute aspects of that reality. Here it is useful to differentiate between realist and subjectivist assumptions.

1. **Realist assumptions** concern the ontological status of the phenomena we assume to constitute social reality and entail the view that they exist, 'out there' independently of our perceptual or cognitive structures and attempts to know. We might not already know its characteristics, but this reality exists, is real, and awaits discovery by us.

2. **Subjectivist assumptions** concern the ontological status of the social phenomena we deal with, which, philosophically, entail the view that what we take to be social reality is a creation or projection of our consciousness and cognition. What we usually assume to be 'out there' has no real independent status separate from the act of knowing. In knowing the social world, we create it. We just probably are not usually aware of our role in these creative processes.

**The chapter so far**

In the last few sections, we have tried to outline some of the philosophical choices that we inevitably have to make when trying to study social phenomena such as organizations. Our philosophical assumptions about ontology and epistemology are always contentious and debatable because that is all they are – assumptions. But we cannot operate without adopting some epistemological and ontological position. The trouble may be that we do not always subject our particular philosophical choices to critical inspection and often make them by default. Major differences over these issues pervade areas such as organization theory and partly account for its diversity. Therefore, it is worth emphasizing that we cannot avoid making philosophical assumptions during our attempts at understanding what is happening, whether this process of perception and knowing is focused on some mundane aspect of our everyday worlds (now there is an assumption!) or upon the concerns of organization theory.

## Mapping some aspects of organization theory's diversity

Although their language and terminology vary, a number of philosophers (e.g., Bhaskar, 1978; Bernstein, 1983) have noted how three different understandings of science are created by different combinations of philosophical assumptions about ontology and epistemology. Each combination is expressed as a particular conception of the relationship between the subject (the knower, such as the scientist, organization theorist or any social actor) and object (what can be known about a specific area or phenomena such as organizations).

So, here we are concerned about outlining how different combinations of these philosophical assumptions influence how organization theorists undertake their subject, including how they:

1. understand what it is they are studying (e.g., organizations)

2. think they can engage with and produce accounts that explain organizational phenomena

3. ask certain kinds of research questions to which they try to provide answers.

Therefore, we are now concerned with explaining how and why the only too evident variation in organization theory happens, including how different schools of thought arise and compete with one another over how to 'do' organization theory. We will describe and explain how these different schools of thought arise because their protagonists deploy different sets of philosophical assumptions about epistemology and the ontological status of social reality. Variation in these philosophical assumptions justify different ways of doing organization theory because they influence how organization theorists understand their relationship with organizations and how they see what organization theory is all about. These philosophical differences are also at the heart of disputes about what we think science is – or should be – and cannot be.

## Positivist protagonists: the truth is out there, and we can objectively know it

For instance, as illustrated in Figure 1.7 (overleaf), there is one very important group of protagonists, often called positivists, who have played a key part in influencing how organization theory has developed. Positivism is the dominant philosophical stance in a great deal of organization theory. Positivists assume that there is a point at which an observer can stand back and objectively or neutrally observe what they understand to be an external reality. In doing so, provided that the correct methodological procedures are followed, positivists think that they can observe without influencing what they observe. This allows the scientist to objectively test theory by gathering data, or the facts that can be collected through observation of an external objective reality. This notion is embedded in the term 'positivism', which was developed by the French philosopher Auguste Comte. For Comte (1853), truth resides in the observer's passive registration of what he called the 'positively given', meaning the facts that we can collect from external reality through observing it. Hence, the truth of competing theories may be assessed through analysis of the extent to which the theory in question corresponds with or is supported by the empirical facts (or data) collected by the scientist from an independently existing reality. These facts are assumed to be 'given' and can be neutrally accessed provided that the correct methodological procedures are followed by the scientist in collecting the necessary *empirical* data from 'out there'.

Hence, the assumption here is that the facts or data can – and indeed, must – be used to objectively test theoretical propositions and their knowledge claims about

**Ideas and perspectives: positivist philosophical assumptions**

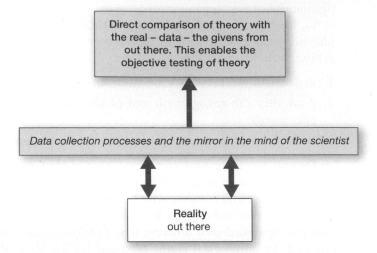

Figure 1.7: Positivist philosophical assumptions – the truth is out there and we can objectively know it.

the world. Those that do not pass this test of empirical evidence may then be rejected as false. This 'empiricist' idea has long been the keystone of much scientific thinking and practice. It is also the keystone of much common sense epistemology – 'the facts speak for themselves'. Without that keystone, positivism collapses. For positivists, if a phenomenon cannot be directly accessed through our sensory apparatus, if it cannot be observed in some way, then we must question whether or not it exists. Things that cannot be observed must be the result of superstition, dogma, myth or fantasy, such as unicorns, ghosts, spirits, UFOs, demons, dragons or gods, and therefore has nothing to do with proper science.

However, our senses – our ability to see, hear, touch, smell or taste – might be misleading; therefore, it is important that scientists remain distanced from the data they collect in order to retain objectivity, avoid bias and avoid the danger of contaminating the data through the very act of collecting them. For positivists, by using the correct methods for collecting the data that await discovery 'out there', they can ensure objectivity.

According to Rorty (1979, p. 46), a leading contemporary philosopher and critic of positivism, this approach metaphorically assumes that there is a 'mirror' in the scientist's mind that just needs to be methodologically polished so that what is out there may be reflected in the scientist's sensory apparatus. Crucial here is the role of language in enabling a neutral representation of reality. We must be able to neutrally describe the facts through language if we are then going to be able to see whether or not these claims about the world do fit the empirical facts that we have discovered and collected from 'out there'.

In sum, positivists assume that it is possible for suitably trained scientists to compare any knowledge claim to the 'real' facts and through this data collection, judge its accuracy and truthfulness. Based upon this comparison to the real, if the theory survives this process of testing, it may then, in principle, be used to guide practice. Conversely, we need to be very wary of theories that have not been or cannot be empirically tested. Hence, positivism combines what we have called an objectivist epistemology and a realist ontology (Figure 1.7).

It is widely agreed that positivism is pivotal to management for two reasons. First, as Thomas (1997) notes, 'Positivism holds the promise of techniques for controlling the world' (p. 693) with which managers expect to be provided. Second, provided that managers appear practically to use neutral scientific knowledge, their subsequent practices are more likely to be authenticated as merely technical activities grounded in their objective representations of reality (Grey, 1997; Grey and Mitev, 1995). They are experts who know things other people do not and are just doing what has to be done. Thus, managerial prerogative – management's right to manage together with the power and social standing that accompanies it – is morally supported by a persuasive claim to an expertise grounded in superior scientific knowledge. In turn, this knowledge depends upon the philosophical assumption (Figure 1.7) that such neutral access to reality is actually possible in the first place.

So, as we noted earlier in this chapter, with the transfer of organization theory into business schools during the 1980s, especially in English-speaking countries, Stern and Barley (1996) argue that there was an increasing promotion of this positivist approach in order to gain credibility amongst students and their new colleagues from other management disciplines. This striving for scientific respectability in positivist philosophical terms also further narrowed organization theory's scope away from complex questions about how organizations impacted upon society to smaller scale problems. These smaller scale problems are more amenable to precise definition and investigation using statistical techniques, centred upon positivist demands for theory testing and the generalizability of findings. Of course, not all positivists have lost this critical edge to their work by adopting a managerialist stance.

For instance, much of Marxist organization theory (e.g., Braverman, 1974) obviously does not have a managerialist mandate and instead attempts to empirically demonstrate how capitalist organizations dominate and exploit employees in different ways. Much of management is thought to be complicit in this process, sometimes being a willing victim, or as in the case of the higher echelons of management, direct beneficiaries. Nevertheless, much of Marxist organization theory is equally positivistic in its approach to social science, the key difference being how Marxists understand the makeup of society and its organizational institutions as being riddled with class-based antagonisms, inequality, exploitation and conflict. Because of these characteristics, organizations and society are generally in need of radical change and transformation. Moreover, organization theory must also try to demonstrate the ongoing existence of this exploitative status quo rather than being the handmaiden of inequality and exploitation and thereby colluding in their maintenance. Given this stance, it would initially seem that there are clear similarities between Marxist theory and critical theory. There are similarities, but there are also significant philosophical differences because critical theory rejects positivism (we shall explore this further later in this chapter).

## Philosophical disputes around the role of the subjective in science

Other disputes also rage with the positivist–modernist approach that lead to some significant differences in how research regarding organizations is undertaken and the kinds of theory that are produced. One key area concerns the importance of human actors' subjective processes of interpreting and understanding what is going on around them in their construction of behaviour in organizations. This issue concerns rival assumptions regarding how we can legitimately explain human behaviour in the social sciences, something that has caused much controversy in areas such as organization theory. This dispute is illustrated in the two types of explanation of human behaviour shown in Figure 1.8.

With type 2 positivist explanations illustrated in Figure 1.8, organization theorists have a direct concern with accessing, understanding and describing our internal logic or frame of reference that, it presumes, leads us to behave in the way we do. How and why we behave the way we do is presumed to be an outcome of how we subjectively make sense of or interpret our surroundings. Human behaviour cannot therefore be explained as the necessary outcomes of, or effects of, external stimuli or causes. Hence, being able to access any actor's subjective cultural world in an objective fashion is the key to any theoretical explanation of that actor's organizational behaviour. However, this 'interpretivist' philosophical stance argues that the actors' subjective realm is not only important to any adequate theoretical explanation of their behaviour but it is also possible to access that realm, describe it and explain members' organizational behaviour in an objective manner. Of course, this process is based upon the provision that the correct methodologies are used.

However, with type 1 positivist explanations, such accessing of actors' subjective, culturally derived perspectives is considered inappropriate. This is because it is presumed that this cannot be done in a direct, objective, neutral manner, regardless of the methodology used. In other words, according to these mainstream positivists, such 'inner' subjective processes are taken to be empirically unobservable and therefore inadmissible as genuinely scientific explanations of what occurs in organizations. Hence, type 1 positivists argue that science must limit itself to the directly observable stimuli that are seen to cause human behaviour, which therefore becomes construed as necessary responses, by preferably using quantitative measures of such phenomena. In doing so, they seek to analyse cause-and-effect relations with little regard for the subjective states of the individuals involved. Investigating human subjective processes, because they are thought to be unobservable, is therefore thought to be dangerous because it might introduce into science theories that are based upon the very guesswork (and possibly, dogma) of which type 1 positivists want to rid science.

Nevertheless positivist organization theory has a significant *interpretive* tradition within it that has a direct interest in building theories out of accessing organizational

**Ideas and perspectives:** The role of the subjective in human behaviour

**Type 1 explanations of behaviour** (according to mainstream positivism)
*Human behaviour is best understood as a necessary response, or effect, directly caused by an external stimulus, or set of stimuli:*

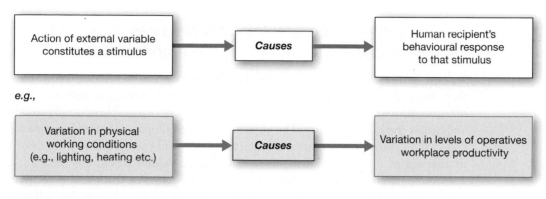

*e.g.,*

*Versus*

**Type 2 explanations of behaviour** (according to interpretivism)
*Human behaviour, or action, is best understood as an outcome of the culturally derived meanings, interpretations and understandings human actors attach to what is going on around them:*

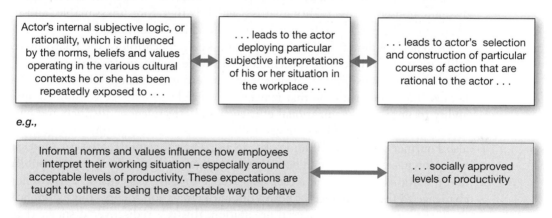

*e.g.,*

Figure 1.8: The role of the subjective in human behaviour.

actor's subjective cultural meanings to explain their actions in varying organizational contexts. Their dispute with type 1 positivists–modernists is therefore more about *what* is important in understanding organizations and the behaviour of their memberships and what is *directly* observable in a neutral fashion. Despite these disputes, important philosophical continuities are found between the two approaches to organization theory. For instance, as Schwandt (1996) puts it, the positivist 'third-person point of view' is retained by interpretivists as they continue to think that researchers can neutrally collect data. It is the source of this data that is different from mainstream positivism (p. 62; see also Knights, 1992; Van Maanen, 1995) in that these interpretive researchers argue that they can neutrally access actors' subjective understandings by using particular methodologies. Hence, they share mainstream positivism's ontological idea that there is a world out there that awaits discovery and epistemological exploration in an objective manner by collecting data – the positively given. The source of this data about the world is the key dispute with mainstream positivism. Around these issues of epistemology and ontology, further philosophical disputes arise within organization theory.

## Epistemological and ontolological disputes: how can we ever know the 'truth' and is there an 'out there'?

As two famous British organization theorists (Grey and Willmott, 2002) explain, there has been some recent erosion of the positivist epistemological approach by organization theorists who have dismissed the possibility of being able neutrally to observe and access the facts of reality. The objectivist epistemological assumption that we can collect data through observation of external reality without contaminating those data by that act of observation is dismissed as both naïve and dangerous. Instead, these epistemologically subjectivist theorists argue that notions of truth and objectivity are impossible, so they must be merely the outcomes of the prestigious, but self-serving, rhetoric engaged in by positivistic social scientists. Positivism creates, according to this philosophical stance, a powerful masquerade that hides the inevitable partiality of the theorist. Crucially, positivists provide their claims about organizations with an aura of detachment and independence that creates the impression that the knowledge being disseminated concerns 'reality as it is', which is therefore unassailable, and hence 'there is no alternative' to the organizational practices it supports.

Elsewhere, Willmott (1998) argues that a key implication of the relatively recent infiltration of a subjectivist epistemological stance in organization theory is the creation of a 'new sensibility' that potentially undermines managerial authority. This is because the popular notion that management's right to manage is founded upon its ability to improve organizational efficiency and effectiveness, justified and enabled by objective analyses of how things really are, has to collapse epistemologically (see also Fournier and Grey, 2000; Locke, 1996). Their inevitably subjective interpretations of what is going on can be no better than any other person's equally subjective interpretations. Despite the recent appearance of this 'subjectivist' epistemological challenge to the dominance of positivism in organization theory, and by implication the questioning of its managerial orientation, this is a rediscovered stance that has long been evident in philosophy (e.g., Foucault, 1977; Habermas, 1972, 1974; Kuhn, 1970; Ortony, 1979; Rorty, 1979).

The argument here is that when we engage with phenomena, we inevitably interpret them using different cultural and linguistic tools that carry social bias based upon our backgrounds. These ways of engaging influence everyone's perception of what we often take to be 'out there'. The idea is that we are not – and cannot be – passive receivers of sensory data no matter what methodology we use to enable this in developing our theories. Hence, the positivist ideal of a neutral, detached observer was a myth. Furthermore, it was a dangerous myth because it allowed people to claim objectivity when none existed. Rather, according to this subjectivist epistemological challenge to positivism, we inevitably apply various inferences and assumptions, which either:

A. Mediate and shape what we see like a set of filters, or lens, leading us to interpret the external social world in particular ways (a stance typical of critical theory, which is discussed in Chapter 8). The truth might be 'out there', but we can never know it.

*Or:*

B. Create what we see, in and through the very act of perception itself (a stance typical of the type of postmodernist theory discussed in Chapter 6). There is no 'out there'. What we take to be truth comes from within us.

---

### Stop and think

Return to the Exercise on page 30. How does how you see the figure illustrate either position A or B above?

---

In either case, what we perceive is a process in which we are active participants, not neutral receivers or passive observers of sensory empirical data, as all positivists have to claim. So, although both positions A and B above entail subjectivist episte-mological assumptions, in each case a very different set of assumptions is being applied regarding the ontological status of social reality.

In other words, the key disagreement between critical theorists and postmodernists is centred upon the ontological implications of their shared subjectivist epistemological commitments. Whereas critical theorists believe there is an 'out there', postmodernists do not. This is something that leads to very different forms of organization theory.

In position A above, which is typical of approaches such as critical theory, the outcomes of research are influenced by the subjective stance of the organization theorist, and his or her way of engaging with organizations. Hence, we are not passive media for the collection of data. Rather, when we engage with the world, we produce different versions of an independently existing reality that we can never fully know. Basically, the truth might be out there, but we can never know it because we always see things through the filters we inevitably deploy in making sense of what is going on. These culturally based, subjective, sense-making processes create reality for us. However, because cultures vary, so, too, does reality for us. People from different cultures live in different socially constructed realities, and we have no effective way of judging between them because we cannot confront them with the facts of 'reality as it is', as positivists demand. Nevertheless, these socially constructed realities guide how we do things, and they have practical consequences.

In this manner, critical theory adopts what is called a 'phenomenalist position' in which, influenced by culturally derived interpretive processes, human knowing shapes our realities. Reality is thus assumed to be a social construction, something we cannot avoid doing. But the versions or images of reality we deploy are always changeable because the social circumstances of their production change. As 'reality for us' changes our organizational practices, our definitions and understanding of organizational problems also change. Of course, this also raises questions regarding whose particular version of reality is dominant in any particular social context and how this impacts on what we do. Moreover, it raises questions regarding why a

**Ideas and perspectives: critical theory**

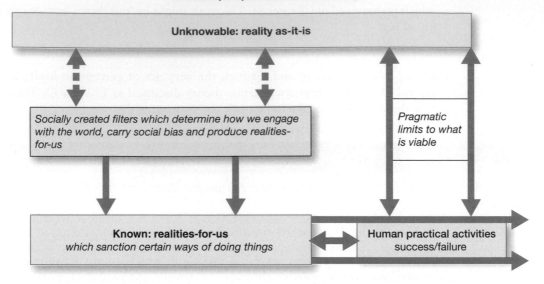

Figure 1.9: Critical theory: the truth is out there but we can never know it.

certain version of reality is dominant and accorded credibility at the expense of the alternatives that are always possible along with the alternative practices that those different ways of knowing enable. Any rendition of reality has practical consequences in that it guides what we know about and what we can do in the world. However, doing practical things, albeit guided by our subjective 'realities for us', does not mean that anything will always work: 'reality as it is' always puts practical limits upon what works or what is viable. In other words, we cannot wish 'reality as it is' away; anything does not work when it comes to our practical endeavours that are guided by our subjective apprehension of the world. This is because the real world will ultimately intervene and constrain what is practically effective, even though we can never directly know what this 'reality as it is' might be and must remain forever stuck in a 'reality-for-us'. The combination of realist ontology and subjectivist epistemology that underpins critical theory is illustrated in Figure 1.9.

## Ideas and perspectives

## Critical theory

The truth about the social world may be 'out there', but we can never know it because we lack a neutral observational language. Therefore, we are always stuck in a subjective socially constructed 'reality for us'. We therefore must try to be aware of how our subjective baggage, which is always operating in some form, influences how we make sense of reality. By interrogating that baggage, through critical reflection, we might be able to change how we make sense of the world, and a range of new interpretations may become possible with their attendant practices. In critical theory, this is often called a critical consciousness. However, in this respect, anything does not go (or work) because the tolerance of reality will always impose pragmatic limits upon what is practically viable when it comes to our reality for us.

Position B, as already mentioned, is a subjectivist ontological and epistemological position typical of approaches such as postmodernism. Here, what we take to be reality is itself created and determined by our subjective acts of perception. Our sense-making literally creates what we see and know about the 'world'. So here, the social world is not there waiting for us to discover it; rather, the act of knowing creates what we perceive. We just assume that it is real and outside of, or separate from, us. So, in contrast to the philosophical position illustrated in Figure 1.9, postmodernist organization theorists have put forward a subjectivist epistemological stance that they combine with a subjectivist ontological stance.

Just as critical theorists do, postmodernists reject positivism as naïve and dangerous because they, too, argue against the possibility of an objective empirical science of organizations. For postmodernists, efforts to develop theories that reveal causal relationships through accumulating objective empirical data are a forlorn hope. This is because the norms, beliefs and values encoded in the academic disciplines of social scientists act to constitute or create what they take to be social reality in the same way that the cultural dispositions of any actor influences what they perceive. So far, this is very similar to critical theory. However, many postmodernists go further in that they argue that in knowing the world, we do not describe what is out there, nor do we create socially constructed versions of what is out there. Instead, we literally create what we take to be reality through that act of knowing. Therefore, everything is *relative* to the eye of the beholder and the subjective means by which we organize what we perceive.

Postmodernists use the term *discourse* to refer to the subjective means by which people organize what they perceive. Discourses are subjective, linguistically formed ways of experiencing and acting and constituting phenomena that we take to be 'out there'. Such discourses are expressed in *all* that can be thought, written or said about a particular phenomenon. Moreover, by creating a phenomenon, discourses influence our behaviour. Therefore, for postmodernists, a discourse stabilizes our subjective apprehension of what is going on into a particular gaze by which we come to *normally* see and know ourselves, others and what we take to be social reality. A dominant discourse that is taken for granted by people and hence is not challenged limits our knowledge and practices and dictates what is legitimate and illegitimate. Inevitably, a dominant discourse excludes alternative ways of knowing and behaving. Alternative discourses and their associated practices are always possible; they are just suppressed. If we change the discourse, we literally change the reality. These always changeable realities are called *hyperreality* by postmodernists. But no discourse is thought to be superior to any other. There are no grounds for choosing between discourses. Everything is relative because there is no appeal to an independent reality to evaluate the truthfulness of our discourses. All there is are discourses; there is nothing beyond them. Hence, the truth cannot be 'out there' because there *is* no 'out there', just different social constructions that appear to be real. So here, social reality becomes an arbitrary output or creation of the organization theorist's and other actors' discursive practices. Ackroyd and Fleetwood (2000) summarize this philosophical stance:

> The social world is constituted completely, or determined by the concepts we hold . . . the social world is constructed entirely by us; it is merely a social construct; there is no extra-discursive realm that is not expressed in discourse; the

social world is generated in discourse. In sum there is held to be no objective social world existing independently of its identification by lay agents and/or social scientists' (p. 8).

This postmodernist stance is illustrated by Figure 1.10.

For the leading French postmodernist Baudrillard (1983, 1993), reality, as an externally existing reference point, is effectively destroyed because it is assumed there is nothing to see 'out there' except for simulations we have created and which appear to be real. Hence, the ontological commitment to reality as an independently existing real reference point for our organization theories is erased. As two British organization theorists have put it, 'the world is not already there, waiting for us to reflect it' (Cooper and Burrell, 1988, p. 100). For Chia (1995; 1996), it follows that any knowledge – organizational or otherwise – has no secure vantage point outside the discursive processes that create our social worlds. However, there is a tendency to externalize, objectify and then forget built into how we are the source of what we assume to be 'out there'. The result is that discursively produced hyper-realities are mistaken for an independent external reality: a 'false concreteness' is accorded to these subjective creations, which then appear as being natural entities 'out there' independent of our apprehension of them. Hence, the concern of the postmodernist is to describe these discursive forms, explore how they have developed and impact upon people, identify how they might change and then ultimately to challenge them so that alternative discourses, which are always possible, might then develop along with their particular hyper-realities. This is a very different agenda for organization theory to that envisaged by, for instance, postivists.

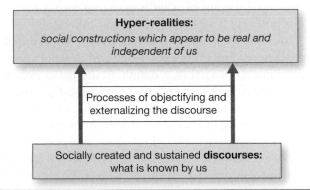

**Ideas and perspectives: postmodernism – the truth cannot be 'out there' since there is no 'out there'**

Figure 1.10: Postmodernism: the truth cannot be 'out there' since there is no 'out there'.

## A few words of warning about the term *postmodernism*

The term *postmodernism* can be used in two very different ways that are mutually antagonistic. Firstly, as we have shown, *postmodernism* can be used to refer to organizational analyses that apply antipositivist postmodern philosophy to challenge how we make sense of organizational phenomena. This approach, as discussed, undermines notions of objectivity and neutrality.

However, an alternative use of the term *postmodern* is often called the period or epochal view. This alternative approach takes as self-evident the notion that all organizations now confront a new time period during which the processes of production, distribution, exchange and consumption have not only dramatically accelerated but have also become increasingly diverse, specialized and temporary. This new historical period is often called the postmodern period, which requires new forms of organization and management. This is a time that arrived after the modern period of capitalist development and signals a change from relative stability to high levels of instability caused by certain recent changes in the world (e.g., globalization or rapid technological change). The result is the development of a form of capitalism, which has drastic implications for how we must organize. Within this period-postmodern view, it is assumed that organizations may be objectively analysed in a positivistic fashion in order to distil the organizational implications of this brave new world of destabilization and uncertainty. The result is a very different approach to organization theory to that which we have so far called postmodernism. It is one in which the theorist aims to produce organizational analyses that are concerned with providing prescriptions intended to help management to cope with the demands of this postmodern epoch (i.e., rational analyses of the implications of the postmodern period to thereby construct possible modes of postmodern management).

So be warned – much confusion can arise here because the same term, *postmodernism*, can be used to refer to two different theoretical approaches that are philosophically antagonistic. One use signifies a major break with positivism, and the second uses positivism to look at organizational change and adaptation in a presumed new period of capitalist development. The second would be dismissed by the first (i.e., the epistemological) group of postmodernists as merely an interesting discourse that leads to certain practices that themselves need to be challenged because they have significant practical consequences for how we organize – if we believe it.

## Overview of the structure and rationale of the book

Although dominated by a managerialist perspective, organization theory is a contested terrain where different schools of thought engage with the phenomena of organization in different ways. In part, this diversity expresses competing assumptions about what lies behind human behaviour and what needs investigating in order to explain it. In part, the diversity is also driven by competing assumptions about ontology and epistemology. These different philosophical stances have become embedded in different ways of researching, analysing and understanding what organizations are about. Our choices regarding these assumptions are ultimately arbitrary; there are no right or wrong philosophical assumptions, just different ones. Hence, one of the aims of this book is to encourage readers to reflect upon these issues and challenge some of their own taken-for-granted assumptions by confronting them with possible alternatives and how they have become embedded in different forms of organization theory.

The different combinations of philosophical assumptions discussed so far and illustrated by Figures 1.3 to 1.6 underlie different approaches to organization theory that are covered in the subsequent chapters of this book. The relationships between these different approaches and how they have a bearing upon the subsequent chapters in this book are illustrated in Table 1.1.

**Table 1.1** Knowledge constituting philosophical assumptions

| Chapter | The Nature of Human Behaviour or Action | Epistemology | Ontological Status of Social Reality |
|---|---|---|---|
| 2. Modernist organization theory: back to the future? | Causally determined | Objectivist | Realist |
| 3. Neo-modernist organization theory: putting people first? | Subjectively meaningful | Objectivist | Realist |
| 4. Neo-modernist organization theory: surfing the new wave? | Influenced by external causes but also subjectively meaningful | Objectivist | Realist |
| 5. Postmodernist organization Theory: new organizational forms for a new millennium? | Influenced by external causes but also subjectively meaningful | Objectivist | Realist |
| 9. The evolution of management as reflected through the lens of modernist organization theory | Influenced by external causes but also subjectively meaningful | Objectivist | Realist |
| 7. Reflective organization theory: symbols, meanings and interpretations | Influenced by external causes but also subjectively meaningful | Subjectivist | Realist |
| 8. Reflexive organization theory: critical theory and psychoanalysis | Influenced by external causes but also subjectively meaningful | Subjectivist | Realist |
| 6. Postmodernism as a philosophy: the ultimate challenge to organization theory? | Discursive | Subjectivist | Subjectivist |
| 10. Perspectives and challenges | <————————————> | | |

## Chapter 2: Modernist organization theory: back to the future?

Underpinning modernism is the notion of the 'ordered world', the notion that chaos and disorder can be managed through human will and intent. In organization theory, this suggests the development of systems, bureaucracies and approaches to management that enable the creation of order in an environment that is fundamentally disordered. Fundamental to modernist organization theory is that we can look at the intellectual world and organizations as systems. This can be seen in two ways. One is that we can look at a whole range of scientific activities, including the development of organization and management theory, as systemically interlinked. This has had a profound effect on the development of organization theory. The other is that we can look at organizations as systems that are more or less complex. A core feature of modernist organization theory is interest in the form of organization – the bureaucracy – and how bureaucracy is located in society. There is a fierce argument here. Is bureaucracy, with its impersonality and amoral approach and the development of the 'bureaucratic mentality', a force for evil, or is it, for these very reasons, the bulwark against chaos and disorder? Thoughtful modernist writers were themselves ambivalent about bureaucracy. Whatever its place in society, bureaucratic organization became the dominant form of design in many societies during the twentieth century with its predominant modernist premise that its form fits the function of effective and efficient organization. In this sense, bureaucracy can be seen as aesthetically satisfying and gives our lives structure and meaning.

## Chapter 3: Neo-modernist organization theory: putting people first?

Although modernism continued through the twentieth century and into the present century to be a powerful force in organization theory and in the development of organizations, a newer form of modernism began to emerge in the first half of the last century. This form of modernism, known as neomodernism, continues to be a pervasive force in organization theory. Neomodernism represents the development of organization theory that is concerned with putting people at the centre of the organization. In doing this, it uses insights and methods from the social sciences to develop a distinctive organization theory that can be applied to issues of management and leadership in organizations. In neomodernism, there is the development of interest in the ways that the values and beliefs of people shape and are shaped by their experience of organizational life, leading to an interest in organization culture, to the ways in which organizations 'need' to be designed around people and to understanding processes of change.

Within neomodernism there are two strong traditions. The human relations approach includes assertion that organizations need leadership and management with a human face in order to create the 'best' environment for people. A different approach, the 'democratic organization' approach, emphasizes concepts of empowerment of all members of the organization.

## Chapter 4: Neo-modernist organization theory: surfing the new wave?

Given that control has always been a central issue for organization theorists, this chapter identifies and explores the different forms of control and their interrelationships, evident in organizations. The chapter initially differentiates between formal and informal control before exploring three forms of formal control: bureaucratic, output based and cultural. It then locates the evolution of new-wave management in the development of cultural forms of control exerted by management over organizations' members. Two different explanations of this apparent development are presented. The first explains new wave management as a necessary response to increasing levels of uncertainty in the operation of many organizations, meaning that traditional forms of control are no longer viable. The second explains its emergence in terms of ideological and rhetorical shifts in management discourse. In exploring this second explanation, the theoretical origins of new-wave management are then elucidated by tracing its perspective back to Durkheim's concept of anomie and how it was subsequently used and applied to organizations by Mayo in the early part of the twentieth century and by North American neo-conservatives in the latter part of that century. Here the humanistic guise of new-wave management is challenged and how it has been expressed by the development of new forms of organization is initially considered.

## Chapter 5: Postmodernist organization theory: new organizational forms for a new millennium?

This chapter introduces the term *postmodernism* and contrasts two different approaches in which it is used: firstly, as a period characterized by increased dynamism and diversity in the environment with implications for how organizations should be designed, and secondly, as a philosophy or way of thinking. Chapter 5 then concentrates on the former and the latter is dealt with in Chapter 6. Chapter 5 traces the history of the term *postmodernism* and shows how postmodernism relates to postfordism, the postindustrial society and the information society, highlighting certain shared characteristics such as increased flexibility and multiskilling, the increased importance of knowledge work, the breakdown of organizational hierarchies, the differentiation of a core and peripheral workforce and the flexible use of labour.

Two themes recur throughout the chapter: firstly, the extent to which these changes are widespread. Although most authors recognize that we have seen a change in some manufacturing practices, some suggest the extent of change has been exaggerated and is based on a parody of what went before. In other words, they believe that fordist styles of production are being presented as far more homogeneous than was ever the case. Others have also pointed to the utilization and refinement of modernist or fordist practices in service industries such as call centres and also in manufacturing industries, which have moved to less industrialized parts of the globe. Hence, the picture of change appears more complex and nuanced. The second core theme concerns the extent to which postmodernity represents a break with the past or whether the practises we see variously defined as postindustrial and postfordist actually reflect a continuation and, in some cases, intensification of modernist organizational practises.

## Chapter 6: Postmodernism as a philosophy: the ultimate challenge to organization theory?

This chapter addresses postmodernism as a philosophy. The focus moves to postmodern theory or philosophy, providing us with a new theoretical position from which to try to make sense of the world around us. The chapter is divided into four sections. The first traces the development of postmodernism, outlines its core elements and differentiates postmodernism from modernism. A recurrent theme in postmodernism that is addressed is the rejection of the modernist 'grand' or 'meta' narrative (see Berg, 1989; Parker, 1992): that it is possible to develop a rational and generalizable basis to scientific inquiry that explains the world from an objective standpoint. The second section of the chapter outlines the work of the three key thinkers or the 'holy trinity' of postmodernism: firstly, Jacques Derrida and his work on the linguistic turn and deconstruction; then Jean Francois Lyotard and his rejection of meta theory; and finally, Michel Foucault and his work on power, knowledge and discourse. Each is examined separately because although they share some assumptions, the focus of their work is somewhat different. However, our aim is not to provide a complete overview of their work but instead try to pick out the core elements that have been used in organization theory. We move on to look at one area where postmodernism has had a huge impact, that of organizational culture, and then finally we address the challenges postmodernism poses for organization theory in the future.

## Chapter 7: Reflective organization theory: symbols, meanings and interpretations

An important strand in the development of organizational theory has been perspectives and theories that emphasis the ways human beings give their world meaning, that they are capable of understanding and reflecting on the complex organizations in which they work. This chapter explores the nature of this approach and its importance. It looks at two key schools (known as the symbolic interaction and phenomenology) that have underpinned the development of this perspective. The chapter then explores how these theories and perspectives help understanding of the ways that individuals and groups construct their organizational identities and the ways these identities become enmeshed in the organizational culture. The significance of these themes and theories is that they can help organizational members to develop deep understanding of, to reflect on, their circumstances in order to learn and develop.

## Chapter 8: Reflexive organization theory: critical theory and psychoanalysis

Although critical theory began to develop as a distinctive approach to understanding society in the 1930s, it was only in the 1980s that it began to become a force in management and organizational studies. Although it takes a radical view of the ways that organizations need to develop in order for them to enable members to be fulfilled as human beings, it enables us to reflect on the ways in which we need to constantly question issues of organizational design, leadership and communication in order to ensure that organizations can be creative and fulfilling places to work. The critical theorists saw psychoanalysis as a theory and method that would enable deep insight into, and exploration of deep issues in, institutions and society. This chapter shows how psychoanalysis enables us to develop deep insights into the ways the unconscious aspects of behaviour can deeply affect organizations and enable the development of practical solutions to these deep problems.

## Chapter 9: The evolution of management as reflected through the lens of modernist organization theory

The explicit aim of a great deal of mainstream organization theory is to meet the presumed needs and concerns of practising managers through conferring the power of control based upon a rigorous analysis and understanding of organizations and their memberships. In contrast, this concluding chapter turns to developing a theoretical understanding of managers themselves as a significant, identifiable organizational group, and management as a separate, hierarchical function in organizations. Hence, this chapter begins with an historical account of how and why management developed in the first place. It then moves on to consider what is called the managerialist thesis and how different interpretations of the significance of the development of management, as a specific function and social group, have impacted upon both how we understand management and how what is called new managerialism has recently developed. The diffusion of new managerialism in the workplace, the form it has taken and its effects upon employees and managers are also related to the rise of new-wave management. The chapter concludes with one contemporary theoretical challenge to managerialism – the economic case for organizational democracy. The theoretical rationale and content of this challenge is then explored as well as how it might founder because of institutional pressures that exist in contemporary organizations.

## Chapter 10: Perspectives and challenges

Here we revisit the perspectives discussed in each chapter by showing how each provides a different analysis of a short case study. We then move on to discuss current challenges to organizational theory, including the debate concerning paradigms and the practical utility of organization theory. This chapter looks briefly at emerging trends in organization theory before concluding with seven questions students of organization theory should reflect on for the field to develop.

## Concluding grid

| Learning outcomes | Challenges to the contemporary organization |
| --- | --- |
| Explore what is meant by the term *theory* by identifying what theories are and what they do. | Theories are pivotal to how we describe, make sense of and explain our experiences. They influence how we behave because they enable us to predict what might happen in different circumstances. Different theories enable us to understand what is going on in different ways and influence what happens to people. They also justify the things that we do and how we do them. |
| Consider how the phenomenon 'organization' has been defined in different ways. | The term *organization* is usually defined in terms of the coordination of people for the achievement of some explicit purpose or common goal. But can or should we assume that it is legitimate to conceive of organizations in this way unless we can assume some consensus amongst people about the purposes of their social interaction? |
| Identify why organization theory is important, especially in terms of how it impacts upon people through influencing their behaviour and practices. | Organization theory is about a significant aspect of our lives and has important practical consequences for how we lead our lives. All organization practices involve the deployment of some form of theory. The key questions are where do these theories come from, who gets to read and write them and what are their effects upon people? |
| Explore the relationship between organization theory and management practice and discuss some of the debates around this issue. | Much, but by no means all, organization theory has been developed to help managers manage. How do managers use these theories intentionally and unintentionally? Moreover, is there a danger that only theories that are ideologically aligned with the presumed perspectives and concerns of the powerful in organizations will prosper? What about the perspectives and concerns of the relatively less powerful in organizations? |
| Describe and explain the apparent diversity of organization theories in terms of competing philosophical assumptions. | Although dominated by a managerialist perspective, organization theory is a contested terrain where different schools of thought engage with the phenomena of organization in different ways. In part, this diversity expresses competing assumptions about ontology and epistemology that have become embedded in different ways of researching, analysing and understanding what organizations are about. Our choices regarding these assumptions are ultimately arbitrary; there are no right or wrong philosophical assumptions. |

## Annotated further reading

Stern and Barley (1996) provide an interesting account of how and why mainstream organization theory has developed both a positivist and managerialist orientation. Although limited to developments in North America, and hence should not be automatically generalized to, for instance, Western European organization theory, they nevertheless make some important observations about the social context in which this body of theory and knowledge has developed. For an outline of the characteristics of positivist organizational research and its continuing relevance to managerial practice, see Hogan and Sinclair (1996). Positivist methods, they claim, enable replicable and generalizable empirical validation to determine whether or not theoretical description, explanation and prediction of organizational behaviour is accurate. The findings are therefore pivotal in promoting organizational effectiveness through guiding managers' interventions into their organizations. However, Hogan and Sinclair's work is limited to appraizing mainstream organization theory.

In contrast, the first three chapters of Burrell and Morgan's seminal work (1979) argue that social theory in general, and organizational analysis in particular, can be understood in terms of a matrix of four paradigms based upon different philosophical assumptions about the nature of social science and the nature of society, which 'generate quite different concepts and analytical tools' (ibid, p. 23). This situation is nicely illustrated by Hassard's (1991) use of Burrell and Morgan's framework for producing four accounts of workplace behaviour in the British Fire Service. Each account was based upon organization theory and methodology consistent with one of Burrell and Morgan's paradigms. However, because of when they were written, both Burrell and Morgan's work and that of Hassard, do not cover fully the recent developments in organization theory.

So, for a cogent explanation of more recent developments in organization theory, we recommend Willmott (1998) in which he explains how there has been some erosion of the positivist consensus by scholars who have dismissed the possibility of a neutral observational language and who argue that notions of truth and objectivity are merely the outcomes of prestigious discursive practises which sublimate partiality. For Willmott, a key implication of this 'new sensibility' is the potential demise of managerialism. This is because any claim that management is founded upon a technical imperative to improve efficiency, justified and enabled by objective analyses of how things really are, epistemologically crumbles.

For a very different view of positivism, we recommend Donaldson (2003), who presents a vigorous defence of positivist organization theory through his critique of what he sees to be the relativistic and destructive incursions of postmodernism. His argument is that any attempt to follow postmodern philosophy is beset by problems because postmodernism, owing to its subjectivist epistemology and ontology, cannot move beyond attacking existing discourses to making a constructive contribution to organization studies.

## Discussion questions

1. There is nothing so practical as a good theory. Discuss with reference to organization theory.
2. Why is Silverman's critique of certain ways of defining organizations, such as that of Schein, so important?
3. How and why does organization theory vary so much?

4. With reference to Stern and Barley's work, explain why the dominant perspective in organization theory is managerialist.

5. Why do critical theorists and postmodernists both reject managerialism?

## References

Alvesson, M. and Willmott, H.C. (1996) *Making Sense of Management: A Critical Introduction*, London: Sage.

Ackroyd, S. and Fleetwood, S. (2000) 'Realism in contemporary organization and management studies', in S. Ackroyd and S. Fleetwood (eds), *Realist Perspectives on Management and Organizations*, London: Routledge.

Bakan, J. (2004) *The Corporation: The Pathological Pursuit of Profit and Power*, New York: Free Press.

Baritz, L. (1960) *Servants of Power*, New York: Wiley.

Baudrillard, J. (1983) *Simulations*, New York: Semiotext(e).

Baudrillard, J. (1993) *Baudrillard Live: Selected Interviews*, M. Gane (ed.), London: Routledge.

Bedeian, A.G. (2004) 'Peer review and the social obstruction of knowledge in the management discipline', *Academy of Management Learning and Education*, 3(2):198–216.

Benton, T. (1977) *The Philosophical Foundations of the Three Sociologies*, London: Routledge and Kegan Paul.

Berg, P.O. (1989) 'Postmodern Management? From Facts to Fiction in Theory and Practice', *Scandinavian Journal of Management*, 5(3):201–217.

Bernstein, R.J. (1983) *Beyond Objectivism and Relativism: Science, Hermeneutics and Praxis*, Philadelphia: University of Pennsylvania.

Bhaskar, R. (1978) *A Realist Theory of Science*, 2nd edn, Brighton: Harvester.

Bhaskar, R. (1989) *The Possibility of Naturalism: A Philosophical Critique of the Contemporary Human Sciences*, 2nd edn, Brighton: Harvester.

Braverman, H. (1974) *Labour and Monopoly Capital: the Degradation of Work in the Twentieth Century*, New York: Monthly Review Press.

Burrell, G. and Morgan, G. (1979) *Sociological Paradigms and Organizational Analysis*, London: Heinemann.

Clegg, S. (ed.) (2002) *Volume 8: Central Currents in Organization Studies*, London: Sage.

Clegg, S. and Hardy, C. (1996) 'Introduction: Organizations, organization and organizing', in S. Clegg, C. Hardy and W.R. Nord (eds), *Handbook of Organization Studies*, London: Sage.

Chia, R. (1995) 'From modern to postmodern organizational analysis', *Organization Studies* 16(4):579–604.

Chia R. (1996) 'Metaphors and metaphorization in organizational analysis: Thinking beyond the thinkable', in D. Grant and C. Oswick (eds), *Metaphor and Organizations*, London: Sage, pp. 127–146.

Comte, A. (1853) *The Positive Philosophy of Auguste Comte*, London: Chapman.

Cooper, R. and Burrell, G. (1988) 'Modernism, postmodernism and organizational analysis: An introduction', *Organization Studies* 9:91–112.

Donaldson, L. (1996) *For Positivist Organization Theory*, London: Sage.

Donaldson, L. (2003) 'A Critique of postmodernism in organization studies. Postmodernism and management: Pros, cons and the alternative', *Research in the Sociology of Organizations* 21:169–202.

Dryzek, J.S. (1995) 'Critical theory as a research programme', in S.K. White (ed.), *The Cambridge Companion to Habermas*, Cambridge: Cambridge University Press.

Fournier, V. and Grey, C. (2000) 'At the critical moment: conditions and prospects for critical management studies', *Human Relations* 53(1):7–32.

Foucault, M. (1977) *Discipline and Punish: The Birth of the Prison*, Harmondsworth: Penguin.

Giddens, A. (1982) *Profiles and Critiques of Social Theory*, London: McMillan Press.

Giddens, A. (1984) *The Constitution of Society*, Cambridge: Polity.

Giddens, A. (1993) *New Rules of Sociological Method*, 2nd edn, New York: Basic Books.

Gill, J. and Johnson, D. (2002) *Research Methods for Managers*, London: Sage.

Grey C. (1997) 'Management as a technical practice: Professionalization or responsibilization', *Systems Practice* 10(6):703–726.

Grey C. and Mitev, N. (1995) 'Management education: A polemic', *Management Learning* 26(1):73–90.

Grey, C. and Willmott, H. (2002) 'Contexts of CMS', *Organization* 9(3):411–418.

Gouldner, A.W. (1959) 'Organizational analysis', in R.K. Merton (ed.) *Sociology Today*, New York: Basic Books.

Habermas, J. (1972) *Knowledge and Human Interests*, London: Heinemann.

Habermas, J. (1974) *Theory and Practice*, London: Heinemann.

Hassard, J. (1991) 'Multiple paradigms and organizational analysis: A case study', *Organization Studies* 12(2):275–299.

Hogan, R. and Sinclair, R. (1996) 'Intellectual, ideological and political obstacles to the advancement of organizational science', *The Journal of Applied Behavioural Science* 32:434–440.

Kassem, M.S. (1976) 'Introduction: European versus American organization theories', in G. Hofstede and M.S. Kassem (eds), *European Contributions to Organization Theory*, Amsterdam: Van Gorcum.

Kanter, R.M. (1989) *When Giants learn to Dance: Mastering the Challenge of Strategy, Management and Careers in the 1990s*, New York: Simon and Schuster.

Keleman, M. and Bansal, P. (2002) 'The conventions of management research and their relevance to management practice', *British Journal of Management* 13:97–108.

Keynes, J.M. (1936) *The General Theory of Employment, Interest and Money*, New York: Harbinger.

Knights, D. (1992) 'Changing spaces: The disruptive impact of a new epistemological location for the study of management', *Academy of Management Review* 17(3):514–536.

Kuhn, T. (1970) *The Structure of Scientific Revolutions*, 2nd edn, Chicago: Chicago University Press.

Lammers, C. J. (1990) 'Sociology of organizations around the globe: Similarities and differences between American, British, French, German and Dutch Brands', *Organization Studies* 11(2):179–205.

Lewin, K. (1951) *Field Theory in Social Science*, New York: Harper and Row.

Locke, R. (1996) *The Collapse of American Management Mystique*, Oxford: Oxford University Press.

Ortony, A. (1979) *Metaphor and Thought*, Cambridge: Cambridge University Press.

Marx, K. (1975) *Early Writings*, Harmondsworth: Penguin.

Parker, M. (1992) 'Post-modern organisations or postmodern organisation theory?', *Organization Studies* 13(1):1–17.

Parsons, T. (1960) *Structure and Processes in Modern Society*, New York: Free Press of Glencoe.

Peters, T. (1992) *Liberation Management: Necessary Disorganization for the Nanosecond Nineties*, London: Macmillan.

Peters, T. and Waterman, R. (1982) *In Search of Excellence: Lessons from America's Best Run Companies*, New York: Harper and Row.

Popper, K. (1967) *Conjectures and Refutations*, London: Routledge and Kegan Paul.

Pugh, D.S. (1977) *Organization Theory*, Harmondsworth: Penguin.

Ramos, A.G. (1981) *The New Science of Organizations*, Toronto: Toronto University Press.

Reed, M. (1985) *Redirections in Organization Analysis*, London: Tavistock.

Rorty, R. (1979) *Philosophy and the Mirror of Nature*, Princeton N.J.: Princeton University Press.

Rose, M. (1978) *Industrial Behaviour*, Harmondswork: Penguin.

Schein, E. (1970) *Organizational Psychology*, 2nd edn, Englewood Cliffs, NJ: Prentice-Hall.

Silverman, D. (1970) *The Theory of Organizations*, London: Heinemann.

Stern, R.N. and Barley S.R. (1996) 'Organizations and social systems: Organization theory's neglected mandate', *Administrative Science Quarterly* 41(1):146–163.

Schwandt, T.A. (1996) 'Farewell to criteriology', *Qualitative Inquiry* 2(1):58–72.

Tranfield, D. and Starkey, D. (1998) 'The nature, social organization and promotion of management research: Towards a policy', *British Journal of Management* 9:341–353.

Thomas A. (1997) 'The coming crisis of western management education', *Systems Practice* 10(6):681–702.

Usdiken, B. and Pasadeos, Y. (1995) 'Organizational analysis in North America and Europe: A comparison of co-citation networks', *Organization Studies* 16(3):503–526.

Van Maanen, J. (1995) 'An end to innocence: the ethnography of ethnography', in J. Van Maanen (ed.), *Representation in Ethnography*, London: Sage.

Weick, K.E. (1989) 'Theory construction as disciplined imagination', *Academy of Management Review* 14:516–531.

Willmott, H.C. (1998) 'Re-cognizing the other: Reflections of a new sensibility in social and organization studies', in R. Chia (ed.), *In the Realm of Organization: Essays for Robert Cooper*, London: Routledge.

# Chapter 2

# Modernist organization theory: back to the future?

## Introduction

This chapter explores one of the key social movements, known as modernism, which continues to influence the development of organizations and organization theory. Underpinning modernism is the notion of the 'ordered world', the idea that chaos and disorder can be managed through human will and intent. It is also a revolutionary world in which old ways of organizing disappear and there is a desire for constant questioning and challenge.

The modernist approach to organizations is based on a belief that if we adopt a rational, scientific approach to organizational life, our organizations can be effective and efficient machines for the delivery of industry, business and public services. A core feature of modernist organization theory is interest in the form of organizations. To the modernist, an organization, like any form of life, is a system that is made up of parts or subsystems. When these are combined, they make a whole that integrates into an organization that is greater than the sum of the parts. Modernists argue that for organizations to be efficient and effective, they need to be designed so that they have a clear structure, a rational sense of order and stability and clear lines of authority and accountability.

One way modernists propose these aims can be achieved is through a bureaucracy. For the modernist the bureaucratic form of organization with its hierarchical sense of order, with its carefully designed structures and ways of working, enables large organizations to respond to a rapidly changing external environment. Bureaucratic organization became the dominant approach to design in many societies during the twentieth century and continues into this century in new forms.

Alongside the development of bureaucracy came an understanding of the idea that the management of organizations through scientific means was of fundamental importance in the development of the ordered, controlled organization. The development of modernist management theory is a topic of such significance that it has a chapter to itself and it is explored in Chapter 9.

## Learning outcomes

- Discuss modernism as a distinctive intellectual and aesthetic movement in the twentieth century.

- Explore the central ideas of modernism in organization theory and relate these concepts to the twenty-first century organization.

- Analyse and explore the ways modernist organization theorists have a particular vision of the nature and being of organizations as ordered, controlled and rational places.

- Analyse and explore the ways modernist organization theorists have a particular vision of the ways that organizations are to be understood and analysed through scientific approaches.

- Discuss the ways in which modernists take different approaches to organization design as a means of developing effective ways of responding to the external environment.

- Discuss the ways in which modernists develop a 'scientific' approach to the understanding of organization culture.

## Structure of the chapter

- The chapter begins by explaining the nature of 'modernism' as one of the key social movements that began in Western societies in the early twentieth century but that has become of global significance. The modernist movement has been deeply influential not only in organizations but also in the creative arts, design and many other aspects of our everyday lives. This theme is illustrated by a discussion of modernist approaches to architecture as a concrete example of the different ways modernism is seen in the world about us.

- We move on to discuss how twentieth century academics developed an understanding of modernism and applied it to organizations. This enables us to explore some of the central issues that underpin the modernist approach to organizations. The most important issue in this chapter is the ways modernists see on the one hand challenge and change, and on the other order, rationality, systems and a scientific approach as key to organization theory.

- We then concentrate on the modernists' belief in the importance of systems as crucial to the understanding and efficient running of organizations. We then explore the ways that modernists see the well-ordered bureaucratic organization as the model for effective organization that can meet the demands of a changing world. We discuss some of the supporting arguments for and against this view. We end this discussion by analysing different approaches in modernism to the design of organizations. The chapter concludes with a review of the modernist understanding of organization culture as something that can be measured, managed and controlled.

## Modernist organization theory in context

## What is modernism?

The way the term *modernism* is used in different contexts is sometimes concrete and definite and sometimes elusive and contradictory. As we shall see as the chapter develops, *modernism* is sometimes used as a term to describe a world of order and rationality that is at the same time challenging and exciting. At other times, it is used to describe a world that is overcontrolled – that needs to be liberated from its dead hand. It can also be used to describe a world in which many are oppressed and elites are able to exercise power.

## Modernism and architecture

In the realm of the creative world, different aspects of modernism are perhaps best seen in architecture. Look at these photographs of buildings shown in Figure 2.1.

Dominant modernism: Trellick Towers, London

Modernism for the people: Park Hill Flats, Sheffield

Democratic modernism: De La Warr Building, Bexhill-on-Sea

Business modernism: Scandinavian style

**Figure 2.1:** Modernist architecture. (*Source:* top left © Hulton-Deutsch Collection/CORBIS; top right © Edifice/CORBIS; bottom left © Michael Nicholson/CORBIS; bottom right © Mikael Andersson/Nordic Photos/Getty Images.)

**Stop and think**

As you explore these photographs of modernist buildings, can you suggest some of the ways they share common features and ways they are different?

The key period for modernist architecture was from the 1930s to the 1980s, but it continues to be a powerful and controversial force. At its heart, modernist architecture is:

- Revolutionary in that it discards ornate architectures of the previous era and uses new materials and technologies to create buildings.
- Highly structured and ordered.
- Tends to be linear and where there are curves, they are designed to provide linkages with the linear. In this design, form always fits function. This means that there is an absence of decoration for the sake of decoration; everything has its place.
- The absence of nonfunctional decoration is a statement of the intellectual rigour of modernism. Every aspect of the design is carefully analysed to ensure that it has a function.
- Modernist architecture, in its search for functionality, purity of form and its appreciation for science and engineering, rejects previous approaches to architecture as overelaborate.
- Modernist architecture is dependent upon scientific approaches to engineering and design. Because of its dependency upon science and engineering, it becomes increasingly professionalized and specialized. At its most creative, it uses materials such as concrete, glass and steel in ways that express the purity of form. But to do this, architects need to have a deep understanding of these materials.
- As it developed, modernist architecture became a global phenomenon, both in developed and in developing nations. It became the universal language of architectural style and design.

This means that in terms of the aesthetic appearance of modernist buildings, there is a choice:

- On the one hand, modernist architecture can have great elegance and purity of line and appearance, so it is like a machine in which people can work, live or create in harmony with their surroundings without distraction.
- On the other hand, the aesthetic of modernism can be 'in your face', brutal and uncompromising in its statement of purpose and dominating in its impact.

This aesthetic is often related to political agendas in which, again, modernism can show two faces:

1. The American sociologist Charles Lemert (1997) discusses the ways the modernist movement in the United States (and indeed in Europe) became the focus for the creation of 'democratic' urban spaces with the belief that by building the biggest and best public housing, planners and architects could eradicate poverty and

human misery. This democratic ideal can also be used to develop public spaces where people can feel at ease with themselves and others, as in the example of the De La Warr building at Bexhill-on-Sea illustrated in Figure 2.1.

2. It can also be a symbol of oppression, of dominance by one group over another. As we can see in Figure 2.1, this can be oppression in the sense that the building itself can be seen as an instrument of power. The very scale of the building and its emphasis on efficiency serve as reminders that the individual member is just a small, insignificant part of the whole machine. This issue is developed in Chapter 7 in an exploration of different forms of modernist architecture as expressions of different approaches to organizations in the world of business and industry. Also, Chapter 6 discusses the idea that the demolition of a particularly monolithic modernist housing estate is claimed to represent the end of modernism and the emergence of the postmodern era.

## What is modernist organization theory?

In many ways, the issues we encounter in modernist architecture are echoed in modernist organization theory. Modernist organization theory both celebrates the nature of the modern organization but is also, at times, a critical exploration of the nature of organization itself.

Listed below are just some of the ways modernist organization theory fits into a general concept of modernism:

1. Modernist organization theory claims to be global; it can be translated into any culture.

2. A large body of modernist organization theory represents a rejection of the past: it represents a new way of understanding organization.

3. Modernist theory can provide support for the development of fair and equitable forms of organization in the sense that the modernist organization has clear lines of authority and order that are based upon logic and reason; it can also be the means for dictators to exercise power. The modernist organization can be portrayed as a force for the general social good; it can be portrayed as evil. It can be aesthetically satisfying or brutalist and 'in your face'.

4. Deeply embedded within modernist organization theory, as it develops, is the professionalization of the language of organization and of management. This 'language' is learnt through business studies courses, MBA programmes and 'management development'.

## The historical roots of modernist organization theory

In its historical context, the roots of modernist organization theory emerge from the 'European Enlightenment project' that dates from the eighteenth century. At its heart, the Enlightenment was an intellectual and creative movement concerned with a new understanding of humanity. It asserts that human beings can be free from the authority of the irrational power of monarchies and religion. We can use our powers of reason to obtain a true understanding of ourselves and society, and through science, the world of nature. The ideal of Enlightenment science is to use sensory observation – sce, touch, taste, hear, smell – to capture the very nature of the world and through the application of 'reason', develop and test theories about the world. The emergence of this scientific approach meant, as it gathered strength, that there was an understanding that we could understand both natural and social phenomena through the lens of science. The development of 'scientism' (which is further discussed in Chapter 8) had a profound effect on all aspects of Western life, including organizations.

## Classical theory of organization

One of the outcomes of the Enlightenment project was the development of thought about the nature of organizations, particularly in business and industry. This gave rise to an important precursor of modernist theory – what is referred to as the classical theory of organizations. There are two streams of thought in classical theory. The first, a sociological and economic approach from the late eighteenth and the early nineteenth centuries, was an exploration of the problems of living in a world in which the factory system was beginning to emerge and commerce, rather than the possession of land, was becoming an increasingly important force in society. The second strand of thought focused on the emergent role of the manager or supervisor as the means of controlling the factory.

It would be useful just to mention the central tenets of classical theory in order to demonstrate its relation to modernist theory. The key interests in classical thought, at least as far as organizations was concerned, were in the changing role of labour and property in shaping organizations and the role of organizations in the transformation of society from agrarian to industrial. The concept of division of labour lay at the very

| Case study | Making pins in Gloucester, England |
| --- | --- |

Pinmaking by hand started in the early 1600s in Gloucester, England. By 1802, there were nine factories in the city employing 1,500 people and exporting pins to North America and Spain.

It was an industry that required the skills of a number of different artisans. Adam Smith, the pioneering economist, considered pinmaking a classic example of the 'division of labour'. Just how many different artisans were involved in the chain of production is controversial. Some manufacturers seem to have managed with six workers, whilst others required up to 25. There may have been a tendency to sub-divide the processes as the eighteenth century went on. The workforce often consisted mainly of women and children who were paid very poor wages.

Several people had attempted the mechanization of pin heading, but finally in 1824, an American named Lemuel Wright patented his machine for making solid head pins. For a number of reasons, the industry in Gloucester declined. (*Source:* Based on www.livinggloucester.co.uk/made/pin)

heart of classical thinking about organizations. As factories developed, employees undertook minute tasks that contributed to the whole in the interests of efficiency. This was captured by the economist Adam Smith in his study of the pin factory that he wrote about in 1776 in *The Wealth of Nations*.

Different writers on organization theory (e.g., Hatch, 1997; Scott, 1964) identify different clusters of writers as belonging to 'classical' and 'modernist' schools of thought. Although the distinction between the two is blurred, it is important to remember that classical modes of thought can be seen to represent the emergence of a materialist, rationalist view of society and organizations that came into its fullest flowering in modernism.

## Stop and think

If you look at developing societies where there is a massive drift of people from agrarian communities into the city, some writers would suggest that this classical approach to organization is to be found in the 'sweatshops' that produce clothing, trainers and other goods. What do you think? We return in later chapters to this topic.

## Modernist organization theory: an overview

Although as we have seen modernism has revolutionary and challenging aspects, much modernist organizational theory emphasizes order, rationality and stability as ways of controlling and managing an ever-changing world. Berman (1983) captures the essence of many writers when he suggests that it is a force for unity and integration. At the same time, modernism also creates new forms of corporate power in which leaders and managers can assume dominant positions in the organization.

There are a number of ways to understand modernist organization theory. One particularly useful approach is to look at it from the interrelated perspectives suggested by one of the leading organization theorists in the United Kingdom, Michael Reed (1993). He uses two terms that were introduced in Chapter 1 (epistemology and ontology) and then discusses 'the technologies' that enable modernism to be embedded in the organization. These three levels are illustrated in Figure 2.2.

We shall look in what follows to the ways in which contemporary writers have explained the nature of modernist organization theory.

### The modernist ontology: the ordered world of the modernist organization

As discussed in the introduction, a definition of ontology is that it is 'the science or study of being' – the way different groups and societies understand the very nature of what it is to be a human being.

**The modernist ontology**
*(what modernists believe to be the very core of organizations)*

For example:

- The world is ordered and there are underlying systems that are there to be discovered.
- Individuals, organizations and societies can be ordered, rational and structured.
- The rational organization is preferable to organizations based on emotion or 'favouritism'.

**The modernist epistemology**
*(what modernists believe to be the way in which we know what are the truths, the facts of organization life)*

For example:

- We can use scientific techniques to understand and control the ways in which we can make our organization ordered and systematic.
- We can rely on the collection of empirical data that enables us to make decisions in a rational way.
- We constantly use systematic devices to understand what is happening in our organization and in the environment.
- We can use performance measures and other scientific means to get the best out of people.
- Truth is reached by rational thought rather than emotion and intuition.

**The modernist technologies**
*(what modernists believe to be the best ways to make sure that organizations are ordered and controlled)*

For example:

- The development of bureaucratic structure that is rational and ordered.
- The development of a management elite that has techniques that enable them to process information and to exercise rational control over members.

**Figure 2.2:** Three key aspects of modernism. (*Source:* Based on Reed, 1993.)

In this sense, the ontological position of modernism is the claims that are made by modernists about the nature of social reality – what exists, what 'reality' looks like, what kinds of 'things' make up reality. A key ontological premise in modernism is that the natural and social worlds are ordered and that the social world in particular can be conducted in a rational, structured manner that is not dominated by emotion. In this sense, the 'world is seen as a system which comes increasingly under human control as our knowledge of it increases' (Parker, 1992, p. 3). According to the sociologist Edward Lemert (1997), modernism can be seen as 'the dominant reality in the worldly affairs of Europe and North America . . . from the first age of explorations in the late fifteenth century through at least the two decades following World War II' (p. 26). In organizational terms, this dominant reality has been expressed in such matters as the way that, even today, many organizations are designed as hierarchical systems with an emphasis on order and control, undertaking processes of long-term, rational, strategic planning in an attempt to control the future.

As the modernist ontology develops, there are two major strands within it. One strand is that organizational life needs to be understood as a place in which rationality prevails. To illustrate this, we can look at the idea of the basic assumptions that may be seen to prevail in many organizations. These are assumptions (common sense ontologies, if you will) that condition the ways members of organizations interact with each other and understand the nature of the organization and the world outside the organization. The organizational psychologist Edgar Schein (1988) suggests that the key basic assumption in modernist organizations would be one based on the idea that human beings are 'rational economic'. This means that:

- The individual exists to strive to achieve personal material and economic reward but within a rational framework. People are rewarded for meeting organizational objectives; the individual has no obligation to others other than enabling *them* to achieve material gain. The rational economic model emphasizes the way the individual is responsible for shaping his or her destiny – but not at the expense of others because organizations depend on people being able to cooperate.

- In private sector business and industry, the rational–economic perspective emphasizes shareholder value. In public sector organizations there is an emphasis on the efficiency and effectiveness of the service.

- At a social level, it is a perspective that emphasizes free market, capitalist endeavour and an enterprise culture. In communist societies, the rational economic model was very important, but in those societies, it was geared toward the growth and development of the 'worker' and the state as the engine of rational economic growth.

The second fundamental issue in the modernist ontology is that we can understand the natural and social worlds as systems. Stars exist as single stars, but they also exist as constellations, systems of stars; the individual person exists in his or her own right and also exists in a system of family, organizational and social systems. The idea of exploring natural and social phenomena as systems is crucial in understanding modernist approaches to organization. The organization theorist Mary-Jo Hatch (1997) suggests that this idea of organizations as systems inspired much of the modern approach to organization theory and helps maintain continued support for modernism because it enables theorists and managers to understand organizations in all their complexity in a holistic, interconnected manner.

The ontological *spirit* of modernism expresses confidence in the future, in technology and in the human ability to create forms that enable progress and adventure. What is exciting about modernism is that it represents the triumph of the intellect over opinion and superstition. It holds promise for liberation from the oppression of living in a society in which people cannot be free from authority. What is threatening about it is that these positive features can themselves come to overwhelm the human spirit. Organizations can become obsessed with the search for data to justify action, what is known as 'paralysis through analysis'. They can become overconcerned with creating 'perfect systems' that do not meet the needs of a rapidly changing market. They can ignore emotion as 'irrational' and then discover that the causes of many of their key problems are deeply concerned with emotion.

The modernist ontology has been criticized in recent years. The writer on organization theory Michael Reed (1993) is typical of writers who suggest that the modernist ontology no longer fits the world of instant global communications and a world of organization in which it is recognized that our emotional lives are as important as our intellectual activity. Although it may well be that some of the more traditional aspects of modernism may be in decline, it is our suggestion that it can still be found in rich variety. The modernist ontology continues to be a pervasive force in the understanding of the nature of organization.

---

**Stop and think**

In this brief description of the ontology of modernism, we have shown a way of organizing in which there is an emphasis on order, the rational, and the objective. As you look at an organization known to you, to what extent would you say that these are important features of the organization? Where do you find them?

---

## The epistemological level: the scientific approach to organization

The term *epistemology* is taken from philosophy, and it draws our attention to a key issue in all our lives – how do we know that what we are hearing, reading, saying or writing is true? How do we discriminate between ideas that we consider 'correct' and those that we think are 'rubbish'? How do we distinguish between what we see as a 'rational' discussion and an 'irrational' argument, the scientific (e.g., astronomy) from the nonscientific (e.g., astrology)? During the course of the day, we are constantly making decisions and behaving toward others based on the ways we construct reality and give meaning to external events.

Modernism is, at heart, optimistic in its search for knowledge; it is based on the assumption that rational principles and practices of knowledge production and evaluation will lead to social progress and personal growth. However, many contemporary writers suggest that this optimistic outcome is not for all members of society. Rather, they suggest that in any typical modernist organization there is an elite of managers and professionals who are able to use their intellect and rationality in the pursuit of their work but that underpinning them are layer upon layer of employees for whom work is essentially boring and tedious (Parker, 1992).

At the core of modernism is a claim to understand nature, the world 'out there', and that the language used to understand organizations is objective, analytical and describes the world of the organization as if it were external from human emotion. The aim of modernist theories, epistemologically speaking, is to portray reality in deep and highly structured ways (Inns and Jones, 1996). From the perspective of contemporary critics of modernism, this means that issues of human action and a human understanding of organizations becomes lost. There is instead of this human understanding, the development of a language that resembles that of natural science. Members who speak this language or discourse are given higher status than those who express themselves in more emotional or intuitive ways or whose way of acting is not seen as 'rational'. This theme is discussed further in Chapter 8.

## Modernist epistemology

In the following example, we have taken some of the key ideas of epistemology and suggested the kind of response that a 'true modernist' might give to the situation:

- We have a view as to what separates 'what we can believe' from 'what we cannot believe'. *As a good modernist, I believe that all organizations need to have tight controls, clear structures, clarity of command and leadership and so on. I can point to many facts and figures and opinions of great writers to justify that belief. As a good modernist, I just cannot believe those writers who say that we ignore the emotional aspects of work at our peril. It is my belief that we should leave our emotions behind us when we come into the organization.*

- What we regard as rational or irrational depends upon the way we understand 'rationality' or 'irrationality'. *As a good modernist, I really believe that all this talk of recognizing the place of emotions in organizations rather than places where people work in clear structures and with clear role descriptions is just air-headed, irrational, romantic nonsense. Emotions are irrational aspects of organization. From my perspective, rational behaviour in organizations consists of collecting data before making key decisions; it is about thinking clearly and analytically about issues.*

- These understandings become so embedded that they are our 'common sense'. *Although I realize that some people criticize my view of organizations my view has stood the test of time. My view of the organizations gives me a comprehensive and coherent understanding of organizational life.*

- When we explore what is going on in the organization these common sense assumptions come into play. *When I am undertaking problem solving or exploring new ways of doing things, I do so through the lens of my modernist approach to understanding, to knowledge. As the philosopher Wittgenstein once said: 'The limits of my language are the limits of my world.' I cannot really understand the world in any other way than in this rational, scientific manner because my whole language is structured around it.*

In this section on modernist epistemology, we have, naturally, concentrated on the modernist. Think about friends and colleagues – and yourself.

Do you know people who you think, epistemologically speaking, are interested in 'the truth' as expressed in facts, figures and rational arguments and in certainty?

Do you have others in your circle that see truth as more about the stories that people tell and see truth in intuition and creativity?

What are the implications for these different approaches to truth in the ways people communicate with each other?

## Two epistemologies

To illustrate the radical differences between epistemologies, Figures 2.3 and 2.4 compare conventional models of Western medical practice and Chinese medicine.

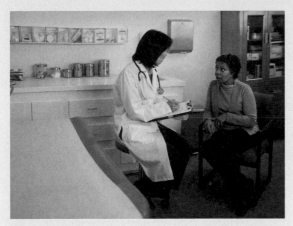

**Figure 2.3:** Modernist medicine. (*Source:* © Sean Justice/The Image Bank/Getty Images.)

Doctors working in a traditional modernist frame claim:

- That they are objective observers of their patients.
- Their collections of empirical data dictate their findings and the theories of medicine.
- That although 'mistakes' can happen, they are corrected by the surveillance of the wider medical community.
- That the scientific stocks of medical knowledge advance as doctors learn more about the social and natural world.

- To advance knowledge, they use strictly scientific methods based on models of natural science that rely on objectivity and quantitative measurement.
- For the modernist, the epistemological position entitles doctors to engage in the search for the essences of being – that they may lay bare the secrets of the universe through genetic engineering and other paths to discovery.
- A key epistemological premise in modernist medicine is that the body is a system but that it is important to attend to the component parts of the system rather than the 'whole system'. This leads to the development of specialisms in health care such as psychiatry, a whole cluster of specialisms in surgery and specialist clinics for the treatment of diseases (Figure 2.3).

**Figure 2.4:** Chinese medicine. (*Source:* © Bruce Hands/Stone/Getty Images.)

Traditional Chinese medicine (Figure 2.4) sees the body as an integrated whole:

- As all parts of the body are linked in obvious or subtle ways, disease may originate locally or in another area of the body caused by an imbalance in the whole system.
- The principal aim of traditional Chinese medicine in treating the whole person is to restore equilibrium between the physical, emotional and spiritual aspects of the individual.

(*Continued*)

Traditional Chinese medicine does not treat specific diseases as such:

- It regards each patient as having a unique pattern of signs and symptoms that constitute a clearly identifiable syndrome or pattern of imbalance.
- This distinctive diagnostic approach means that each patient is treated on an individual basis.

These two approaches to medicine illustrate, in some ways, diametrically opposed approaches to organization theory. The Western doctor may well be compared with the modernist approaches to the organization – the stress on rationality and scientific process in making decisions, the reliance on the expert (in organizations the manager or the management consultant), and the idea that management and organization can be regarded as 'science'. The Chinese approach to medicine reflects a different tendency in organization and management in the sense of looking for the uniqueness of situations, looking for balance between the physical, emotional and spiritual aspects of the organization. These are approaches to organization explored in Chapters 7 and 8 – reflective and reflexive approaches to the organization.

## The technologies: how modernists get things done

As we have seen, for the true modernist, organizations are at their best when they are orderly and rational places – but also with the potential for excitement and challenge. For them to exist in that state of challenging rationality, managers need to be able to develop an understanding of what is happening inside and outside the organization through the application of scientific methodologies. The next step is to make sure that organizations can operate and get on with their work. The processes that 'make it happen' are the technologies of modernism, the means, by which the modernist agenda is implemented in the organization.

Contemporary writers point to two key technologies that underpin modernism: *bureaucracy* and *modernist processes of management*. The term *bureaucracy* is discussed further in the course of this chapter. It refers to the core structure of the organization. The idea of bureaucracy is based upon the premise that organizations can operate *effectively and efficiently* through a clear sense of hierarchy and authority in organizations. In the bureaucratic organization every person is aware of the nature of his or her role and the tasks that are associated with that role. People are also aware of their status – from the most junior through to the chief executive – so that they are aware of their responsibilities and their place in the structure of authority in the organization.

This sense of order in the bureaucracy is accompanied by an understanding that organizations can be managed *effectively and efficiently* by people who understand that 'managing' is a special skill, who have a clear sense of the nature of the 'business' and who can make sure that these purposes can be fulfilled. The nature of 'modernist management' is discussed extensively in Chapter 9.

There is a tendency amongst contemporary writers to emphasize the negative effects of these technologies. Many writers from the early 1980s onward suggest that modernism encourages high levels of control in organizations. They argue that because the modernist form of organization has become so pervasive, that our lives become totally controlled by the organization (Burrell, 1998). This has happened both through the forces of bureaucracy and through the imposition of managers whose primary purpose is to control. In a paradoxical way, the modernist organization that we created in the first place in order to try to control a disordered world ends up by controlling us.

The sense that organizations are places in which we have to act in a disciplined way is heightened through systems and processes of management. The writer on organizations and management Gibson Burrell (1998) points to the ways information technology (IT) and IT networking can be seen as analogous to Foucault's (1977) image of the panopticon. This was a form of prison building first devised in the early nineteenth century. It has a central hub from which the rows of cells radiate providing warders with a total surveillance of the inmates 'that induces in the inmate a state of conscious and permanent visibility' (p. 202); the prisoners feel that they are constantly being watched. These issues and the implications of the idea of the panopticon are discussed in more detail in Chapter 6. The feeling of powerful control and constant surveillance that can be experienced in the modernist organization is captured in the Case study below.

## Case study — Automobile Association to log call centre staff's trips to loo in pay deal

David Hencke, Westminster correspondent
Monday 31 October 2005
*The Guardian*

Nearly 3,000 AA call centre staff are to be monitored by computers to ensure they do not take too many breaks, in a move forming part of a performance-related pay deal whereby workers get a total of 82 minutes' free time, to include lunch, tea breaks and visits to the lavatory. The GMB union criticized the move, which expects staff to make up lost time, saying workers were being treated 'like battery hens'. The motoring organization is the latest company to introduce dataveillance, a form of electronic tagging, to check on employees. Some supermarket suppliers have asked staff to put mini-computers on their arms so they can be directed to pick up goods faster from shelves. . . . The AA's new working practices are part of a planned £12m savings scheme which expects car breakdown personnel and insurance sellers – who earn about £13,000 a year – to be 'online' for 85% of the time they are at work. In the system, similar to that used in India by US firms to monitor call centre workers, the computer will flag when an employee is away from the desk. Conversations, calls and mealtimes can all be recorded.

*Source: Guardian Unlimited © Guardian Newspapers Limited 2005*

## Stop and think

Based on your own experience of organizations do you think that this view of organizations as concerned with surveillance and control is valid, or do you think it is an exaggerated view of the modern organization?

## The chapter so far

What we have tried to do in the chapter so far is to achieve two objectives:

1. The first is to give some context for the term 'modernism' by exploring the ways that the main tenets of modernism – the concern for order, rationality and systems – can be seen in the world around us.

2. We then developed an overview of three key aspects of modernism. We looked at its ontological underpinnings with the desire for order, rationality and the notion that we can create organizations that meet these needs. We saw how in terms of epistemology, knowledge and information are accumulated in a scientific manner and can be quantified. To make it all happen within the organization we saw how the design of the organization – the bureaucracy– was fundamental. We also mentioned that the other aspect of 'making it happen', the nature of management, would be dealt with in more detail in Chapter 9.

From these two explorations, we have derived some core characteristics of modernist organization theory. We could summarize these as a number of propositions:

• That the design of organizations needs to accord with the principles of system and rational order.

• That modernist organization theory sees change as inevitable but it can be undertaken in ways that are rational and essentially ordered. This is in the context that modernism is not just about order and rationality; it is also about change and indeed excitement.

• That individuals and groups in their relationship to the organization can be conceived as components of the machine.

• That although many of the critics of modernism believe that it has passed its sell-by date, many of the technologies of management and processes of organizational development continue to be underpinned by modernism.

To the modernist, however, the criticisms that modernism is obsessed with surveillance and control go against the rationality of the organization as a well-ordered machine that includes a stress on the creation of effective and efficient relationships between members and activities. The modernist would argue that it is preferable to develop ways of controlling the system so that it does not control us.

In the next part of this chapter, we shall pick up the key themes suggested by contemporary writers on modernism in order to develop an understanding of how modernist ways of thinking about organizations developed and the ways they continue to present challenging perspectives for today's organizations.

## How modernist organization theory continues to influence the understanding and exploration of organizations: the organization as system

In this section of the chapter, we will explore a fundamental aspect of modernist organization theory – the organization as a system. The core modernist themes of rationality and order and the search for knowledge that can be ordered in a 'scientific' manner are underpinned by systematic approaches. This can be thought of as:

- the need to categorize and prioritize data, information, facts and actions
- the need to diagnose problems in an ordered manner
- the need to see how different aspects of the organization interrelate with each other.

For modernists such as Chester Barnard (1938), the influential writer on fields as diverse as computer science, public administration, economics and philosophy, 'organizations are the least 'natural', most rationally contrived units of human association' (p. 4). For the organization to operate efficiently, there need to be means for the coordination of activities, and these need to be built into the system. Barnard realized that organizations are made up of individual humans with individual motivations and that every large organization includes smaller, less formal groupings whose goals need to be harnessed to those of the whole. The responsibility for the achievement of this is management's.

## General Systems Theory

The idea that the organization is a system has its roots in the more general proposition that *all* aspects of the natural and social world can be described as systems. This concept, called General Systems Theory, is generally attributed to the Viennese theoretical biologist Ludwig von Bertalanffy (1901–1972). This concept was developed during the 1950s and beyond into developing new understandings of the ways that society is organized within the social sciences and was a core aspect of modernist Organization Theory. General Systems Theory, as Bertalanffy and his followers developed it, was an approach to understanding the fundamental nature of 'systems'. This is the idea that biological organisms from the simple amoeba right through to a complex society are systems. They are 'systems' because they are made up of a number of different parts – the subsystems – that depend on each other and are related to each other, sometimes in very simple ways and sometimes in complex ways.

As we shall discuss later in this chapter, some systems can seem to be relatively 'closed' so that they seem to exist *relatively* independently of the outside world. Most systems are 'open' in the sense that they exist within an external environment to which they adapt and change. Most systems suffer disturbances from time to time. Something happens outside the system, or there is a change inside it. As disturbances occur, the cells in the organisms, the subsystems of the organization, change in order to adjust to the new circumstances. In General Systems Theory they do this adjustment in order to maintain the system as a whole. This relates to the idea that all systems want to attain a position of equilibrium; they have a sense of natural balance. If an organization grows and develops too quickly, it will become overheated and overcomplex; if an organization begins to wither and decline, it will lose support and resources and be unable to thrive. Overheated and failing organizations need, according to systems theory, to be able to re-establish equilibrium.

| Biography | **A key figure in systems thinking: Kenneth Boulding (1910–1993)** |
|---|---|

Kenneth Boulding was born in Edinburgh, Scotland, in 1910 but spent most of his career in the United States. He established his early career as an economist at a number of universities. As his work developed, he became increasingly interested in the idea that there could be a fusion of key ideas in biology and economics to produce what came to be known as 'evolutionary economics'. This concern to look at the human aspects of economics was reflected in his interest in ethical, religious and environmental issues in relation to economics. He was also a passionate advocate for the integration of the social sciences and the development of an understanding of the link between the social sciences and the study of organizations. He died in 1993.

The task of General Systems Theory was a very broad one, namely, to deduce the universal principles that are valid for systems in general. General Systems theorists believed that because there are basic similarities in the components of any system that they can create systems models that could be applied to any scientific endeavour from, for example, physics to organization theory. This desire to create overarching models and systems to explain everything lies at the heart of the modernist approach. Although interest in General Systems Theory really started in the years after World War II, it has remained a powerful force in the development of organization and management theory.

In a landmark article published in 1956 in the American journal *Management Science*, Boulding took the core proposition of General Systems Theory and argued that a fundamental link exists between the approaches to systems that are to be found in natural science and in different types of organization.

## General Systems Theory builds hierarchies of knowledge that relate to different levels of sophistication in understanding organizations

Boulding's key contribution to the development of General Systems Theory, as far as modernist organization theory is concerned, was to arrange fields of knowledge in a hierarchy of complexity. He derived nine levels of complexity of systems. Table 2.1, which is derived from Boulding's thinking, shows these nine levels. The second column shows the ways that the levels relate to science in a general way. In the third column, we have added to Boulding's model a very brief indication as to how these levels relate to different sorts of organization. Level 1 represents subsystems that make up the system as a whole; level 2 represents the classical approach to organization (as it is found in a twentieth century organization) already discussed; levels 3 and 4 lie at the heart of the modernist understanding of the organization. The remaining levels in Boulding's model take us beyond the modernist conception of organization into other theories and systems of organization that are discussed in later chapters of this book.

**Table 2.1** Hierarchy of science and organization theory

| The hierarchy | General systems theory | Organization theory |
|---|---|---|
| Level 1: **Frameworks** | The basic static patterns that are to be found in the natural world – simple systems, the shape of phenomena, the map, the anatomy of the human being. | This is the basic system – the goals of the organization, the ways the organization adapts to changes, the way the organization members integrate with each other and so on. |
| Level 2: **Clockwork** | Moving from the static to the **machine-like dynamic**. A world of 'harmony and invention', of 'cause and effect', of engineering, of the search for equilibrium. | This is a very smooth-running organization in which everything is in its place, everyone knows his or her role and the external environment does not change significantly, so there is no major turbulence to disturb the production. |
| Level 3: **Thermostat** | This level represents the start of the transmission and interpretation of information in which the system itself defines 'equilibrium' – a sophisticated machine. | Here members begin to communicate about the nature of their work. Internal and external pressures cause limited change, and it is the role of managers to make sure that the organization maintains its stability. |
| Level 4: **The open system** | The beginning of life as the organism interacts both with its environment and within itself in complex (and sometimes unpredictable ways); it can maintain itself and reproduce. | The organization is becoming much more dynamic and there is much more change going on as the external environment changes, but the organization still operates as a system. |
| Level 5: **The botanical gardens** | The cells of life are differentiated, and there is greater complexity. Information seeking and communication occur between the different cells. | The organization is a 'living system' with considerable diversity. The organization occupies its own niche in the natural order and can either grow or die. This theme is discussed in Chapter 3. |
| Level 6: **The zoo** | The animal world – information seeking, structuring (limited) knowledge and degrees of interpretation. Greater levels of unpredictability of behaviour – the 'herd instinct'. | The organization is a place in which there are real human beings, but at this level, they behave in ways that conform to their group identity – 'workers', 'managers' or 'leaders'. This theme is discussed in Chapter 3. |
| Level 7: **The individual world** | The development of self-consciousness, the reflective ability. Language, ability to symbolize, to communicate. | Organizations are places that are made up of individuals with their own needs and desires; if organizations are effective, they are good at meeting these individual needs. This theme is discussed in Chapter 7. |
| Level 8: **The social world** | The relationship of the individual to social organizations and society; the development of culture. | Organizations are places in which groups and the social element are very important. Effective organizations recognize this. This theme is discussed in Chapter 8. |
| Level 9: **The transcendental** | Asking 'impossible questions' about the meaning of life – the spiritual dimension. | Organizations are places where members can achieve the true meaning of life, where they can reach their potential. This theme is discussed in Chapter 8. |

*Source:* Based on Boulding (1956).

In the next part of this chapter, we have taken three of the levels discussed by Boulding and show how they are of considerable importance in the development of modernist organization theory and the ways they are of relevance in contemporary organizations. We start with an introduction to the key elements of a human, social system and relate this to organization.

## The basic systems of the organization: what every human system must have to survive

As this part of the chapter develops, we shall give a number of examples of organizations as systems. To give a flavour of the idea of systems in organizations we start by referring to one of the key concepts suggested by the sociologist Talcott Parsons. He suggested that every human system – from the individual to the family to the organization to the society itself – needs four key components for it to survive (Parsons, 1951). These are called the functional imperatives (Figure 2.5).

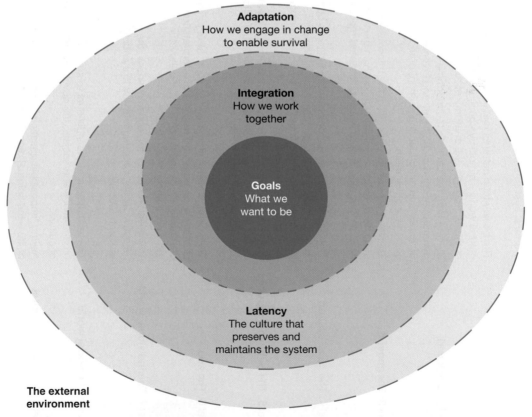

**Figure 2.5:** What every organization needs: the functional imperatives. (*Source:* Based on Parsons, 1951.)

| Biography | **A key figure in systems thinking in the social sciences: Talcott Parsons (1902–1979)** |
|---|---|

Talcott Parsons was born in 1902. He was one of the leading sociologists of his generation. He began his career as a biologist and later became interested in economics and sociology. He studied in Heidelberg, Germany. He taught sociology at Harvard University from 1931 until his death. He published many books and articles, including what was probably his greatest academic achievement, *The Social System*, in 1951. As with many other authors of that period, he wanted to integrate all the social sciences into a science of human action. As a social scientist, he could be described as a modernist in the sense that his work emphasizes the nature of order in society and his search for the ways different aspects of society serve a function or purpose. He argued that the crucial feature of societies, as of biological organisms, is that they are systems that seek to preserve a stable state of being or equilibrium. He died in Munich in 1979.

The key components that organizations need to have in order for them to function effectively are:

- They have a set of **goals**. This means that the organization is aware of its core purposes, why it exists and what it wants to achieve. When an organization has this sense of its goals, it then has a sense of equilibrium, a sense that it is not becoming overheated on the one hand or failing to thrive effectively on the other. In modernist organizations the part of the organization that is responsible for setting these goals is usually the senior management. At the same time, organization members have their personal goals and an awareness of the goals and aspirations of friends and colleagues (Sorge, 2002). In this sense, we can imagine the organization as having within it this rational, ordered, hierarchical design with everything in its place – a magnificent clockwork mechanism – that is, to a greater or lesser extent, affected by the strengths and limitations of the ways human beings live within the system.

- There are means by which **integration** of the different groups and subsystems in the organization takes place. These processes of integration ensure that members are able to work together in a cooperative manner. In many modernist organizations, this becomes the key work of the administrative staff or of the IT infrastructure.

- They have what Parsons called **latency**. This is something that is hidden from view; it is part of the 'taken for granted' aspect of the organization but is where the established patterns in the system are maintained and kept safe; it is the culture of the organization. These are also the processes that are deeply embedded in the organization of managing conflict.

- Processes of **adaptation** are built into the organization. This means that the organization can change in order either to maintain equilibrium or move to a higher state of equilibrium. In modernist organizations functional departments enable this to happen. It can be the marketing department aware of changes in the external environment, the human resources department of shifts and changes within the organization and so on.

Within the modernist view of the world, the important aspect of these four functional imperatives is that if they are in place they give to organizations (or any human system) a sense of order and balance so that even processes of change are regulated and planned and do not push the organization too far from its equilibrium. From a systems perspective, these four functional imperatives represent the basic building blocks of any human system. They represent level 1 of Boulding's model.

The next part of the chapter looks at the ways these core elements are expressed in different levels of modernist organization from a 'simple' organization (Boulding's level 2) through to a more complex organization (Boulding's level 4).

## The organization as simple machine

Boulding suggests that systems operating at level 2 do so in a simple dynamic manner 'with predetermined, necessary motions'. Boulding (1956) adds that 'physical and chemical and most *social systems* do in fact exhibit a tendency to equilibrium – otherwise the world would have exploded or imploded long ago' (p. 198). If we look at an organization as a simple system, it will, if it is working well, have a set of clear goals, the members will live in an atmosphere that is strongly controlled and the different parts of the organization will be tightly integrated through sets of rules and procedures to make sure that all the activities are coordinated. In this situation, the work of the manager is to prevent dysfunction, to prevent the organization from falling out of balance. Because so much emphasis is placed on control and integration, it is likely to be slow to adjust to processes of change and adaptation; the organization feels like it is relatively closed off from the outside world until a major tremor causes it to go completely out of equilibrium. This is illustrated in the Case study.

### Case study    Keeping the regularities at Boulding's level 2

Many years ago, the author of this chapter worked for a large company that made breakfast cereals. He worked in a small department that was responsible for unpacking packets of cereal that had gone past their 'sell-by date' so that the contents could be reprocessed to be sent on to make animal food. The packs to be emptied arrived in the morning, and we would work on them all day. The product of our labours – empty packets and vats of recycled cereal – were taken away at the end of the day. The work was regular, ordered and mechanical. We, the human operators, were little machines.

Actually, the whole factory was rather like that. It was very ordered, very regular. There was little excitement. Producing fresh cereal and emptying the stale packs was an ordered affair that nowadays is almost entirely mechanized.

The role of managers was to create systems that kept the organization in balance, to maintain a high level of control, so that the system worked like clockwork. Many of the managers were engineers, and they used the logic and rationality of their engineering background to create order and stability. As we worked away on our packing and unpacking machines, we were constantly aware of the supervisors making sure that we were producing at the required rate.

Because the company had (still has) an international reputation, its market was quite stable; in many ways, it felt like quite a closed system in which we lived and worked. Some years later, the external environment in which the company operated became much more competitive, and processes of adaptation began to develop and emerge. The company became a more open system.

Two elements make this simple system attractive. It gives the illusion to managers that they can achieve control of the 'clockwork' mechanism, and it gives members the feeling that if the machine is working effectively, all will be well. Even if there are days when things go wrong, the 'clockwork' will take the organization back to the equilibrium.

The essence of the simple systems thinking is captured by the view that relatively closed organizations protect the technical core – the part of the organization that produces or manufactures the goods or services – from external pressures. The writers on organization theory Lee Bolman and Terence Deal (1997) write that in these relatively closed organizations 'The name of the game was efficiency, internal control of the means of production'. (p. 235). In many ways, this organization is a very sophisticated version of the pin factory, the classical organization discussed earlier.

### Stop and think

These relatively closed systems are still common in organizations either as organizations, or more usually as departments existing within larger, more complex systems. Can you identify departments or organizations of this type? What are their strengths and limitations?

## Level 3: 'Get the structure and systems right so that all is in balance'

The kind of organization described above as a 'simple system' (relatively closed from its external environment) is a mechanical place that spends so much energy on maintaining itself that it is not at all effective at managing change. One of the key issues in the simple system is that integration is managed through rules and procedures. As organizations become more complex, there is a greater need for information to flow between the different parts of the system. Two sorts of information become of high importance at this level. The first is information from the external environment. This includes information about customers and competitors that comes via marketing and sales; it includes information about suppliers to the organization of goods and services that comes via the production department. The second information flow

## Example: keeping the information flowing

Imagine an organization that has been going through major change in structure, culture and in the upgrading of its premises. During the change process, managers needed to be constantly in touch with senior management in order to understand the nature of the change in order to reduce any damaging effects within the department. The key issue is to ensure that information is flowing at all levels of the organization to make sure that the process of change is controlled. The sorts of information contained in the communication would be financial, concerned with staffing levels; the effectiveness of the business processes; and information from customers, suppliers and even shareholders. This information enables managers to maintain a level of control, to ensure that nothing spirals into becoming a big problem. In this sense, managers try to understand the different forces in the situation that are helping and hindering the change process. Managers are working hard to ensure that there is balance within the organization to take account of changes in the outside environment.

that is important is internal to the organization. This is the flow from department to department, from manager to staff and to senior management. This preoccupation with developing flows of information and ways of interpreting them became one of the preoccupations of the modernist approaches to organization.

As the organization goes through this process of change, there is a need, from the modernist perspective, to ensure that the flow of information is controlled. One of the key images used to describe this idea of controlled information is to regard the organization as a cybernetic system. This is a term taken from engineering; *cybernetic systems* are communications and controls in living and mechanical systems that are built into the system. A sophisticated IT network is a cybernetic system in the sense that it provides information and control. The system produces data that can be measured and are 'objective' and 'rational'. The sorts of information that are used in organizations to make decisions would be part of the cybernetic system. This information is considered vital to the success of the organization and its managers in that it enables them to fulfil their responsibility for the guidance and steering process of the organization.

According to one of the most influential writers on the development of complex systems in organizations, Ralph Stacey (2001), some of the key features of the application of cybernetic systems theory to organizations include the following:

- It is the application of the engineer's idea of control to human activity. Although flows of information have become very important in making decisions, the emphasis is on the organization as machine. The exchange of information is not the same as the essentially human act of communication.

- It assumes that *organizations* can have goals and can achieve high levels of self-control and self-regulation as long as the appropriate systems and information flows (called *feedback loops*) are in place.

- These feedback loops work in a circular form. If members of staff give to their manager information about areas where things are going wrong, then they will expect information back from the manager in order to undertake their work effectively. However, because the information flows are carefully controlled, there is an assumption that for everything that happens in the organization there is a straightforward relationship between 'cause and effect'.

- There is a clear boundary between the system and the environment. It is not completely open to the environment; rather, the environment only 'meets' the system at local, predetermined points such as senior management or the marketing department.

- The cybernetic system seeks equilibrium, so that success is determined by the extent to which there is stability, a sense of consistency and harmonious operation, although the system can allow for a degree of conflict between the subsystems.

From a modernist management perspective, managers may be seen as being like a 'thermostat', exercising control through the information flows. They are responsible for interpreting and understanding the information that moves the organization to the desired state of equilibrium. It presupposes that managers are similar to engineers who use techniques to control and manage the human elements. Senior managers keep a close eye on the environment and attempt to make adjustments within the organization that enable it to maintain environmental equilibrium. The successful management group is one that maintains equilibrium and whose change efforts are geared toward the achievement of a new state of equilibrium and do not engage in major disruptive change. In this situation, the work of the manager is to prevent dysfunction, to prevent the organization from falling too far out of equilibrium.

However, at this level, the organization is operating as a most elegant machine. Managers act according to well-established courses of action in order to preserve the equilibrium or are careful to ensure that movement to an 'improved' level of equilibrium is carefully planned.

## Stop and think

There is an assumption at this level that organizations can be treated as very elegant and sophisticated machines. What do you think are the strengths and limitations of this view?

## Level 4: 'The machine is alive! – well, almost'

It is at this level that Boulding talks of the presence of a 'living system'. We are looking at the 'open' system with well-defined inputs and outputs between the organization and its environment and with a clear relationship between the internal arrangements and the external environment.

In the previous section, we discussed the way that the idea of organizations as cybernetic systems had been used in a somewhat narrow, engineering-based way. The American academic and consultant to large corporate organizations Robert Pascale (1990) takes the idea of the cybernetic system to another level. He refers to 'a well known law of cybernetics – the law of requisite variety – which states that for any system to adapt to its external environment, its internal controls must incorporate variety into its internal processes' (p. 14). He further suggests that this principle of requisite variety is linked to the concept of innovative organizations, a theme to be pursued in later chapters. However, for our current purposes, there are two key distinguishing issues at this level – self-maintenance and self-reproduction. From an organizational perspective, self-maintenance of the organization (its ability to sustain itself) comes from the variety of ways the organization can respond to the environment. The idea of self-reproduction means that the organization can grow, develop and form new divisions and structures in a responsive manner.

To show how this type of systems approach can be developed, the model presented in Figure 2.6 is one that explores an open systems perspective.

These are the key issues explored by the model in Figure 2.6:

- The **core vision and mission** are the stated reasons that underpin the core purpose of the organization; they define the purpose of the organization (i.e., its goals). The **ideology** is concerned with the ways the organization pursues its goals.
- The **leadership** of the organization is a key subsystem. The leader is the 'captain of the ship' who upholds the core values of the organization and ensures that strategies are in place for their implementation.

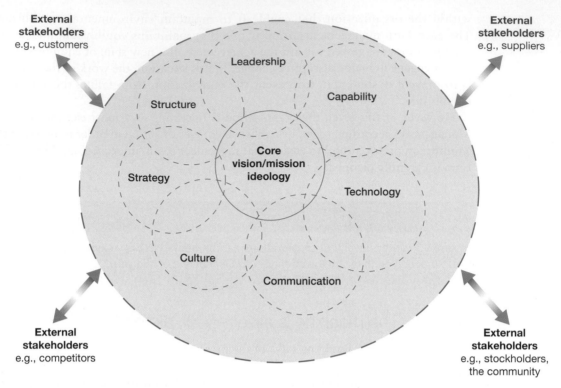

**Figure 2.6:** A systems model.

- The core **capability** valued in the organization are the kinds of expertise or the sorts of qualities that are expected at different levels or functions in the organization.

- The **technology** ranges from the IT infrastructure through to the kind of technologies used in manufacturing through to the ways in which members are expected to relate to the technology. In some organizations, the technologies are considered vehicles that enable the members to work more effectively; in others, the technology seems to control the members.

- How is **communication** handled in the organization? How do the information flows take place so that there are feedback loops to allow appropriate decisions to be made?

- The **culture** of the organization includes how modernists see the culture or organizational climate as a subsystem that, when the organization is working in equilibrium, preserves and maintains the values and goals of the organization.

- The ways **strategy** is developed in the organization and the strategy itself. In some organizations, for example, the strategy is prepared by senior managers at a set period and becomes the document by which members are expected to live; in others, strategy is emergent and is something in which many members of the organization can participate.

- The **structure** of the organization is the way in which the organization is designed. In modernist terms, does the design of the organization fit the purpose?

- This model also includes elements of the **environment** so that it becomes a vehicle for the exploration of the relationship between it and the organization.

| Case study | An organization looks to the future |
|---|---|

The author of this chapter was invited to undertake a consultancy project for the board and senior management of a large organization, and we agreed that an open systems approach would be useful to explore some of the key issues of change and adaptation that confronted it. We worked together over a period of three days.

During the first day, we spent a good deal of time exploring the changing nature of the customers, suppliers and shareholders. We also looked at the ways the organization was affected by its competitors and the other organizations with which it collaborated. The group began to think about the ways the external environment would affect the internal systems of the organization.

To do this, on the second day, we began to use the systems model. After some discussion of the way the model works, the members of the group split into smaller groupings. The chief executive and a couple of his colleagues were to discuss 'vision' and 'leadership'; the IT director led a small group to discuss 'technology' and 'communication'; the HR director and colleagues discussed 'capability' and 'culture'; and the marketing director with some colleagues discussed 'strategy' and 'structure'.

Their task was twofold. The first was to do a diagnosis of the way that each of the systems on which they were working was operating right now. Then their second task was to think through how each of the systems 'should be', bearing in mind the changing environment in which they were placed.

When each of the groups had completed the task, they came together to explore each of the subsystems and then to create a 'whole picture' of how they thought the organization needed to be in order to deal with its external environment. The whole group then began to discuss the ways they would ensure that their new understanding of the organization could be put into place.

What was important for them was the idea that they could look at their organization as a whole. It was also important for them to realize that all those subsystems did not need to fit together in a perfect manner and that some conflicts between them could be quite creative.

| Stop and think | Using the open systems model |
|---|---|

One of the key uses of the systems approach discussed above is to use it as a device for undertaking a diagnosis of issues in the organization. Using the model outlined above, develop a diagnosis of an organization (or a department) known to you. The organization you discuss could be either a formal organization or an informal organization such as a group of students living in the same accommodation. As you do this, try to get beneath the surface.

The level that we have just explored, the fourth, is the 'living organization', but it is not 'human'. The organization is not yet populated with living, breathing, sentient human beings with their own agendas and preoccupations.

Although the organization is an open system, it does not have the capability to be reflective, to have an emotional and intellectual engagement with itself and its environment. To reach this level, we move beyond the fourth level of organization. These are developments in organization theory discussed in later chapters.

## The chapter so far

### Why modernists love systems theory

From a modernist perspective, interest in systems theory is understandable. It displays a fascination with the key concerns of modernism.

- These concerns include:

  - the search for order and rationality

  - the establishment of control over knowledge through control of flows of information and the ability to assemble data in ways that are rational and ordered

  - the desire for the whole picture

  - the modernist love of hierarchy

  - a passion to understand what is happening in the organization

  - the search for cooperation and collaboration within organizations and the avoidance of conflict.

- The systems approach to organizations provides theorists and managers with an opportunity to align organization theory with the natural sciences. This means that they can legitimate the use of scientific and engineering principles as a means of establishing order and control in organizations.

- Systems theory provides a rich opportunity to develop an understanding of core operating principles that apply to all organizations.

- It provides an intellectually rigorous structure for the exploration of organizations.

- When we reach open systems theory, we can explore the relationship between the organization and its external environment. This provides a rational framework for dealing with the uncertainties that a fickle fate throws at organizations.

### And why contemporary writers are sceptical of systems theory

Critics suggest that an excessive faith in the theory can lead people in organizations down some wrong paths. The organization theorists Michael Harrison and Arie Shirom (1999) suggest:

- The search for rules and regulations that would 'cure' situations where there are problems between subsystems can lead to major problems. Instead of searching for new rules, it is better for managers to take a pragmatic approach.

- If an organization were in perfect fit between the subsystems for more than a moment, then it would be stagnant because there is no dynamic for change.

- Even if the fit between different subsystems is not as good as it might be, limited fit may be no bad thing because a lack of fit can lead to some useful conflicts.

- Organizations are dynamic, and the shapes of the subsystems and their relationships with each other are constantly on the move.

- A well-aligned organization can become unresponsive. This issue can be significant particularly for larger, more mature organizations that become satisfied with their elegant organizational design.

We have seen that, from a modernist perspective, organizations are systems that seem to float in their environment. At the lower levels of systems thinking, they are quite enclosed into themselves with, it would seem, little connection with the wider environment. As we enter into the higher levels and organizations develop into 'open systems', they can be seen to be closely linked with their external environment. In the next section, we will explore the nature of the relationship between the modernist organization and the society around it. Before we do that, however, this is a brief intellectual biography of one of the leading modernist organization theorists of our age to give a flavour of the depth of modernist thought.

| Biography | A thoroughly modern modernist: Lex Donaldson |
|---|---|

One of the leading modernist writers in organization theory is Lex Donaldson, who is currently professor of organizational design at the Australian Graduate School of Management in Sydney, Australia. In an article written in 2005, he discusses his intellectual background. He writes that he has steadily argued for positivism (the ability to measure things rather than speculate about them) and functionalism (that everything in organizations should have a purpose). This stems from a lifelong commitment to taking a scientific view of organizations. He explains that his positivist view of organizations is based on his use of quantitative methods, the search for cause and effect, and a view that we can measure and determine the forces that place pressure on organizations. He is a functionalist in the sense that he believes that organizations are created and maintained in order to fulfil tasks that cannot be accomplished by individuals alone. Managers and their organizations make choices, and in doing so, tend to act rationally. They are aware of contingencies, and they develop structures to meet those contingencies (to be discussed later). His view is that organizations, as open systems, can quickly move out of equilibrium into disequilibrium and that, even though there is rationality in the system, organizations can lose functionality for periods of time.

## How modernist organization theory underpins conventional understandings of the relationship between organizations and society

At the very heart of the modernist organization lies the idea of the bureaucracy. A bureaucratic organization is one that is created and designed so that every position in the organization needs to be filled by people who are experts and specialists in the work that they do. Thus, if the post is that of administrative assistant, whose main work is maintaining the IT files on personnel in the organization, the person must be an expert in that. If the post is that of chief executive with responsibility for the organization's strategy, then the person appointed to that post will be expert in that work. At the heart of bureaucracy is the notion that when one works for the bureaucratic organization, the members undertake their work in an impersonal and impartial manner: they follow the rules without personal fear or favour. As the next sections unfold, we shall explore this key concept, but for the moment, think of the idea of bureaucracy as a controlled and ordered way of organizing people so that they can produce their work with the maximum efficiency.

| Biography | **Great figures in the social sciences:** **Max Weber (1864–1920)** |
|---|---|

Max Weber was born in 1864 into a prosperous German bourgeoisie family. He went to the University of Freiberg in 1881, where he enrolled as a student of law. According to his biographers Hans Gerth and C Wright Mills (1948), Weber became a member of the duelling club where he learnt to hold his own in drinking bouts as well as duels. He became a member of academic staff at the University of Heidelberg, but after a period of depression, he went on an extended visit to the United States, an experience he found intellectually both exhilarating and depressing. He found the very nature of American life exciting after the rather suffocating experience of 'old Europe'; on the other hand, he was appalled by the human waste and poverty that he found in abundance. After this experience, he returned to Heidelberg, where he continued writing and other scholarly activities. During the World War I, he established and ran hospitals in the Heidelberg area, experiencing bureaucracy from the inside. His biographers comment that he suffered from long periods of deep depression and that his life oscillated between neurotic collapse, travel and work. He was held together, they suggest, by a profound sense of humour and his strong sense of personal integrity. He died in 1920.

Although Max Weber's work helps us to understand the modernist age and modernist organizations, his work as one of the foundation figures of modern sociology makes him exempt from easy classification. The range of his writing is enormous. In addition to his classic work on bureaucracy discussed in this chapter, Weber wrote about science and politics, the nature of power, religion and society, his experience of the United States, and the social structures of societies as diverse as Germany and 'Chinese intellectuals'.

One of the ways Weber differs from the modernist stance, according to the American sociologist Stephen Kalberg (1997), is that he was not interested in defining general laws of history and social change and then trying to explain all specific developments by deduction from these laws. Instead of this 'natural science' approach, he advocated an approach in which the sociologist tries to understand the reality that surrounds our lives. In this sense, he would take the uniqueness of a case or development – for example, bureaucracy – and seek to identify what caused this uniqueness.

At the start of the twentieth century, Weber (1922) wrote that in the modern world:

> The (need for) speed of operations . . . is determined by the peculiar nature of modern means of communication. . . . The extraordinary increase in the speed by which public announcements, as well as economic and political facts, are transmitted exerts a steady and sharp pressure in the direction of speeding up the tempo of administrative reaction towards various situations. The optimum of such reaction time is normally attained only by a strictly bureaucratic organization (p. 214).

For Weber, the development of bureaucracy was revolutionary in the sense that it was responsible for the destruction of ways of organizing that were irrational such as the rule of the monarch, the feudal rights of the lord of the manor, the rule of the dictator and tyrant or the rule of the mob. The growth of bureaucracy leads, he suggests, to 'a "rationalist" way of life' that 'furthers the domination of "rational matter of factness" and "the personality type of the professional expert"' (Weber, 1922, p. 240). On the negative side, Weber was fatalistic about the development of economic materialism – the search for economic and financial reward – of which bureaucracy is a key component. He referred to the life of machine production and materialism as an imprisoning 'iron cage' (Weber, 1904, p. 1264). He suggests that the 'objective indispensability' of bureaucracy 'means that the mechanism . . . is easily made to work for everybody who knows how to gain control over it' (Weber, 1922, p. 229).

This means that if people whose aims are not for the social good can gain command of the bureaucratic machine, they can distort its purpose. This has led to one of the key debates about bureaucracy: is it essentially immoral, amoral or moral? There is a further discussion of the implications of the issues surrounding control in Chapter 4.

## Is bureaucracy immoral?

Although the bureaucratic structure is supposed to be strictly impersonal and rational it is at the same time not totally free of emotion. The sociologist Robert Merton observed that the discipline required to work in a bureaucracy is supported 'by strong sentiments which entail devotion to one's duties, a strong sense of the limitation of one's authority . . . and methodical performance of routine activities' (Merton, 1968, p. 252). As Merton observed, these commitments to the ordered life can lead to severe problems – the desire for order becoming more important than the primary purpose of the organization, leading to the development of the 'bureaucratic virtuoso, who never forgets a single rule' (Merton, 1968, p. 253).

Weber (1920), in a public lecture, asked his audience to imagine a world – private and public organizations – dominated by bureaucratic organization and rational organization. This is a world in which 'the performance of each individual worker is mathematically measured, each man becomes a little cog in the machine and aware of this, his one preoccupation is whether he can become a larger cog' (p. 335). When he looked at the processes of bureaucracy in his own society, he saw that the leadership and senior management layers were dominated by 'timidity' – what we today call the *apparatchiks*, 'the suits' – 'who need "order" and nothing but order' (p. 362).

In this sense, bureaucracy is seen as a form of social organization that depends on 'the routine application of mundane discipline, which becomes progressively sanctified and normalized' (Bos and Willmott, 2001). As the bureaucracy becomes a way of life, its members become increasingly detached from taking a moral perspective on what they are doing. This argument has been powerfully articulated by writers such as the sociologist Zygmunt Bauman. He argues (1989) that as the bureaucracy develops its routines and 'rational' approaches to decision making, notions of the 'moral impulse' become dampened so that members can engage in the most horrific acts. This is a theme to which we return in Chapter 6.

In order to illustrate his thesis, Bauman discussed bureaucratic engagement in the Holocaust as a particular feature of the modernist understanding of the world, and indeed other writers have taken up the argument that bureaucracy and the bureaucratic personality are essentially guided only by the rationality of bureaucratic necessity. The social historian David Cesarani (2004) writes that it is important to understand Eichmann (one of the key architects of the Holocaust) not as an evil person but as a bureaucratically 'normal' person who used bureaucratic means to undertake purposes that *others* see as evil but were not seen as such by the perpetrators. He argues that Eichmann and many others used their bureaucratic expertise in such matters as categorizing in detail the sorts of person who 'should' be sent to the concentration camps. The 'bureaucrats' created detailed lists of those who were sent to the camps, and organizing the transportation of people to the camps and the resources and so on were matters that required bureaucratic expertise. After the basic premise had been accepted that there were certain categories of people who 'should be assigned' to concentration camps, the rest was a bureaucratic exercise. Cesarani suggests that Eichmann 'managed genocide in the way that any Chief Executive of any corporation would run a multinational company'. It is suggested that in this process of 'bureaucratic normalization', members' moral responsibilities are placed under an anaesthetic because this helps them to deal with the uncertainties of life; if we can deny that emotions exist, we never have to deal with them (Bos and Willmott, 2001).

There is, however, an alternative to this fatalistic view. If we return to Weber's (1922) public lecture with which we started this section, he suggests that the key question is not how to stop bureaucratization but rather, 'What will come of it?' (p. 362). It is at this point that Weber comes to discuss the idea that the inevitability of bureaucracy can be controlled and its negative effects reduced by human will and intention. He asks the key question, 'What can we oppose to this machinery in order to keep a portion of mankind free from this parcelling-out of the soul, from the supreme mastery of the bureaucratic way of life'? (p. 362). Although Weber does not answer this question, it suggests attention to the development of intellectual and emotional intelligence and reflectiveness in the development of organizations – an issue that is discussed in Chapter 8.

The sociologist Richard Sennett (2006) puts forward a view that contrasts with this bureaucratic fatalism. He suggests that even when the bureaucracy appears to be very restrictive of freedom, members can negotiate and give new meanings to the 'things they are told to do' so that they can construct their own realities within the bureaucracy. Living within the bureaucracy gives people a framework of time to work and to be with others that members can find satisfying and that 'bureaucratic structures provide the occasion for interpreting power, for making sense of it on the ground; they thus can give people a sense of agency' (p. 36). Paul du Gay (2000) suggests that writers such as Bauman, in their powerful opposition to bureaucracy, have actually misunderstood Weber's concept of bureaucracy. Crucially, du Gay argues that the 'objectivity' required of the bureaucrat is not an impersonal dehumanized matter, but rather, it is the 'trained capacity to treat people as individual cases . . . so that the partialities of patronage and the dangers of corruption might be avoided' (p. 42). The historian Robert Locke (1996) points to instances in which enlightened bureaucrats in nineteenth century Germany drove forward social reforms that would not have happened in the prevailing society. We shall explore some of the profound advantages that bureaucracy can bring in the next two sections.

# Form fits function: how modernist organizational theory challenges the relationship between individuals, groups and the organization through bureaucracy and hierarchy

Beyond the views that bureaucracies can be stifling or that they can be so driven by logics of efficiency and control that they become machines for the delivery of the wishes of those in power, there is a third view. This is that bureaucracies can be the engines of change and development. Bureaucracies can rise to new challenges that make the work of members more purposive; people who work in bureaucracies can make their work more interesting and develop their organizations (Blau and Scott, 1963). This perspective on bureaucracy as an agent of change is a reminder of Weber's view that bureaucracy was the very engine by which the modern age would be able to respond to the issues of change and turbulence that characterize it.

## Bureaucracy as thing of beauty

At the start of this chapter, we suggested that modernism could take several forms from the brutal to the elegant. The Italian sociologist of organizations Antonio Strati (1999) suggests that concepts such as aesthetics, exploring organizations from the perspective that they are artistic achievements that can be admired for their beauty, have been ignored by researchers. He suggests that many organization theorists have perpetuated the story that life in the organization is an emotion free zone in which members do not exercise emotional or aesthetic judgements about their lives in organizations.

One writer who has taken up this challenge, George Frederickson (2000), a professor of public administration at the University of Kansas, argues that the bureaucratic experience can be aesthetically 'beautiful'. He argues that this sense of aesthetic satisfaction can be found for those who value the sense of precision, harmony, routine and ritual that can be found in the bureaucracy. Furthermore, he suggests that the sense of order, fairness, the fixing of responsibility and leadership can be experienced as beautiful because it engenders trust, predictability and a sense of fairness amongst all levels of members. He argues that it is possible in a bureaucratic organization to achieve high and honourable purpose so that members can feel that they are professionally, intellectually and emotionally engaged. Frederickson argues that looking at bureaucracy as potentially beautiful – using the lens of aesthetics – is useful in the sense that it directs attention to more qualitative, subjective ways of understanding organization and leads to a more crafted, less deterministic way of designing organizations. We return to a discussion of organization aesthetics as an emergent theme in organization theory in Chapter 10.

## Bureaucracy and rules

This aesthetic approach also points to the ways that members can optimize their effectiveness and levels of satisfaction and commitment to the organization. This may be illustrated by looking at one aspect of bureaucracy – its propensity to generate 'rules'. As Bozeman and Rainey (1998) suggest, the conventional thinking (both academic and in popular writing) is that bureaucracies, particularly in the public sector, are 'machines for the production of rules'.

However, their research reveals that there is a much more complex situation in relation to these debates. They suggest that when managers believe that they lack the support of their senior managers, they will make up rules so that the rules protect them from uncertainty. They also found that when managers were in a situation in which decisions were not recorded in a formal manner, they wanted 'more rules' so they believed that they had a clear structure within which they were taking decisions. They suggest, incidentally, that these needs for rules are stronger in private sector organizations because the levels of uncertainty these managers experience are greater. Paradoxically, the fewer formal bureaucratic rules, the more the need for the development of informal rules.

In some respects, the research by Bozeman and Rainey echoes the earlier seminal work of the sociologist Alvin Gouldner (1954). In his exploration of bureaucracy in industrial organizations, he suggests that it is important to understand the patterns of bureaucratic form in different organizations. He suggests, for example, that in the large organization he studied, there were three dominant patterns:

1. **Mock bureaucracy:** These are rules that exist in the organization but there is an 'informal agreement' between members that nobody will really obey them. These are often, Gouldner suggests, rules that are 'imposed' by an external body (which could be headquarters) that 'insiders' agree (implicitly) are 'unnecessary'. An example is that there can be stern rules about health and safety that come from the head office that are experienced by managers and employees at the local level as quite impractical. These rules would impede their work, so both parties ignore them – until something goes seriously wrong.

2. **Representative bureaucracy:** These are rules that all members agree are important and significant for the successful operation of the organization and that meet individual and group needs. For example, in the industrial plant that Gouldner studied, the safety rules were highly bureaucratized, but *all* members thought that strong adherence to them was important because they had been agreed between the management and the unions in what was felt to be a fair and balanced way.

3. **Punishment-centred bureaucracy:** This is where one party seeks to impose rules on others and where compliance of the other party is based on either the fear of punishment or the expectation of reward for compliance. An example of this is when a union develops strict procedures for health and safety that are irksome to management but are imposed upon them as part of a negotiated deal. In this case, management implements the rules because they have to but without a sense of commitment to them.

Constant scrutiny of the processes by which the bureaucratic 'rules' of the organization are generated can also play an important part in processes of change. In his exploration of bureaucratic rule making in a university, Schulz (1998) suggests that a practical way of getting change to happen in organizations is to abolish the old rules and replace them with new ones.

## The virtuous bureaucracy

We have tried to show in this section that many of the problems that people attribute to bureaucracies and bureaucratic rules are connected with the ways that members operate the bureaucracy. The organization psychologist Elliott Jaques (1990) argues that the *ideal* design for organization is bureaucratic and hierarchical *as long as the design is fit for purpose*. He argues that what is wrong with bureaucracy is not the form per se but rather that, in many organizations, those who are responsible for the design of the organization – the senior management – do not really understand how to craft it effectively. He argues that an effectively designed bureaucratic structure enables members of the organization to be entirely clear about the patterns of accountability in the organization. This means that members can have clarity about who is responsible for the tasks to be performed and who is responsible for the processes that are to be undertaken in the organization. In this way, he suggests, thoughtful managers living within the hierarchy can develop a deeper understanding of the nature of management and its purpose.

## Modernist themes in organizational design

### Modernist bureaucracy as a key challenge to organization design

During the past 20 years or so, there have been powerful debates (discussed particularly in Chapters 5 and 6) that the fundamental nature of organization is changing and that organization theory has to adapt to these changes. The argument is that modernism and the bureaucratic design that goes with it is dead. We shall suggest in this section that although the traditional centralized bureaucracy of public sector organizations is changing, it is replaced by new forms of bureaucracy.

Weber conceptualized two modes of bureaucracy. In the public services, for the purposes of fulfilling the purposes of government, there is 'bureaucratic authority'; in the private domain, there is 'bureaucratic management'. During the 1990s, however, there emerged what is called new public management. This meant a significant shift towards a new approach to the organization of public services such as health care, universities, schools, and government and municipal authorities. New public management represented a movement from a public service understanding of modernism to one based on the principles of business and industry. Although the impact of new public management is strongest (as its name implies) on forms of management in public services (discussed extensively in Chapter 9), it has implications for organization design.

From a modernist perspective, we have seen that bureaucracy provides the conditions for organizational efficiency. Weber (1922), that sceptical observer of the development of modernism and bureaucracy, suggests that the bureaucratic, modernist organization provides 'precision, speed, unambiguity, knowledge of the files [in contemporary terms, IT strategy], continuity, discretion, unity, strict subordination, reduction of friction and of material and personal costs' (p. 214). In design terms, new public management stresses the achievement of principles of efficiency. This means that decision making necds to be based on logic and rationality and decisions can be quantified. It also means that organizational processes are best designed to be linear – one thing after another – rather than complex. It also implies understanding problems involves reducing them to their basic elements. In universities, for example, students work on *modular* courses, in which they *accumulate credits*. These individual *modules* have hours of teaching and learning allocated to them on the basis of the number of credits they offer, and each module has specific learning and assessment outcomes. This reduction of the student's experience to core elements is in the spirit of the 'new modernism' (Jaffee, 2001). The search for efficiency also involves separation between those who think and act strategically in the organization and those who implement those strategies.

Some writers see the emergence of new public management in a favourable light. Peter Bogason, who is professor of public administration at Roskilde University in Denmark, wrote in 1998 that Scandinavian local government is increasingly changing its organizational pattern. It is moving away from the principles of centralized bureaucratic control that were held sacred after the reforms of the 1960s and 1970s – reforms that made local government the building block for the welfare 'state' – toward being decentralized and fragmented. This is making room for new styles of management and organization such as contracting out and similar market-like arrangements. Because the services are delivered at a local level, there have been democratic initiatives that place service users in command of service institutions. He suggests that there is a movement from central bureaucratic control to patterns of collaboration between organizations. These forms of organization design are discussed in later chapters.

On the other hand, there is an argument that the development of new public management will lead to the destruction of the very heart of public service organizations. By this, the critics of this new modernism mean that hospitals, schools, universities and social services will become increasingly similar to fast food restaurants for the delivery of services. For the critics of the 'new modernism', organizations come to resemble fast food outlets such as McDonalds.

## Too efficient for its own good: The McDonaldization of everything

George Ritzer is a professor of sociology at the University of Maryland. In 1993, he wrote *The McDonaldization of Society*, which many critics of the 'new modernism' took as a rallying call. This is an extract from an interview he gave in 1997.

*You have described the McDonaldized society as a system of 'iron cages' in which all institutions come to be dominated by the same principle. So what sort of world would you like us to be living in?*

Well, obviously (laughter) . . . . . a far less caged one. I mean the fundamental problem with McDonaldized systems is that it's other people in the system structuring our lives for us, rather than us structuring our lives for ourselves. I mean, that's really what McDonald's is all about. . . . Humanity is essentially creative and if you develop these systems that are constraining and controlling people they can't be creative, they can't be human.

*Do you think that the issue should be broadened to include more than just the specific case of McDonald's?*

Yeah, see for me it's that they've set in motion something which is so much bigger than they are. . . . In Weber's theory of rationalization and in Weber's model was the bureaucracy, the German bureaucracy, and we're living in an extension, a massive extension of that process with a new model in the fast food restaurant.

*Source:* www.mcspotlight.org/people/interviews/ritzer_george.html

Table 2.2 tries to capture some of this complexity. We look at the ways that an organization such as a university can have within it elements that on the one hand can lead to McDonaldization and on the other have elements within it of the 'new modernism' that help it to be more effective in its work.

The idea that public sector organizations would benefit from a more clearly 'new modernist' approach to management and leadership is fundamental to the ideas of new public management. For some writers, the link between these approaches to organization and McDonaldization are inevitable; for others the relationship between this form of organization and actual practice are much more complex. Writers such as Prichard and Willmott (1997) suggest that the fatalistic view is questionable and they reflect a view that the McDonaldization thesis is not appropriate. Their core argument is that organizations are actually very complex and that within them there can be many discourses, of which this new modernism, with its emphasis on the technologies of bureaucratic and management control, is only one. At the heart of the debate is the extent to which new forms of organization (to be discussed in later chapters) will replace the modernist form or the extent that 'new modernism' will actually prevail as a dominant organizational form.

## Contingency theory and organization design

Debates about the design of organization have occupied an important strand in modernist organization theory. In the United Kingdom, a group of organization theorists based mainly at the University of Aston during the 1970s were preoccupied by a number of questions that were captured in a paper published in 1973 by Derek

**Table 2.2** Fatalism and optimism in the 'new' modernist organization

| Key issues in the 'new modernist' approach | 'Fatalistic McDonaldization' thesis that modernist organization reduces organizations to machines | The new modernist organization provides structure and meaning to organizations |
| --- | --- | --- |
| Decision making based on **logic and rationality**. | All decisions are based on 'the logics of efficiency' so that individual or group or professional creativity and initiative are squeezed out. The university becomes a 'machine' in relation to its delivery. | There are aspects of the university in which logic and rationality can provide an important framework. Lack of logic can lead to favouritism and judgements based on political power of particular stakeholders. |
| Key features of organizational life can be expressed in a **linear manner**. | An organization dominated by 'rules' and procedures that do not allow complexity. The development of 'templates' that mean that there is only 'one way' of developing new programmes or determining the 'value' of research. | Many decision-making processes can be made in a linear matter. This achieves a level of transparency in our practices and enables us to routinize many practices that were previously overcomplicated. |
| Decisions can be **quantified**. | Increased reliance on performance standards and attempts to assess quality through quantification. Activities become increasingly controlled by quantification (e.g., time allocations for teaching, research). | Performance standards enable members to get a good picture of how well (or poorly) we are performing. At a group level, it enables us to acknowledge those who are 'doing the business' and to punish those who are not. |
| Understanding problems and making decisions involves a search for the basic elements. | Key activities are reduced to their smallest units, so we think of teaching as 'modular' and that within the 'module', we are expected to specify 'learning outcomes' and 'assessment outcomes' as if they were 'mechanical outcomes from teaching with the student as passive recipient. | The search for 'the basic elements' enables us to really get to grips with what we are really doing. It enables us to design our teaching and research with a greater degree of precision. |
| There is a split **between thinking and doing**. | Senior management determines the strategic direction; academic staff believe they are robbed of autonomy and creativity. | This is actually about boundaries. It is legitimated that senior management takes responsibility for its work and staff members take responsibility for theirs. Staff members 'doing' teaching and research require considerable intellect, and they should be left alone to get on with their work. |

Pugh, a member of the Aston Group. The first was to ask if there were any general principles of organization design and structure that would apply to all organizations. The second was to ask if the context – the contingencies faced by an organization such as size, ownership, location and technology – determine the appropriate design. The third issue was to try to understand the extent to which management have latitude in the extent they can design their organization or if design is driven either by general principles or the contingencies in which the organization is placed.

The conclusion from this study was to identify the importance of organizational context, the contingencies that influence design. This research suggested strongly that although such features as the personality of the chief executive, historical crises or government policies play their part in organization design 'context is more important than is generally realized' (Pugh, 1973, p. 34). The implication for management, he suggests, is that given the amount of information available to them, managers will be able to be sensitive to changes in contingencies that can occur before internal adjustments need to be made.

One of the key contingencies identified by the Aston School is that as organizations increase in size, they inevitably become more formal in design terms, as revealed by a proliferation of rules and formal written documents. The means of controlling employees also become more formal as the possibilities for interaction between employees and supervisors become more remote. They also argued that growth in size also tends toward a greater controlling interest by the organization centre (Jones, 1996, p. 92). This increasing formality is an aspect of what the modernist organization theorist Lex Donaldson (2005) has called 'bureaucratic contingency', the idea that bureaucracy does not just happen but rather comes from a number of considerations or contingencies that are part of the design process. The number of employees affects the degree to which an organization is bureaucratic; it is the appropriate design for large organizations with repetitive operations and where decision making can be made through the application of rules. Donaldson suggests that in large organizations that try to have simple, nonbureaucratic structures, senior managers can become overwhelmed by the decisions they have to make.

Donaldson (1996) also argues that contingency theory is a synthesis between modernist theories of organization and neo-modernist approaches (discussed in Chapter 3). He suggests that this approach has considerable power in the analysis of the relationship between organizations and their environment. For example, the traditional modernist approach to contingency theory is that writers try to find general rules that would explain what was happening in particular organizations. The Scandinavian academic Gustavsen (1992) developed a neo-modernist approach. Here the researcher begins with developing an understanding of the ways that, at a local level, organization members constructed their patterns of competencies and capabilities within the contingencies that they faced. He then explored the ways the members themselves generalized from the particular experience.

## How modernist organization theory develops an understanding of organizational culture

One of the key themes explored in different chapters of this book is organizational culture. This has become a very important theme in organization theory, and writers from different backgrounds have come to very different conclusions about its nature.

This section will show how modernists developed a distinctive understanding of this theme after a brief review of different approaches to organization culture.

## Organization culture as a key theme in organization theory

A common definition shared by the vast majority of writers is that organization culture is concerned with the ways members of organizations develop an identity, share values and create a common understanding of what their organization is about. As we shall see in various chapters, the development of the concept of organizational culture is a rich and complex story with many twists and turns that are connected with the ways different theorists of organization have understood the nature of culture.

Some writers believe that organization culture is something that is built into the organization as a subsystem. This is essentially the modernist view of culture discussed below. This perspective has influenced the more 'people-centred' view of organizations – neo-modernism – discussed in Chapter 3. In this view, organization culture is seen as complex sets of values that people hold about themselves and their organization. Emerging from this concern with values came a perspective that management could 'control' employees through culture. The idea of the 'corporate culture' is discussed as a feature of 'new-wave' management in Chapter 4.

Other writers believe that culture is something that members create and that it emerges out of the everyday interactions between people. In this tradition, organizations are made up of many 'cultures', and although there may be a dominating culture at any particular time, it is a temporary dominance. This is essentially the view of organization culture discussed in Chapters 7 and 8.

A third tradition in organization theory asserts that the concept of organization culture is essentially ambiguous and fractured and that other models of culture are attempts to impose a model of order where no order exists. This is essentially the postmodern view of culture discussed in Chapter 6.

## The modernist tradition in organization culture

In the modernist tradition, organization culture is one of the underlying systems of the organization and is something that when it is in a state of equilibrium – when the organization is operating effectively – preserves and maintains the values and goals of the organization. Although the word *culture* is used by recent modernist writers, they also use the word *climate* to describe it. The use of this word is interesting in that it describes a condition that is remote from human intervention; it is something that the organization actually *has* as part of its atmosphere, although, for modernists, it can be managed. The term *climate* also conveys the idea that it is something that can be measured in a scientific way, that data can give a rational picture of the state of the climate at any one time.

Daniel Denison (1996), an academic at the University of Michigan, notes that modernists are interested in the surface aspects of culture or climate, aspects that can be directly observed and can be generalized over a wide area of organizations. They are interested in such things as the way that offices are designed, the ways people work with each other and the kinds of 'facts' about the organization that can be gained from surveys and questionnaires. Organization theorists who work within this tradition believe that culture can be compared across organizations and different societies so that ultimately there can be a 'grand theory' of culture that 'explains' it as a universal phenomenon. For managers, the development of these general explanations of culture means that they can compare their culture or climate with that of other organizations. The overall perspective of this modernist approach is that organizational culture is a key organizational subsystem. Some of these issues can be seen in the Case study below. This is a description of the approach taken by a management consultancy company, Momentum, to organization climate.

## Case study        Climate surveys

'A climate survey is just that: it provides the equivalent of a meteorological situation map of an organization, indicating if cold fronts or anti-cyclones are on the way. Staff members are invited to supply views in complete confidence and anonymity. This provides managers with information on issues across the organization and in specific areas or divisions. The results often act as a catalyst for setting the strategic direction of the organization.

The survey's value springs from the anonymity the process provides. This enables it to unearth issues – positive as well as negative – that may have gone unnoticed and unrecognized.

Momentum has effectively administered climate surveys to a wide range of both private- and public sector organizations. We have developed a successful approach involving our own technology. This allows us to use one, or a combination of, paper-based, email or internet survey vehicles.

Our approach typically pursues the following process:

- survey questionnaire development
- analysis
- climate survey results
- following up
- survey questionnaire development.

Questionnaires are customized to your organization's requirement, with key 'factors' and related questions all agreed in consultation with you. Factors used by most organizations include things such as strategic direction, customer service, remuneration, job satisfaction, turnover and so on. As well as this, a range of demographic factors are also usually used. Some of these include length of service, gender, role, location, division and education level.

### Analysis

Our industrial psychologists specialize in statistical survey techniques. They carry out a comprehensive analysis of the data to identify significant trends and patterns from the factors targeted in the survey.

*(Continued)*

## Case study    (Continued)

### Climate survey results

As soon as a full analysis of both qualitative comments and quantitative information has been completed by staff, these are presented in a very simple yet informative format. This might include:

- a summary and overview of the survey response
- a comparison against past survey data
- benchmarking against other organizations
- outcomes and trends of each factor which the questionnaire was designed to measure
- survey data graphs and response statistics
- comments and feedback from staff
- order of priority of each question.

### Following up

Probably the most important part of this process is showing staff that action has been taken to address the issues raised. To this end, we provide workshops and facilitation kits to managers. These contain resources such as Over Head Transparencies, handouts, a facilitators' guide as well as a response sheet, so that staff can participate in identifying solutions to the issues raised.'

*Source:* Momentum Consultancy

The modernist perspective on organization culture is that it can be explored within the rules of natural science. There is an interest in generating 'general theories' of culture; it falls clearly within a systems approach, and culture is a 'functional imperative' within organizations. Key writers in this perspective, such as Denison, argue that there is a growing synthesis between this approach and the more 'human' approaches (to be discussed in Chapter 3), although the modernist approach retains its distinctive claim that it can develop frameworks for understanding organizational culture that has application to all organizations (Denison and Mishra, 1995).

## Conclusions: does modernist organization theory still provide challenges for new visions of the organization?

The starting point to this chapter was to look at 'modernism' as a dominating force in many aspects of social and cultural life during the twentieth century. There is, however, a major difference between discussions of modernism in theories of culture, the arts and architecture, and in organizations. In organization theory, the ideas of modernism were dominant for much of the twentieth century. The writers on organization theory Philip Hancock and Melissa Tyler (2001) suggest that historically interest in the 'modern' had previously been largely just taken for granted – it was the dominant story in town, organizationally speaking. The language of modernism provided theorists and managers (largely through the development of business schools) with dominance in the development of organization theory, with its 'promise' that modernism can improve organizational life (Hassard, 1996).

As the chapter developed, we saw that the underpinning core philosophy of modernism provides a strong underpinning to contemporary organizations. Indeed, in the case of new public management it has become, in some respects, a key discourse in the conduct of large public sector organizations. The continuing power of modernism as paradigm is, of course, controversial – for some writers, it represents the continuing dominance of a managerial elite supported by a stifling bureaucracy; for others, it is a means of developing an ordered organization in an unstable world.

## Concluding grid

| Learning outcome | The modernist challenge |
| --- | --- |
| Discuss modernism as a distinctive intellectual and aesthetic movement in the twentieth century. | To what extent does modernism continue to be a valued part of everyday life in architecture and the creative arts in your society? |
| Explore the central ideas of modernism in organization theory and relate these concepts to the twenty-first century organization. | Do modernist approaches to understanding issues of effectiveness and efficiency of organizations continue to be powerful in your society? |
| Analyse and explore the ways in which modernist organization theorists have a particular vision of the nature and being of organizations as ordered, controlled and rational places. | The concept of bureaucracy provides boundaries, structures and a sense of order and accountability that is essentially democratic. What is the role of bureaucracy in organizations in your society? Is its role diminishing or growing? |
| Analyse and explore the ways in which modernist organization theorists have a particular vision of the ways that organizations are to be understood and analysed through scientific approaches. | Systems theory has broadened the scope of organization theory by developing linkages between organization theory and other modes of scientific endeavour. What are the ways that systems theory influence organizations to gather and communicate information (e.g., IT strategies)? |
| Discuss the ways in which modernists take different approaches to organization design as a means of developing effective ways of responding to the external environment. | What has been the impact of new forms of modernism – new public management and McDonaldization – in organizations in your society? |
| Discuss the ways in which modernists develop a 'scientific' approach to the understanding of organization culture. | What is the value of developing an understanding of the 'climate' of an organization? |

## Annotated further reading

A book that gives an interesting overview of the modern condition of mind and life from the Enlightenment to the present day may be found in the book by John Jervis (1998) *Exploring the Modern*.

For a powerful view of the way a contemporary modernist came to his position and what it looks like, read Donaldson (2005). It is an interesting read from someone who is prepared to label himself as an extremist.

If you are interested in the moral debates about bureaucracy, the DVD/video *Conspiracy* is a chilling account of a meeting that took place during World War II about what came to be known as the 'final solution'. The film uses minutes that were taken at the meeting. It is a quite horrifying account of the ways evil ends can be pursued through 'neutral' bureaucratic means. A DVD/video that takes a different perspective, stressing the role of personal responsibility, is Stanley Kramer's 1961 film *Judgment at Nuremburg*.

A recent book that, in a compelling manner, puts forward a vigorous defence of bureaucracy as highly relevant to today's organizations is by Paul du Gay (2000) titled *In Praise of Bureaucracy: Weber, Organization, Ethics*.

## Discussion questions

1. Choose three examples of modernism in the arts and design and discuss them from aesthetic and practical perspectives. To what extent do the general ideas about modernism appeal to you in the twenty-first century? From your observation, how do these general ideas fit into your ideas about organizations in the twenty-first century?

2. Assess the claim that within modernism you can find order and stability and a rational approach to the world of organizations. Is this view still sustainable given the extent of globalization, diversity and complexity in the twenty-first century?

3. Can we make moral judgements about modernism?

4. Undertake a systems analysis (as in the model presented in this chapter) of an organization known to you. Estimate the value of systems analysis as an approach to understanding key features of organizational life.

5. Assess the debates about bureaucracy and evaluate the ways the bureaucratic form fits (or fails to fit) the functions of the contemporary organization.

6. As we have seen, whereas some writers represent the ideas of new public management as the only way to make large organizations truly responsive to the needs of contemporary society, others see it as a destructive force. What is your opinion?

## References

Barnard, C. (1938) *The Functions of the Executive*, Cambridge, MA: Harvard University Press.

Banman, Z. (1989) *Modernity and the holocaust*, London: Polity Press.

Berman, M. (1983) *All that is Solid Melts Into Air: The Experience of Modernity*, London: Verso.

Blau, P.M. and Scott, W.R. (1964) *Formal Organizations: A Comparative Approach*, London: Routledge & Kegan Paul.

Bogason, P. (1998) 'Changes in the Scandinavian model. From bureaucratic command to interorganizational negotiation', *Public Administration* 76(2):335–354.

Bolman, L.G. and Deal, T.E. (1997) *Reframing Organizations: Artistry, Choice, and Leadership*, San Francisco: Jossey Bass.

Bos, R.T. and Willmott, H. (2001) 'Towards post dualistic business ethics: Interweaving reason and emotion in working life', *Journal of Management Studies* 38(6):769–793.

Boulding, K.E. (1956) 'General systems theory: The skeleton of science', *Management Science* 2(3):197–208.

Bozeman, B. and Rainey, H.G. (1998) 'Organizational rules and the "bureaucratic personality"', *American Journal of Political Science* 42(1):163–189.

Burrell, G. (1998) 'Modernism, postmodernism and organizational analysis: The contribution of Michel Foucault', in A. McKinlay and K. Starkey (eds), *Foucault, Management and Organization Theory: From Panopticon to Technologies of Self*, London: Sage.

Cesarani, D. (2004) *Eichmann: His Life and Crimes*, London: Heinemann.

Denison, D.R. (1990) *Corporate Culture and Organizational Effectiveness*, New York: John Wiley & Sons.

Denison, D.R. and Mishra, A.K. (1995) 'Toward a theory of organizational culture and effectiveness', *Organization Science* 6(2):204–223.

Donaldson, L. (1996) 'The normal science of structural contingency theory', in S. Clegg, C. Hardy and W.R. Nord (eds), *Handbook of Organization Studies*, London: Sage.

Donaldson, L. (2005) 'Following the scientific method: How I became a committed functionalist and positivist', *Organization Studies* 26(7):1071–1088.

du Gay, P. (2000) *In Praise of Bureaucracy: Weber, Organization, Ethics*, London: Sage.

Frederickson, H.G. (2000) 'Can bureaucracy be beautiful?', *Public Administration Review* 60(1):47–53.

Foucault, M. (1977) *Discipline and Punish: The Birth of the Prison*, London: Penguin Books.

Gerth, H.H. and Mills C.W. (1948) 'Introduction: The man and his work', in H.H. Gerth and C. Wright Mills (eds), *From Max Weber: Essays in Sociology*, London: Routledge and Kegan Paul.

Gouldner, A. (1954) *Patterns of Industrial Bureaucracy*, New York: The Free Press.

Gustavsen, B. (1992) *Dialogue and Development*, Assen/Maastricht: Van Gorcum and Stockholm: The Swedish Centre for Working Life.

Hancock, P. and Tyler, M. (2001) *Work, Postmodernism and Organization: A Critical Introduction*, London: Sage.

Harrison, M.I. and Shirom, A. (1999) *Organizational Diagnosis and Assessment: Bridging Theory and Practice*, Thousand Oaks, CA: Sage.

Hassard, J. (1996) 'Exploring the terrain of modernism and postmodernism in organization theory', in D.M. Boje, R.P. Gephart, Jr. and T.J. Thatchenkery (eds), *Postmodern Management and Organization Theory*, Thousand Oaks, CA: Sage.

Hatch, M.J. (1997) *Organization Theory: Modern, Symbolic and Postmodern Perspectives*, Oxford: Oxford University Press.

Inns, D.E. and Jones, P.I. (1996) 'Metaphor in organization theory: Following in the footsteps of the poet?', in D. Grant and C. Oswick (eds), *Metaphor and Organizations*, London: Sage.

Jaffee, D. (2001) *Organization Theory: Tension and Change*, New York: McGraw Hill.

Jaques, E. (1990) 'In praise of hierarchy', *Harvard Business Review* 68(1):127–133.

Jervis, J. (1998) *Exploring the Modern*, Oxford: Blackwell Publishers.

Jones, F.E. (1996) *Understanding Organizations: A Sociological Perspective*, Toronto: Copp Clark Ltd.

Kalberg, S. (1997) 'Max Weber's Sociology: Research Strategies and Modes of Analysis', in C. Camic (ed.), *Reclaiming the Sociological Classics: The State of the Scholarship*, Oxford: Basil Blackwell.

Lemert, C. (1997) *Postmodernism Is Not What You Think*, Oxford: Blackwell Publishers Ltd.

Locke, R.R. (1996) *The Collapse of the American Management Mystique*, Oxford: Oxford University Press.

Merton, R.K. (1968) *Social Theory and Social Structure*, New York: The Free Press.

Parker, M. (1992) 'Postmodern organization or postmodern organization theory', *Organization Studies* 13(1): 1–17.

Parsons, T. (1951) *The Social System*, London: Routledge and Kegan Paul.

Pascale, R. (1990) *Managing on the Edge: How Successful Companies Use Conflict to Stay Ahead*, Harmondsworth: Penguin.

Prichard, C. and Willmott, H. (1997) 'Just how managed is the McUniversity?', *Organization Studies* 18(12):287–316.

Pugh, D.S. (1973) 'The measurement of organization structures: Does context determine form?' *Organizational Dynamics* Spring:19–34.

Reed, M.I. (1993) 'Organizations and modernity: Continuity and discontinuity in organization theory', in J. Hassard and M. Parker (eds), *Postmodernism and Organizations*, London: Sage.

Ritzer, G. (1993) *The McDonaldization of Society*, Newbury Park, CA: Pine Forge.

Schein, E. (1988) *Organizational Psychology*, Englewood Cliffs, NJ: Prentice-Hall.

Scott, W.G. (1963) 'Organization theory: An overview and an appraisal', in K. Davis and W.G. Scott (eds), *Readings in Human Relations*, 2nd edn, New York: McGraw-Hill.

Sennett, R. (2006) *The Culture of the New Capitalism*, London: Yale University Press.

Schulz, M. (1998) 'Limits to Bureaucratic Growth: The Density Dependence of Organizational Rule Births', *Administrative Science Quarterly* 43(4):845–876.

Sorge, A. (2002) 'Organization', in A. Sorge (ed), *Organization*, London: Thomson Learning.

Stacey, R.D. (2001) *Strategic Management and Organizational Dynamics: The Challenge of Complexity*, 3rd edn, Harlow: Financial Times/Prentice Hall.

Strati, A. (1999) *Organization and Aesthetics*, London: Sage.

Weber, M. (1904) 'The Protestant ethic and the spirit of capitalism', in T. Parsons, E. Shils, K.D. Naegele and J.R. Pitts (eds) (1965), *Theories of Society: Foundations of Modern Sociological Theory*, New York: The Free Press.

Weber, M. (1920) 'Some consequences of bureaucratization', in L.A. Coser and B. Rosenberg (eds) (1989), *Sociological Theory: A Book of Readings*, 5th edn, Prospect Heights, IL: Waveland Press.

Weber, M. (1922) 'Bureaucracy', in H.H. Gerth and C. Wright Mills (1948) *From Max Weber: Essays in Sociology*, London: Routledge and Kegan Paul.

# Chapter 3

# Neo-modernist organization theory: putting people first?

## Introduction

As we saw in Chapter 2, classic modernism continues to be a powerful force in organization theory. However, a newer form of modernism – known as neo-modernism – emerged in the first half of the past century to challenge in particular the place of the 'human' in organizations. Neo-modernism is 'neo' in the sense that it is an organization theory that is concerned with putting people at the heart of the organization; it is 'modernist' in the sense that it assumes that effective 'organizations' are fundamental to human progress. The neo-modernists are interested in the ways in which the values and beliefs of people shape and are shaped by their experience of organizational life. This leads to their interest in organization culture, in the ways that organizations 'need' to be designed around people and in understanding processes of change.

Within neo-modernism there are two key traditions. The first is the 'human relations' movement that was closely associated with Harvard Business School. As it developed, it was underpinned by the belief that insights from the social sciences such as psychology, sociology and anthropology can be used to create practical theories about the most effective ways to create a relationship between people and organizations. In the human relations tradition, organizations need leadership and management with a human face in order to create the 'best' environment for people. A different tradition within neo-modernism, that of the 'democratic organization' emphasizes the idea of empowerment of *all* members of the organization. This tradition is discussed briefly in this chapter and is returned to in Chapters 8 and 9.

## Learning outcomes

- Explore the development of neo-modernism as a 'practical' organization theory based on insights and methodologies of the social sciences with a concern for its practical application in organizations.

- Discuss the human relations school as a pervasive example of neo-modernist organization theory and philosophy.

- Examine the Hawthorne Studies as a classic piece of applied organizational research within the neo-modernist tradition.

- Discuss how neo-modernist organization theory challenges understandings of the relationship between organizations and society.

- Explore the development by neo-modernists of an understanding of organization culture.

- Discuss how neo-modernist organization theory develops challenges in the design and development of organizations.

## Structure of the chapter

- The chapter begins with a discussion of the key ideas that lie behind the idea of neo-modernism. We show how it developed, particularly in the United States, as an attempt to bring together the social sciences into a distinctive organization theory with a focus on people in organizations, which would have practical applications for managers in organizations. We show how this idea is used to demonstrate a number of ways that the neo-modernist approach is important in contemporary organizations. We then consider one of the dominant approaches to neo-modernist organization theory – the human relations school that developed at Harvard Business School in the United States of America. This leads to a discussion of the Hawthorne Studies as one of the major research projects undertaken by Harvard Business School that has had a lasting influence on the development of organizational research. After this overview of the development of neo-modernism, we discuss the way that it challenges understandings of the relationship between organizations and society, how it developed an understanding of organizational culture and a particular approach to the management of change.

## Neo-modernist organization theory focuses attention on the human issues in organization

This chapter shows how a body of organization theory known as neo-modernism emerged during the 1920s largely out of concerns that modernist organization theory (see Chapter 2) failed to explain the place of 'the human' in the organization. The advocates of neo-modernism rejected the idea that people in organizations only work for economic reward and that their primary motivation for working more productively is for even greater reward. They believed that people work in organizations for a variety of reasons – economic reward, individual satisfaction, membership of a social group, 'belonging' to an organization, having a say in the running of the organization – and for organizations to be *effective*, account needs to be given to these different aspects of human motivation. Although some of the principles of neo-modernism changed over time, there were two enduring concerns in the movement:

1. They applied the approaches and methodologies of social science to organizations. The neo-modernists looked to psychology, sociology and anthropology as the core bodies of theory from which they developed their understanding of organization and management.

2. They saw that in order to develop effective organizations, there was the need to integrate the person into the organization. The neo-modernists are 'modernist' in the sense that they understand the notion of 'organization' as a cornerstone to human activity. The early proponents of neo-modernism came from the United States and were called the 'human relations' school, which during its long history, has undergone peaks and dips in its fortune. Thus, the British sociologist Michael Rose, writing in 1976, suggested that although the human relations movement had considerable intellectual diversity, it was by the 1970s 'in disgrace'. This was largely because of the way it emphasized the importance of management and because it had come to be seen as a means by which employees could be manipulated to work more effectively for organizations. At the same time, developments of the human relations school continue to be a powerful force in English speaking, and to a lesser extent, European thinking about the relationship between an organization and its members.

A different strand of neo-modernism in American and European thought emphasized ideas of democracy and participation in organizations as opposed to the more conventionally 'hierarchical' approaches of the human relations school. These ideas about democratic organization represent a bridge between neo-modernism and radical theories of organization, and they are discussed in greater length, particularly in a European context, in Chapters 8 and 9.

## 'There is nothing so practical as a good theory'

When the social psychologist Kurt Lewin (1951) observed, 'There is nothing so practical as a good theory' (p. 169), he was suggesting that as organization theory develops, there is a need to integrate theory with practice. This reflects a belief in modernist and neo-modernist thought that theory should have a direct application to the development of organizations. Through this link between theory and practice, neo-modernists argue, organization members can undertake key tasks such as leadership and management, developing the relationships between organization members, and the design of organizations, in a sophisticated and crafted manner. Although all the theories discussed in this text enable the development of understanding of organizations, they do so in a diversity of ways – some are 'practical'; others encourage reflection, a critical understanding of organizations or an exploration of the very fundamentals of organizational life.

The following section concentrates primarily on, as a key example of neo-modernism, the ways the human relations school has developed as a 'practical theory', although the section also mentions the democratic strand in neo-modernist thought. This school had (for reasons to be discussed later) the development of a relationship between the academic world and business and industry as a distinctive part of its mission and purpose.

## How Roethlisberger developed a 'practical' organization theory

One of the key thinkers and researchers of the human relations school, F.J. Roethlisberger, provided, in a paper written in 1948, an indication of the way organization theory could develop as a scientific approach to the issues that confront people (especially managers) in organizations.

Chapter 1 described the ways organization theory has developed into a distinctive social science discipline so that it is a body of thinking and writing that tries to describe, explain and influence what goes on in organizations. We also saw that within 'organization theory', there are many differences and conflicts between the different

| Biography | Jules Roethlisberger 1894–1974 |
| --- | --- |

Fritz Jules Roethlisberger was one of the founders of the 'human relations' movement based at Harvard University Business School that we discuss in a later section. He was born in 1894 and died in 1974.

He was, according to Eric Dent, an assistant professor at George Washington University, deeply interested in the exploration of the actions of members of organizations. One of the outcomes of this was the research and writings that were based on what came to be called the 'Hawthorne Experiments' (or Hawthorne Studies), which are discussed in a later section. Roethlisberger was fascinated by language and its role in written and oral communication – why do we choose one word rather than another?, why does the CEO send a memo about one situation but not another? In many ways, his approach to organizations was that of an anthropologist, exploring the patterns of communication, the values and the deeper social structures of organization life. He blended this with a practical approach, with the idea that managers could also be anthropologists of organizational life, so that they, too, could understand the deeper human issues. Roethlisberger was not entirely comfortable with the tensions in his academic life between his intellectual research interests and the culture at Harvard Business School, which had a close relationship between the 'academic' and 'business' worlds, although he was a key member of the Harvard MBA programme. He was probably the first person, in 1958, to coin the expression 'organization behaviour' (Dent, 2000).

schools of thought. Roethlisberger asks two fundamental questions: How do we develop an organization theory that enables the development of the human aspects of organization? and How can organization theory explore issues such as leadership, motivation, the development of groups and culture so that members can be more effective in their work? He argues that such a theory needs three components:

1. **Explore and synthesize in a variety of ways insights from the social sciences.** If, for example, we were undertaking research into the ways an organization is managing change, we could use insights from anthropology to explore issues of culture change; psychology to be aware of the ways teams work together; and sociology to understand issues of power, authority and conflict.

2. **The second component is** what we referred to in Chapter 1 as the epistemological perspective, and that is, to **use the methodologies and techniques of the social sciences.** In the interests of developing a socially scientific approach to the exploration of organizations, we need to have a range of methods that will provide an objective

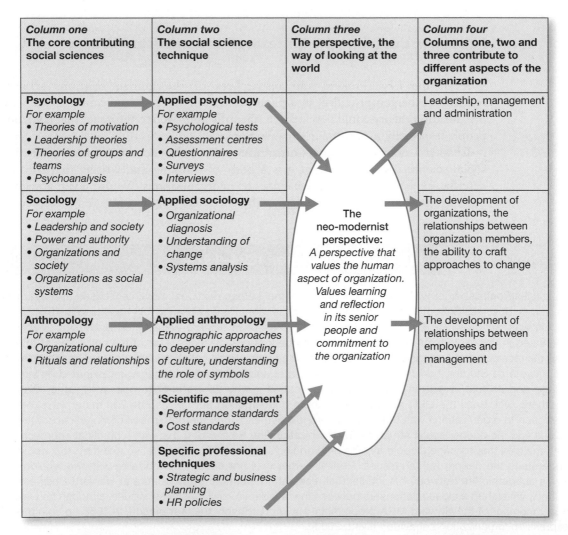

Figure 3.1: From science to application – a systems model. (*Source:* Adapted from Roethlisberger, 1948.)

view of the organization. These methods can range from the qualitative methods such as the close ethnographic observation of people in their work settings through to quantitative approaches such as questionnaires and surveys and even 'experiments'.

3. **The third component is** what we referred to in Chapter 1 as the ontological perspective, **the way we see and understand the very nature of what it is to be human.** For the neo-modernist there are two key aspects to this. On the one hand, their ontology is humanistic. They place 'the human' as central in the order of nature. They also believe that humanity is different from the 'natural' world and that it therefore needs to be studied and understood in ways that are different from the world of nature. In place of the ontology of rationality and order of the modernists, the humanist ontology stresses the role of values and culture in the development of the organization.

A key aspect of the neo-modernists' ontological position is that the human world can be understood from a systems approach. In this sense, they are similar to the modernists (discussed in Chapter 2). The human world is underpinned by systems. As we shall see, an organization's design and development can be explored using a systems approach, and culture can be explored as a system. This ontological position is the means by which the neo-modernists can *reflect* on the ways theory and practical action can be integrated.

This approach is expressed in Figure 3.1, which is an adapted and updated version of Roethlisberger's 1948 model.

As the model develops, you can see how there is an integration of various elements that contributes to an organization theory that claims to be both rigorous and provides practical application to organizations.

## Column 1: The core contributing social sciences

The social science bases of neo-modernism lie in different combinations of psychology, sociology and anthropology. Some of the authors associated with this tradition are psychologists interested in developing theories of individual motivation and leadership qualities. Others take a more sociological approach in their interest in the relationship between organization members and their society, yet others have an anthropological take on organizations in their interest in 'shared values' and culture. These are not just issues for the academic or researcher. An understanding of these core contributing social sciences is also important for managers and leaders because these social sciences provide the core underpinning to the development of understanding of the human issues in organizations.

## Column 2: The techniques for analysis

Different combinations of the scientific techniques and methods that come from these social science disciplines provide different approaches to diagnosis and understanding. In the case of the analysis of individual motivation, for example, survey and questionnaire methods derived from psychology have been used to 'measure' members' feelings about the forces that motivate and demotivate them in the workplace. Sociological methods such as interviews have been used to develop insights into members' under-standings of organizational 'culture', and anthropological approaches of participant observation have been used to develop understanding of the deeper myths and stories that people tell of their organization. From a neo-modernist perspective, these tech-niques of analysis and understanding of the human features of organization are just as important as the quantitative approaches to data analysis.

From a practical organizational perspective, Roethlisberger suggests that **methods that are derived from scientific management and 'professional techniques'** can play a part in the development of means of evaluating performance. By this, he means that as part of the repertoire of techniques that managers have available to them, the rafts of performance standards and measures of success or failure can be used to measure organizational effectiveness. The sorts of 'professional techniques' used include many different techniques and methods that marketing, human resource and other professionals use. However, what is important about using these methodologies is, from a neo-modernist perspective, to use them with a 'human face'. If, for example, the organization has performance targets to meet, they should not be treated as absolutes in a mechanistic manner but rather as targets that are the basis for informed discussion about how they are to be achieved.

## Column 3: The neo-modernist perspective

The social sciences and the techniques are filtered through the lens of the neo-modernist perspective. The perspective is the way that the different theories are integrated and are developed to produce a 'practical' theory of action that can be applied to organizational issues. Within neo-modernism, this perspective is expressed primarily through the human relations school and its later developments or through the ideas of what is known as democratic neo-modernism. At the heart of these perspectives:

1. **Human relations** is concerned with problems of communication and understanding between individuals and groups and between groups. It is also concerned with the problems of 'securing action and cooperation' (Roethlisberger, 1948, p. 106) within organizations and the 'maintenance of individual and organizational equilibrium' through processes of change. This emphasis on cooperation and equilibrium relates back to some of the modernist assumptions that underpin neo-modernism. One of the key themes in neo-modernism is that organizations need to be orderly human systems in which conflict needs to be carefully controlled. The maintenance of a sense of equilibrium means that people are not pushed too far out of their 'comfort zones' in times of change, so they can concentrate on their effective membership of the organization. From a more critical perspective, the sociologist Stewart Clegg (1990) suggests that the stress on the ways that leaders and managers 'manipulate internal characteristics such as employee morale, motivation and teamwork' (p. 51) in order to affect outputs causes it to be a relatively closed systems approach because it tends to ignore the external environment

   Roethlisberger suggests that the human relations approach accords with scientific principles because it has a clear method, can ask 'useful' questions, has organizing principles so that a holistic view of the organization can be gained and it can develop simple 'theories and hypotheses' to enable learning and development.

2. As an example of the **democratic perspective,** we can cite what the Norwegian academic Haldor Byrkjeflot calls the 'Nordic tradition'. This perspective places great emphasis on worker involvement and workplace democracy than does the human relations approach. There has been a strong emphasis on the development of intellectual and emotional capability at all 'levels' (rather than in just the managers and leaders) in the organization in Nordic countries over a number of years. This interest in the potential of all members of staff was more deeply embedded in managerial culture in these countries at an earlier period than in many other Western countries. For historical reasons, the creation of an atmosphere in which the organization can rely on loyalty and commitment is considered less risky in Nordic countries than in many others (Kreiner and Mouritsen, 2003). This democratic perspective also has its place in the United States. The development of the democratic perspective provides a link between neo-modernism and more radical approaches to organization theory discussed in Chapter 8; the implications of this perspective for management are discussed in Chapter 9.

## Column 4: Contributions to business and management

The aim of neo-modernism is to provide a practical theory for the development of the human aspects of organization. Roethlisberger saw that there were three ways this organization theory could make a difference. They are:

1. The development of new approaches to the management and leadership of organizations.

2. The development of both staff and organizations; the development of processes of change that take into account the human factor.

3. The development of improved relationships between different 'levels' in the organization.

These three contributions have had a profound effect on the development of organizations, and they will be discussed as the chapter unfolds.

This model can be used in a number of ways. Roethlisberger suggested that one approach is to look at a number of approaches to developing organizations that are reflected in organization and management texts and to develop an understanding of how these approaches are developed.

## Four combinations of science, scientific technique and the neo-modernist approach reach different parts of the organization

This section will show how neo-modernist organization theory has had a powerful effect on the development of organizations. Roethlisberger had the view that his model could be used at different 'levels' in order to look at different approaches to core issues in organizations, and we have adapted his ideas to focus on four levels:

1. **Level 1 – Developing the organization:** At this level, we can see how neo-modernists use a range of theories from the social sciences and use core ideas in neo-modernism

to develop an understanding of the human processes involved in change in organizations. This level points to the importance of culture and design of organizations in the change process.

2. **Level 2 – Managing the human resource:** This level includes the ways that psychology together with neo-modernist perspectives leads to approaches to human resource management.

3. **Level 3 – 'We are a people-centred organization':** The ways that human relations philosophy can develop an organization that looks to create an organization that members believe 'cares' for them.

4. **Level 4 – The world of the management guru:** This level is a warning about the rise of the management guru, the 'expert' who emphasizes the 'people factor' in organizations.

In the discussion of the four levels that follows, we have concentrated on the human relations school because it provides the clearest articulation of the ways these levels may be found both in the literature and in organizations.

## Level 1: Developing the organization

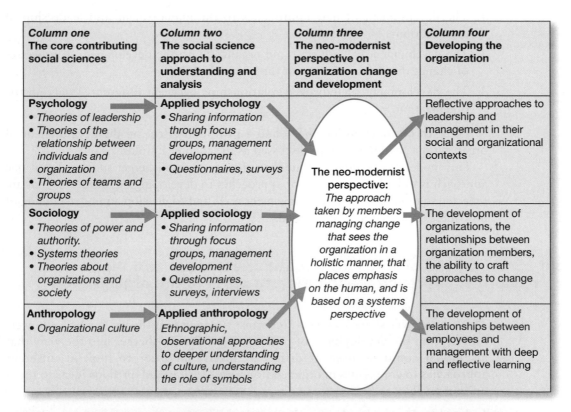

| *Column one*<br>**The core contributing social sciences** | *Column two*<br>**The social science approach to understanding and analysis** | *Column three*<br>**The neo-modernist perspective on organization change and development** | *Column four*<br>**Developing the organization** |
|---|---|---|---|
| **Psychology**<br>• *Theories of leadership*<br>• *Theories of the relationship between individuals and organization*<br>• *Theories of teams and groups* | **Applied psychology**<br>• *Sharing information through focus groups, management development*<br>• *Questionnaires, surveys* | **The neo-modernist perspective:** *The approach taken by members managing change that sees the organization in a holistic manner, that places emphasis on the human, and is based on a systems perspective* | Reflective approaches to leadership and management in their social and organizational contexts |
| **Sociology**<br>• *Theories of power and authority.*<br>• *Systems theories*<br>• *Theories about organizations and society* | **Applied sociology**<br>• *Sharing information through focus groups, management development*<br>• *Questionnaires, surveys, interviews* | | The development of organizations, the relationships between organization members, the ability to craft approaches to change |
| **Anthropology**<br>• *Organizational culture* | **Applied anthropology**<br>*Ethnographic, observational approaches to deeper understanding of culture, understanding the role of symbols* | | The development of relationships between employees and management with deep and reflective learning |

**Figure 3.2:** Designing and developing an organization. (*Source:* Based on Roethlisberger, 1948.)

This is the richest of all the combinations of elements because it provides a crucial focus on the ways organizations can be designed and developed (Figure 3.2). As we shall discuss later, the approach known as organization development is based on the application of social sciences ranging from psychological theories through to anthropology in different combinations according to the situation. It is based upon the idea that before an organization undergoes major development, members need to understand at a deep level the current state of the organization. They do this through processes of diagnosis based on the social sciences. Some of the typical means of this kind of exploration are mentioned in Column 2.

In terms of its perspective, organization development is a humanistic and systems-based approach. Because of its emphasis on the need to gain the commitment of the members and because it looks at the organization as a system, it is an approach that is planned over a long time scale. From a human relations perspective, in this process of design and development, there is an emphasis on the key role of top management and on the development of an organizational vision as a means of integrating people with the organization. From both a human relations and democratic perspective, organization development emphasizes the empowerment of people, organization learning and the collaborative crafting of design and development (French and Bell, 1999).

## Level 2: Managing the human resource

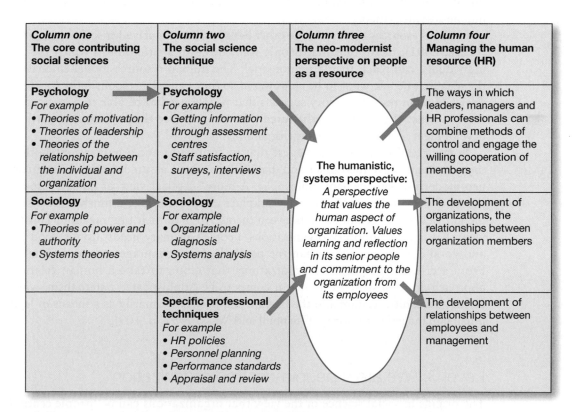

**Figure 3.3:** Managing the human resource. (*Source:* Based on Roethlisberger, 1948.)

At the heart of human relations lies a key issue: that organizations are able to get members to achieve specified standards of performance, but they can do so because members are committed to those standards. Managers need not only set standards but also ensure that people 'accept them logically, understandingly and emotionally' (Roethlisberger, 1948, p. 105).

In the fullness of time, this notion of creating commitment to standards becomes part of the role of human resource management, and with it the professionals 'who are dedicated to leveraging HR practices . . . that create value and deliver results' (Ulrich, 1997, p. 234). Within neo-modernist human resource management, there are basically two approaches. The American academic Raymond Miles initially addressed these in an influential paper in 1965, and it has been extensively developed in the human resource literature since then. The first approach is developed from the human relations theory and the second from 'human resource theory'.

The human relations approach, according to the writers on organization theory Bolman and Deal (1997), is concerned with developing the relationship between the individual and the organization through such strategies as good pay, security, promotion from within, training and 'sharing the fruits of organizational success' (p. 141). This approach has a strong emphasis on the idea that the organization is committed to employees and their emotional satisfaction. This is associated with a sense of celebration that comes with working for a successful company. Those who live within the human relations tradition, such as the psychologist Chris Argyris (1998), express impatience with contemporary concepts of empowerment that lie at the heart of human resources theory.

Human resources theory, on the other hand, assumes a drive for self-actualization (Jaffee, 2001), the notion that people want to be in a situation in which they, as individuals, can reach their true potential. The human resource model emphasizes the idea that people want to be empowered so they can take responsibility for themselves. Human resource theory suggests that people need to be able to participate in the ways that their work is structured. Human resource theory moves toward the development of a more democratic organization.

Bolman and Deal (1997) suggest that in contemporary organizations both of these strategies have their place and that effectiveness is assured through a long-term neo-modernist management philosophy. A more sceptical view of human resource theory is that in the contemporary workplace, employees take a much more instrumental view of the relationship between themselves and their organization. This is a view that in contemporary organizations, people's primary needs are for good pay and good conditions rather than the psychological advantages of empowerment. From a critical perspective, organizations that claim to take a human relations approach do so in such a way that it comes to be 'sophisticated paternalism, where caring, humanity, welfare and the like are emphasized primarily as a means of legitimizing managerial authority' (Turnbull and Wass, 1997, p. 109).

## Level 3: 'We are a people-centred organization'

The origins in social science of the view that organizations can be 'people centred' come at least in part from an emerging understanding that organizations are rich and complex arenas in which understanding members' emotional lives is of crucial

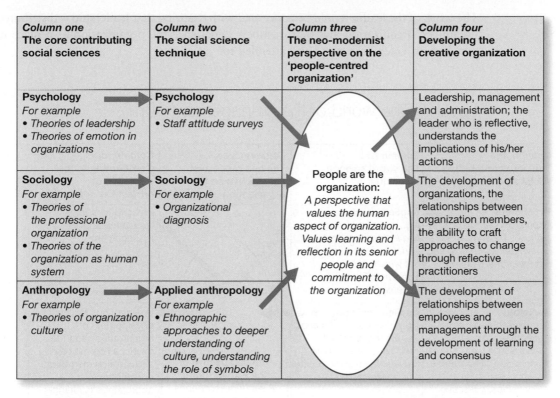

**Figure 3.4:** We are a people-centred organization. (*Source:* Based on Roethlisberger, 1948.)

importance. In the people-centred organization, the actions of management and leaders are infused with a core belief in the creation of a sense of trust and openness to learning and development. This focus on 'people' has a clear purpose. It is directly related to the ability of senior management to *gain and sustain* the commitment of employees and the ability of employees to *give* 'commitment'. This concept lies at the heart of human relations in modern organizations (Fincham, 2000).

This interest in the 'people-centred' organization has also, within the human relations perspective, led to the rise of a particular form of leadership. This type of leader symbolizes the aspirations of the organization and its members. This kind of leader believes he or she can have a major impact on the organization by empowering organization members. It is an approach to leadership that emphasizes leaders' personal characteristics and the way they create organizational settings within which they enact their leadership. (Hunt, 1991). They operate on the basis that their vision and the intellectual stimulation they provide will enable subordinates to succeed beyond their own expectations by persuading them to overcome their own self-interests and to focus on the organization's vision (Conger and Benjamin, 1999). We return in later chapters to these issues.

Neomodernist democratic approaches to leadership are rather different from this. As we show in Chapter 8, there is a suspicion of the very concept of 'leadership' and an expectation that the leader would symbolize the values of democratic organization.

The work of the leader would be concerned with ensuring that leadership is distributed within the organization and that members experience the organization as a place in which their 'voices' are heard and attended to.

## Level 4: The world of the management guru

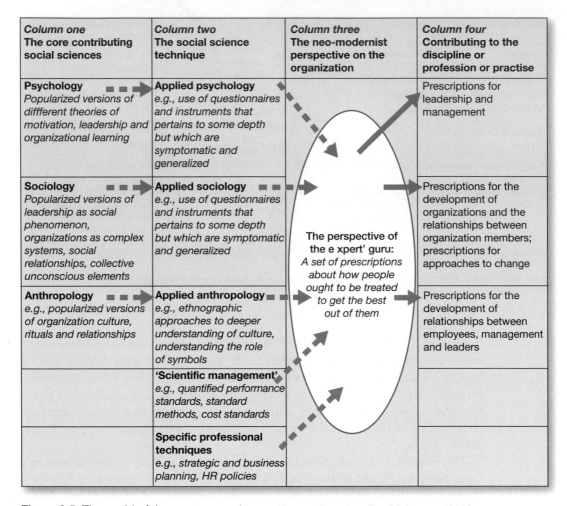

| Column one<br>The core contributing social sciences | Column two<br>The social science technique | Column three<br>The neo-modernist perspective on the organization | Column four<br>Contributing to the discipline or profession or practise |
|---|---|---|---|
| **Psychology**<br>*Popularized versions of diffferent theories of motivation, leadership and organizational learning* | **Applied psychology**<br>*e.g., use of questionnaires and instruments that pertains to some depth but which are symptomatic and generalized* | | Prescriptions for leadership and management |
| **Sociology**<br>*Popularized versions of leadership as social phenomenon, organizations as complex systems, social relationships, collective unconscious elements* | **Applied sociology**<br>*e.g., use of questionnaires and instruments that pertains to some depth but which are symptomatic and generalized* | **The perspective of the e xpert' guru:**<br>*A set of prescriptions about how people ought to be treated to get the best out of them* | Prescriptions for the development of organizations and the relationships between organization members; prescriptions for approaches to change |
| **Anthropology**<br>*e.g., popularized versions of organization culture, rituals and relationships* | **Applied anthropology**<br>*e.g., ethnographic approaches to deeper understanding of culture, understanding the role of symbols* | | Prescriptions for the development of relationships between employees, management and leaders |
| | **'Scientific management'**<br>*e.g., quantified performance standards, standard methods, cost standards* | | |
| | **Specific professional techniques**<br>*e.g., strategic and business planning, HR policies* | | |

**Figure 3.5:** The world of the management guru. (*Source:* Based on Roethlisberger, 1948.)

Roethlisberger's (1948) description of this level is, from a twenty-first century perspective, highly prescient. It was for him the most problematic of all the ways the neo-modernist approaches to organizations can operate. He writes that this approach attempts to give people rules for 'success' on how to get other people to do what you want them to, on how to be 'happy' and 'human' at the same 'time' (p. 106). He notes how this approach can be neatly packaged and marketed but 'misses completely the tremendous complexity of the problems with which the field of *human relations* is concerned' (p. 106). The writers on organization theory David Knights and Hugh Willmott (1999) show how core themes in human relations have become distorted by prescriptive, recipe-driven approaches to change and business processes and the ways these approaches exploit organization members (Figure 3.5).

The processes by which management gurus communicate their 'solutions' to organizational challenges are captured by the organization theorist Andrew Huczynski (1996). He suggests that many managers and leaders find that their organizations are enormously complex and that they 'need' someone to lead them through this difficulty into a simpler world. What they find helpful are sets of relatively simple recipes, prescriptions that tell them how they 'ought' to run their organizations or to fire their imagination with new ideas. In this sense, the 'management guru' is seen to be attractive. Typically, the management guru brings into the presentation a smattering of theory and is powerful in advocating the core philosophy or idea with strong ideas as to how he or she will improve the organization. Within the human relations tradition, favourite themes of the 'gurus' have been leadership, motivation of employees and organization culture. They have been particularly influential in the development of the 'new-wave' ideas discussed in Chapter 4. The ideas of the guru are transmitted in many different media. Gurus appear on TV, produce texts (sometimes referred to as 'airport lounge' books) that are immediately accessible, and appear as conference speakers.

## Example: A tale for our times – the guru speaks

The stage is set. There is a simple lectern and a large screen. The audience consists of more than 200 senior managers and leaders who have paid a considerable fee to be present at the event, a presentation on 'Be a better leader'. They are seated at round tables with a dozen colleagues.

The lights go down, and the guru enters onto the well-lit stage. In a previous life, she was an academic at a distinguished university. But over time, she discovered that she had a story to tell, and she knew that she could tell it well. She walks to the podium. The audience is expectant. She receives the sort of applause that would greet a great singer. The audience settles down. She begins her story. Her PowerPoint presentation takes us through the presentation bullet point by bullet point. There are jokes that are received with bursts of laughter, there are personal anecdotes with which the audience identifies, and there are moments when you can see other members of the audience nodding sagely in agreement with some key point. When the guru tells us that our organizations cannot perform properly because our leadership is inadequate, we agree with her (even though it is us she is criticizing). She then tells us a 'better way' to perform our leadership. As she takes us through this route, we begin to feel better because we feel sure that what she is saying makes sense, although there are one or two sceptical members of the audience who think that her ideas about leadership are really rather old-fashioned.

From Roethlisberger's point of view, the development of prescriptive recipes that were neatly packaged in order to provide solutions to organizational problems was highly problematic in that they presented 'easy solutions' to difficult problems. It is through the example of the 'guru' with its superficial exploration and explanation that he is making a claim for the seriousness of the development of an organizational theory that has depth in its application of the insights from social sciences through the lens of the neo-modernist perspective.

## The chapter so far

So far, we have looked at the nature of neo-modernism and how it differs from but is also related to modernist organization theory. It is modernist in the sense that the organization's goals and purposes are of primary importance and in the sense that neo-modernists want to provide practical solutions to organizational issues.

What was new in this perspective was that 'people' (the human factor) were given high prominence. We also see in neo-modernism the rise of an interest in an empirical, social science-based understanding of organizations. We have also seen that there is a tension within neo-modernism between the human relations approach with its emphasis on commitment to the organization and more democratic approaches with their emphasis on empowerment.

These themes were discussed through an exploration of Roethlisberger's model, which shows how there can be a relationship between:

- Different **social sciences** that provide the intellectual core of neo-modernist approaches to organization theory.

- The **techniques of social science** that provide a sound empirical base for the study of organizations.

- A **core organizational philosophy**, ontology or belief about the nature of organization that provides a lens through which the exploration can occur. This core organizational philosophy is humanistic in that it places the human as central to all activity and is based upon the idea that organizations are systems.

- The **application** of these to different features of organizational life such as the quality of leadership, the development of organizations, and the management of people.

We have shown how these four dimensions give rise to a number of core themes, practical theories for organizations – the development of organizations, managing the human resource, the 'people-centred organization' and the rise of the management guru – that have been influential in the development of the contemporary organization.

In the course of the chapter, we have mentioned on a number of occasions the human relations school as one of the crucial movements within neo-modernism. In the next section, we shall turn the focus on the development of this school and show how its ideas and approach to research in organizations became one of the key bodies of organization theory during the twentieth century.

## The human relations school as an example of neo-modernist organization theory

### How 'human relations' begins

This story[1] goes back to the 1920s, just after World War I. In the United States, some four million workers were on strike – it was a period of great industrial and business unrest. In a more global setting, there was the great influenza pandemic (which killed

---

[1]The following story of the development of a movement and a manifesto is based upon an extended case study by Ellen O'Connor (1999b), the title of which gives a good indication of where this section is taking us – 'The politics of management thought: A case study of the Harvard Business School and the human relations school'.

some 8,000,000 people), the rise of the communist system, developing mass inflation in some European economies and attempts to recover from the war. There was also (just as happened after the World War II) physical and philosophical reconstruction – an attempt to 'rethink who we are'.

In the sphere of what we would now call organization theory, there was in the United States a conflict between two distinct views. Part of the 'philosophical reconstruction' movement consisted of thinkers who were concerned to establish 'industrial democracy'. These ideas are discussed briefly in this chapter and in greater depth in Chapters 8 and 9. Other theorists, however, opposed this position. They took a position that was antidemocratic and that stressed the authority of leadership and management. They believed that democracy placed too much faith in the intellectual capacity of labour to value democratic approaches to the workplace. The way that this latter view achieved dominance in American thinking for many years is an interesting example of the way a particular organization theory can be aligned to the interests of business and industry. One of the leading writers in this tradition was Elton Mayo.

The continuing influence of Mayo's thought, particularly over issues of control through the organization culture, are discussed in Chapter 4.

In 1927, Mayo was recruited into Harvard Business School. Many senior industrialists already respected Mayo's work. There was a feeling that Mayo's human relations approach, combined with his belief that organizations were best run by a management elite, was a good combination. What was more, his intellectual capabilities as a polymath – sometime moral philosopher, industrial psychologist and sociologist – were considered impeccable, although academics from later generations believed that Mayo showed neither the patience nor scepticism that proper social research demands (Rose, 1978). Mayo's ability to recognize emergent social problems and to popularize explanations and solutions 'turned him into a kind of human relations superstar' (p. 114). This collaboration persisted for many years between the business school, distinguished academics, and business and industry. It provided powerful support for the idea that there can be a way of managing organizations that is centred on people but within the context of strong leadership. In many respects, the tradition that the development of theory needs to be aligned to the interests of business and industry continues within Harvard Business School and its publications today.

## What is the human relations school?

This story shows that during the 1920s and 1930s in the United States, a sustained attempt to develop a *movement* in organization theory began to appear. As discussed in an earlier section, what was novel about the development of this school was that it represents a synthesis of social sciences, the techniques associated with those social sciences and a particular perspective about the nature of the relationship between members of organizations and their organizations. Then, crucially, there was a concern to apply the insights from this synthesis into business and industry.

As the human relations school developed as a body of theory and research, a number of themes began to appear that, as the movement evolved, contained some conflicting elements but overall a coherent view of the world. This may be seen in the definitions of the human relations school that can be seen in the following Ideas and perspectives box.

## Some definitions of the human relations school

*Modern society faces two interrelated crises.* On the one hand, economic activity is showing evidence of *an alarming and a growing trend towards instability*; whilst, on the other hand *the mass of industrial workers are failing to take their place as an integral part of the industrial society*, thus further threatening the social and economic structure. (Whitehead, 1935, p. 1) . . . It is a disaster of the first magnitude that industrialists and their employees have devoted their talents to evolving countless devices for the better cooperation of labor without ever emphasizing *the one essential condition for success: a secure and adequate relationship within the working group for each and every individual involved* (p. 10).

Human Relations *is a field of research, teaching and practice, just as is the field of medicine.* While the professors at Harvard did not pretend to be businessmen, or even men of action, *they felt that they and the businessmen had a kindred interest and a kindred approach. Both theorist and practitioner were interested in the process of getting cooperative action in organized human activity* (Schoen, 1957, p. 92).

The latest manifestation of the human relations school has been to emphasize 'the development of *"the cultures of excellence approach"* that places an emphasis on such matters as organizational commitment, transformational leadership and the development of teams' (Grint and Case, 2000, p. 38).

These different definitions of the human relations approach show that the approach attempts to be an integrative and scientific approach to understanding the ways human activity is in a complex relationship with social and organizational features. The first of the definitions, from T.N. Whitehead, one of the leading associates of Elton Mayo, reflects the early concern in the human relations school that industrial societies were on the point of collapse into either anarchy or extremist, totalitarian forms of society. The best way forward in dealing with this was to make organizations into havens of safety within which members can find meaning through their working groups.

The second definition, from the American academic Donald Schoen, reflects the way the human relations school reflected the application of social science to business and industry in developing an understanding of the ways behaviour in organizations could be organized. The third definition, from two UK academics Keith Grint and Peter Case, reflects the way the human relations approach has moved into an exploration of the ways organizational culture can be developed in order to ensure that there is commitment to the organization. It also reflects the idea that although the human relations school as a *distinctive movement* began to go into a decline in the 1970s, as mentioned earlier in the chapter, its underpinning assumptions continued to be influential in the development of neo-modernist organization theory.

## The human relations school develops

As the human relations school developed, it went through a number of phases. These phases reflected intellectual shifts because between the different disciplines that constitute it, new understandings of the nature of business and industry came into being. And,

Grint and Case (2000) suggest, national and international events and trends affected the school although some of the core themes endured. As we have seen, the origins of human relations lay in concerns about what appeared to be the more 'irrational' aspects of individuals and groups that had the potential to cause social turbulence and disorder. However, when these symptoms are analysed and understood through the human relations lens, it is revealed that peoples' 'real' concerns are about the nature of their lives in organizations and that it is the work of managers and leaders to create those conditions. These themes continue to be reflected in the work of contemporary neo-modernists. For example, James Champy, chair and CEO of a leading management consultancy, and Nitin Nohria, an associate professor at Harvard Business School, write that for many employees, there is a loss of meaning and connectedness as organizations go through enormous change. The organization needs a 'soul to energize it and principles to guide it. This is the challenge. Managers must rise to it, for they are the force at the centre of the storm' (Champy and Nohria, 1996, p. 265).

After World War II, Grint and Case suggest, the neo-human relations school emerged. There was a shift away from the sociological concerns about the nature of industrial society toward a more psychological perspective. In the context of the United States, the fears that the business and industrial society could be *radically* disturbed by an 'irrational' workforce had largely receded. The key social question was how organizations exist in a 'free and democratic society' and reflect the needs of the individual. This resulted in programmes that encouraged limited degrees of employee participation in decision making and emphasized that there was an obligation on organizations to develop the 'quality of working life'. There was an emphasis on the ways *individuals* should be enabled to develop and learn through their work in organizations. This emphasis on individual achievement to achieve organizational goals is a concept that recurs in neo-modernist writing with, at its zenith, the 'individualized corporation', a prescription that:

> Companies can and must capitalize on the idiosyncrasies – and even the eccentricities – of people by recognizing developing and applying their unique capabilities (Ghoshal and Bartlett, 1998, p. 241).

We would add, however, that this seems to be a rather narrow concept of individualism. It is underpinned by the notion that the person needs to be 'at one with' the conditions of organizational life. It is akin to a bargain with the organization and the individual – the former gives the latter opportunities to grow as long as this growth is within boundaries. Individualistic anarchy or full democracy it is not.

In the course of this chapter, we have emphasized the core idea that neo-modernism is based on the idea that there can be 'practical theories' that can be used in order to manage the human aspects of organization. As the human relations school developed, the idea that their theories should come from empirical research was of crucial importance. A key experience in the development of organization theory as we know it today occurred during the period 1927 to 1932, when there were a number of 'experimental studies' conducted at the Hawthorne Works of the Western Electric Company in Chicago. This research enterprise was crucial in the development of organization theory. This was the first *major* social science study to demonstrate the possibility of the empirical study of organizations and to develop theories of organization that would have practical implications for business and industry.

## The Hawthorne Studies as a classic example of applied organizational research within the human relations tradition

Mayo was the leading researcher and investigator in these studies. The Western Electric Company that had undertaken some research into the productivity of its workers had approached him. Mayo built up the research connection between the company and Harvard Business School. The 'Hawthorne Studies' resulted in numerous academic papers and publications, the most famous of which was written by Mayo's colleague Fritz Roethlisberger and Bill Dickson, who worked for Western Electric. First published in 1939, the study of the Hawthorne experiments, *Management and the Worker*, became a core text for managers for many years after its publication, although its reputation within the academic community varied from a degree of enthusiasm to condemnation of its underpinning ontological position and its research methodologies and methods.

The studies began with observations of five workers and ended up with studies of about 20,000 individual workers. The starting point was to explore the relationship between conditions of work and the incidence of fatigue and monotony amongst workers.

Their starting point, with five workers in an experimental group and five in a control group, was that behaviour could be studied through setting up an 'experiment' to test the hypothesis that workers' output was affected by the physical conditions in which they work. The researchers anticipated that 'exact knowledge could be obtained about this relation by establishing an experimental situation in which the effect of variables like temperature, humidity and hours of sleep could be measured separately from the effect of an experimentally imposed condition of work' (Roethlisberger and Dickson, 1939, p. 3). They were in for a surprise.

## The Relay Assembly Test Room

The 'experiment' took place in the Telephone Relay Assembly Test Room. In this room, illustrated in Figure 3.6, women put together some 35 small parts into an 'assembly fixture' that was then secured by four machine screws. The various component parts were put in front of the workers in small bins. The operators selected the components from the bins and assembled them with considerable skill. Each relay took about 1 minute to assemble, and each operator assembled some 500 relays each day in what was a highly repetitive task.

For the purposes of the research, there were two groupings of women. One was the group that worked in a 'normal' manner assembling the relays. This was the control group. The other group was the group on whom the 'experiments' were performed. During this research, the investigators altered rest pauses, changed the pattern of supervision, experimented with shorter working days and weeks, tested hypotheses for fatigue and monotony, experimented with wage incentives and so on. Each of these 'experiments' was carefully recorded and tabulated. Out of this series of experiments, it was realized that the 'variables' that affect worker performance are much more complex than had previously been thought.

**Figure 3.6:** The 'experimental' Relay Assembly Test Room used in the Hawthorne Studies. (*Source:* Courtesy of AT&T Archives and History Center, Warren, NJ.)

When the researchers began their work in the Relay Assembly Test Room, they had anticipated that there would be a straightforward relationship between the core issue they were investigating – the physical conditions in which the women worked (as exemplified by the level of illumination) and their level of productivity. As the investigation proceeded, however, instead of getting 'definite answers', the researchers found that they needed to restate the problems and develop new hypotheses and ideas. In one of the most famous of the 'experiments', for example, they eventually generated five hypotheses that gave some explanation for their 'astonishing' finding that whatever the level of lighting or rate of rest pauses, the level of productivity of the women increased during the course of the experiment.

By the end of this piece of work, the key issues that they took forward for further investigation included such practical issues as the effects of fatigue, monotony and economic incentives on productivity. They also placed great significance on the social issues involved in the quality of supervision because during the 'experiment', the supervisors and the women had achieved much more satisfactory working relationships than was normally the case in the test room. It was indeed this social aspect that dominated their investigation in the Bank Wiring Room and that subsequently became an important theme for the human relations school.

## The Bank Wiring Observation Room

The second major site chosen was the Bank Wiring Room in 1931. The basic purpose of this research was to study the informal organization of a large factory workshop. In this case, the researchers attempted to study the men in the shop using more naturalistic observational methods rather than the 'experimental' method in the Relay Assembly Test Room.

In the Bank Wiring Room, the task was complex but repetitive. Three wiremen (for each piece of equipment) attached cables to sets of wires to terminals in a series of 'banks' that were separated by insulators. When the wiring was done, the solder man took over to complete the actual task. As each level of the equipment was completed, it was inspected and tested for any defects. The inspector then completed a quality control form. In the observation room, there were two inspectors to look over the work of the three teams of wiremen (Roethlisberger and Dickson, 1939).

## Research and the development of neo-modernist organization theory

As the researchers proceeded with their work, they encountered a number of dilemmas and issues, many of which still preoccupy research into organizations. Some of the key issues that are discussed in *Management and the Worker* include:

- **Giving an account of the research:** Given the longitudinal nature (over a period of five years) of the study, they had a choice of presentation of the research. They could take a **sequential approach** to the study, taking each stage and discussing its implications and the leads they were to follow and the conclusions they drew – rather like one of those tales of forensic detective discovery that uncovers the story in an emergent manner complete with false starts and dead ends. Alternatively, they could develop a **grand narrative** at the end of the study, telling a 'smoothed out' story that would present the findings in a systematic and logical manner.

  They chose the emergent sequential approach. They seemed happy to expose the 'human imperfection' of their work. They wanted to describe what actually happened, to 'picture the trials and tribulations of a research investigator . . . and thus allow future investigators to see and profit from the mistakes which were made'. They were also spared 'the task of having to strengthen weak places and make their façades more imposing' (Roethlisberger and Dickson, 1939, p. 4).

- **Relating observations to theory:** As they presented their materials, the researchers made a conscious decision to separate the 'facts observed' from the 'methods, working hypotheses, theories or conceptual schemes used by the researchers'. The original 'facts of observation' and their verification were what really counted. They claimed that existing theories from sociology or psychology were regarded by them as 'part of the working equipment' (Roethlisberger and Dickson, 1939, p. 5), so they only included for discussion those theories that assisted the search for more 'facts' or to make better interpretations. They were attempting to create a 'conversation' between the 'facts' that they were observing, their interpretation of those 'facts' and theories drawn from the social sciences.

At the same time, however, working within their neo-modernist human relations perspective restricted the range of interpretation possible. There is, for example, very little human relations 'theory' that relates to employees and management being in an *instrumental, economic* relationship with each other. Indeed, human relations theory deliberately avoids such explanations, so 'economic theories' are ignored in the interpretation of the research (Jones, 1996). As the organization theorist Gareth Morgan (1997) observed, if we look at the world of organization through the lens of *any* perspective or body of theory, we gain powerful insights into organizations but also get a distorted picture. As Morgan suggests, the way of seeing created through the theory becomes also 'a way of *not* seeing' (p. 5). When we use a theory to look at organizations, we look for the things that theory points us toward but also exclude features that are not within its gaze.

- **The relationship between researcher and subject:** This relationship between the researchers and the subjects of the research has another implication. Roethlisberger and Dickson (1939) discuss the ways the women in the first experiment (the Relay Assembly Test Room) were initially deeply suspicious of the researchers. They thought that they might be victimized by the researchers (or the managers). As the experiment went on and the women encountered different conditions, they relaxed, made comments that they enjoyed the relative freedom from control in the 'laboratory' that was the Relay Assembly Test Room. This effect, the awareness of being researched and its impact on the subjects' behaviour became known as the 'Hawthorne effect' (Johnson and Duberley, 2000). It is suggested, however, that the Hawthorne effect tends not to be long lasting and that subjects rapidly return to more routine behaviours (Berg, 2001). However, another way of looking at the phenomenon is to ask: what is the effect of the researcher on the subject telling us about the situation and peoples' understandings? For example, what was it in the culture that caused the women at first to fear intimidation and then later on to enjoy the presence of the researchers?

- **Ethical issues in the research – whose side are we on?** The researchers were aware that many of their readers would be staff at Western Electric, the company that sponsored the research, and that they had an obligation to them and indeed to the company itself. As Strati (2000) notes, much of the work of the human relations researchers was commissioned by management. Roethlisberger and Dickson (1939) write that the researchers felt that they could 'best fulfil their obligation . . . by maintaining a spirit of scientific objectivity, by being faithful to the data before them and by presenting them, in so far as they were humanly capable of doing so, free from bias' (p. 4). They add, perhaps a tad naïvely in our more sceptical age, that through this objectivity, they could represent to employees the purpose of the enquiry and 'the sincere desire on management's part to understand better the facts of human behavior, their own as well as their employees' (p. 4). From a contemporary perspective, the researchers, in their collaborative stance with management, entered muddy waters, ethically speaking. An example of this is the way some less cooperative workers in the Relay experiment were replaced by management with more compliant employees (Wilson, 2004).

## Why the Hawthorne Studies were so important

Although the Hawthorne Studies have been subjected to sometimes fierce criticism methodologically and ethically, they represented a crucial phase in the development of an empirically 'social scientific' approach to the understanding of organizational life. They also represent an important stage in the development of an organization theory that is grounded in an understanding that action in organizations is based on the 'humanness of being'.

As this neo-modernist tradition has developed, it has become akin to the Dutch academic Cas Vroom's (2002) concept of a dynamic, learning approach. He suggests that both the processes of organization that are to be studied and the theories that are generated about organizations are part of a learning process. In this sense, he suggests, the production of 'definitive theories' (of, for example, motivation or leadership) is a waste of time; what is more important is to create an interaction between those who are involved in the development of theory and those who are actually involved in the processes of organization.

### Stop and think

This account of the Hawthorne Studies demonstrates a synthesis between a range of social science theories, techniques and their exploration through the human relations perspective. How do the issues discussed in this section relate to any research project or work that you may be undertaking?

As this part of the chapter progressed, we have given a general overview of the human relations school. We have shown how at its heart, this perspective is concerned with problems of communication and understanding between individuals and groups, between groups, and crucially, the relationship of these to the organization.

This core theme is now to be developed by a closer exploration of the ways the ideas of the human relations school and other neo-modernists are influential in developing an understanding of the relationship between organizations and society.

## How neo-modernist organization theory challenges understandings of the relationship between organizations and society

The issue of the relationship between the individual, society, and the organization is one that preoccupied the French sociologist Durkheim, who had a profound influence on the early human relations writers (Starkey, 1998). He saw individuality as something natural in society but found great difficulty in what he identified as individualism in extreme, 'rampant, pathological forms' (Cuff, Sharrock and Francis, 1998, p. 71), just as he felt that subordination to collective forms of life was problematic. He looked for balance between the expression of individuality and conformity; this is a key issue in neo-modernism. From the human relations perspective, the organization (as a key aspect of the social system in modern societies) replaces traditional support mechanisms such as the family, the church or the local community (Pugh and Hickson, 1989). This leads, within human relations, to a preoccupation with ideas that focus on core issues of the extent to which the individual 'needs to be' committed to the organization, not only for the benefit of the individual and the organization but also for society.

## A puzzle – is it is better to 'belong' or to be an 'individual'?

### Ideas and perspectives

## Making sure that work has meaning

Human relations philosophy seeks to create conditions in which work feels that it has a purpose, not only in an economic sense but in a moral sense as well. As a crucial example of this, as icon of the human relations approach, is the psychologist Fred Herzberg's (1968) seminal paper on motivation. In this paper, he stresses the notion that economic factors (salary) are a 'hygiene' factor; insufficient salary causes dissatisfaction. What really 'motivates' people to improve are feelings of achievement, recognition, having satisfying tasks to perform, feelings of responsibility and the potential for advancement and growth, all of which are features that give meaning to life at work.

### Continuity in neo-modernist thinking

It is interesting to note that Herzberg's 1968 paper was reprinted in the *Harvard Business Review* in January 2003 with the editor's comment: 'Herzberg's work influenced a generation of scholars and managers – but his conclusions don't seem to have fully penetrated the American workplace, if the extraordinary attention still given to compensation and incentive packages is any indication'.

As we have already seen, the human relations school began its life with a fundamental concern about the nature of society. There was also a concern to move beyond the view found in modernist thinking that employees are machines who only work for economic and purely instrumental reasons. Robert Woods Johnson, a businessman writing in the *Harvard Business Review* in 1949, captured the view that 'workers have human hearts and minds. They love and are loved. They have their moments of noble desire. But for the most part their lives are not spectacular. . . . Their first demand upon society is that they be treated as human beings, not like machines' (p. 528). To a contemporary reader, this might well seem to be patronizing; in its context, it represented a leap forward in attitudes towards the employee.

It follows that the human relations approach in organizations would be instrumental in developing a sense of belonging – not only belonging to the group, the organization, but also to society itself. A human relations approach has a bigger purpose than just making organizations more effective; it also encourages an attitude in people such that 'service to society, as well as to personal interest, becomes important. Teamwork and cooperation follow' (Johnson, 1949, p. 524).

In their impatience with the 'country club' approach, Blake and Mouton express a view that concentration on people without full attention to the tasks they 'should'

## The organization as 'country club'

The idea of the people-centred organization is controversial. Many years ago, the psychologists and management consultants Robert Blake and Jane Mouton (1964) developed their 'management grid'. Their work gained considerable popularity because it provided managers with a means to understand the implications of their 'management style' and to develop their performance. Their organization, Grid International, continues to provide consultancy and research and their key text, *The Managerial Grid: Key Orientations for Achieving Production Through People*, has been reprinted many times.

They saw the 'best' organizations as those that combine attention to people with attention to the core tasks (i.e., the production of the goods and services that are the primary purpose) of the organization. They had a low opinion of organizations, which they termed 'country clubs', that paid too much attention to people at the expense of the core task. They write:

> At its heart the core management philosophy would be benign, thoughtful, valuing people with a strong emphasis on gaining commitment and motivation with a pretence of democracy. The elements of control and day-to-day management would be operated in a collaborative way, with managers backing off if employees 'objected' if they experienced the controls as onerous. It would be a pleasant place in which to work as long as things are going well.

Within this organization there is an avoidance of pressure, managers persuade rather than impose and members avoid conflict. There is a high emphasis on communication – members (including senior managers) often live in open-plan offices – although there is a low emphasis on creativity for this often comes from disagreement and tensions. . . . In the longer term this organization is built on shifting sands as it will inevitably and inexorably be overtaken by competitive elements – and because conflict is essentially suppressed within the organization there may well be a tipping point at which the conflict breaks out.

They argue that in the long term, organizations such as this cannot, 'in a profit-motivated economy', survive. But 'more important is the threat they create toward the long-term erosion of a free-enterprise way of economic life' (Blake and Mouton, 1964, pp. 57–80).

What do you think are the underlying assumptions that underpin Blake and Mouton's description about the nature of organizations that concentrate on its members, and what are the assumptions that they make about the relationship of this kind of organization to society?

perform is a fatal distraction. This idea is echoed in this polemic from an anonymous editorial feature in the *Harvard Business Review*:

> The world's work has to be done, and people have to take responsibility for their own work and their own lives. The cult of human relations is but part and parcel of the sloppy sentimentalism characterizing the world today (Anonymous, 2001, p. 160).

This writer goes on to suggest that most great advances are made by individuals and that trying to keep everybody happy results in conformity, in failure to build individuals. This leads to mediocrity. So, the anonymous author concludes, 'Let's treat people like people, but let's not make a big production of it' (p. 160).

The case study presented below focuses on some of the advantages and disadvantages of the development of a feeling of 'belonging' to an organization.

| Case study | Great programmes – and he made people happy |
|---|---|

Greg Dyke was the Director General of the British Broadcasting Corporation who resigned from the BBC in 2004 in controversial circumstances. On his departure this report appeared in a newspaper:

> Those seeking an insight why hundreds of BBC staff downed tools in protest at Greg Dyke's departure should read the e-mail he sent before leaving Broadcasting House for the last time. 'I hope that, over the last four years, I've helped to make it a more human place where everyone who works here feels appreciated. If that's anywhere near true I leave contented, if sad', he wrote. . . . 'Happy staff a happy BBC make', he once said, claiming that when he left he wanted people to say, he made great programmes, and the people making them had a great time.

*Source:* Excerpt from an article by Jason Beattie, 30 January 2004 © *The Scotsman.*

His predecessor as director general, John Birt, had been a very different character. He was known to be a somewhat austere person who was a strong believer in the ideas of the new public management discussed in Chapter 2. He brought to the BBC a strong belief in creating 'internal markets' between the commissioning of programmes and their production, performance targets, the idea that departments should operate as cost centres and a strong emphasis on management.

When Dyke was appointed in 2000, one of his first acts was to make a speech to 400 managers, which was then relayed to the entire staff. In this speech, he outlined his vision of a happy, loving and united organization that would move away from what were seen as the divisive elements of Birt's time.

He left the BBC after the Hutton report into the death of the Iraq weapons expert David Kelly. In this report, the BBC had been severely criticized because one of its senior reporters had not reflected accurately the incidents that led up to Kelly's death. Dyke's supporters are of the opinion that he (and the BBC) had been victims of a political agenda. His critics suggest that he had been too eager to defend the reporter and the BBC – his 'people centredness' had got the better of him.

In many respects, Dyke's approach to running the BBC took the very qualities that critics of this approach to commitment to the organization condemn and turned them on their head. His understanding was that benign, collaborative, persuasive, communicating styles of managing and leading would lead to creativity; his opponents thought that this concern for commitment was not enough and that his leadership needed the stern hand of authority and control.

## Longing to belong: too much commitment

The tensions found in the development of a balance between society, individual and the organization may be seen in those who overidentify with the organization, for whom the organization is their complete sense of being. The writer on organizations Henry Mintzberg (1998) describes these as 'missionary organizations'. These organizations are held together by a culture that stresses values and beliefs that are shared by all the members. The American management consultant James Collins and the professor of organization behaviour and change Jerry Porras (2000) examined 18 exceptional and long-lasting companies in order to discover what made them so successful. They found that these organizations have a very powerful sense of themselves with a strong set of core values that may be termed a *visionary organizational ideology*. They are pervaded by the neo-modernist ethos that commitment is a means of ensuring success.

---

### Ideas and perspectives

## Organization man

Some suggest that the issues of commitment present difficult issues. One of the most outstanding texts on this was William H. Whyte's *The Organization Man*. This book was originally published in 1956 at a period in American history when ideas of commitment and conformity to the values of the organization were very powerful and when the ideas of the human relations school were being applied in organizations.

In a gender-specific way (the members of the organizations about which he writes were male), he discusses the development of the idea that work has to have a deep meaning and the growth of what he calls the social ethic:

> By Social Ethic I mean that contemporary body of thought which makes morally legitimate the pressures of society against the individual. Its major propositions are three: a belief in the group as the source of creativity; a belief in 'belongingness' as the ultimate need of the individual; and a belief in the application of science to achieve the belongingness. . . . By applying the methods of science to human relations we can eliminate obstacles to consensus and create equilibrium in which society's needs and the needs of the individual are one and the same. Essentially it is a utopian faith. Superficially, it seems dedicated to the practical problems of organizational life. . . . It is the long term promise that animates its followers, for it relates techniques to the vision of a finite achievable harmony (Whyte, 1960, p. 11).

### The organization person

When we look at the literature on organization and management theory (until recent times), it is worth noting the pervasive use of the words 'man' and 'he'. In the United Kingdom, for example, it is noteworthy that management and leadership are characteristically presented 'as a "masculine" pursuit, as if masculinity itself was a universal, unchanging quality' (Roper, 1994, p. 21). However, in an American organization that has a strong sense of vision that also values diversity, '"vision and diversity can work hand in hand". Some of the most cult-like visionary companies have received accolades as being the best major corporations for women and minorities. Merck (a global research-driven pharmaceutical company), for example, has a long record of accomplishment of progressive equal opportunity programs. At Merck, diversity is a form of progress that nicely complements its deeply cherished core: "You can be any color, size, shape, or gender at Merck – just as long as you believe in what the company stands for"' (Collins and Porras, 2000, p. 137).

## A reminder – the human relations approach is not the only neo-modernist story in town

In this section of the chapter, we have concentrated on the impact of the human relations approach in the development of an understanding of the relationship between the organization and society. If, however, we take the ideas of 'democratic organization' in the United States and Europe, we find a somewhat different relationship between individuals, organizations and society. As mentioned already in this chapter, the idea of democracy in organizations refers to the idea that all members of the organization can participate in the decision-making processes. These issues are discussed in Chapter 8.

### The chapter so far

In this section, we have shown that one of the key aspects of neo-modernism is an understanding that we cannot understand what goes on in organizations without considering the social context in which they are set. The human relations perspective says that, in some respects, the organization can serve as a defence against the alienating processes that prevail in society. By contrast, in another neo-modernist tradition, we see that democracy in organizations is a reflection of systems and structures that exist in society.

We suggested at the start of this section that there is an emphasis in neo-modernism on the issues of values and commitment to the organization. We also mentioned that a core aspect of the neo-modernist approach is the development of a culture that can contain and express these values and that can attract commitment them. This theme of the development of organization culture has been a key theme in neo-modernist thinking.

## How neo-modernist organization theory challenges understandings of organization culture

From the neo-modernist perspective, organization culture is concerned with what Roethlisberger and Dickson (1939) called the 'social organization' by which they meant the 'patterns of relations between members of the organizations together with the objects that symbolize these relations' (to be discussed later). Organization culture is, for the neo-modernist, the aspect of the organization in which members' social values and norms about such things as the nature of the individual and the group and norms coexist alaongside organizational values and norms. It is the organizational subsystem in which the employee 'must seek to satisfy his[sic] need for a secure position within a stable group' (Whitehead, 1935, p. 2). In this sense, neo-modernist ideas about organizational culture seek to humanize and even partially (or wholly, in the case of democratic neo-modernism) democratize the work environment so that employees can 'feel good' about themselves and their work environments (Knights and Willmott, 1999).

In historical terms, the human relations interest in culture goes back to an interest in 'social organization' already mentioned. In the United Kingdom, the first sustained discussion of 'organization culture' appeared in 1951 in Elliott Jaques' *The Changing Culture of a Factory*. Growth in interest in organization culture was slow. Texts that mentioned 'culture' tended to do so in relation to cultural communication in dealing with people from other nations, although there was an acknowledgement that anthropologists had 'long claimed that a knowledge of culture is valuable' to the manager and indeed that people in business were beginning to take this claim seriously (Whyte, 1969, p. 167). This interest did not reach fruition until the 1980s. In 1982, Terrence Deal and Allen Kennedy produced the first edition of their book *Corporate Cultures: The Rites and Rituals of Corporate Life*. This was followed a couple of years later by the first edition of Edgar Schein's *Organization Culture and Leadership* (1992) to be followed by many other writers that come from a wide variety of perspectives and theoretical positions.

Of that first edition, Schein (1992) wrote: 'There was a great interest in understanding and managing culture because it was perceived to be not only a concept that could explain many organizational phenomena but also something that leaders could manipulate to create a more effective organization' (p. xi). There are three strands to this comment. There is the neo-modernist desire to understand and explain organizational culture, to develop a practical theory of organizational culture. Secondly, there is the human relations idea that understanding culture can lead to improved management of culture. The third idea is that culture is something that leaders could manipulate. This takes the development of organization culture into the 'new-wave' approaches discussed in Chapter 4 in which culture is used as a means of establishing control over members. Although in the literature on organizational culture some writers are clearly in the human relations tradition, and others are clearly new wave, the boundaries between human relations approaches and the new-wave approaches can be blurred.

The organization theorist Dennis K. Mumby (1988) describes the neo-modernist approach as one that is 'pragmatic'. In this pragmatic perspective, the culture is something that the organization *has* as an organization subsystem. It is there to be discovered by perceptive members so that they can 'assess the degree to which shared meaning systems are detrimental or beneficial' (p. 8) to the organization. From a neo-modernist pragmatic perspective, there are times when it is possible to attempt to create and develop a uniform organization culture with an idea that all members of the organization live and breathe in the same culture. More often, however, Mumby suggests that pragmatic managers (or in a democratic organization, the members) use ideas and models of culture to try to develop an existing organizational culture. In this approach to managing organization culture, the approach is to acknowledge that different groups in the organization – for example, marketing, human resources, production and so on – live in somewhat different 'cultures' and then to work toward as strong a level of cultural sharing as is possible.

There are two major strands in the pragmatic approach to organization culture both of which have been influential in contemporary debates.

## Creating a culture that gives meaning to work

The first strand is connected with the desire to create organizations that are meaningful for those who work in them. A key aspect of the human relations school is that the organization is a place in which there is a shared 'sense of moral order and social collectivity' (Starkey, 1998, p. 126). In the earlier human relations literature, there is a strong emphasis on the organization 'a highly developed and closely co-ordinated system of interhuman activities. It is logically defined by an economic purpose. And to achieve that purpose it requires great and continuing social cohesion' (Whitehead, 1935, p. 6). In the later human relations literature, there is more of an emphasis on the *interplay* between the individual and the organization and the idea that people get a sense of identity through social recognition gained in the workplace (Knights and Willmott, 1999). Identification within the organization can be gained through a culture that respects the psychological contract between the individual and the group and the organization.

This understanding of organization culture led ultimately (alongside other influences) to the development of the 'corporate culture' model that pervaded much of the management literature of the 1990s and into the present. The British organization theorists David Knights and Hugh Willmott (1999) suggest that the emphasis on members' feelings of belonging to the organization through shared values has taken over from more traditional ways of managing behaviour such as hierarchy and structure. Because this emphasis on shared values developed into an interest in *manipulating* them so that they begin to be used to *control* behaviour with specific tools and techniques of cultural control, it tips over into new-wave approaches discussed in Chapter 4.

---

### Ideas and perspectives

#### *Psychological contract* gives work meaning

The psychological contract is the extent to which we see a relationship between the values that we hold as individuals and those that we identify as inherent in the culture of the organization. It is the extent to which we feel we can legitimately meet the expectations 'the organization' places on us and the extent to which 'the organization' can have legitimate expectations of us. The psychological contract reflects our beliefs and assumptions about the nature of work and life and our understanding of the 'culture' of the organization (Boyatzis and Skelly, 1995). In these terms, a 'good' psychological contract is when we experience high compatibility between individual values and those of the organization; a 'poor' psychological contract is when we feel low compatibility – when individuals feel abused by 'the organization' or 'the organization' feels that its members, as individuals, are 'taking advantage' of it.

## Developing understanding of culture

The second strand in the development of pragmatist neo-modernist thinking was in the development of an *understanding of the nature* of organization culture. As the Hawthorne Studies proceeded, Roethlisberger and Dickson way back in 1939 realized that a crucial step in the interpretation of the attitudes of employees and supervisors was to get beneath the surface attitudes of members to get to a deeper level – the 'meaning or function' of these attitudes – such as looking at the values that lie behind what people say. This insight contributed to the development of an understanding of organization culture that pervades 'pragmatic' theory.

This approach has led to the rise of models that enable managers to undertake exploration of, and then 'manage', culture. The American academic and writer on organization communications Philip Clampitt (2005) shows why this emphasis on values and the role of the manager in understanding them is so important:

> The effective leader teaches employees what the corporation values, why it is valued and how to transform values into action. Education of this sort requires special skills. Employees, like students, do not always see the value of what they are doing until after they have done it. They may tire, get discouraged, or even resist. Yet, the thoughtful manager overcomes these hindrances while engendering commitment to corporate values and inspiring employees to enact them. They view the values as DNA which should be replicated throughout the organization. Ultimately, the values must move from objective statements to subjective realities (p. 55).

In this quotation, we can see some of the core elements of the human relations approach to neo-modernism with also some hints of a more controlling 'new-wave' interest. It is interesting to notice the primary importance Clampitt gives to the leaders and managers as the 'holders' of the values and the culture and the way he depicts employees as somehow wayward and need to be 'educated' into the corporate values. There is also contained here a notion that in some way, the corporate values are 'objective', factual statements of the way the organization 'should be', so that corporate values become the organizational 'truth' and the key to success is that the members of the organization internalize those values.

## Developing a 'practical theory' of organizational culture

At the start of this chapter, we discussed that one of the key features of neo-modernism is the way it takes theoretical perspectives from the social sciences; uses methods from these social sciences; and using a neo-modernist perspective, presents 'practical' ideas that can be applied in organizational contexts. The development of neo-modernist approaches to organizational culture has been drawn mainly from particular traditions in anthropology and sociology. They also look at culture as one of the subsystems of the total organizational system but in a different way from the modernists. In the discussion of the modernist understanding of culture, it was represented as a subsystem along with the other subsystems. To the neo-modernist, organizational culture is represented as a subsystem that permeates the others. It is the 'social glue' that binds the other subsystems together – or in times when there are differences in values between members of the organization, it can be the source of dissent and differences. This may be illustrated by this representation of the open systems model discussed in Chapter 2 (Figure 3.7).

In the neo-modernist tradition, organization culture is described as a system with different levels, from the more superficial aspects to the deeper. The organizational psychologist Schein (1992) suggests that culture can be found at three levels. At the surface level are what he calls *artefacts*. These are the visible aspect of the culture such as the physical environment, the language that members use, their appearance and other 'phenomena that one sees, hears, and feels when one encounters a new group with an unfamiliar culture' (p. 17). An important issue that Schein raises is that although phenomena at this level are easy to observe, they can be difficult to decipher; they can provide clues to deeper levels but can also be deceptive. At the second level are the *espoused values*. These values that are shared within the group or organization enable members to reduce uncertainty in crucial areas of their operation. The third, deepest layer is what he calls the *basic assumptions*. These are values, beliefs about 'what works' that have become so taken for granted by members that they are rarely, if ever, questioned. They are assumptions that members make that guide their behaviour.

The model presented in Figure 3.8 echoes some aspects of Schein's model of culture but also contains different elements. It is a model that can be used to explore and understand the culture of a group, department or even, when there is a relatively uniform culture, an organization.

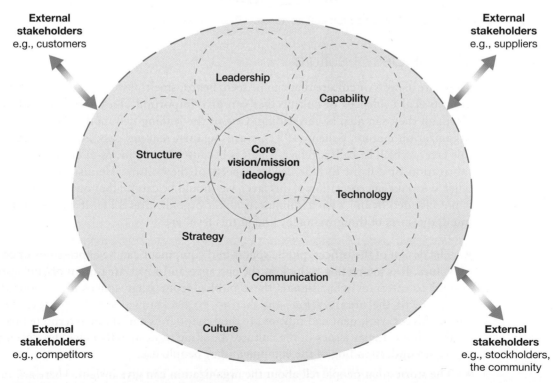

**Figure 3.7:** Neo-modernist open systems.

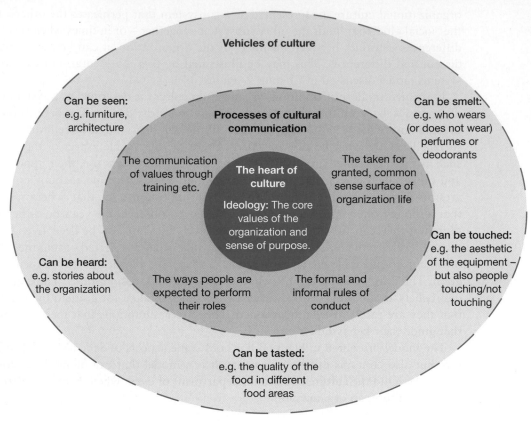

**Figure 3.8:** Three layers of organization culture. (*Source:* Based on McAuley, 1994.)

## The vehicles of culture

These are aspects of culture that can be seen, heard, smelt, tasted and touched. These are physical evidences of culture that can give important clues about the culture, although they can also be misleading. One of the leading neo-modernist writers on organization culture, Schein (1992), warns against making easy interpretations of this layer (which he calls artefacts). This is because these vehicles of culture can be a fabrication or a front to hide deeper aspects of the culture. He also suggests that when we make interpretation of this layer, we should be careful that our interpretation is not clouded by our own assumptions about organizational life. If we bear this in mind, the sorts of thing we might find at this level are:

- **The design of the offices, public spaces and equipment can be expressions of core values.** It is interesting to look at the entrance and foyer area of an organization and to interpret what signals these public, front stage spaces give about the nature of the organization and then to go backstage. Are the places where employees work neat and tidy, or are they chaotic? What can be interpreted from this about deeper issues in the culture? Looking at design also includes developing an understanding of the equipment that people use.

- **The stories that people tell about the organization can give insight.** There are various forms of storytelling. There are the 'official stories' about the organization

## Example: The computer as icon

In the offices of the publisher of this text, most of the staff uses the standard personal computer (PC). However, not 'the designers'. They use Apple Macs. They have stacks of magazines about them and talk about how magnificent their computers are in comparison with the mundane PC. From the point of view of the designers, their computers differentiate them from other members of staff; from a corporate point of view, letting the designers access the Apple Mac is a symbol of the respect given to the creativity of the designers.

that are reflected in the marketing literature and in documents such as the corporate plan. Then there are the stories that people tell about the organization that reflect the ebb and flow of the organization's history – these are referred to as the *organizational sagas* that tell the story of how the organization has achieved what it has achieved. There are also the organizational heroes (who personify the organizational values) and the villains (those who have failed the organization in some way). In approaches to organization culture that discuss it as something that an organization *is* rather than something the organization *has* as subsystem, the concept of stories becomes much more powerful; this is discussed in Chapter 7.

- **Issues of smell, touch and taste can tell us something about deeper issues.** In many organizations, these can be subtle but important. In the matter of 'smell', most organizations aim to be neutral, but there can be issues about who wears (or does not wear) perfumes and deodorants at work – and indeed, some organizations have 'rules' about not wearing perfumes. In relation to touch, there is the extent to which there are 'rules' about who can touch who and where they can touch. In some organizations, any idea that one person can actually touch another would be strictly forbidden; in others, touch (within boundaries) is seen as quite a legitimate way of expressing the working relationship.

## The processes of the communication of culture

This second layer takes us to the ways the culture is communicated between members. This level includes features such as:

- The ways the **rituals** of everyday organization life are handled. A key example of this is the way regular formal meetings are conducted, the way the agenda is created and the extent to which it is followed, the patterns of power and who gets heard (and ignored) in the meetings, and the sense of order (or disorder) that pervades the meeting.
- The ways new members are **socialized** into the organization and **are expected to perform their roles.**
- The **taken-for-granted, 'common sense'** aspects of organizational life. Over time, many of the ways we work in the organization become 'common sense' so that we no longer question them. They become routine, and we communicate these ways of doing our work to others as 'the right way' to do them. This can be a very important aspect of cultural communication. This is illustrated in the Case study.

## Case study

### How the taken-for-granted, common sense assumptions can become problematic

Common sense assumptions about the nature of the organization can become deeply embedded within the organization culture. Paul Bate, director of the Centre for the Study of Organizational Change at the University of Bath, undertook a major study of the culture of senior management at British Rail a few years before the system was privatized. British Rail was responsible for the railway system of the United Kingdom. It had been established in 1948 but had a long history of operation.

As an example of this, Bate showed the way British Rail senior management had a number of key cultural taken for granted axioms, which he called the 'isms'. In order to uncover these 'isms', Bate and his colleagues interviewed senior management and undertook many hours of studying and interpreting transcripts of meetings. They found that although these 'isms' were on the surface logical and reasonable, they had complex negative impacts. Bate points out that the 'isms' can be 'so locked up in their inner logic that they have little time for "here and now" realities' (Bate, 1994, p. 121), so they can be powerful aspects of the culture that resist change.

These 'isms' included:

- **Segmentalism:** Structurally, it was quite sensible for this large organization to operate in a divisional manner with differentiation between different groups and modes of operation. However, in cultural terms, this habit of division was deeply disadvantageous because members of divisions began to see themselves as 'barons' with their own fiefdoms in a state of constant feud with the other 'barons'.

- **Isolationism:** Historically, the railways had operated separately from other industrial groups – it saw itself as different. This was useful in that it enabled it to 'get on with the business' – but culturally, the habits of isolationism meant that there was a lack of connection with development in other businesses and industries. This was reflected in, for example, the fact that railway technology was not able to take advantage of technological advances in the aerospace industry that might be useful.

- **Elitism:** The railways were run in a disciplined manner with clear elites to provide guidance and a clear command structure. Although this was functional in an industry in which safety needs a clear command structure, it was culturally dysfunctional in that the contributions to the business of many who were lower down in the hierarchy were unacknowledged.

- **Fashionism:** Given the way that the industry valued its history, this 'ism' was a bit of a paradox but it involved the idea of 'an obsession with the new and the newfangled' (Bate, 1994, p. 118) techniques of business and management. At a superficial level, this was useful in that it was seen as a way of dealing with symptomatic problems, although at a deeper cultural level, it meant that initiatives were not sustained. There was little understanding of 'taking the long view'.

- **Structuralism:** Constant restructuring was seen as the way to solve organizational problems. From a cultural point of view, this was dysfunctional because it meant that organizational members, especially within the management cadre, could not establish a strong view of who they were.

- **Pragmatism:** The culture of senior management valued people of action, people who could get things done. People were measured on the basis of achievement rather than their intellectual quality. This anti-intellectual culture became problematic when situations occurred that required deep thought. An example of this was in the development of overall strategic direction for the rail industry; decisions were often taken that were ad hoc and not thought through.

These powerful 'isms', or metaphors, were not really understood by senior management until Bate and his colleagues, on the basis of detailed exploration of the 'language in use' of senior management, revealed it.

The diagnostic work done by Bate and his colleagues had a profound effect on senior management at British Rail because understanding of these dysfunctions meant that the board could begin to work on them. Ironically, the privatization of the system in 1995 meant that some of these manifestations of dysfunction (especially segmentalism) returned, although many others have changed as the 'new history' of the railway system has developed.

## The 'heart of culture'

This is the deepest level of culture and is concerned with the core values and purposes of the organization, what has come to be known as the **organizational ideology**.

The leading exponents of the idea of the organization based on a strong core ideology in recent years have been Collins and Porras, whose text *Built to Last: Successful Habits of Visionary Companies* is now in its third edition since its original publication in 1994. For the purposes of their study, they chose organizations in the United States that were regarded as 'premier institutions', that were 'widely admired', had made an 'indelible imprint on the world in which we live', had multiple generations of chief executives, had gone through a number of 'product life cycles' and had been 'founded before 1950' (Collins and Porras, 2000). They chose some 18 visionary companies, including 3M, American Express, General Electric, Hewlett-Packard, IBM, Johnson and Johnson, Sony and the manufacturers of leading-edge pharmaceuticals, Merck.

Collins and Porras (2000) suggest that the core ideology is a combination of core values and purpose. By the *core values*, they mean the 'essential and enduring tenets – a small set of general guiding principles' (p. 73) These are, at their heart, concerned with the issues of how members behave toward each other, the ethical values held within the organization, those core values that will not be affected by short-term expediencies. By *purpose*, they mean the 'organization's fundamental reasons for existing beyond just making money', essentially concerned with the core vision of the organization.

To achieve this at an organizational level, they suggest that the organization create powerful symbols that reinforce the ideology. These symbols can be expressed through intense socialization into the organization, through the processes of internal promotion, unique 'language', clear signs as to what is tolerated ('honest mistakes') and not tolerated (actions that breach the ideology) (p. 136) and the physical layout of the premises. Collins and Porras discuss the delicate balance between preserving the ideological core through the development of a cult-like devotion to the organization and the need for innovation and creativity.

Collins and Porras concede that ideological organizations can fall from grace; they can go through bad periods. They recover when they recover their original ideology. Mintzberg, Ahlstrand and Lampel (1998) suspect that many of the core issues that confront managers 'exist below the level of conscious awareness' (p. 266). Roethlisberger and Dickson observed (1939, v) that 'the logics of the ideological (aspects of the) organization express only some of the values of the social organization' (p. 568) – basically that the ideological organization cannot encompass all behaviour and attitudes in the organization and runs the danger of becoming an ideal that becomes divorced from reality as it is experienced by members.

## A different (European) view on core values

It is interesting (as a manifestation of different cultures in organization theory) to contrast the expository style of Collins and Porras with the somewhat quieter style of the European writer Arie de Geus (1997). He had been responsible for planning coordination for the Royal Dutch/Shell Group. He became interested in the identification of the underlying features that led to corporate longevity – in the case of his study, he looked at companies that had survived *as sizeable businesses* for at least as long as Royal Dutch/Shell (founded in the 1890s); some of the companies in the study were more than 200 years old. What he found was that these long-lasting companies had four characteristics in common:

1. These companies had a culture that was sensitive to their environment. They were closely in tune with their own society. Although many of the companies were international in their scope, they were able to identify with the local.

2. They were cohesive with a strong sense of identity. Members (and suppliers) believed that they were all part of one entity. As with the visionary company, promotions took place from within, and apart from moments of crisis, 'the management's top priority and concern was the health of the institution as a whole' (p. 6).

3. They were 'tolerant,' especially with regard to 'activities on the margins: outliers, experiments, and eccentricities within the boundaries of the cohesive firm, which kept stretching their understanding of possibilities' (p. 7).

4. The culture was conservative in financing. He suggests that they practised frugality and did not risk capital without careful assessment. They valued the idea of having money available to give them flexibility and generally tried to avoid the use of third-party financiers.

**Stop and think**

Are there fundamental differences between Collins and Porras' essentially American view of the values driven ideological organization and the European view expressed by de Geus?

## A tale of two cultures

In the Case study that follows, a student on our master's course in materials and management wrote of his experiences of the contrasting cultures in a steel plant in England and a similar plant in one of the Scandinavian countries.

| Case study | The culture of steel-making in England and Scandinavia[2] |

The student who wrote this is a graduate engineer in a steel plant in England who undertook a long secondment in Scandinavia. In this account, he dips in and out of the three levels of culture to come to some interesting and contrasting conclusions.

'During my time working with The Anglo-Scandinavian Steel Company I have been fortunate enough to work in different countries, including a secondment to work as a research and development engineer in Scandinavia. This opportunity gave me first hand experience of understanding the differences between organizational cultures within a multinational company.

'In my experience, a key cultural contrast between the UK and Scandinavia, within The Anglo-Scandinavian Steel Company, is the value placed upon the employee as an integral part of the organization. UK organizations, not just my own, offer very little to the employee other than what is stipulated within their contract, everything else must be bought or earned – which is not necessarily a bad philosophy if it means getting the most out of an individual.

'In Scandinavia on the other hand, parallel employees receive far greater privileges than their UK counterparts do – a contrasting technique that perhaps makes the individual happier day-to-day and therefore more willing to attend work in the first place! To cite an example, coffee breaks in Scandinavia are taken as half hour outages in a working day, away from the place of work in a coffee room fully catered for complete with cakes and fruit paid for by the company. Coffee breaks in the UK consist of a trip to the vending machine, taking it back to your desk to drink it whilst you continue working. I feel privileged if I find the machine is on free vend – but this is usually only when it is broken!

'The second cultural level, the processes of communication, is equally contrasting within the different geographical locations of The Anglo-Scandinavian Steel Company. The day-to-day ways of going about routines and rituals are extremely different. In the UK, it is commonplace to work late and put in extra hours for no extra financial reward. I adopted this ritual when I started working in Scandinavia but soon stopped when I realized I was locked in the building and all of the lights had been switched off at 6pm! It is almost unheard of to work beyond the standard working day in Scandinavia.

'Office culture within The Anglo-Scandinavian Steel Company UK business areas is open-plan and team orientated, whereas in Scandinavia it is cell-based with everyone located in their own personal space. This may support why they have more formal breaks in the day to socialize as when they work, they work alone. In the UK the open-plan office layout allows for continual communication that at times can have its downside due to the regularity of distraction. The cell-based office culture creates a more formal atmosphere; I have experienced much more formal and hierarchical role-appropriate behaviour in Scandinavia than I have in the UK where junior vice-presidents can be as approachable as a parallel colleague.

---

[2] This case study is reproduced by kind permission of the student and his company, the name of which has been changed.

*(Continued)*

**Case study** **(Continued)**

'An important aspect of the core values is around issues of the nature of employment. The cultural difference is that in the UK you feel your job is safe until the next round of redundancies, whereas in Scandinavia, employees feel they have a job for life. The emphasis in the Scandinavia is usually focused around increasing employee numbers to support an expanding business as opposed to the mentality of slashing jobs and expecting less people to produce more output as is commonly found in the UK manufacturing sector.

'I believe that the core values of the UK steel industry culture developed out of its physical presence, size and stature within the communities of major population centres. On this basis the industry gained its reputation based upon the cultural vehicles of history, tradition, size and importance. This perception is supported by the impression those on the outside have of the industry. They do not know it as an industry with core ideologies and assumptions. The public sees it as a loud, dirty, aggressive animal with a traditional industrial heritage. The reality is the contrary. Yes, it is heavy industry; however, it operates today with precision engineering, high health, safety and environmental standards and competitive marketing strategies, similar to that of any light and commercial industry.

'In contrast, I believe the steel industry culture in Scandinavia developed initially through its core values. In doing this it focused upon developing and establishing methods, practices and organizational procedures before concentrating on the physical aspects of growth and domination. Scandinavian steel manufacturing is not found amidst the major population centres of the home countries, they are found in modest locations, relatively hidden and secluded, and have steadily advanced with technology that is arguably more advanced than that found in the UK today.'

**Stop and think**

Use the model of culture to undertake a diagnosis of an organization known to you. Be creative in thinking about the items that can go into the three layers. When you have done the analysis, think about the strengths and weaknesses of using a model like this.

Within the neo-modernist tradition, we see an interest in the concept of what we now call 'organization culture' as a key feature in the effective development of the organization. Within neo-modernism, there are two key strands. One is the careful diagnosis and understanding of culture – a scientific approach to the study of culture. The second strand is the concern with attempts to ensure that there is a match between culture and organizational purpose. This goes back to Roethlisberger and Dickson's (1939) comment that 'the limits of human collaboration are determined far more by the informal than by the formal organization' and that collaboration involves 'social codes, conventions, traditions, and routine or customary ways of responding to situations' (p. 568). This insight leads to a perspective on culture that is realist, purposive and not just a component of organizational life but central and that culture *can be* an engine for organizational effectiveness.

## How neo-modernist organization theory develops challenges in the design of organizations

Aligned with the interest in organization culture neo-modernists are also interested in the design of organizations – indeed, these are inextricably intertwined. For the neo-modernist, design is not only about structure; it is also about the processes by which the structures and design is achieved. Within neo-modernism, there are two approaches. The first, the processual approach (Whittington, 2001), takes the view that if the organization gets its internal design to be strong, it can withstand whatever pressures are placed on it from the external environment. The second, that of organization development, stresses the idea that in crafting issues of change in the organization adherence to social science theories and methodologies provide a crucial underpinning.

## The processual perspective

This approach to organizational design emphasizes the notion that members need to understand and develop the core distinctive competencies that characterize and differentiate the organization. Organization design (as a key component of strategy) is geared toward 'the long-term construction and consolidation of distinctive internal competences' (Whittington, 2001, p. 25). Within the neo-modernist tradition, there is an emphasis on the development of what is known as the *learning organization* as the key means of developing capability.

As far as management and leaders are concerned, a key design issue is the development of structures and systems that enable learning. Thus, Roethlisberger suggested way back in 1951 that 'What industry and business must have in their supervisory and executive groups are more educated groups – not more trained seals' (p. 50). By the 1990s, the idea of organizational learning had become more democratic. It extended into the idea of the learning organization. This, according to one of the leading American writers on this concept, Peter Senge (1990), is distinguished from the more traditional 'controlling organization' because *all* the members will have mastery of 'certain basic disciplines' (p. 5). These disciplines include:

1. The ability to understand organizations as systems so that members can understand the ways that all aspects of organizations are interconnected.

2. The development of what he calls 'personal mastery' so that members are engaged in a process of continuous development in terms of their vision, focus of their energies and of seeing reality objectively.

3. The development of understanding of our common sense 'mental models' so that we can become more open to the thinking and influence of others.

4. The building of a shared vision so that members create strong commitment to the future of the organization and its values.

5. The development of team learning on the grounds that Senge believes that teams rather than individuals are the fundamental learning unit in organizations.

Senge sees the development of the learning organization rising from changing understandings of the nature of work and our relationship to it. He believes there is a movement from the instrumental idea that people work for financial gain toward a situation in which organizational members are more concerned to gain intrinsic emotional and spiritual rewards from work. Writers such as de Geus (1997) and Whittington (2001) see the need for learning to be a key component of organizational design as arising from the development of the 'knowledge economy' – 'the shift to knowledge as the critical production factor and the changing world around the factories' (de Geus, 1997, p. 20)

These approaches to the issues of learning, participation and empowerment and their relationship to the democratization of the workplace as organizational design provides the springboard for a rich and diverse literature on the nature of the political relationship between management and employees to be discussed in Chapter 8. Suffice it to say for the purposes of this chapter that from a Northern European perspective, whereas studies indicate that in English-speaking countries, 'participation is elitist (i.e., driven by management) and the distribution of power is authoritarian' in the Scandinavian countries, there tends to be 'egalitarian participation and democratic distribution of power' (Westenholz, 2003, p. 50).

## Design and development

We have seen that for the neo-modernist the social sciences combined with intelligently applied social science methodologies all presented through the lens of a neo-modernist perspective are placed at the service of 'the organization' in order to improve it. Not only does this process relate to culture and design, but it also relates to processes of change. Within the neo-modernist tradition, the major lever for change is through the process known as organization development (OD). It is based upon behavioural science, and its scope ranges from leadership and group dynamics to strategy, organization design and interorganizational relations. This crafted process of planned change is an adaptive process for planning and implementing change rather than a blueprint for getting things done (Cummings and Worley, 2001).

Some of the key definitional features of organization development include:

- It is top-management supported and is a long-range effort to improve an organization's capacity to solve problems and its ability to renew itself.
- It emphasizes effective diagnosis and management of organization culture.
- It is about how people and organizations function and how to get them to function better.
- It applies to the strategy, structure and processes of an entire system such as an organization, a single plant of a multiplant firm, a department or a work group.

Organization development is potentially a valuable approach to change provided it is viewed within the wider organizational and social context and the organization development programme is seen as a means rather than a goal in itself (Wilson,

1993). However, if the organization development initiative enables members of the organization to manage change in its many complexities and in ways that facilitate and develop understanding of the organizational vision and create commitment to it then, its supporters suggest, the process of change becomes embedded in the organization (Paton and McCalman, 2000).

In addition to organization development, some other approaches to change are neo-modernist. These include:

- **Whole-systems approach:** This approach is based on sociological theory and methods for developing understanding of change processes. There is an emphasis on the idea that the organization is a community. In this approach, all the members of the organization (or department) meet together in one place. With an external consultant operating as a facilitator, the members go through a series of experiences that encourage reflection amongst all the members. In this situation, there is an emphasis on the processes of change and the ways that people work together during the time of change and afterwards (Darwin et al., 2002).

- **Assessment centres and leadership development** are used as means of assessing the potential capabilities and the development of organizational members. Their roots lie in psychology and the use of psychological instruments such as questionnaires and interviews so that both the organization and the individual can gain insight into the skills, behaviours and attitudes that are appropriate within the organization.

- The development of **mentoring** in recent years as a key means of integrating the individual into the organization has been an important application of neo-modernist approaches. This approach has its roots in psychology. The idea of the 'experienced' manager mentoring the 'newer' member of staff through the helping interview falls well within the neo-modernist notion of working with the individual to become integrated into the organization.

In these approaches to change, we can see that the combination of social science techniques and neo-modernist thinking about the role of the group and the individual in the organization has led to a range of approaches. It should be emphasized that there is clear water between these neo-modernist and the more prescriptive approaches to change that are characteristic of new-wave approaches discussed in Chapter 4. In recent years, approaches to planned change such as business process re-engineering have become popular. In these approaches, according to Gunge (2000), employees are 'promised' that they can become empowered, liberated from the normal constraints of organizational bureaucracy and so on, but Gunge suggests:

> Re-engineering (that is process improvement) is conducted in an instrumental, top-down and goal directed fashion. . . . But how can a change process conducted in accordance with the existing rules of organizing produce a break with these very rules? How can an organizational change programme, which is based on hierarchical authority, possibly lead to an organization where people are empowered in any substantive way? (p. 121).

By contrast, organization development is geared toward a more genuine model of empowerment. Although the neo-modernist approach has within it a view that management is the 'higher authority', especially in the management of change, it does *not* 'seek to transform employees into disciplined subjects of a managed corporate culture where the mantras of empowerment, commitment, involvement, team working and customer service are repeatedly recited' (Knights and Willmott, 1999, p. 139).

## Conclusions: does neo-modernist organization theory exercise challenges for new visions of the organization?

At the start of this chapter, we mentioned that the neo-modernists have had their vicissitudes in terms of reputation. Neo-modernism developed in a number of different forms, but perhaps its key achievement is a notion that we can combine insights from social science and the rigour of the methods associated with these social sciences and integrate them through the lens of humanistic philosophy in order to develop organizations.

In this chapter, we showed how the human relations school rose to dominance as organization theory because it:

1. Created a clear and identifiable approach to understanding the core human issues of organizations.
2. Appealed to business and industry because it seemed to offer solutions to major issues of motivation and commitment.

We have also seen that at the heart of neo-modernism are preoccupations about the relationship between the organization and the society in which it is located and the ways the social world abuts onto the culture of the organization. Throughout the chapter, we have shown how neo-modernism lives on in the development of organizations. This can be summarized by relating the learning outcomes from the start of the chapter to some of the accomplishments of neo-modernism.

| Learning outcome | Challenges to the contemporary organization |
| --- | --- |
| Explore the development of neo-modernism as a 'practical' organization theory based on insights and methodologies of the social sciences with a concern for its practical application into organizations. | What do you think of the claim that neo-modernism is one of the key organization theories because it takes seriously the ways the social sciences can be used in order to develop 'practical theories'? |
| Discuss the human relations school as a pervasive example of neo-modernist organization theory and philosophy. | Bodies of organizational theory such as motivation, the humanizing of management, the importance of values and organization design developed through the neo-modernist perspective. What is their relevance to the twenty-first century organization? |

| | |
|---|---|
| Examine the Hawthorne Studies as a classic piece of applied organizational research within the neo-modernist tradition. | These studies generated, in a reflective way, some core issues that pervade the ways we do empirical organizational research today. They ask challenging issues such as:<br><br>• When we report our research, should we tell it like a smoothed-out story, or tell it like it was?<br><br>• How do we create a 'good' relationship between the empirical research and the relevant theory?<br><br>• What is the requisite relationship between the researcher and the subject of research?<br><br>• What ethical issues do we encounter in our research, and how do we resolve them?<br><br>To be sure, the answers they gave to these issues are not always all that satisfactory; what **is** important is that they reflectively asked the questions and set the challenges. |
| Discuss how neo-modernist organization theory challenges understandings of the relationship between organizations and society. | The neo-modernists acknowledged the real significance of organizations as a key component of the social structure. What is your opinion of their thinking that organizations have some social responsibility in society and that this needs to be considered alongside the search for economic success? |
| Explore the development by neo-modernists of an understanding of organization culture. | The neo-modernists were one of the key movers in the development of interest in the concept of organization culture with a particular interest in the idea that an organizational culture can be developed and sustained that meets the needs of both members and the business. |
| Discuss how neo-modernist organization theory develops challenges in the design and development of organizations. | Neo-modernists bring to our attention two crucial issues. The first is the key issue that design needs to be able to take account of the processes by which members of the organization learn and develop. The second issue is that organizations can go through processes of change and development in a manner that takes advantage of the social sciences. To what extent do these approaches take account of increasing organizational and environmental complexity? |

## Key resources for future development

In the course of the chapter, we have mentioned that the human relations school has not always enjoyed a high reputation amongst academics. For an interesting critique of the human relations school (including the Hawthorne Studies), you could look at Rose (1978). Unfortunately, this book is out of print, but it should be held by university libraries.

A very interesting article that explores the work of Mayo, particularly his contribution to the development of human resource management, is O'Connor (1999a).

There have been many texts in the neo-modernist tradition on organization culture. One of the most comprehensive and less prescriptive examples is Schein (2004).

A useful overview of organization development and other neo-modernist approaches to change in can be found in French and Bell (1999).

## Discussion questions

1. In this chapter, we have suggested that on the one hand, attending to 'the human factor' is of crucial importance in the development of organizations and on the other that all this attention to the social distracts attention from individual creativity and 'getting on with the job'. What do you think?

2. What are the key issues and problems that you would associate with the neo-modernist view that organization theory is built from the social sciences and its methodologies placed through the filter of a neo-modernist perspective with a strong emphasis on **application** into organizations?

3. How do the 'research issues' that arise from the Hawthorne Studies relate to issues of researching organizations in your own experience?

4. Neo-modernists understand that organizations 'should be' tightly integrated into the society in which they are located. What do you see to be the advantages and disadvantages of this position?

5. Undertake a diagnosis of the culture of an organization known to you using the model. Assess the value of the insights the diagnosis provides on the nature of the culture.

6. In modernism, the key view of organization design is that 'form follows function'. In neo-modernism, the emphasis is on process and the achievement of design processes that enable learning and development. Can these two views be reconciled?

7. Neo-modernists believe that organization development paves the way to human participative processes of change; its critics claim that it is a form of 'social engineering' that is dominated by senior management perspectives on the organization. What do you think?

## References

Anonymous. (2001) 'Enough about people', *Harvard Business Review* 79(2):160.

Argyris, C. (1998) 'Empowerment: The Emperor's new clothes', *Harvard Business Review* 76(3): 98–105.

Bate, P. (1994) *Strategies for Cultural Change*, London: Butterworth/Heinemann.

Berg, B.L. (2001) *Qualitative Research Methods for the Social Sciences*, Boston: Allyn and Bacon.

Blake, R.R. and Mouton, J.S. (1964) *The Managerial Grid: Key Orientations for Achieving Production Through People*, Houston: Gulf Publishing Company.

Bolman, L.G. and Deal, T.E. (1997) *Reframing Organizations: Artistry, Choice and Leadership*, 2nd edn, San Francisco: Jossey-Bass.

Boyatzis, R.E. and Skelly, F.R. (1995) 'The impact of changing values on organizational life – the latest update', in D. Kolb, J. Osland and I.M. Rubin (eds) *The Organizational Behavior Reader*, 6th edn, Englewood Cliffs, NJ: Prentice Hall.

Champy, J. and Nohria, N. (1996) 'Epilogue – The eye of the storm: The force at the center', in J. Champy and N. Nohria (eds) *Fast Forward: The Best Ideas on Managing Business Change*, Cambridge, MA: Harvard Business School Press.

Clampitt, P.G. (2005) *Communicating for Managerial Effectiveness*, 3rd edn, Thousand Oaks, CA: Sage Publications.

Clegg, S.R. (1990) *Modern Organizations: Organization Studies in the Postmodern World*, London: Sage.

Collins, J.C. and Porras, J.I. (2000) *Built to Last: Successful Habits of Visionary Companies*, 3rd edn, London: Random House Business Books.

Conger, J.A. and Benjamin, B. (1999) *Building Leaders: How Successful Companies Develop the Next Generation*, San Francisco: Jossey Bass.

Cuff, E.C., Sharrock, W.W. and Francis, D.W. (1998) *Perspectives in Sociology*, 4th edn, London: Routledge.

Cummings, T.G. and Worley, C.G. (2001) *Organization Development and Change*, 7th edn, Cincinnati, Ohio: South-Western College Publishing/Thomson Learning.

Darwin, J., Johnson, P. and McAuley, J. (2002) *Developing Strategies for Change*, London: Financial Times/Prentice Hall.

Deal, T. and Kennedy, A. (1982) *Corporate Cultures: The Rites and Rituals of Corporate Life*, Reading, MA: Addison-Wesley.

de Geus, A. (1997) *The Living Company: Habits for Survival in a Turbulent Business Environment*, Boston: Harvard Business School Press.

Dent, E.B. (2000) *The Messy History of OB&D: How Three Strands Came to be Seen as One Rope*, Draft article, Retrieved June 2006 from http://polaris.umuc.edu/~edent/OBD.HTM.

Fincham, R. (2000) 'Management as magic: Reengineering and the search for business salvation', in D. Knights and H. Willmott (eds), *The Reengineering Revolution: Critical Studies of Corporate Change*, London: Sage.

French, W.L. and Bell, C.H. (1999) *Organization Development: Behavioral Science Interventions for Organizational Improvement*, Upper Saddle River, NJ: Prentice Hall.

Ghoshal, S. and Bartlett, C.A. (1998) *The Individualized Corporation: A Fundamentally New Approach to Management*, London: Heinemann.

Grint, K. and Case, P. (2000) '"Now where were we?" BPR lotus-eaters and corporate amnesia', in D. Knights and H. Willmott (eds), *The Reengineering Revolution: Critical Studies of Corporate Change*, London: Sage.

Gunge, S.P. (2000) 'Business Process Reengineering' and 'The New Organization', in D. Knights and H. Willmott, *The Reengineering Revolution: Critical studies of corporate change*, London: Sage Publication.

Herzberg, F. (1968) 'One more time: How do you motivate employees?' *Harvard Business Review* 46(1):53–63.

Huczynski, A.A. (1996) *Management Gurus: What Makes Them and How to Become One*, London: International Thomson Press.

Hunt, J.G. (1991) *Leadership: A New Synthesis*, Newbury Park, CA: Sage Publications.

Jaffee, D. (2001) *Organization Theory: Tension and Change*, London: McGraw Hill International Edition.

Jaques, E. (1951) *The Changing Culture of a Factory*, London: Heinemann.

Johnson, P. and Duberley, J. (2000) *Understanding Management Research*, London: Sage.

Johnson, R.W. (1949) 'Human relations in modern business', *Harvard Business Review* 27(5):521–541.

Jones, F. E. (1996) *Understanding Organizations: A Sociological Perspective*, Toronto: Copp Clark Ltd.

Knights, D. and Willmott, H. (1999) *Management Lives: Power and Identity in Work Organizations*, London: Sage.

Kreiner, K. and Mouritsen, I. (2003) 'Knowledge management as technology: Making knowledge manageable', in B. Czarniawska and G. Sevón (eds), *The Northern Lights – Organization theory in Scandinavia*, Copenhagen: Copenhagen Business School Press.

Lewin, K. (1951) *Field Theory in Social Science: Selected Theoretical Papers*, D. Cartwright (ed.), New York: Harper & Row.

McAuley, M.J. (1994) *Managing Your Enterprise Book 4*, Bristol: NHS Training Division.

Mintzberg, H., Ahlstrand, B. and Lampel, J. (1998) *Strategy Safari: A Guided Tour Through the Wilds of Strategic Management*, London: Prentice Hall.

Miles, R.E. (1965) 'Human relations or human resources?', *Harvard Business Review* 43(4):148–158.

Morgan, G. (1997) *Images of Organization (2nd Edition)*, London: Sage Publications.

Mumby, D.K. (1988) *Communication and Power in Organizations: Discourse, Ideology and Domination*, Norwood, NJ: Ablex Publishing Corporation.

O'Connor, E.S. (1999a) 'Minding the workers: The meaning of "human" and "human relations"', in E. Mayo (ed.), *Organization* 6(2):223–246.

O'Connor, E.S. (1999b) 'The politics of management thought: A case study of the Harvard Business School and the human relations school', *Academy of Management Review* 24(1):117–132.

Paton, R.A. and McCalman, J. (2000) *Change Management: A guide to effective implementation*, 2nd edn, London: Sage Publications.

Pugh, D.S. and Hickson, D.J. (1989) *Writers on Organizations*, 4th edn, Harmondsworth: Penguin Books.

Roethlisberger, F.J. (1948) 'Human relations: Rare, medium, or well-done?', *Harvard Business Review* 26(1):521–542.

Roethlisberger, F.J. and Dickson, W.J. (1939) *Management and the Worker: An Account of a Research Program Conducted by the Western Electric Company, Hawthorne Works, Chicago*, Cambridge, MA: Harvard University Press.

Roper, M. (1994) *Masculinity and the British Organization Man Since 1945*, Oxford: Oxford University Press.

Rose, M. (1978) *Industrial Behaviour: Theoretical Developments Since Taylor*, Harmondsworth: Penguin Books. (Currently out of print.)

Schein, E. (1992) *Organization Culture and Leadership*, 2nd edn, San Francisco: Jossey-Bass.

Schein, E. (2004) *Organizational Culture and Leadership*, 3rd edn, San Francisco: Jossey-Bass.

Schoen, D.R. (1957) 'Human relations: Boon or bogie?' *Harvard Business Review* Nov/Dec: 91–97.

Senge, P. (1990) *The Fifth Discipine: the art and practice of the learning organization*, London: Century Business.

Starkey, K. (1998) 'Durkheim and the limits of corporate culture: Whose culture? Which Durkheim?', *Journal of Management Studies* 35(2):125–136.

Strati, A. (2000) *Theory and Method in Organization Studies: Paradigms and Choices*, London: Sage Publications.

Turnbull, P. and Wass, V. (1997) 'Marksist management; sophisticated human relations in a high street retail store', *Industrial Relations Journal* 29(2):98–111.

Ulrich, D. (1997) *Human Resource Champions: The Next Agenda for Adding Value and Delivering Results*, Boston: Harvard Business School Press.

Vroom, C. (2002) 'Organization structure', in A. Sorge (ed.) *Organization*, London: Thomson Learning.

Westenholz, A. (2003) 'Organizational citizens – Unionized wage earners, participative management and beyond', in B. Czarniawska and G. Sevón (eds), *The Northern Lights – Organization Theory in Scandinavia*, Copenhagen: Copenhagen Business School Press.

Whitehead, T.N. (1935) 'Human relations within human groups', *Harvard Business Review* 14(1):1–13.

Whittington, R. (2001) *What is Strategy – and Does It Matter?*, London: Thomson Learning.

Whyte, W.F. (1969) *Organizational Behavior: Theory and Application*, Homewood, IL: Richard D. Irwin, Inc. & The Dorsey Press.

Whyte, W.H. (1960) *The Organization Man*, Harmondsworth: Penguin Books.

Wilson D. C. (1993) *A Strategy of Change: Concepts and Controversies in the Management of Change*, London: Routledge.

Wilson, F. (2004) *Organization Behaviour and Work*, 2nd edn, Oxford: Oxford University Press.

# Chapter 4

# Neo-modernist organization theory: surfing the new wave?

## Introduction

This chapter deals with a significant aspect of all organizations – the processes by which organizational members attempt to influence and control each other over what gets done, and how those things are done, when they are done, where they are done and by whom they are done. As illustrated in previous chapters, because our everyday participation in organizations usually entails the surrender of some of our individual autonomy to what appears to be an external and usually hierarchically ordered collective will, control has been a pivotal issue for organization theorists since the late 1800s and the publication of the seminal work of Max Weber (1947) concerning the development of bureaucracy. Indeed as Pfeffer (1997) more recently observed, control is an 'essential problem of management and organization' (p. 100).

From the point of view of management trying to influence the behaviour of subordinates, how control is attempted in organizations seems to be gradually changing. Or at least according to what is called new-wave theory, it has to change in order for organizations to be more efficient and effective. Indeed, one key development in the past 20 years directly related to new-wave theory seems to have been the development of forms of control located in culture management, including the ways managers attempt to influence the norms, beliefs and values of employees so they work in a manner that is in line with managers' perceived requirements for efficient and effective task performance. To understand this possible development, it has to be put into the context of alternative forms of control in order to gauge how – and if – culture management is a significant theoretical development and change in how organizations are practically organized.

## Learning outcomes

- Differentiate formal control from informal control.

- Identify the different types of formal control that are deployed in organizations and how they operate so as to influence employee behaviour.

- Locate new wave management theory in the development of what has been called cultural, clan or normative control.

- Review different theoretical explanations as to why a shift in control toward the cultural, in many organizations, may have happened.

- Investigate the philosophical origins and underlying assumptions of new-wave management.

## Structure of the chapter

- This chapter begins by defining new-wave theory and outlining its origins in relation to debates about control. It then illustrates how any attempt at controlling or influencing the behaviour of subordinates is an extremely complex process because of the unpredictability of members' responses to any attempt at influencing their behaviour and, most significantly, because of the operation of what is called the *informal organization*.

- The chapter then turns to a further layer of complexity that is created by how different types of formal control operate. This is used to illustrate how cultural management, the hallmark of new-wave management, is operationalized by managers and how it is different to other types of control.

- Two competing explanations of the apparent spread of culture management are then considered: one that explains its emergence as a necessary response to changes in organizations' environments, and one that focuses upon changes in managerial ideologies and discourses, which is further examined by looking at the theoretical and philosophical origins of new-wave management. The chapter concludes by considering the significance of culture management in contemporary organizations.

## The origins of new-wave management

For a long time, many organization theorists, using an array of different perspectives, have considered that understanding the structures and processes of different forms of control was the key to understanding the ways different types of organizations operate. Some might appear to be primarily concerned with advising managers upon how to make labour more tractable in the pursuit of economic efficiency (e.g., Ouchi, 1981; Tannenbaum, 1962), others are more concerned with describing and documenting how different forms of control operate in different social contexts (e.g., Etzioni, 1965), and still others seem to focus upon the unanticipated consequences of attempts at control (e.g., Gouldner, 1954, 1965) or, in some cases, critiquing the whole process from a Marxist stance (Braverman, 1974; Clawson, 1980; Edwards, 1979).

A key issue here is that, during different historical periods, different forms of control have been intentionally used by organizational elites in trying to consolidate and extend their influence over the behaviour of subordinates in the workplace. Indeed, the interplay of economic and cultural forces, the climate of relations between managers and employees, together with the changing nature of work, have all been associated with causing changes in the control strategies in use (Edwards, 1979) and variation in how control is theorized and discussed (Barley and Kunda, 1992). Regardless of the forms of control at play, organizational elites have encountered a vast array of responses from subordinates that seem to range from various kinds of conforming behaviour, through to subtle and often covert forms of resistance and organizational misbehaviour, through to outright active rebellion (Ackroyd and Thompson, 1999; Ezzamel, Willmott and Worthington, 2001; Jermier, Knights and Nord, 1994; McKinley and Taylor, 1998).

Since the early 1980s, it seems that we have witnessed the emergence of new forms of control, or, perhaps more accurately, certain control strategies have become more prominent and widespread as a means of disciplining employees (Sturdy, Knights and Willmott, 1992; Wilkinson and Willmott, 1995). In 1989, Stephen Wood dubbed this phenomenon 'new-wave management'. Wood derived this name from a recently published book by a respected organization theorist, Gareth Morgan, titled '*Riding the Waves of Change: Developing Managerial Competencies for a Turbulent World*' (1988). In a surprising departure from his usual approach to organization theory, Morgan had based his text upon the thoughts and ideas of 20 North American executives regarding the managerial competencies required for the coping with the waves of organizational, technological and environmental change leading into the twenty-first century. The surfing metaphor was intended to capture the process of dealing with the rapid changes that were presumed to confront organizations and with which senior managers must cope. The suggested strategies included:

- creating and communicating a shared vision
- creating flatter less hierarchical organizations
- generating flexibility and freedom by giving employees autonomy through empowering them
- promoting entrepreneurship and risk taking amongst managers based upon their reading of the environment and anticipating change

- developing skills of remote management so that management control may be exerted from a distance
- building flexible organizations around small groups or teams.

Pivotal to these strategies was changing corporate culture and reframing members' cognitions so that innovation, learning and creativity are encouraged because 'gone is the old-fashioned notion of hierarchy in which one member directs the activities of other members' (Morgan, 1988, p. 129).

Of course, Morgan was not the first organization theorist to put forward such prescriptions. But it is interesting to observe how these theoretical ideas were being articulated by his executives, and this is worth considering in relation to the concept of the double hermeneutic covered in Chapter 1 of this book.

Originating primarily in North America, new-wave management appears to have emerged out of attempts to secure enhanced competitive advantage by emulating what were thought to be the adoptable aspects of Japanese organizations' apparent competitive advantage (Pascale and Athos, 1982; Vogel, 1979), and from trying to identify and replicate existing indigenous 'excellent' American management practices (e.g., Peters and Waterman, 1982).

Here a key belief was that the apparent success of Japanese industry since World War II lay in the cultural roots of their managerial system. For some American theorists (e.g., Ouchi, 1981; Ouchi and Jaeger, 1978), American management's cultural roots lay in individualism, which gave rise to antagonistic workplace relations. On the other hand, Japanese culture emphasized collective consensus, interdependent cooperation and deference to paternalistic authority figures. Because traditional sources of affiliation (e.g., the church, the family) were thought to be in decline in the United States, the workplace needed to become a source of social stability and cohesion. This new way of managing was dubbed theory Z. This combined what was thought to be the best of American and Japanese management practices and prescribed a flattening of organizational hierarchies and an emphasis upon cultural control; the devolution of some decision making to employee teams and an increase in employee participation; the elimination of organizational status differences and barriers; and a move toward lifetime employment for certain employees. Although many commentators disputed the appropriateness of theory Z, especially its paternalistic elements, to an American cultural context (e.g., England, 1983), the promotion of 'strong' organizational cultures as sources of social affiliation and solidarity began to be seen as a key source of competitive advantage. This notion is still evident today in many organizations to the extent that cultural management has become a normal, everyday aspect of the their operations that is almost unnoticed because it is so unexceptional.

So, regardless of the source of inspiration, a key outcome was the emergence of a focus upon the management of the cultural dimensions of organizations as a decisive control strategy in order to create cultural homogenization and facilitate the social integration of members so as to create 'strong cultures' that promoted the kind of employee behaviour that enhanced productivity, quality, flexibility and so on. In this manner, *culture management* became more synonymous with *culture change* rather than its maintenance. For some writers, these developments necessarily entailed the demise of bureaucracy because the control afforded by the latter 'stifle[d] initiative and creativity' in an atmosphere that was 'emotionally repressive' (Kanter, 1989,

p. 280), a situation that was seen to be increasingly uncompetitive because of certain changes that were presumed to be ongoing in Western economies. So, this apparent shift in control began to be associated with a decisive break with the past through the predicted (e.g., Heydebrand, 1989) and perceived (e.g., Heckscher and Donnellon, 1994) development of postbureaucratic forms of organization whose emergence was often seen as a strategic response to the perceived need for certain forms of labour-led flexibility in times of high uncertainty (Clegg, 1990).

In Chapter 5, we will turn to the development of these notionally new postbureaucratic, or postmodern, organizational forms. In this chapter, we focus upon understanding and explaining the perceived shift in control that is often thought to have taken place in many of the organizations in which we work. In order to do this, we must begin by identifying the different types of control in organizations and how they operate. Because the focus of this chapter is upon new-wave management theory, our primary aim is to establish how cultural control differs from and relates to alternative control strategies.

## Control in organizations

Here we are concerned with what may be called *formal control*. This is where organizational elites develop social and technical arrangements purposely aimed at influencing the work behaviour of subordinates in desired directions. Obviously, this is based upon the assumption that it is possible to systematically control organizational relationships. Indeed, we all experience formal control processes, albeit in different ways, whether we are attending university lectures, giving those lectures or working eight-hour 'continental shifts' in a Sheffield steelworks. Sometimes these processes are very subtle and barely noticeable because they are so much a normal part of our everyday lives and expectations. As such, formal control refers to everyday hierarchical processes and practices whereby attempts are made to ensure that members' *potential* labour power is realized in relation to their organizational tasks. However, establishing formal control over human beings is a very uncertain issue, with many unintended consequences, basically for three reasons.

### Unpredictable behaviour

How people react to any attempt at controlling their organizational behaviour is often somewhat unpredictable. Their conformity to managers' plans and requirements cannot be engineered in the same way we might use physical resources to construct a building by arranging bricks, concrete, steel and so on according to preformulated plans drawn up by an architect. In part, this is because people do not automatically respond to others' instructions as if they were inanimate marionettes automatically responding to the manipulations of the puppet master. People are not passive recipients of external stimuli, such as the directions of supervisors and managers backed up by different kinds of reward and punishment. Instead, they react variably to events based upon how they understand what is going on. In other words, human beings possess agency: their behaviour is guided by their active sense-making, and this can lead to unintended and often unpredictable consequences. In doing so, people reflect upon, interpret and give meaning to what is going on around them, and they might do this in different ways, with different behavioural outcomes. Hence, trying to organize others and control aspects of what they do is always somewhat unpredictable because of human agency.

Human agency involves some very complex processes. For instance, impacting upon our subjective apprehension of what is going on are the ways people routinely communicate and negotiate different understandings of their organizational experiences with each other in different social contexts. These variable social processes are a pivotal influence upon any actors' self-awareness, generation, evaluation, selection and enactment of particular courses of action (see Burr, 1995; Silverman, 1970). They might choose to obey, ignore, subvert or actively resist the demands placed upon them by managers; they might also completely misunderstand these instructions. So, control over employee behaviour is always problematic, especially because people always retain at least the potential to resist control strategies – something that makes attempts at managing their behaviour in precise directions often unrealizable in practice. Whether or not they exercise that power to resist may largely depend upon how they *perceive* themselves in relation to organizational contexts, especially with regard to their own needs or interests and the possibilities of meeting them, which in turn depends upon the dynamics of the social processes outlined above (see also Young, 1989). One outcome of such unpredictability, that to a degree results in ongoing patterns of (mis)behaviour, is often called the 'informal organization'.

## Informal control: organizational misbehaviour?

As we have just implied, formal control is not the only type of control that operates in organizations. There are also controls that are located in the informal organization:

> . . . the practices, values, norms beliefs, unofficial rules, as well as the complex network of social relations, membership patterns and centres of influence and communication that developed within and between constituent groups of the organization under the formal arrangements but that were not specified by them (Roethlisberger, 1968, p. 262).

Informal control is often covert and hidden from the uninitiated. This is because it arises spontaneously out of everyday social interaction, whereby social pressure is tacitly (and sometimes overtly) exerted upon the individual to conform to a group's unwritten rules about appropriate conduct. Here the informally organized and sanctioned ways of behaving may, or may not, be inimical to the demands emanating from the formal organization. Indeed, formal attempts at securing control may well founder when they confront the individual and collective intransigencies that emanate from informal social relations (see the following case study).

**Case Study**

**An insight into organization theory in action:
The sociology of trench warfare**

**Stop and think**

In organizational terms, what is going on in Figure 4.1? Now read below.

**Figure 4.1:** A snapshot taken by a British Officer showing German and British troops fraternizing on the Western Front during the Christmas truce of 1914. (*Source:* IWM Q11718.)

## Informal organization in the military: 1914–1918

Ashworth (1968) uses an array of documentary sources, including participants' memoirs, diaries, and letters as well as battalion histories and the papers of military elites, to develop what he calls a 'sociology of trench warfare'. As Ashworth points out, often the distances separating the opposing trenches were small (usually around 100 to 300 yards, but often less), which allowed direct communication between soldiers on opposing sides across 'no man's land'. For Ashworth, this possibility was a pivotal influence upon how an informal military organization arose amongst many of the armies involved in trench warfare, including the British, Irish, French, German and Bulgarian. Ashworth's work gives a most vivid description of an informal organization's opposition to the norms and demands of the formal organization amidst the most desperate of circumstances. It is also a testament to human survival and ingenuity.

## The formal structure of relationships

According to Ashworth (1968), the formal British military organization required that, in all circumstances, interaction between the soldier and the enemy had to be governed by the norm of offensiveness. Here:

> The exemplary soldier, in terms of elite values, was the soldier who, on his own initiative, instigated action likely to cause the enemy deprivation. The object of war was to eliminate the enemy both physically and morally . . . the 'offensive' or 'fighting' spirit . . . limited only by fatigue, orders to the contrary or the shortage of weapons and ammunition (p. 409).

Military elites systematically tried to instil this norm into combatant officers and troops during training and in formal face-to-face situations.

> During these socialization processes, 'The state and military organizations had equipped the soldier with an image of the enemy which . . . provided a surrogate motive for violence . . . as a subhuman thing capable of all conceivable crimes . . . to maximize the differences between the soldier and his foe' (pp. 420–421).

Although it is important not to forget that World War I entailed horrendous casualty rates on all sides, especially during mass infantry attacks, Ashworth shows how the opposing troops, when given the chance, would informally negotiate cooperative arrangements that saved lives.

## The informal structure of relationships

Ashworth's evidence suggests that in many sectors of the front line, for long periods of time, warfare was not governed by the official offensive norm. Instead, the informal 'live and let live principle' dominated:

> A collective agreement between front-line soldiers of opposing armies to inhibit offensive activity to a level mutually defined as tolerable. This understanding was tacit and covert; it was expressed in activity or non-activity rather than in verbal terms. This norm was supported by a system of sanctions. In the positive sense it constituted a system of mutual service, each side rewarded by the other by refraining from offensive activity on the condition, of course, that this non-activity was reciprocated. Negatively, violations of the norm were sanctioned (p. 411).

For instance, violations of the norm resulted in retaliation by the opposition until the norm was re-established. However, within respective armies, sanctions also operated in the form of 'group disapproval . . . against those individuals whose activities were defined as too offensive' (p. 415). The result was a ritualized and routinized structure of often perfunctory and mutually acceptable offensive activity well below that prescribed by military elites as appropriate – yet sufficient to give the appearance of animosity to the uninitiated. Importantly, this informal structure also served as a means of communication between opposing sides. Front-line officers colluded in maintaining this cooperation because it was equally in their interests to do so: just as with their subordinates, the informal norm also increased their chances of survival. This common interest transcended the 'institutionally defined differences between officers and other ranks' (p. 420) and simultaneously drove a wedge between lower-ranking combatant officers and staff officers – those senior officers being far removed from any physical danger. Ashworth illustrates this state of affairs in series of quotations from participants.

- All patrols – English and German – . . . pretend that they are Levites and the other is a good Samaritan, and pass by on the other side, no word spoken (p. 412).
- It is only common courtesy not to interrupt each others' meals with intermittent missiles of hate (p. 413).
- The only activity with which the battalion had to contend was sniping. . . . On the left the Germans amused themselves by aiming at spots on the walls of cottages . . . until they had cut a hole (p. 413).
- If a Frenchman had orders to throw bombs several times during the night he agreed with his 'German comrade' to throw them left and right of [the German's] trench (p. 413).
- The most unpopular man . . . is the trench mortar officer . . . he discharges the mortar over the parapet into the German trenches. . . . The whole weight of public opinion in our trench is directed against it being fired from anywhere at all (p. 415).

As we have indicated, it is important to not underestimate the sheer horror of trench warfare and the terrible casualties suffered – especially when a large-scale offensive was happening – something that displaced the informal organization. For instance, on 1 July 1916, during the first day of the Somme offensive, the British army alone sustained 60,000 casualties, with some 20,000 of these fatalities. To get some idea of a British soldier's chances of surviving this particular carnage, the casualty rate in the battalion of one of this book's author's grandfather, on this day, meant that there were only around 60 survivors out of more than 600 men.

The informal behaviour of opposing troops during trench warfare is analogous to a form of employee 'misbehaviour'. Ackroyd and Thompson (1999) argue that employee 'misbehaviour' and resistance to formal control have been, and continue to be, endemic to organizations. They locate such behaviour in the articulation of employees' interests and identities as well in the development of what they call 'informal self-organization'. Although the latter developed so as to promote and protect those perceived interests, managers have often tolerated, used and depended upon it (see Fortado, 1994) through, for instance, the unplanned creation of tacit, reciprocal, social and economic exchanges with employees, which Gouldner (1954, 1965) originally called an *indulgency pattern*. As Gouldner found, managers connived with employees to ignore the regulations, commands and orders from their hierarchical superiors because it was in their interests to do so. However, it is important to realize that perhaps certain changes to how organizations assert control over employees may have restricted the possibilities of informal organization. As Ackroyd and Thompson (1999) observe:

> A combination of organizational restructuring and management action has now 'penetrated' informal self-organization and modified older forms of shop floor autonomy. Old-style work limitation or other things that employers like to call 'Spanish practices' may not be appropriate or feasible in new conditions. But as we have demonstrated, modified forms of self organization remain the bedrock of employee action (p. 163).

### Stop and think

How does Ashworth's account of trench warfare illustrate an indulgency pattern between front-line officers and other ranks in the trenches?

### The chapter so far

Establishing formal control over the membership of any organization is an inherently complex process because how people respond to attempts at influencing their behaviour is always somewhat unpredictable. This is because of human agency and how human agency is often expressed in and through the informal organization.

## Complexity and the problem of implementation

Formal control processes are in themselves complex and therefore inherently difficult to implement. At risk of some oversimplification, there are four key elements in any formal system of control (see also Otley and Berry, 1980):

1. Objectives, for some chosen aspect of task performance, must be set so as to define what ought to be happening.
2. There must exist a means by which the chosen aspect of task performance is monitored and evaluated in relation to those objectives so as to identify deviant and conforming task performances.
3. There must be some disciplinary apparatus for trying to correct deviations from what is expected.

4. There must be some means for rewarding, in an appropriate manner, task performances that meet expectations so as to reinforce that behaviour so that it will be repeated.

However, how each element is designed in practice can vary considerably. For instance, an array of different types of formal control may be used to influence subordinates' behaviour by focusing upon different aspects of their task performance. One way of understanding how these different types of formal control within organizations operate is illustrated by Figure 4.2. This shows the operation

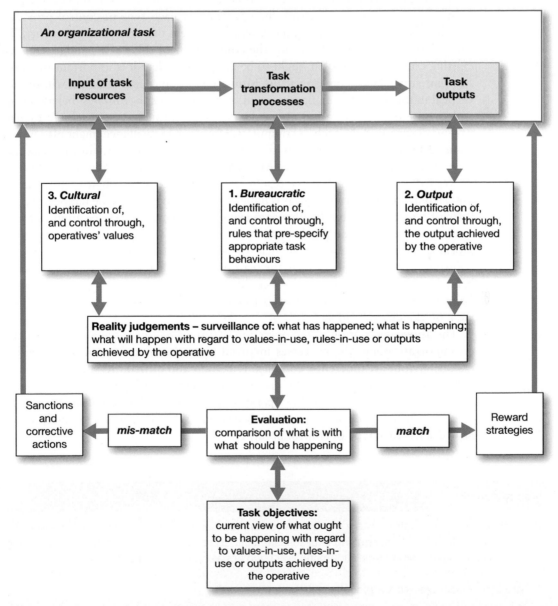

**Figure 4.2:** The operation of three types of control in relation to an organizational task. (*Source:* Adapted from Johnson et al., 2001; also see Otley and Berry, 1980.)

of three important types of formal control in relation to the conduct of an organizational task:

1. **The input of task resources** (e.g., human skills, human values or attitudes, technology, capital, raw materials), which are combined together by . . .
2. **The task transformation processes** (e.g., people working in teams or individually etc.) combine task inputs together to create a variety of . . .
3. **Task outputs** (e.g., goods and services, profits or losses, satisfied or dissatisfied customers, environmental pollution, scrap).

Although focusing upon different aspects of an organizational task, in principle (if by no means always in practice), the operation of each type of control provides a particular (re)presentation, or image, of some aspect of organizational reality. This surveillance potentially allows for the comparison of this reality judgement with existing conceptions of what ought to be happening. Here it is important to emphasize that surveillance comes in many forms. For instance, surveillance will often be vertical in the sense that managers might try to observe subordinates' behaviour and collect and store information about their task performance, increasingly by using various electronic aids, such as computers. However, surveillance might also be horizontal and involve peer review with team members formally monitoring aspects of each others' task performance (see McKinley and Taylor, 1998; Sewell, 1998).

Regardless of its form, if the results of surveillance are evaluative comparisons that signal a match between what is happening and what should be happening, some form of reward (often but by no means exclusively financial) may be administered so as to reinforce such desirable behaviour on the part of the operative so that it will be repeated. However, when a mismatch is signaled by the comparison processes, task controllers could then investigate the reasons behind such a deviation from desirable behaviour. Notionally, this analysis could then allow them to identify and apply the appropriate corrective actions so as to ensure that operatives' behaviour will get back on the desired course.

The above description of the operation of any of the three types of control raises an important point: the processes involved in establishing control over members' task behaviour are inherently complex, uncertain and difficult to successfully implement. For instance, if any of the operations illustrated in Figure 4.2 are missing or done ineffectively, the control in operation may not be able to ensure the required level of influence over operatives' task behaviour. With these issues in mind, we shall now discuss each type of control in turn.

---

**Stop and think**

With reference to any control system with which you are familiar, for instance how your behaviour on a course of study you are undertaking is assessed, think about what aspects of the task are being controlled (e.g., inputs, processes or outputs) and try to answer the questions below.

1.  Are there clear objectives in place for the system?
2.  Are these objectives appropriate to the nature of the task being controlled?

3. Are these objectives operationalized in terms of clearly signaled expectations regarding task outputs, task processes or operative's values?

4. When people meet those expectations, are they rewarded?

5. If they are rewarded, are these rewards valued and perceived as fair by recipients?

6. If a mismatch occurs, is the system capable of signaling those deviations to controllers in a timely fashion?

7. If a mismatch is signaled by the system, does someone, firstly, have the information to select corrective actions, and secondly, the authority and motivation to implement those actions?

Questions 1 to 7 can serve as an initial check upon the operation of any control system: if any of your answers to these questions is no, then the control system is potentially ineffective.

Consider Ashworth's example of trench warfare in terms of questions 1 to 7. In control terms, why were senior officers often failing to instil the official norm of offensiveness in combat troops?

## Three types of formal control

### Bureaucratic control

Bureaucratic control entails the development of impersonal rules and procedures so as to influence the task transformation element by specifying what operatives should do, how, where and when. As we have seen in Chapter 2, Weber (1947) thought that a framework of intentionally established and impersonal rules to govern task performance was one of the most distinctive features of the bureaucratic administrative systems. For Weber, this entailed the subordination of members to the precise calculation of the means by which specific ends might be achieved, something that he called *formal rationality*. These rules, sometimes expressed as orders from above, are rationally designed by hierarchical superiors who occupy their posts on merit because they have more knowledge, experience and expertise than those below them in the organization. Such rules serve to remove from operatives choice or discretion with regard to how to do their work. So, the creation of a body of rules and procedures, backed up by various means of monitoring members' subsequent behaviour along with sanctions so as to ensure members' compliance, serves to preprogramme members' task performance. In other words, bureaucratic controls serve to constrain the range of members' behaviour, increase the predictability of their actions and increase the probability that perceived organizational requirements dominate that behaviour. Bureaucratic control of labour processes results in modern forms of work study and industrial engineering that use various techniques for deriving standard times, standard methods and planned and standardized work flows with detailed divisions of labour and job descriptions (Hales, 1993; Littler, 1982). Often, as in fordism, this entails the application of technology (e.g., the assembly line) to preprogramme the pace, sequencing and nature of labour processes (e.g., Cooley, 1980; Gartman, 1979) in which the rules are built into, and expressed, by the technology in use. The result is that control becomes more impersonal because the hierarchical authority relations it articulates become embedded in everyday social, technical and physical arrangements between members.

Numerous problems may arise with bureaucratic modes of control when they are badly managed. For instance, Heckscher and Donnellon (1994) argue that there is a danger that rules tend to accumulate because when mistakes are made, another rule is created with no subsequent way of removing that rule. Indeed, rules can become 'sanctified', with their strict observation becoming an end in itself, rather than being perceived as a means to achieve ends. Merton (1940) originally called this problem 'goal displacement' because means become ends in themselves, and hence following the rules becomes an overriding concern rather than doing a job effectively. Often people in bureaucracies realize this is happening and to do their jobs effectively and efficiently, often choose to ignore the rules when it suits them (see Blau, 1955) rather than to disrupt the organization. Indeed, it is also worth remembering that sometimes 'working to rule' is a tactic used by employees to put pressure on management during industrial disputes because of the disruption it causes!

Besides such bureaucratic 'disfunctions', a significant issue is that bureaucratic controls are only viable when task continuity exists (Offe, 1976) – that is, when those who create and administer the rules know what should be done, how, where, when and so on, and can thereby remove the conception of how to do tasks from their execution by operatives. However, Perrow (1967) has argued that when tasks are complex, unpredictable and unanalysable, for whatever reason, this knowledge may not exist, and therefore tasks cannot be subjected to bureaucratic hierarchical ordering. If such task–discontinuity exists, it becomes necessary to develop alternative forms of control that can leave the transformation process to the discretion, experience and intuition of the operative. We shall return to this issue later in this chapter.

## Output control

Output control entails trying to influence task performance by prescribing what operatives should achieve by completing a task, rather than trying to preprogramme transformation processes by specifying how they should do the task (see Figure 4.2). In Ouchi's (1979) terms, output controls focus upon the after-effects of operatives' behaviour rather than the actual behaviour itself. This entails the operationalization of the objectives set for the activities under control into a set of metrics or indicators. These devices allow observation and measurement of specific task outputs achieved by the operative and thereby enable the assessment of the extent to which those activities are attaining the objectives set for the task. For any given task, there are always a wide number of possible objectives that can be used for control purposes. Inevitably, output-based controls select only some of these possibilities. By giving prominence and visibility to only particular aspects of task performance, output controls create meaning and impose it upon task performance by defining what is good or bad performance, thereby transmitting to the operative what is valued by the 'organization'. Although this makes task performance available for inspection, evaluation, classification and action, it also excludes alternative possible definitions of any given performance by hiding their relevance through suppressing their potential visibility. Such partiality can cause numerous problems in organizations, particularly when inappropriate behaviours are inadvertently encouraged by control systems that only measure a narrow range of outputs (see Lawler and Rhode, 1976).

To avoid such problems, Kaplan and Norton (1990, 1996) have, for instance, developed the notion of a 'balanced scorecard' that helps controllers select a range of objectives that can be operationalized into metrics by performance measurement systems and will provide more comprehensive information. Their approach aims to measure performance in terms of four sets of indicators relating to different aspects of the organization. These include financial considerations such as costs and profits, customer relations and customer satisfaction, internal business processes that need to be excelled at, and the ability of the organization to learn, change and improve. However, even the balanced scorecard has to choose a limited number of performance dimensions for its attempts at surveillance and control and in so doing can ignore the complexities of organizational work – for instance, relationships with the local community or with suppliers of goods and services seem to be relatively underrepresented in the fourfold scheme. Mabey and Salaman (1995) make a slightly different point. They observe that with any output based control system there is often a failure:

> . . . to appreciate the subtlety of organizational life . . . [that] risk[s] shattering subtle structures of tacit but critical employee commitment by substituting a simplistic set of objectives. It carries the danger that if the system does 'work', in the sense that people focus on those elements of performance that have been selected and highlighted by the organization, the results may not at all be desirable: a pre-existing pride in skill and work might be replaced by a contractual focus (p. 193).

Such calculative compliance may be exacerbated by the hierarchical processes through which people are rewarded for apparent success, or punished for apparent failure, as signaled by the output based system. Here those being controlled tend to engage in defensive forms of impression management so as to appear competent in terms of the criteria that derive from the objectives that have been set – indeed, it is in their interests to do so. Problems that they might associate with the control system, that might threaten this presentation of oneself as competent, may be hidden or rationalized away. Indeed, when organizational changes occur, that mean that the output controls are focusing on the wrong performance dimensions, people may have become unwilling or unable to challenge the continuing relevance and importance of particular objectives through which control over task performance is implemented (see Duberley et al., 2000).

### The chapter so far

We have described two forms of formal control purposively designed by hierarchical superiors in order to influence the behaviour of subordinates. These we have called the bureaucratic and the output, which either try to regulate the task transformation process by the articulation of rules or focus upon what is achieved through task performance. This sets the scene for the third type of formal control, the cultural, which attempts to influence key aspects of what employees bring with them to task performance: their values and beliefs.

## Cultural control

Cultural control entails an attempt to influence what employees subjectively bring with them to their work and it is central to what Wood (1989) has called 'new-wave management'. It focuses upon aspects of the input element in Figure 4.2 through the orchestration and transmission to employees of specific emotions, norms and values that are congruent with what management perceives to be important for the tasks at hand. The emphasis is upon the generation and maintenance of a shared culture throughout the organization so that all are committed to the goals prescribed by management to create, for example, 'a culture of excellence' (Peters and Waterman, 1982).

Although cultural, normative or clan (the terms are interchangeable) control is a key characteristic of new-wave management, it has also been associated with the evolution of human resources management during the late 1980s (see Fox, 1990; Guest, 1987, 1991). Hence, cultural control not only entails identification, prescription and transmission of the values deemed appropriate, it also involves the highly problematic assessment of whether or not organizational members actually possess those values (see Figure 4.2).

---

### Stop and think

In the earlier case study, Ashworth gives an account of how formal control was attempted over British troops during World War I.

1. What type(s) of formal control were involved here?
2. Why were they often failing to instil 'offensive norms' amongst front-line troops?
3. Could an alternative type of control been used to make the troops more 'offensive'?

---

As Kunda notes (1992, p. 2), instead of overtly focusing upon members' actual behaviour or the outcomes of that behaviour, these more hidden forms of formal control focus upon the basic value premises which surround members' behaviour and decision making so as to normatively regulate the employees' consciousness. Indeed, a variety of production systems that gained some prominence during the 1990s, such as teamworking (Barker, 1993; Buchanan, 2000; Mueller, 1994; Sewell, 2001), total quality management (Knights and McCabe, 1998; Tuckman, 1994; Wilkinson et al., 1992) and lean production (Ezzamel et al., 2001; Wickens, 1992; Womack et al., 1990), all entail concerted attempts at orchestrating and disseminating management inspired values. Kunda (1992) describes such normative control as:

> The attempt to elicit and direct the required efforts of members by controlling the underlying experiences, thoughts and feelings that guide their actions. Under normative control, members act in the best interest of the company not because they are physically coerced, or purely from an instrumental concern with economic rewards. . . . Rather they are driven by internal commitment, strong identification with company goals. . . . Thus, under normative control, membership is founded not on the behavioural or economic transaction traditionally associated with work organizations, but, more crucially, on an experiential transaction, one in which symbolic rewards are exchanged for a moral orientation to the organization (p. 2).

So, for Kunda, the concept of culture has both cognitive and affective dimensions. It refers to what members know and emotionally feel about their organization and their work. Thus, normative cultural control is based upon establishing 'intense emotional attachment and the internalization of clearly enunciated company values' (Kunda, 1992, p. 10). Therefore, controllers must attempt to ensure that subordinates internalize – or have already internalized – the values, beliefs and attitudes that are deemed to be supportive of the organizational goals set by hierarchical superiors. Performance evaluation then becomes a matter of assessing members' organization behaviour through reference to the manifestation of sanctioned cultural mores and sentiments.

If the evolution of bureaucratic controls can be seen as an attempt to regulate out of existence the informal organization, in many respects, cultural control may be seen as an attempt to capture and reshape the informal organization by realigning employees' values so that they fit what senior managers deem to be necessary so as to ensure efficient and effective organization. Hence, with regard to our earlier trench warfare example, this would entail the relevant military elites successfully socializing combat troops into the norm of offensiveness and driving out, what was from their point of view, the inappropriate informal 'live and let live principle'. In other words, a key aim of cultural control is to change the informal organization so that this aspect of organizational life works in concert with, rather than against, the perceived requirements of organizational elites. However, as Kunda (1992, p. 5) also observes, the danger is that people are manipulated and coerced without being aware of it – a very insidious form of control. In contrast, bureaucratic controls are much more overt, and people are much more aware of what is going on.

For Anthony (1994), 'bureaucratic control, from the perspective of the controllers, unfortunately leaves subordinates free, partly because they possess their own cultural defences. So the defences must be broken down' (p. 92). As soon as these cultural defences are broken down, informal peer group pressure upon the individual member is redirected and begins to marshal management-approved norms. So, one possible result of cultural control may be that the formal and informal organizations are not readily distinguishable: informal organizing is formally prescribed, and 'culture' replaces 'structure' as an organizing principle (Kunda, 1992, p. 30). Another possible result is 'an overcoming of the division between the "personal life", values and beliefs of employees and the impersonal demands of corporations for greater productivity and quality' (Willmott, 1993, p. 63). So, if the appropriate values are subscribed to, a common sense of purpose or 'moral involvement', activated through emotion and sentiment, develops, which makes the constant surveillance and supervision of employees by managers, as a means of external control, redundant (Barker, 1993; Mitchell, 1985). Ironically, this alternative source of discipline and control over the employee reduces the need for some tiers of management, thereby contributing to the delayering of organizations (an issue we shall return to in Chapter 9). Indeed, the aim is for employees to exercise 'responsible autonomy', which:

> attempts to harness the adaptability of labour power by giving workers leeway and encouraging them to adapt to changing situations in a manner beneficial to the firm. To do this, top managers give them status, autonomy, and try to win their loyalty to the firm's ideals (the competitive struggle) ideologically (Friedman, 1977, p. 5).

So, in a paradoxical way, responsible autonomy seems to mean some autonomy without autonomy because employees have to align themselves with the organization's 'ideals' as defined by senior managers. Here, because employees have assimilated management-sanctioned cultural norms, they can be trusted to exercise self-discipline, discretion and initiative regarding their job performance in a manner that is supportive of managerial aims and objectives (see also Burawoy, 1979, 1985). Of course, achieving such an ideal end state requires managers to engineer changes in members' cultures based upon some tacit theoretical understanding of what Kunda (1992) calls 'the structural causes and consequences of cultural forms and their relationship to various measures of organizational effectiveness' (p. 8). In other words, for management to successfully change the configurations of employee culture(s) in this manner, they must not only have a clear understanding of the nature of existing employee cultures but also an understanding of how and why these have arisen in the first place, how these cultural dimensions impact on organizational effectiveness and what cultural elements need to change in order to improve effectiveness. Finally, management also needs to understand how it can intervene to promote change in the direction it desires. Of course, all this would be a tall order for even the most sophisticated professional social anthropologist to undertake (never mind managers not actually educated in social anthropological theory and methodology), many aspects of which they would also consider to be grossly unethical because to intervene in indigenous cultures, in order to change them in line with the social anthropologist's own cultural mores, would be condemned as a form of cultural imperialism. This is an important ethical point apparently lost upon many new-wave theorists.

## The new wave in action: managing cultural change

Much new-wave theory has been concerned with understanding how cultures get established in the first place. Usually a focus here (Kotter and Heskett, 1992; Schein, 1992) is upon the pivotal role played by the founder of the organization who, we are told, creates the culture by enacting and implementing his or her personal beliefs and values in the form of business strategies and management philosophies. For instance, we are told that the culture of Hewlett-Packard is as it is because of the influence of Hewlett's and Packard's own values (Kotter and Heskett, 1992; Peters and Waterman, 1982). The culture becomes embedded in the organization according to what is rewarded and what is communicated via the founder-leader's attention to particular priorities and goals. Other members learn and adopt this culture, especially when it seems to work well. Accordingly, the culture evolves as members attempt to meet the demands emerging from the organization's environment and to meet the needs of internal coordination and integration. Of course, this is a very top-down management view of cultural formation that underplays the diversity of cultural forms one is more likely to find in organizations. This diversity derives from the numerous different sources of social influence that any employee will encounter, both inside and outside the organization. So, as we shall discuss later, what seems to be the focus of this managerialist stance is *corporate culture* rather than *organizational culture*. This top-down view is replicated when it comes to managing culture change where it is even more important to differentiate the two theoretical definitions of what we are referring to by the concept of culture in this context.

A concern to engineer the homogenization of the cultural aspects of organizations, so as to establish common ways of thinking and feeling that are approved of by senior management, is illustrated by the advice Cummings and Huse (1989) give to managers who are embarking upon cultural change programmes. Here they put forward a five-stage model for managing the process:

1. Start from a **clear strategic vision** so as to provide purpose and direction.
2. Senior managers need to be **committed** to the new values and exert pressure.
3. Senior managers must communicate the new culture through **symbolic leadership** – their actions and behaviour must articulate the new values.
4. **Support the changes** through modifying structures, information and control systems and management style.
5. **Change the membership** through recruitment, redundancy, induction, training and so on.

Although approaches to engineering cultural change vary (see Brown, 1995, for an overview) Cummings and Huse's model presents several key elements. In order to guide organizational change, senior managers must deliberately articulate a corporate vision and mission statement that codifies their perceptions of the organization's long-term purpose and character, along with a supportive range of goals and core values underpinned by behavioural norms (Martin, 1995; Watson 1994). An example of such a vision and mission statement is provided below.

## Example: Microsoft's mission and values

Microsoft's mission: To enable people and businesses throughout the world to realize their potential.

### Delivering on Our Mission

The tenets central to accomplishing our mission stem from our core company values:

### Broad Customer Connection

Connecting with our customers, understanding their needs and how they use technology and providing value through information and support to help them realize their potential.

### A Global, Inclusive Approach

Thinking and acting globally, enabling a diverse workforce that generates innovative decision making for a broad spectrum of customers and partners, innovating to lower the costs of technology, showing leadership in supporting the communities in which we work and live.

### Excellence

In everything we do.

### Trustworthy Computing

Deepening customer trust through the quality of our products and services, . . . accountability, and our predictability in everything we do.

*(Continued)*

## Example: (Continued)

### Great People with Great Values

Delivering on our mission requires great people who are bright, creative, and energetic and who share the following values:

- Integrity and honesty.
- Passion for customers, partners and technology.
- Open and respectful with others and dedicated to making them better.
- Willing to take on big challenges and see them through.
- Self-critical, questioning, and committed to personal excellence and self-improvement.
- Accountable for commitments, results, and quality to customers, shareholders and employees.

### Innovative and Responsible Platform Leadership

Expanding platform innovation, benefits, and opportunities for customers and partners, openness in discussing their future directions; and working with others to ensure that their products and our platforms work well together.

### Enabling People to Do New Things

Broadening choices for customers by identifying new areas of business; incubating new products; integrating new customer scenarios into existing businesses; exploring acquisitions of new talent and experience; and integrating more deeply with new and existing partners.

At Microsoft, we're committed to our mission of helping our customers scale new heights and achieve goals they never thought possible.

*Source:* Microsoft. http://www.microsoft.com/mscorp/mission.

### Stop and think

How does the above mission and value statement express the following?

1. Core values to which Microsoft is committed.
2. The core purpose of the firm.
3. Visionary goals that Microsoft will pursue to fulfil its mission.

Following Anthony (1994), it is useful here to differentiate *corporate* culture from *organizational* culture (see also Chapter 3). Whereas the former refers to the values and meanings espoused by senior management, the latter refers to the probably diverse cultural patterns that exist in an organization – the informal organization. In Cummings and Huse's model, therefore, culture change–management is about the propagation of the corporate at the expense of the organizational.

However, as Linstead (1999, p. 93) notes there may be some cynical duplicity in the exposition of corporate culture because it may entail a concerted attempt to engineer the consent of the workforce by the popularization of either the values held by senior management or the values the latter prescribe for others but do not share.

Nevertheless, it is important not to underestimate the pressures upon all managers to consistently act out the espoused values at the heart of the cultural changes they are charged with propagating. As Hope and Hendry (1995) observe, the new management behaviour 'requires an investment of "self" rather dogged mimicry of behaviour and values set down in the corporate handbook. If the self is not engaged then power is reduced, for the required behaviour is distanced from the person itself' (p. 63). Moreover, employees may be alert to any disparity between management's cultural rhetoric and its apparent everyday behaviour to the extent that employees may use the espoused values underpinning prescribed cultural change to challenge and rectify the inauthenticity signified by such lapses in managers' performance of their corporate script (see Rosenthal et al., 1997).

So, having established what they want in employees, senior managers then have to change existing values and meanings when they do not match the corporate culture. The subsequent cascading downward of this prescribed culture often entails reorganization of the workplace to ensure that those with the required values (at least at the public level of testimony) are in positions of influence, as role models, so that they can communicate values both symbolically in their everyday leadership (see Grugulis et al., 2000; Pattison, 1997) and through their establishment of corporate rites, ceremonies, slogans, stories and myths that in effect tell employees how they should behave. Other means of cultural dissemination and maintenance might include team briefings, quality circles, house journals and the organization of various social activities that entail 'cultural extravaganza' inside and outside the workplace. An example of cultural extravaganza, which illustrates a symbolic importance, is enthusiastically described by Deal and Kennedy (1982).

> Mary Kay Cosmetics stages 'seminars' that are lavish multimillion dollar events at the Dallas convention center . . . awards for the best sales are given – pink Buicks and Cadillacs. One year the cars simply 'floated' down into the stage from a 'cloud' – a weighty touch of hoopla that produced over-whelming response from the crowd. At the end of this extravaganza everyone understands that the challenge of the company is sales (p. 74).

Such rather bizarre events entail the manipulation of symbols to reinforce what is wanted and approved of. Other ways of manipulating symbols might include the very architecture of buildings. For instance, at Nike's corporate headquarters in Portland, Oregon, employees approach the main buildings along a rocky road that symbolizes the journey from an uncertain past to a more promising – Nike – future. The actual buildings themselves are each adorned with sporting icons, past and present (e.g., Sebastian Coe, Steve Cram, Karl Lewis) whose excellence at their sports the employee is expected to emulate in a passion for his or her work. These headquarters are where the sportswear designers, amongst others, work – but there is no production facility. It is a self-contained world with its own gyms, hairdressers, restaurants and so on where employees are encouraged to spend long hours and be inspired by the successes of those sporting heroes.

Other processes of communication and social interaction might, as Dent (1995) observed in one (British) National Health Service hospital, entail some spatial reorganization by physically locating managers close to those they wish to influence so as enable them informally to nurture and sustain the desired cultural changes. This approach to reorganization seems to reflect Deal and Kennedy's (1983) advice that a 'hero' who is committed to the new culture should be in charge of the change process. However, these change processes also must entail 'transitional rituals' in which 'people mourn old ways, renegotiate new values and relationships and anoint heroes' (p. 175).

Alongside these tactics there is a further concerted attempt by management to influence the value premises of members' behaviour by trying to restructure their attitudes and beliefs through the use of an array of human resource management practises (Guest, 1998; Hope and Hendry, 1995; Legge, 1995; Wood, 1989). For instance, induction, training, appraisal and reward systems are formally realigned to reinforce displays of culturally acceptable behaviour by members. Meanwhile, managers may also attempt to alter the composition of the workforce through the use of sophisticated recruitment and selection techniques, which include assessment centres, psychometric tests, personal history inventories and indices of loyalty and other attitudes. The aim of such preemptive control is to ensure that the attitudinal and behavioural characteristics of new employees fit the prescribed culture thereby excluding alternative values (Ogbonna, 1992; Townley, 1989, 1994). Simultaneously, redundancy may be used to eliminate alternative values by removing employees who are seen to be unable or unwilling to embrace the specified culture (Dobson, 1989). For instance, one of this book's authors was told by a post-experience student that her organization was going to select people for redundancy on the basis of interviews aimed at identifying whether or not staff knew the corporate vision and mission statement. Of course, identifying those cultural deviants might be much more problematic despite the often hidden forms of surveillance that might be used to assess employees' conformity to approved norms (Sewell and Wilkinson, 1992). This is because people might be alert to the need to appear to subscribe to the culture and give off the appropriate signals without actually assimilating the specified cultural norms (see the next Stop and think box).

In sum, culture change management is presented as a technocratic exercise directed by expert senior managers. It is a technical process that involves the application of management recipes derived from new-wave theory, which is done to less knowledgeable others whose existing values and beliefs are thought to be somehow problematic and therefore in need of remedial treatment. Underlying this approach is the assumption that culture is what Smircich (1983) calls a 'critical variable' that may be directly controlled and managed. However, as she also points out, such an assumption ignores how cultures arise spontaneously out of everyday social interaction, and people will resist attempts by management to manipulate these processes. So, for instance, although culture change–management has been fashionable for some time, it is difficult to judge the impact of management interventions aimed at reshaping organizational cultures so that those employees become committed to management approved goals rather than just going through the motions so as appear to conform to such requirements. According to Johnson and Gill (1993), this is because commitment implies the employee's 'internalization of management-derived and sanctioned beliefs, norms and values, in the sense that they become part of the core of the individual's perceptual world; thereby they develop into moral obligations (moral involvement) that impel autonomously particular forms of behaviour' (p. 36). To put it bluntly if employees are committed – they do what they do because they think it is the 'right' thing to do – discipline is based upon 'peer pressure and more crucially, internalized standards of performance' (Kunda, 1992, p. 90). Therefore, for cultural control to be judged as being successfully in place, internalization of the prescribed cognitive and affective system must have occurred. However, the development of such inner convictions is only one of three possible

## Stop and think

Drawing upon Kelman's (1961) work, Johnson and Gill (1993) point out that compliance:

. . . is the mode of conforming behaviour of a person who is motivated by a desire to gain a reward or avoid a punishment. Such behaviour lasts only as long as the promise or threat of sanction exists. On the other hand 'identification' is a conforming response to social influence brought about by a desire to be like the people who are exerting the influence upon the individual. It therefore entails emotional gratification through emotional attachment to 'significant others'. In contrast to 'internalization', 'identification' does not necessarily involve the development of internal moral imperatives within the individual. However, such imperatives may develop as the individual adopts the beliefs, norms and values of the significant others in his/her perceptual world, thereby producing what Kelman specifically defines as 'internalization' (pp. 34–35).

As Willmott (1993) observes, very often the result of culture management programmes is:

. . . selective calculative compliance. In which case, employee behaviour is (minimally) congruent with 'realizing' the values of the corporation, but only in so far as it is calculated that material and/or symbolic advantage can be gained from managing the appearance of consent. . . . However, mere compliance is insufficient since it signals a failure to mobilize the emotional energies of staff in ways that inspires them to embody and live out the corporate values (p. 537).

A conundrum here is that any manifest employee behaviour that overtly conforms to management's attempts at reshaping shop floor cultures could be the expression of compliance, identification or internalization. Indeed, as Ogbonna (1992, p. 82) notes, the deep-seated attitudes of individuals are not readily observable. However, for Kunda (1992), the experience of cognitive dissonance may mean that compliance eventually beaks down into other forms of conformity:

. . . members who, under pressure, publicly espouse beliefs and opinions they might otherwise reject tend to adopt them as an authentic expression of their point of view . . . Over time, cognitive and emotive dissonance may blur the boundary between performers' perception of an acted role and the experience of an 'authentic self' (p. 156).

Potentially, this implies that culture management can change organizational cultures in line with management requirements by reshaping employees' understanding of themselves and their organizational roles.

1. In terms of control, what are the different behavioural implications of each form of conformity?
2. How can managers ever know which form of conformity is being enacted by employees?
3. Conversely, how can employees ever know that managers are being authentic in their performance of approved corporate cultural scripts?

overtly conforming responses to social influence; the other two are 'compliance' and 'identification', which have major implications for the kind of control that is being established over members' behaviour (see below).

There are many examples of employees' *appearing* to respond as expected and seeming to willingly participate in the processes of culture management, sometimes to the extent that managerial prerogative is extended to new areas of the employees' lives by instilling responsible autonomy (e.g., Barker, 1993; Casey, 1995; Grugulis et al., 2000; Kunda, 1992; Rosenthal et al., 1997). However, as we have already noted, employees are not culture-free before management's attempts at normative control: employee cultural terrains are always already occupied and expressed in and through the informal organization.

For instance, with specific regard to the propagation of the enterprise culture, Du Gay (1996, pp. 160–161) notes how managerial attempts at inscribing employees with particular sets of values cannot completely close off the processes of the production of meaning and identity which derive from different cultural aspects of their lives, both inside and outside work. As Linstead and Grafton-Small (1992, p. 344) incisively put it, the effects of culture management will always be unpredictable because corporate cultures are similar to texts that employees read and make sense of, and in so doing bring their awareness of alternative cultural texts that enter the corporate text, 'changing its nature and reproducing it as they consume it'. For Du Gay (1996), because employees are not mere automatons, the social complexities at play here can create the conditions for resistance to management's attempts at control, through, for instance, the (often covert) reassertion of traditional employee cultures (see also Anthony, 1994; Covaleski et al., 1998). In other words, there is always at least the *potential* for competition over the employee's allegiances, and hence resistance to management normative control, from an array of cultural sites with which the employee has social contact. These alternative sites include the informal work group, occupational groups, class memberships, political affiliations, trade unions, professional memberships, the local community, ethnic groupings, gender and so on. Potentially, these alternative cultural sites constitute rival social localities in which socialization of the employee might take place and in which the employee's subjective sense of identity might be formulated.

The result may be that culture management initiatives often fail to engage with the employee's self-identity and instead, the conformity that is engendered may be based upon cynicism and calculative compliance rather than the holy grail of internalization and commitment. Moreover, when management seeks to invoke employee commitment, 'It is likely to be asking for impossible outcomes from those whose conditions of labour lack the necessary characteristics of autonomy and trust that would lead to making those "investments"' (Warhurst and Thompson, 1998, p. 12). Although this point might mean that the possibility of 'successful' cultural change is more likely with certain types of 'core' employees, especially in knowledge-intensive companies with highly paid, highly educated employees who have secure jobs and who engage in forms of self-management (Alvesson, 1995), it also means that when attempts at cultural change are accompanied by downsizing, outsourcing and delayering, as is often the case, they are all the more likely to fall upon fallow ground (Hope and Hendry, 1995).

---

**The chapter so far**

In the previous sections, we have elucidated key aspects of a third formal control – the normative, clan, or cultural. How this form of control is implemented in practice has been considered through looking at how management might attempt to engineer cultural change as well as how they might try to maintain desirable cultures. However, the management of cultural change is highly unpredictable because alternative sites of cultural influence will always be present.

---

## A theoretical explanation of a possible shift in control: a new historical configuration?

Many proponents of new-wave organization theory (see Berg, 1989; Thompson, 1993) appropriate elements of what is called the context or period explanation of the disfunctions of bureaucracy to justify their prescriptions for organizations. For instance, a still popular notion, shared by many organization theorists that has been enthusiastically appropriated by many politicians (see Clarke and Newman, 1997), arose in the late 1980s and early 1990s. This notion is that organizations now confront a time of discontinuous and accelerating social, economic and technological change along with heightened levels of competition on a global scale. This period has been variously dubbed the end of organized capitalism (Lash and Urry, 1987), the age of unreason (Handy, 1989), the postmodern world (Clegg, 1990) and postcapitalism (Drucker, 1993). Regardless of the label used, the uniting theme is one of tremendous change as we enter a new historical configuration. For instance, it is argued that the processes of production, distribution, exchange and consumption have not just dramatically accelerated but have also become increasingly diverse, specialized and temporary – a destabilized 'casino capitalism' (Bluestone and Harrison, 1988) of 'globalization and relativization' (Robertson, 1992), of 'intensified risk' (Beck, 1992), of 'heterogenization' (Daudi, 1990), of 'time-space compression' (Harvey, 1989) and of 'BLUR' (Davis and Meyer, 1998). These different commentators emphasize the significance of different destabilizing disturbances, but they all appear to agree upon three things that constitute fundamental challenges to how organizations are managed.

1. Shifts towards globalization, a postindustrial information age and new patterns of work are not just irreversible but are also gaining speed.
2. Uncertainty is now pervasive in contemporary society because 'along with the growing capacity of technical options grows the incalculability of their consequences' (Beck, 1992, p. 21).
3. These developments have important repercussions for work organizations as managers face up to finding new ways of coping with the uncertainties that partly derive from a need for continuous rapid adjustment to a market environment that seems to have become permanently more complex, turbulent and unpredictable than in the past.

Although this notion that we have entered a new historical configuration that has devastating implications for organizations has attracted some scepticism (e.g., Du Gay, 2000;

Thompson 1993), much commentary (e.g., Hastings, 1993; Heckscher, 1994; Osbourne and Gaebler, 1992; Perrone, 1997) presents the view that the main casualties of destabilization are public and private sector bureaucracies.

The reasoning behind this view and the espoused aim of dismantling the apparently now obsolete bureaucracy is well rehearsed and circulates largely around the argument that bureaucracies are dependent upon a hierarchical ordering of knowledge – that people higher up in the organizational hierarchy must know precisely what people lower down the hierarchy should do. For instance, for it to be possible to establish controls based upon the specification of behaviour through rules that programme employees' tasks, it is necessary for proper and desirable task behaviour to first be recognizable. As we have illustrated, the construction of rules and specifications serves to preprogramme employees' tasks and enable the monitoring and evaluation of their actual task behaviours with reference to what has been deemed to be appropriate. However, when the appropriate behaviour may be unknown or unknowable 'the observations of actual behaviour are of no use for control purposes' (Ouchi, 1978, p. 175). Indeed, when tasks are complex and unpredictable, it is impossible to create predetermined rules to facilitate the regulation of employee behaviour. Indeed, for many tasks, it may be vital to allow employees to exercise their own discretion – the ability to choose to do the tasks according to how an employee sees the demands of the situation. The ability to exercise discretion and initiative is something that bureaucracy may remove or prevent unless it is somehow informally circumvented by the cooperation of managers and employees (see Blau, 1955).

For instance, Kelly (1985) argues that when an organization has a continuous, standardized and homogeneous throughput, as in the early days of car manufacturing (e.g., the black Model-T Ford motor car), a bureaucratic approach could be an extremely efficient way of organizing work. However, when:

> . . . demand became unpredictable, in quantity and quality, when markets were diversified worldwide and thereby difficult to control, and when the pace of technological change made obsolete single purpose production equipment, the mass production system became too rigid and too costly (Castells, 1996, p. 154).

So, where mass markets for goods and services are in decline or no longer exist, and thus where there is a heterogeneous, rapidly changing and unpredictable throughput of goods and services, and therefore tasks become, in Clegg's (1990) terms, increasingly de-differentiated (see the next Ideas and perspectives box) what may be required is a more functionally flexible, committed, itinerant and skilled workforce capable of exercising discretion so as to cope with the uncertainties created by fluctuations in product and technology. Indeed, an array of theorists have argued that control through the monitoring of compliance with procedures and rules becomes increasingly problematic as task transformation processes become unanalysable and nonpreprogrammable (Ouchi, 1979, 1981; Perrow, 1967), emergent (Mohrman et al., 1990), de-differentiated (Clegg, 1990) and characterized by task discontinuity (Offe, 1976). Such a situation requires employees who are capable of creatively and flexibly dealing with unpredictable production variances where and when they arise (Jackson and Wall, 1991) rather than merely complying with preformulated rules and procedures, or the direct supervisory commands, of management.

## Ideas and perspectives

## Clegg's (1990) argument

*Modernity* was characterized by:

Stable mass (i.e., *undifferentiated*) markets and patterns of consumption, which resulted in a constant predictable throughput of goods and services. This allowed management to bureaucratize labour processes and *differentiate* (i.e., divide-up) labour processes through deskilling and a micro-division of labour that specified what employees should do, how, where and when.

**Versus:**

*Postmodernity* is characterized by:

Unstable niche (i.e., *differentiated*) markets and patterns of consumption, which results in a variable unpredictable throughput of goods and services. This requires management to *de-differentiate* (i.e., put back together) labour processes so that employees have a wide range of skills that they can flexibly deploy as unforeseen demands arise.

In other words, such a situation requires employees to use their discretion, flexibly deploy a wide range of skills and manage for themselves how tasks are done – something that in turn might entail 'delayering' because those layers of management whose function it was to directly control and supervise employee task behaviour are no longer required because that function is now devolved to the self-managing employee (Shaw and Schneider, 1993).

Although it has been widely claimed that such flexibility might not be possible with bureaucratic controls (Badham and Matthews, 1989; Hammer and Champy, 1993; Piore, 1986), some enhancement of flexibility may be achievable by using them in conjunction with flexible, advanced manufacturing technologies (Adler, 1993; Smith, 1989; Wickens, 1992). Alternatively, Hertog and Wielinga (1992) argue that one way organizations might react to complexity and turbulence is to retain bureaucracy but enlarge the organization's information processing capacity through vertical information systems that provide more detailed information more rapidly. By more effectively predicting change in an organization's environment through this enhanced scanning, information gathering and analysis facility, it could be possible to predict requisite organizational changes and implement them in a bureaucratic fashion that allows for timely adaptation. However, they also identify a second approach that entails the abandonment of bureaucracy through processes of 'organizational renewal' that dissolve the bureaucratic distinction between 'thinking and doing'. According to Hertog and Wielinga (1992), problems of organizational 'dissonance' occur when vertical control and information systems are being implemented in organizations that are attempting renewal and hence require employees who can exercise discretion and initiative.

Ouchi (1979, p. 175) argues that more consonant with such 'organizational renewal' would be the use of output controls because, as we have already shown, they focus upon the 'after effects' of task performance rather than try to preprogramme the transformation process itself. Hence, output control can ensure control while leaving the everyday accomplishment of tasks to the judgement and discretion of employees. However, output controls rely upon the ability to measure the consequences of employee task performance accurately and fairly. So where organizational activities involve the undertaking of variable or non-routine tasks and take place in environments that are complex and rapidly changing, they become characterized by high degrees of uncertainty and unpredictability. When outputs become difficult to measure and standards that are appropriate and equitable difficult to devise, there is the danger that the objectives being operationalized and imposed become rapidly out of date or have been inappropriate from the outset. This problem is described by Mabey and Salaman (1995) when they observe the identification of outputs that may be measured and rewarded:

> [It] may be possible in an organization which enjoys a relatively stable internal and external environment, but where greater turbulence is experienced it is possible that objectives and hence performance dimensions targeted today may be inapplicable tomorrow (p. 194).

As Ouchi (1979, 1980, 1981) has observed, when controllers have neither the expert knowledge about how tasks should be performed nor the ability to measure performance in terms of outputs in a valid and reliable manner, a viable alternative means by which formal control might be established is through members' commitment to the collectivity on the basis of shared beliefs and values – clan, normative or cultural control. Hence, if one accepts the idea that we now live in an increasingly destabilized world, an explanation of a shift toward cultural control (if this has indeed happened) becomes evident. We can illustrate this issue by further drawing upon the work of Perrow (1967) and Ouchi (1979). From their work, it is possible to identify two sets of contextual factors related to task outputs and transformation processes, whose interaction influence forms of control that are viable in different circumstances. This interaction is represented by the matrix illustrated in Figure 4.3.

- In quadrant 1, tasks are routine, analysable and predictable, and outputs are stable and measurable; therefore, both output and bureaucratic controls are viable.
- In quadrant 2, tasks are exceptional, unanalysable and unpredictable, but outputs are stable and measurable; therefore, because tasks are not preprogrammable, output controls are viable, but bureaucratic controls are not.
- In quadrant 3, tasks are routine, analysable and predictable, but outputs are unstable and unmeasurable; therefore, bureaucratic controls are viable but output controls are not.
- In quadrant, 4 we find the most problematic situation because the ability to select and measure outputs is low and tasks are exceptional. Therefore, both output and rule-based controls are unsuitable. It is under these conditions where cultural controls may the only viable source of control because they offer the opportunity for fostering control on the basis of shared values and goals and the development of strong feelings of solidarity – opportunities that do not depend upon selecting measurable outputs or detailed knowledge of the employee's tasks.

Nature of task transformation processes

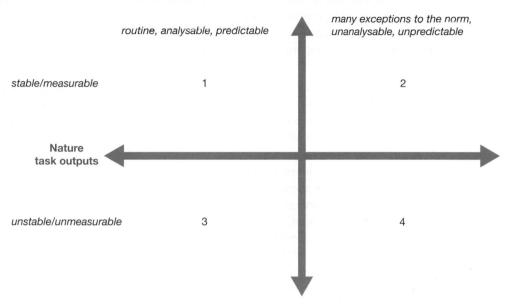

Figure 4.3: Factors impacting on the viability of different forms of control.

- Importantly, because of this lack of dependency upon task and output knowledge, control invested in shared cultural attributes is potentially viable in any of the quadrants illustrated in Figure 4.3. As Kunda (1992, p. 220) observes, such normative controls often can, and do, build upon and complement, rather than replace, alternative forms of control.

**Stop and think**

Using the matrix in Figure 4.3, identify examples of occupations with which you are familiar that fit into each of the four cells. What are the control implications for each example according to the model – but what happens in practice?

Hence, as we noted earlier, one possible explanation of the rise of new-wave management and its fixation with cultural control lies in how other forms of control are increasingly unviable because of changes in the nature of the tasks that many employees do because of destabilization. This apparently new reality of disorder, uncertainty and increasing complexity signifies a break with a more certain and stable past and has spawned new social and institutional forms that, for Clegg, 'require management' (1990, p. 15). Hence, the main casualties here are bureaucratic organizations because they are deemed incapable of coping with this new world order. As Osbourne and Gaebler (1992) put it in their highly influential book:

In this environment, bureaucratic institutions – public and private – increasingly fail us. Today's environment demands institutions that are extremely flexible and adaptable. It demands institutions that deliver high-quality goods and services squeezing ever more bang out of every buck. It demands institutions that are responsive to their customers, offering choices of non-standardized services; that lead by persuasion and incentives rather than commands; that give their employees a sense of meaning and control, even ownership. (p. 15).

So, pivotal to new-wave management is the notion that the strategic challenges that now confront organizations demand postbureaucratic organizations that are characterized as being knowledge based (e.g., Grant, 1996) or knowledge intensive (e.g., Blackler, 1995) but close to the customer (e.g., Peters and Waterman, 1982), in which formal levels of hierarchy are reduced through delayering (e.g., Shaw and Schneider, 1993) and decentralization (e.g., Hastings, 1993) and have been networked so as to create more permeable boundaries with their environments (e.g., Jarillo, 1993). These organizations require functionally flexible high-performance workforces (Applebaum et al., 2000), that are empowered so as to be capable of exercising discretion in a responsible fashion and be able to cope with discontinuous change (Volberda, 1998; Wood, 1999), developments that have supposedly undermined the traditional management tenets of a bygone, more stable and predictable era when bureaucracies once thrived, and may well be a direct threat to some managers.

## The chapter so far

In the previous section, we have reviewed one possible theoretical explanation of why output and bureaucratic forms of control may no longer be appropriate for many organizations. This idea that we now live in a period of heightened uncertainty might explain why cultural control has become such a significant area of concern and discourse for both managers and organization theorists. However, there is an alternative theoretical explanation to which we now turn.

## An alternative theoretical explanation: movements in managerial discourse?

It appears to be a condition of modernity for every generation to believe it is in the midst of revolutionary change

(Jaques, 1996, pp. 18–19).

In the previous sections, cultural control has been presented largely as a potential replacement of, or at least a reinforcement of, output and bureaucratic forms of control in organizations. This may be seen as a *contingent necessity* (i.e., a demand that has to be accommodated) if we accept that increasing levels of turbulence and uncertainty mean that many organizational settings are becoming too complex and ambiguous to be managed through the use of output and bureaucratic control. However, Ouchi (1980) also argues that although the costs of developing what he called 'clan' (i.e., cultural) control may be high, these costs are more than recovered by the savings that accrue from:

1. A reduction in the need for performance monitoring, measurement and evaluation once the appropriate values have been internalized.
2. Perceived differences of interest should be minimized by the establishment of a common culture.

Hence, there is a clear tendency in much new-wave literature to present cultural control as unproblematically superior because it is taken to generate, through emotional and sentimental manipulation, internalized self-discipline expressed as feelings of commitment to 'the organization' – employee behavioural outcomes that alternative forms of control, with their focus upon compliance to external sources of reward and punishment, cannot systematically deliver. So, in relation to their alternatives, cultural controls are often presented as generally, rather than contingently, more effective and efficient because they can reduce bureaucratic impedimenta, flatten hierarchies, cut administrative costs, increase productivity and crucially, increase the agility and responsiveness of organizations to an increasingly destabilized business environment (e.g., Kanter, 1989; Peters, 1989).

Here there is a danger of overly rationalizing management decision making and the choices that are made with regard to different strategies of control – that senior managers, by deploying economically rational calculation, seek to consciously seek out and implement efficiency-optimizing solutions to secure unambiguous organizational goals in the discharge of their fiduciary responsibilities to shareholders (in the case of the private sector). Such assumptions about management behaviour are dubious because they treat managers as if they are all-knowing, yet servile, agents of capital's interests – a characterization that has been widely questioned and exposed by both theoretical and empirical research (Buchanan and Badham, 1999; Cappelli et al., 1997; Grint, 1995; Jackall, 1988; Watson, 1994). A result of this characterization is that descriptions of changes in control and prescription about these processes get entangled. Another result is an analysis that explains the evolution of normative control to be a necessary, progressive, response to demands arising from the need for efficiency and competitive advantage in changing organizational circumstances propelled by the destabilizing disturbances noted above.

In contrast, Barley and Kunda (1992) eschew such determinism by pointing to how the propagation of managerial 'ideologies of control' come in repeated historical 'surges'.

## Stop and think

Barley and Kunda (1992) claim that normative (i.e., cultural or clan; as we have said, the terms are interchangeable) control is nothing new because it has happened before. If this is the case, does this mean that the prior explanation, put forward by some organization theorists, of organizational change in terms of progressive, efficiency-seeking shifts in control in response to changing organizational circumstances, is not sustainable?

In assessing this question, also think about what is implied by the quote from Jaques (1996) above.

In defining what they mean by ideology, Barley and Kunda (1992) point out how all theorists have to make assumptions, often unwittingly, about the nature of the phenomena with which they deal (see also Chapter 1). In management theory, the resultant discourses refer to corporations, employees and managers and the 'means by which the latter can direct the other two' (p. 364). With reference to North America, Barley and Kunda use historical information to document how, since the 1870s, management discourse has oscillated five times between what they call normative control and rational rhetoric of control (see the Ideas and perspectives box below).

Barley and Kunda (1992) proceed to argue that the different ideologies of control themselves express culturally based assumptions that have conceptually constrained the imagination of the managerial community to what amounts to a dichotomy.

## Ideas and perspectives

## Barley and Kunda (1992)

**Rational control:** is defined as bureaucratizing work processes and a utilitarian appeal to what was construed as the employee's economically rational self-interest. Rational modes of theorizing surged from 1900 to 1923 with scientific management and again with systems rationalization from 1955 to 1980.

Key assumptions are:

1. **Organizations:** Perceived as machines, either mechanical or computational, that can be analysed, assembled and reassembled in terms of a set of component parts.
2. **Managers:** Expert systems designers who marshal a body of empirical knowledge to analyse an organization's problems.
3. **Employees:** Rational actors who comply with the control demands of the system on the basis of their calculation of economic interest and benefit.
4. **Control:** Exercised by manipulating systems.

**Normative control** is defined as the idea that managers could regulate employee behaviour by attending to their thoughts and emotions. Normative modes of theorizing surged from 1870 to 1900 with industrial betterment, again from 1925 to 1955 with human relations and again from 1980 to the (then) present day with organization culture and quality.

Key assumptions are:

1. **Organizations:** Collectivities that are, or should be, the location of shared values and moral involvement.
2. **Managers:** Leaders who set an example to inspire and motivate employees.
3. **Employees:** Social beings who would perform their work diligently when they were committed to a collectivity whose ideals they valued.
4. **Control:** Exercised by shaping employees' emotions and values.

During each surge to prominence, the particular ideology being propagated is considered to be at the cutting edge of managerial thought, *if not necessarily* at the level of management practice.

However, they demonstrate how economic cycles have determined when new surges in management theorizing happen. Although each surge in management theorizing was championed by specific groups 'whose interests were thereby advanced' (p. 393), they conclude that in practice, rationalist thinking is usually dominant, but normative factors receive more attention at certain points in time. Generally, they hypothesize that:

> . . . one might argue that rational rhetoric should surge when profitability seems most tightly linked to the management of capital. Conversely, normative rhetoric should surge when profitability seems to depend more on the management of labour (p. 389).

They suggest that managers will be 'attracted to rhetorics that emphasize rational procedures and structures when profits hinge easily on capital investment and automation' (p. 391) but will shift to normative rhetorics, emphasizing the motivation of labour, when returns on capital seem to be in decline during economic downswings.

However, they emphasize that:

1. They do not claim that rational and normative ideologies alternately become dominant according to economic cycles; rather, the rational has always tended to be theoretically prevalent and more closely linked to actual managerial practice.

2. Rationalism will sometimes fuel an interest in and be tempered by normative theorizing because it may be seen to provide a means of reducing employees' negative reactions to scientific management or fordism and other attempts at bureaucratizing labour processes illustrated in earlier chapters.

## The chapter so far

As we have shown in the previous section, although Barley and Kunda raise the issue of ideological change, as they acknowledge, a question that remains unanswered is how these ideological shifts impact upon managerial practices. Does practice vary with ideology – that is, do they covary? If they do not, does this mean that the surges in different ideologies are merely different rhetorical window dressings? In Chapter 6, we will explore these questions by analysing the development of postbureaucratic organizational forms and how they articulate aspects of new-wave management theory. In the rest of this chapter, we will explore the theoretical origins and philosophical assumptions of new-wave management so as to examine the ideological dimension of these questions in more detail.

## The theoretical origins of new-wave theory

As we have illustrated, an effect of new-wave theory has been to cultivate a fixation with culture and charismatic leadership as the determinants of entrepreneurial success, efficiency and competitive advantage. Often these developments are portrayed as liberating, as trusting and empowering employees by creating organizational changes that free them from the authoritarian excesses of direct managerial control (e.g., Dean and Evans, 1994; Peters, 1992; Pfeffer, 1995; Simons, 1995). However, if we look at the theoretical origins of the new wave, a very different ideological picture emerges.

As Barley and Kunda (1992), indicate corporate 'culturism' is not anything new because it can at least be traced to Mayo's Durkheimian interpretation of the Hawthorne Studies and the subsequent popularization of human relations (see also O'Connor, 1999; Ray, 1986; Silver, 1987; and Chapter 2 of this book). Indeed, despite their reticence about their own theoretical underpinnings, Peters and Waterman (1982, p. 5) admit to 'tapping' into Mayo's ideas and clearly their view that 'man [sic] is strikingly irrational' (p. 86) lends force to this admission. So, here it is important to begin with how Mayo (1919, 1933, 1949) drew attention to the role of emotions and sentiments in the regulation of workers' behaviour by arguing that human cooperation at work had always relied upon the evolution of a 'nonlogical social code'. But as Durkheim (1933/1893) had observed about what he classified as the traditional mechanism of social order (i.e., mechanical solidarity – see the Ideas and perspectives box opposite), this social code, based upon shared values and the order it bestowed upon employees had disintegrated under the pressures generated by social and technological change. In particular, Mayo (1919) thought that the spread of political liberalism, with its stress upon individualism and democracy, had created 'a condition of perilous instability' (p. 41). As Barley and Kunda (1992) put it, the perceived problem became expressed as 'the practical issue of how to prevent anomie construed as a lack of commitment while reaping the benefits of the very rationalization that exacerbated anomie' (p. 389).

Here we can trace the new wave via Mayo and Durkheim back to Hobbes' (1962/1651) antidemocratic philosophy (see also O'Connor, 1999). Hobbes pessimistically assumed that people in their 'natural state' are inherently lazy,

| Biography | **Elton Mayo (1880–1949)** |
|---|---|

George Elton Mayo was born in 1880 in Adelaide, Australia. Before fully embarking upon a university career as an academic, Mayo worked as a journalist, a lecturer at a Working Men's College in London and a manager of a publishing business in Adelaide. He was appointed as a lecturer in philosophy and education at the University of Queensland in 1912 where he worked until 1923. He then moved to the United States to eventually take up a post at the University of Pennsylvania before becoming professor of industrial research at Harvard Business School until 1947. He is probably best known for his involvement in the Hawthorne Studies and his subsequent book, *The Human Problems of an Industrialized Civilization* (1940). In this and other work, Mayo put forward the idea that employees' work performance is partly dependent upon social issues, especially with regard to how work satisfaction lay in recognition and a sense of belonging rather than merely upon monetary rewards. A key implication of this stance was that a lack of attention to human relationships was a significant gap in most existing management theories and that managers need to develop a means of harnessing the informal organization so that it worked in concert with, rather than against, their intentions. These ideas were closely associated with the human relations school of organization and management theory. Mayo formally retired in 1942 to a life in England, where he spent the subsequent years giving talks, writing books and getting involved with the fledgling National Institute for Industrial Psychology. He died in 1949 in Surrey.

## Durkheim, *anomie* and neo-conservativism

At the end of the nineteenth century, the leading French sociologist Emile Durkheim (1933/1893) argued that one effect of the devastating economic, social and technological changes that he saw to be accompanying rapid industrialization and urbanization was the development of an increasingly complex, specialized and differentiated hierarchical division of labour. This had effectively destroyed the traditional social order, which he called 'mechanical solidarity': the subordination of the individual to uniform systems of shared values, beliefs and sentiments located in the common experience of an undifferentiated rural population. Durkheim argued that a new social order, which he called organic solidarity, based on contractual relationships engendered by the interdependence demanded by an increasingly differentiated division of labour, had failed to develop properly. For Durkheim, these developments had sown the seeds of moral anarchy and conflict, especially in the economic sphere, because the old moral order based upon a uniformity of beliefs in society and its institutions disintegrated without any alternative form of control to replace it. The resultant disequilibrium was characterized by what Durkheim called 'anomie', 'a breakdown in the cultural structure' (Merton, 1957, p. 162). As Anthony (1994, pp. 75–76) helpfully elaborates, *anomie* is a Greek term meaning 'a condition of lawlessness in which the law is defined in the broadest sense as the canons and norms of the society in which the individual lives. *Anomie* is a condition of moral lawlessness . . . the cause of social disorder . . . the condition in which the person is outside moral and therefore cultural control'. Although Durkheim thought that the normless situation he observed was transient, he also believed that new norms of behaviour, expressed as a collective morality and social cohesion, would have to be constructed in order to eradicate *anomie* and the serious damage it inflicted upon society.

Durkheim's analysis is not just an interesting historical curiosity; it also has been a significant, if largely unacknowledged, influence upon both recent political developments and upon management practice.

For instance, it is interesting to note how in the United States, neo-conservatives tacitly deploy *anomie* in their analysis of changes in society and their remedies. In the recent BBC documentary series *The Power of Nightmares* (2004), neo-conservativism was associated with the political philosophy of Leo Strauss. Strauss thought that the prosperous liberal American society he observed during the 1950s and 1960s contained the seeds of its own destruction – selfish individualism and moral relativism meant that individuals pursued their own interests and undermined the shared values that held society together. For Strauss, the social disintegration that liberalism had unleashed could only be halted by restoring a shared moral framework, with meaning and purpose to people's lives. This could be done by recreating the 'necessary illusion' that the United States was a unique nation whose destiny was to battle against 'evil' in the world. Strauss was highly influential upon a group of disenchanted students who rose to power in subsequent Republican administrations and who became dubbed neo-conservatives. In this documentary, their neo-conservative ideology is portrayed as making the claim that American society is under assault by the forces of liberalism, which are disrupting society and destroying its traditional bonds located in the family, the church and so on, so that a moral lawlessness is endemic. Based upon such an analysis, part of the neo-conservative solution to this perceived 'pathological problem' was an attempt to create a sense of social solidarity that would drive out such immorality by inventing an external threat – an enemy in whose face American society could morally unite. In this fight against the evils that were trying to destroy the United States, the first threat identified by neo-conservatives during the 1980s was the USSR, which, according to this documentary, posed no direct military threat (as the then Reagan government was repeatedly told by the CIA) and whose economy was in a state of near collapse. By the 1990s, the USSR had indeed collapsed from within;

*(Continued)*

## Ideas and perspectives    (Continued)

therefore, the neo-conservatives had to seek out a new threat so as to pursue their antiliberal agenda and drive out what they construed as moral lawlessness.

During the late 1990s, the Democratic president, Clinton, became the victim of a concerted campaign of vilification that presented him and liberalism as an internal threat. However, after the turn of the century, a new external threat was eventually provided for the subsequent neo-conservative Bush administration by former allies within radical Islamic fundamentalism, who, ironically, had been supplied with arms and financial support by the United States during the Reagan presidency in their fight against the USSR in Afghanistan. Also included in this new threat were relatively secular 'rogue' states, such as Iraq, who were accused of possessing weapons of mass destruction and of aiding terrorism: accusations that have since been disproven since the American-led invasion of 2003.

### Stop and think

It is a remarkable coincidence that anomic analyses of the problems organizations face and their solution through culture management also arose (or re-emerged) during the same period when neo-conservativism came to the fore as a political force in the United States. Why might this be the case? What is the relationship between new-wave management and neo-conservativism?

aggressive, egotistical, hedonistic and greedy. Driven by these natural appetites and impulses, life before the development of society's controls was 'solitary, poor, nasty, brutish and short' as people attempted to acquire dominion over others. Because of these inherent propensities, if it were not for the (unnatural) controls provided by society and its institutions, Hobbes' 'commonwealth' or 'state' and the power of the sovereign, life would be inevitably 'a war of all against all'. According to Lukes (1978), this Hobbesian outlook informs Durkheim's concept of *anomie* – an observation from which we can infer that through *anomie*, Hobbes also tacitly informs new-wave management. For Hobbes, 'man [sic] is a bundle of desires, which need to be regulated, tamed, repressed, manipulated and given direction for the sake of social order . . . coercion, external authority, and restraint are necessary and desirable for social order and individual happiness. . . . (Lukes, 1978, p. 145). In other words, the 'problems' that arise in society and its institutions are judged to be caused by what amounts to a situation of under control in which the pathological impulses, at the heart of 'human nature', have been allowed freedom of expression. As Lukes notes, 'Anomic man is, for Durkheim, the unregulated man who needs rules to live by, limits to his desires, "circumscribed tasks" to perform and "limited horizons" for his [sic] thoughts' (p. 141). These philosophical assumptions drive Mayo's subsequent Durkheimian analysis of work organizations and the remedies he puts forward, which in turn are articulated by new-wave management.

Mayo thought that the anomic pressures that he claimed plagued and threatened society, by letting loose primitive human instincts, also engendered the development of employee behaviours that were inimical to the expert exercise of authority by sovereign managers. However, he argued that it was possible for management (who somehow were, and are, exempted from these pressures) to reintegrate the irrational employee 'who had no understanding of his [sic] real needs' (1940, p. 183). By encouraging conformity to the appropriate norms, as defined by managers, managers could engineer employee consent. In sum, the argument runs something as follows:

- Employees are primarily irrational beings who are also motivated by a sentimental desire for social acceptance by their work group peers.

- Informal work group norms arise out of social interaction; however, there is no guarantee that these norms will be consistent with management objectives – indeed, given human nature, they are unlikely to be so.

- Managers can influence these social processes without changing the material conditions of the employee's work.

- Through *their* leadership skills, managers can develop organizations as places of shared values, thereby shaping employee attitudes and perceptions to managers' own ends so as to ensure that the direction of *their* organizations was determined by *them*.

So, in essence, Mayo equated organizational effectiveness with the establishment of socially cohesive collectivities that exhibited what amounted to Durkheim's mechanical solidarity. This is reflected in the 'integration' (Meyerson and Martin, 1987) perspective articulated by new-wave management, which regards culture as a mechanism of control that, when suitably managed, becomes a vehicle for efficiency, effectiveness and competitive advantage. This can be compared with Myerson and Martin's other two perspectives, which can also inform how we understand the cultural dimension to organizations (see the following Ideas and perspectives box).

## Ideas and perspectives

## Meyerson and Martin's alternative views of culture

### Differentiation perspective

People who adopt this perspective assume that organizations are characterized by a multiplicity of cultures that in themselves are consensual, consistent, coherent, stable wholes. From this view, although any cultural form entails some social control over members because of the subjectivity it endows in members through processes of socialization, this 'is not a form of social control created and manipulated by management, but a process in which management, workers and the community at large participate alike' (Meek, 1988, p. 462). Hence, because of the spontaneity involved here, the ability of management to control through homogenization is severely curtailed because resistance from alternative cultural sources is inevitable.

### Fragmentation perspective

People adopting this perspective assume that organizational cultures are multiplicitous, inconsistent, ambiguous and constantly changing. Thus, organizational members will have membership of different cultures in different organizational settings; hence, one's identity becomes fragmented. According to this perspective:

... consensus, dissensus and confusion coexist making it difficult to draw cultural and subcultural boundaries. An ambiguity paradigmic view of culture then, would have no universally shared integrating set of values, save one: an awareness of ambiguity itself (Martin and Meyerson, 1988, p. 117).

The integration perspective is further illustrated in recent new-wave discourse in which 'strong', internally consistent, organizational cultures are deemed to be essential for successful corporate performance by persistently impressing upon the employee an ethos of excellence, customer care, quality and so on (see Harris, 1996; Kotter and Heskett, 1992; Peters and Waterman, 1982; Porras and Collins, 1994). As Ray notes (1986, p. 295), people are assumed to be 'emotional, symbol-loving and needing to belong to a superior entity or collectivity'.

However, there is also an emphasis upon economic performance in a period of increasing destabilization; therefore, for example, what counts is the development of 'only cultures that can help organizations anticipate and adapt to environmental change . . . [These] will be associated with superior performance over long periods of time' (Kotter and Heskett, 1992, p. 44). Here Kotter and Heskett claim that their empirical evidence suggests that unadaptive corporate cultures are characterized by managers who are risk averse, parochial and behave so 'politically and bureaucratically' (p. 51) that they are incapable of changing 'their strategies quickly to adjust to or take advantage of changes in their business environment' (p. 51). In contrast, they claim that in adaptive corporate cultures, managers deeply care about all constituencies (customers, stockholders and employees) but are especially customer focused and are prepared to take risks and initiate changes (p. 51). In other words, the development of strong cultures is not a universal panacea; it is only specific forms of strong culture that provide competitive advantage. Kotter and Heskett's findings have implications for the concerns voiced by some theorists that strong cultures may produce conformist behaviour that is intolerant of any deviance and therefore prevent creative adaptation and change (see Coopey and Hartley, 1991, pp. 26–28).

As in the new-wave literature, not any old form of social cohesiveness (i.e., strong culture) would do for Mayo (1919) – and certainly not ones based upon trade union membership and the like, which might present a competing claim upon employees' values and sentiments. Rather, management must control these processes and, in particular, avoid transplanting the 'collective mediocrity' (p. 57) created by notions such as workplace democracy by ensuring that 'in all matters . . . the widest knowledge and the highest skill should be sovereign' (p. 59). A key management skill was the manipulation of employees' non-logical sentiments so as to replace the destroyed traditional bonds of community and thereby sublimate what Mayo called 'man's fundamental rottenness' (p. 16). Therefore, Mayo (1949) advocated that management should develop communication and interpersonal skills such as leadership and counselling as therapies to redeem anomic workers from their collective psychosis and nurture the 'desire and capacity to work better with management' (pp. 74–75). As Alvesson and Willmott (1996) note, irrational employee sentiment is thus transposed from being a disruptive problem that needed to be eradicated to being an '*untapped resource* for securing improved levels of commitment and productivity' (p. 111; emphasis in original).

Mayo's heritage is illustrated and extended by the new-wave view. If the appropriate values and attitudes are internalized by the maladjusted worker through management's remedial interventions, a common sense of purpose and moral involvement, activated through emotion and sentiment, develops that makes the constant surveillance of employees, as a form of control, redundant. In this idiom, the now ubiquitous term 'culture' substitutes Mayo's 'non logical social code' in various attempts at rationalizing the 'irrational,' thereby ensuring that employee subjectivities become a resource available for the pursuit of corporate imperatives. As Anthony (1994) observes:

> The current concern with cultural management could be interpreted as the last great gamble. . . . in which the free market solves its problems of relationships with people by seeking to enclose them completely within its own material ethos (p. 76).

This statement is vividly portrayed in Du Gay's work (1996), in which he shows how through new-wave management, employees have recently become inscribed by an ethos of enterprise that blurs the distinction between the identities of consumers and employees so that both are now constituted as autonomous, responsible, calculating individuals seeking to maximize their worth through acts of choice in a market-based world. Hence, employees' perceptions of themselves are being realigned so that they are responsive to the demands of global competition. Within this ethos:

> an active, 'enterprizing' consumer is placed at the moral centre of the market based universe. What counts as 'good', or 'virtuous', in this universe is judged by reference to the apparent needs, desires and projected preferences of the 'sovereign consumer'. Thus, an enterprise culture is a culture of the customer, where markets subordinate producers to the preferences of individual consumers. Success and failure in this market based universe are supposedly determined by the relative ability of competing producers to satisfy the preferences of the enterprizing consumer (Du Gay, 1996, p. 77).

So, for new-wave theorists, when bureaucracy fails, its replacement by cultural forms of management control is necessary so as to avoid a situation of undercontrol and the Hobbesian 'war of all against all' that would then be let loose. In effect, as with Hobbes, a radical individualism paves the way for what amounts to authoritarian organizational governance, albeit often articulated in a humanistic guise. For instance, during the past two decades, we have been repeatedly told that charismatic leaders are now needed who will inspire and enthuse subordinates with 'visions of business' (Champy, 1995, p. 17) so that they 'fall in love' with the company (Harris, 1996) and thereby ensure 'corporate discipline, cooperation and teamwork' (Kanter, 1989, p. 10). These notions tacitly articulate Hobbes' view that absolute rulers can gain power by persuading everyone that it is 'reasonable' to entrust that power to them (1962/1651, p. 227). Thus, hierarchy and management prerogative are effectively reinforced, and in some cases, according to Pattison (1997), sanctified through the senior manager's heroic role as charismatic cultural custodian and saviour who forestalls the socially corrosive effects of *anomie* once held in check by the calculative compliance afforded, to some degree, by the now apparently obsolete bureaucratic regimes whose viability has been destroyed by the destabilizing disturbances noted earlier.

For commentators like Armstrong (2000), particular 'new' forms of organization, such as the learning organization, are therefore 'naught but a Hawthorne light bulb with a dimmer switch, intended to stimulate productivity regardless of its chameleonic brilliance' (p. 359). We turn to these new organizational forms in Chapter 5. We will also return to the influence of new-wave theory upon managerialism in Chapter 9.

## Conclusions

If one thing is clear, it is that there has been a great deal of talk and writing about organizational and corporate culture since its (re)emergence as a focus for management control during the early 1980s. However, this is not a mere historical curiosity. Today, talk of culture management is a routine feature of organizational life and is a concept that is widely discussed and taught on management and organization theory courses as a technocratically viable means of influencing the ways members think, feel, act and perceive themselves and others. The apparent intention here is to pass on this know-how (see, for example, Kotter and Heskett, 1992) and to engineer 'strong' cultures that fit the organizations' requirements, as defined by senior management, through creating internal alignment to ensure business success and organizational efficiency – high performance is the holy grail – or is it a forlorn hope? As Willmott (2003) has recently commented:

> While the expectations about the effectiveness of corporate culturism have no doubt been lowered and qualified, the basic philosophy of pseudo or managerial humanism continues to be invoked – perhaps for want of an ideologically acceptable alternative for the 'best practice' of managing 'human resources' (p. 80).

In this chapter, we have located these debates within the issue of control in organizations. In doing so, we have explored the three different types of formal control that may be found in the organizations in which we work: First, the bureaucratic; second, the output based; and third, the normative, clan or cultural. Throughout the chapter, we have emphasized how it is crucial to understand the operation of these controls in their complex social contexts. We have also showed how the development of new-wave management theory has been organized around the promise of cultural control in which the (senior) manager becomes 'an engineer' of the employee's 'soul' (Rose, 1992) so that 'the private selves of members have become part of the "contested terrain"' (Kunda, 1992, p. 221). This mission necessarily entails concerted attempts at culturally penetrating, reconstructing and disciplining the informal level of organizations so that one potential source of 'misbehaviour' and opposition becomes realigned behind senior management's espoused aims.

Of course, in practice, how effective cultural control is at securing employee commitment remains open to question for two reasons. First, cultural control cannot foreclose alternative sources of cultural influence upon employees that may be sources of resistance to that control. Second, how could one ever know whether overt displays of behaviour, which conform to the cultural expectations that have been cascaded down by management, are a product of employees' internalization of those norms or are an outcome of some other conforming subjective stance, such as calculative compliance?

Here we have also considered two rival explanations of what has been called the 'cultural turn' in organizations (Thompson and Findlay, 1999) – one that focuses upon management's quests for efficiency-optimizing solutions to the problem of control in conditions of destabilization; the other in terms of ideological and rhetorical change. The question that neither explanation answers is the extent to which, in practice, there has indeed been a shift in control away from bureaucratic and output-based controls to the normative. Indeed, rather than replacing alternative forms of control, perhaps what we have witnessed in recent years is often best seen as attempts at adding a further dimension of formal control that complements and extends the bureaucratic and output-based forms (see Delbridge, 1998) to embrace what was once an exclusively informal aspect: a possibility that has significant implications for how we understand the appearance of 'new' organizational forms – to which we now turn.

## Concluding grid

| Learning outcomes | Challenges to contemporary organizations |
|---|---|
| Differentiate formal control from informal control. | How can we formally capture and redirect the informal organization or sometimes how can we eliminate the informal organization so that it is no longer a source of resistance to hierarchical control?<br>How resilient is the informal organization to contemporary assaults upon its integrity? |
| Identify the different types of formal control that are deployed in organizations and how they operate so as to influence employee behaviour. | Are bureaucratic and output-based forms of control still appropriate in contemporary organizations, especially if we now confront a time of unpredictable change that confronts all organizations? |
| Locate new wave management theory in the development of what has been called cultural, clan or normative control. | How can the cultural norms and mores of employees be socially engineered so they are supportive of senior management's aims for the organization, and how could anyone ever know if such a programme of change had actually been successful? |
| Review different theoretical explanations as to why a shift in control toward the cultural, in many organizations, may have happened. | Which explanation is the most viable?<br>1. The failure of bureaucratic organizations to enable adaptation to a new period of instability and change.<br>2. Ideological shifts in management rhetoric that have little actual impact upon how organizations are managed except in the ways they explain to themselves and significant others what they are attempting to do. |
| Investigate the philosophical origins and underlying assumptions of new-wave management. | Is there anything new about 'new'-wave management because it can be historically traced back to Mayo's adaptation of Durkheim, whose analysis in terms of *anomie* is simultaneously shared by North American neo-conservatives? |

## Annotated further reading

For a superb analysis of subversion, resistance and the informal organization that uses an array of classical social science sources to examine issues such as recalcitrance, sabotage, labour turnover, pilferage, humour and sexuality in the workplace, the reader should turn to Ackroyd and Thompson (1999). A useful and wide-ranging general introduction to studying organizational culture can be found in Martin (2002). For a more managerialist stance on these issues, which has the virtue of some theoretical sophistication, see Kotter and Heskett's work (1992). Meanwhile, Kunda's (1992) ethnographic study of a 'high-tech' corporation still provides one of the most interesting and theoretically informative accounts of the role of cultural control in the workplace. This should be read in conjunction with Anthony's (1994) critical and accessible analysis of the practical difficulties of culture management and the considerable dangers that lurk therein. For a devastating critique of the culture management literature and its theoretical stance, Willmott's (1993) article is superb. He has revisited this work in a recent article (2003), which should be read after the 1993 paper. For a comprehensive review of the literature on organizational culture, we strongly recommend Alvesson's (2002) exploration of several alternative perspectives, which includes an emancipatory view that derives from critical theory the focus of Chapter 8 in this book.

## Discussion questions

1. What are the implications of the informal organization for how managers should manage?
2. Why have cultural or normative forms of control become so significant in contemporary organizations?
3. Discuss the following statement: 'Culture management will always fail because of the informal organization.'
4. How does culture management express North American neo-conservative ideology?
5. Discuss the following statement: 'There is nothing new about new-wave management.'

## References

Ackroyd, S. and Thompson, P. (1999) *Organization Misbehaviour*, London: Sage.

Adler, P.S. (1993) 'Time and motion regained', *Harvard Business Review* Jan/Feb:97–107.

Alvesson, M. (1995) *Management of Knowledge-Intensive Companies*, Berlin/New York: de Gruyter.

Alvesson, M. (2002) *Understanding Organization Culture*, London: Sage.

Alvesson, M. and Willmott, H.C. (1996) *Making Sense of Management: A Critical Introduction*, London: Sage.

Anthony, P. (1994) *Managing Culture*, Buckingham: Open University Press.

Applebaum, E., Bailey, T., Berg, P. and Kalleberg, A.L. (2000) *Manufacturing Advantage: Why High-Performance Work Systems Pay Off*, Ithaca, NY: ILR Press.

Armstrong, H. (2000) 'The Learning Organization: Changed Means to an Unchanged End', *Organization* 7(2):355–361

Ashworth, A.E. (1968) 'The sociology of trench warfare 1914–18', *The British Journal of Sociology* XIX(4):407–423.

Badham, R. and Matthews, J. (1989) 'The New production systems debate', *Labour and Industry* 2(2):194–246.

Barker, J.R. (1993) 'Tightening the iron cage: Concertive control in self-managing teams', *Administrative Science Quarterly* 38:408–437.

Barley, S.R. and Kunda, G. (1992) 'Design and devotion: Surges of rational and normative ideologies of control in managerial discourse', *Administrative Science Quarterly* 37:363–399.

Beck, U. (1992) *Risk Society*, London: Sage.

Berg, P.O. (1989) 'Postmodern Management? From Facts to Fiction in Theory and Practice', *Scandinavian Journal of Management* 5(3):201–17.

Blackler, F. (1995) 'Knowledge, knowledge work and organizations: An overview and interpretation', *Organization Studies* 16(6):1021–1046.

Blau, P.M. (1955) *The Dynamics of Bureaucracy*, Chicago: Chicago University Press.

Bluestone, B. and Harrison, H. (1988) *The Great U-Turn*, New York: Basic Books.

Braverman, H. (1974) *Labour and Monoploy Capital: The Degradation of Work in the Twentieth Century*, New York: Monthly Review Press.

Brown, A. (1995) *Organizational Culture*, London: Pitman.

Buchanan, D. (2000) 'An eager and enduring embrace: The ongoing rediscovery of teamworking as a management idea', in S. Proctor and F. Mueller (eds), *Teamworking*, London: Prentice-Hall International.

Buchanan, D. and Badham, R. (1999) *Power, Politics and Organizational Change: Winning the Turf Game*, London: Sage.

Burawoy, M. (1979) *Manufacturing Consent: Changes in the Labour Process under Monopoly Capitalism*, Chicago: Chicago University Press.

Burawoy, M. (1985) *The Politics of Production*, London: Verso.

Burr, V. (1995) *Introduction to Social Constructionism*, London: Routledge.

Cappelli, P., Bassi, L., Kahtz, H., Knoke, D. and Osterman, M. (1997) *Change at Work*, Oxford: Oxford University Press.

Casey, C. (1995) *Work, Self and Society*, London: Routledge.

Castells, M. (1996) *The Rise of the Network Society*, Malden, MA: Blackwell.

Champy, J. (1995) *Reengineering Management*, London: Harper Collins.

Clarke, J. and Newman, J. (1997) *The Managerial State*, London: Sage.

Clawson, D. (1980) *Bureaucracy and the Labour Process: The Transformation of US Industry, 1860–1920*, New York: Monthly Review Press.

Clegg, S.R. (1990) *Modern Organizations: Organizations in the Postmodern World*, London: Sage.

Cooley, M. (1980) *Architect or Bee*, Slough: Langley Technical Services.

Coopey, J. and Hartley, J. (1991) 'Reconsidering the case for organizational commitment', *Human Resource Management Journal* 1(3):18–32.

Covaleski, M.A., Dirsmith, M.W., Heian, J.B. and Samuel, S. (1998) 'The calculated and the avowed: techniques of discipline and struggles over identity in Big Six public accounting firms', *Administrative Science Quarterly* 43(2):293–327.

Cummings, T.G. and Huse, E.F. (1989) *OD and Change*, St. Paul: West.

Daudi, P. (1990) 'Conversing in management's public place', *Scandinavian Journal of Management* 6(3):285–307.

Davis, S. and Meyer, C. (1998) *BLUR: The Speed of Change in the Connected Economy*, Reading, MA: Addison-Wesley.

Deal, T. and Kennedy, A. (1982) *Corporate Cultures: The Rites and Rituals of Corporate Life*, Reading, MA: Addison-Wesley.

Deal, T. and Kennedy, A. (1983) 'Culture: A new look through old lenses', *Journal of Applied Behavioural Science* 19(4):497–507.

Dean, J.W. and Evans, J.R. (1994) *Total Quality: Management, Organization and Strategy*, St. Paul: West.

Delbridge, R. (1998) *Life on the Line in Contemporary Manufacturing*, Oxford: Oxford University Press.

Dent, M. (1995) 'The new national health service: A case of postmodernism?' *Organization Studies* 16(5):875–899.

Dobson, P. (1989) 'Changing culture', *Employment Gazette* 647–650.

Drucker, P.F. (1993) *Post-Capitalist Society*, New York: Harper and Row.

Du Gay, P. (1996) *Consumption and Identity at Work*, London: Sage.

Du Gay, P. (2000) *In Praise of Bureaucracy*, London: Sage.

Durkheim, E. (1933/1893) *The Division of Labour in Society*, New York: The Free Press.

Edwards, R. (1979) *Contested Terrain: The Transformation of the Workplace in the Twentieth Century*, New York: Basic Books.

England, G.W. (1983) 'Japanese and American management: Theory Z and beyond', *Journal of International Business Studies* 14(3):131–142.

Etzioni, A. (1965) 'Organizational control structure', in J.G. March (ed.), *Handbook of Organizations*, Chicago: Rand McNally.

Ezzamel, M., Willmott, H. and Worthington, F. (2001) 'Power, control and resistance in "the factory that time forgot,"' *Journal of Management Studies* 38(8):1053–1079.

Fortado, B. (1994) 'Informal supervisory social control strategies', *Journal of Management Studies* 31(2):251–274.

Fox, S. (1990) 'Strategic HRM: Postmodern conditioning for the corporate culture', *Management Education and Development* 21(3):192–206.

Friedman, A.L. (1977) *Industry and Labour*, London: Macmillan.

Gartman, D. (1979) 'Origins of the assembly line and capitalist control of work at Ford', in A. Zimbalist (ed.), *Case Studies on the Labor Process*, New York: Monthly Review Press.

Gouldner, A.W. (1954) *Patterns of Industrial Bureaucracy*, New York: Free Press.

Gouldner, A.W. (1965) *Wildcat Strike*, New York: Harper.

Grant, R.M. (1996) 'Toward a knowledge-based theory of the firm', *Strategic Management Journal* 17(Winter):109–122.

Grint, K. (1995) *Management: A Sociological Introduction*, London: Taylor Francis.

Grugulis, I., Dundon, T. and Wilkinson, A. (2000) 'Culture control and the "culture manager": Employment practices in a consultancy', *Work Employment and Society* 14(1):97–116.

Guest, D.E. (1987) 'Human resource management and industrial relations', *Journal of Management Studies* 25(4):503–521.

Guest, D.E. (1991) 'Personnel management: The end of orthodoxy'. *British Journal of Industrial Relations* 29(2):194–175.

Guest, D.E. (1998) 'Beyond HRM: Commitment and the contract culture', in P. Sparrow and M. Marchington (eds), *Human Resource Management: The New Agenda*, London: Pitman Publishing.

Hales, C. (1993) *Managing Through Organization*, London: Routledge.

Hammer, M. and Champy, J. (1993) *Re-engineering the Corporation*, London: Nicholas Brearley.

Handy, C.B. (1989) *The Age of Unreason*, London: Business Books.

Harris, J. (1996) *Getting Employees to Fall in Love with Your Company*, New York: Amacon.

Harvey, D. (1989) *The Condition of Postmodernity: An Enquiry into the Origin of Social Change*, Oxford: Basil Blackwell.

Hastings, C. (1993) *The New Organization*, London: McGraw-Hill.

Heckscher, C. (1994) 'Defining the post-bureaucratic type', in C. Hechsher and A. Donnellon (eds), *The Post-Bureaucratic Organization: New Perspectives on Organizational Change*, London: Sage.

Heckscher, C. and Donnellon, A. (eds) (1994) *The Post-Bureaucratic Organization*, London: Sage.

Hertog, F. den, and Wielinga, C. (1992) 'Control systems in dissonance: The computer as ink blot', *Accounting, Organizations and Society* 17(2):103–127.

Heydebrand, W. (1989) 'New organizational forms', *Work Employment and Society* 16(3):323–357.

Hobbes, T. (1962/1651) *Leviathan*, Cambridge: Cambridge University Press.

Hope, V. and Hendry, J. (1995) 'Corporate culture – Is it relevant for organizations of the 1990s?', *Human Resource Management Journal* 5(4):61–73.

Jackall, R. (1988) *Moral Mazes: The World of Corporate Managers*, Oxford: Oxford University Press.

Jackson, P.R. and Wall, T.D. (1991) 'How does operator control enhance performance of advanced manufacturing technology?', *Ergonomics* 34(10):1310–1311.

Jaques, R. (1996) *Manufacturing Consent*, London: Sage.

Jarillo, J.C. (1993) *Strategic Networks: Creating the Borderless Organization*, Oxford: Butterworth-Heinemann.

Jermier, J.M., Knights, D. and Nord, W.R. (eds), (1994) *Resistance and Power in Organizations*, London: Routledge.

Johnson, P. and Gill, J. (1993) *Management Control and Organizational Behaviour*, London: Paul Chapman/Sage.

Johnson, P., Cassell, C., Close, P. and Duberley, J. (2001) 'Performance evaluation and control: Supporting organizational change', *Management Decision* 39(10):841–850.

Kanter, R.M. (1989) *When Giants Learn to Dance: Mastering the Challenges of Strategy, Management and Careers in the 1990s*, London: Unwin Hyman.

Kaplan, R.S. and Norton, D.P. (1992) 'The balanced score card: Measures that drive performance', *Harvard Business Review* 69(1):71–79.

Kaplan, R.S. and Norton, D.P. (1996) 'Using the balanced score card as a strategic management system', *Harvard Business Review* 73(1):75–85.

Kelly, J. (1985) 'Management's redesign of work: labour process, labour markets and product markets', in D. Knights, H. Willmott and D. Collinson (eds), *Job Redesign*, Gower: Aldershot.

Kelman, H. (1961) 'The process of opinion change', *Public Opinion* 25:57–78.

Knights, D. and McCabe, D. (1998) 'Dreams and designs on strategy: A critical analysis of TQM and management control', *Work, Employment and Society* 12(3):433–456.

Kotter, J. and Heskett, J. (1992) *Corporate Culture and Performance*, New York: The Free Press.

Kunda, G. (1992) *Engineering Culture: Control and Commitment in a High Tech Corporation*, Philadelphia: Temple University Press.

Lash, S. and Urry, J. (1987) *The End of Organized Capitalism*, Cambridge: Polity Press.

Lawler, E.E. and Rhode, J.R. (1976) *Information and Control in Organizations*, London: Goodyear.

Legge, K. (1995) *Human Resource Management: Rhetorics and Reality*, Basingstoke: Macmillan.

Linstead, S. (1999) 'Managing culture', in L. Fulop and S. Linstead (eds), *Management: A Critical Text*, Basingstoke: Macmillan Press.

Linstead, S. and Grafton-Small, R. (1992) 'On reading organization culture', *Organization Studies* 13(3):331–355.

Littler, C. (1982) *The Development of the Labour Process in Capitalist Societies*, London: Heinemann.

Lukes, S. (1978) 'Alienation and anomie', in P. Laslett and W.G. Runciman (eds), *Philosophy Politics and Society*, Oxford: Blackwell.

Mabey, C. and Salaman, G. (1995) *Strategic Human Resource Management*, Oxford: Blackwell.

Martin, J. (1995) 'Organizational culture', in N. Nicholson (ed.) *Blackwell Encyclopedic Dictionary of Organization Behaviour*, Oxford: Blackwell.

Martin, J. (2002) *Organizational Culture*, London: Sage.

Martin, J. and Meyerson, D. (1988) 'Organizational cultures and the denial, channeling and acknowledgement of ambiguity', in L. Pondy, R.J. Boland and H. Thomas (eds), *Managing Ambiguity and Change*, New York: Wiley.

Mayo, E. (1949) *The Social Problems of an Industrial Civilization*, London: Routledge and Kegan Paul.

Mayo, E. (1933) *The Human Problems of an Industrialized Civilization*, Boston: Harvard Business Press.

Mayo, E. (1919) *Democracy and Freedom: An Essay in Social Logic*, Melbourne: Macmillan.

McKinley, A. and Taylor, P. (1998) 'Through the looking glass: Foucault and the politics of production', in A. McKinley and K. Starkey (eds) *Foucault, Management and Organization Theory*, London: Sage.

Meek, V.L. (1988) 'Organizational culture: Origins and weaknesses', *Organization Studies* 9(4):453–473.

Merton, R. (1940) 'Bureaucratic structure and personality', *Social Forces* May:560–568.

Merton, R. (1957) 'Social Theory and Social Structure', New York: Free Press.

Meyerson, D. and Martin, J. (1987) 'Cultural change: An integration of three different views', *Journal of Management Studies* 24(6):623–647.

Mitchell, T. (1985) 'In search of excellence versus the hundred best companies to work for in America: A question of values and perspective', *Academy of Management Review* 10(2):–355.

Mohrman, S.A., Ledford, G.E. and Mohrman, A.M. (1990) 'Conclusion: What we have learned about large-scale organizational change', in Mohrman, S.A. et al. (eds), *Large-Scale Organizational Change*, San Francisco: Jossey-Bass.

Morgan, G. (1988) *Riding The Waves of Change: Developing Managerial Competencies for a Turbulent World*, San Francisco: Jossey-Bass.

Mueller, F. (1994) 'Teams between hierarchy and commitment: Change strategies and the "internal environment"', *Journal of Management Studies* 31(3):383–403.

O'Connor, E.S. (1999) 'Minding the Workers: The Meaning of "Human" and "Human Relations" in Elton Mayo', *Organization* 6(2):223–246.

Offe, C. (1976) *Industry and Inequality*, London: Edward Arnold.

Ogbonna, E. (1992) 'Organization culture and human resource management: Dilemmas and contradictions', in P. Blyton and P. Turnbull (eds), *Reassessing Human Resource Management*, London: Sage.

Osbourne, D. and Gaebler, T. (1992) *Re-inventing Government*, Reading, MA: Addison-Wesley.

Otley, D.T. and Berry, A.J. (1980) 'Control, organization and accounting', *Accounting, Organizations and Society* 5(2):231–244.

Ouchi, W.G. (1979) 'A conceptual framework for the design of management control systems', *Management Science* 25:833–848.

Ouchi, W.G. (1980) 'Markets, bureaucracies and clans', *Administrative Science Quarterly* March:129–141.

Ouchi, W.G. (1981) *Theory Z: How American Business Can Meet the Japanese Challenge*, Reading, MA: Addison-Wesley.

Ouchi, W.G. and Jaeger, A.M. (1978) 'Type Z organizations: Stability in the midst of mobility', *Academy of Management Review* 3(April):305–314.

Pascale, R. and Athos, A.G. (1982) *The Art of Japanese Management*, Penguin: Harmondsworth.

Pattison, S. (1997) *The Faith of Managers*, London: Cassell.

Perrone, V. (1997) 'The coevolution of contexs and structures: The N-form', in T. Clark (ed.), *Organization Behaviour: Essays in the Honour of Derek S. Pugh*, Ashgate: Aldershot. Hants.

Perrow, C.A. (1967) 'A framework for the comparative analysis of organizations'. *American Sociological Review* 32:194–208.

Peters, T. (1989) *Thriving on Chaos*, London: Pan.

Peters, T. (1992) *Liberation Management*, London: Macmillan.

Peters, T. and Waterman, R.H. (1982) *In Search of Excellence*, London: Harper and Row.

Pfeffer, G. (1995) *Competitive Advantage Through People*, Boston: Harvard Business School Press.

Pfeffer, G. (1997) *New Directions for Organization Theory*, Oxford University Press: Oxford.

Piore, M.J. (1986) 'Perspectives on labour market flexibility', *Industrial Relations* 25(2):146–166.

Porras, J. and Collins, J. (1994) *Built to Last*, New York: Harper Business.

Ray, C.A. (1986) 'Corporate culture: The last frontier of control', *Journal of Management Studies* 23(3):287–297.

Robertson, R. (1992) *Globalization*, London: Sage.

Roethlisberger, F.J. (1968) *Man-In-Organization*, Cambridge, MA: Belknap Press/Harvard University Press.

Rose, N. (1992) *Governing the Soul: The Shaping of the Private Self*, London: Routledge.

Rosenthal, P., Hill, S. and Peccei, R. (1997) 'Checking out service: Evaluating excellence, HRM, and TQM in retailing', *Work, Employment and Society* 11(3):481–503.

Schein, E.H. (1992) *Organization Culture and Leadership*, 2nd edn, San Francisco: Jossey-Bass.

Sewell, G. (1998) 'The discipline of teams: The control of team based industrial work through electronic and peer surveillance', *Administrative Science Quarterly* 43:406–469.

Sewell, G. (2001) 'What goes around, comes around: inventing a mythology of teamwork and empowerment', *Journal of Applied Behavioural Science* 37(1):70–89.

Sewell, G. and Wilkinson, B. (1992) 'Empowerment or emasculation: Shopfloor surveillance in a Total Quality Organization' in P. Blyton and P. Turnbull (eds), *Reassessing Human Resource Management*, London: Sage.

Shaw, D.G. and Schneider, C.E. (1993) 'Making Organization Change Happen: The Keys to Successful Delayering', *Human Resource Planning* 6(1):1–18.

Silver, J. (1987) 'The ideology of excellence: Management and neo-conservatism', *Studies in Political Economy* 24(Autumn):105–129.

Silverman, D. (1970) *The Theory of Organizations*, London: Heinemann.

Simons, R. (1995) 'Control in the age of empowerment', *Harvard Business Review* 73(1/2):80–88.

Smircich, L. (1983) 'Concepts of culture and organizational analysis', *Administrative Science Quarterly* 28:339–358.

Smith, C. (1989) 'Flexible specialization, automation and mass production', *Work, Employment and Society* 3(2):203–220.

Sturdy, A., Knights, D. and Willmott, H. (eds) (1992) *Skill and Consent*, London: Routledge.

Tannenbaum, A.S. (1962) 'Control in organizations', *Administrative Science Quarterly* 7:236–257.

Thompson, P. (1993) 'Postmodernism: Fatal distraction?' in J. Hassard and M. Parker (eds), *Postmodernism and Organizations*, London: Sage.

Thompson, P. and Findlay, T. (1999) 'Changing the people; social engineering in the contemporary workplace', in A. Sayer and L. Ray (eds), *Culture and Economy After the Cultural Turn*, London: Sage.

Townley, B. (1989) 'Selection and appraisal: Reconstituting "social relations"', in J. Storey (ed.) *New Perspectives on Human Resource Management*, London: Routledge.

Townley, B. (1994) *Reframing Human Resource Management: Power, Ethics and the Subject at Work*, London: Sage.

Tuckman, A. (1994) 'The yellow brick road: Total quality management and the restructuring of organizational culture', *Organization Studies* 15(5):727–751.

Vogel, E.F. (1979) *Japan as Number One*, New York: Harper and Row.

Volberda, H. (1998) *Building the Flexible Firm: How to Remain Competitive*, Oxford: Oxford University Press.

Warhurst, C. and Thompson, P. (1998) 'Hearts, hands and minds: Changing work and workers at the end of the century', in P. Thompson and C. Warhurst (eds), *Workplaces of the Future*, London: Macmillan.

Watson, T. (1994) *In Search of Management*, London: Routledge.

Weber, M. (1947) *The Theory of Social and Economic Organization* (first published 1924), Glencoe, IL: Free Press.

Wickens, P.D. (1992) 'Lean production and beyond: The system, its critics and the future', *Human Resource Management Journal* 3(4):75–89.

Wilkinson, A. and Willmott, H. (eds) (1995) *Making Quality Critical*, London: Routledge.

Wilkinson, A., Marchinton, M. and Goodman, J. (1992) 'TQM and Employee Involvement', *Human Resource Management Journal* 2(4):1–20.

Willmott, H. C. (1993) 'Strength is ignorance; Slavery is freedom: Managing culture in modern organizations', *Journal of Management Studies* 30(4):515–552.

Willmott, H.C. (2003) 'Renewing strength: Corporate culture revisited', *Management*, 6(3):73–87. Available at: http//www.dmsp.dauphine.fr/Management.

Womack, J., Jones, D. and Roos, D. (1990) *The Machine that Changed the World*, New York: Macmillan.

Wood, S. (1989) 'New wave management?' *Work Employment and Society* 3(3):379–402.

Wood, S. (1999) 'Human resource management and performance', *International Journal of Management Reviews* 1:367–413.

Young, E. (1989) 'On naming the rose: Interests and multiple meanings as elements of organizational culture', *Organization Studies* 10:187–206.

## Suggested reading

Atkinson, J. (1984) 'Manpower strategies for flexible organizations', *Personnel Management* 16(8):28–31.

Badarocco, J.L. (1991) *The Knowledge Link: How Firms Compete Through Strategic Alliances*, Boston: Harvard University Press.

Blau, P.M. (1964) *Exchange and Power in Social Life*, New York: John Wiley.

Bolton, M., Malmrose, R. and Ouchi, W. (1994) 'The organization of innovation in the US and Japan: neo-classical and relational contracting', *Journal of Management Studies* 21(5):653–679.

Bush, J.B. and Frohman, A.L. (1991) 'Communication in a network organization', *Organization Dynamics* 20(2):23–36.

Carlisle, J.A. and Parker, R.C. (1989) *Beyond Negotiation*, Chichester: Wiley.

Child, J. (1987) 'Organizational design for advanced manufacturing technology', in T. Wall et al. (eds), *The Human Side of Advanced Manufacturing Technology*, Chichester: Wiley.

Coriat, B. (1980) 'The restructuring of the assembly line: A new economy of time and control', *Capital and Class* 11(1):34–43.

Culbert, S.A. and McDonough, J.J. (1986) 'The politics of trust and organizational empowerment', *Public Administration Quarterly* 10(2):171–188.

Grabner, G. (ed.) (1991) *The Embedded Firm – On the Socio-Economics of Industrial Networks*, London: Routledge.

Gray, B. (1985) 'Conditions facilitating interorganizational collaboration', *Human Relations* 38(10):911–936.

Hamel, G. (1991) 'Learning in international alliances', *Strategic Management Journal* 12:83–103.

Hancock, P.G. (1997) 'Citizenship or vassalage? Organization membership in the age of unreason', *Organization* 4(1):93–111.

Hopwood, A. (1974) *Accounting and Human Behaviour*, London: Prentice-Hall.

Jorde, T.M. and Teece, D.J. (1989) 'Competition and cooperation: Striking the right balance', *California Management Review* 31(3):25–37.

Kanter, R.M. (1994) 'Collaborative advantage: The art of alliances', *Harvard Business Review* 72(4):96–108.

Lawless, M.W. and Moore, R.A. (1989) 'Interorganizational systems in public service delivery: A new application of the dynamic network framework', *Human Relations* 42(12): 1167–1184.

Lorenz, E. (1991) 'Neither friends nor strangers: Informal networks of subcontracting in French industry', in G. Lorenz, J. Frances, R. Levacic and J. Mitchell (eds), *Markets, Hierarchies and Networks: The Co-ordination of Social Life*, London: Sage.

Lynch, R.P. (1993) *Business Alliances Guide*, Chichester: Wiley.

MacNeil, I.R. (1985) 'Relational contract: What we do and not know', *Wisconsin Law Review* 483–525.

MacNeil, I.R. (1978) 'Adjustment of long-term economic relations under classical', neo-classical and relational contract law', *Northwestern University Law Review* 854–905.

Miles, R.E. (1989) 'Adapting technology and competition: A new industrial relations for the 21st century', *California Management Review* 31(2):9–28.

Miles, R.E. and Snow, C.C. (1984) 'Fit, failure and the hall of fame', *California Management Review* 26(1):10–28.

Miles, R.E. and Snow, C.C. (1986) 'Organizations: New concepts for new forms', *California Management Review* 28(3):62–73.

Miles, R.E. and Snow, C.C. (1992) 'Causes of failure in network organizations', *California Management Review* 34(2):53–72.

Powell, W.W. (1990) 'Neither market nor hierarchy: Network forms of organization', *Research in Organizational Behaviour* 12:295–336.

PricewaterhouseCoopers. (1999) *Global Top Decision Makers' Study on Process Outsourcing,* New York: PricewaterhouseCoopers, Yankelovitch Partners, Goldstain Consulting.

Ritzer, G. (1993) *The McDonaldization of Society*, London: Pine Forge.

Rousseau, D.M. and Parks, J.M. (1993) 'The contracts of individuals and organizations', *Research in Organization Behaviour* 15:1–43.

Snow, C.C., Miles, R.E. and Coleman, H.J. (1992) 'Managing 21st century network organizations', *Organizational Dynamics* 21(4):5–20.

Stiles, J. (1994) 'Strategic alliances: Making them work', *Long Range Planning* 27(4):133–137.

Stinchcombe, A. (1986) 'Contracts as hierarchical arrangements', in A. Stinchcombe and C.A. Heimer (eds), *Organization Theory and Project Management*, Oslo: Norwegian University Press.

Sydow. J. (1992) 'On the management of strategic networks', in H. Ernst and V. Meier (eds), *Regional Developments and Contemporary Industrial Response*, London: Pinter.

Teubner, G. (1991) 'The many headed hydra: Networks as higher order collective actors', in S. McCahery, S. Picciotto and C. Scott (eds), *Corporate Control and Accountability: Changing Structures and Dynamics*, Oxford: Oxford University Press.

Turpin, D. (1993) 'Strategic alliances with Japanese firms: Myths and realities', *Long Range Planning* 26(4):11–16.

Whittaker, A. (1992) 'The transformation of work', in M. Reed and M. Hughes (eds), *Rethinking Organization*, London: Sage.

Wickens, P.D. (1987) *The Road to Nissan*, Basingstoke: MacMillan.

Williamson, O. (1985) *The Economic Institutions of Capitalism*, New York: The Free Press.

Wood, S. (1986) 'The cooperative labour strategy in the U.S. auto industry', *Economic and Industrial Democracy* 7(4):415–448.

# Chapter 5

# Postmodernist organization theory: new organizational forms for a new millennium?

## Introduction

There has been a proliferation of the use of the *post-* prefix in recent times. Sociology and organization theory texts have, for example, discussed post-industrialism, post-fordism, post-capitalism, post-humanism, post-Marxism, post-feminism, the post-market society, the post-economic society, the postcollectivist society, the postbourgeois society and so on. In the next two chapters, we will explore the meaning of postmodernism and consider the different ways it is defined. This chapter will address the notion of postmodernism as a period in time that comes 'after modernism' and has particular features. This chapter will explore the implications of those features for organization theory.

## Learning outcomes

- Outline the nature of the postmodern condition.

- Discuss the relationship between postmodernism, post-industrialism and post-fordism.

- Examine the implications of the postmodern epoch for organizational design and theorizing.

- Discuss the concept of the 'flexible firm' and the implications of this for the experience of people at work.

## Structure of the chapter

- The chapter begins with an introduction to the concept of postmodernism and highlights the debate surrounding the relationship between economic and cultural change and the history of the term. Although some writers differentiate *postmodernism* from *post*-industrialism, in this chapter, we have taken *postmodernism* to be an overarching term that incorporates post-industrialism, the information society and post-fordism.

Our next section outlines post industrialism and the information society, examining the changes in society and organizations suggested by each. We then move on to address post-fordism. Three schools of thought concerning post-fordism are introduced and evaluated. Finally, the chapter looks at the work of Stewart Clegg and Paul Heydebrand, who outline the features of postmodern organizational forms in detail.

## What is postmodernism?

There are two core strands to postmodernism that differ dramatically. One sees post-modernism or postmodernity as a period of time that comes after the modernist period in history. The other takes a more philosophical perspective and considers post-modernism to be a new way of viewing the world, a new philosophy. We will deal with the first of these perspectives in this chapter and the second in the next chapter. They are dealt with separately because they are fundamentally different. The first focusses on changes that have happened or are happening in the world and looks at the implications for individuals, organizations and societies. The second perspective, as we will discuss in the next chapter, focuses more on the way we understand the world about us.

Postmodernity or postmodernism as it is used here thus refers to a new historical era. It has been described in a variety of ways. Some authors address cultural changes, par-ticularly focusing on changes in architecture, art and music. Postmodern architecture has received particular attention. Here the modernist notion of form fitting function, central to modernism as discussed in Chapter 2, has been eschewed in favour of dis-unity and contradiction. Thus, in *Learning from Las Vegas*, Venturi et al. (1972) praise the postmodern architecture of Las Vegas for its use of popular material and its indif-ference to unity (see Figure 5.1 below). A postmodern style is also apparent in the Sainsbury Wing of the National Gallery in London, which uses a pastiche of styles such that it is 'an architecture of richness and ambiguity rather than clarity and purity' (Ghirardo, 1996, quoted in Butler, 2002, p. 90).

**Figure 5.1:** Postmodern pastiche architecture in Las Vegas.
(*Source:* © Pete Saloutos/CORBIS.)

Similarly, in art and music, the division between high and low art is broken down. An example, according to Butler, is the symphonies *Low* and *Heroes* by Philip Glass, which draw on the work of David Bowie and Brian Eno, thus bringing together classical and popular music. We will develop these ideas further in the next chapter. For now, suffice it to say that postmodernity is characterized by a movement away from the grand designs of the past. Some see it as a move toward a disposable, consumerist society: 'Tesco ergo sum' – 'I shop; therefore, I am.' This is neatly illustrated by the quote from Tyler Burden, the main character in the film *Fight Club* (2000):

> We're consumers. We're byproducts of a lifestyle obsession. Murder, crime, poverty – these things don't concern me. What concerns me is celebrity magazines, television with 500 channels, some guy's name on my underwear, Rogaine, Viagra, Olestra.

The example below develops this idea, giving a tongue-in-cheek forecast of the future from the *Times* newspaper, which suggests that branding and consumerism will reign supreme in the not-too-distant future.

In contrast to the cultural sphere, others examine economic transformations and changes in the way that production is organized – this is often called late capitalism, post-fordism or flexible specialization. As we shall see, these descriptions have some clear commonalities, notably a preoccupation with new technology, consumerism

## Ideas and perspectives

## Society of the future?

It is the year 2015. Mr and Mrs Texaco – having cooked on their Aganaught, a meal to a Jules Oliver recipe, of chicken killed at the press of a button in their cook space that morning – saunter down to the pub where they drink beer from intelligent glasses that tell them when they've had enough. . . . Today at Nokia school Mr and Mrs Texaco's children spent a uniform free right brain day learning, art, drama and creative studies. . . . walking down the high street past the vodapod and the Starbucks shaped like a coffee mug, the Texacos find the faith centre a sanctuary, as it is the only place in town free from commercial branding or sponsorship. Like most of their neighbours Mr and Mrs Texaco are paid to change their name to advertise a product. The Texacos, like the majority of the country, are in the creative industry. Mr Texaco has several jobs, some of which used to be hobbies. He has turned his skill as a former graffiti artist into designing T-shirts, and creates at least four slogans a week. . . . Mrs Texaco who is deputy editor of *Trend Week* has her work space kitted out as the café bar of a hamlet in the Carpathians. . . . On the streets the yob is a creature of the past. New style ASBOs (artistically sterile behaviour orders) channel useless aggression into creative work, like doing customized carpaints for anyone from an eco-warrior to a rapper.

*Source:* Adapted from an article by Alan Hamilton, *The Times*, 1 October 2005, p. 28.

## Stop and think

- To what extent do labels or brands affect you and your behaviour?
- To what extent would having a fashionable brand make working for a company more desirable?

Ideas and perspectives

## Organization as carnival

In short, today's organizational images stink. Not just those that derive from the military (kick ass and take names) and pyramids (heavy, steep, immobile), but even the new 'network', 'spiderweb', 'calder mobile'. These modern notions are a mighty step forward, but they still miss the core idea of tomorrow's surviving corporation: Dynamism.

How about company as carnival?. . . say carnival and you think energy, surprise, buzz, fun. The mark of the carnival – and what makes it most different from a day at most offices – is its creative dynamism. Dynamism is its signature, the reason we go back. To create and maintain a carnival is never to get an inch away from dynamic imagery. As chief, you must feel the dynamics in your fingertips. . . .

The practical point for the firms' leaders: constantly using dynamic imagery, thinking of yourself as running a carnival and stomping out all forms of static thinking and imagery will help you toward the right stricture and strategy for these woozy times.

To wit: if you don't feel crazy, you're not in touch with the times.

*Source:* Peters (1992), pp. 15–18.

and organizational flexibility. Thus, in writings on postmodernity, we see many critiques of modernist forms of organization typified by bureaucracy. Often these treat bureaucracy as a terminally ill organizational form incapable of responding to the needs of the dynamic environment of the late twentieth century (Hecksher, 1994). In its place is the notion of a radically different form of organization, with a variety of new names: the postbureaucratic organization (Hecksher and Donnellon, 1994), the postentrepreneurial organization (Kanter, 1989), the postmodern organization (Clegg, 1990), the virtual organization (Nohria and Berkley, 1994), the self-designing organization (Weick and Berlinger, 1989), the federal organization (Handy, 1989), the intelligent enterprise (Quinn, 1992) and the organization as carnival (Peters, 1992) – see below. All the authors propose their model as developmentally more advanced forms of organization. Yet, as we will discuss in the following sections, the extent to which these forms exist in practice is open to debate. Before we move on to look at this, though, we must first examine whether postmodernism constitutes anything new and track the historical development of the term in order to understand the various ways it has been applied.

## Is postmodernism anything new?

One of the problems that exists when trying to examine postmodernity as a period in time is that there is much debate as to whether the postmodern period represents something new – a break with or change from modernism – or whether it is actually just an extension of modernism. Some sociologists, such as Zygmunt Baumann, argue that it is 'fully fledged, viable social system which has come to replace the "classical" modern capitalist society and thus needs to be theorized in its own terms' (Baumann, 1988). Others argue that the distinction is not so clear and that the postmodern form is emerging but at the moment is still a rather vague conceptualization.

Key writers in this area, such as American anthropologist David Harvey (1989) and Marxist professor of literature Frederic Jameson (1992), suggest that rather than seeing postmodernism as a break or rupture with modernism, we should maintain awareness of the basic continuity between society today and that which preceded it. Jameson characterizes postmodernism as the 'cultural logic of late capitalism'. In other words, it represents the changes in culture that correspond to the economic move into late capitalism. Following the analysis of Marxists such as Mandel, he lists the features of late capitalism as:

- the transnational business enterprise
- the new international division of labour
- new relationships in international banking and stock exchanges
- new forms of media interrelationship
- computers and automation
- the flight of production to advanced underdeveloped areas of the world.

Along with these factors come social consequences such as 'the emergence of yuppies' and 'gentrification on a now global scale' (cited in Kumar, 1995, p. 115).

Similarly writers such as Scott Lash, a professor of cultural studies, stress that postmodern society is linked with changes in production – thus, *postmodernism* is the term we use to describe the culture that complements a shift to post-industrial modes of production. Postmodernism, according to Lash, can be seen as a process of dedifferentiation, or bringing together (Lash and Bagguley, 1987). Thus, the social and cultural realms become more interwoven, with, for example, status being conferred increasingly by the display of cultural symbols; and culture and commerce also interpenetrating each other, which can be seen in the central role of advertising in contemporary culture and the ways sporting and artistic events have become big business (see the example below).

## Example: McDonald's goes for gold with Olympic sponsorships

Houston Rockets All-Star Yao Ming is a global spokesman for McDonald's, the Official Restaurant of the 2004 Olympic Games

ATHENS – Flashbulbs popped and adoring fans applauded as Venus Williams took the microphone during a promotional appearance in Athens on Friday to recount her many childhood dreams that have come true – winning two Olympic medals and four Grand Slam titles, competing alongside sister Serena and, finally, partnering with McDonald's at the Olympic Games. 'As a child', Williams said, 'I always dreamed of becoming a McDonald's athlete'.

For a four-year investment estimated at $65 million, McDonald's has been designated the Official Restaurant of the 2004 Olympic Games. As such, it is the only brand-name restaurant in the Olympic

*(Continued)*

Example: (Continued)

**Figure 5.2:** Business sponsoring sport. (*Source:* © J Gross/Getty Images Sport/Getty Images.)

athletes' village, main sports complex and press center, ensuring that virtually no Olympic athlete, fan or journalist starts the day without passing by a McDonald's.

While McDonald's has used the Olympics to sell its burgers and fries in the United States for decades, the fast-food giant is thinking globally now. And its global marketing strategy is in full swing in Athens, where the 2004 Games serve as a vehicle to extend its reach and portray its menu as part of a healthy lifestyle.

Among its high-profile pitchmen is China's Yao Ming, the No. 1 pick of the 2002 NBA draft and star of China's Olympic basketball team. With an eye toward further expansion into China, McDonald's signed Yao as its first global ambassador earlier this year. That is also why McDonald's chose to announce in Beijing, host of the 2008 Olympics, that it had extended its Olympic sponsorship through 2012. The company plans to increase the number of McDonald's in China by 65 percent, from 600 to 1,000, in time for Opening Ceremonies of the 2008 Games.

*Source:* Reprinted from Clarke, L. *Washington Post* 4 August 2004, p. E01.

Harvey also extensively documents the shifts in cultural and economic spheres to show how the move to postmodernism is correlated with a move to what he terms *flexible accumulation* in the economic sphere. One of the most important aspects of the new capitalist approach is that it greatly increases rates of innovation. Thus, he argues that postmodern developments are a response to 'the more flexible motion of capital (which) emphasizes the new, the fleeting, the ephemeral, the fugitive, and the contingent in modern life, rather than the more solid values implanted under fordism' (Harvey, 1989, p. 74). Thus, there is a sense that in the postmodern world, change is all around, and we are living in a more dynamic environment, where time and space are compressed so that we can travel very long distances in short time periods, which has changed the way global space is understood.

Although these writers refer to postmodernism in cultural terms as a consequence of the current mode of economic production, Kumar (1995) sees the situation more holistically. He criticizes the split between culture and society and suggests that they should be seen together and that we should consider postmodernity as a spirit that permeates culture and society: 'Postmodernism appears an attribute of all aspects of society and it seems unwise, at least initially, to privilege any one part as cause or determinant' (p. 120). This is the approach taken in this chapter, and postmodernism is seen as an overarching theme that incorporates concepts such as post-fordism and the information society.

## The history

Although seen as a recently new phenomenon, the term *postmodern* has been in use for nearly 100 years. Although Welsch (1988) discusses how Rudolf Pannwitz used the term as early as 1917 to describe the collapse of moral values in contemporary European Culture, Arnold Toynbee is commonly cited as the originator of the term in the sense of postmodernity as a new period of time. In 1954, he used the term 'post modern age' to discuss the period in time post-1875, which he saw as characterized by wars, social turmoil and revolution – a 'time of troubles' (Best and Kellner, 1991). In the 1950s, there was an increased level of interest in the notion of a postmodern age with writers such as Rosenberg and White (1957), Mills (1959) and Drucker (1957) highlighting the challenges of the new 'postmodern' world. Some, such as Drucker, saw the postmodern age in positive terms, with new technology and new modes of organizing providing the possibility of the end of poverty, incorporating new opportunities for all. Others, such as Mills, were more critical, considering the possibilities of the postmodern age actually reducing the level of freedom for individuals. A more detailed exposition of the postmodern era comes from Barraclough (1964). He proposes that the new postmodern age is constituted by revolutionary developments in science and technology, a new imperialism, a transition from individualism to mass society, and new forms of culture. Similarly, Etzioni (1968) considered the possible dangers such as loss of community as well as possible benefits from new technologies being developed to solve social problems and enable people to lead better lives.

However it has been defined, postmodernism has always had its proponents and detractors. Detractors, often characterized as cultural conservatives, focus on the crisis of Western civilization with societies in decline, facing change and revolution. The proponents are far more optimistic. They can be divided into social and cultural wings (Best and Kellner, 1991). Whereas the social optimists see the postmodern world as offering a new affluent society, the cultural wing affirms the liberating features of new postmodern cultural forms, enabling the combination of the classical with the popular, high with low art. There is clearly much diversity of opinion concerning what *postmodernism* means, whether it is a good or bad thing and its implications for organizational design. In the next sections, we look in more detail at some of the core concepts used to explain the postmodern epoch.

### The chapter so far

This section has outlined some of the core features of the postmodern epoch, including the historical development of the concept. In the next section, we will address post-industrialism and the information age. Post-industrialism is often subsumed under the heading postmodernity, being seen as an aspect of the postmodern age, with the terms being used interchangeably or, as discussed earlier, it is sometimes seen as the economic and social corollary of postmodern culture.

## Post-industrialism and the information society

From the 1970s, there has been much talk of post-industrialism and the information society. Change has most definitely been in the air, with writers such as Francis Fukyama, the influential American political economist, declaring the 'end of history' and French sociologist Alain Touraine suggesting we face the end of industrial society. But as one period appears to come to an end, concepts have emerged to explain the new contemporary society. Thus, writers such as Alvin Toffler, Daniel Bell and Peter Drucker have made great claims for the time of change that societies in the West have been going through. Perhaps the most famous description of these changes has come in the work of Daniel Bell on post-industrialism. Bell defines a post-industrial society thus:

> A post industrial society is based on services. Hence it is a game between persons. What counts is not raw muscle power, or energy but information. The central person is the professional, for he is equipped, by his education and training, to provide the kinds of skills which are increasingly demanded in the post industrial society. If an industrial society is defined by the quantity of goods as marking a standard of living, the post industrial society is defined by the quality of life as measured by the services and amenities – health, education, recreation and the arts – which are now deemed desirable and possible for everyone (Bell, 1974, p. 127).

Table 5.1 outlines the theory of social development put forward by Bell.

It is difficult to know whether commentators such as Bell are arguing that we now live in a post-industrial society. When the concept was first introduced, it was put forward as an ideal type, against which it would be possible to assess the emergence of particular changes in society. However, subsequent use of the term, both by Bell and others, suggests that the construct has come to be seen as reality (Smart, 1992).

**Table 5.1** Bell's stages of societal development

| Stage of development | Major technological innovation | Principal economic activity | Social systems | Date of origin |
|---|---|---|---|---|
| Pre-agrarian | | Hunting/gathering | Simple tribal nomadic | Origin of mankind (2 to 4 million years ago) |
| Agrarian | Metal working | Farming | Rural settlements | c. 7000 BC |
| Industrial | Steam power | Manufacturing | Industrial cities | c. AD 1800 |
| Post-industrial | Computer | Services | Suburban communities | AD 1965 |

*Source:* Sadler (1988, p. 4.)

Essentially, for Bell, the term *post-industrial society* refers to changes in the sphere of production arising from developments in science and technology. Smart summarizes the five main changes constituting the move to post-industrialism as:

1. A relative shift of emphasis from goods production to service provision in the economic sector and an increase in health, education, research and development and government agencies in particular.

2. A growth in numbers and influence of a professional and technical class.

3. The primacy of theoretical knowledge as a resource for innovation and policy.

4. Control of technology and technological assessment.

5. The creation of a new intellectual technology (Smart, 1992, p. 33).

Bell was particularly concerned with the change in society away from a social structure based upon the production of goods toward one that gave primacy to theoretical knowledge. He saw this change as both derived from and driving the changes listed above. Thus, writers such as Masuda and Naisbitt discuss the coming preeminence of knowledge capital over material capital in the economy (Masuda 1981, 1985; Naisbitt 1984). As Naisbitt (1984) comments: 'We now mass-produce knowledge in the way we used to mass produce cars . . . knowledge is the driving force of the economy' (p. 7). Knowledge work is understood to comprise the creation

Biography       **Daniel Bell (1919–   )**

Daniel Bell attended City College, in 1939. He was Henry Ford II professor emeritus of the social sciences, Harvard University; scholar in residence of the American Academy of Arts and Sciences; past professor of sociology, Columbia University; co-founder of *The Public Interest Magazine*; former member of the editorial board of *Fortune*; and former editor of *The New Leader*.

Bell was among the original *New York intellectuals*, a group of anti-Stalinist left-wing writers. Bell is an influential sociologist and social theorist; author of numerous books, including *The Coming of the Post Industrial Society* (1973), *The End of Ideology* (1960) and *The Cultural Contradictions of Capitalism* (1976). The latter two appeared on the *Times'* Literary Supplement's list of the 100 most important books of the second half of the twentieth century.

of knowledge, the application of knowledge, the transmission of knowledge and the acquisition of knowledge. Employees are likely to engage in knowledge work to the extent that they have the ability, motivation and opportunity to do so. The task of managing knowledge work is focused on establishing these conditions. Organizational characteristics such as transformational leadership, job design, social interaction and organizational culture are identified as potential predictors of ability, motivation and opportunity (Kelloway and Barling, 2000, p. 287). A new type of worker, 'the knowledge worker', emerges as a result of the use of technology to upgrade the knowledge content of existing jobs and the creation of new kinds of jobs in the knowledge sector. The case study below gives an example of the move toward post-industrialism in the Norwegian shipping industry.

| Case study | Post-industrialism in Scandinavian shipping |
| --- | --- |

Although Norway's ocean-going fleet continues to shrink in size, its leading banks and ship finance houses have undergone a steady growth in international activity. Scandinavia's leading banks Nordea and DnB Nor now count themselves among the world's top three arrangers of loans to the shipping industry, with this growth set to continue. There is of course no direct link between the Norwegian duos' growing international shipping commitments and the decline of the Norwegian registered fleet with 3.3m dwt or almost 8% of flagged tonnage lost in the second quarter from a year earlier. However the contrast in fortunes exemplifies that it is in the midst of something akin to its own version of post-industrial decline.

*Source:* Lloyds List International (2005) *Special Report – Ship Finance,* Issue 59011.

Drawing on the work of Bell, Sadler (1988) differentiates three ways of analysing the changes being wrought by the post-industrial age: changes in the social order, changes in the economy and changes in technology. He posits a new social order involving four key changes:

1. Changes in attitudes, values and beliefs, including attitudes to work and authority and the balance between exploitation and the conservation of the earth's resources.
2. Changes in social institutions, most importantly, the family.
3. Changes in social structure, particularly the disappearance of many traditional occupational groupings.
4. Changes in lifestyle.

Similar to other writers, Sadler focuses on the move from manufacturing to services as the most obvious economic aspect of the move to post-industrialism. He argues that knowledge is the central resource of the new economy, claiming three distinctive characteristics for knowledge compared with other resources:

1. It cannot be consumed in the way capital and labour can.
2. It is hard to protect.
3. Its impact on the economy is hard to quantify.

With regard to information technology, he considers the ways new technology will enable the development of new products and new production processes, which will change the shape of organization. Sadler provides a useful analogy when he talks about the development of the new post-industrial society as a fabric being woven with many threads, including globalization, the dominance of the service sector, changes in lifestyles and the development of new technologies. Thus, we can see the overlap of many concepts such as postmodernism, post–industrialism and the information society. He argues that the fabric is still in the process of being woven but, once completed, society will have been radically transformed (Sadler, 1988).

Alvin Toffler is somewhat more dramatic than Bell or Sadler in his analysis of change and the emergence of a post-industrial society although he dislikes the term

## Ideas and perspectives

## The post-industrial social order

According to Sadler (1988), it is not so common nowadays to find the nuclear family household in the sense of a married couple with two children living at home together. He lists some of the variants:

- Two people, not married, living together with no children.

- Two people, married or not married, living together but with children of both current and previous marriages or cohabitations.

- Single parents living with children of a marriage broken by death, divorce or desertion (the parent is usually but not always female).

- Traditional households in which there may be more than two children and, in addition, one or more living-in grandparent.

- Single persons living alone not yet having reached retirement age.

- Single persons of the same gender sharing accommodation (with or without sharing a sexual relationship).

- Single persons (usually students or young workers) of different genders sharing the same accommodation but without sexual involvement with each other.

- Retired persons living alone, either married couples or a widow (more common) or widower (less common).

- Some kind of commune (this is still quite rare).

According to Sadler, although the children of the emerging post-industrial society will tend to come from a bewildering array of backgrounds, they will share some values and expectations: they will tend to put individuals before organizations, and they will not take orders or subject themselves to bureaucratic rules as easily as their parents. They will expect to be consulted about issues and will be discriminating and discerning consumers.

### Stop and think

- Do you think it necessarily follows that we will become more individualistic? Why should this be the case?

- Think about your own family background. To what extent do you think this has impacted on your relationships with organizations?

- How do you think organizations will need to change to deal with children of the post-industrial age?

*post-industrial* because it fails to capture the full extent of the transformations being faced and tends to use terms such as the *information society* instead. Toffler (1971) is an American 'futurist'. He came to fame with the publication of his book *Future Shock*, in which he uses a three-stage model of societal change from agricultural to industrial to super-industrial stages of development. According to Toffler, we are now experiencing the latter, characterized by an accelerating pace of change in every-day life that is producing less permanent relationships, a breakdown in bureaucratic structures and the emergence of new flexible organizational forms. This is producing a new society, one in which we will confront an increasing proliferation of choice in the sphere of economic production and consumption and a fragmentation of cultures and communities. In his later book, *The Third Wave*, Toffler (1984) develops his thesis and argues that we are currently in the grip of the third wave, which is confronting the core attributes of all second-wave societies, which can be attributed to both capitalism and socialism, both of which he sees as in terminal decline. Changes occurring in respect of energy; production and distribution systems; social institutions and relationships; and culture, communications and politics represent the foundations for a possible new civilization (Smart, 1992). Toffler talks about the emergence of the 'prosumer' who produces for self consumption and includes

1. Consumers who are amateurs in a particular field but who are knowledgeable enough to require equipment that has some professional features ('professional' + 'consumer') – for example, the new generation of digital film equipment is designed for the prosumer, the consumer who thinks of himself as a semi-professional.

2. People who help to design or customize the products they purchase ('producer' + 'consumer').

3. People who create goods for their own use and also possibly to sell ('producer' + 'consumer').

Their emergence is seen as an important aspect of the move to third-wave civilization, alongside homeworking in the 'electronic cottage', and an end to the process of market expansion. According to Toffler, the home will be the site of much more economic (and social) activity. Workers will be increasingly linked to organizations with information and communication technology, enabling them to work more flexibly. For those working within organizations and not from home, it has been suggested they will see seven key trends: the organization will be organized around process, not task; a flat hierarchy; team management; performance measured by customer

## Biography    Alvin Toffler (1928–    )

Alvin Toffler is an American author and one of the world's best-known futurists. A former associate editor of *Fortune* magazine, his early work focused on the impact of technology. Toffler invented the term 'future shock' to describe the 'dizzying disorientation brought on by the premature arrival of the future'. He also wrote the books *The Third Wave* (1984), *Powershift: Knowledge, Wealth, and Violence at the Edge of the 21st Century* (1993) and *Creating a New Civilization: The Politics of the Third Wave* (1995). Toffler works in close intellectual partnership with his spouse, Heidi Toffler, who has coauthored many of his works.

satisfaction; rewards based upon team performance; maximization of contacts with suppliers and customers; and the retraining of staff at all levels (Castells, 1996, p. 164).

## The virtual organization

These issues bring us to the concept of the virtual organization. This became popular around 15 years ago. Virtual organizations are electronically networked organizations that transcend conventional organizational boundaries with information technology–enabled linkages both within and between organizations. In its simplest form, however, virtuality exists where information technology is used to enhance organizational activities, which reduces the need for physical or formalized structures. The concept can be challenging for us in terms of our understanding of what an organization is because our image of organizations is often based upon their physical elements. A virtual organization may have no physical location. People may not work together in one site. According to Charles Handy (1994), this poses a serious managerial dilemma: how do you manage people who you do not see? He suggests that trust will be key. There may be unintended human consequences of the move to homeworking and the virtual organization such as a loss of community and a sense of isolation. There will be a need for workers to make sense of work and its relationship to non-work in this new context. An often-cited example of the virtual organization is Verifone, which manufactures and services electronic credit card payment systems. Taylor (1995) argues that four aspects define the Verifone business model:

1. **Global reach:** Verifone has no corporate headquarters, recognizes no national origin and is at home everywhere in the world.
2. **Location independence:** Employees from the CEO down spend a lot of time travelling. One third of Verifone's 2,500 staff is away from the office at least half the time.
3. **Electronic knowledge network:** All corporate information is available online worldwide for immediate access. The company's top 250 people, for example, track sales down to the last week, day and hour using Revwatch.
4. **Time compression:** Verifone calls it the *culture of urgency*. The CEO claims that Verifone has achieved a 24-hour workday. Software projects, for example, routinely follow the sun. Programmers working in Bangalore, Paris, Dallas or Honolulu ship code back and forth to keep the development process moving while they are sleeping.

Thus, it is argued that information technology enables companies such as Verifone to maximize flexibility through the development of virtual linkages within the company. In addition, the erosion of boundaries between firms made possible by information technology has seen the development of new organizational forms, including networking and alliances. These enable organizations to outsource aspects of their production and other functions to other companies if they can do these more efficiently, as we will discuss in the following sections.

More recently, Castells, in his extensive three-volume study *The Information Age* (2000a, 2000b, 2004), examines a wide range of issues such as crime, new social and political movements, personal and collective identities, the status of women and marriage and families, alongside economic and cultural changes. The common theme

## Case study          Vehicle rescue – a virtual organization?

Run into problems on the motorway and if you're a member of the Automobile Association (AA), a vehicle recovery organization, the person taking your anxious call for help may very well be talking to you from their spare bedroom. The AA has over 140 home based call handlers who between them sort out 2.25 million breakdown calls from stricken motorists each year. Having started a pilot project with a group of nine home based employees in late 1997, the AA rapidly expanded its telework programme, in the process closing down its centre in Leeds and the breakdown side of its Newcastle call centre. The AA argues that using homeworkers allows for much greater flexibility in rostering (homeworkers typically work the early morning and late afternoon and evening 'drive-time' shifts with time off in between) helps to retain staff and improves productivity. In order to pay for the technology, the workers have to be 1.5 times as productive as site staff. Their performance is closely monitored. The magic figure is 12.6 calls per hour. This statistic together with other measures such as 'clear-up time' for calls and time taken for breaks, is recorded by the company's automated call distribution system.

Employees are split into seven teams, each with their own team manager. A staff league table is produced monthly. This means individual performance is very much public knowledge – just to make it absolutely clear workers who under-perform see their efforts highlighted in red on the handouts. In between meetings managers can communicate with team members by sending messages via AA's electronic information services system. Each teleworker has also been equipped with a fax machine. There are no email or video-conferencing facilities and team managers do not require teleworkers to check in by phone before starting work.

*Source:* Bibby (2002).

## Stop and think

- What do you see as the advantages and disadvantages of this kind of working?
- What do you think are the implications of using technology to monitor and control people in their own homes?

running through his analysis is the information technology revolution and the associated compression of time and space. Castells' work has been important in highlighting the different directions in which information society theory has moved. Initially, writers focused on the way organizations and those currently in power might use information technology. Castells argues there has been a shift in emphasis from technology to people, consideration of the multiple and diverse uses of the internet. Increased attention has been given to how the oppositional groups in society (such as anti-globalizers) can make use of such tools (Castells, 2004, pp. 145–167). Also, there have been illuminating accounts of some of the more unexpected effects of outsourcing made possible by global telecommunications – for example, the relocation of call centres to India.

Similar to other theoretical approaches discussed in this chapter, the information society has both advocates and critics. The advocates see information technology as offering the opportunity to transform the way we work and liberate individuals from bureaucratic organizations (Ducatel et al., 2000; Toffler, 1984). The critics, on the other hand, see a more sophisticated method of control and exploitation. Some critics of Bell go further. For example, Webster (1995) suggests that Bell's whole thesis of the post-industrial society is misguided because it relies on a false dichotomy between manufacturing and services. Thus, it is suggested that the service sector is helping to sustain the manufacturing sector through producer services such as banking, marketing and distribution. Furthermore, Noon and Blyton (2002) argue that there has been an expansion not just in service work but also of service products. For example, instead of using public transport, people drive cars, which also impacts on manufacturing. Noon and Blyton propose that this more complex picture of social and sectoral change suggests a continuity of economic development rather than a dramatic structural shift. This further leads them to question Bell's separation of the structural and the cultural.

Although most would accept that information technology has fundamentally changed the ways we live and work, writers such as Kumar (1995), Nowotny (1982) and Rosenbrock (1985) argue that the post-industrial society does not constitute a change of the magnitude of the industrial revolution. Kumar quotes Hammelink, who argues that:

> The information society is a myth developed to serve the interests of those who initiate and manage the information revolution: the most powerful sectors in society, its central administrative elites, the military establishment and global industrial corporations (Kumar, 1995, p. 31).

## The chapter so far

In this section, we have examined the post-industrial or the information society. We have outlined the core aspects of the change from industrial to post-industrial society, including the emergence of knowledge workers. In the next section, we move on to discuss post-fordism, a sometimes overlapping and similarly contentious term.

## Neo-fordism, flexible specialization and post-fordism

The term *fordism* refers to a particular mode of organizing that is typified by the motor industry in the United States. Its central element is mass production, linked to mass consumption. Large volumes of a standard product are produced, and technology is used in such a way that jobs are deskilled. Allied to this are high wages and the reshaping of working class culture to provide the mass market for goods being produced (Bagguley, 1989). Because the market for mass-produced goods cannot expand indefinitely – there is a limit to the number of standardized cars or white goods that a person might wish to own – an initial solution is what has come to be known as neo-fordism. According to Crook et al. (1992), this involves:

- **Diversification:** Expansion into or merging with companies in adjacent product markets or the cultivation of new product markets. The outcome is even larger scale – conglomerate companies with equally saturated markets.

- **Internationalization:** Extension of economies of scale by expansion beyond the domestic market (however, global markets also have their limits).
- **Intensification:** The intensive application of technology, especially hard automated technology to reduce costs (however, demand for standardized consumer durables tends to be inelastic at low price levels).

Crook et al. (1992) suggest there is widespread agreement across the ideological spectrum that even neo-fordism met the limits of the global market around 1970, bringing about a crisis of saturated demand and reduced levels of employment. This creates a vicious circle as the failure of businesses, because of insufficient demand, creates further unemployment, which in turn depresses demand. Thus, it is argued that a new mode of production was required, and we have moved into a post-Fordist epoch characterized by:

> ... broad job descriptions and labour flexibility allied with the fragmentation of markets ... implying 'multiskilling' on the one hand and participation on the other. In the realm of consumption, greater choice and variety are preferred, gone is the option of one version of one model (Bagguley, 1989, p. 7).

Organizations have increasingly sought to differentiate their products, to add value to them, either through changes in the products themselves or in the ways they are branded and advertised.

Table 5.2 illustrates the main differences between fordism and post-fordism.

It is possible to differentiate three schools that have contributed to the debate on neo- and post-fordism: 1) the regulation school, typified by the work of French economist Michel Aglietta (1987), which is generally classed as neo-Fordist; 2) the institutionalist school, typified by the work of Michael Piore and Charles Sabel (1984) in their seminal work *The Second Industrial Divide*, and 3) the managerialist school exemplified in the work of British sociologist Atkinson (1984). The next section outlines each of these approaches and considers their strengths and weaknesses.

**Table 5.2** Fordism vs. post-fordism

|  | **Fordism** | **Post-fordism** |
| --- | --- | --- |
| Markets | Mass consumption | Fragmented, niche markets |
| Technology | Dedicated | General |
| Production | Assembly line | Batch |
| Workers | Semi-skilled | Multiskilled |
| Management | Taylorist | Human relations |
| Unions | General or industrial | Absent or company union |
| Industrial relations | Centralized | Decentralized |

## The regulation school

The regulation school is typified by the work of Aglietta (1987), who focuses on the development of neo-fordism. For Aglietta, the demise of fordism has arisen as a result of its own success. Assembly lines were as efficient as it was possible to make them, with three factors limiting further productivity gains:

1. Increases in the balance delay time. Individual tasks take different amounts of time to complete, which can create blockages and delays in the process of production. As tasks become increasingly fragmented, more time is spent by workers simply doing nothing.
2. The effects of intensified labour on the physical and mental health of workers, which can lead to absenteeism.
3. Collectivization of work breaks the link between individual effort, output and reward.

Aglietta sees the solution in terms neo-fordism, a mode of organizing that develops and refines fordism, fine tuning it to meet the needs of the current environment rather than negating its fundamental principles. This incorporates the transfer of production to lower cost parts of the world economy and the development of more sophisticated systems of machines that effectively control their own operations. Thus, fordism will be increasingly confined to less developed areas of the world economy – for example, the newly industrializing countries of South East Asia and South America. This has been the subject of some criticism as multinational corporations have sought to move their production, or indeed service provision, to areas with much cheaper labour costs (see the example below).

## Example: Offshoring financial services

**Insurer plans to save £10m in Indian job shift**

Royal & Sun Alliance is shifting more than 1,000 jobs to India in a move designed to save the UK's second-largest general insurer at least £10m a year. The news follows last month's announcement from rival Aviva, which plans to double its 'offshoring' capacity in India to 7,000 by 2007.

RSA, which has large operations in Halifax, Liverpool and Sunderland, said no decision had been taken on where the axe would fall. Duncan Boyle, RSA UK chief executive, said the establishment of an offshore presence was part of an operational review designed to cut costs and standardize procedures. The majority of the jobs would be lost through natural wastage. RSA has undergone a restructuring over the past two years in an attempt to return to profitability, including selling businesses and reducing the amount of premium it takes in. This has reduced its UK headcount from 20,000 to 11,000. Trade unions reacted angrily to the latest round of cuts, calling on Tony Blair to do more to halt the growing outsourcing trend. More than 100,000 jobs in the financial services industry could be lost to Asia by 2007.

*(Continued)*

(Continued)

David Fleming, Amicus national secretary, said: 'This announcement clearly shows that offshoring presents an unprecedented threat to UK jobs and the economy.' RSA's Bangalore facility will be operated by Accenture, the consultants that already manage the insurer's IT systems. A host of other insurers, including Aviva and Prudential, and bank groups HSBC and Barclays, have established Indian operations, which usually handle call centre and back-office functions. Foreign companies have been quick to exploit India's cheap, flexible and often highly qualified labour force, although there is evidence of a growing resentment among UK consumers against companies that move operations offshore. More than 40 per cent of customers surveyed by Troika, a financial services consultancy, said they would switch their bank or insurance company if the provider was rerouting calls to India. Some groups have even sought to score a competitive goal by distancing themselves from off-shoring rivals.

An advertising campaign from National Westminster Bank, part of Royal Bank of Scotland, is appealing to customers to switch their accounts because NatWest employs only UK-based call centre staff. Mr Boyle accepted there was a 'bit of emotion' about offshoring but said customer reaction to an RSA trial had been positive. Offshoring has also become a political issue in many countries, with the exception of the UK, where the government has shied away from commenting on the issue.

*Source*: Robert Orr (2004) *Financial Times* 12 October.

The example above highlights one way in which service work is being moved to developing countries. For many years we have seen the use of cheap labour in developing countries to manufacture goods. Many well-known companies, particularly those involved in the manufacture of clothing, have been extensively criticized for their use of Fordist techniques combined with cheap, unregulated labour abroad. Increasingly there has also been the movement of service work to the developing countries and some skilled work such as IT services.

Although Taylorist techniques are used in developing nations, in the more developed world, according to Aglietta, we will see the expansion of flexible manufacturing systems (FMS). An FMS links flexible manufacturing cells, each of which is made up of a number of computer numerically controlled machines, together by a single control and transportation system. It also incorporates the use of computer-aided design (CAD); computer-aided planning (CAP) and computer-aided manufacture (CAM). Aglietta suggests that this automation enables the centralization of planning of production but decentralization of the units of production. Using this technology, workers can be organized into semi-autonomous work groups; however, unlike others, which we will discuss, Aglietta does not see this as increasing multiskilling but focuses instead on the potential for further deskilling and work intensification. Although regulation theorists such as Aglietta see neo-fordism as a solution to the crisis of fordism, others see it as the first step away from fordism toward a new mode of production, which they termed *flexible specialization* (Piore and Sabel, 1984; Sabel, 1982). Before we move on to address this, however, we must first briefly deal with the criticisms of Aglietta's work. Firstly, he has been criticized for providing an imprecise definition of neo-fordism and secondly, for overgeneralizing the concept of fordism, showing insufficient concern with service industries and batch production in manufacturing.

## Institutionalist school

During the 1970s and 1980s, Italian and other commentators began to document what they called 'the third Italy'. This was differentiated from the first Italy of mass production and the second Italy of the economically underdeveloped south. The third Italy was a dynamic area of small firms and workshops in the central and northern areas of the country. The main element differentiating production here from other areas was what has been termed 'productive decentralization and social integration' (Brusco, 1982). The third Italy is composed of groups of artisan type firms, combining highly skilled workers and high technology producing sophisticated goods. A collaborative, collective character of relations within the firm was complemented by the same cooperative relationships between firms.

Two American academics, Michael Piore and Charles Sabel, have extensively discussed the move from mass production to 'flexible specialization', which they call the second industrial divide. Similar to Aglietta, their approach is based upon the premise that mass production is unable to meet the demands of an increasingly differentiated marketplace; however, they provide more detail of the move to post-fordism. In contrast to Aglietta, they emphasize the role of the market in the emergence and development of fordism. They see the development of mass production as the outcome of social struggles, as a 'technological paradigm' that provides a particular view of what constitutes efficient production technology that is dominant throughout society (Piore and Sabel, 1984, pp. 44–47). Because mass production was seen as such a successful approach in the United States, it was widely copied elsewhere. Piore and Sabel identify five factors that created the crisis of mass production:

1. Industrial unrest giving rise to wage inflation.
2. The floatation of exchange rates, which destabilized world markets.
3. The first oil shock, which fuelled inflation and led to the industrialization of certain developing countries.
4. The second oil shock, which led to price inflation and recession.
5. High interest rates and debt crisis.

These five factors linked with structural trends to create a crisis (Piore and Sable, 1984, p. 183). To resolve this, they argue, there are effectively two ways to reinvigorate mass production: either a restructuring of organizations away from the bureaucratic model or the development of a completely new industrial system constituted by many smaller specialized companies – a system they called 'flexible specialization'.

## Restructuring organizations

There are four key features of this strategy: 1) the introduction of computers, which makes the monitoring of individual workers more possible; 2) the redesign of workstations to enable workers to carry out multiple tasks; 3) the rotation of workers within groups; and 4) allowing work groups responsibility for tasks such as inspection. In many respects, the approach suggested here is very similar to Aglietta's neo-fordism.

## Flexible specialization

Piore and Sable (1984) define flexible specialization as:

> . . . . a strategy of permanent innovation: accommodation to ceaseless change, rather than effort to control it. This strategy is based upon flexible – multiuse – equipment, skilled workers; and the creation, through politics, of an industrial community that restricts the forms of competition to those favouring innovation (p. 17).

This leads to the re-emergence of craft forms of organization in regional economies built around a network of small decentralized firms which work alongside each other in a harmonious balance of competition and cooperation to provide an innovative environment, including high levels of participation and empowerment of the workforce. Flexibility derives from both the machinery and the workforce, which includes multiskilled 'craft' workers. The characteristics of flexible specialization include:

1. Small-scale production of a large variety of goods, a strategy whose viability has been increased in recent decades by the introduction of information technologies that improve the cost competitiveness of small-batch production.
2. Strong networks of small producers that achieve efficiency through specialization and flexibility through collaboration.
3. Representation of workers' interests through strong unions that bargain over wage norms at the national level and seek cooperative solutions to work organizations and flexible deployment of labour locally.
4. Municipal governments that provide collective goods and services, thereby reducing costs and encouraging cooperation (Applebaum and Batt, 1994, p. 37).

It has been argued that the move to flexible specialization is, at least partly, responsible for the revival of small firms. However, Sabel (1989) points to the use of flexible specialization by large firms as well. An often cited example is Benetton, the Italian clothing company. In each of the Benetton shops, specially controlled electronic cash registers constantly transmit full data about sales – type of article, colour, size and so on. This information is received centrally and forms the basis for decisions about design and production. Benetton's main production facilities are complemented by a network of more than 200 subcontractors – small firms usually employing between 30 and 50 workers, providing additional flexibility of volume. Thus, it has been argued that Benetton has reduced the response time to market changes to ten days (Kumar, 1995, p. 45; Murray, 1987).

Another, slightly less flattering, example is provided by Richard Sennett (1998) in his book *The Corrosion of Character*. Sennett discusses a Greek bakery in Boston that had been taken over by a huge food conglomerate. Yet he argues this is no mass production operation. Instead, it works according to Piore and Sabel's flexible specialization, using sophisticated reconfigurable machines. There is a great deal of flexibility in production. One day the bakers might make a thousand loaves of French bread, the next a thousand bagels, depending on immediate market demand in Boston. The composition of the workforce has also changed: although the bakery was once all male, this is no longer the case. One of the Italian workers was a girl barely out of her teens; another was a woman with grown children. Workers come and go throughout the day. Sennett describes the bakery as a 'tangled web' of part-time schedules for the women and a few of the men, and the old night shift replaced by a much more flexible labour time. The power of the bakers' union has eroded in the shop; as a result, the younger workers are not covered by union contracts, and they work on a contingent basis as well as on flexible schedules. Most strikingly, given the prejudices that Sennett discusses regarding the way the bakery had previously been organized, the shop-floor foreman is black. But sadly, Sennett comments:

> What is truly new is that in the bakery I caught sight of a terrible paradox. In this high tech, flexible workplace where everything is user-friendly, the workers felt personally demeaned by the way they work. In this baker's paradise, that reaction to their work is something they do not themselves understand. Operationally everything is so clear; emotionally so illegible (Sennett, 1998, p. 68).

Here Sennett highlights a criticism of post-fordism and flexible specialization, which we shall return to later: although advocates argue that this approach to organization will be more satisfying and motivating to the workforce, this does not always appear to be the case.

This is not the only criticism of the concept of flexible specialization. Karen Legge (1995), a well-known critical commentator on human resource management issues, identifies a tendency of protagonists of flexible specialization to leap from describing a conceptual model to normative prescriptions of what organizations should do – prescriptions that often ignore the specific contexts and histories that have supported the development of these organizations and regions. Furthermore, she argues that their innovative practices are contextually specific and could not be transferred successfully to markets requiring high levels of capital investment. Legge (1995) also suggests that the re-emergence of the craft worker is overstated, partly because the protagonists of this model have focused almost exclusively on manufacturing industry. On the contrary, she points to evidence in the service sector that technology is being used to deskill and routinize jobs.

Additional criticisms include that the concept is ill-defined and therefore difficult for other researchers and theorists to test. Wood (1989) in particular makes the point that it is hard to know what actually constitutes flexibility: is it the ability to produce alternative styles of the same model car, different models or indeed different products? It has also been suggested that the Fordist stereotype is somewhat exaggerated and that, for example, a variety of different manufacturing technologies have coexisted within 'Fordist' production systems. A further criticism is developed relating to the way the market is conceived in flexible specialization. Thompson and McHugh (1991), in their critique of the model, point out that rather than responding to the needs of the market, large multinational companies often manipulate demand through sophisticated advertising. Finally, writers such as Amin (1989) question the extent to which these small innovative organizations owe at least some of their success to the exploitation of semi-skilled workers. Thus, although some authors celebrate the idea of flexible specialization, others deride it as 'bundled-together disparate, speculative economic and social changes' (Thompson, 2003, p. 361) or 'an expression of hope' rather than a reality (Clarke, 1990, p. 75).

Next we move on to the third, and equally contentious, approach to post-fordism highlighted by Lash and Bagguley: the managerialist school.

## The 'managerialist' school

This line of analysis has been principally developed by Atkinson (1984). It should not be confused with managerialism as discussed in Chapter 9 because here we focus purely on the flexibility debate. Atkinson builds his model of 'the flexible firm' on dual labour market analysis, although he makes no explicit reference to this body of literature. Figure 5.3 outlines the various groups of workers that Atkinson believes will constitute the flexible firm. Fundamental to Atkinson's model is the differentiation between a core and a peripheral workforce, which, he argues, employers use to achieve the requisite level of production or service required by the market.

Core workers are multiskilled and essential to the organization's activities. They have high salaries and permanent contracts. They are *functionally flexible* in that they can be moved around the organization as the need arises. *Functional* or *internal flexibility* thus refers to the employer's ability to redeploy workers. This is often accomplished through the use of 'high-performance work systems', which means workers operate together in teams and are empowered to participate in decision making. Workers are multiskilled, and various strategies are used to enhance their commitment to the organization – for example, tying their compensation to organizational performance through profit-related bonuses (Kalleberg, 2003).

The periphery includes the part of the workforce that can be easily adjusted to meet fluctuations in demand – what some have labelled 'disposable workers' (Rosenberg and Lapidus, 1999). It can be split into two key types of flexibility: numerical flexibility and distancing. *Numerical flexibility* comprises several kinds of 'nonstandard' employment relations, including part-time, temporary workers and on-call staff, who are on the company payroll but have relatively weak ties with it. *Distancing* involves subcontracting operations that were previously performed within the organization. It can include both high- and low-skill workers and has been used extensively by some organizations (see the British Telecom case study on page 222) to cope with peaks in demand, although as the case study demonstrates,

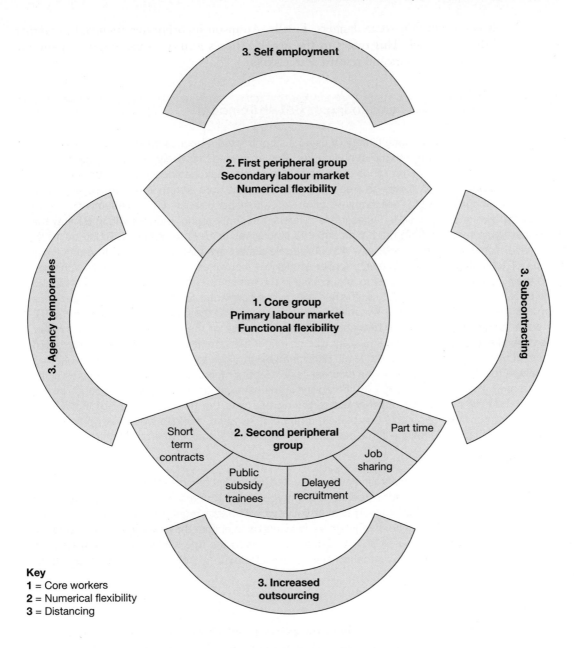

**Figure 5.3:** Atkinson's flexible firm. (*Source*: After Atkinson, 1984.)

it is not without some dangers. Finally, Atkinson incorporates *financial flexibility* into his model. This refers to the organization's ability to use pay to encourage desired behaviours and reward scarce skills.

## Case study    Subcontracting at British Telecom

British Telecom (BT) has had a long history of using subcontracted labour to meet contingencies that could not be addressed by the internal labour market. This expanded massively though during the early to mid-1990s. For example, the presence of contract labour in the field engineering function grew from less than 10 to about 10,000. It was an area of work in which the core–periphery argument was often invoked. In the labour market for telecommunication skills, postliberalization, BT had effectively played the role of supplier of suitably skilled telecoms engineers. The 'right sizing' process within BT saw the staff-in-post figure reduced from more than 245,000 employees in 1990 to around 130,000 by 1996. One 'release' scheme alone in 1992 saw 40,000 people depart from BT in one year. In many ways therefore BT ultimately became its own supplier of 'flexible' non-direct labour. The release schemes flooded the external market in parallel to an increase in the demands put on contractors, who tapped into the pool of labour created by BT. By the mid-1990s, the contractor firms had begun to experience problems in their capacity to supply suitable labour consistent with the demands put on them by BT. The market for such skilled labour had tightened, and because of the winding down of the major release schemes, the supply of ex-BT workers was no longer being replenished. This was exacerbated as the stock of ex-BT workers began to reach pensionable age. The very flexibility that was invoked as an advantage to BT of engagement in the external flexible labour market began to undermine the utility of reliance on it. Problems emerged with the ability of the external labour market to respond quickly enough to changes in demand. Further exacerbating this was the free movement of individuals between contractor firms and cable companies. In the first instance, workers who took up contracts with other – potentially competing – firms became unavailable to BT, thus exacerbating the shortage of suitable labour

The deregulation of the employment relationship, reflected in the shift to a greater reliance on the external labour market, can be characterized by the emergence of a number of ironies. Notably, the opportunity to pursue the flexibility advantages associated with a less regulated supply of labour was predicated upon the prior existence of regulatory mechanisms to ensure the creation and reproduction of skills and not simply the absence of institutional obstacles to the free working of the market. The problems that emerged within this situation were associated with a lack of regulation over labour supply and skill reproduction.

There is great debate about the extent to which organizations have adopted one or both of these forms of flexibility. Some writers (e.g., Osterman, 2000) argue that the use of policies geared toward developing high commitment in core workers is well diffused. This is supported in the United Kingdom by a survey that took place in 2002 (and written up in White et al., 2004, *Managing to Change? British Workplaces and the Future of Work*). About one half of respondents believed that employees have been asked to carry out a greater variety of tasks in the past three years. The survey also suggested that working in teams has increased, which, the authors suggest, reflects 'intelligent flexibility' through more versatile and interchangeable employees. Generally, although empirical studies are inconclusive and are in the service sector, particularly in areas such as call centres, it would appear that Fordist approaches are alive and well (Frenkel, 2003; Frenkel et al., 1998). With regard to

**Table 5.3** The incidence of part-time work in European Union member states

| Member state | Total % 1992 | Total % 2002 | Male % 1992 | Male % 2002 | Female % 1992 | Female % 2002 |
|---|---|---|---|---|---|---|
| Austria | 12.6 | 18.9 | 3.6 | 5.1 | 24.5 | 35.7 |
| Belgium | 12.7 | 19.4 | 2.3 | 5.9 | 28.9 | 37.7 |
| Denmark | 23.0 | 20.6 | 10.7 | 11.0 | 37.1 | 31.4 |
| Finland | 10.4 | 12.4 | 7.3 | 8.0 | 13.7 | 17.1 |
| France | 13.1 | 16.2 | 3.8 | 5.0 | 25.2 | 29.7 |
| Germany | 14.5 | 20.8 | 2.7 | 5.8 | 30.9 | 39.5 |
| Greece | 4.5 | 4.5 | 2.6 | 2.3 | 8.1 | 8.1 |
| Ireland | 9.1 | 16.5 | 3.8 | 6.5 | 18.7 | 30.5 |
| Italy | 5.5 | 8.6 | 2.5 | 3.7 | 11.2 | 16.7 |
| Luxembourg | 6.5 | 11.7 | 1.0 | 1.8 | 16.2 | 26.4 |
| Netherlands | 34.8 | 43.8 | 15.2 | 21.5 | 64.4 | 72.8 |
| Portugal | 7.2 | 11.3 | 4.1 | 7.1 | 11.1 | 16.4 |
| Spain | 6.0 | 8.0 | 2.2 | 2.6 | 13.8 | 17.0 |
| Sweden | 20.5 | 21.4 | 6.8 | 11.2 | 36.0 | 32.9 |
| United Kingdom | 22.9 | 25.0 | 6.3 | 9.4 | 43.8 | 44.0 |
| **Total %** | **14.2** | **18.2** | **4.2** | **6.6** | **28.8** | **33.5** |

*Source*: European Foundation for the Improvement of Living and Working Conditions (2004).

numerical flexibility, on the other hand, a great deal of evidence suggests that this has increased, although the prevalence of these arrangements varies across industries and across countries. For example, Table 5.3 shows the incidence of part-time work in Europe.

A cross-country analysis shows the incidence of part-time work is more widespread in the countries of northern Europe than in those of southern Europe. According to the European Foundation for the Improvement of Living and Working Conditions (EFILWC), these national differences are caused by a combination of factors, including differences in the state of the economy, the labour market, the organization of childcare, education, and tax and social security benefits. However, a general trend is visible in that part-time work has increased in all member states for both men and women in the period 1992 to 2002, with the exception of men in Greece and women in Sweden and Denmark.

In addition, research in the United Kingdom shows that the proportion of those employed on temporary contracts also increased from about 5% in the early 1990s to 6.7% in 1999 (Hoque and Kirkpatrick, 2003), and according to Drucker (2002), the Swiss company Adecco places almost 700,000 temporary workers daily with businesses all over the world. He estimates that every day as many as 10 million workers are 'temps' across the globe. The 1990s and early 2000s also witnessed an expansion in the numbers of professional or managerial workers entering temporary or part-time contracts. There remains some debate as to whether these employees find themselves marginalized in the same way as other members of the periphery (Mallon and Duberley, 2000). As the Ideas and perspectives box below illustrates, although writers discuss the poor employment situation of temporary workers, workers do not all necessarily experience it this way. Thus, some writers have stressed the celebration of the individual's liberation to pursue his or her own 'portfolio' or 'boundaryless' career. The transition to portfolio work (and other more boundaryless forms of career) has been widely heralded as a contemporary career transition (Handy, 1994). This involves individuals selling a variety of their skills to a number of employers on a range of different employment and contractual arrangements. Thus, the individual takes charge of his or her career and seeks to develop a range of sellable skills to maintain employability given the demise of employment security (e.g., Arthur and Rousseau, 1996). Security for an individual, it is suggested (see, for example, Mirvis and Hall, 1994), should be anchored, not in a particular

## Ideas and perspectives

## The experience of temporary work for *some* women

It is generally assumed that women doing temporary work are exploited and have a 'weak commitment' to the labour market (Hakim, 1995). They are seen as poorly paid and having reduced entitlements to employee benefits and trade union protection. However, the following quotes come from interviews by Casey and Alach (2004) with female temps in a range of occupations:

> I like to travel a lot, usually about two months every year. Temping is really good because it allows me to save for the trip. . . . I like temping and I know that full time employment just wasn't for me. I couldn't just sit in an office from nine to five. I need more hours in the day to do my own thing (Navindra, age 24).

> There's a lot of freedom in temping to just up and go, you know. Because as a temp to a degree you are your own boss. I mean . . . you can state when you want to work and when you don't want to work. Would I go back permanent? . . . no I don't think so. . . . When you're a temp there's always a threat that if you're a good temp you can just turn around and walk away. And I think people tend to value that, you know, they sort of respect you a bit more. I tend to get more respect as a temp for my abilities (Susan, age 39).

> We temps are lucky because we can choose. And we don't get taken into a room every two or three weeks and asked what we've done, and how many products we've sold and get ticked off (Beth, age 58).

> Since I've been temping my stress levels have gone down a lot from when I had a permanent job . . . you just don't have to get involved . . . when you leave at the end of the day that's it! Even on long-term assignments you can still retain that distance of mind (Linda, age 39).

### Stop and think

How would you explain these attitudes? What are the implications for employers?

organization, but in one's own portable skills and employability. Hence, people are encouraged to weaken their ties with organizations. Instead of a relationship built upon mutual commitment and continuity, a more transactional relationship is advocated that is based upon short-term, measurable exchanges. The career should become something managed by the individual rather than the organization. Indeed, Harvard Business School academic Rosabeth Moss Kanter predicts the demise of the bureaucratic career, as we will discuss in Chapter 9, and in its place, a flourishing of career forms more associated with professional and entrepreneurial work.

## The flexible firm – critique

This concept of the flexible firm has been the target for a large amount of critical debate (for example, see Legge, 1995; Pollert, 1988, 1991; Thompson and McHugh, 1991). It has been suggested that the flexible firm is more of an ideological prescription than an observation of changes currently happening in organizations. There are two core areas that are raised for critique. The first relates to the conceptual weakness of the model. It is hard to draw clear lines between the core and the periphery. For example, how do we define core workers: is it purely on the basis of having secure employment? As Pollert points out, whereas some workers may have job security but may not be regarded as core to the organization, others may be very important to the organization's functioning but work on part-time or fixed-term contracts. Similarly, Hyman (1991) makes the point that it is too simplistic to equate core workers with high levels of skill and peripheral workers as unskilled or inflexible. Figure 5.4 (overleaf) cross-classifies the core–periphery distinction with the degree of control that workers have over their skills and market situation. Although simplistic, this shows that although some workers in the periphery of the organization have low skill and little control, others have high skill levels and considerable autonomy over their work. Similarly, not all those in the core enjoy high levels of autonomy. Some workers who might be classified as core (e.g., attendants in fast food establishments) may have few skills and relatively low security.

The assumption of the use of functional and numerical flexibility together has also been challenged. Some studies have found either a negative or nonexistent relationship between functional and numerical flexibility in organizations (see, for example, Calas and Smircich, 1999; Capelli, 1995); others have suggested they can coexist (Gittelman, 1999). Some writers point to the ways the flexible firm model extends and intensifies labour market segregation by gender, race and age. For example, Sennett (1998) discusses the impact of the compression of working life and suggests this has created an emphasis on youth. He quotes a recent issue of the *California Management Review*, which sought to explain the positives of youth and the negatives of age in flexible organizations. It did so by arguing that older workers have inflexible mindsets and are risk averse, as well as lacking the sheer physical energy needed to cope with the demands of life in the flexible workplace. Drawing on the work of Newman, he quotes an advertising executive: 'If you're in advertising, you're dead after thirty. Age is a killer.' Similarly, a Wall Street executive told her, 'Employers think that if you are over forty you can't think anymore. Over fifty and they think you're burned out.' Sennett

| Relationship to employer | Degree of worker control | |
|---|---|---|
| | High | Low |
| Core | High firm-specific skills; high security with employer<br><br>Examples: autonomous jobs in standard employment relations | Low skills, low security with employer<br><br>Example: regular, part-time, routine jobs |
| Periphery | Highly portable skills; effective occupational association; high security with an occupation<br><br>Examples: high-skilled independent contractors and consultants; high-skilled temporary help agency employees | Non-transferable skills; weak occupational association; low security with employer or occupation<br><br>Examples: short term hires in routine jobs; low-skilled temporary help agency employees |

**Figure 5.4:** Dimensions of labour market segmentation. (*Source*: Kalleberg, 2003.)

argues these prejudices serve several purposes. For instance, they target older workers for dismissal during corporate reengineering (Sennett, 1998, p. 93).

Others have also pointed to the darker side of the flexible firm. Atkinson himself worries that widespread uptake of the model and increased use of the core–periphery distinction would mean that an individual's pay, security and career opportunities would increasingly be secured at the expense of the employment conditions of others, often women, more of whom will find themselves permanently relegated in dead-end, insecure and low-paid jobs (Atkinson 1984). Similarly, (Gorz 1999, p. 45) makes the point that post-fordism produces its elite by producing unemployment; the latter is the precondition for the former.

Although we might imagine that workers in the core of organizations are the lucky ones, that may not be the case because more flexible forms of organization are often associated with flexible labour practices and work intensification. According to Green (2003), work intensification can take two forms: the extension of working time and more intensive effort. For example, books such as Harrison's *Lean and Mean* (1994) articulate the dark side of flexible production and confront the positive images generally put forward for flexible, team-oriented organizations. Also, Thompson (2003) discusses the psychological insecurity experienced when an organization has downsized to its core workforce and subcontracted peripheral work to outsiders:

> Those that survive rationalization and downsizing are left to bear the costs, not just of low morale but of increased workloads and threats to their pensions, damaging perceptions of the effort bargain and psychological contract in the process (Beynon et al. 2002, quoted in Thompson, 2003, p. 366).

Thus, as with post-industrialism, the post-Fordist model is attacked on three fronts:

1. By those who question it conceptually as a way of explaining the changes occurring in society.
2. By those who question the empirical data that supports such a transition.
3. By those who point to the perhaps unintended consequences of a move to such forms of work organization.

### The chapter so far

Having broadly defined postmodernism and post-industrialism earlier, this section examined the concept of post-fordism. Three alternative approaches were outlined and evaluated. We will now finish this chapter by discussing writers who have explicitly examined the concept of the postmodern organization.

## Postmodern organizations – the work of Stewart Clegg and Paul Heydebrand

In this final section, our aim is to examine writers who have specifically looked at the emergence of postmodern organizational forms. The most developed exposition of postmodern forms of organization comes in the works of Paul Heydebrand (e.g., 1989) and Stewart Clegg. Rather than examining macro-level changes in society, the aim of these two writers is to 'focus on these tendencies through the embeddedness of economic action' (Clegg, 1990, p. 180). In other words, they examine the nature of contemporary organizational forms.

Heydebrand analyses the literature on Japanization and the post-industrial society to develop a somewhat tentative model of postmodern organizational forms. He suggests that the 'ideal type' postmodern organizational form would be:

- small
- using computerized technology
- functionally decentralized
- participative
- clan (Ouchi, 1981) approaches toward control. This kind of control does not focus on monitoring behaviour or outcomes; rather, the various individuals share common values, and their activities and outcomes are 'controlled' by their own value systems in absence of any explicit organizational controls
- informal
- having a strong corporate culture to integrate people with the organization's mission.

Unlike some of the other writers we have discussed, Heydebrand does not see postmodern organizational forms as a break from modernism or a complete move away from rationality. Rather, he sees postmodern organizations as a pragmatic response to current economic and social conditions, an alternative approach to try to achieve rationality in more dynamic and uncertain environmental conditions. Clegg further develops these ideas. He argues that even in the postmodern age, organizations still require management but that traditional modernist, bureaucratic forms of organization do not capture the organizational patterns of contemporary South East Asian, and particularly Japanese, organizations. He suggests that post-modernism points to a more organic, less differentiated type of organization than those dominated by the bureaucratic designs of modernity:

> Where modernist organization was rigid, postmodern organization is **flexible**. Where modernist consumption was premised on mass forms, postmodernist consumption is premised on **niches**. Where modernist organization was premised on technological determinism, postmodernist organization is premised on **technological choices** made possible through 'de-dedicated' microelectronic equipment. Where modernist organization and jobs were highly differentiated, demarcated and deskilled, postmodernist organization and jobs are highly de-differentiated and **multiskilled**. Employment relations as a fundamental relation of organization upon which has been constructed a whole discourse of the determinism of size as a contingency variable increasingly give way to more **complex** and **fragmentary relational forms,** such as subcontracting and networking (Clegg, 1990, p. 181; emphasis added).

Unlike some other writers, Clegg does not set out to persuade the reader that postmodernism or postmodern organizational forms are necessarily a good thing. Rather, he argues that whether postmodern organizations turn out to be seen as dynamic and refreshingly pluralistic or another attempt at totalitarianism control depends upon the triumphs and failures of diverse institutional forms of power and knowledge in the making of the postmodern world.

Derived from Jacques (1989), Clegg (1990) draws on seven organizational imperatives in his analysis of postmodern organizations. Although his focus in this analysis is largely on Japanese organizations, he also cites examples from Europe, such as the much referred to 'third Italian' fashion industry and also French bread making. The seven organizational imperatives are:

### 1. Articulating mission, goals, strategies and main functions

Japanese firms tend not to adopt the conglomerate approach common in the United States and United Kingdom. As a consequence, there is more internal coherence, a well-focused mission and a strong, homogenous internal culture with high levels of employee commitment. Research and production are integrated through overlapping teams. Work practices are flexible, involving team work, job rotation and a skilled and constantly reskilling workforce. Central to these practices is long-term employment security for the workforce.

## 2. Arranging functional alignments

In Japanese enterprises, the functional alignment of activities is achieved by extensive use of the market principle through subcontracting and a (quasi) democratic principle through self-managed teamwork taking place within an overall structure of hierarchy and private ownership. Within the self-managed teams, work roles overlap, and the task structure is continuous, in which workers allocate tasks internally. The greater flexibility of workers extends to the technological design of work itself. Production lines are organized to be more flexible, allowing operatives to perform a number of tasks rather than just one.

## 3. Mechanisms of coordination and control

Clegg (1990) identifies two aspects to this power in the organization and power around the organization. In terms of power in the organization, he discusses how although the personalization and particularization of power appear quite normal in the Asian region, Japanese superiors are expected to make their subordinates accept the practice of groupism so that trust is constituted that transcends particularisms, binding each person to the love of the enterprise. This high level of commitment is matched by high levels of empowerment, enabled through the widespread use of communication of information. Flexibility and empowerment extend throughout the organization's structure across all levels and functions. Managers tend not to specialize in the same way as US or UK managers. Instead, management rotation ensures a cadre of management generalists who have a good level of understanding of the various aspects of the business.

With respect to power around the organization, this concerns the ways organizations are connected. In the West, Clegg (1990) argues, this takes place primarily through mechanisms of 'interlocking dictatorships' and the share market. In contrast, Japanese enterprises operate under relatively stable capital market conditions. The Ministry of International Trade and Industry (MITI) has an important role in vertically coordinating enterprises. In addition, the state plays a proactive role in developing industry policy with respect to new and declining branches of industry to support the development of national capitalism.

## 4. Constituting accountability and role relationships

Japanese organizations tend to focus on group accountability. Dedifferentiation appears to be in place, which means that workers tend to be multiskilled. Skill formation is oriented toward the organization rather than individually achieved, which ties the workers more closely to the organization.

## 5. Planning and communication

A focus on the long term is central to Japanese organizations. Clegg (1990) outlines the different accounting systems and their impact on managerial behaviour. By applying different financial measures, he argues that Japanese firms are able to undertake long-term capital investment that US and UK firms would not be able to justify.

### 6. Relating rewards and performance

Japanese organizations focus on improving organizational performance rather than individual performance. Two guiding rules for reward are identified in Japanese firms: 1) a single individual is never rewarded alone and 2) the expressive dimension of rewards is emphasized; thus, there is use of symbolic rewards.

### 7. Achieving effective leadership

Leadership provides organizational values that serve as a basis for the development of mutual trust and commitment. Thus, the role of leadership in the postmodern organization is to inculcate appropriate values throughout the organization – to manage the organizational culture.

Much of the description from Clegg (1990) corresponds broadly with the descriptions of post-Fordist or post-industrial organizations. The differences relate to the extent to which Clegg draws particularly on Japanese organizations as providing the model underlying this transformation in organizational forms. His comparison of modern and postmodern organizational forms is depicted in Figure 5.5.

Clegg (1990) stresses that the schema he develops is indicative and sensitizing, providing clues as to what to look for to assess organizational diversities rather than a model that could be easily applied. He also makes the point that national context

| | Modernity | Postmodernity |
|---|---|---|
| *1. Mission goals, strategies and main functions* | | |
| | Specialization | Diffusion |
| *2. Functional alignments* | | |
| | Bureaucracy | Democracy |
| | Hierarchy | Market |
| *3. Coordination and control* | | |
| | *In organizations* | |
| | Disempowerment | Empowerment |
| | *Around organizations* | |
| | *Laissez faire* | Industry policy |
| *4. Accountability and role relationships* | | |
| | Extra-organizational | Intra-organizational |
| | Skill formation | |
| | Inflexible | Flexible |
| *5. Planning and communication* | | |
| | Short term techniques | Long term techniques |
| *6. Relation of performance and reward* | | |
| | Individualized | Collectivized |
| *7. Leadership* | | |
| | Mistrust | Trust |

**Figure 5.5:** Clegg's postmodern versus modern organizational forms. (*Source*: Clegg 1990: p. 203.)

is important and that the pattern of organizational features he describes to some extent depends upon the development of postwar Japanese society. Furthermore, he recognizes that although he has put forward one version of Japanese organization that he calls postmodern, not all organizations in Japan would fit this model because they would have to be organized to deal with specific contingencies in terms of size, technology and so on. Thus, Clegg shows that organizational forms depend upon particular contingencies and the institutional frameworks within which organizations are situated. The case study below discusses Toyota, often put forward as the archetypal Japanese organization.

| Case study | Toyota – the postmodern or post-Fordist motor manufacturer? |
|---|---|

The rise of the Japanese car manufacturers to positions of global dominance in the decades following the World War II is well known. In recent years, despite the well-publicized troubles of some companies such as Nissan, other Japanese car makers, most notably Toyota, have sustained and even increased their global competitive advantage.

This competitive advantage is based on a corporate philosophy known as the Toyota Production System. The system depends in part on a human resources management policy that stimulates employee creativity and loyalty but also, importantly, on a highly efficient network of suppliers and components manufacturers.

Toyota and other foreign car makers have successfully penetrated the US market and established a world-wide presence by virtue of its productivity. Toyota's philosophy of empowering its workers is the centrepiece of a human resources management system that fosters creativity and innovation by encouraging employee participation and engendering high levels of employee loyalty.

Much of Toyota's success can be attributed directly to the synergistic performance of its policies in human resources management and supply-chain networks. The evolution of Toyota's network system approach can be traced to the period immediately following the World War II when the economic outlook was uncertain and human, natural and capital resources were in limited supply. Toyota's president, Toyoda Kiichiro and, later Ohno Taiichi, the real architects of the Toyota Production System (TPS), developed a highly efficient production system later characterized as 'lean production'. Toyota's methods paralleled those of Henry Ford several decades earlier, although Toyota's approach to both product development and distribution proved to be much more consumer-friendly and market-driven.

### Supply chain management

Engineering and component fabrication account for around 85% of the direct cost of the manufacturing process associated with car production. Outsourcing plays an increasingly important role for both domestic and foreign car makers as companies attempt to 'externalize' many of these direct costs and minimize market risk, while at the same time realizing the benefits of using specialized suppliers.

Supply chain relationships among Asian manufacturers are based on a complex system of cooperation and equity interests. In both Japan and Korea, cooperation and asset concentration are encouraged, and antitrust prohibitions are far less restrictive than in the USA.

*(Continued)*

## Case study          (Continued)

Importantly, both government and culture play a major role in Asian manufacturing and distribution practices. Asian values, more so than in Western cultures, traditionally emphasize the collective good over the goals of the individual. This attitude clearly supports the synergistic approach of supply chain management and has encouraged concern for quality and productivity.

### Determining factors in productivity

Toyota's approach to product development and production was different from the path taken by other foreign manufacturers. First, Toyota made a strategic commitment at the outset to produce automobiles exclusively. Second, Toyoda Kiichiro believed the company would fare better if it selectively borrowed technologies and practices from established car makers without being bound by the restrictions that direct technology transfer would have imposed on the company. In effect, Toyota borrowed the best concepts and practices from elsewhere and then developed what was needed to satisfy customer demand. Customer satisfaction has remained the focal point of Toyota's strategic initiatives since the 1950s.

Several specific factors, or components, have been cited as underlying Toyota's success, including:

- A world-class network of suppliers in both Japan and, more recently, in the USA.
- A highly efficient and effective just-in-time (JIT) inventory system that is heavily dependent upon the coordination of its supplier network.
- A state-of-the-art assembly system incorporating the latest robotic technology. Toyota plants in Japan and North America have both won the World-wide Platinum Plant Quality Award.
- An effective and efficient human resources management system, the cornerstone of which is a high level of employee loyalty and commitment to quality.

The outcome of such strategic architecture, based on careful analysis of a company's resources and competencies, in addition to the orchestration of these strategic resources and competencies over time, can be seen in the measures of productivity for lean versus non-lean automotive companies.

*Source:* Adapted from Vaghefi (2002) *Financial Times* 5 September.

## Stop and think

- Using Clegg's (1990) template, would you classify Toyota as a postmodern organization?
- To what extent do you think Toyota's model of organization is transferable to other countries?

As mentioned earlier, Clegg (1990) is critical in his analysis of postmodern organizational forms. He expresses concern for the divisive nature of the core–periphery split and also makes the point that:

> If Japan represents one possible path towards postmodernity, it is clear that there have been winners and losers in this development. To recap, the winners have been men in the internal labour markets in the big name companies and the enterprise group networks. The losers have been women and those, more than two thirds of all workers, who are outside the core labour market (p. 206).

However, Clegg does not really deal with the issue that over the past 30 years, many comparative surveys have found Japanese managers and employees far less satisfied with their jobs than their Western counterparts (Meek, 2004), or indeed the recent social problems of *karoshi* (death from overwork) and *ijime* (bullying) in Japanese workplaces, suggesting that Japanese workplaces may not be the idyllic place for the core workforce we are led to believe.

A further indirect criticism of the work of Clegg and Heydebrand comes from the work of Crook et al. (1992) who suggest that any attempt to define the postmodern organization simply in terms of a new set of organizational imperatives fails to grasp the nature of postmodernization as a process of dedifferentiation that manifests itself across the whole organizational spectrum. Thus, Clegg could be criticized for over-looking the very fragmentation that is at the heart of the postmodernization process (Hancock and Tyler, 2001).

Many of the criticisms of postmodern organizational forms are similar to those concerning post-industrialism and post-fordism. For example, critics comment on the lack of both conceptual clarity and empirical evidence for what is an argument of empirical change and the ways writers can slip from the descriptive into the prescriptive (Thompson, 2003). Others suggest it is merely a new, ill-defined term developed to revive interest in the field with little to recommend it (Parker, 1993). It is certainly easy to see overlap between what Clegg calls the postmodern organization and others such as Hecksher and Donnellon (1994) call the postbureaucratic organizational form. Hecksher and Donnellon outline the following 11 features of the ideal type postbureacratic organization:

1. Consensus through institutionalized dialogue rather than acquiescence to authority and rules.

2. Influence by persuasion rather than official position.

3. Influence based upon mutual trust and interdependence rather than narrow self- or departmental interest.

4. Integration through a strong emphasis on organizational mission rather than formal job definitions and rules.

5. Sharing of information rather than hoarding and hiding information.

6. Organizational behaviour and action based upon principles rather than formal rules.

7. Consultation and communication based upon the problem or the project rather than a formal chain of command.

8. Verification of qualifications and expertise through open processes of association and peer evaluation rather than formal credentials and official position.

9. Looser organizational boundaries that tolerate outsiders coming in and insiders going out rather than the insular 'organization man/woman' emphasis.

10. Evaluation, compensation and promotion based upon public and negotiated standards of performance rather than rigid objective criteria.

11. Expectations of constant change based upon continual assessment rather than expectations of permanence based upon the assumption of a fixed set of appropriate procedures (pp. 25–28).

As with the post-industrial and post-Fordist models, there is debate concerning the extent to which organizations that map exactly onto this ideal type really exist. A common example cited of postbureaucratic organization is Danish hearing aid company Oticon. The chief executive decided in 1990 that the company should be fundamentally restructured and that 'All paper would go, all jobs would go, all walls would go'. Thus, it is claimed Oticon was transformed into what was called a 'spaghetti organization'. The spaghetti organization had no formal structure; the only structure was provided by projects with the additional dimension that all staff members were multiskilled. Thus, people were no longer members of departments. Teams were formed, disbanded and reformed again as the work required. Oticon's employees no longer had traditional offices; along with the organization chart, Oticon physically eliminated its walls. Employees had a desk and a computer, but the location of that desk could change, and every individual was expected to be able to move within five minutes. This is an impressive example of an organization moving toward postbureaucracy, and there are others that discuss, for example, the move toward postbureaucracy in the public sector evident in the rise of contracting and public–private partnerships in which local authorities and hospitals collaborate with private sector businesses in the provision of services. It is clear, however, that organizations rarely manage to do away with bureaucracy totally, and although much maligned, elements of bureaucracy remain. For example, even at Oticon, the approach was modified after 1996 to avoid unexpected costs that had been incurred, including problems of coordination and employee time allocation (Child, 2005).

## Conclusions

The aim of this chapter has been to examine some of the theoretical explanations for the changes we are witnessing in contemporary work organizations and society more generally. We have addressed post-industrialism, postmodernity and post-fordism and made the point that although some writers differentiate the terms sharply, others use them interchangeably. Additionally, there are certain core characteristics such as increased flexibility and multiskilling, the increased importance of knowledge work, the breakdown of organizational hierarchies, the differentiation of a core and peripheral workforce and the flexible use of labour.

Two themes recur throughout the chapter: the first is the extent to which these changes are widespread. Although most authors recognize that we have seen a change in some manufacturing practices, some suggest the extent of change has been exaggerated and is based upon a parody of what went before. In other words, Fordist styles of production are being presented as far more homogeneous than was ever the case. Others have also pointed to the utilization and refinement of modernist or Fordist practices in service industries such as call centres and also in manufacturing industries that have moved to less industrialized parts of the globe. Hence, the picture of change appears complex and nuanced. The second core theme concerns the extent to which postmodernity represents a break with the past or whether the practices we see variously defined as post-industrial and post-Fordist actually reflect a continuation and, in some cases, intensification of modernist organizational practices. Foucault, a writer we will be talking about in much more depth in the next chapter, comments on the tendency to see the present as fundamentally different to anything that went before:

> Here I think we are touching on . . . one of the most harmful habits in contemporary thought . . . the analysis of the present as being precisely, in history, a present of rupture, or of high point, or of completion or of a returning dawn. . . . I think we should have the modesty to say to ourselves that, on the one hand, the time we live in is not the unique or fundamental or irruptive point in history where everything is completed and begun again. We must also have the modesty to say, on the other hand that . . . the time we live in is very interesting; it needs to be analyzed and broken down, and that we would do well to ask ourselves, 'what is the nature of our present?' . . . with the proviso that we do not allow ourselves the facile, rather theatrical declaration that this moment in which we exist is one of total pedition, in the abyss of darkness, or a triumphant daybreak, etc. It is a time like any other, or rather, a time which is never quite like any other (Foucault, 1983, p. 206, quoted in Smart, 1992).

Thus, although protagonists outline the fundamental changes occurring in society, detractors argue that we are witnessing a development of capitalist society rather than a move to a new kind of societal form. Kumar (1995), however, makes the important point that perhaps it is hard to recognize an epochal shift when going through it. Would commentators of the day have recognized the industrial revolution as it took place? Perhaps we are witnessing the first steps to large-scale change, which, by its very nature, will be messy, protracted and painful. Thus, depending upon whose analysis you accept, society in the West remains staunchly modern, has undergone a complete shift into postmodernity or is embarking on some journey between the two. Whatever may be the case, this chapter has highlighted some of the changes that seem to be happening within work organizations. In the next chapter, we move to a totally different perspective on postmodernism. There we will look at postmodern philosophy and the challenges it poses for organization theory.

## Concluding grid

| Learning outcomes | Challenges to contemporary organizations |
|---|---|
| Outline the nature of the postmodern condition. | The debate concerning whether postmodernity is a change in culture that corresponds to changes in late capitalism has been considered. The key features of postmodernity have been highlighted, which pose the following challenges: to what extent has society become based upon services, where knowledge is seen as a source of competitive advantage between organizations? Are cultural and business spheres merging? What is the impact of this upon organizations? To what extent are companies resituating manufacturing processes to the developing world? What are the implications of this for organizations in both the developed and developing world? |

*(Continued)*

## Concluding grid (Continued)

| Learning outcomes | Challenges to contemporary organizations |
| --- | --- |
| Discuss the relationship between postmodernism, post-industrialism and post-fordism. | *Postmodernism* has been used as a term that captures changes conceptualized as both post-industrial or post-Fordist. How widespread are these changes? Have Fordist approaches been superseded? |
| Examine the implications of the postmodern epoch for organizational design and theorizing. | The chapter examines the implications for organizations with regard to issues such as flexible specialization, the flexible firm and the nature of postmodern organizations. To what extent are the characteristics of these organizations, including decentralization, multiskilled workforces, flat hierarchies and niche markets, present in today's organizations? |
| Discuss the concept of the 'flexible firm' and the implications of this for the experience of people at work. | Four approaches to flexibility have been outlined: functional flexibility, numerical flexibility, distancing and financial flexibility. How relevant is this model to today's organizations? The model has been critiqued in three ways: <br><br> 1. By those who question its validity as a model of the changes occurring in society. <br><br> 2. By those who question the empirical data that support a transition to the flexible firm. <br><br> 3. By those who point to the consequences of a move to such forms of work organization. <br><br> To what extent are these critiques valid? Do flexible firms as identified by Atkinson exist in practice? |

## Annotated further reading

If you wish to examine the themes discussed in this chapter further good texts to draw on are those by Harvey (1989), Smart (1992) and Kumar (1995). Hancock and Tyler (2001) also provide an excellent chapter that focuses explicitly on the impact of these macro-level debates on work organizations.

## Discussion questions

1. Compare and contrast the three different approaches towards post-fordism.
2. Watch the film *The Full Monty*. To what extent does the situation faced by the ex-steelworkers in Sheffield, England depicted in the film compare with industrial workers in your home town/city?

What retraining would you suggest to enable these people to become part of the knowledge economy?

3. Examine the relationship between business and sport by choosing one international sporting event and try to identify how many sponsorship deals are evident.

4. Debate the pros and cons of outsourcing production to developing countries. Consider the perspectives of producers, consumers and workers in the developed countries and workers in developing countries.

5. According to Drucker, in the past workers relied on capitalists as they owned the tools of their labour. In the knowledge society, employees – that is, knowledge workers – own the tools of production. It is the knowledge investment that determines whether the employee is productive or not. What are the implications of this for relations between workers and organizations? What do you believe will be the key challenges of managing knowledge workers?

## References

Aglietta, M. (1987) *A Theory of Capitalist Regulation: The US Experience*, London: Verso.

Applebaum, E. and Batt, R. (1994) *The New American Workplace*, Ithaca, NY: ILR Press.

Amin, A. (1989) 'Flexible specialization and small firms in Italy: Myths and realities', *Antipode* 21:13–34.

Arthur, M. and Rousseau, D. (1996) *Boundaryless Careers: A New Employment Principle for the New Organizational Era*, New York: Oxford University Press.

Atkinson, J. (1984) 'Manpower strategies for flexible organizations', *Personnel Management* August.

Bagguley, P. (1989) *The Post-Fordist Enigma: Theories of Labour Flexibility*, Lancaster University.

Barraclough, G. (1964) *An Introduction to Contemporary History*, Baltimore: Penguin.

Baumann, Z. (1988) 'Is there a postmodern sociology?' *Theory, Culture and Society* 5:217–237.

Bell, D. (1973) *The Coming of the Post Industrial Society: A Venture in Social Forecasting*, New York: Basic Books.

Bell, D. (1974) *The Coming of the Post Industrial Society,* New York: Basic Books.

Bell, D. (1960) *The End of Ideology: On the Exhaustion of Political Ideas in the Fifties*, Collier Books.

Bell, D. (1976) *The Cultural Contradictions of Capitalism*, New York: HarperCollins.

Best, S. and Kellner, D. (1991) *Postmodern Theory: Critical Interrogations*, New York: The Guilford Press.

Beynon, H., Grimshaw, D., Rubery, J. and Ward, K. (2002) 'The restructuring of career paths in large service sector organisations: delayering, upskilling and polarisation', *The Sociological Review* 50(1):89–116.

Bibby, A. (2002) Home start. *People Management* 10 (January).

Brusco, S. (1982) 'The Modena model: Productive decentralization and social integration', *Cambridge Journal of Economics* 6:167–184.

Butler, C. (2002) *Postmodernism: A Very Short Introduction*, Oxford: Oxford University Press.

Calas, M. and Smircich, L. (1999) 'Past postmodernism? Reflections and tentative directions', *Academy of Management Review* 24(4):649–671.

Capelli, P. (1995) Rethinking employment, *British Journal of Industrial Relations* 33:563–602.

Casey, C. and Alach, P. (2004) 'Just a temp? Women, temporary employment and lifestyle', *Work, Employment & Society* 18(3):459–480.

Castells, M. (1996) *The Rise of Network Society*, Blackwells: Oxford.

Castells, M. (2000a) *The Information Age: Economy, Society and Culture, vol I: The Rise of the Network Society*, Oxford: Blackwell.

Castells, M. (2000b) *The Information Age: Economy, Society and Culture, vol II: End of Millenium*, Oxford: Blackwell.

Castells, M. (2004) *The Information Age: Economy, Society and Culture, vol III: The Power of Identity*, Oxford: Blackwell.

Child, J. (2005) *Organization*, Oxford: Oxford University Press.

Clarke, S. (1990) 'New Utopias for Old: Fordist Dreams and Post Fordist Fantasies', *Capital and Class* (42):131–155.

Clegg, S. (1990) *Modern Organizations: Organization Studies in a Postmodern World*, London: Sage.

Crook, S., Pakulski, J. and Waters, M. (1992) *Postmodernization: Change in Advanced Society*, London: Sage.

Drucker, P. (1957) *Americas Next Twenty Years*, New York: Harper & Brothers.

Drucker, P. (2002) 'They're not employees; they're people', *Harvard Business Review* February.

Ducatel, K., Webster, J. and Herrmann, W. (2000) *The Information Society in Europe: Work and Life in an Age of Globalization*, Lanham: Rowan and Littlefield.

Etzioni, A. (1968) *The Active Society*, New York: The Free Press.

European Foundation for the Improvement of Living and Working Conditions (2004) *Part-time Work in Europe*, Dublin: European Foundation for the Improvement of Living and Working Conditions: 20.

Foucault, M. (1983) 'The subject and power', in H. Dreyfus and P. Rabinow (eds), Michel Foucault: *Beyond structuralism and hermeneutics*, Chicago: University of Chicago Press.

Frenkel, S.J. (2003) 'The embedded character of workplace relations', *Work and Occupations* 30(2):135–153.

Frenkel, S.J., Korczynski, M., Tam, M., and Shire, K. (1998) 'Beyond bureaucracy? Work organization in call centres', *International Journal of Human Resource Management* 9:957–979.

Ghirardo, D. (1996) *Architecture After Modernism*, New York: Thames & Hudson.

Gittelman, M. (1999) *Flexible Working Practices: Where They Are Found and What Are Their Labour Market Implications*, Paris: OECD Employment Outlook.

Gorz, A. (1999) *Reclaiming Work*, Cambridge, United Kingdom: Polity.

Green, F. (2003) 'The rise and decline of job insecurity', University of Kent working papers, October.

Hakim, C. (1995) 'Workforce restructuring in cross-national perspective', *Work, Employment & Society* 9:379–388.

Hancock, P. and Tyler, M. (2001) *Work, Postmodernism and Organization*, London: Sage.

Handy C. (1989) *The Age of Unreason*, London: Arrow.

Handy, C. (1994) *The Age of Paradox*, Cambridge, MA: Harvard Business School Press.

Harvey, D. (1989) The *Condition of Postmodernity: An Enquiry into the Origins of Cultural Change*, Cambridge MA: Blackwell.

Harrison, B. (1994) *Lean and Mean: Why Large Firms Will Continue to Dominate the Global Economy*, London: Guilford Press.

Hecksher, C. (1994) 'Defining the post-bureaucratic type', in C. Hecksher and A. Donnellon (eds), *The Post bureaucratic Organization: New Perspectives on Organizational Change*, London: Sage.

Hecksher, C. and Donnellon, A. (eds) (1994) *The Post-Bureaucratic Organization: New Perspectives on Organizational Change*, London: Sage.

Heydebrand, R. (1989) 'New Organizational Forms', *Work and Occupations* 16(3):323–357.

Hoque, K. and Kirkpatrick, I. (2003) 'Non-standard employment in the management and professional workforce: Training, consultation and gender implications', *Work Employment and Society* 17(4):667–689.

Hyman, R. (1991) 'The fetishism of flexibility', in B. Jessop, H. Kastandiek, K. Nielsen and O. Pederson (eds), *The Politics of Flexibility*, Cheltenham: Edward Elgar.

Jacques, E. (1989) *Requisite organization: The CEO's Guide to Creative Structure and Leadership*, Gower: Aldershot.

Jameson, F. (1992) *Postmodernism or the Cultural Logic of Late Capitalism*, Durban, North Carolina: Duke University Press.

Kalleberg, A. (2003) 'Flexible firms and labour market segmentation: Effects of workplace restructuring on jobs and workers', *Work and Occupations* 30(2):154–175.

Kanter, R.M. (1989) *When Giants Learn to Dance: Mastering the Challenges of Strategy, Management, and Careers in the 1990s*, New York: Simon & Schuster.

Kelloway, E.K. and Barling, J. (2000) 'Knowledge work as organizational behavior', *International Journal of Management Reviews* 2:287–304.

Kumar, K. (1995) *From Post-Industrial to Post-Modern Society*, Oxford: Blackwell.

Lash, S. and Bagguley, P. (1987) *Labour Flexibility and Disorganized Capitalism*, Lancaster, UK: Department of Sociology, University of Lancaster.

Legge, K. (1995) *Human Resource Management: Rhetorics and Realities*, London: Palgrave.

Mallon, M. and Duberley, J. (2000) 'Managers and professionals in the contingent workforce: A challenge for HRM', *Human Resource Management Journal* 10(1):33–47.

Masuda, Y. (1981) *The Information Society as Post-Industrial Society*, Bethesda, MD: World Futures Society.

Masuda, Y. (1985) *Computopia. The Information Technology Revolution*, Oxford: Basil Blackwell, pp. 620–634.

Meek, C. (2004) 'The dark side of Japanese management in the 1990s: Karoshi and ijime in the Japanese workplace', *Journal of Managerial Psychology* 19(3):312–325.

Mills, C.W. (1959) *The Sociological Imagination*, Harmondsworth: Penguin Books.

Mirvis, P.H. and Hall, D. (1994) 'Psychological success and the boundaryless career', *Journal of Organizational Behaviour* 15:365–380.

Murray, F. (1987) 'Flexible specialisation in the third Italy', *Capital and Class* 33:84–95.

Naisbitt, J. (1984) *Megatrends: Ten New Directions Transforming Our Lives*, New York: Warner Books.

Noon, M. and Blyton, P. (2002) *The Realities of Work*, Basingstoke: Palgrave.

Nohria, N. and Berkley, J. (1994) 'The virtual organization: Bureaucracy, technology and the implosion of control', in C. Hecksher and A. Donnellon (eds), *The Post-Bureaucratic Organization: New Perspectives on Organizational Change*, London: Sage.

Nowotny, H. (1982) *The Information Society: Its impact on the Home, Local Community and Marginal Groups. Information Society: For Richer for Poorer*, Bjorn-Anderson, Amsterdam: North-Holland Publishing, pp. 97–113.

Osterman, P. (2000) 'Work organization in an age of restructuring: Trends in diffusion effects on employee welfare', *Industrial and Labour Relations Review* 53:179–196.

Ouchi, W. (1981) *Theory Z: How American Business Can Meet the Japanese Challenge*, Reading, MA: Addison Wesley.

Parker, M. (1993) *Life after Jean-Francois? Postmodernism and Organizations*, J. Hassard and M. Parker (eds), London: Sage, pp. 204–212.

Peters, T. (1992) *Liberation Management*, New York: Pan.

Piore, M. and Sabel, C. (1984) *The Second Industrial Divide: Possibilities for Prosperity*, New York: Basic Books.

Pollert, A. (1988) 'Dismantling flexibility', *Capital and Class* 34:42–75.

Pollert, A. (1991) 'The orthodoxy of flexibility', in A. Pollert (ed.), *Farewell to Flexibility*, Oxford: Blackwell.

Quinn, J.B. (1992) *The Intelligent Enterprise*, New York: The Free Press.

Rosenberg, S. and Lapidus, J. (1999) 'Contingent and non-standard work in the United States: Towards a more poorly compensated, insecure workforce', in A. Felstead and N. Jewson (eds), *Global Trends in Flexible Labour: Critical Perspectives on Work and Organizations*, London: Macmillan.

Rosenberg, B. and White, D. (1957) *Mass Culture*, New York: The Free Press.

Rosenbrock, J. (1985) *A New Industrial Revolution? The Information Technology Revolution*, T. Forrester, Oxford: Basil Blackwell.

Sabel, C.F. (1982) *Work and Politics: The Division of Labor in Industry*, New York: Cambridge University Press.

Sabel, C.F. (1989) 'Flexible specialization and the re-emergence of regional economies', in P. Hirst and J. Zeitlin (eds), *Reversing Industrial Decline? Industrial Structure and Policy in Britain and Her Competitors*, Oxford: St. Martin's Press, pp. 17–69.

Sadler, P. (1988) *Managerial Leadership in the Post Industrial Society*, Aldershot: Gower.

Sennett, R. (1998) *The Corrosion of Character*, New York: Norton.

Smart, B. (1992) *Modern Conditions, Postmodern Controversies*, London: Routledge.

Taylor, W. (1995) 'At Verifone it's a dog's life (and they love it)'. Retrieved June 2006, from www.fastcompany.com/online/01/vfone.html.

Thompson, P. (2003) *Postmodernism-Fatal Distraction? Postmodernism and Organizations*, J. Hassard and M. Parker (eds), London: Sage, pp. 181–204.

Thompson, P. and McHugh, D. (1991) *Work Organizations a Critical Introduction*, London: Macmillan.

Toffler, A. (1971) *Future Shock*, London: Pan Books Ltd.

Toffler, A. (1984) *The Third Wave*, New York: Bantam.

Toffler, A. and Toffler, H. (1995) *Creating a New Civilization: The Politics of the Third Wave*, Atlanta: Turner.

Vaghefi, M.R. (2002) *Creating Sustainable Competitive Advantage: The Toyota Philosophy and Its Effects*, Retrieved June 2006, from www.ft.com, 5 September 2002.

Venturi R., Izenour, S. and Brown, D.S. (1972) *Learning from Las Vegas*, Cambridge, MA: The MIT Press.

Webster, F. (1995) *Theories of the Information Society*, London: Routledge.

Weick, K. and Berlinger, L. (1989) 'Career improvisations in self-designing organizations', in M. Arthur and B. Lawrence (eds), *Handbook of Career Theory*, New York: Cambridge University Press.

Welsch, W. (1988) *Unsere postmoderne Moderne*, Weinheim: VCH Verlagsgesellschaft (Original 1986).

White, M., Hill S., Mills, C. and Smeatan, D. (2004) *Managing to Change? British Workplaces and the Future of Work*, London: Palgrave.

Wood, S. (1989) *The Transformation of Work?*, London: Unwin Hyman.

# Chapter 6

# Postmodernism as a philosophy: the ultimate challenge to organization theory?

## Introduction

As we discussed in the previous chapter, since the early 1980s, 'postmodernism' has attracted considerable interest from academics in the social sciences. Despite this attention, the term *postmodernism* remains notoriously difficult to define. As Gellner (1992) argues, 'it is not altogether clear what the devil it is. In fact clarity is not conspicuous amongst its marked attributes'. Indeed, the philosopher and novelist Umberto Eco (1989), himself classified as a postmodern writer largely because of his novel *The Name of the Rose*, has written of postmodernism: 'I have the impression that it is applied today to anything the users of the term happen to like' (p. 65). Postmodernists are an eclectic group. Others have argued that there are probably as many forms of postmodernism as there are postmodernists (Featherstone, 1988, p. 207).

In the previous chapter, we focused on one interpretation of postmodernism – the notion that organizations now face a postmodern era of change and uncertainty. The authors we dealt with in Chapter 5 highlight changes in the environment and the search for new ways of organizing or new organizational forms. In this chapter, our focus moves to postmodern theory or philosophy. This provides us with a new theoretical position from which to try to make sense of the world around us. Some students find this a more difficult approach to get to grips with. To some extent, this is a result of the very complex language used by postmodernists. However, an added difficulty stems from the fact that postmodernism refers to a wide and diverse body of work in which postmodernists reject a single correct position in favour of a variety of perspectives that emphasize ambivalence and indeterminacy. Thus, diversity is valued – and this runs counter to any notion of unifying these different understandings into a single, all-encompassing explanation.

The aim of this chapter is to overcome some of that ambiguity and try to draw out the core strands of postmodernist theory as it applies to, and has been used in, organization studies.

## Learning outcomes

- Understand the main features of postmodern approaches to understanding.

- Evaluate the contributions of key thinkers in the area.

- Analyse the impact of postmodernist theory on organization theory and the study of organizational culture in recent years.

- Discuss the challenges that postmodernism holds for the future of organization theory.

## Structure of the chapter

- In order to explore postmodernism, the rest of the chapter is divided into four sections. The first traces the development of postmodernism, outlines its core elements and differentiates postmodernism from modernism. Section two outlines the work of the three key thinkers or the 'holy trinity' of postmodernism. Firstly, we look at Jacques Derrida and his work on the linguistic turn and deconstruction; then Jean Francois Lyotard and his rejection of metanarrative; and finally, Michel Foucault and his work on power, knowledge and discourse. We are examining each separately because, although they share some assumptions, the focus of their work is somewhat different. However, our aim in this chapter is not to provide a complete overview of their work but instead try to pick out the core elements that have been used in organization theory. In section three, we move on to look at one area where postmodernism has had a huge impact, organizational culture. This has already been considered in the previous chapters, and here we will show the different approach taken in a postmodern perspective on culture. Finally, in section four, we address the challenges that postmodernism poses for organization theory in the future.

## What is postmodernism?

Postmodern theory seems to have developed in continental Europe, particularly France and Germany. According to Hancock and Tyler (2001), the term *postmodernism* seems to have originated in the late nineteenth century when it was used to describe certain new avant-garde art forms. As discussed in the previous chapter, it became far more common during the 1960s and 1970s. Butler (2002) considers Carl Andre's rectangular pile of bricks, *Equivalent VIII* (1966), as a typically postmodern object. Because this lacks any features to sustain itself, it inspires us to ask questions about its context rather than its content; to ask, 'What is the point of this?' Thus, similar to Duchamp's fountain (see the example below), 'It tests our intellectual responses and our tolerance of the works the art gallery can bring to the attention of its public' (Butler, 2002, p. 3). In other words, it encourages us to question what art is.

### Example: Duchamp's fountain[1]

Marcel Duchamp's fountain pictured in Figure 6.1 caused quite a stir in the art world. It is an example of what Duchamp called a 'ready made.' The 'readymades' were Duchamp's attempt to make works of art that were not 'of art.' These are claimed to be experiments in provocation that attempt to break with artistic tradition and develop a new kind of art that provokes the observer to participate and think. The fountain was conceived of for a show promoting avante-garde art and was submitted using the pseudonym R. Mutt. It was a prank that was meant to taunt the show's avant-garde organizers. For some of them, the idea of equating art with a toilet fixture was too much, and the fountain was 'misplaced' for the duration of the exhibition. Later Duchamp defended the piece against complaints of plagiarism by replying that it did not matter if Mr Mutt made the urinal – he chose it, and by removing its usual significance, he created a new thought for the object!

More recently, Duchamp's fountain has come to be revered. It came top in a poll of 500 art critics in 2004. According to art expert Simon Wilson, it 'reflects the dynamic nature of art today and the idea that the creative process that goes into a work of art is the most important thing – the work itself can be made of anything and can take any form'. (*BBC News*, 12 January 2004.)

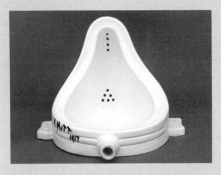

**Figure 6.1:** Duchamp's fountain.
(*Source:* © Tate, London, 2006.)

[1]Duchamp's fountain is often categorized as surrealist. The fact that it is now often discussed as postmodern is an interesting example of how postmodernism seems to pull in a wide variety of different approaches and perspectives.

Although we are used to seeing the term *postmodern* in relation to art and architecture, according to postmodern management academic Boje (1999), it has also been seen in the natural sciences from the 1960s onward. Best and Kellner (1997) provide a comprehensive overview of the interdisciplinary development of postmodern science, arguing that many of the developments are centred around chaos and complexity theory (see, for example, Cilliers, 1998). Thus, it could be argued that postmodernism is very much a philosophy of our age, drawing from and impacting on a wide variety of different areas.

In Chapter 2 on modernism, we discussed the enlightenment and the desire to progress through the development of theories that explain the world around us. A recurrent theme in postmodernism is a rejection of the modernist 'grand' or 'meta' narrative (see Parker, 1992) that it is possible to develop a rational and generalizable basis to scientific inquiry that explains the world from an objective standpoint. For instance, as we will discuss later, Lyotard (1984) defines the postmodern 'as an incredulity towards metanarratives' (p. xxiv), and American anthropologist David Harvey (1989, p. 10) suggests that it entails a rejection of overarching propositions that assume the validity of their own truth claims. In particular, Lyotard (1984), Bauman (1989) and Burrell (1997) attack the 'fallen' Enlightenment metanarrative of science as the source of human progress and emancipation through rational control located in reliable knowledge. For Lyotard, the promise of the Enlightenment to emancipate humanity from poverty and ignorance died in the Nazi concentration camps and the Stalinist gulags. Indeed, Bauman and Burrell both argue that, because the Nazis relied so heavily on modernist ideas such as rationality and bureaucracy (as discussed in Chapter 2), it is hard to see how these modernist ideals can guarantee modernism's promise of bringing the greater good. Accordingly, progress and emancipation are seen by postmodernists as self-legitimizing myths, as delusions based upon yet another metanarrative. It is worth noting, though, that this thesis has been questioned recently on a number of grounds, not least the specious equation of modernity with totalitarianism, and debate as to the extent to which the Nazi regime operated along completely bureaucratic lines (Rowlinson and Carter, 2002).

The rejection of metanarratives means that this chapter will not provide new models of organizational forms or theories of organization, like those we saw in previous chapters. Instead, postmodern philosophy concentrates much more on critiquing and deconstructing existing theories than constructing new ones. In some ways, then, postmodernism is defined as the direct opposite of modernism. However, the critique provided by postmodernists can be a somewhat caricatured account of modern cultural and theoretical practices. For example, Harvey objects to the assimilation of a wide variety of modern architectural forms to the debacle of housing projects such as Pruitt-Igoe (see the example below) and points out that the metanarratives decried by postmodernists were much more open, nuanced and sophisticated than critics admit (Harvey, 1989, p. 115).

## Example: Modernism and the Pruitt-Igoe housing development

The federally funded Pruitt-Igoe housing project in St. Louis was designed by St. Louis architects George Hellmuth and Minoru Yamasaki in 1951. It was thought to be the epitome of modernist architecture – high-rise, 'designed for interaction' and a solution to the problems of urban development and renewal in the middle of the 20th century. It was devised by experts and imposed upon society as a typical modernist glorification of privileged knowledge. Pruitt-Igoe opened in 1954 and was completed in 1956. It included 33, 11-storey buildings on a 35-acre site. It did not, however, prove successful, and soon residents were complaining of mice, cockroaches, broken lifts, high crime rates and so on.

*(Continued)*

## Example: (Continued)

In his 1970 book *Behind Ghetto Walls*, sociology professor Lee Rainwater condemned Pruitt-Igoe as a 'federally built and supported slum'. His study outlined the failure of the housing project, noting that its vacancies, crime, safety concerns and physical deterioration were unsurpassed by any other public housing complex in the nation.

The first of the Pruitt-Igoe buildings was demolished on 16 March 1972, at 3.22pm, a point in time that American architect Charles Jencks claims heralded the beginning of the postmodern era. The failure of Pruitt-Igoe represents to many the failure of modernist thinking and high-tech solutions to social problems (rational planning built on objectivist models of human behaviour).

**Figure 6.2:** Pruitt-Igoe and the end of modernity. (*Source:* © Bettmann/Corbis.)

## Postmodernism: the core elements

Although there is much ambiguity, four core propositions have been identified in postmodern theory (Hancock and Tyler, 2001). We have translated these into simple language below:

1. We cannot assume that there is such a thing as pure reason or that by gaining more knowledge the human race will necessarily progress.

2. The language we use actually shapes what we see and feel. It provides us with a framework through which we understand and make sense of the world.

3. There is no such thing as pure knowledge. What we see and what we know depend upon the context in which we operate and the language available to us.

4. We must recognize that there are many different views of any situation and that we should attempt to find out different perspectives, particularly those from less powerful people, who may not normally get the chance to put across their perspectives.

These propositions are of key importance to understanding postmodernism and as we will see in later sections, they permeate the work of various postmodern writers.

---

## Example: Organizations and Tamara

In Hollywood a play called *Tamara* puts the audience in a very different position than traditional theatre. In *Tamara*, Los Angeles' longest running play, a dozen characters unfold their stories before a walking sometimes running audience. *Tamara* enacts a true story taken from the diary of Aelis Mazoyer. It is Italy, 10 January 1927, in the era of Mussolini. Gabriele d'Annunzio, a poet, patriot, womanizer, and a revolutionary who is exceedingly popular with the people is under house arrest. Tamara, an expatriate Polish beauty, aristocrat and aspiring artist is summoned from Paris to paint d'Annunzio's portrait. Instead of remaining stationary, viewing a single stage, the audience fragments into small groups that chase characters from one room to the next, even going into bedrooms, kitchens and other chambers to chase and co-create the stories that interest them the most. If there are a dozen stages and a dozen storytellers, the number of storylines an audience could trace as it chases the wandering discourses of *Tamara* is 12 factorial (479,001,600)! No audience member gets to follow all the stories since the action is simultaneous, involving different characters in different rooms and on different floors. At the play each audience member receives a 'passport' to return again and again to try to figure out more of the many intertwined networks of stories. *Tamara* cannot be understood in one visit . . . two people can even be in the same room and – if they came there by way of different rooms and character sequences – each can walk away from the same conversation with entirely different stories.

*Source:* From Boje (1995).

Boje uses *Tamara* as a metaphor for organization, showing how the meaning of events depends upon the locality, the prior sequence of stories and the transformation of characters in the wandering discourse. So, for example, although managers may sit together at a meeting, their interpretations and perspectives may be very different as a result of their previous interactions and experiences. Each of us can gain only a partial, context-specific view of any particular situation.

---

Table 6.1 gives a broad-brush analysis of the core differences between modernism and postmodernism. It is fairly typical for the two to be represented in this way. However, to have such a table depends upon binary oppositions, which, as we will show later, is most definitely not in line with the postmodern approach. Therefore, the table (and others that follow using the device of binary opposition) should have a warning sign attached to it. By presenting modernism and postmodernism as binary oppositions, it is easy to make clear distinctions between the two (and postmodernists would argue, see one as privileged in relation to the other) when in reality, the picture is far more complex. It is perhaps better to think of each element as a continuum and to recognize that a particular author or piece of research may sit at different points on each element of the continuum, in some ways more modernist and in others more postmodernist.

**Table 6.1** Modernism versus postmodernism

| Modernity | Postmodernity |
| --- | --- |
| Consensus | Dissensus |
| Universality | Multiplicity |
| Generalizability | Localization and contextualization |
| Totalizing | Diversity |
| Stability | Impermanence |
| Suppression of difference | Pursuit of difference |
| Macropolitics | Micropolitics |
| Centering | Marginality |
| Continuities | Discontinuities |

*Source:* Adapted from English (1998, p. 433), originally published in Best and Kellner (1997).

## Postmodernism and organization theory

As discussed in the introduction to this book, organization theory is a relatively young and fast-developing field. Postmodernism increasingly attracted the interest of organizational theorists from the late 1980s with the publication of a series of articles in the journal *Organization Studies* by UK academics Robert Cooper and Gibson Burrell (Burrell, 1988; Cooper, 1989; Cooper and Burrell, 1988). This developed out of an increased disillusionment in certain quarters with positivist approaches toward studying organizations and the functionalist assumptions upon which much organization theory was based. Thus, the 1970s and 1980s saw the development of interpretive and social constructivist approaches toward understanding organizations (see Chapter 4). Hancock and Tyler (2001) also point to the increasing radicalization of organization theory through the work of writers such as Burrell (1980) and Clegg and Dunkerley (1980), who highlighted the importance of considering power when analysing organizations.

This background meant that organization studies was fertile ground for the development of a new approach, and although some have suggested that academics may have been jumping on a bandwagon to further their careers (Alvesson, 1995) and others question the true level of diversity of the field (Reed, 1996), most would agree that postmodernism has posed significant challenges for organization theory.

Although there is a great deal of disagreement between various postmodern writers, they have been organized by some commentators into two groups, variously called either hard or soft (Watson, 1993, cited in Parker, 1995) or sceptical and affirmative (Rosenau, 1992). According to American theorist Rosenau, the sceptical postmodernists offer a powerful critique of modernism. They present a pessimistic view, arguing that the postmodern age is one of fragmentation, disintegration, malaise and meaninglessness (see Table 6.2 for an illustration). Sceptics are antirepresentational; they argue that the language we use constitutes reality rather than representing it. So, language is not neutral; rather, the words we have available to

**Table 6.2** Affirmative versus sceptical postmodernism

| | Affirmative | Sceptical |
|---|---|---|
| **Differences** | | |
| View of social science | Approach toward social science is descriptive not prescriptive. Research from this perspective concentrates on unusual aspects of organization and is underpinned by novelty and reflexivity; researchers are encouraged to consider their influence upon the research process. | Argues that the universe is impossible to understand, so attempts to build a postmodern social science are futile. There is no hope of developing a universalistic organization theory. The world is seen as fragmented and disrupted |
| Role of author | Reduces the power of the author, without completely undermining him or her. The author continues to have a small role as interpreter. The author should attempt to reflect on his or her role in the construction of the text. | Author has little clout and no authority. Readers will have different interpretations of what is written, and these are as valid as the author's interpretation. Consciously strives to cultivate an 'indefinite unsettled text' – there is ambiguity concerning the meaning of the text. |
| Method or epistemology | Criticizes and seeks to revise modernist epistemology and methodology. Rejects absolute relativism; focuses on the margins and the excluded within organizations and society. | Antirepresentational. Impossible to map social world. At the most extreme form of this perspective, ethnography, anthropology and sociology are merely literary endeavours – they cannot generate theory and should be judged on their literary appeal. Renounces efforts to construct new knowledge; focuses instead on deconstruction and critique. |

**Similarities**

**Role of reader**

Postmodern texts are more open and less definitive. Readers would be expected to sort out the meaning of texts for themselves and to accept that whatever conclusions they reach may be of little value to anyone else. There is a recognition that meaning is context specific.

**Political orientation**

Internally heterogeneous and diverse, postmodern writings do not prescribe particular political views. Inherently they are neither left nor right wing

*Source*: Adapted from Rosenau (1992).

use shape the way we interpret things. In other words, as we will discuss later, language is all we have – there is not a separate reality that exists outside the language we use to describe it.

Affirmatives, on the other hand, although agreeing with the sceptic's critique of modernity, offer a more hopeful, optimistic view of the postmodern age. These theorists are in many ways similar to critical theorists. Rosenau (1992) suggests that writers from this perspective are either open to positive political action or content with the recognition of 'visionary, celebratory, personal non-dogmatic projects' (p. 16). There is much more optimism and a concern to change the status quo than is seen from the sceptical standpoint. That said, these two groupings are by no means mutually exclusive, and there is a great deal of interchange between them. Based upon the work of Rosenau, Table 6.2 highlights the key differences and some similarities between them.

Readers should recognize, however, that not all postmodernists will agree on these core themes. Some may take more extreme positions that others – that is the beauty (and the bane!) of postmodernism – it is a mixed group with lots of different contributors, taking alternative perspectives. But then, as we discovered in Chapter 2, the same could be said to some extent for modernism. Fundamental to postmodern research, though, is the desire to challenge the content and form of dominant models of knowledge and also to produce new forms of knowledge through breaking down disciplinary boundaries and giving voice to those not represented in the dominant discourses (Giroux, 1992, p. 56): in other words, focusing studies on areas of organizations that have not traditionally been examined or those who may be marginalized. This will be explored more in the sections that follow. First, though, because there is a good deal of overlap and confusion between the two, we need to deal with the thorny issue of the relationship between postmodernism and poststructuralism.

## Poststructuralism and postmodernism

In Chapter 5, we considered the various 'post-'s available. It is particularly important here to consider the distinction between postmodernism and poststructuralism; this is not easy. The relationship between postmodernism and poststructuralist philosophy has been expressed in a number of different ways (see, for example, Bauman, 1992; Calas and Smircich, 1999). Hatch (1997) sees postmodernism evolving out of the poststructuralist movement of the 1960s. There are certainly many linkages.

Central to poststructuralism is a focus on language. Poststructuralism considers the social world to be the outcome and the product of language. In other words, from a poststructuralist perspective, the distinctions we make are not necessarily real but are produced by the language we use. This, according to Hancock and Tyler (2001), means that poststructuralism provides a philosophical basis to challenge the absolute claims to knowledge that, as discussed in Chapter 2, provide the basis for the modernist worldview. Thus, the relationship between postmodernism and poststructuralism is a complex and intimate one; some authors are defined as both postmodern and poststructuralist, and others as one but not the other. Parker (1995), for example, distinguishes between self-avowed postmodernists such as Lyotard and Baudrillard and poststructuralist writers such as Derrida and Foucault. He argues that postmodernists have a tendency to appropriate other thinkers who might be better understood and used in other ways. He argues that the conflation of poststructuralism and postmodernism is one example of this and one that tends to conceal the sophisticated defence of critical affirmation contained within Derrida's writing in particular (p. 555). Other organization theorists, though, such as Hassard (1996) and Boje et al. (1996), stress the importance of both Foucault and Derrida to the development of postmodernism. Thus, we are left in an intriguing position where it is hard to clearly delineate poststructuralism and postmodernism. What we can be certain of, though, is that whatever their differences, a focus on language, subjectivity and knowledge is central to both approaches.

### The chapter so far

In this first section, you have been introduced to the fundamental principles of postmodernism. You should also be aware of the two different approaches to postmodernism: sceptical and affirmative. One of the core issues we have outlined is the sheer diversity of the field and the different labels attached to various authors. We will now explore that further by looking at three important theorists.

## Three key thinkers of postmodernism

### Jacques Derrida: the linguistic turn and deconstruction

Deconstruction lies at the heart of a postmodern approach toward organizational analysis. Similar to many other aspects of postmodernism, defining deconstruction is no easy task. Hundreds of pages are devoted to the issue of what deconstruction is and how it is done. The first author to use the term was Derrida, although it has since been explored by a number of others, including Culler (1990), Johnson (1981) and Hillis-Miller (2002). In this chapter, we concentrate on the work of Derrida because it is with him that deconstruction is most associated. Central to Derrida's work is the view that meaning includes identity (what something is) and difference (what something is not). He combines two senses of the term difference – to differ in space and to defer in time – to produce what he calls *difference*, that the meaning of

### Biography    Jacques Derrida 1930–2004

Born and brought up in Algeria, Derrida moved to Paris at the age of 19 to complete his education. He was a controversial figure – to his supporters, he was the embodiment of the rebel philosopher, attacking the traditional approaches to literature and philosophy. Detractors, on the other hand, saw his work as frivolous and obscure. For example, in 1992 staff at Cambridge University protested against plans to award him an honorary degree.

Derrida taught at a number of very prestigious schools, including the Sorbonne, the Ecole Normale Superieure and the Ecole des Haute Etudes. He was also professor of philosophy and comparative literature at the University of California, Irvine. His first book published in 1962 was on Husserl's geometry (1989), but *Of Grammatology, Speech and Phenomena* (1967a) and *Writing and Difference* (1967b) were published in Paris. Since then, he wrote extensively on language, art, ethics and politics. The work that first made Derrida's international reputation was *Of Grammatology*. Although the topic, writing, seemed uncontroversial, it delivered a challenge to the tradition of Western philosophy. He also campaigned for the rights of immigrants in France, against apartheid in South Africa and in support of dissidents in communist Czechoslovakia.

a word 'is derived from a process of deferral to other words . . . that differ from itself' (Gergen, 1992, p. 219). If the meaning of one word can only be attained by looking at its relationship to others (e.g., in a dictionary), then the accomplishment of meaning is continually deferred as each consultation of the dictionary merely leads to further words, which in turn have to be looked up (see the Ideas and perspectives box below). According to Derrida, such unending deferral means that communication is *polysemous* and the meaning of words cannot be pinned down. Thus, there are always deferred and marginalized meanings within any communication that can be revealed in a text by a reader. Martin (1992) argues that *difference* is a useful way of thinking about organizations because it reveals perspectives that would otherwise be excluded. *Difference* implies that something is understood in a certain way because of what it (apparently) is not. We get a better picture of what is there by thinking about what is absent.

The postmodernists' acknowledgement of the power of language to shape what we see (sometimes called the *linguistic turn*) means that what we take to be knowledge is constructed in and through language. Knowledge has no secure vantage point outside such sociolinguistic processes. Hence, what Italian philosopher and politician Gianni Vattimo calls the 'myth of transparency' (1992, p. 18), of unmediated access to reality, is an illusion. Rather, language and the social negotiation of meaning need to be illuminated to show how they influence our perceptions. We will return to the issue of knowledge in the next section.

For postmodernists, 'reality' can have an infinite number of attributes because there are as many realities as there are ways of perceiving and explaining. A traditional view is that language is capable of expressing ideas without changing them, that in the hierarchy of language, writing is secondary to speech and that the author

---

## Ideas and perspectives

## Polysemous or multiple meaning

Kenneth Gergen, a writer on social constructionism (1992, p. 219) provides the following example of corporate rationality whose meaning at first sight seems self-evident but whose polysemous aspects means that it could mean virtually anything.

'Let's be logical about this; the bottom line would be the closing of the Portsmouth division' does not carry with it a transparent meaning. Rather, its meaning depends on what we make of words like 'logical', 'bottom line' 'closing' and the like. These meanings require that we defer to still other words. What does the speaker mean by the term 'logical' for example? To answer we must defer to other words like 'rational' 'systematic' or 'coherent'. . . at the outset it is clear that that there are many meanings for such terms . . . they have been used in many contexts and thus bear 'the trace' (in Derrida's terms) of many terms. For example 'logical' can also mean 'right thinking', 'conventional' or 'superior'. Which does the speaker really intend? . . . each term employed for clarifying the initial statement is itself opaque until the process of *differance* is again set in motion. 'Right thinking' can also mean 'morally' correct, 'conventional' can also mean 'banal', and so on. And in turn these terms bear the traces of numerous others in an ever-expanding network of significations (cited in Johnson and Duberley, 2000, p. 97).

of a text is its source of meaning. Derrida challenges these assumptions and disputes the idea that a text has an unchanging, unified meaning. For instance, Derrida critiques what he calls logocentricism by arguing that for every 'fixed' idea, there is also an 'absent' idea. In other words, how we make sense of the world inevitably entails partiality because by interpreting experience in a particular way, we inadvertently exclude alternative renditions. Here he is pointing to how a 'logos' legitimates and stabilizes particular ways of viewing things and modes of engagement while excluding other possibilities. Unity and consistency are maintained at the expense of separation and contradiction.

Deconstruction is concerned with breaking down such unity. It involves:

> Demystifying a text, tearing it apart to reveal its internal, arbitrary hierarchies and its presuppositions. . . . A deconstructive reading of a text seeks to discover its ambivalence, blindness and logocentricity (Rosenau, 1992, p. 120).

As the term implies, deconstruction is the dismantling of constructions – or more precisely, linguistic constructions. It derives from literary criticism in which texts are analysed to reveal their inherent contradictions, assumptions and different layers of meaning. All texts therefore contain elements that counter their author's assertions. For deconstructionists, any body of knowledge can be treated as a text that can be deconstructed. Here deconstruction attempts to demonstrate how any claim to truth – for instance, whether made by scientists or theologians – is always the product of social construction and therefore relative.

Often this involves identifying the assumptions that underpin and thereby produce the truth claim. These assumptions are then challenged through their denial and the identification of the 'absent' alternatives whose articulation produces an alternative rendition, or re-reading, of reality. Hence, deconstruction denies that any text is ever settled or stable: it can always be questioned as layers of meaning are removed to reveal other meanings or interpretations that have been suppressed. It leads to questions about *how* something becomes seen as factual and about the consequences of such privileging. The result is a relativistic position because deconstruction does not get the deconstructor closer to a 'fixed', or privileged, truth. As Vattimo (1988) argues, deconstruction is not designed merely to unmask error as that assumes that truth exists. At most, it offers alternative social constructions of reality within a text, which are themselves then available to deconstruction and thereby are not allowed to rest in any finalized truth. Thus, 'deconstruction deconstructs itself, and at the same time creates another labyrinthine fiction whose authority is undermined by its own creation' (Hillis-Miller, 1981, p. 261). Deconstructors do not wish to override one interpretation because another one is better or correct. On the contrary, they seek to show how a multitude of different interpretations can be supported by the same text.

## The process of deconstruction

Derrida does not provide clear guidelines as to how deconstruction should be undertaken. Different authors suggest alternative approaches to the process. For example, Cooper (1989) suggests that when undertaking deconstruction, the search is for gaps and instabilities in time, space and text. Typically, this follows two movements called *overturning* and *metaphorization*. Cooper argues that because of the Western way of thinking texts are structured around binary opposites in which one term dominates the other. Overturning involves examining a text for binary oppositions and challenging these. So, looking at a text, a deconstructionist would examine where binary oppositions (e.g., good/bad, strong/weak, black/white, male/female) are either explicitly or implicitly being used and would consider whether one is being privileged over the other. But Cooper points out that Derrida is careful to emphasize the potential pitfall of overturning the higher term and simply replacing it with the lower term, which then becomes the higher term. He argues it is necessary to engage in a process of metaphorization, the second stage of deconstruction. This involves recognizing that any positively valued term (e.g., *civilization* or *normal*) is defined only by contrast to a negatively valued second term (e.g., *barbarism* or *abnormal*). The relationship is one of mutual definition in which the individual terms actually inhabit each other; therefore, undecidability underlies this second movement of metaphorization. Deconstructors must embrace this indeterminacy and give up any attempt to gain an understanding of the 'true' meaning of the text.

An alternative approach comes from Boje and Dennehy (1994), who provides a seven-step process through which to undertake deconstruction. They argue that a text must be interrogated with the following questions:

1. **Define the dualities:** Who or what are at opposite ends in the story? This could involve making a list of any bipolar terms that are used in the story, even if only one side is mentioned. For example, in male-dominated organization stories, men are central, and women may be unmentioned.

2. **Reinterpret:** What is the alternative interpretation of the story? Any story is one interpretation from a particular point of view. It usually has some form of hierarchical thinking in place; see if you can reinterpret this.

3. **Rebel voices:** Deny the authority of the one voice. Who is not being represented or is underrepresented? What voices are subordinate or hierarchical to other voices? For example, in descriptions of organizations, support workers are often ignored.

4. **Other side of the story:** What is the silent or underrepresented story? Reverse the story by putting the bottom on top, the marginal in control or the back stage up front. For example, reverse the male centre by holding a spotlight on its excesses until it becomes a female centre. In telling the other side, the point is not to replace one centre with another but to show how each centre is in a constant state of change and disintegration.

5. **Deny the plot:** What is the plot? Turn it around.

6. **Find the exception:** What is the exception that breaks the rule? State the rule of the story in a way that makes it seem extreme or absurd.

7. **What is between the lines:** What is not said? What is the writing on the wall?

8. **Resituate:** The point of doing 1 to 7 is to find a new perspective, one that resituates the story beyond its dualisms, excluded voices or single viewpoint. The idea is to reauthor the story so that a new balance of views is attained (Boje and Dennehy, 1994, p. 340).

**Binary oppositions in practice: it's good to talk**

As discussed, one typical procedure of deconstruction is its critique of dualisms or binary oppositions because it is argued that in all classic dualities of Western thought, one term is privileged over the other, with the second term seen as secondary, derivative or even parasitic. For example:

- speech over writing
- presence over absence
- unity over difference
- fullness over emptiness
- meaning over meaninglessness
- life over death.

In a paper presented to the Market Research Society's annual conference, Monty Alexander (1995) co-founder with Virginia Valentine of the innovative marketing agency Semiotic Solutions, discusses his firm's use of binary opposites in their work on British Telecom's (BT) 'It's Good to Talk' Campaign. Central to their analysis was a distinction between *big talk* and *small talk*.

| Big talk | Small talk |
|---|---|
| Important | Unimportant |
| Male | Female |
| Serious | Trivial |
| Official, proper | Unofficial, improper |

In helping BT to define its strategy, Alexander and Valentine sought to challenge these values: 'In order to justify and legitimize female usage of the phone and to encourage greater usage by men – a campaign was needed which raised the status of small talk, by emphasizing the emotional, rather than the rational benefits of communication' (Alexander, Burt and Collinson, 1995, p. 279).

*Source:* Taken from Tietze et al., 2003, p. 24.

**Stop and think**

Think of an organization that you know well:

- Can you identify any binary oppositions that are used to describe workers?
- What assumptions underpin these oppositions?

## The use of deconstruction in organization theory

Deconstruction has become an increasingly popular method for analysing organizations and organizational texts. As early as 1984, Frug offered a deconstruction of bureaucracy, showing that the conceptions of bureaucracy used by organization theorists are structured around the binary oppositions of subjectivity/objectivity. More recently, examples of this method include the work of Kilduff (1993), who deconstructs March and Simon's (1958) classic organizational text to identify the gaps and silences, showing the Tayloristic assumptions underpinning the text. Kilduff argues that although the explicit text of the book *Organizations* appears to offer a stark contrast between a model of employee as machine and a model of employee as decision maker, the subtext undermines this dichotomy. Kilduff deconstructs the text to show that the machine analogy has been updated from a labouring machine to a computing machine. Both types of machine can be programmed to perform precise iterations, and both are readily replaceable by actual machinery. Similarly, Carter and Jackson (1993) deconstruct motivation theory, particularly expectancy theory. They make the point that they are not interested in discovering whether the theory is 'true'; instead, they seek to highlight its internal contradictions and underlying assumptions.

One of the most famous examples of deconstruction in organization studies was undertaken by Joanne Martin (1990). She deconstructed a speech from the CEO of a company she was researching. An extract of the speech is given below.

> We have a young woman who is extraordinarily important to the launching of a major new [product]. We will be talking about it next Tuesday in its first world-wide introduction. She has arranged to have her caesarean [operation] yesterday in order to be prepared for this event (p. 139).

Martin provides a deconstruction of this showing the inconsistency of the president's claims to helping women and the fact that this woman is praised for altering the timing of the birth of her child. She goes deeper, though, focusing on multiple interpretations of the story's language, including what is not said. Martin's deconstruction focuses on the connotations of the metaphors and puns, revealing unstated assumptions and sexual taboos implicit in the story's language. For example, Martin shows how the first phrase in the story, 'We have a young woman,' implies a very high degree of corporate control; it could have been said as, 'We employ a young woman.' Martin argues that the phrase 'having a young woman' is also a sexual pun that has male heterosexual connotations that are repeated in other puns throughout the story. Martin develops her analysis by exploring the hidden assumptions held in the text by making two small changes – the central character is changed from a woman having a caesarean to a man having a heart bypass operation. She argues that this small change has a huge impact – the structure of the story, its metaphor and the puns no longer made sense – thus, she reveals the hidden workings of gender-based ideology (Martin, 1992).

## Case study | Deconstructing Disney

A typical postmodern work also comes from Boje (1995), who has done a great deal of work deconstructing Disney as a storytelling organization. Here he gives one example of stories we are told. In early versions of the official story, Walt came up with the idea and drew Mickey Mouse on the way back from New York on a train, and his wife Lillian is said to have suggested the name Mickey (in preference to Mortimer). In 1948, Walt recalled how Mickey Mouse 'popped out of his mind onto a drawing pad' (Hollis and Sibley, 1988, p. 15, quoted in Boje, 1995). Boje discusses how Walt mythologized Mickey in the official version of the Disney history, which featured himself as a struggling artist who befriended a family of mice. One of the mice (Mickey) became so tame that it would climb up onto Walt's drawing board to be fed scraps of food. In the official Disney story, Ub Iwerks and Roy Disney are marginal characters, as are cartoonists such as Kinney; scriptwriters such as Charles Shows; and story creators such as Babbitt, Sorrell and Hilberman. However, other accounts suggest it was Ub Iwerks who did the early artwork, created Mickey and perhaps even created the famous Disney signature. The point here is not that the Disney version is untrue but that it marginalizes and eliminates many characters with stories worth telling (Boje, 1995).

## Problems with deconstruction

Although increasing in popularity, deconstruction is not without its critics. One issue is that Derrida gives little instruction about how to do deconstruction. He does not want it reduced to a simple set of techniques. This is perhaps understandable but it leaves the process shrouded in mystery. Another concern is that postmodernists may accord themselves some sort of privileged position, implicitly assuming that they are somehow able to stand outside the discursive knowledge – power relations that embed everyone else (Johnson and Duberley, 2000). Thus, they are able to deconstruct texts to show their true meaning. This criticism may be unfair, though, because most deconstructionists would argue that they only seek to put forward alternative interpretations and would never seek to find the 'true' meaning of a text because this is not possible. Others critique deconstruction as a way of developing the field of organization studies because of its essentially negative perspective. For example, Alvesson (1995, p. 1055) comments that although deconstruction is 'philosophically waterproof', if all organization theorists adopted it they would work within a very restricted space: if all people became converts then everyone would be involved in the deconstruction of others' deconstructions . . . it starts and ends with 'writers write about writers for other writers' (Castoriadis, 1992, p. 16). Derrida's work has also been criticized by writers such as Butler (2002, p. 8) for his seeming ignorance of other philosophers in his earlier works.

The 'theory' of deconstruction has also been revealed to have within it a number of contradictory elements (Clegg and Hardy, 1996). Firstly, deconstructionists argue against theory building, yet they advance a theoretical position. Secondly, deconstructionists seek to deconstruct the tools of logic, reason and rationality, yet they seek to do so with these very tools. Finally, deconstructionists argue against privileging any position, yet if their theory (that holds no theory can be true for everyone) holds for everyone, even for the person who mistakenly believes deconstruction false, then the theory does what it says cannot be done – it privileges itself as a universal theory. It establishes some basis for truth that transcends its own confines.

Finally, although Boje (2002) suggests that the new postmodern science would recombine science and ethics, Feldman (1998) claims deconstruction poses serious difficulties for the discipline of organization theory because its calls for an 'opening of cultural and linguistic forms will destabilize already unstable ethical structures' (p. 60). Thus, there is a concern that the implicit relativism of postmodernism is dangerous in terms of ethics. We will return to the issue of relativism at the end of the chapter because this is a hotly debated issue. Now we turn to an area of postmodernism closely related to deconstruction. This is the idea, linked to Lyotard, that the very nature of knowledge has changed in the postmodern age.

## J.F. Lyotard and the nature of knowledge

In organization theory, Lyotard's most often cited work, *The Postmodern Condition: A Report on Knowledge* (1984) is often said to represent the beginning of postmodern thought in the social sciences. Originally written for the Quebec government, it examines knowledge, science and technology in advanced capitalist societies such as the United Kingdom, France and the United States. Lyotard argues that as societies enter the post-industrial phase, the condition, character and status of knowledge are altered. Lyotard traces the changing condition of knowledge from the premodern to the postmodern condition, represented in Table 6.3.

As mentioned earlier, Lyotard famously defines postmodernism as an incredulity toward metanarratives, which he defines as totalizing stories about history and the goals of the human race that ground and legitimate particular forms of knowledge and cultural practices. A metanarrative can include any grand, encompassing story or framework. Examples of metanarratives include:

- Many Christians believe human existence is inherently sinful although capable of redemption and eternal peace in heaven.

- The enlightenment theorists believed that rational thought, allied to scientific reasoning, would lead inevitably toward moral, social and ethical progress.

**Table 6.3** The changing condition of knowledge

| Premodern | Modern | Postmodern |
|---|---|---|
| Knowledge is largely narrative, storylike. Narratives such as religion and myth constituted knowledge by virtue of their function in transmitting sets of rules that constitute the social bond. Narratives legitimate themselves through the function of social unity. | Scientific knowledge is based on verification, falsification and proof. The criterion of legitimation is truth – in other words, does the theory correspond with the facts of reality? | Incredulity toward metanarratives. The new basis of knowledge is the optimization of input to output. A shift of emphasis from the ends of action to their means. Knowledge is not valued depending upon whether it is true or not but by its exchange value. Knowledge is a commodity to be sold. The criterion of legitimation is efficiency. |

*Source:* Based on Lyotard (1984).

- Marxists believe that human existence is alienated from its species being, although capable of realizing its full potential through collective democratic organization (http://en.wikipedia.org/wiki/metanarrative).

The two metanarratives which Lyotard sees as central to modernism are:

1. The idea that history progresses toward social enlightenment and emancipation.
2. Knowledge progressing toward totalization (Lyotard, 1984).

This incredulity toward metanarratives is combined in Lyotard's work with a recognition of the contingency of all claims as to what constitutes knowledge. Thus, it is argued, we need to 'search for new modes of representing knowledge in a world devoid of any firm ontological, epistemological or ethical foundations' (Hancock and Tyler, 2001, p. 20). Concomitant with the demise of the grand metanarrative, Lyotard suggests a return to the 'petit recits' or 'little narrative' of the everyday. Thus, research in organization studies would focus on the stories of organizational lives in terms that emphasize the contextual nature of their character, with no intent to develop overarching theories or explanations.

---

**Stop and think**    Organizational stories

In their book *Experiencing Organizations*, Fineman and Gabriel (1996) provide stories or 'petits recits' from a variety of students on placement in organizations. These stories cover things such as how they were inducted into the organizations, their experiences of conflict and disillusionment and how they became aware of the prevalence of power and politics in organizations.

- What kinds of 'stories' would you tell a researcher if they asked you about your organizational life at the moment?
- To what extent would these be generalizable?
- How would these differ from the stories you may have told last week or last year?

---

According to Lyotard, modernism is being called into question by the new technologies of the current era. For example, he highlights the ways new methods of data collection, storage and distribution are possible with new computer packages and databases. He believes these changes are bringing about a revolution in the same way that earlier changes in technology brought about the Industrial Revolution. He further claims that post-industrial capitalism has shifted social values away from truth and justice toward efficiency. Lyotard argues that this shift implies a transition from a concern with what is true to a concern for the usefulness or market value of knowledge – its *performativity*. Hatch (1997) argues that the rhetoric of organizational efficiency that is so often discussed in practitioner and academic circles is a result of the redefinition of knowledge. Thus, what we consider to be knowledge within and about organizations has changed and reflects new technologies that enable us to collect and hold different sorts of information.

Lyotard has much in common with other postmodern writers in that he calls into question the individual's capacity to reason and asserts the importance of non-rational forces such as emotion on decision making. In his later work (Lyotard, 1988), he is concerned with the problem of legitimation and how narratives justify or legitimate themselves in order to take on the status of something more than mere stories (Jones, 2003). Using Wittgenstein's idea of language games, he attempts to show that reason and representation cannot explain everything. Thus, the postmodern world is composed of many fragmented language games that control the moves that can be made within them by reference to narratives of legitimation that are deemed appropriate by their respective institutions. An example of what happens if an individual ignores these legitimation narratives is given in the example below, which examines the Velikovsky controversy.

## Example: The scientific metanarrative

An interesting example from Burrell (1997) shows how science, as metanarrative, blocks out other stories and prevents other voices from being heard. He tells the tale of the Velikovsky controversy in the 1960s. In 1958, Velikovsky, a Russian born psychiatrist, wrote a book called *Worlds in Collision*, which asserted that around 3,500 years ago, the planet Venus was somehow ejected from the planet Jupiter as a comet. Comet Venus then started moving around the solar system, and as it did so, its gravitational field pushed other planets out of their orbits or changed their rotation. Velikovsky attributed many of the disasters recorded in ancient times to the strange interaction between Earth and Venus. His evidence and theory were drawn from a close reading of ancient Hindu, Jewish and Biblical material, which saw the solar system to have been profoundly disturbed around 4000 BC by a cataclysmic event. Providing the evidence consonant with entry of a new planet into the solar system at this time, Velikovsky maintained that Venus was this new planet and would exhibit surface features very unlike the ones predicted by those followers of the stable planetary view.

Velikovsky's theories did not fit in with modern astrophysics, and he was criticized by most scientists. He was dismissed as a crackpot, and some attempted to silence him by putting pressure on the publishers not to publish *Worlds in Collision*. However, Velikovsky made a much better job of predicting certain aspects of the planet Venus, such as its surface temperature, than specialists in NASA or leading universities. According to Burrell, the disciplinary power of scientific disciplines is tremendous, and this example is just one of many (1997, pp. 190–191). But it highlights that the primacy of a particular form of (scientific) knowledge is not necessary in the interests of anyone other than those with access to that knowledge.

In his later work, such as *The Differend: Phrases in Dispute*, Lyotard (1988) develops the philosophy of language that underpins his ideas about postmodernism. He examines how injustices can take place in the context of language. A differend is a case of conflict between parties that cannot be equitably resolved for lack of a rule of judgement applicable to both – in other words, the parties cannot agree on some criterion or rule that can be used to judge their dispute. A victim of the differend is someone who has lost the power to present a wrong – he or she may be prevented from speaking by force. Alternatively, this person may be able to speak but in that speech be unable to present the wrong done in the discourse of the rule of judgement (Woodward, 2002). Lyotard uses the example of revisionist historian Faurisson and his demand for proof that the Holocaust actually happened. Faurisson will only accept proof of the acceptance of the gas chambers from witnesses who were themselves victims of the gas chambers. Of course, there are no such witnesses because those that were present in the gas chambers died. This is an example of how the differend produces a 'catch 22' because there are two alternatives: either there were gas chambers (in which the victims of them died) or there were not, which leads to the same conclusion: there were no gas chambers. The case is a differend because the harm done to the victim cannot be presented in the standard of judgement upheld by Faurisson. In the organization studies arena, writers such as Jackson and Carter (1998) have used Lyotard's notion of the differend to shed light on the language games, linguistic closures and silencing that accompany the language of management gurus.

Although often cited, the work of Lyotard has been less directly influential in organization theory than that of Derrida or Foucault (Casey, 2002). In particular, Jones (2003) bemoans the lack of attention in organization studies to Lyotard's concern with ethics, justice and politics. He argues that rather than pigeonhole Lyotard as a postmodernist, attention should be shown to the continuity between Lyotard and a Weberian or Frankfurt version of concern with instrumental rationality, which we discussed in Chapter 2.

Fundamentally, Lyotard questions whether we can have overarching theories of organization. In particular, his work draws attention to the relationship between language and knowledge and the impact of new technologies upon what we consider to be knowledge. The relationship between language, knowledge and power is explored further by Michel Foucault, probably the most cited of the postmodern theorists, who we turn to next.

## Foucault: postmodernism, discourse, knowledge and power

Although classified by some as a poststructuralist and not a postmodernist, Foucault is included here because he is often referred to in texts on postmodernism in organization studies, and his ideas are often appropriated by writers from that perspective. Foucault's ideas developed out of Marxist and linguistic structuralism and were

| Biography | Michel Foucault, 1926–1984 |
| --- | --- |

French philosopher, psychologist, social critic. Born in 1926 in Poitiers, his father was a surgeon who wanted him to follow in his footsteps. In 1960, he published his first landmark work, *Madness and Civilization*, in which he argued that madness as we know it is an invention of the Age of Reason. Starting in 1970, he was a professor of history of systems of thought at the College de France. Foucault's major works include *The Order of Things* (1966), *The History of Sexuality* (1976–1984), and *Discipline and Punish: The Birth of the Prison* (1975). Broadly speaking, his work can be divided into two phases. The first phase, often described as his archaeological work, addresses the ways discourses establish rules for constituting areas of knowledge. The second phase is described as genealogical (Fairclough, 1992). In this phase, he was interested in the relationships between power, knowledge and language.

applied to a wide variety of topics, including madness, medicine, punishment and sexuality. A central theme of his work was the power relations involved in the control of what constitutes reason, knowledge and truth. Foucault's ideas developed and changed over the course of his writing, which sometimes makes him hard to characterize. As he argues:

> I never think quite the same thing as my books are experiences. . . . An experience is something that one comes out of to be transformed. . . . Each book transforms what I was thinking when I finished the previous book. I am an experimenter not a theorist (Foucault, 2000, pp. 239–240).

But when pressed to explain his wide ranging interests, he commented:

> What I have studied are the three traditional problems: (1) What are the relations we have to truth through scientific knowledge, to those 'truth games' which are so important in civilization and in which we are both subject and objects? (2) What are the relationships we have to others through those strange strategies and power relationships? And (3) what are the relationships between truth, power, and self? I would like to finish with a question: What could be more classic than these questions and more systematic than the evolution through questions one, two, and three and back to the first? I am just at this point (Foucault, 1988, p. 15).

Through his various writings, Foucault exposes the fact that all disciplines, whether they are scientific, legal, political, or social, operate through a network of self-legitimizing power and knowledge. Power and knowledge are interlinked. He further maintains that power/knowledge functions in a way that makes its version of truth obvious to its participants. He critiques the project of the modern human sciences by showing that their claims to objectivity are impossible in a domain in which truth itself is always a discursive construct. Any given historical period shares unconscious formations that define the right way to reason for the truth. For an example of how this can exclude certain groups and give power to others, see the example below.

## Example: Privileged access to the truth?

Consider the Romans. By which of course we mean Roman men. They considered themselves only to have sworn an oath if they held their testicles in their hands at the moment of swearing. The evidence of women and eunuchs could not be believed under the law for they were not capable of being fully trusted. It was only 'real' men, in swearing upon their potency, who were therefore expected to tell the truth . . . the possession of truth was much more assured if one possessed testicles (Burrell, 1997, p. 12).

Here Burrell shows how in that particular context, women were not seen as legitimate holders of the truth. For your view to be trusted, you had to possess testicles. In more recent times, the Velikovsky controversy discussed previously shows how scientific disciplines may disregard information from those who do not follow their conventions.

In his writings, Foucault differentiates three ways of viewing power:

1. **Sovereign power:** This is embodied in the sovereign who has unlimited power over his or her subjects. When crimes are committed, they are punished in a dramatic fashion. Thus, power is something that is exercised intermittently, as something negative that prevents as well as prohibits. Foucault suggests this kind of conception of power developed out of monarchic rule and argues that we should consider the following two types of power.

2. **Disciplinary power:** This attempts to place people under continuous surveillance rather than subject them to specific physical punishments. It has been of increasing interest in organizational theory (e.g. Burrell, 1988; Townley, 1995). Foucault discusses Jeremy Bentham's panopticon (outlined in Chapter 2) as an exemplar of disciplinary power. As discussed earlier, the panopticon was a circular building with a centrally elevated watchtower around which a number of cells radiated (see the Ideas and perspectives box below). The idea of the panopticon was that those within the cells know that they cannot avoid the gaze of the observer and were always potentially being watched. Therefore, the principle of surveillance was internalized. Inhabitants of the cells would monitor their own behaviour, and in this sense, the functioning of power becomes automatic rather than a conscious effort from an external being. Foucault uses this to show that power does not just mean compelling us to act. We are not necessarily compelled to act as we do by some external agency. Instead, through society's disciplines of schools, hospitals, prisons and the military, we have internalized it to become self-governed or 'normalized'.

   The example below highlights the surveillance systems operated in most call centres. It has been argued that these forms of surveillance operate along similar principles to the panopticon, encouraging employees to become self-disciplining subjects.

## Ideas and perspectives

## Bentham's panopticon

The **Panopticon** (Figure 6.3) is a type of *prison* building designed by the philosopher Jeremy Bentham. The concept of the design is to allow an observer to observe (*-opticon*) all (*pan-*) prisoners without the prisoners' being able to tell if they are being observed or not, thus conveying a 'sentiment of an invisible omniscience':

The architectural figure incorporates a tower central to an annular building that is divided into cells, each cell extending the entire thickness of the building to allow inner and outer windows. The occupants of the cells . . . are thus backlit, isolated from one another by walls, and subject to scrutiny both collectively and individually by an observer in the tower who remains unseen. Toward this end, Bentham envisioned not only venetian blinds on the tower observation ports but also mazelike connections among tower rooms to avoid glints of light or noise that might betray the presence of an observer.

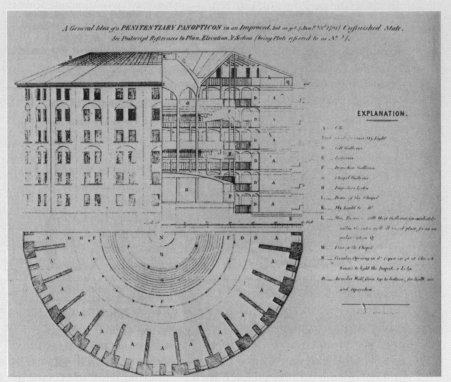

**Figure 6.3:** Panopticon blueprint by Jeremy Bentham, 1791.

3. **Biopower:** In all the books of his last period, Foucault seeks to show that Western society has developed a new kind of power – a new system of control that traditional concepts of authority are unable to understand and criticize. Instead of focusing on individuals, biopower focuses on the body and targets whole populations – for example, through attempts to define the range of sexual responses and types of sexual identities that are possible within particular social contexts.

## Example: Disciplinary power in call centres

The Real Time Adherence Module . . . continuously monitors Automatic Call Distribution (ACD) real time messages associated with each ACD position. These messages indicate when an agent signs in and out, initiates an incoming or outgoing call, and enters after call wrap up . . . the software constantly tracks each agent's actual work state and compares it to the schedule. The moment a discrepancy arises . . . the agent's name and the amount of time involved is noted and each notification or alarm is colour coded to show the nature of the problem . . . supervisors can create detailed alarm summary reports on the agents they have been monitoring. Supervisors can see an agent's status at any given moment and take appropriate action to meet the others' performance objectives.

*Source:* TCS Management group publicity, quoted in Taylor and Bain, 1999, p. 108.

**Stop and think**

Computer surveillance techniques such as those used in call centres are often likened to the panopticon.

- To what extent do you think this is a valid comparison?
- Can organizations achieve the same levels of control as 'total institutions' such as prisons and asylums?
- How much opportunity do you think there is for individual and collective resistance in organizations such as call centres?

In traditional organization theory, power has often been seen as a resource that is held by a particular group or individual. Foucault disputes that anyone can hold power. Instead, he argues that power relations are extremely widespread in human relationships. These relationships host a whole range of power relations that may come into play among individuals, within families, in educational relationships, in political life and so on (Foucault, 1984). Thus, managers do not create discipline through their actions or strategies. They are as much disciplined as their subordinates: 'Disciplinary power is invested in, transmitted by and reproduced through all human beings in their day to day existence' (Burrell, 1988, p. 227).

Central to Foucault's approach is the notion of *discourse*. Discourses are sets of ideas and practices that condition our ways of relating to and acting upon particular phenomena: a discourse is expressed in all that can be thought, written or said about a particular topic, which by constituting the phenomenon in a particular way, influences behaviour. Thus, discourses are similar to what Kuhn (1970) calls *paradigms* in that they structure knowledge and practice by producing rules that put boundaries around what can be articulated.

Discourses are social constructions, and the existence of a reality independent of their knowledge constitution is at best precarious. For Foucault, all aspects of life are subject to observation, investigation and regulation through the media of discourse. In effect, the history of science is one of how particular discourses have come to dominate particular contexts and thereby dictate what counts as knowledge and what does not. Over time, discourses change, and *genealogy* is the analysis of the conditions that make it possible for a particular discourse to develop and the analysis of the processes by which discourses change and adapt. The point is, however, that all the knowledge we have is constructed in and by some discourse. As we will discuss in the concluding chapter, discourse has become an increasingly important concept in organization studies – for example, the journals *Organization Studies*, *Academy of Management Review* and *Organization* have all produced special issues devoted to the issue of discourse in the past few years.

A useful way of thinking about and analysing or deconstructing a particular discourse has been developed by Jackson and Carter (2000, p. 66). They argue that discourses define *who* can speak, about *what* issues, in *which* contexts and *styles* (how) and for *what* reasons.

Foucault does not identify the exercise of power with any particular class or group. Power is not seen as being possessed by conscious agents, whether they are individuals or collectivities. People exist within webs of power and, like knowledge, power is

**Stop and think**    Management discourse – the discourse of enterprise

Du Gay has highlighted the development of a discourse of enterprise within UK management. Within this discourse, the consumer is at centre stage, seen to 'dictate production, to fuel innovation; to be creating new service sectors in advanced countries, to be driving modern politics; to have it in their power to save the environment and protect the future of the planet' (Gabriel and Lang, 1995, p. 1). At the heart of the enterprise discourse, Du Gay and Salaman (1992) argue, the language of the market reigns supreme as 'the only valid vocabulary of moral and social calculation' (p. 662). Thus, we see the reconceptualization and renaming of students, passengers, recipients of social services and patients all as 'customers' (Irvine, 2000; Neuberger, 1999). At first glance, this would appear to be a process of homogenization: it could be argued that this relabelling serves to obscure the unique qualities that distinguish these different groups. However, it could be argued that this discourse emphasizes above all the notion of the empowered individual (as opposed to the more impotent collective), prioritizing and celebrating individual autonomy and personal choice (Cohen et al., 2003).

Think about this discourse. Consider the different assumptions that might underlie treating someone as a patient or a student and treating them as a customer. How might doctors or teachers have to respond differently? Using Carter and Jackson's approach, think about:

- *Who* does it empower to speak?
- About *what* issues?
- In *which* contexts?
- *How*?
- For *what* reasons?

seen to be the outcome of and to reside in discourses themselves. In Cooper's (1989) terminology, knowledge and power 'inhabit each other'. For Foucault (1980), 'the exercise of power perpetually creates knowledge and, conversely, knowledge constantly induces effects of power' (p. 52). For instance, the ability to deploy a particular scientific discourse reflects a command of knowledge of a particular domain (Layder, 1994).

In the case of management, this ability is used in relation to people who lack such a command and who have no socially legitimate claim to such knowledge. In a sense, the deployment of any discourse is seen as empowering those people with the right to speak and analyse while subordinating others who are the object of the knowledge and disciplinary practises produced by the discourse. The disempowered collude in the establishment of this power relationship in two ways. Firstly, they accept the authority of discourse speakers to analyse and categorize, thereby empowering them. Secondly, the discourse defines and constrains the identities of the disempowered to the extent that they engage in self-surveillance and correction of their behaviour toward the norms it articulates. Thus, not all people are equal within the web of power relations that defines them. A psychiatrist is able to define a patient's state of mental health in terms of a body of medical and psychological knowledge.

The patient, on the other hand, generally has to accept the doctor's diagnosis. Similarly, the manager can define the employee's performance.

It is important to recognize, though, that Foucault was not suggesting that power and knowledge are the same thing but that they are found together. His aim was to show us that no knowledge is impartial, not even expert knowledge such as medicine, law or indeed management. Instead, Foucault highlights how:

> ... *the ways in which knowledge is gained through ostensibly objective techniques of measurement, enumeration and classification, in reality, form the basis of an instrumental rationalism that seeks to render human beings useful, disciplined and docile* (Sewell, 2000, p. 407).

This has been applied to organization theory in a number of ways. For example, Townley (1994) has shown how human resource management (HRM) can be seen as 'a discourse and set of practices that attempt to reduce indeterminacy involved in the employment contract' (Townley, 1994, p. 518) through the discipline of subjects. Townley argues that the seemingly mundane techniques of HRM actually form a panopticon. They categorize and measure tasks, behaviour and interactions and therefore make them visible and more governable. In a similar vein, Baldry et al. (1998), among others, have shown how the discourse of teamworking can be used as an insidious form of control. This relates back to issues talked about in Chapter 4 on cultural control, in which people's behaviour is controlled through the development of particular group norms. Foucauldian analyses have also been seen in a wide variety of works in other areas of organization theory – for example, organizational identity (Philips and Hardy, 1997) and strategy (Knights and Morgan, 1991).

## Criticisms of Foucault

Although contested by some (e.g., Barrat, 2002), criticism has been made of Foucault's earlier work that his analysis of power focuses at 'some impersonal realm beyond the reach of the productive activities of human beings' (Layder, 1994, p. 111). The human self is not given any active role; rather, human subjectivities are constituted by the play of power, discourse and practice (Newton, 1998). Therefore, it has been argued that Foucault does not give humans much of an active role in shaping their own identities. Instead, these are determined by discourse. Reed (1998) is particularly critical of this, complaining:

> It is very difficult, if not impossible to shake off 'Foucaultland'. We escape Weber's iron cage of bureaucratic rationalization and Marx's immutable laws of capitalist development only to be trapped, indeed trap ourselves, within a Foucauldian disciplinary society where we become incarcerated within a total organizational world in which we play no conscious or active role in the making (p. 198).

In his later work, Foucault shifts attention to the ability of individuals to define their own identity, but according to both Best and Kellner (1991) and Layder (1994), he fails to deal adequately with both sides of the structure/agency problem.

Foucault has also been criticized for underestimating the importance of macro aspects of power such as state or government power and for his lack of empirical grounding. That said, his analysis of the interlinkage between knowledge and power has had a huge impact on organization studies. He has been influential in the development of research in areas such as workplace surveillance and the control of human sexuality in organizations, and his concept of discourse has been an increasingly popular one.

In the next section, we briefly return to one area of organization theory that has burgeoned in the past two decades: organizational culture. We introduced the concept of culture in Chapter 3, returned to it from a new-wave perspective in Chapter 4 and will examine it again from a symbolic interactionist perspective in Chapter 7. We now want to highlight the different approach taken in a postmodern study of culture. We will not reiterate definitions of culture here because they were given in earlier chapters.

## The chapter so far

We began this chapter by outlining postmodernism and identifying its core features. The previous section has looked at the work of three core thinkers in postmodernism: Derrida, Lyotard and Foucault. We have explored issues such as the important role played by language in constructing what we see, the purpose and process of deconstruction, the link between knowledge and power and how various forms of knowledge come to be seen as legitimate, and the concept of discourse.

## Organizational culture

Although studies of organizational culture proliferate and have been undertaken from a variety of positions, it has been argued that a defining feature of postmodernism is an 'overriding concern with the increasing role of culture in shaping and defining the nature of social relations. Indeed for many culture has itself been perhaps irrevocably postmodernized' (Hancock and Tyler, 2001, p. 111). Thus, although culture was the subject of study some time before the arrival of postmodernism on the scene in organization theory, postmodernism has brought with it new ways of understanding and researching organizational culture.

Schultz (1992) identifies three core challenges that postmodernism presents to the literature on corporate culture. Firstly, postmodernism questions the modernist assumption of culture as patterns of meanings and values located at the depth of the organization, which are expressed through a variety of symbols and artefacts. Instead, postmodernism transforms these assumed expressions of profound culture into hollow rituals based upon the rupture between form and content. Second, postmodernism questions the notion of corporate culture as a vehicle for the specific identity of organizations. Rather, from a postmodern point of view, corporate culture has been used as a way of developing copies of the same culture in numerous different organizations and has destroyed the last remnants of organizational originality. Finally, postmodernism strikes against the new-wave assumption discussed in

Chapter 4 that corporate culture is able to regulate the behaviour of the members of the organization through meaningful events and internalized knowledge. Instead, postmodernism focuses on the seductiveness of corporate culture to act through aesthetics, renewal and illusions.

From a modernist perspective, much of the debate in the literature on corporate or organizational culture concerns whether it should be seen as an artefact or root metaphor – in other words, whether it is something the organization has or something the organization is and whether it can be managed or not. Postmodernism steps outside this debate. According to Schultz, it challenges both the pragmatic construction of culture as a variable and the theoretical construction of culture as a metaphor because 'they are both trapped in the modernist claims for depth, uniqueness and meaningful actions' (Schultz, 1992, p. 16). In other words, both approaches seem to suggest culture as a unifying feature. Similarly, Jeffcutt (1993) shows how postmodernism challenges both corporate functionalist and symbolic interpretive approaches to culture because they share a commitment to establishing a definitive understanding or last word on the nature of organizational reality through a process of closure that privileges particular readings and voices while suppressing and denying alternative articulations (Jeffcutt, 1993, p. 38). From a postmodern perspective, there can be no unified or unifying organizational culture.

As a result, Schultz (1992) sees culture as 'a catalyst of the tensions between modernism and postmodernism' (p. 29). He argues that these tensions may lead to a notion of culture as two faced: one face, as shown in Chapter 4, seeming to regulate, limit and direct the actions of organizational members, and the other to license individuals and groups to act autonomously and spontaneously in the seductive game of cultural forms.

So how do we understand and examine postmodern organizational culture? The most engaging use of a postmodern perspective with regard to organizational culture comes from Joanne Martin (1992), who, to a large extent, typifies her fragmentation view of organizational culture as postmodern. Here, ambiguity is brought to the foreground. There is no attempt to find cultural consensus; rather, there is a recognition of multiple interpretations and a complexity of relationships between different aspects of culture. From this perspective, culture is defined as:

> . . . a web of individuals sporadically and loosely connected by their changing positions on a variety of issues. Their involvement, their subcultural identities and their individual self-definitions fluctuate, depending on which issues are activated at a given moment (p. 153).

Martin and Meyerson (1988) also use the metaphor of a web to explain culture from this perspective. They point out that individuals can be seen as nodes on the web, connected by shared concerns to some but not all the surrounding nodes. When a particular issue becomes salient, one pattern of connections becomes relevant. That pattern would include a unique array of agreements, disagreements, and domains of ignorance (p. 117). From this perspective, culture is loosely structured. Although some people may share some values, these are not universally shared, and culture emerges dynamically as people experience events. Culture can no longer be seen as 'the glue' that holds the organization, or at least parts of it, together. Instead, it is dynamic, fractured and ambiguous – culture as kaleidoscope. If we are to accept such a definition, the question then becomes how do researchers represent such a loose and fragmented culture?

Martin (1992) uses Derrida's concept of difference in her analysis of culture, arguing that studies should examine absences as well as presences. For instance, she comments that most organizations have a prodigal son story that concerns a fairly high-ranking executive who at one time left the organization under some kind of cloud but was later welcomed back and forgiven. A cultural analysis of General Motors (GM) showed that this was not the case there, presumably because executives who leave that organization are rarely welcomed back. Martin makes the point, though, that whereas the absence of the prodigal son story has been noted in studies of GM, the possibility of a prodigal daughter story is never mentioned. In her interpretation, this absence can be understood with reference to the wider social context. Both organizational and domestic life tend to have gender segregated roles – it is likely that few women at GM have held a sufficiently high rank to qualify for the prodigal role!

Therefore, from a postmodern perspective, any representation of culture should show multiplicity, difference and discontinuity. In a research project aimed at describing an organization's culture, there should always be a concern to question the author's inevitably inaccurate representation of the views of participants, and participants in the research should be encouraged to speak for themselves in the text. However, this is not without problems because even doing this will not fully remove the authority of the author who studies a particular culture, including choosing what to include and what to exclude (Martin, 1992).

Currently, it appears that organization culture remains a contested area. The postmodern approach has brought to it an understanding of the need to look for ambiguity, to examine what takes place at the margins, where people who do not get much attention or who are not seen as core staff operate, and recognition of the multiple perspectives that will exist within any organization. It has also brought an increased recognition of the relationship between the researcher and the researched (Johnson and Duberley, 2000) and the development of new methods of studying organizational culture – for example, as text that can be deconstructed.

---

**Stop and think**    University culture

Universities are made up of a wide range of groups. There are undergraduate students, full- and part-time postgraduate students, lecturers, professors, support staff, people working in central administrative departments, cleaners, security guards, gardeners, information technology specialists and so on.

- Think about how you would define the culture of a university you have attended or currently attend.
- Can you think of any alternative explanations? Would other people experience the culture in the same way as you?
- Can you see contradiction in different aspects of the culture?
- Think in particular about marginalized groups or people who are seen as less important. How might they experience the culture differently?

**The chapter so far**

Having examined the nature of postmodernism and some of its core theorists, the previous section has looked at the application of postmodernism to organizational culture. Here we have seen that the focus on difference and indeterminacy means that it is impossible from a postmodern perspective to assume one unified organizational culture. The challenges postmodernism has posed for organizational culture are also relevant to other aspects of organizational theory, and these are outlined in the section that follows.

## The challenges of postmodernism to organization theory

In order to summarize the chapter and pull together the challenges that postmodernism holds for organization theory, we have taken as our basis Kilduff and Mehra's (1997) discussion of the five problematics of postmodernism. These are closely interrelated and can be seen to follow on from each other.

### Problematizing normal science

As discussed, postmodernists reject metanarratives. This raises a fundamental challenge: From a postmodern perspective, what is the purpose of organization theory? Indeed, can there be an organization theory?

From a postmodern perspective, researchers should not be searching for grand theories or overarching theoretical propositions that explain organizational processes. Rather, the focus should be on gaining an understanding of a situation at a particular point in time, recognizing that this is only one of a number of possible understandings. There is no longer a search for the truth. Postmodern theory can be used instead to try to challenge dominant understandings and to develop the capacity for reflection and reflexivity in managers and citizens (Gephart et al., 1996, p. 359). There is no desire to come to a final end point, an overarching theoretical explanation; rather, postmodern 'theory' is used to challenge existing practices and deconstruct accepted wisdom.

### Problematizing truth

Because what counts as truth is not fixed, the pursuit of truth becomes deeply problematic as a goal of social science. According to Kilduff and Mehra (1997), this suggests increased research attention to how individuals make sense of, experience, construct and maintain social worlds and how those social constructions take on the appearance of certainty. This is an important issue and raises another challenge for organizational theory: to further develop ways of accessing how people make sense of situations and how these develop over time. This would seem to promote the use of in-depth qualitative research methods such as interviews and participant observation to study organizations. However, rather than seeking to unify and homogenize peoples' experiences, organization theorists would be searching for conflicts, contradictions and ambiguity, trying to understand the processes through which particular discourses have developed and hold sway at a particular point in time. These conflicts would exist between different peoples' interpretations but also within individual accounts of organizational experience (El-Sawad et al., 2004). Instead of searching for unifying threads to pull together peoples' stories, organization theorists would celebrate the diversity and complexity.

## Problematizing representation

The representational mode of analysis in organizational theory has been criticized by many writers. For example, Degot (1982) argues that although it is generally thought that organization theorists study organizations that exist 'out there' in the real world, in his view, the organization is a cultural object that is the product of a prior model. Pointing to the work of people such Katz and Kahn and the Aston studies, he argues that what the theorist sees is not the model as a representation of the organization but the organization as a representation of the model (Burrell, 1988). In other words, the way that theorists conceptualize and design tools to measure aspects of organization dictates what they will see.

From a postmodern perspective, no method is capable of achieving an objective representation of facts. Instead, scientific methods are invoked in an attempt to persuade the reader. Postmodern researchers should seek to make their research methods clear and explain their own involvement. Organization theorists should look for relevance, surprise, challenge and discovery. This could be seen as incredibly liberating because for some researchers it means that no research method is considered to have privileged status (Gergen and Thatchenkerry, 1996). Researchers can adopt a mix-and-match approach, using methods with quite different underlying assumptions. That said, the majority of postmodern researchers in organizational theory choose to adopt a qualitative approach. In particular, ethnography is popular because it enables the researcher to give voice to those not represented in the dominant discourse (Linstead, 1993). The roles of researchers and writers come to the fore here, and it is incumbent upon them to reflect on their own roles in organizational research and the assumptions they bring to their analyses, recognizing, however, that they have no objective base from which to do so.

## Problematizing writing

Postmodernists see all texts as suitable for deconstruction. There is recognition that science and social science is a rhetorical activity, with texts intended to persuade. Thus, the role of writers is in some ways magnified as their rhetorical skills become more important. Organization theorists need to 'sell' their particular version of reality. In other ways, their role is negated in the sense that they may suggest one interpretation, but there is no reason why their interpretation should be accorded any more status than any of the rest of us. Their work should be open to deconstruction. Thus, organizational theorists need to find ways to open up texts for multiple readings and to involve participants, readers and audiences in the production of research. Interestingly, though, although this should make texts more accessible, postmodern writers have often been criticized for their obscure language.

## Example: Playing language games

Late in 1994, New York University physicist Alain Sokal submitted a sham article to the cultural studies journal *Social Text,* in which he reviewed some current topics in physics and mathematics and with tongue in cheek, drew various cultural, philosophical and political morals that he thought would appeal to fashionable postmodern academic commentators on science who question the claims of science to objectivity. The editors of *Social Text* did not detect that Sokal's article was a hoax, and they published it in the journal's Spring/Summer 1996 issue. The hoax was revealed by Sokal in an article for another journal, *Lingua Franca*, in which he explained that his *Social Text* article had been 'liberally salted with nonsense', and in his opinion was accepted only because '(a) it sounded good and (b) it flattered the editors' ideological preconceptions'. Newspapers and newsmagazines throughout the United States and Britain carried the story. Sokal's hoax was not merely a joke, though, and served a public purpose: to attract attention to what Sokal saw as a decline of standards of rigour in the academic community, and for that reason, it was unmasked immediately by the author himself.

For fun, you can access a web-based piece of computer programming by Andrew Bulhak of Melbourne, Australia: the Postmodernism Generator. Every time you visit it, at http://www.cs.monash.edu.au/cgi-bin/postmodern, it will spontaneously generate for you, using faultless grammatical principles, a new postmodern discourse, never before seen. Each of these is essentially nonsense, although the obscure language used means that it can look very impressive to the uninitiated!

## Problematizing generalizability

From a postmodern perspective, the aim of social science is not to develop laws that can be generalized from one context to another. As a research goal, this would be doomed partially because of the complex historically specific context of research. As with the first problematic, this leads to the question: What is the purpose of research? For some, it may be the pleasure of the text; for others, it may be to impact on practice. Kilduff and Mehra (1997) make the point that as we progress, we become more aware of our own ignorance, because rather paradoxically, we 'know more and doubt what we know' (Richardson, 1998, p. 358). From a Lyotardian perspective, researchers may choose to focus on 'petits recits', or from a Derridean perspective, upon deconstruction. Whatever, they will not be aiming to develop the explanatory frameworks of the modernist age.

Organization theorists need to keep these problematics and challenges in their minds. We would also add an additional challenge that seems central to postmodernism and that is to study unusual or perhaps unspoken aspects of organization. Hancock and Tyler (2001) and Burrell (1997) have shown how postmodern theorizing has been applied to aspects such as emotion and sexuality in organizations, issues that received little attention from modernist approaches. A challenge from this perspective is to further open organizations for investigation, highlighting previously unconsidered aspects, shining a torchlight on hidden aspects of organization and giving voice to those silenced in traditional organizational theory. Hence, postmodern researchers may challenge our conceptions of organizations by focusing on areas and groups of people that have previously been ignored.

## Postmodernism and the spectre of relativism

Finally, it would be impossible to complete a chapter on postmodernism without some discussion of relativism and the challenges it poses for the development of organization theory from a postmodern perspective. This has been a very hotly contested debate that we can only cover briefly here, but it is covered in more depth in Johnson and Duberley (2000).

Central to most of our discussion of postmodernism have been the ideas that there is no objective reality and that language is not independent of reality. With no external reality, we are left in a difficult position from which to make moral judgements. Thus, critics of postmodernism attack its relativism, arguing that a postmodernist perspective makes it impossible to prioritize or compare values, to make choices between moral alternatives. In a scathing attack on postmodernism, Parker (1995) argues: 'If all truths are relative, then those of the dictator deserve as much consideration as those of the victims in mass graves and the bureaucrats who keep the files' (p. 576).

If there is no possibility of judging between different interpretations because there are no independent criteria upon which to judge, then it follows that there are no criteria through which we can engage in any form of criticism of the status quo. Critique becomes either a contentious exercise because all that happens is a pointless comparison of incompatible views or the critic's unsustainable assertion of a privileged viewpoint. Indeed, under the mantle of relativism, it is difficult to see how anyone can have anything to say that is significant, never mind critical. Any intervention, organizational or otherwise, implies the exercise of choice based upon some kind of evaluative criteria. This leads some to question whether organization theory has a purpose at all. Child (2004) suggests that such a perspective, if it were to become dominant, would lead us to a kind of 'Hobbesian world in which everyone would be at war with everyone else. . . . [it] espouses anarchy and threatens an eventual loss of freedom, which is ironic in view of its aspirations'. In addition, it must be remembered that moral relativity is not a suspending of all theories. Rather it *is* a theory, something that postmodernists claim to reject.

Others, particularly those who might define themselves as affirmative, moderate or critical postmodernists, however, have attempted to take a less extreme position. For example, Rosaldo (1989) argues that dismantling the objectivism of modernism, rather than supporting a nihilistic land where anything goes, actually enables organization theorists to create a space for ethical concerns in an area where morals and

| Case study | Child labour in India |
|---|---|

Bangles are a big business in India. Millions of bangles, made by children in the dark rooms of Ferozabad's slums, are bought and sold each year.

Children begin work making bangles as young as 4 years old. Many children work 8–10 hours a day in dark unventilated rooms. Boys traditionally do the 'jhalai' work, flattening bangles into a level plane over gas flames and girls do 'judai' joining the bangles together. Children earn about Rs 30 (50 pence) for producing on average 4,500 bangles each day.

Fast spinning mills and gas flames release glass particles into the air, and as a result a large percentage of the children working in the bangle industry develop tuberculosis. These children are rarely cured of pneumonia and bronchitis, because they are never removed from the environment that causes the disease.

It is estimated that over 75,000 children work in the bangle industry in Ferozabad town, out of an estimated 1.5 million children who work in the north Indian state of Uttar Pradesh.

*Source:* UNICEF, 2005. www.unicef.org.uk/publications/pdf/ECECHILD2_A4.pdf

| Stop and think |
|---|

It has been argued that if we take a relativist line, then any behaviour is justifiable and there are no absolute grounds from which to criticize. Do you think relativism may be a problem for organization theory?

Consider the implications of this for:

- the minimum wage
- sweatshops in developing countries
- equal opportunities legislation.

values are rarely debated. Others, such as Tietze et al. (2003) and Boje (2000), would tend to agree. It appears, at the end of the day, that the view one holds with regard to relativism depends, in part at least, upon the way one defines postmodernism. Thus we leave postmodern philosophy in an appropriate place with lots of challenges and questions and few answers.

# Conclusions

This chapter has outlined the core concepts of postmodernism and provided an overview of three important theorists. After a brief examination of the impact of postmodernism on the study of organizational culture, we have finished by debating the fundamental challenges of postmodernism to the development of organization theory. The grid below links back to the learning objectives of this chapter to highlight the main areas covered.

# Concluding grid

| Learning outcomes | Challenges to the contemporary organization |
|---|---|
| Understand the main features of postmodern approaches to understanding. | The main features of the postmodern approach include:<br><br>• a rejection of metanarratives<br>• a rejection of the belief in pure reason<br>• the recognition of language as constitutive of reality<br>• the pursuit of difference.<br><br>What are the implications of these for how we study organizations? |
| Evaluate the contributions of key thinkers in the area. | Three key thinkers have been addressed in this chapter:<br><br>• Derrida's contribution has been discussed in terms of the important role of language and the process of deconstruction.<br>• Lyotard's contribution has been assessed in terms of his rejection of grand narratives and his articulation of how injustices can take place in the context of language.<br>• Foucault's contribution has been considered in relation to his ideas about discourse, power and knowledge. Each of these has implications for the study of organizations and the development of organization theory. |
| Analyse the impact of postmodernist theory on organization theory and the study of organizational culture in recent years. | The impact of deconstruction has been examined, and the growing importance of discourse as an analytical tool in organization theory has been addressed.<br>The implications of a postmodern reading of culture have been considered in terms of diversity and the fragmentation view of culture, and the need to understand culture as a 'kaleidoscope'? |
| Discuss the challenges that postmodernism holds for the future of organization theory. | This includes the fundamental challenge of whether it is possible to have a postmodern organization theory because of the rejection of grand theories – although we also have to deal with the issue that the argument that there cannot be grand theory is indeed itself a theory! Other challenges to the development of theory concern issues such as the impossibility of objectivity, the role of the author and the problem of relativism – that everything depends on context. |

## Annotated further reading

For those who would like to explore these issues in more depth, a very good starting point would be Best and Kellner (1991). Other useful texts include Rosenau (1992). For an excellent review of postmodernism and studies of work and organization, see Hancock and Tyler (2001), which goes into much more depth on the issues covered here and also has interesting chapters on emotion and sexuality as new subject areas in organization theory. Smart (1993) also gives a good overview of postmodernism.

## Discussion questions

1. Using the methods suggested by Boje and Dennehy, deconstruct the corporate values statement of The Body Shop PLC, available at http://www.uk.thebodyshop.com/web/tbsuk/values.jsp

2. Think about an organization that you know well. How would you describe the culture? If possible, talk to other people from different groups within the organizations. Consider their different perspectives on the culture.

3. One aspect of postmodernism is to give voice to those traditionally silenced in organizations. Who would you consider to be silenced in your organization? Why?

4. It has been suggested that the discourse of teamworking reflects the contemporary zeitgeist. Using the method put forward by Carter and Jackson, how would you analyse or deconstruct this discourse?

5. Conduct a debate for and against relativism.

6. To what extent can a postmodern perspective on organization theory give managers insight into the conduct of their working lives?

## References

Alexander, M., Burt, M. and Collinson, A. (1995) *Big Talk, Small Talk: BT's Strategic Use of Semiotics in Planning Its Current Advertising*, London: Market Research Conference.

Alvesson, M. (1995) 'The meaning and meaninglessness of postmodernism: Some ironic remarks', *Organization Studies* 16(6):1047–1075.

Baldry, C., Bain, P. and Taylor, P. (1998) 'Bright Satanic offices: Intensification, control and team Taylorism', in P. Thompson and C. Warhurst (eds), *Workplaces of the Future*, London: Macmillan, pp. 163–183.

Barrat, E. (2002) 'Foucault, foucauldianism and human resource management', *Personnel Review* 31(1/2):189–204.

Bauman, Z. (1989) *Modernity and The Holocaust*, Ithaca, NY: Cornell University Press.

Bauman, Z. (1992) *Intimations of Postmodernity*, London: Routledge.

Best, S. and Kellner, D. (1991) *Postmodern Theory: Critical Interrogations*, New York: The Guilford Press.

Best, S. and Kellner, D. (1997) *The Postmodern Turn*, London: The Guilford Press.

Boje, D.M. (1995) 'Stories of the storytelling organization: A postmodern analysis of Disney as "Tamaraland"', *Academy of Management Journal* 38(4):997–1035.

Boje, D.M. (2000) *Postmodern Organization Science: Narrative Ethics, Tamara and the Binary Machine*. Retrieved June 2006, from http://www.zianet.com/boje/tamara/papers/Boje_response_to_Weiss.html.

Boje, D.M. (2002) *Theatres of Capitalism*, San Francisco, CA: Hampton Press.

Boje, D.M. and Dennehy, R. (1994) *Managing in the Postmodern World: America's Revolution against Exploitation*, Dubuque, IA: Kendall/Hunt.

Boje, D.M., Fitzgibbons, D.E. and Steingard, D.S. (1996) 'Storytelling at *Administrative Science Quarterly*', in D.M. Boje, R.P. Gephart, Jr. and T.J. Thatchenkery (eds), *Warding of the Postmodern Barbarians Postmodern Management and Organization Theory*, Thousand Oaks, CA: Sage, pp. 60–94.

Burrell, G. (1980) *Radical Organization Theory, The International Yearbook of Organizational Studies*, in D. Dunkerley and G. Salaman (eds), London: Routledge and Kegan Paul.

Burrell, G. (1988) 'Modernism, postmodernism and organizational analysis 2: The contribution of Michel Foucault', *Organization Studies* 9:221–235.

Burrell, G. (1997) *Pandemonium: Towards a Retro-Organization Theory*, London: Sage.

Butler, C. (2002) *Postmodernism: A Very Short Introduction*, Oxford: Oxford University Press.

Calas, M. and Smircich, L. (1999) 'Past postmodernism? Reflections and tentative directions', *Academy of Management Review* 24(4):649–671.

Carter, P. and Jackson, N. (1993) 'Modernism, postmodernism and motivation, or why expectancy theory failed to live up to expectations', in Hassard and M. Parker (eds), *Postmodernism and Organizations,* London: Sage, pp. 84–100.

Casey, C. (2002) *Critical Analysis of Organizations: Theory, Practice, Revitalization*, London: Sage.

Castoriadis, C. (1992) *Philosophy, Politics, Autonomy: Essays in Political Philosophy*, Oxford: Oxford University Press.

Child, J. (2004) Brief reflection on postmodernism. Personal correspondence to J. Duberley, Birmingham.

Cilliers, P. (1998) *Complexity and Postmodernism: Understanding Complex Systems*, London: Sage.

Clegg, S. and Dunkerley, D. (1980) *Organization Class and Control*, London: Routledge and Kegan Paul.

Clegg, S. and Hardy, C. (1996) 'Conclusion: Representations', in S. Clegg, C. Hardy and W. Nord (eds), *Handbook of Organization Studies*, London: Sage, pp. 676–708.

Cohen, L., Musson, G. and Duberley J. (2003) 'Entreprising professionals: Scientists, doctors and their customers'. *International Journal of Entrepreneurship and Innovation*, February 2004, pp. 15–24.

Cooper, R. (1989) 'Modernism, post modernism and organizational analysis 3: The contribution of Jacques Derrida', *Organization Studies* 10(4):479–502.

Cooper, R. and Burrell, G. (1988) 'Modernism, postmodernism and organizational analysis', *Organization Studies* 9(1):91–112.

Culler, J. (1990) *On Deconstruction: Theory and Criticism after Structuralism*, London: Routledge.

Degot, Vincent (1982): 'Le Modele de l'Agent et le Probleme de la Construction de l'Object dans les Theories de l'Entreprise', *Social Science Information/Information Surles Sciences Sociales* 21(4–5):627–664.

Derrida, J. (1989) *Edmund Husserl's Origins of Geometry: An Introduction,* Nebraska: University of Nebraska Press.

Derrida, J. (1967a) *Of Grammatology, Speech and Phenomena*, Baltimore: John Hopkins University Press.

Derrida, J. (1967b) *Writing and Difference*, Chicago: University of Chicago Press.

Du Gay, P. and Salaman, G. (1992) The cult(ure) of the customer, *Journal of Management Studies* 29(5):615–633.

Eco, U. (1989) *Postscript to the Name of the Rose*, London: Harcourt Brace.

El-Sawad, A., Arnold, J. and Cohen, L. (2004) '"Doublethink": The prevalence and function of contradiction in accounts of organizational life', *Human Relations* 57(9):1179–1203.

English, F.W. (1998) 'The postmodern turn in educational administration: apostrophic or catastrophic development?' *Journal of School Leadership* 8:426–447.

Fairclough, N. (1992) *Discourse and Social Change*, London: Polity.

Featherstone, M. (1988) 'In pursuit of the postmodern: An introduction', *Theory, Culture and Society* 5(2–3):195–217.

Feldman, S. (1998) 'Playing with the pieces: Deconstruction and the loss of moral culture', *Journal of Management Studies* 35(1):59–79.

Fineman, S. and Gabriel, Y. (1996) *Experiencing Organizations*, London: Sage.

Foucault, M. (1960) *Madness and Civilisation*, New York: Random House.

Foucault, M. (1966) *The Order of Things*, New York: Pantheon.

Foucault, M. (1975) *Discipline and Punish: The Birth of the Prison*, New York: Pantheon.

Foucault, M. (1976) *The History of Sexuality*, New York: Harper and Row.

Foucault, M. (1980) *The History of Sexuality*, (trans. Robert Hurley), Vol. 1, New York: Vintage Press.

Foucault, M. (1984) 'The ethics of the concern for self as a practice of freedom', in S. Lotringer (ed.) *Foucault Live (Interviews 1961–1984)*, New York, Semiotext(e).

Foucault, M. (1988) 'Truth, power, self: An interview with Michel Foucault', in L.H. Martin (ed.), *Technologies of the Self: A Seminar with Michel Foucault*, London: Tavistock, pp. 9–15.

Foucault, M. (2000) 'Interview with Michel Foucault', in J. Faubion (ed.), *Power*, New York: New York Press.

Frug, G.E. (1984) The ideology of bureaucracy in American law, *Harvard Law Review* 97(6):1276–1388.

Gabriel, Y. and Lang, P. (1995) *The Unmanageable Consumer: Contemporary Consumption and Its Fragmentation*, London: Sage

Gellner, E. (1992) *Postmodernism, Reason and Religion*, London: Routledge.

Gephart, R., Thatchenkerry, T.J. and Boje, D. (1996) 'Conclusion: Restructuring organizations for future survival', in D. Boje, R. Gephart and T.J. Thatchenkerry (eds), *Postmodern Management and Organization Theory*, Thousand Oaks, CA: Sage.

Gergen, K. (1992) 'Organization theory in the postmodern era', in M. Reed and M. Hughes (eds), *Rethinking Organization*, London: Sage, pp. 207–226.

Gergen, K. and Thatchenkerry, T.J. (1996) 'Organization science as social construction: Postmodern potentials', *The Journal of Applied Behavioural Science* 32(4):356–377.

Giroux, H.A. (1992) *Border Crossings: Cultural Workers and the Politics of Education*, New York: Routledge.

Hancock, P. and M. Tyler (2001) *Work, Postmodernism and Organization*, London: Sage.

Harvey, D. (1989) *The Condition of Postmodernity: An Enquiry into the Origins of Cultural Change*, Cambridge, MA: Blackwell.

Hassard, J. (1996) 'Exploring the terrain of modernism and postmodernism in organization in organization theory', in D.M. Boje, R.P. Gephart, Jr. and T.J. Thatchenkery (eds), *Postmodern Management and Organization Theory*, Thousand Oaks, CA: Sage.

Hatch, M.J. (1997) *Organization Theory*, Oxford: Oxford University Press.

Hillis-Miller, J. (1981) 'The disarticulation of the self in Nietzsche', *The Monist* 64(April): 247–261.

Hillis-Miller, J. (2002) *Speech Acts in Literature*, Stanford, CA: Stanford University Press.

Hollis, R. and Sibley, B. (1988) *The Disney Studio Story*: UK, Octopus.

Irvine, D. (2000) Medical regulation – Modernisation continues, *Consumer Policy Review* Mar/Apr.

Jackson, N. and Carter, P. (1998) 'Labour as dressage', in A. McKinlay and K. Starkey (eds), *Foucault, Management and Organization Theory*, London: Sage, pp. 49–64.

Jackson, N. and Carter, P. (2000) *Rethinking Organizational Behaviour*, Harlow: Pearson.

Jeffcutt, P. (1993) 'From interpretation to representation', in J. Hassard and M. Parker (eds), *Postmodernism and Organizations,* London: Sage, pp. 25–48.

Johnson, B. (1981). *The Critical Difference*, Baltimore: Johns Hopkins University Press.

Johnson, P. and Duberley, J. (2000) *Understanding Management Research: An Introduction to Epistemology*, London: Sage.

Jones, M. (2003) *On Studying Organisational Symbolism*, Thousand Oaks, CA: Sage.

Kilduff, M. (1993) Deconstructing organizations, *Academy of Management Review* 18:13–31.

Kilduff, M. and Mehra, A. (1997) 'Postmodernism and organizational research', *Academy of Management Review* 22(2):453–481.

Knights, D. and Morgan, G. (1991) 'Strategic discourse and subjectivity', *Organization Studies* 12(2):251–274.

Kuhn, T. (1970) *The Structure of Scientific Revolutions*, 2nd edn, University of Chicago Press.

Layder, D. (1994) *Understanding Social Theory*, London: Sage.

Linstead, S. (1993) 'From postmodern anthropology to deconstructive ethnography', *Human Relations* 46(1):97–120.

Lyotard, J.F. (1984) *The Postmodern Condition: A Report on Knowledge*, Manchester: Manchester University Press.

Lyotard, J.F. (1988) *The Differend: Phrases in Dispute*, Manchester: Manchester University Press.

March, J. and Simon, H. (1958) *Organizations*, New York: John Wiley.

Martin, J. (1990) 'Deconstructing organizational taboos: The suppression of gender conflict in organizations', *Organization Science* 1(4):339–359.

Martin, J. (1992) *Cultures in Organizations: Three Perspectives*, Oxford: Oxford University Press.

Martin, J. and Meyerson, D. (1988) 'Organizational cultures and the denial, channelling, and acknowledgment of ambiguity', in L.R. Pondy, R.J. Boland and H. Thomas (eds), *Managing Ambiguity and Change*, New York: Wiley, pp. 93–125.

Neuberger, J. (1999) 'Do we need a new word for patients?' *British Medical Journal* 318:1756–1758.

Newton, T. (1998) 'Theorizing subjectivity in organizations: The failure of foucauldian studies', *Organization Studies* 19(3):415–447.

Parker, M. (1992) 'Post modern organizations or postmodern organization theory?' *Organization Studies* 13(1):1–17.

Parker, M. (1995) 'Critique in the name of what? Postmodern and critical approaches towards organizations', *Organization Studies* 16(4):553–564.

Phillips, N. and Hardy, C. (1997) 'Managing multiple identities: Discourse, legitimacy and resources in the U.K. refugee system', *Organization* 4(2):159–185.

Rainwater, L. (1970) *Behind Ghetto Walls*, Chicago: Aldine Publishing Co.

Reed, M. (1996) 'Organizational theorizing: A historically contested terrain', in S.R. Clegg, C. Hardy and W. Nord (eds), *Handbook of Organization Studies*, London: Sage, pp. 31–56.

Reed, M. (1998) 'Organizational analysis as discourse analysis: A critique', in D. Grant and T. Keenoy (eds), *Discourse and Organization*, London: Sage, pp. 193–213.

Richardson, L. (1998) 'Writing: A method of inquiry', in N. Denzin and Y. Lincoln (eds), *Collecting and Interpreting Qualitative Methods*, Thousand Oaks, CA: Sage.

Rosaldo, R. (1989) *Culture and Truth: The Remaking of Social Analysis*, Boston: Beacon Press.

Rosenau, P.M. (1992) *Postmodernism and the Social Sciences: Insights, Inroads and Intrusions*. Princeton, NJ: Princeton University Press.

Rowlinson, M. and Carter, C. (2002) 'Foucault and history in organization studies', *Organization* 9(4):527–547.

Schultz, M. (1992) 'Postmodern pictures of culture: A postmodern reflection on the 'modern notion' of corporate culture', *International Studies of Management and Organization* 22(2):15–36.

Sewell (2000) 'Foucault, management and organization theory: From panopticon to technologies of the self', *Administrative Science Quarterly* 45(2):406–409.

Smart, B. (1993) *Postmodernity*, London: Routledge.

Taylor, P. and Bain, P. (1999) 'An assembly line in the head: Work and employee relations in the call centre', *Industrial Relations Journal* 30(2):101–117.

Tietze, S., Cohen, L. and Musson, G. (2003) *Understanding Organizations Through Language*, London: Sage.

Townley, B. (1994) *Reframing Human Resource Management: Power, Ethics and the Subject at Work*, London: Sage.

Townley, B. (1995) 'Managing by numbers: Accounting, personnel, management and the creation of a mathesis', *Critical Perspectives on Accounting* 6(6):555–575.

Vattimo, G. (1988) *The End of Modernity: Nihilism and Hermeneutics in Postmodern Culture*, London: Polity Press.

Vattimo, G. (1992) *The Transparent Society*, Cambridge: Polity Press.

Watson, T. (1993) *In Search of Management*, London: Routledege.

Woodward, A. (2002) 'Jean Francois Lyotard', *The Internet Encyclopedia of Philosophy*. http://www.iep.utm.edu/l/Lyotard.htm

# Chapter 7

# Reflective organization theory: symbols, meanings and interpretations

## Introduction

Imagine that you have been at a meeting of the executive team of your organization to discuss some issue of great importance to yourself, to the others at the meeting and to the organization. During its course, many controversial issues are raised, but by the end, agreements are made and differences are left for later. Afterwards you talk about the meeting with others who were there. You realize that you have agreement with some of them about what happened. With others, however, it is almost as if they were at a different event. As far as they are concerned, that meeting has a different meaning from yours. They have interpreted incidents in ways that are radically different from your interpretation. What you heard as a deep and damaging argument during the meeting they understood as constructive debate. When the managing director intervened to make a decision, you felt her interruption as a symbol of her power and need to control; others thought her contribution as a symbol of her admirable qualities of quiet decision making.

The underlying theme of this chapter is: how do we give meaning to the complex events that confront us in organizational life? When we see objects, hear stories, smell perfumes, taste food, touch materials, how do we interpret them so that they mean something to us? How do we create and communicate our understanding of 'reality' in organizational settings? What are the processes by which we seek to negotiate with others the different meanings that we give to events and processes in everyday organizational life? In this chapter, we will look at a number of theories and perspectives that explore these issues.

The development of understanding of meaning and interpretation is related to two key issues in contemporary organizational theory. The first is concerned with the ways we make meaning through symbols that capture our understanding of reality. The study of this ability to make meaning through the interpretation of symbols has given the body of theories to be explored in this chapter the title of *interpretavist* theories. The second key idea is that members of organizations can find profound value in *reflection* about the deeper issues of organizational life. The development of reflective approaches to life and work in organizations requires the ability to stand apart from the rush and crisis of everyday life and develop intellectual and emotional understanding.

## Learning outcomes

- Define what is meant by 'reflective' organization theory.

- Compare and contrast how different strands of interpretavist, reflective organization theory sheds light on how organization members give meaning to their lives at work.

- Discuss the ways individuals develop a sense of self in organizations.

- Assess how these theories provide insights into how individuals and groups create their organizational identities.

- Explore how these different theories enrich our understanding of organizational culture.

- Examine the ways these theories challenge our understandings of the design of organizations.

## Structure of the chapter

- In this chapter, we discuss two approaches to the interpretation and understanding of organizations, both of which have had an important impact on the development of organization theory. Although we shall, in this chapter, discuss ways these themes are interrelated, historically they come from quite different traditions; the implications of difference and interrelationship will be developed as the chapter progresses. Both these approaches emphasize the ways readers can use these theories of organization in order to *reflect* on their own circumstances, both personal and organizational.

## What it means to be reflective

There has been a tradition in organization theory, especially when it has been aligned to management theory, of *prescriptive* outcomes so that managers can be presented with a clear, well-defined set of approaches that gives them the 'best way' to manage people and organizations. You will have found this expressed most strongly in the discussion of new-wave organization theory in Chapter 4. A different tradition in the development of organization theory has been that of the *reflective* attitude.

At its heart, the reflective attitude is important to those who research organizations, those who develop organization theory and those who are members of an organization (and many of us are all three of these, formally or informally). It is a belief that organization theory and research in organizations should enable the researcher, the theorist and organization members (individuals and groups) to achieve a full understanding of their situations through the process of reflection. This involves the development of a self-critical consideration of assumptions and consistent exploration of alternative interpretative frameworks. This has major implications:

1. **Understanding the link between 'empirical information' (the facts and figures) and the interpretation of that information.** This relates to the idea that the same

### Ideas and perspectives

## The reflective attitude

One of the first writers on the reflective attitude was the highly influential writer Donald A. Schön in his book *The Reflective Practitioner* (1991, originally published in 1983). He explores some of the key dilemmas that face professionals – doctors, scientists, engineers, lawyers, managers and so on – in their organizational activity and in their role in society. He argues that by the 1980s, the very idea of 'the professional', at one time the pillar of society, had come under profound question and that professionals were suffering a crisis of confidence. At the heart of this, he argues, was the problem that the 'knowledge base' – what the doctor learns in medical school, for example – of the traditional profession is not sufficient to meet the new complexities of contemporary life. It is too specialized, too focused on the development of technical expertise.

Schön suggests that one of the key ways of dealing with this profound problem is through the development of 'reflection in action.' It is through reflection, he suggests, that the professional can 'surface and criticize the tacit understandings that have grown up around the repetitive experiences of a specialized practice, and can make new sense of the situations of uncertainty or uniqueness which he may allow himself to experience' (p. 61).

What this means for the manager is that as she undertakes her MBA and then works in an organization, her whole approach to management typically becomes a matter of accepted 'common sense'. She no longer thinks deeply about the ways she deals with staff, with the ways she makes decisions and so on; it has become her routine. Undertaking reflection as part of her everyday life causes her to think about these routine ways of doing things without disabling her ability to act. Reflection slows her down and enables her to deal more effectively with new and uncertain situations.

'information' can be given many interpretations. For the organization theorist, this multiplicity of meaning means that the researcher needs to possess the ability to capture the complexity of interpretation in the development of theory; for the organization member, it means understanding that many features of the situation are not what they seem to be.

2. **Understanding that the language that people use is typically not as straightforward as it might seem.** As organizations develop, members characteristically build up 'common sense' ways of talking about events and processes.

## Example: The managing director talks

This is an excerpt from comments made by the managing director of a division of a professional services organization. He was talking to the executive at their weekly formal meeting. The six monthly financial figures had just been received, and they were disappointing:

> We've not done at all well although not as badly as some of the other divisions; they've got real problems. We need to develop quite rapidly our recovery plan. We need to have a post-mortem with people, investigate what's gone wrong with your areas and we need to develop a recovery plan. You know we've got a clear vision of where we want to get to and we've got to stick with it.

As we shall discuss as the chapter unfolds, our language is pervaded by metaphor. The image of 'the vision' points the group to something to which it can aspire; the word suggests the nobility of the enterprise. The common sense language that members use relates to specific contexts that they all 'understand' as organizational members. The members of the executive know that in *this* organization, the metaphors 'recovery plan' and 'post-mortem' indicate that there is going to be some 'blaming' of the failure onto specific groups of staff. The way people talk is embedded in the history of the organization. The references to how other divisions have fared is 'understood' by members of the executive to refer to past rivalries and conflicts with other divisions. The managing director is appealing to a sense of *schadenfreude*, that perverse pleasure that members can take in the downfall of others.

The language we use is geared toward creating an image of how we understand the truth rather than the truth itself. For the researcher and organization theorist, this involves the understanding of the language-in-use in its context; for the organization member, this involves development of understanding of the deeper issues of language and communication in the organization (Alvesson and Deetz, 2000) so they can act in an informed manner. In the example given above, one of the members of the executive, later in the meeting, discussed with the managing director the way that he had talked of undertaking a 'post-mortem'. There was a useful discussion of the need to avoid 'blame' and focus on the issues – and indeed, that the very term 'post-mortem' was inappropriate. This modest clarification of the common sense understanding of the language proved fruitful.

The development of reflection is closely linked to contemporary ideas that explore the development of emotional and spiritual intelligence to improve the quality of leadership and management. This involves the development of self-awareness, self-control, motivation of self and others, and skill in dealing with social situations (Goleman, 1998). At an organizational level, this is a recognition that emotions are an important aspect of the ways people at all levels relate to organizational tasks and processes and that there is a need to develop approaches that understand the emotional aspects of work and issues of organizational change (Huy, 1999). Underpinning this need to be reflective about our lives in organizations is an understanding that organizational life can be dysfunctional and problematic for its members. The development of reflective emotional intelligence means that managers can develop the ability to identify aspects of organizational life that are emotionally toxic, that 'drains vitality from individuals' and that need to be handled in 'healthy and constructive ways' (Frost, 2004, p. 111).

From the point of view of organizational theory, then, the reflective approach is one that gets the researcher closer to deeper, more truthful, understanding of the ways organization members develop and understand their organizational world. From the point of view of the organizational member, this reflective attitude provides people with a richer understanding of core issues of organizational life. In a practical manner, it enables members to act in organizational life in ways that are considered and thought through. In Chapter 8, we will discuss the ways a number of primarily European theories take this reflective process one step further – into the *reflexive* process or attitude.

In the following sections, we shall look at a number of theories and perspectives that have informed and contributed to the development of reflective organizational theory. These approaches are concerned with the ways humans can act together, collectively; can give meaning to their lives in organizations; and develop and interpret symbols, metaphors and stories that enable them to develop meaning and share understandings of the world. The first of these approaches developed in the United States and is known as symbolic interactionism.

## Working and acting together: symbolic interactionism

A couple talking together, a group of people undertaking a task, an organization committed to producing goods and services are all examples of collective action. How this ability to act in a collective way happens is the core subject matter of symbolic interactionism.

What is important about this is that it emphasizes that organization members can be purposive in the ways that we make meaning and work together to achieve that shared definition of the situation – or fail to reach an agreement. It takes us away from any view of the human being that we are essentially passive actors tossed about by the vicissitudes of fate. It also emphasizes that we can choose to *reflect* on our actions and our situation.

The origins of symbolic interactionism in the early years of the twentieth century are strangely reminiscent of the growth of the neo-modernist human relations school in Harvard, discussed in Chapter 3, in that both developed from a particular university and both had formidable leaders in the development of the approach.

## Symbolic interactionism

These are some of the key issues that symbolic interactionism seeks to answer. They are taken from one of the key writers on symbolic interactionist theory, Becker (1977):

> The theory of symbolic interaction takes as its central problem this question: How is it possible for collective human action to occur? How can people come together in lines of action in something we can call a collective act? By collective act we should understand not simply cooperative activities in which people consciously strive to achieve some common goal, but any activity involving two or more people in which individual lines of activity come to have some kind of unity and coherence with one another (p. 290).

### 'The Chicago school'

Although the symbolic interactionist movement developed in other American universities (so that the term 'Chicago school' is more about a movement than an actual geographical location), its most famous home was the department of sociology at the University of Chicago.

In the early years of the twentieth century, distinguished scholars were appointed to the department. One of these was Robert E. Park. His interest, developed from working with the great German sociologist Georg Simmel, was in the meanings that we give to everyday life – what might be called the ignored, common sense, 'trivial' (but enduring) aspects of living. These include the ways humans are 'sociable', create relationships, hold conversations and shape their actions. His interest in the processes of everyday behaviour led to a consideration of the relationship between the individual and the society. Park began to analyse the processes by which we take on and shape, by virtue of our own qualities and personalities, the roles that we occupy. This eventually led to a third interest – the idea that institutions (e.g., religious groups, business organizations) develop because of internal and environmental changes (Matthews, 1977). These interests were taken on by later generations of academics within the department.

Another key member in these early years was George Herbert Mead, who came to Chicago with a somewhat different perspective from Park's. For our purposes, his key contribution was his concern with the notion that human consciousness emerges from interaction and that the high level of human development comes from a synthesis of the biological, psychological and sociological circumstances that surround our development. These features that differentiate the human from other species enable us to reflect on our experiences and to give them meaning – the reflective process (Meltzer et al., 1975).

A second wave of scholars in the 1960s and 1970s developed the earlier interests of Park and his colleagues into the various forms of symbolic interactionism that will be discussed in this chapter. Writers such as Erving Goffman, Howard Becker, Anselm Strauss and many others to be discussed later in the chapter came to prominence. Unlike the neo-modernist academics in Harvard Business School whose focus was entirely on organizations, the symbolic interactionists were sociologists with a wide interest in society and its institutions. However, Everett Hughes' seminal work *Men and Their Work* (and note the gender specificity – so typical of its time) published in 1958 focused attention on organizations and began work towards an organization theory derived from symbolic interactionism.

Although there were many other influences on the Chicago school as it developed, this interest in the everyday construction of life endured. Although the world in which we live is one of 'change, movement, instability and conflict', the mystery is that it 'never quite fell apart; beneath the disorder lurked "natural" principles of organization which kept it, if not healthy, at least functioning and a certain natural vitality which kept it alive and lively, lurching from one state of disequilibrium to another' (Matthews, 1977, p. 120). It is that mystery that sociologists who wish to 'understand the social world from the point of view of the social actor' (Bulmer et al., 1997, p. 251) would want to uncover.

An important aspect of the development of the Chicago school is that it can be seen to be particularly American in its development. It has within it an understanding that people live in an 'open society' that is not constrained by deep and enduring class divisions. In many respects, it captures aspects of the fondly held myth of the 'American way of life' – respect for the individual and a belief in flexibility and mobility (Shaskolsky, 1970, quoted in Meltzer et al., 1975). Despite this American flavour, the Chicago school has developed a theoretical perspective on organizations that is deeply influential and has universal appeal. Some of the key issues that emerge from the Chicago school and their contribution to organization theory are discussed in later sections of this chapter. In what follows, we explore some of the core ideas, the basic assumptions, that lie behind symbolic interactionism.

## The processes of making and sharing meaning

The symbolic interactionists developed a network of ideas and propositions about the ways we make and share meaning. They emphasized the ways we as human beings are able to actively construct and create symbols of the world in which we live. This construction of the world is *individual* to the extent to which we have different personalities and experiences that filter experiences in particular ways, but it is also *social* in the sense that we share (or fail to share) meanings and interpretations.

The aim of symbolic interactionism is not to penetrate to the depths of *individual* thought and action. As a social science, its aim is instead to develop an understanding of the statements made by actors acting collectively, in small or large groupings, based upon specific interactions. It explores the ways members give meaning to situations and from this, to develop insights that can be related to other interactive situations so that an overall theory of social interaction can be developed (Cossette, 1998).

## The basic assumptions of symbolic interactionism

Symbolic interactionists make a number of assumptions about the nature of the individual, how individuals interact with others and how we undergo processes of change. These core principles – the ontological underpinning – were captured by the

## The symbol

The Swedish academics Mats Alvesson and Per Olof Berg see symbols as 'instruments to create order out of chaos' (1992, p. 85). They say that a symbol always represents something different from or something more than itself so that:

- *The corporate logo* is more than just a sign; it is a symbol of the way 'the organization' would like to be seen. The logo is an expression of 'the brand' that characterizes the organization; it is a symbol of its identity.

- *Special parking spaces for top management* are more than just parking spaces; they are a symbol of power and authority.

- *The ways formal meetings are handled* are more than just places where decisions are made; they are symbols of social relationships and, at a deep and often hidden level, the values and priorities of members.

- *Corporate plans* are more than a plan for the next period; they are symbols of the organization's sense of its place in the world.

- *Offices in which colleagues pile papers around them where there is officially a 'tidy desk' policy* are more than just untidiness; they can be a symbol of discontent or indifference to the 'petty rules' of the organization.

- *Architecture, statues, interior design and decoration* are all symbols that, in different organizational contexts, have different meanings. In the United Kingdom, for example, there have been occasions where expensive contemporary statues have been erected on hospital grounds. For some, they symbolize the notion that hospitals can be aesthetically pleasing places; for others, they symbolize the ways health care can be wasteful of money.

Symbols are the objects, stories, sayings, tastes and smells that give us (as couples, groups, organizations) a sense of identity, that give us meaning and structure. We do not always agree about the *interpretation* of the symbol (and this can be a source of profound and deep conflict), but we recognize its power to capture meaning.

American sociologist Norman Denzin (1971). The model in Figure 7.1 captures the essence of these assumptions and we then discuss why these ideas are important in contemporary organization theory. These assumptions can also be looked at as *a process* by which individuals and groups learn and develop through their interaction. The symbolic interactionists refer to a process such as this as a 'career' with the idea that if all goes well, any interaction or sharing of meaning has a beginning, a middle and an end. It is important to note, however, that although the model is presented in a linear fashion, the everyday processes of making meaning and communicating do not necessarily happen in this orderly way.

As the individual grows and develops and communicates with others, he or she:

1. **Is capable of self-reflective thought and action:** This refers to the idea that it is part of our human capability to be *reflective*. In organizational terms, this

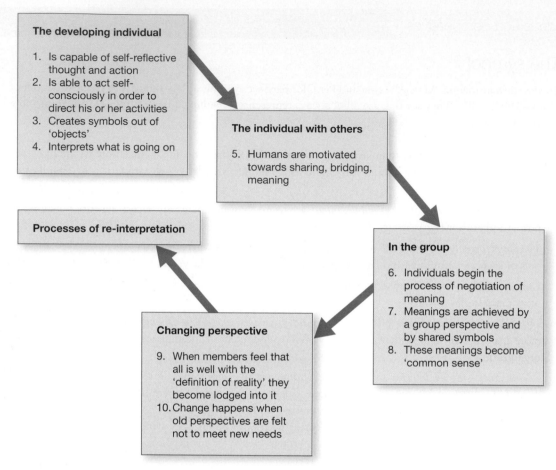

**Figure 7.1:** The processes of making meaning – a symbolic interactionist approach. (*Source:* Based on Denzin, 1971.)

means that *all* members of the organization *are capable of* making sense of their own actions, both as individuals and as members of their group. The implication of this is that in organizations, there are different understandings of what is happening. This view contrasts with the view in modernist thinking (in Chapter 2) that most members of organizations are driven by the desire for individual economic success. It also contrasts with the view discussed in Chapters 3 and 4 that managers are 'superior beings' who need to harness the commitment of employees to the values and purposes of the organization.

2. **Is able to act self-consciously in order to direct his or her activities:** Not only are we capable of reflective thought, but we can also consciously choose to act in certain ways. We are not corks tossed hither and thither by the vicissitudes of fate or by our genetic inheritance. In organizational terms, this points toward the idea that organizations are pluralistic, with different ways of acting and behaving. Pluralist perspectives in organization theory say that in any one organization, we can find many different ways of thinking and acting amongst individuals and groups. This is an important theme that is discussed in later sections

of the chapter. This contrasts with unitarist theories that suggest that thinking and acting in organizations is uniform and directed to organizational goals so that people who do not behave in this way are regarded as *deviants*.

3. **Creates symbols out of 'objects':** Denzin suggests that an 'object' is anything toward which action can be organized. This may be illustrated by an example. At one time, spaces in the car park of the office in which the author[1] works were 'allocated' on the basis that any employee could use the car park until it was full. Then there was a change in policy so that allocation was based on strict criteria. This meant, as it worked out, that most occupants of it were senior management. There were various reactions to this from the somewhat embarrassed pleasure of those who had a guaranteed space to the deep resentment of those who saw the new policy as 'yet another' symbol of what they saw as the increasing split between 'management' and 'staff'.

    In organizational terms, this implies that such 'objects' as business plans, vision statements, the spaces in which people work, the technologies of everyday life such as the PC (or Apple Mac) and the modes of dress adopted, are all symbols to which different groups (or individuals) give different meanings.

4. **Interprets what is going on:** As we go about our everyday business, doing what we do, we interpret our own actions and the actions of others. The interpretations that we give to events and people can be quite different as between different individuals and groups and this can lead to conflicts. It should be added that awareness of the self and of others is not evenly distributed across the population; we may have colleagues whose interpretive ability is to all organizational intents and purposes minimal (they are 'insensitive') yet others whose awareness of the other is somewhat overwhelming (oversensitive).

As individuals work with others:

5. **Humans are motivated toward sharing, bridging meaning:** Human beings are interested in the process of discovering the meanings that others give to 'objects' and situations and are frequently engaged in the process of working toward understanding the other.

As the group develops:

6. **Individuals begin the process of negotiation of meaning:** As we work together, we negotiate the 'meaning' of other members of the group and the 'objects' that are part of the group's life. After a while, we develop a group consensus as to the meaning. In this process, the language that people use becomes 'a dynamic reality that is shaped by events which it, in turn, helps shape' (Cossette, 1998, p. 1368). An example of this is the way members of a committee may initially have a struggle to develop a shared understanding of the purposes and processes of their committee. They negotiate over the meaning and significance of 'the agenda', what should or should not be included as 'standing items' and so on. Over a period, however, there is characteristically the development of shared, stable definitions of the key issues.

---

[1]During the course of this chapter, the author has deliberately chosen to give examples that relate to his professional and managerial organizational life. This is in the spirit of the reflective tradition and is done in the hope that it will illustrate the issues that are discussed in the chapter.

7. **Meanings are achieved through the development of a group perspective – joint action rests on ability to grasp direction of the act of others:** If things are going well, individuals develop through interaction a group understanding of the situation. Because of this, they can act together toward a joint effort at understanding and action. The development of the group perspective and the processes leading to joint action are likely to have within it a degree of conflict and disturbance. A conflict-free group would have difficulty in establishing a clear identity and consciousness of itself; it would not be able to develop a distinctive group structure (Denzin, 1971). The absence of conflict leads to collusion and the destruction of the group – the Abilene paradox (Harvey, 1988) discussed in Chapter 8.

8. **These meanings become the group's common sense:** As soon as the group has achieved this level of shared perspective, the core issues that are its business become part of the group's common sense. There is acceptance of the meaning of, for example, 'the agenda', the importance of 'the finances', the significance of 'thinking strategically' and so on. When the meanings become shared, they become 'symbols'. The group also develops 'rules' and 'codes' that are taken-for-granted aspects of the interaction. These rules and codes relate to the roles of the members of the group, who has 'the right' to talk most (and who is regarded as marginal, whose voice does not count), the relative formality or informality of conduct in the group and so on.

As time goes by, the group may begin to go through change:

9. **When members feel that all is well with the 'definition of reality', it becomes the 'truth':** Both as individuals and groups, we can become very comfortable with the way we are. As individuals, we can think that our understanding of reality and of ourselves is one that is true and correct. As a group, we may believe that we are doing our business efficiently and effectively. There is no need to change; we have our lives sorted. This can be an important feature of organization life in the sense that it can be important, even in periods of major change, to be able to identify those quiet areas in the midst of the storm that are undertaking their business effectively because they know what they are supposed to be doing. On the other hand, groups (and individuals) can become complacent, unable to see that there is stormy weather on the way.

10. **Change takes place when old perspectives fail to meet new needs:** But then there are occasions when our way of looking at the world no longer fits the circumstances in which we find ourselves; we are motivated to change. In organizational terms, this means that we are capable of developing new understandings of social objects and our environment.

As change takes place, so there are processes of reinterpretation. This takes us through to the developing individual.

As you read these assumptions that underpin symbolic interactionism, it is important to remember that although they are all part of a process of reflective learning, they do not happen in the straightforward, sequential manner presented. As we go through everyday life, we encounter many groups and situations, and this leads to complex patterns of learning and development. In addition, even when we enter a group for the first time, we carry into that group meanings and definitions that come from our previous history and experience (Knights and Willmott, 1999).

**Stop and think**

As you look through these assumptions and processes that the symbolic interactionists associate with learning and development, how do they fit with your experience? Do you think the core assumptions hold true to you? Can you think of occasions when the development of a shared meaning has gone wrong? Could you identify from the model above where problems and issues that caused things to go wrong arose?

## Strengths and weaknesses of the symbolic interactionist understanding of organizations

### Strengths

Symbolic interactionist theory suggests that human beings are capable of applying reason and logic to situations, capable of intentional action and of reflecting on their circumstances. In this sense, the ideas that lie behind symbolic interactionism help us to develop understanding of the ways members place themselves within their organization.

Beyond this, symbolic interactionism gets us to explore key organizational issues of the nature of organizational reality. They suggest that our understanding of reality is 'mediated through symbols' so that our 'taken for granted sense of reality and selfhood is seen to be held together by a precarious set of symbols with which we just happen to have identified' (Knights and Willmott, 1997, p. 74). The importance of this is that it points to the way meaning in organizational life is constantly the subject of negotiation and that beneath the apparently solid exterior of the organization, there lie the shifting sands of a constantly changing understanding of organizational 'reality'.

### Weaknesses

The British organization theorists David Knights and Hugh Willmott (1999) suggest that in its interest in the processes of the achievement of consensus, the symbolic inter-actionists ignore the deeper contradictions that the person (or the group) can encounter in the development of its identity. Symbolic interactionism presents a model of 'self-consciousness' that 'appears overly abstracted and detached from the "lived experience" of human beings with bodily desires' (p. 73). They suggest that this smoothes people out so that the symbolic interactionists avoid discussion of deep and enduring conflict. They also claim, along with many other writers, that symbolic interactionism ignores the deeper, more emotional aspects of the self. Although symbolic interactionists acknowledge that the constructions of reality created by individuals and groups may not be rational and that interaction may have hidden aspects as well as the overt 'purpose', it deals with the surface aspects of interaction rather than the emotional content of it.

As an example of this, from a symbolic interactionist perspective, activities such as 'accomplishing a task, exchanging a greeting, eating a meal or making love' are regarded as processes by which individuals act together. They negotiate, fit together 'disparate, conflicting and often incomplete plans of action into a package of meanings that, at least for the moment of activity, provides a basis for interaction. This feature of the joint action suggests that interaction may have a variable career' (Denzin, 1971, p. 264) – it can fail as well as succeed. Although this provides a plausible account of the development of the ways people act together to accomplish their work, it is interesting to note the way that Denzin brackets together 'accomplishing a task' with 'making love' – as if they were of the same emotional content (which, of course, they may be for some).

As we shall see in later sections, despite these weaknesses, the symbolic interactionist perspective provides a powerful body of theory for the reflective exploration of key organizational issues. In the next section, we turn to theories that take us to another depth in this journey of reflective organization theory. Although, as we saw in the discussion of the rise of the Chicago school, symbolic interactionism had its roots in nineteenth century European sociological thought, it developed as a particularly American approach to understanding the ways we create and share meaning through the symbols of everyday life. Within European thought in organization theory, interest in the way that we symbolize organizations came initially from a different intellectual set of sources, although in recent years there has been a degree of synthesis of these perspectives, both in the United States and in Europe.

## The chapter so far

As the chapter has unfolded, we have discussed a core theme in the theories to be discussed here. This is the idea that habits of reflection can be an important part of the members' lives in organization. Reflection is the ability to stand apart from everyday organizational life in order to understand some of the deeper issues that confront it. One of the key issues that confront organizational members lies in the ways we understand and interpret the actions and communications of others. To initiate an exploration of this issue, we looked at one of the key theoretical perspectives that throws light on the processes by which we communicate and collaborate – symbolic interactionism. We discussed the ways this theory has developed a number of strands and that at the heart of the theory is the idea of the 'symbol.' We have seen that although there is much in symbolic interactionism that helps us to understand, in a reflective way, the ways we communicate, it says little about the ways we can understand the emotional aspects of life. In the next section, we look at an approach that claims to give insight into emotional understanding.

## Phenomenology reaches the emotions

The British organization theorist Yannis Gabriel (2000) suggests that symbolic interactionists believe that myths, stories and symbols gives *clues* about the nature of social reality in organizations; phenomenologists see stories everywhere. Such things

Ideas and perspectives

## Phenomenology

The literature on phenomenology is vast and highly complex. This definition is meant to give just an indication of phenomenology in organizational life.

**Phenomenological approaches** are concerned with the description and understandings of the everyday experience of organizational members without imposing on these experiences theories or presuppositions – letting the experience 'speak for itself'. The great German phenomenologist Husserl's slogan was – 'Back to the things themselves'. Underpinning phenomenology are processes of reflection in order to achieve understanding of the ways members make sense of their organizational life. In phenomenology, there is no such thing as 'the truth' as something out there, external from human experience. Instead of searching for 'the truth', phenomenologists explore perceptions, fantasies, stories, myths, sagas and so on in order to develop understanding of the meanings that members give to everyday and extraordinary features of their lives.

This means that we can reach a deeper 'truth' – an understanding of the ways members' structure and communicate the meaning that they give to their organizations. Although 'meaning' starts with the individual shaping his or her world, phenomenologists are interested in the ways we share meaning – intersubjectivity.

(Based on Urmson and Rée, 1991.)

As we shall see later in this chapter, phenomenologists are 'scientific' in the sense that they have procedures and processes for developing an understanding of everyday experience.

as strategies, business plans, performance appraisals, all the artefacts of organizational life are stories. Phenomenology claims to give a reflective understanding of organizations because of its approach to the ways members give meaning to their organizations through conversation, metaphor and storytelling.

A phenomenological approach to organizations provides an understanding of 'interior', deeper meanings, the emotions and values that are part of the person's experience of organizational life. The roots of phenomenology's claim for a deeper understanding of human experience lies in its development as a philosophy and as a key theoretical position in sociology that can be applied to organization theory. The core thinkers in the development of phenomenology were, in Europe, the German philosopher Edmund Husserl (1859–1938), and in the United States, the philosopher George Herbert Mead (1863–1931). The key aspects that underpin phenomenology are that it illuminates the nature of human experience and as a method it provides a detailed description of human experience. What it does is to take 'the individual human being as the centre of a system of coordinates on which the experience of the world is mapped' (Luckman, 1978, p. 8). It is also 'reflective' in that it makes human experience the core of all our understanding of the world. In this sense, 'objects' – the things that surround us such as telephones, the desk at which we work – are given meaning through our consciousness. This means that 'reality' is something that is represented by our minds – the meaning of the telephone does not exist without our consciousness of it. However, because of the physical existence of reality, we can confirm its existence by looking at it on the desk and see it as a telephone (Strati, 1999).

## Example: The room is prepared for the important visitor

In the intervening hours the castle had come to life like a device whose mechanism has been wound up and reset: not only the furniture, chairs and sofas liberated from their linen shrouds, but also the paintings on the walls. . . . Logs were piled on the hearth ready for a fire for it was the end of summer and after midnight the cold mist spread a damp breath through the rooms. *All of a sudden the objects seemed to take on meaning, as if to prove that everything in the world acquires significance only in relation to human activity and human destiny* (from Sándor Márai's novel *Embers* originally published in Hungary in 1942).

### Stop and think

This is clearly a romantic way of depicting the way we give meaning to the objects in our environment. Can you think of places in your own experience that have achieved this kind of meaning and significance? Or are most of the offices and places where we work so anonymous that it is difficult to give them any significance? Why do some people like to bring into their workplace photographs and other objects and display them on their desks?

In this sense, organizations can be seen as places in which members are capable of making meaning, capable of cooperation and able to choose. As organizations develop, Strati suggests, there are intertwining aspects of the 'formal' organization (its structures and its rules) and the informal in which 'customs, cognitions, social norms, ideals, folklore and institutions' (p. 87) play an enduring part. These informal aspects of members' organizational lives give the formal aspects meaning and significance so that the formal is embedded in the informal and the informal embedded in the formal.

### Case study        Phenomenology in action

In this case study, the writers on organizations Anne Wallemacq and David Sims were acting as organizational facilitators to a small group of managers. They wrote of this experience of using a phenomenological approach in a paper published in 1998.

Three managers from small business organizations came for help to the authors of this case study. These managers came from organizations that had gone through significant change – in one case, a merger; in another, product diversification; and in the third, an internal crisis – and they were looking for improved ways of managing change. During the change process, things had gone wrong, and the vision of their organizations that they held in their heads seemed no longer very appropriate.

The facilitators believed that the best way forward was to undertake with the managers a process of sense making. Their aim was to enable the managers to achieve an 'operating vision' of their firm that would allow them to understand what was going on and to cope with the major changes. The facilitators' core task was to act as a 'mirror' to the managers, reflecting their *way* of saying what they said. They also discovered, through the language in use and the physical features of the organizations (e.g., the design of offices) the basic images that members relied on to think about and act in their organizations.

The facilitators then offered a number of concepts – as for example presentation of different forms of organization structure – that helped the managers to begin to surface a number of the basic beliefs they held about organizational life. This helped members to uncover the 'hidden metaphors' – the aspects of organizational life that are normally hidden beneath the 'rational' order of things.

One of the managers gave an example of this. She had founded a small firm that provided intensive training in information technology. The firm grew rapidly, and as it grew, she created new branches in different parts of Europe. Thinking it through in a rational manner, each branch was structurally 'a copy' of the original company. As time went by, the number of branches grew, but the founder felt increasingly marginalized as all the new branches went their own way. As the managers discussed this situation with each other and with the facilitators, it became clear that there was, beneath the rational story of the development of new branches, another story. This second story was a 'hidden metaphor'. This 'hidden metaphor' was that the owner had been going through the biological process of cellular division. The 'mother cell' (the owner) had duplicated itself, and in doing so, had replicated the new cells in exactly the same form as the original. For her, the problem was that these new 'cells' all asserted their independence; they were her 'children' who had 'grown up'. When they visited the company, this image of the owner as 'mother' was reinforced. She tried to create a family atmosphere: when she visited the branches she insisted on tidying up and so on.

These two stories – the rational story of the successful company opening new branches modelled on the original company structure and the story of the founder as 'mother' – sit alongside each other. They do not exist without each other. As each of the managers talked through their issues, it was realized that all of them had various stories operating at different levels.

The outcome of this reflective way of looking at their understanding of themselves as managers and their organization was they were able to look at their situations from a very different perspective. By the end of the process, they no longer felt trapped in the processes of change but rather felt that they could manage themselves – and others – through the process in a more proactive manner.

### Stop and think

This account looks at the way people experience their organizational life at a number of layers. There is the layer of everyday reality in which people make rational decisions. There are also deeper stories expressed as 'hidden metaphors'. Reality is composed of many different stories that we tell about our organizations, some on the surface and some hidden from view. What would you see as the advantages and disadvantages of this approach within organizations known to you?

The phenomenological view of organization involves the development of an understanding that 'exterior' aspects of behaviour and 'interior' emotions and values are interlinked. It also implies that the stories that we tell about organizations, those aspects of organizational life that are rational and those that are irrational, are at some deep level all integrated and intersect with each other. This complexity means that 'knowledge' about our organizations 'has to be perpetually created and re-created in social, symbolic and interactive relationships' (Røyrvik and Wulff, 2002, p. 155).

So, in everyday life, there is this level of perpetual creation and recreation as we talk to each other and create new symbols and meanings, retell the stories in new contexts and reveal 'hidden metaphors' in different ways. Lying alongside this is another everyday world – the world of 'common sense' reality. This is the part of our organizational world that we 'take for granted'. This study of the everyday world of common sense takes us to another perspective, ethnomethodology.

## Ethnomethodology: understanding organizational 'common sense'

The origins of ethnomethodology were primarily in the United States with its key author Harold Garfinkel. The tradition of this kind of study has been developed in the United Kingdom by a group of writers influenced by Wes Sharrock and his colleagues at the University of Manchester.

In his original and highly influential studies, Garfinkel (1976) got his students to engage in a variety of activities in which the taken-for-granted common sense assumptions were put under question. In one situation, for example, he asked his students to:

> . . . engage someone in conversation and to imagine and act on the assumption that what the other person was saying was directed by hidden motives which were his real ones. They were to assume that the other person was trying to trick them (p. 51).

When he discussed this with the students, the vast majority found the assignment difficult and actually found the conversation very difficult to handle – because it ran

### Ideas and perspectives

## Ethnomethodology

At its heart, ethnomethodology is the study of the 'common sense' methods that members use to solve problems, make decisions, make sense of their situations and undertake fact finding in their everyday lives. They are the 'quite ordinary, familiar, unsurprising ways that people enquire into and determine the reality of various things' (Cuff et al., 1998, p. 163). In this perspective, 'the study of an organization must begin with the study of its use by members' in the sense that when we become a competent member of organizations we display, adhere to and develop a sense of order that enables us to conduct our everyday business (Manning, 1971, p. 244).

so directly against their common sense assumptions about the nature of trust in conversation. In another situation:

> Students were asked to spend from fifteen minutes to an hour in their homes imagining that they were boarders and acting out this assumption. They were instructed to conduct themselves in a circumspect and polite fashion. They were to avoid getting personal, to use formal address, to speak only when spoken to (p. 47).

The reactions of the families to this varied considerably. In some cases, they took the student's behaviour as a joke or that the student 'wanted something'. However, in the vast majority of cases, family members were astonished and bewildered by this change in behaviour. The general feeling was that the student's polite behaviour had disturbed the 'common sense' assumptions that family members make of each other.

This exploration of the common sense assumptions that members make about the ways they make decisions and about the ways we interact with each other helps us to understand three key issues that are central to ethnomethodology.

1. The first of these, according to the Swedish writers on organizational research Mats Alvesson and Kaj Sköldberg (2000), is concerned with *membership*. This is the ability to speak the 'natural language' of the group. When the students were using formal address with their families, they were no longer using the natural language of the family; to be a competent member is to show that you can 'speak the speech' of the group.

2. The second of these concepts is *accountability*. This is concerned with the way we recount our actions reflectively in a common sense way. When we describe to colleagues what happened in a meeting, for example, we tell it as a story with a beginning, middle and end. If we construct the meeting as 'serious', we tell the story of the meeting in a 'serious' manner.

3. The third of these concepts is to do with the way that in most organizational situations, we are able to create and sustain 'rules of conduct' that are common sense ways of enabling conversations to take place – although there can be occasions where we cannot 'find the rules' and the interaction ends up in embarrassment and difficulty.

One of Sharrock's doctoral students, Alex Dennis (2001), provides an interesting example of this kind of study in an organizational setting. He explores detailed transcripts of interactions between different members of staff concerning the everyday decision making of staff in a hospital stroke unit. He examines the way that staff make decisions about patients, how they weave their way through formal 'operating procedures' that may conflict with what is happening before them, how one member of staff who is a doctor reconciles his 'doctorly' background with being a member of a multidisciplinary team.

The intellectual roots of ethnomethodology come from phenomenology in the sense that ethnomethodology explores the ways we develop our understanding of the world from the microprocesses of everyday interaction from which come our common sense knowledge and understanding of the world. The last of the perspectives is the way these common sense understandings are captured in the symbols, myths and stories of organizational life.

## Organizational symbolism

Since the mid 1970s, the development of understanding of the ways in which symbols lie at the heart of organizational life has become an important strand of organizational theory through the concept of organizational symbolism. The development of this approach came particularly from Scandinavia. The first major text on the topic was written by Gunnar Westerlund and Sven-Erik Sjöstrand in 1979. The Swedish organization theorists Alvesson and Berg (1992) write that the supporters of this approach claim that it creates a new understanding of organizational 'reality' that is far different from the sorts of approach that the modernists (discussed in Chapter 2) or the neo-modernists (discussed in Chapter 3) put forward. Indeed, some of the organization symbolists regard themselves as to be firmly placed within the postmodern movement (discussed in Chapter 6), although Alvesson and Berg are sceptical of this claim.

The organizational symbolists share with the symbolic interactionists and the phenomenologists the idea that within any organization, there are many versions of 'reality' as individuals and groups develop different symbols or use the same symbols but give them different meanings. What is different, however, is that whereas the symbolic interactionists tend to assert that members create symbols in specific organizational settings to meet specific needs, the organizational symbolists believe that individuals and groups import into the organization symbols and meanings from their wider society. An example of this is the way that we look at 'leadership' as a symbol. For the organizational symbolist, the way we look at the 'leaders' in the organization as a symbol is an outcome of our prior experience of 'leaders' from other organizations, from literature and movies, from our everyday social life. These issues are taken up in the discussion of culture in a later section of this chapter.

The organizational symbolists are also interested in the idea of looking at organizations as an aesthetic experience. The Italian organization theorist Antonio Strati (1999) writes of the way we use our senses of hearing, sight, touch, smell and taste and our capacity to make aesthetic judgements in order to 'assess whether something is pleasant or otherwise, whether it matches our taste or otherwise, whether it "involves" us or leaves us indifferent or even repelled' (p. 2). The development of a distinctive 'aesthetic perspective' in organization theory is discussed in Chapter 10.

### The chapter so far

As this chapter has developed, we have looked at a number of perspectives that are concerned with the ways we symbolize the world around us. We looked in particular at the worldview of the symbolic interactionists and the ways they suggest we explore and develop meaning in organizational life. We then looked at a somewhat different approach, that of phenomenology. Here the claim is that in developing understanding, there is an exploration of the meaning-in-context of members and that lying alongside the surface 'reality' there lie other stories. We also looked at the ideas that underpin ethnomethodology as an approach to uncovering the common sense everyday realities of organizational life. We concluded with a brief review of 'organizational symbolism' as a perspective that focuses on these issues as they relate to organizations. Some of the core issues that are contained within phenomenology and ethnomethodology take us into issues that are discussed in Chapter 8, and it is important to note that some of the writers in the organization symbolism school claim to be, philosophically, postmodern in their approach (discussed in Chapter 6).

There is some evidence that many (but by no means all) writers within these perspectives are developing an understanding of each other. For the purposes of this chapter and the development of an understanding of the ways these interpretavist, reflective perspectives and theories present challenges to organizational theory, we shall deal with them together unless the approaches present conflicts that are particularly useful to explore.

## The ways in which individuals develop a sense of self in organizations

During the twentieth century, there was ambivalence amongst writers on organizations about the nature of the individual in organizational life. At one end of the scale, there is the sternly modernist view (discussed in Chapter 2) that the individual was a sophisticated machine devoid of emotion and sentiment. Then there emerged the view (discussed in Chapter 3) that individuals are emotional and sentient beings with a longing to 'belong' to the organization that would give their lives meaning and commitment. In other chapters of this text, you will find many other versions of the relationship of the self to the organization. In this section, we explore an understanding of the self in organizations based on the idea that the 'self' emerges out of an existing understanding of the 'self' (who I am) *and* out of interaction with others.

### The self as dramatic artful creation

Within the symbolic interactionist movement, Goffman perhaps best developed this sense of self as artful creation. He looks at interaction as a form of drama in which we undertake impression management – the process by which we wish to impress others that we are worth listening to and that our ideas and beliefs are valid and truthful.

| Biography | **Erving Goffman (1922–1982)** |
| --- | --- |

Erving Goffman was born in Canada in 1922 and died in Philadelphia in 1982. He studied at the University of Edinburgh and started his academic career at the University of Chicago, where he spent a brief period and then had a distinguished career at a number of universities in the United States. Although his work falls within the symbolic interactionist tradition, he is generally regarded as something of a maverick member. His work relies strongly on his observation of people in their ordinary settings. The book that first brought him to the attention of a wider public was *The Presentation of Self in Everyday Life* (1959). His fascination with the ways people make sense of their everyday lives was reflected in a number of works, including *Frame Analysis* (1974) and in *Forms of Talk* (1981). His interest in the nature of organizations was reflected in *Asylums* (1974), a study of organizations such as prisons, convents and monasteries, and psychiatric hospitals that exist as closed communities. He believed that the study of these organizations had implications for 'open' organizations in which most of us work.

At the heart of this aspect of his work is the notion that whenever 'I' am in interaction with others, 'I' engage in a constant process of discovering information about them, and they are also in a constant process of discovering information about me. This is done in a context of prior knowledge about each other; prior knowledge of where we come from, socially speaking; the rules that we have about gender; and so on.

When 'I' am in communication with others there are, Goffman (1959) suggests, two key elements. At one level is what 'I' provide as the conscious performance that 'I' am controlling carefully to manage an impression of myself. This is the presentation of myself as a credible, competent person. 'I' need to project an image of myself so that 'you' will find me to be a person in whom you can put your trust, so that 'you' can believe that my account of reality is one that you will find to be plausible. On the other hand, 'you' will be searching for the 'given-off' signals – those features of my performance that present me as not quite the person I wish to present. We are like actors in a drama – except that the 'script' is constantly improvised and much more liable to break down or to take unexpected directions than in the theatre.

## Example: Given and given off signals in a meeting

This is an account of an incident during a meeting in a professional services organization:

The other day, I was in a meeting where I really wanted to present the case that a particular programme I lead was truly marvellous, but at the back of my mind was a sense of doubt about it. I started the presentation in fine voice. All was in control. However, a minute or so into my presentation, I realized that there were hesitations, little contradictions, unexpected lowering of the voice as I lost a degree of confidence in what I was saying. If *I* noticed my 'given offs', I am sure that the others, who I wished to impress, did, thus discrediting the confidence of the 'given' performance.

Goffman's model of interaction as drama has rich implications for organizational theory and the ways we conduct ourselves in organizational life. This includes the way we arrange the setting in which our performance takes place. This not only relates to the ways status is symbolized in the organization through the physical surroundings but also the ways we present ourselves. This can relate, for example, to issues of who works in shared offices and who works in their own office – and in the case of the latter, who gets an office with a good view and who gets an office with a view of the back of the building. It can also relate to forms of dress. In many organizations, it seems to be the case that staff can dress relatively informally, but when they reach a certain level (which varies from organization to organization), they are expected to dress more formally (they become 'a suit' – or even more pejoratively, a 'grey suit').

## Negotiating the way between the self and the organization's rules

In most organizations, there is a negotiation between the ways the individual wishes to present himself or herself and the norms of the organization, although some organizations are stricter than others. Goffman suggests that there are important ways that these fronts are negotiated, especially when people are working in team or group situations.

## Example: 'Mohican worker can return to airport job'

A Stansted Airport worker has been told his job is safe after facing the axe over his Mohican-style haircut. Ryanair check-in clerk John Graham, 22, breathed a sigh of relief yesterday when Swissport bosses told him he could return to work. . . . 'We have agreed to negotiate a much more transparent dress code policy'. Mr. Pearce (the Trade Union representative) said there was some confusion over how much hair gel employees were allowed to use and that he would be meeting Swissport bosses to devise a clearer definition next week.

*Source: © Essex Chronicle,* 25 February, 2005.

This example from an airport near London that is primarily geared toward economy flights to Europe illustrates that in the presentation of 'front', there can be interesting flashpoints between what the individual considers 'fashionable' and what the organization considers respectable.

The development of the front, in organizational and everyday life, involves understanding the rules of conduct that are embedded in the situations we encounter. A rule of conduct is a 'guide for action that is recommended not because it is pleasant, cheap or effective, but because it is suitable or just' (Goffman, 1972, p. 48). The rules of conduct become part of our common sense, and when we are committed to them, they also become an important part of our self-image, our organizational identity. This development of the front and the organizational identity can, for some members, be easily attained so that they enter the organization seamlessly, as if to the manner born. For others, the transition into the organization is arduous as they go through a difficult process of socialization into it (a process to be discussed in a later section). And of course, there is the extent to which we choose to go into organizations that suit our own understanding of what we want from organization life. In some cultures, there is a sense that we can match aspiration to organization; in other cultures, the sense of choice is much more restricted.

## Example: To be a 'good professor'

This is an account of his everyday life given by a university professor who lectures and manages a group of research colleagues:

If I wish to be seen as a 'good (or competent) lecturer' I would wish to be seen as someone who fulfils not only the overt *obligations* of a lecturer (e.g., marking assignments on time) but also the covert aspects. These include the implicit rules of conduct shared by colleagues in relation to 'how we behave towards' students and colleagues in relation to degrees of intimacy and distance. Additionally, if I am performing those obligations, I will have an *expectation* that others will reciprocate

*(Continued)*

## Example: (Continued)

so that they display a conception of me that agrees with my self-image as one who 'buys into' the rules of conduct.

When I was giving a lecture to a final year undergraduate group the other day I tried to fulfil the overt obligations through presenting the lecture in a straightforward manner, gave each member of the group a handout, provided them with a PowerPoint presentation. In terms of the implicit rules of intimacy and distance – well, I greeted students who were late with a teasing amiability, during the lecture invited comments and discussion (which did not happen but it was my attempt to engage with them), at times engaged in 'tiny chats' with members of the group, and made a few asides that were designed to be 'spontaneous' humorous reflections on what was going on. The management of 'distance' came in part from the formal set-up of the lecture situation and from the observation of clear boundaries – when the lecture finished I (and the students) switched off attention to each other, I (and they) became anonymous.

As the lecture started at 0900 hours the students were passive but seemed to 'buy in' to my performance. They would, from time to time, acknowledge what was happening in relation to my little attempts to enliven the scene without it disturbing their conception of the lecture (at that time of the day) as a place in which they could 'quietly learn' or gently slumber (but not *show* that they were asleep since that might be taken to show contempt for the situation).

As I go through my organizational day I notice that I go through these performances – as colleague to other academic colleagues, as manager in meetings, as member of academic staff talking through issues with administrative colleagues. There are also moments of 'informality' when I have a 'moment of flirtation' (in a deeply respectful way) with someone I rather like. Some of the serious meetings are handled in a deeply serious manner. In other meetings there can be quite 'personal' but humorous comments and teasing in the midst of the seriousness. In other meetings I can put on an impression of submission as a means of impressing management. This is a way of convey- ing that I am listening to the other's every word although some interpret this behaviour on my part as ironic, a comment on the other's seriousness. In all these performances there is a mixture of me as the 'professional' and my idiosyncratic interpretation of the extent to which I can bring a fondly held impression of my 'self' into the situation.

Of course as I write this I realize that all may be delusion – that instead of seeing these as credible performances students and colleagues see laid before them something rather pathetic – or menac- ing. In the performance of the drama but in the absence of critical reviews one can never be sure. . . .

### Stop and think

This issue of impression management and the display of competence is an important topic. What are the ways that people known to you undertake this impression management? Have you noticed people who apparently are utterly careless of these issues of impression management and displays of competence? Do they 'get away with it', or is their utter carelessness *their own* form of impression management? How do you manage the impression you make on others?

## Developing the organizational identity

Although the literature on the development of identity in the symbolic interactionist movement is rich and complex, four themes are of particular significance. What fol- lows is a summary of some of the key issues.

## Theme 1: Role making and role taking

The first of these is concerned with a bundle of issues about the *nature and development of the concept of role* in organizations. In modernist literature, the idea of the role tended to be something rather fixed. For example, the role of 'manager' was circumscribed in an official definition, the role description, from which departures would be regarded as a deviation. Within symbolic interactionism, however, the concept becomes much more fluid. No role can exist without other roles to which the particular role is orientated, and roles are negotiated around a set of implicit rules. That is to say, within the organization, there may well be a generalized concept of 'the manager', and this may be captured in such documents as the 'role description' but on a day-to-day basis, enactment of the role of 'manager' is a performance that is based (to a greater or lesser extent) upon the basis of an understanding of:

1. the way the individual 'manager' wishes to perform the role
2. the way the other person (as role holder) wishes the role of 'manager' to be performed
3. the way the other person wishes to perform his or her own role.

In this sense, the performance of a role is a combination of 'role taking' and 'role making'. In role taking, the person acts 'in the perspective supplied in part by his [sic] relationship to others whose actions reflect roles that he must identify' (Turner, 1962, p. 23). What happens when 'I get it right' when I am role taking is that 'I' am properly orientated to the role performance of the other and their expectations of me; my performance matches the expectations of the other, and the other's performance matches my expectations. When I get it wrong, I miscalculate either the other's understanding of his or her role performance or of his or her role relationship with me.

---

**Ideas and perspectives**

## Getting it wrong, organizationally speaking

One of the roles taken by the writer is that of a relatively senior middle manager. In terms of personal style, I have developed over many years a self-presentation that is somewhat self-deprecating with a love for irony. Soon after I was appointed to my management role, I became engaged in conversation with a very senior manager. The meeting went seriously wrong. The feedback I received later was that my self-deprecating presentation was taken seriously as a sign of lack of competence, and my sense of irony was taken as a sign that I was not committed as strongly as I should be to the purposes of the meeting. There was also a hint that my treatment of the senior manager of the university as an equal was inappropriate. What I had to learn (take on in the role) was a more serious manner, to display commitment and to observe the (unwritten) protocols of deference and demeanour that are important in dealing with senior managers.

**Stop and think**

Can you think of a situation in which you presented yourself in a manner that did not meet the expectations of the other, even though you felt sure that it was a credible self-presentation? Were there any consequences of this? Typical organizational situations you might like to think about are interviews, undertaking a presentation or interaction with a colleague or manager.

The other side of the coin – role making – is the process by which the person constructs the role. Turner (1962) suggests that most roles:

> . . . 'exist' in varying degrees of concreteness and consistency, while the individual confidently frames his behavior as if they had unequivocal existence and clarity. The result is that in attempting from time to time to make aspects of the role explicit he is creating and modifying roles as well as merely bringing them to light' (p. 22).

In this sense, role making is akin to improvization in jazz. There is a core theme that is capable of variation, but within boundaries. In jazz and in organizational settings, performances can run along an axis from 'safe' (and possibly with an implication that the performance is somewhat boring) through to 'developmental' (in which the performance is seen to be fresh, providing a novel interpretation of the role) through to the 'bizarre' (in which the performance is seen as 'too idiosyncratic' to be 'reliable').

## Example: A psychiatrist does some role making

During the 1970s, Dr Mendoza was a distinguished consultant psychiatrist who worked at a psychiatric hospital with an international reputation. He had been thinking deeply about his medical practice. He came to realize that something that alienated him and his colleagues from the patients was the use of specialist psychiatric language. He decided to undertake some extreme role making. This took the form of 'talking' with the patients and with colleagues using ordinary, lay language. Initially, this was greeted with a degree of shock. Many of his psychiatrist colleagues saw the behaviour as bizarre – indeed, some thought that he was going through a psychiatric disturbance. Eventually, however, others began to see that this was a useful way of interacting with patients. Some 20 years later, a profound change in medical training in the United Kingdom is that doctors have the development of effective communication with patients as part of their core curriculum. That which was at one time regarded as bizarre role making is now embedded within the role.

In organizational terms, these concepts of role making and role taking throw considerable light on issues of interpersonal relationships. An example of this, to be developed further in the discussion of culture below, is the ways that managers develop understandings of the needs to collaborate. The author of a number of texts on organizations as dramas, James Bryant (2002) suggests that on the one hand, managers face the challenge of working effectively with others in order to benefit their customers and to cope with challenges in their global marketplace. In Goffman's terms, the *character* of management is collaborative. However, the enactment of collaboration involves many tensions at many different levels. Bryant suggests that an understanding of these tensions – the 'conditions of performance' in Goffman's terms – needs to be understood if networks of collaboration are to be truly developed.

The ability of organization members to undertake role making and role taking is intimately bound up with the ways members see themselves and others as 'competent'. In this sense, members of organizations have some concern to display their competence. A presentation of the self that leads to the person to be seen as a 'competent member' generally leads to an assessment of that person which concludes that continued investment in him or her is worthwhile or that he or she is placed for promotion or at the very least is placed to maintain employment in the organization (McAuley, 1994). The Swedish academic Jörgen Sandberg (2000) researched the ways that some 50 engineers in the department of engine optimization at the Volvo Car Corporation understood what constituted 'competence' amongst this group of highly skilled personnel. What he found was that 'workers' knowledge, skills, and other attributes used in accomplishing work are preceded by and based on their conceptions of work' so that competence is assigned on the basis of members' understanding of the nature of their work. What Sandberg is suggesting is that although formal role descriptions may have sets of attributes in them that describe what it is to be a 'competent' manager, doctor, scientist and so on, what counts is the way members construct in their everyday lives attributes of competence in assessing their own and others' activities.

## Theme 2: Socialization into the organization or profession

A second key theme is the ways members are socialized into an organizational role or identity. Within symbolic interactionism, this interest in the ways that people become organizational members or members of their profession arose out of a preoccupation with personal and group change in adult life. You may remember that when we introduced symbolic interactionism at the start of the chapter, we suggested that people begin to change, as individuals and groups, when old perspectives and ways of understanding no longer fit new situations. In the development of understanding of the processes of socialization, the sociologist Howard Becker suggested that there are two key questions.

The first is the consideration of the organizational context of personal change:

What kinds of situations do the socializing institutions place their new recruits in, what kinds of responses and expectations do recruits find in these situations, and to what extent are these incorporated into the self? (Becker, 1977).

| Biography | **Howard S. Becker (1928–    )** |
|-----------|----------------------------------|

Howard S. Becker was born in Chicago, Illinois in 1928. He studied for his doctorate at the University of Chicago and worked there at the same time as Erving Goffman and Anselm Strauss. He currently divides his time between San Francisco and France. In addition to his academic career, he was a jazz musician and an exhibition-rated photographer.

His range of publications was enormous. For many people, one of his most famous books is *Outsiders* (1963). This was a key study in the ways that people and social groups become labelled as 'deviants' and the consequences that this has for them and for those who apply the labels. He also wrote extensively on the processes of socialization into professions and on the nature of professions as well as on the development of sociological theory.

In many organizations, some of the overt signals and situations that are used to socialize members include:

- **Mentoring and coaching:** These are the processes by which newcomers to the organization are placed with more senior members in order to enable the newcomer to develop understanding of the ways the organization 'does things' (coaching) and develops its understanding of the core processes of the organization (mentoring).

- **Management development:** These are the processes by which 'new' managers are developed into the role.

- **Appraisal and performance review:** Formal appraisal sessions are often a process by which members can feel rewarded for undertaking tasks and processes in an organizationally appropriate way and be reminded when they have strayed from the path of appropriate behaviour.

In addition, in covert ways, the sorts of situations that socialize members include both at the organizational and the group levels:

- Signals of approval or disapproval that are given in informal settings. This might include on the one hand a smile or friendly gesture or on the other a frown or 'being ignored' when the normal behaviour from the other is a greeting.

- The 'quiet word' that 'We don't do things the way you just did that'.

- Nicknames, especially when they are used to indicate that the person named is in some way or other a deviant or politically powerful.

The second question that Becker suggests is of crucial importance in this process of socialization to understand the inner processes of organizational socialization: what is happening to the individual as he or she is 'going through' the socialization process? The sorts of features that are important here include:

- What *meaning* do I give to the sorts of covert and overt situations and signals mentioned above? Do I see them as indicative of an organization that meets my own self-ideal, an organization in which I would really like to work? Do they indicate that I should be suspicious? Do the ways that these socialization efforts are conducted indicate that 'they are a bunch of idiots'?

- How do the 'official' overt situations fit in with what I see happening within the group that I feel closest to, and *their* 'culture'?

- To what extent do the 'socialization situations' that I am encountering fit with my own desire for autonomy or conformity?

### Stop and think

You might like to think how these issues of 'personal preference' in the socialization process are important to you. For example, the extent to which one wants to 'fit in' to the organization (or that part of the organization one is entering) and the extent to which one wishes to preserve autonomy from it can lead to interesting tensions. Can you think of situations in which you have been in conflict with efforts to socialize you into organizational values you have thought to be ridiculous?

In relation to the issue of the organizational context, Becker suggests that we can infer from the symbolic interactionist literature a basic model of how members are socialized into the organization. Although the process of socialization may appear to be relatively straightforward, the outcomes are likely to be complex.

The ways that socialization happens in organizations are related to the social networks that are part of organizational members' lives. An example of this is the case of information technology professionals working for large information technology-based organizations. From an organizational perspective, it was desirable to retain these professionals on long-term contracts in order to maintain a degree of stability. However, within the social networks of these professionals, the general view was that they owed no loyalty to the organization and that it was preferable to 'follow the money'. In some respects, this 'freelance' view was entirely rational; in other respects, it was a shared value of the network not entirely borne out by the evidence. Longer term commitment to the organization could yield rewards in relation to salary, status and security.

The process of socialization is likely to be a collective experience rather than an entirely individual one. In organizational terms, this means that in terms of the 'socialization situations', members of the organization go through these either as groups (as in management development) or as individuals experiencing a shared, institutionalized process (as in mentoring). Amongst the local group of colleagues, the individual is entering into the 'group culture', the shared experience of 'becoming' a competent member.

An example of the way these three issues are interrelated may be found in leadership development programmes that are designed to socialize senior members of organizations into an approach to leadership roles that is seen by the organization to be desirable. Selected personnel attend a series of modules provided by organizations that provide 'leadership development'. Many of these organizations undertake this process through exercises that take place out of doors that are then discussed and processed by an experienced facilitator indoors. An example of this approach is given in the box below.

## Example: Leadership development

**The Leadership Trust**

The Leadership in Management (LM) programme is an intensive five-day course aimed at identifying and exploring the fundamental aspects of good leadership, communication and team building.

Through a combination of project work and review, central presentations, activities (climbing, caving or sub-aqua diving) and personal feedback, the LM programme recreates the complex challenges and changing context of the business world in the 'safe' environment of The Leadership Trust.

In order to ensure maximum benefit from attending, delegates are encouraged to consider their own personal and corporate learning objectives. Upon receipt of a booking, all delegates will be directed to our web-based pre-course briefing service.

*(Continued)*

## Example: (Continued)

**Delegate Profile**

The LM programme is designed to develop the personal leadership skills of those at director and middle-senior management levels.

Delegates are grouped into teams of six to nine individuals from different organizations, facilitated by course tutors and led by the overall course director.

*Source:* www.leadership.co.uk

It is interesting to observe the complexity of response to attendance on the programme when members return to their organization. For some, it is either the confirmation of 'what they already knew' – that the concept of leadership espoused by the programme (and endorsed by the organization) is entirely legitimate and one to which they would wish to adhere. For others, the programme is the beginning of a journey of enlightenment as they attempt to relate the issues from the programme into their lives at work. For others, the programme is 'interesting' but not experienced as particularly relevant to their lives. In addition, there are those for whom the programme is a form of indoctrination into a particular 'way of being' that is the opposite of their identity as a member of the organization. Paradoxically, for some members of the group, the stressful environment of the programme and the novelty of the situation may reinforce existing behaviours and attitudes rather than changing them (Grant, 1996) – they re-enter their organization with an enhanced conviction that their way of 'being a leader' was the right way all along.

### Theme 3: The career

These themes of role and socialization are closely connected with the concept of the *career*. This is based on the idea that as we go through the process of 'being' in the organization (or in life generally), we go through a continuing series of experiences, each of which has a cycle or trajectory.

### Ideas and perspectives

## The trajectory

The sociologists Anselm Strauss and Juliet Corbin (1990) write about the processes of 'managing' patients who have chronic illnesses as they go through the trajectory of their condition.

This trajectory can be brief or extended; each of the stages may well have quite different timelines. It starts with the patient's growing awareness that all is not well, to the diagnosis of the condition, to a state of crisis for the patient, to the stage of acute (i.e., not long lasting) illness, from stability of the condition to instability, to deterioration and ultimately the death of the patient. Strauss' work was very influential in the development of understanding amongst medical and nursing staff of appropriate care interventions at each of these stages.

The idea of the trajectory has found wide use. Figure 7.2 is an example of a 'trajectory of change' that looks at the different stages that a person (or group or even organization) can go through in the process of change.

Although these depictions of the trajectory can appear to be quite mechanistic, the timelines for the various stages are not predetermined. In addition people, can become 'stuck' at any one stage of the process. We can work with colleagues who are 'stuck' in depression from changes that took place many years ago.

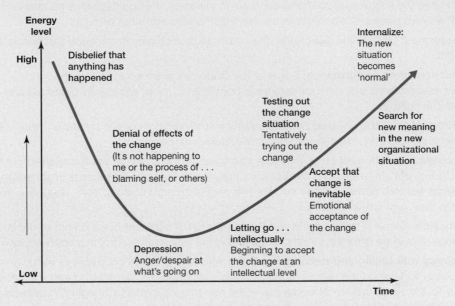

**Figure 7.2:** A trajectory of change. (*Source:* From Hayes, J., *The Theory and Practice of Change Management*, 2002, Palgrave, reproduced with permission of Palgrave Macmillan.)

Within symbolic interactionist research, there was a fascination with the ways that professionals become socialized into their profession, with studies, particularly in the 1950s through to the 1980s, of the development of medical and nursing students in particular. This research is a way of thinking about the challenges of the development of organizational and professional identity that continues to be influential.

## Example: Was it like this for you?

During the 1960s, the sociologist Fred Davis (1968) studied student nurses in a nursing college in the United States. At that time, all the students were women and they lived a fairly enclosed existence. They had many rituals and ceremonies to symbolize the stages of their career as students. The stages of the career were, in broad outline:

- **Initial innocence:** They came into college with a view that they would be 'curing' sick patients. They had high ideals about the nature their career.

*(Continued)*

## Example: (Continued)

- **Their experience was different from their expectations:** They were spending a lot of time in class; they had not seen patients. There was a discrepancy between their high ideals and what was going on. Initially, this was not talked about amongst them, but after a while this became a shared pain.

- **'Psyching out':** This was a period of adjustment when the students experienced lack of fit between goals and the means of achieving the goals. This state is known as *anomie*. The American sociologist R.K. Merton suggests that when people are in this state, they go through a number of responses to it. These are the sorts of *anomic responses* that the students went through:

  - **Conformed:** Despite the discomfort, they stuck to their studies in the hope that things would get better.

  - **Ritualized their performance:** Some of the students continued to attend the classes, handed in their assessments, but were there more in body than in mind, essentially detached and alienated from the college.

  - **Retreated from the college:** Some students actually left the college because it was not meeting their goals and they could not reconcile themselves to the means.

  - **Innovated:** A pattern of behaviour was that some of the students set themselves out to be the 'lecturers' pet'. In befriending the lecturers, they learnt the route to success in achieving what the college wanted. Some of these secrets they would communicate to their struggling colleagues; some they kept to themselves.

  - **Rebellion:** Some of the students adopted a position of constant questioning, of demanding that 'things should be different' in the college and in the way that their training was developing.

- **Preliminary role taking and making:** For those who stayed in the college, this was a period when they began to take on the role of 'student nurse', although this does not mean that they all conformed to the same pattern of behaviour – the role making involved bringing in aspects of themselves into the performance. They began to use the 'language of nursing' but often with joking gestures that this language was not *their* language. They were beginning to take on a new 'common sense' understanding of what it is to be a nurse.

- **Sustained role taking and making:** At this stage, they began to adopt in a sustained way the language of nursing and the 'professional demeanour' expected of the nurse that was a graduate from the college.

### Stop and think

If at some stage in your life, you have been a 'student' or undergone induction into a profession, how does the above compare with that experience? Does this concept of the career ring true in your experience, or is the actual experience much more ambiguous and uncertain?

## Theme 4: The power of the professional symbol

In the 1960s Howard Becker produced a seminal paper called *The Nature of a Profession*. In this paper, he takes up a number of themes that come from the thinking of previous writers on the nature of the professionals, and he captures many of the issues that were around in the Chicago school at the time. These preoccupations came to be known as the 'professional project', an explanation of the ways that the label 'professional' is a means to the acquisition of power and influence (Macdonald, 1995); these same considerations could be applied to the 'management and leadership projects'.

Becker suggests that there had been a long tradition in the social sciences of attempts to define the nature of the professional. Traditionally, they are depicted as people who possess specialized skills that require prolonged training and study. Success as a professional was measured by quality of service rather than financial reward. In this traditional view, the work of professionals is regulated by a professional body in order to maintain the professional service and to enforce a code of ethics. However, Becker suggests, these traditional definitions are fraught with ambiguity.

Becker's (1977) crucial suggestion is, in understanding the nature of the profession, that we 'view *profession* as an honorific symbol in use in our society and analyse the characteristics of that symbol' (p. 93). He suggests that when we look at the 'great professions' (medicine and the law) we do so with a sentimental gaze; we attribute to them an idealism that is not realistic given our everyday experience of the way in which they work. This is why so many groups, including management, wish to achieve professional status. They wish to bask in the glory of the label 'professional'. As far as the professional is concerned, the collective possession of the symbolic label of 'professional' gives them a justification for their claims to autonomy in the conduct of their work and a remit to control the activities of others. This is because no outsider can judge their work or their assessments of the situation because outsiders have not been exposed to the prolonged training of the professional.

The prizes of autonomy and control have been two of the key drivers for occupational groups to achieve professional status, especially in the context where they practise in large organizations rather than in small professional practices. The way that professionals of all sorts – medical practitioners, lawyers, accountants, scientists and engineers, marketing and human resources, to name but a few – assert their professional status on the one hand and 'fit into' the organizations in which they practise their profession continues to be an issue of considerable importance.

## Stop and think

Becker's key thinking on this issue of professionals was written in the 1970s. To what extent do you think these issues regarding the place of professionals in organizations have changed since he wrote that article? On the one hand, there are ways in which our 'respect' for professionals has declined – but maybe there are ways in which we are now, given the advances in technology and knowledge that are part of professional life, even more deferential to them. What do you think?

Throughout this chapter, we have tried to show how these insights from reflective organization theory can help us to develop understanding of the self, the group and the organization. This proposition can be taken a step further in the sense that we can understand identity as being not only about reflection and self-examination. These are the processes by which individuals and the organization can come to question key issues about their identities – who they are and what they stand for. It is through these processes, according to the writers on organization culture Mary Jo Hatch and Majken Schultz (2002), that members can engage in active processes of change. They suggest that these issues of personal, group and organizational identity need to be explored in the context of understandings of the organization culture. This provides a useful link with the next section.

> **The chapter so far**
>
> **Characters in search of an identity**
>
> In this section, we have explored some of the ways that key issues of identity in organization are shaped and developed. We have discussed the ways we construct our identities and conduct ourselves in organizational life. We have suggested that our identities are lodged in the performances that we give in organizational and everyday life and that the development of these performances (and their interpretation by others) involves understanding the rules of conduct that are embedded in the situations we encounter. We explored a bundle of issues about the *nature and development of the concept of role* in organizations and suggested that the performance of a role is a combination of 'role making' and 'role taking'. We also discussed the ways people become organizational members or members of their profession through socialization via direct and indirect processes.

# Understanding organization culture through symbols

## Introduction – two ways of exploring culture

As discussed elsewhere in this book, there are, within organization theory, radically different approaches to the exploration of organization culture. At one end of the spectrum, there is the view that an organization *has* a culture or organizational climate as discussed in Chapter 2; at the postmodern end of the spectrum, discussed in Chapter 6, there is a view that within the organization, 'culture' is highly fragmented and dispersed.

The perspective on culture discussed in this section is the *subjectivist* or *interpretavist* perspective. In this approach, culture is that which is conceptualized, understood, by either the organizational member or the researcher through his or her subjective experience. What this means is that 'organization members, as social actors, actively participate in the construction of organizational reality through organizational symbolism, in its various forms' (Mumby, 1988, p. 12). At its most radical, this subjectivist approach dissolves the whole concept of organization culture so that it becomes, as an idea, problematic, as discussed in Chapter 6. The theories and perspectives discussed in this section, however, enable us to understand the ways that organization members develop meaning and significance in their organizational lives, the ways that they develop symbols that capture the essence of their organizational lives.

## Communicating cultures

As suggested earlier in this chapter, the claim of writers in the phenomenological tradition is that it can 'write meaning, and its close relative emotion, back into the study of organizations' (Gabriel, 1991, p. 857). The key interest in this approach is in the nicknames, jokes, stories, myths and sagas that pervade organizational life. According to organization theorist Yannis Gabriel, different forms of communication represent members' attempts to 'humanize organizations and strengthen the individual in his/her daily engagement with them'. For those who feel that they have power in the organization, these stories and myths provide a means of preserving their sense of authority; for those who feel powerless, they help, Gabriel suggests, to make organizational live bearable. This conceptualization of culture as serving a function for organizational members separates it from the postmodern view of culture discussed in Chapters 6. The postmodern view sees culture as emergent text 'involving authors, readers, texts and other texts' (Linstead and Grafton-Small, 1992, p. 350) that is concerned with difference rather than shared meaning.

Many writers have developed understanding of the role of nicknames, jokes, stories, myths and sagas in the development and communication of cultures. In the following, we mention some of the core ideas.

1. **Jokes and nicknames:** The psychoanalyst Sigmund Freud suggested, in a book written in 1916, that there are two kind of jokes. The first is what he called 'innocent jokes'. These are jokes that do not make any particular point and where the joke is an end in itself. The second type of joke has a purpose, it is 'tendentious', to use Freud's (1976) term. Such jokes can run the risk of offending listeners and 'run the risk of meeting with people who do not want to listen to them' (p. 132), but they can bring great pleasure as well. Purposive jokes enable people to express difficult emotions or their anger in a way that is more acceptable than the straightforward expressions of feelings. Wherever there are purposive jokes, there are usually three parties involved. These parties to the joke are the teller of the joke, the listener to the joke and the person who is the focus of the joke.

   It is interesting to observe the ways that these general principles, especially with regard to jokes that are purposive, are acted out in organizations. Phiup Bougen (1994), an academic at Madrid Business School, writes of the way that accountants are the subject of stereotypes and humour. In many organizations, the accountant is seen to be a stern figure who exercises control through the budgets, and the jokes and stereotypes are ways of dealing with the perceived threat that they pose; the jokes are essentially hostile. Bougen also shows the ways that the humour changes over time as perceptions of the character of 'the accountant' as professional change. In her study of young managers studying for a qualification the academic, Irena Grugulis (2002) found that they used humour as a way of dealing with the stress of assessment and the possibility of failure. At a deeper level, humour allows them to criticize the course and the qualification so that their hostility to the situation is not 'personal'. They use humour to deal with the complexity of the situation without committing themselves to any serious action. In this sense, humour acts as a defence against the anxiety that they found in the situation.

   In many ways, nicknames are jokes captured in a word. They may, in Freud's terms, be innocent or purposive. In a paper on the use of nicknames in organizations, the American academic Bruce Fortado (1998) suggests that their use has a number of functions that can be interpreted from their context. Nicknames can be used to identify character defects in senior people; they help to bond colleagues together. In particular, they can be a form of bonding for people who feel that they are 'deviants' from the 'normal' order in the organization. The nickname, for these people, is a way of gaining some feeling of control in difficult situations. Nicknames serve the function, Fortado argues, of developing members' social control of situations, of developing camaraderie amongst the group, of socialization into the group. They are an important aspect of labelling and identifying others and creating and sustaining negative or positive images of the other.

## Example: Joking nicknames

Because jokes and nicknames are understood in a particular context, they can be difficult to explain. But an example that comes to mind is this from the author's experience.

One of our senior male managers was nicknamed 'the fat controller'. This name comes from a series of books for children written by the Reverend Wilbert Awdry about a mythical railway. The nickname captured feelings that some of his colleagues had about him as a somewhat dominating person. In a similar vein, one of the senior female managers was known as 'the head girl'. Again, this image goes back to children's books about schools and the way in which the 'head girl' was seen as a somewhat dominating person.

What is perhaps interesting is the ways in which these names could be used with affection for most of the time but could sometimes be used with an edge of aggression when these characters were experienced as being *too* bossy or imperious.

2. **Stories, myths and sagas:** The range of what is meant by the term 'stories' is considerable. It ranges from 'corridor gossip' to tales told about victories or defeats within the organization, to accounts of meetings through to public proclamations by the chief executive on the future of the organization. In his study of storytelling, Gabriel (2000) created a detailed taxonomy of stories. His main classifications included:

   1. Comic stories in which the teller of the story is a deserving victim or comes out of the story as a foolish person. This includes incidents in which the teller made a mistake.

   2. Comic stories in which the teller of the story is a survivor, shows a good sense of humour in adversity or plucks victory out of adversity.

   3. Romantic stories in which the teller talks of love and affection. Sometimes these stories were 'romantic' in the sense that customers or hospital patients had expressed great appreciation for the care that they had received. They were also more directly 'romantic' in that there were stories of love and affection between members of the organization.

   We would add, however, another type of story. These are the 'serious stories' that can be spoken or written that represent the different representations of the different groups in the organization – management, trades and professional unions that advocate their different perspectives. From a management perspective, these can take the form of rules and procedures, business plans or strategic documents. When senior management of an organization works toward the development of a corporate culture, of the sort that was discussed in Chapter 4, that emphasizes the idea that all members share a set of core values, they are developing a story, a 'grand narrative' about the organization. This theme is developed in Chapter 6.

A major theme in the study of stories has been to understand them as ways that members give their work and their lives meaning. As we saw in Chapter 3, the idea of the corporate culture can have great appeal for the kind of person who wants to work for an organization that 'provides' strong core values. Their story is more or less the same as the corporate story. On the other hand, some members may gain meaning from their work by constantly complaining about the organization and its ways. Their 'stories' are, organizationally speaking, tales told by dissidents. Between the 'true believer' and 'the dissident', there are likely to be many shades of organizational story, including 'innocent' stories told just for the fun of it. As Gabriel (1991) points out, stories are not 'the truth' but are there to be interpreted, their deeper meaning to be discerned from the context of the story.

One of the most important areas of study in the interpretavist approach to organization culture has been into the idea of the *myth*. A myth can be regarded as a 'bundle' of stories that when taken together make some overall sense, although it is often the case that we do not realize until we have moments of reflection that we have created a 'myth'. They are best looked at as explanations of core aspects of organizational life that people hold to be 'good enough'. Myths can be complex and interwoven, and as new myths develop, they become deeply interwoven with the existing 'mythic reservoir' (Røyrvik and Wulff, 2002). They are stories with a veiled meaning that people tell to each other in the organization. The myth sustains people in the belief that their version of the organizational story is correct. This approach to culture has particular appeal in the Scandinavian countries (Czarniawska and Sköldberg, 2003). Myths provide 'sign posts' that can lead organization members and theorists toward the ways that relationships are structured in organizations; understanding myths and rituals can help organizations develop.

## Case study — Pervasive myths in an engineering consulting company

Scandiaconsult, a Scandinavian consulting engineering company, had been going through a period of rapid growth after it had undertaken a number of mergers and acquisitions. As a consulting company, its aim was to provide sophisticated solutions to large engineering projects. The authors of a case study, Emil Røyrvik and Egil Wulff (2002), worked with top management and project workers in project situations and through interviews to develop understanding of their stories and the everyday issues and problems. In the course of their work, they uncovered two key myths that pervaded the organization:

- **How the company initiated new projects:** A key activity for a consulting organization such as Scandiaconsult is the ability to acquire and generate new projects; they are the life blood of the organization. In this case, there were pervasive 'myths' held by people responsible for getting new projects. On the one hand, there was the myth that the company could only get projects through pure and 'objective' invitations for tender. This is the idea that when the company received an invitation to submit a tender for a project, those responsible for submitting the tender would design the document so that it would be of high quality but also be the most competitive tender. On the other hand, there was a myth that new projects were best gained through the development of long-term relationships and networks with organizations that needed the services of Scandiaconsult. The

*(Continued)*

issues that were contained within these two myths are very complex. Through the uncovering of the myths and discussion of them, members of the organization developed a new understanding of these myths and developed improved approaches to making choices as to how new projects should be approached.

- **The ideal form of organization for the company:** In this case, there were again two basic 'myths' (with many positions between). On the one hand, there was the 'myth' that the company should be organized around the geographical location of its regional branches. In this way of organizing, the teams of consultants would be multidisciplinary and able to provide an immediate service to clients within the region. On the other hand, there was a prevailing myth that the company should be organized around the different professional and technical disciplines. This was on the basis that the work that they performed required a high level of expertise and the constant development of professional knowledge and that this was best achieved by the co-location of the different disciplines. The issues and dilemmas that were contained within the myths of organization were complex and involved many dilemmas for organizational members. As in the first example, uncovering the myths led to a better understanding of the dilemmas and choices that could be made.

*Source: Based on Røyrvik and Wulff (2002)*

What is important in the myths is that they contain rational and non-rational elements *and* that within them there are elements about core values and the emotional commitments of members to the organization, their professions and their own sense of being. Strati (1999) suggests that organizations are not pervaded by a single myth that is well defined but rather the outcome of each member's account of the relationship between the individual and the organization; the myths display the intensity of their feelings with regard to their everyday organizational life that they construct and reconstruct.

Myth making occurs not only at the local organizational level; within organization and management theory there have developed myths about organizations and organizational life. With perhaps a hint of mischief, the Swedish organization theorist Barbara Czarniawska-Joerges (1992) reports of the way in which writers on corporate culture such as Deal and Kennedy (1982), discussed in Chapter 4, convey a 'myth' of organizational life. This mythology tells heroic stories of leaders who succeeded against all the odds, of the American dream of heroic entrepreneurial leadership *and also* paradoxically, talks of organizations as places in which values are shared within a view of 'corporate culture'. These myths provide managers and leaders with a sense of aspiration, an emotional buzz that ultimately, the organization can be 'managed'.

| Case study | Contrasting myths of an organization |

An interesting feature of the growth of the 'guru academic' (discussed in Chapter 3) has been the extent to which they can extol the virtues of organizations that exemplify the approach to organizational success that they advocate. One of the leading guru academics is Gary Hamel. He is founder and chair of an international management consultancy company, visiting professor of strategy and international management at London Business School and the Thomas S. Murphy Distinguished Research Fellow at Harvard Business School.

An example of the way a myth of organization can be created was Hamel's text *Leading the Revolution* (2000) in the course of which he mythologized the now disgraced energy and communications organization, Enron. The underpinning set of beliefs that this myth of Enron supports is that the American approach to conducting business is the very engine of change and progress. It is interesting to look at just some of the images and metaphors that Hamel uses to construct the myth:

- Enron . . . has '*again and again reinvented*' themselves.
- It '*revolutionized* international power plant development.'
- 'Enron's leaders know that you can't *pioneer* new markets without taking some risks.'
- 'Enron's *pro-entrepreneur* culture.'
- Building teams depended on the 'willingness of top-notch Enron people to *uproot* their careers *almost overnight*' (p. 219).
- Most Enron workers have '*self directed careers*' (p. 220).
- 'You can't build a *forever restless, opportunity seeking company* unless you're willing to hire *forever restless, opportunity seeking individuals*' (p. 221).
- 'There's also a chance for *some serious wealth creation*' (p. 259).
- The company has '*out-sized aspiration*' (p. 221).
- Enron had 'a *passion* to make markets . . . more efficient . . . a *vibrant* internal market . . . Highly motivated *entrepreneurs.*
- *Fluid organizational boundaries* (Hamel's emphasis, p. 222).

Hamel's mythology may be contrasted with this alternative 'myth' (written by a journalist, Madeleine Bunting, for the *Guardian* newspaper in 2002) that is highly critical of Enron and celebrates its demise. In this version, the underpinning core values that support the myth is that advanced capitalism is essentially corrupt and corrupting.

'Enron provides a *textbook case* of how *corporate power* subverts the political process. . . . It's *mucky stuff*, and *heads will roll*, but it's also a very familiar theme'. The Enron story 'spells the end not just to some nasty *pork-barrel politics* but to an *ideologically driven vicious corporate model*. . . . This vision of a *Darwinian dog-eat-dog market*' drove Enron. The company relied on 'a *near fundamentalist faith*' in the market so that '*true believers*' claimed there were simply no limits to its application.

Enron became the example par excellence of how, in the late 90s US corporate culture *highjacked and inverted* 60s radicalism. *Business guru* Gary Hamel praised Enron's activists (who) lived the rule of 'creative destruction' in which all conventional assumptions were to be challenged. . . . *It bred a culture of breathtaking arrogance* that Enron could do the impossible.

(In both of the extracts, the emphases, unless otherwise indicated, are from this chapter's author.)

From the interpretavist perspective jokes, nicknames, stories and myths are core aspects of organizational life. The ways in which they interrelate, sustain and create change to the rich and complex cultures of organizations. They tell us of important issues that members confront on a daily basis, about power and influence (or the lack of it), decision making (or feelings of impotence), issues about control (or lack of it) and so on.

## Negotiation of meaning influences organizational design

In this last section, we will discuss the ways that interpretive understandings of organizations illuminate the ways organizations are designed. In conventional organizational theory the structure of organizations is something that comes from formal processes of organizational design. An interpretive perspective shows, however, that lying alongside the formal structure, members can develop very different understandings of organizational design. We shall explore one particular perspective – the Arena concept developed by Strauss et al. (1964). This concept demonstrates how members use language and symbols in order to create a shifting design of their organization.

At the core of the concept of *negotiated order* is the idea that although the official structure of the organization is based upon a hierarchical or network or matrix model, what *actually* happens is significantly based upon processes of *negotiation*.

Strauss and his colleagues initially developed the idea of the negotiated order from their seminal study of seven psychiatric units in hospitals in the United States. At one extreme were units in which the emphasis was psychotherapeutic, where all members of the unit – doctors, patients, nurses, physiotherapists and so on – were strictly equal in their rights and there was no hieratical distinction made about the mode of care. At the other extreme were units in which the hierarchy was strictly defined as between doctors, nurses and patients. Other units occupied positions between these extremes. The issue that interested Strauss and his colleagues was: why is it that, given that each unit has the same types of staff and the same types of patient, they had such different structures and arrangements for the treatment of patients?

## Ideology, rhetoric and negotiation

Strauss and his colleagues were deeply aware of the nature of power and politics in organizations. They observed that in many organizations, position in the hierarchy was important and that position could be used as part of the process of negotiation. In many (but not all) of the psychiatric units, the medical staff were able to impose their definition of the situation onto the situation. They used their professional

---

Biography  **Anselm Strauss (1916–1996)**

Anselm Strauss was born in 1916 and died in San Francisco in 1996. He studied at the University of Chicago for both his masters degree and his PhD but spent most of his academic career (from 1960) at the University of California. Much of his writing was within the symbolic interactionist tradition. Indeed, he believed that, with due modesty, the ideas discussed in this section represented an extension of the Chicago school. He was one of only a few members of the Chicago school who took a direct interest in organizations. His interests in sociology were extensive, although for a time he tended to concentrate on the sociology of medicine and the medical system. It was from this that he developed the theories of negotiation and negotiated order that became central to his thinking. His interest was also in the development of methodologies for social science research. In 1967, he wrote with Barney Glaser a text on qualitative research, *The Discovery of Grounded Theory*, which is still in print. He developed his approach to research methods (with Juliet Corbin) in a number of influential texts.

# Professional ideologies, professional rhetoric: the negotiated arena

The key to this issue lies in what Strauss calls the different *professional ideologies* held by the staff. Professional ideologies are derived from the type of training and subsequent experiences that the professional has had. The psychiatric and nursing staff placed themselves into well-defined ideological camps, and their identities were firmly lodged in those ideologies. Strauss uses the term 'professional' in a broad sense to include any member of staff who has a particular understanding of the issues.

For example, some psychiatrists have a 'medical' ideology. By this, they would believe that the only way to treat patients effectively would be by giving them the right drugs, and when appropriate, the administration of electric shock treatment. Holding this ideology, with its emphasis on accurate diagnosis, means that the psychiatrists see themselves as having absolute control over the fate of the patient and the right to issue precise instructions to staff. This ideology also involves the dismissal of other forms of treatment, such as psychotherapy, as being unscientific.

At the other extreme are the psychiatrists who believe in psychotherapeutic methods of treatment. This involves an ideology that involves concepts of equality as between the parties involved in treatment and may regard the 'medical' model as not getting to the roots of the patient's problems (the psychotherapeutic psychiatrist believes the medical model to be relatively good at treating symptoms but poor at treating causes). Nurses and others also hold to treatment ideologies, and these can be very powerful in determining the pattern of care given to patients.

This professional ideology is expressed through the *professional rhetoric*. This term is used to describe the specialist language (the jargon) that members learn during the course of their training and socialization into the role. In the psychiatric units, all the different professionals had their own professional rhetoric. Staff who trained in schools where there was an emphasis on the medical model had a professional rhetoric that was different from those trained in schools where there was an emphasis on psychotherapeutic approaches. The exploration of the idea that the professional rhetoric can be explored as a discourse is discussed in Chapter 6.

When the nurses, psychiatrists, physiotherapists and others work together in order to discuss problems and issues they enter the *professional arena* in which the different groups of staff use their rhetoric in order to promote their particular ideology. This idea of the professional arena can be extended to any working group. If you take, for example, a board meeting of a manufacturing organization, the professional arena would consist of such professionals as marketing, production, sales, human resource and so on.

## Stop and think

Take an organization (or department) known to you. What would you see as the key ideologies in relation to the tasks that need to be undertaken? In the situation you are exploring, are there conflicts that make work difficult, or do the different ideologies and rhetorics make for an exciting life? If you think that there is little or no ideological difference between members, what are the consequences?

rhetoric (their esoteric, specialized language) to achieve that definition. However, as a rule, in order for the professional rhetoric to be effective, it needs to be accompanied by careful presentation of self. If the person's language is too esoteric, too much bound up in the language of the profession, he or she runs the danger of being thought of as narrow, not having the broad picture. If on the other hand, the person's language it too 'popular', he or she may be thought of as being 'incompetent' in the performance of their professional tasks and therefore unreliable as a colleague.

In some of the units that Strauss and his colleagues studied, the doctors did not have it all their own way. There were occasions when the nursing staff exercised the dominant ideology. They used their professional rhetoric to push the medical staff into methods of treatment with which the latter did not entirely agree. Typically, what happened in a case of this sort was that the medical staff, for career reasons, tended to work in some of the units for a shorter period than the nursing staff. In these cases, the nurses had a high degree of 'local knowledge' of the patients and their circumstances. In this situation, the nurses could bring their experience to bear as part of their professional rhetoric to counter the proposals of the doctors. Because members with high local knowledge *tended* to be more conservative in their ideas about therapy (largely because they had become insulated to the conditions on the ward), they would use arguments such as: 'We tried that before, and it didn't work then' if the doctors introduced new ideas.

This process of negotiation can also be seen in other aspects of work, characteristically, in terms of task allocation. Generally, people in work organizations have such documents as job descriptions that describe the nature of their contribution to the organization. However, it is typically the case that these descriptions are somewhat fuzzy around the edges; they rarely if ever describe exactly the sort of rights and responsibilities to be allocated to the various types and grades of people in the organization. They usually set a minimum level of performance, and the sociologist is generally interested in the ways in which people use these rules in order either to restrict or improve their work situations. Amongst the sorts of activities and negotiations in this area that Strauss discusses we find:

1. **Task gaining:** This is when a staff group would actively search out new tasks to perform because the task would give them, for example, prestige or a place nearer the 'centre of things'.

2. **Task offering:** A staff group would offer tasks because it enables them to be rid of irksome duties or it might mean that they are not inconvenienced. When there is offering, there might also be *task refusal*. Relevant people have recourse either to the rules of the organization or to legal constraints to prevent them either from being obliged to take on a task they do not want to perform or to deny the possibility of a person's taking on a task they would want to undertake.

3. **Task stripping:** This occurs when a person wants to take away a task from another. This could be because the first person wants to perform the task himself or herself, feeling that it is rightly his or hers. Alternatively, it could be because the first person feels that the second is performing the task incompetently.

4. **Task maintenance** is the attempt by the person who is threatened by the task stripper to maintain stability in the tasks performed. Again, this may be done either by recourse to the rules or by claiming that 'It has always been the case that I perform this task'.

These activities are undertaken because organizational members want to control the various aspects of their work and negotiate to make this possible. They stake claims and counterdemands and engage in 'games' of give and take in order to achieve satisfactory outcomes for themselves and their groups.

## Arenas and games

The idea that organizations can be looked at as arenas is analogous to the view that they can be looked at as an 'ecology of games'. Many years ago, the American sociologist Norton Long (1958) argued that the activities that people undertake in any particular situation could be looked at as a serious and profound game. The game provides the players with a set of goals that give them a sense of success or failure in their activities. These evolving games also provide members with clear roles and help them to develop strategies and political tactics. The ability to understand the behaviour of an individual or group depends upon the ability to understand the game in which that person or group is involved. The important issue here at all levels from individual to corporate is the development of competence in the games.

## Example: The rules of the game

This is from a conversation with a senior divisional manager:

When we have meetings of the senior management group, it is interesting to observe the way things get played out. I noticed the other day how neatly Lindsey, who looks after research and development, got for herself quite a useful place on the marketing group. But then it's fascinating how they all play their roles. I love the way the executive tries to dominate the senior managers on the board and then the way that the senior managers create alliances with different members of the executive. And then it's interesting who has a voice and who is ignored. I have a feeling that the human resources guy will not be a member of the group much longer; he's such a wimp. The other thing I notice is the way we talk about head office, the way we feel we've always got to do it their way and if someone gets too rebellious about that way they get stamped on by the others.

The negotiated arena approach to organizational design does not deny the power of hierarchy or other forms of authority in organizations. It is fascinating to look at the ways in which people *use* their position in the hierarchy (whether senior or junior), *use* their 'job descriptions', *use* their professional rhetoric, *use* their understanding of their personal power and so on in order to attempt to influence their place and the place of others in the organization.

Organizational members work together in webs of negotiation. At the start of this chapter, we discussed the idea that one of the fundamental assumptions behind symbolic interactionism was that when members of a group (or a department or even an organization) feel that all is well with the current definition of reality, they become 'lodged' into it. Change happens when old perspectives are believed not to meet new needs. In this sense, aspects of the everyday design of the organization can be seen as an emergent structure. If members come to believe that the game is not one that is yielding the results, or as people leave the organization and newcomers join, then the arena itself has the potential for change.

## Conclusions

In this chapter, we have looked at the ways that key theories and perspectives from sociology have made major contributions to organizational theory and provide challenges to other theories of organization. These perspectives challenge modernism and neo-modernism in the sense that they get beneath the prescriptive approaches to organizations that ultimately pervade these theories. They challenge postmodernism in the sense that these perspectives do not deny the reality of organizational life; they enable people to reflect in practical ways on the nature of their experience in organizations. The symbolic interactionists and the phenomenologists took a lead in the development of interpretative methodologies in the social sciences generally and in organizations in particular.

Interpretivists, particularly in the later Chicago school, were not interested in the development of a 'grand theory' that explains everything in the social world. Rather, their interest was in the development of theories that were empirically grounded and that provided ideas and propositions about the ways we create and communicate meaning. According to the sociologist Martin Bulmer (Bulmer et al., 1997), the perspectives presented in this chapter bring theoretical ideas and empirical data together so that the theory and the data illuminate each other – and sometimes sparked new directions of investigation through their confrontation.

Crucially, however, what the perspectives and theories presented in this chapter do is to present organizational members with propositions and methods that enable them to reflect deeply on issues of personal and organizational identity, on the nature of organizational purposes and the ways we give meaning to organizational life. These processes of reflectiveness and self-examination are there to enable the organization to develop and undergo change in intellectually rigorous and thoughtful ways. Some of these issues are summarized below where we match the learning outcomes of the chapter against the challenges these represent to organizational members.

## Concluding grid

| Learning outcomes | Challenges to the contemporary organization |
| --- | --- |
| Define what is meant by 'reflective' organization theory. | The development of reflective ability enables deeper understanding of key organizational issue and it enables informed action. |
| Compare and contrast how different strands of interpretavist, reflective organization theory sheds light on how organization members give meaning to their lives at work. | Enables us to understand the ways that members give diverse and complex meanings to their organizational world. |
| Discuss the ways individuals develop a sense of self in organizations. | Enables us to develop deeper insights into the ways that members actually experience the world of their organizations. |

Assess how these theories provide insights into how individuals and groups create their organizational identities.

The challenge that these perspectives give is to develop our understanding of the ways that members structure their organizational lives.

Explore how these different theories enrich our understanding of organizational culture.

Develops a deeper understanding of the underlying cultural beliefs that members hold about the organization.

Examine the ways these theories challenge our understandings of the design of organizations.

Enable organizational members to reflect on the ways that the patterns of negotiation actually help the organization develop or may be dysfunctional.

## Annotated further reading

The key ideas and perspectives that lie behind 'reflection' as an important organizational activity are contained in Donald Schön (1991). Although this book concentrates on the significance of reflection for members of professions such as medicine and engineering, it also has profound lessons for the practice of management.

If you are interested in the development of the Chicago school and in the work of Howard Becker visit his web page at http://home.earthlink.net/~hsbecker/

If you find the ideas of Goffman interesting, you might find the American film *Primary Colors* (director, Mike Nichols, 1998) both entertaining and instructive. It is a satirical study in impression management as it explores the fictionalized experiences of a candidate for the US presidency.

Goffman's book, *The Presentation of Self in Everyday Life* (1959), gives a very good insight into his overall approach to the development of identity and the processes by which we manage meaning.

Gabriel's (2000) *Storytelling in Organizations: Facts, Fictions, and Fantasies* is an authoritative account of stories in organizations. In particular, his classification of the types of story told by members in organizations provides very useful insights.

## Discussion questions

1. At the start of the chapter, we developed a model that underpins symbolic interactionism. This model took us through a number of 'stages' in the processes of individual and group meaning making and the ways we develop symbols. What do you see as the strengths and weaknesses of this model?

2. Some describe the work of Goffman as 'cynical' in its emphasis on impression management and its absence of notions of the 'true self'. Others feel that in his exploration of 'impression management', Goffman is actually describing key human abilities in making and communicating meaning. What do you think?

3. If you look at your own experience and those of colleagues, what are the key features that lie behind the development of your identity as, for example, a student or manager?

4. In our discussion of culture in this chapter, we have explored the reflective, interpretavist approach to this important topic. We ended the section, however, by putting forward the view that all the different perspectives on culture presented in this text have value. From what you have read so far in this chapter and others, do you think that this synthesizing view is useful, or do you prefer a purist view that one of the perspectives is superior to others? What influenced your preference?

5. In the section on 'design of organizations', we expressed the view that the negotiated order can be as important as the formal structure of the organization (e.g., hierarchy, network or matrix) in determining the ways that people and organizations undertake their work. Do you think that this view is useful?

# References

Alvesson, M. and Berg, P.O. (1992) *Corporate Culture and Organizational Symbolism: An Overview*, Berlin: Walter de Gruyter.

Alvesson, M. and Deetz, S. (2000) *Doing Critical Management Research*, London: Sage.

Alvesson, M. and Sköldberg, K. (2000) *Reflexive Methodology. New Vistas for Qualitative Research*, London: Sage.

Becker, H.S. (1963) *Outsiders: Studies in the Sociology of Deviance*, New York: The Free Press.

Becker, H.S. (1977) *Sociological Work: Method and Substance*, New Brunswick, NJ: Transaction Books.

Bougen, P.D. (1994) 'Joking apart: The serious side to the accountant stereotype', *Accounting, Organizations and Society* 19(3):319–335.

Bryant, J. (2003) *The Six Dilemmas of Collaboration*, Chichester: John Wiley.

Bulmer, M., Thomas W.I. and Park, R.E. (1997) 'Conceptualizing, theorizing and investigating social processes', in C. Camic (ed.), *Reclaiming the Sociological Classics: The State of the Scholarship*, Oxford: Blackwell Publishers.

Bunting, M. (2002) 'Fall of the arrogant', *The Guardian*, 28 January.

Cossette, P. (1998) 'The study of language in organizations: A symbolic interactionist stance', *Human Relations* 51(11):1355–1379.

Cuff, E.C., Sharrock, W.W. and Francis, D.W. (1998) *Perspectives in Sociology*, 4th edn, London: Routledge.

Czarniawska, B. and Sköldberg, K. (2003) 'Tales of organizing: Symbolism and narration in management studies', in B. Czarniawska and G. Sevón (eds), *The Northern Lights – Organization Theory in Scandinavia*, Copenhagen: Copenhagen Business School Press.

Czarniawska-Joerges, B. (1992) *Exploring Complex Organizations: A Cultural Perspective*, Newbury Park, CA: Sage.

Davis, F. (1968) 'Professional socialization as subjective experience', in H. Becker (ed.), *Institutions and the Person*, New York: Aldine.

Deal, T.E. and Kennedy, A.A. (1982) *Corporate Cultures: The Rites and Rituals of Corporate Life*, Reading, MA: Addison Wesley.

Dennis, A. (2001) *Making Decisions About People: The Organizational Contingencies of Illness*, Aldershot: Ashgate Publishing Ltd.

Denzin, N.K. (1971) 'Symbolic interactionism and ethnomethodology', in J.D. Douglas (ed.), *Understanding Everyday Life: Toward the Reconstruction of Sociological Knowledge*, London: Routledge & Kegan Paul.

Fortado, B. (1998) 'Interpreting nicknames: A micropolitical portal', *Journal of Management Studies* 35(1):14–34.

Frost, P.J. (2004) 'Handling toxic emotions: New challenges for leaders and their organization', *Organizational Dynamics* 33(2):111–128.

Freud, S. (1976) *Jokes and their Relation to the Unconscious*, Harmondsworth: Penguin Books.

Gabriel, Y. (1991) 'Turning facts into stories and stories into facts: A hermeneutic exploration of organizational folklore', *Human Relations* 44(8):857–875.

Gabriel, Y. (2000) *Storytelling in Organizations: Facts, Fictions, and Fantasies*, Oxford: Oxford University Press.

Garfinkel, H. (1976) *Studies in Ethnomethodology*, New York: Prentice Hall.

Glaser, B. and Strauss, A.L. (1967) *The Discovery of Grounded Theory: Strategies for Qualitative Research,* New York: Aldine.

Goffman, E. (1959) *The Presentation of Self in Everyday Life*, New York: Doubleday.

Goffman, E. (1972) *Interaction Ritual: Essays on Face-to-Face Behaviour*, Harmondsworth: Penguin University Books.

Goffman, E. (1974) *Asylums*, Harmondsworth: Penguin Books.

Goffman, E. (1974) *Frame Analysis: An Essay on the Organization of Experience*, Harmondsworth: Penguin Books.

Goffman, E. (1981) *Forms of Talk*, Oxford: Basil Blackwell.

Goleman, D. (1998) 'What makes a leader?' *Harvard Business Review* 76(6):92–102.

Grant, D. (1996) 'Metaphors, human resource management and control', in C. Oswick and D. Grant (eds), *Organization Development: Metaphorical Explorations*, London: Pitman Publishing.

Grugulis, I. (2002) 'Nothing serious? Candidates' use of humour in management training', *Human Relations* 55(4):387–406.

Hamel, G. (2000) *Leading the Revolution*, Cambridge, MA: Harvard Business School Press.

Hatch, M.J. and Schultz, M. (2002) 'The dynamics of organizational identity', *Human Relations* 55(8):989–1018.

Harvey, J.B. (1988) 'The Abilene paradox: The management of agreement', in J.B. Harvey (ed.), *The Abilene Paradox and other Meditations on Management*, San Francisco: Jossey-Bass.

Hayes, J. (2002) *The Theory and Practice of Change Management*, Basingstoke: Palgrave.

Hughes, E. (1958) *Men and Their Work*, Glencoe, IL: Free Press.

Huy, Q.N. (1999) 'Emotional capability, emotional intelligence, and radical change', *Academy of Management Review* 24(2):325–345.

Knights, D. and Willmott H. (1999) *Management Lives; Power and Identity in Work Organizations*, London: Sage.

Linstead, S. and Grafton-Small, R. (1992) 'On reading organizational culture', *Organization Studies* 13(3):331–355.

Long, N.E. (1958) 'The local community as an ecology of games', *American Journal of Sociology* 64(3):251–255.

Luckman, T. (1978) 'Preface', in T. Luckman (ed.), *Phenomenology and Sociology: Selected Readings*, Harmondsworth: Penguin Books Ltd.

Macdonald, K.M. (1995) *The Sociology of the Professions*, London: Sage.

McAuley, J. (1994) 'Exploring issues in culture and competence', *Human Relations* 47(4): 417–430.

Manning, P.K. (1971) 'Talking and becoming: A view of organizational socialization', in J.D. Douglas (ed.), *Understanding Everyday Life: Toward the Reconstruction of Sociological Knowledge*, London: Routledge & Kegan Paul.

Márai, S. (2002) *Embers*, London: Penguin Viking.

Matthews, F.H. (1977) *Quest for an American Sociology: Robert E. Park and the Chicago School*, Montreal: McGill-Queen's University Press.

Meltzer, B.N., Petras, J.W. and Reynolds, L.T. (1975) *Symbolic Interactionism: Genesis, Varieties and Criticism*, Boston: Routledge & Kegan Paul.

Mumby, D.K. (1988) *Communication and Power in Organizations: Discourse, Ideology, and Domination*, Norwood, NJ: Ablex Publishing Corporation.

Røyrvik, E.A. and Wulff, E. (2002) 'Mythmaking and knowledge sharing: Living organizational myths and the broadening of opportunity structures for knowledge sharing in a Scandinavian engineering consultant company', *Creativity and Innovation Management* 11(3):154–164.

Sandberg, J. (2000) 'Understanding human competence at work: An interpretative approach', *Academy of Management Journal* 43(1):9–2.

Schön, D.A. (1991) *The Reflective Practitioner: How Professionals think in Action*, Aldershot: Ashgate Arena.

Shaskolsky, L. (1970) 'The development of sociological theory in America – A sociology of knowledge interpretation', in L.T. and J.M. Reynolds (eds), *The Sociology of Sociology*, New York: McKay.

Strati, A. (1999) *Organization and Aesthetics*, London: Sage.

Strati, A. (2000) *Theory and Method in Organization Studies: Paradigms and Choices*, London: Sage.

Strauss, A., Bucher, R., Ehrlich, D. and Sabshin, M. (1964) *Psychiatric Institutions and Ideologies*, Glencoe, IL: Free Press.

Strauss, A. and Corbin, J. (1990) 'Trajectory framework for management of chronic illness', in A. Strauss (ed.), *Creating Sociological Awareness: Collective Images and Symbolic Representation*, New Brunswick, NJ: Transaction Publishers.

Turner, R.H. (1962) 'Role-Taking: Process versus Conformity' in A.M. Rose (ed.), *Human Behaviour and Social Processes: An Interactionist Approach*, London: Routledge and Kegan Paul.

Urmson, J. and Rée, O.J. (1991) *The Concise Encyclopedia of Western Philosophy and Philosophers*, London: Routledge

Wallemacq, A. and Sims, D. (1998) 'The struggle with sense', in D. Grant, T. Keenoy, and C. Oswick (eds), *Discourse and Organization*, London: Sage.

Westerlund, G. and Sjöstrand, S.-E. (1979) *Organizational Myths*, New York: Harper & Row.

# Chapter 8

# Reflexive organization theory: critical theory and psychoanalysis

## Introduction

One of the fascinating things about organizations is the common sense ways that people who work in them carry on with their lives. Some of us regard the place in which we work as a source of great enjoyment. Others take a view that work is for economic reward in order to enjoy life outside the organization. For others, work is a source of oppression and fear. In all these situations, members *generally* accept that the circumstances in which they work are to be taken for granted. However, at a deeper level, there are many 'power plays' enacted (sometimes consciously and sometimes unconsciously) that profoundly affect our relationship to organizations. Beneath the surface, undercurrents of deep emotion affect the ways we work in organizations and the ways organizations relate to their wider society. In this chapter, we will explore some of these aspects of organizational life.

The main goal of this chapter is to develop understanding of what are called reflexive approaches to organizations. This word 'reflexive' carries the idea that when we explore deeper issues of organizational life, we can also develop new ways of acting and thinking about issues such as power and control and with issues of communication and emotion. Both critical theory and psychoanalysis (the core subjects of this chapter), as they are applied in organization theory, are concerned with the development of organizations that enables people to be fulfilled emotionally and intellectually.

- Explore the development of critical theory as a challenging perspective in organization theory.

- Trace the development of psychoanalysis as a challenging perspective in organization theory.

- Examine the ways that critical theory and psychoanalysis come together to provide reflexive insights into the nature of organizations.

- Discuss how critical theory and psychoanalysis challenge understandings of the relationship between the organization and society.

- Discuss how critical theory and psychoanalysis challenge the individual, the group and the organization.

- Examine how critical theory and psychoanalysis develops challenging perspectives on organization culture.

- Explore how critical theory and psychoanalysis present challenging perspectives for organizational design.

- Discuss how critical theory and psychoanalysis challenge understandings of leadership and management.

## Structure of the chapter

- The chapter begins with an overview of critical theory. When it started life as an intellectual force in the 1930s, critical theory was an approach that explored the social world in a way that was sceptical, that asked questions about features of society that we normally take for granted. In the 1980s, a number of writers began to relate the core ideas of critical theory to the exploration of management and organizations. It takes a radical view of the ways that organizations need to develop in order for them to enable members to be fulfilled as human beings.

- The chapter continues with a discussion of the ways psychoanalysis develops challenges to many of the conventional assumptions about organizations. Although psychoanalysis started in the late nineteenth century as an approach to the exploration of the inner world of the individual as it developed, there emerged an approach to understanding deeper issues in organizations and society. We then show how the critical theorists used psychoanalysis as a way of enabling us to reflect in a deep way on core aspects of organizational life. We then move on to discuss the ways that psychoanalysis and critical theory enable us to reflect on the ways we need to constantly question issues of organizational design, organization culture, leadership and communication in order to ensure that organizations can be creative and fulfilling places in which to work.

## The development of critical theory as a challenging perspective in organization theory

The critical theorists from their start in the 1920s (with a break in the 1930s, when they moved to the United States) and their return in the 1950s are closely associated with the University of Frankfurt in Germany, where they founded the Institute for Social Research. The key writers are referred to as the Frankfurt school.

## Critical theory as seen by the Frankfurt school

At its heart, critical theory is an exploration of core aspects of society and organizations. It asks profound questions about the very nature of contemporary society; it works toward an understanding of the ways communications between people become distorted by the processes of power that are part of our everyday, taken-for-granted experience. It is reflexive in the sense that critical theory proposes that if we use our intellectual and emotional resources, we can overcome what they identify as the major flaws in society and organizations. As critical theory developed, it contained insights from a very wide range of intellectuals and scholars, particularly the work of Karl Marx, Max Weber, Sigmund Freud and German philosophers such as Immanuel Kant, all of whom, in their different ways, posed fundamental questions about the nature of 'reality' and how we experience it.

## Some key influences in the development of critical theory

The writings of Karl Marx (1818–1883) were highly influential on critical theorists because of his exploration of the nature of the development of contemporary society. Marx witnessed and developed a critique of a society in which there was, with the development of business and industry, the growth of a division between the owners of business and industry and those who worked in them. As the twentieth century progressed and as labour gained strength through trade unions and legislation, there was a general tendency in Western societies for employees to be absorbed into the capitalist organization, although critics of the development of the 'globalized capitalist economy' suggest that the problems of powerless and alienated workers have been transferred to developing countries. From a different perspective, the German sociologist Max Weber (1864–1920) was also a key influence on the development of critical theory. He was preoccupied with the development of advanced Western capitalism and institutions such as bureaucracy that characterize the world of business and industry. These marked a clear revolutionary difference between the modern world and feudal, agricultural societies. We discussed his contribution to the development of the idea of bureaucracy in Chapter 2.

There are two major themes that critical theorists take from these writings. The first, which is chiefly associated with Anglo-American thought, is that business organizations exist in order to maximize shareholder value. This means that the focus of business is to maximize the level of dividend for the owners. This is a view of society

## Capitalism and advanced capitalism

In Marxist thought, the development of capitalism was one stage in a historical process so that the economic structure of capitalistic society grew out of feudal society. In an essay in the work *Capital*, which he wrote with Frederick Engels in 1886, he wrote that as capitalist industrial and business society develops, the 'owners' of business and industry (the means of production) gain power in society and those who work (the proletariat) become increasingly powerless and alienated from society. As the foundations of capitalism reach maturity, capital (i.e., money in the form of shareholding and private ownership) becomes increasingly concentrated in the hands of the few. The workers become dominated by 'the conscious technical application of science, the methodical cultivation of the soil' so that their work is measured entirely in terms of its efficiency. However, as this process continues, the workers are increasingly gripped by 'misery, oppression, slavery, degradation, exploitation; but with this too grows the revolt of the working-class' (1965, p. 1248). Ultimately, the concentration of capital and the oppression of the workers collapses. The German philosopher Georg Hegel (1770–1831) influenced Marx's thinking. Hegel suggested that there was a relationship between the activity of human labour and the growth of self-knowledge. It is through work and by imposing our own designs on nature that we come to understand our true humanity (Connerton, 1976). Marx turned this idea on its head. He argued that in capitalist societies, because of the way we are dominated by the means of production, we become estranged from ourselves. Far from discovering ourselves through work, we lose any sense of self.

A different view of the development of capitalism was taken by another key influence on the critical theorists, Max Weber. In an essay published in Germany in 1920, he wrote that capitalist economic action 'rests on the expectation of profit by the utilization of opportunities for exchange, that is on (formally) peaceful chances of profit' (1920a). This search for profit can be found in many societies and in many different forms. However, the particular form of capitalism that emerged to full flowering in the eighteenth and nineteenth centuries that is known as Western, advanced, 'high' or rational capitalism comes from the conjunction of particular circumstances. At the heart is 'the rational capitalistic organization of (formally) free labour' – workers are not 'tied' to the land as peasants or by obligation to their 'masters'. The development of the idea of the 'rational industrial organization' (discussed in Chapter 2) that lies at the heart of rational capitalism emerges from 'the separation of business from the household . . . and closely connected with it rational book keeping' (1965, p. 1256). As with Marx, he saw that a strong influence on the development of modern capitalism has been the rational *application* of scientific knowledge. He believed that the particular emphasis on rationality in modern capitalism emerged from Western culture. One of a number of aspects of culture was an unintended consequence of the rise of Protestantism in Western Europe. He suggests that there were two crucial elements to Protestant religion. The first was a stern, austere, ascetic attitude to pleasure and seriousness, the idea that 'impulsive enjoyment of life, which leads away from work in a calling and from religion, was the enemy of rational asceticism' (1965, p. 1260). The second crucial element of the Protestant ascetic attitude was that it 'condemned both dishonesty and impulsive avarice' so that although the pursuit of wealth as an end in itself is 'highly reprehensible . . . the attainment of it as a fruit of labour in a calling was a sign of God's blessing' (1965, p. 1261). As rational capitalism develops, it no longer needs the support of the Protestant ascetic and the idea of the 'calling' so that 'in the field of its highest development, the United States, the pursuit of wealth, stripped of its religious and ethical meaning, tends to become associated with purely mundane passions, which often give it the character of sport' (1965, p. 1265).

that critical theorists find highly unsympathetic and is one for which they would wish to find alternatives. A somewhat different view that is more associated with Northern European thinking is that although shareholders are important, they are but one of a complex of stakeholders in the organization, including customers, employees, suppliers, the wider society and so on. Although to the critical theorist this is a somewhat more acceptable form of organization, they would wish to develop it in order to promote ideas of democratic organization that are discussed in later sections. The key issue within modern critical theory is: how do we create within this context societies and organizations that enable *all* members to be able to 'be human', to fulfil their true potential? Although some traditions within critical theory are fiercely anti-capitalist, there is also a tradition that capitalism is the world in which we live (at the moment), so what is the best way in which we can make it work?

If Marx and Weber were concerned with the development of society, the work of Freud (1856–1939) was deeply influential in the way that we understand the role of the unconscious in everyday life, and, from the perspective of the critical theorists, the ways we communicate with each other, a theme to be developed in this chapter.

Lying beneath all these issues of society and the individual is the work of Kant (1724–1804) and philosophers who followed in his tradition whose basic theory is that we give the world meaning as we interpret and understand the world about us. For Kant, it is part of human nature that when an object, opinion, fact or story confronts us we do not passively take it from eye to brain, as it were. Rather, we automatically select, organize and interpret our experience of external reality so that all we can have knowledge of is the 'how the world appears in our consciousness via the filtration and order imposed by our a priori mental forms' (Johnson and Duberley, 2000, p. 66). These a priori mental forms can be thought of as our mindset, our common sense ways of understanding the world. We are not, however, victims of these established a priori forms of thinking. We can come to understand through rational thinking the nature of these ways of thinking; this is the process of *reflexive thought* discussed later in the chapter.

These influences came together during the early years of the Frankfurt school in the 1920s and 1930s. Despite mass unemployment in Germany, a rising middle class was becoming more prosperous. From the perspective of the critical theorists, however, this prosperity came at a profound psychological and cultural cost. What they saw was that people were suffering a loss of personal identity as they became increasingly anonymous. They were becoming more detached from society as they lost their sense of community.

From the perspective of critical theorists, the reification of human experience led to an increasingly decadent culture that encouraged intellectual passivity and conformity. The period from 1919 to 1933 – known as the Weimar Republic in Germany – was brilliantly captured by novelists, artists and filmmakers of the time (referred to in the Annotated further reading at the end of the chapter). In the later part of this period, severe economic crises and the underlying social issues saw the rise of Nazism in Germany.

During the 1930s, the members of the Frankfurt school moved, in the face of the growing Nazi threat, to the United States and returned to Germany in 1949. They came into intellectual prominence in the late 1960s during the period of social upheaval that assailed Western Europe and the United States at that time. The reason

| Biographies | **Some key figures in the Frankfurt school** |
|---|---|

The membership of the Frankfurt school was quite diverse. These vignettes present an intellectual portrait of just a small number of them but provide a hint as to the range of their interests.

**Theodor Adorno** was born in Frankfurt in 1903 and died in 1969. He studied both philosophy and musical composition. He became the co-director of the Frankfurt Institute for Social Research. His interests ranged from empirical social research and the sociology of culture to the philosophy of aesthetics. He was particularly interested in how popular culture and consumerism affects people in capitalist societies.

**Max Horkheimer** was born in Stuttgart in 1895 and died in 1973. He was the director of the Institute for Social Research (the home of the Frankfurt school) in the 1930s and was responsible for its relocation to New York in 1935 and its return to Frankfurt in 1949. As his work developed, he was concerned that in the contemporary world, there had been a decline in thinking in a critical way about the nature of society. He thought that contemporary society was becoming obsessed with commercial values. He was also concerned that we had come to use ideas of 'rationality and reason' in a very narrow sort of way – that we were coming to use rational means in order to achieve usually unquestioned ends. This is an important issue in organizations in which we can see the use of 'scientific management' as the means to achieve production or services, but where the goals of the organization (e.g., shareholder value) may be essentially non-rational.

**Herbert Marcuse** was born in 1898 and died in 1979 and was a key member of the Frankfurt school. In 1934 he left Germany and emigrated to the United States, where he lived for the rest of his life. Not only a philosopher, he was a man of action. He joined the Office of Secret Services and became the head of the European bureau during World War II and worked for the US government until the 1950s, when he returned to intellectual work. Probably his most famous work was *One Dimensional Man*, which was a wide-ranging critique of both capitalist and communist societies. Over the years, he became increasingly influential as he traveled widely, and he became a major force in intellectual life in the United States. His work even gained the attention of the mass media. Throughout his life, he was in favour of revolutionary change and defended new forms of radical opposition to the status quo.

**Erich Fromm** was born in Frankfurt in 1900 and was a member of the Frankfurt school from its early days. He was brought up in a religious Jewish community and trained in psychoanalysis in Berlin. He emigrated to the United States in 1932, where he taught in a number of universities. He was regarded by many as a radical thinker, particularly in the way he developed fresh insights into the interrelationship between psychology and sociology. He believed strongly in the role of emotion and insight in human development. He thought dangerous those leaders 'who use only their brains and whose hearts have hardened. Critical and radical thought will only bear fruit when it is blended with the most precious quality man is endowed with – the love of life' (Fromm, 1973, p. 453). He wrote more than 20 books, and he died in 1980.

**Jürgan Habermas** was born in 1929 and is considered by many to be one of the leading contemporary critical theorists. He is emeritus professor of philosophy at the University of Frankfurt. One of his key intellectual preoccupations is how, in modern industrial and business societies, we tend to be very good at using 'scientific approaches' to ensure that organizations have the means to achieve the goals of the organization, but we do not really ask the deeper questions about the goals of organizations (or indeed a whole range of social issues). Throughout his work, he is interested in developing understanding of the deeper issues of human communication in order to find ways that humans can communicate with each other with greater integrity and truthfulness. As we shall see during this chapter, his interests are wide ranging – philosophy, the nature of communications, architecture as symbol of the modern age, the nature of democracy and so on. His most recent book, published in 2001 and titled *The Future of Human Nature*, explores the implications of genetic engineering and the ways our understanding of genetics can have profound implications for the ways we see ourselves and the nature of identity.

## Ideas and perspectives

## Reification

The Hungarian critical theorist George Lucaćs (1922) used the term 'reification' to capture the way that the push toward rationality in capitalist society and the desire for the mass production of goods and services causes 'human beings' to become anonymous 'things'. There are two sides to this. Objectively, reification is experienced when we become, in modern organizations, a 'job description' with expected 'outputs' that are determined impersonally and that carry a certain value expressed in the salary or wage. Our work is determined by the job description, and we are easily replaced. Subjectively, when we feel that our work lacks meaning, we feel alienated from the tasks that confront us and from others.

The term 'reification' is also used to describe the way terms such as 'organization', 'vision', 'goals' and 'strategy' are used in organizations to suggest that there is some higher order phenomenon that is detached from human activity. It gives these words an air of neutrality as if they were not the creations of real human beings.

that critical theory became an intellectual force in Western Germany is because it was seen to provide support for an attack on what academics and the more intellectual students saw as the emergence of a society that was *driven* by 'the compulsive force of a commodity dominated society' (Connerton, 1980, p. 2). This is a picture of society in which people are driven by the need to possess goods and organizations are designed to maximize 'customer satisfaction', a society dominated by supermarkets, hypermarkets, shopping malls and, today, internet shopping.

## Example: 'Property is theft'

The year 1968 was characterized throughout Western Europe and the United States by an atmosphere of revolution and change. Some of this was expressed in violent forms. In Germany, for example, the Baader-Meinholf was a group of people who were devoted to violent forms of action; they were deeply influenced by the ideas of people such as Che Guevara who believed that social change could only come out of total disruption. Others took a view that protest was best taken by quieter forms of direct action. One form of this was to attack ideas about property and our need to possess goods. To illustrate this, we have taken this extract from a lecture by the distinguished Nigerian poet and playwright Wole Soyinka. During the 1960s, he had placed himself in exile from Nigeria and was undertaking a lecture tour in Europe. He writes:

> I observed this pattern of 'direct action' at work most notably in Frankfurt University. A student who took a parked bicycle, motor-bike, or motor car that belonged to another did not consider it an act of theft. He kept it and returned it at his leisure, or simply kept it for as long as it took him to acquire a more attractive or convenient one, abandoning the former hundreds of kilometres from where its owner last saw it. Libraries bewailed their helplessness as students took away books and never returned them, often returning to exercise their right to borrow some more. Others felt that the shelves of bookstores should be open to the acquisitive mood of the reader.

Students felt quite noble in raiding the accounts of a parent or guardian – or indeed the neighbourhood store. All property is theft – and that, take note, included intellectual property. In short, plagiarism was no crime (Soyinka, 2004).

*Source:* Excerpt from Reith Lecture 2004.[1]

## Stop and think

In this excerpt, we have a particular view about the growth of the 'consumerist society' and the 'best' way to resist it. As you look around your society today, to what extent do you feel that people see consumerism as important – and is there still resistance to it? How do you think this resistance is expressed? On the other hand, has this consumerist view now become entirely respectable?

[1]The Reith Lectures are an annual event that is broadcast by the BBC on Radio Four (the leading speech station of the BBC). They are considered prestigious, and they represent dominant themes in society. The lectures by Wole Soyinka may be found at http://www.bbc.co.uk/radio4/reith2004.

There were two aspects of critical theory that were thought to be important by those intellectuals who took place in the protests of the late 1960s who wanted radical change in society. The first theme was the idea that we need to break down the way organizations and society are currently designed so that they enable the production of goods and services at the expense of peoples' 'instinctual drives'. This is known as the 'emancipatory interest' in critical theory. It is a view, to be explored during the chapter, that on the one hand, there is the human being who is 'naturally' inclined to be rational and collaborative, and on the other hand, there are social and economic forces that we feel we cannot control that 'push' us into problematic patterns of behaviour. These latter, according to Habermas, are the forces from which we need to be emancipated so that we can free ourselves from the false ideas of consumerism and self-centredness towards self-development and autonomy (the idea that we can work in a collaborative way with others). As we shall show, many of the critical theorists have a basically optimistic view of human nature; if we are freed from the chains of living in a consumerist, production-driven society we would behave cooperatively and organically in relation to each other.

## Example: From relative emancipation to oppression

Ruth, one of the students on our undergraduate course, was talking about working for a call centre for the past four years. The centre provided a specialist service for the promotion of pharmaceutical goods to doctors and hospitals. When she started, the centre staff, who were all young, worked in teams. They were able to chat with each other between calls and worked well together collaboratively. They were able to use their intelligence in gauging the effectiveness of the calls. They enjoyed their work even though it was sometimes quite stressful. A new manager was appointed. She thought that this way of working was *inefficient*, so cubicles were installed to separate the staff from each other. Although this has increased the number of calls, the number of staff who are leaving the centre to find other employment has also increased.

The second theme was that critical theory provided an intellectual basis for the establishment of a more *direct* way of understanding the world. The argument that they put forward is that as Western society develops, we live more and more in a world where our everyday experience is distorted by communications. This happens at many levels in organizations. One of the most powerful examples of this is in the way that the very nature of organizational life is presented in corporate plans and communications and indeed in many texts about organizations as they present a view of organizations *as if* they are 'perfect'.

---

**Ideas and perspectives**

## The textbook and the world of experience

The American writer and teacher Howard Schwartz (1990) discusses a problem he had in teaching organizational behaviour to MBA students who were also managers in business organizations. He wanted them to explore the gap between the ways organizations are depicted in most management textbooks and in the sorts of documents about strategy that are produced within organizations, and the world of their daily experience in organizations.

He asked his MBA students to picture an organization they knew well. Then he described two organizational worlds:

- The first was based on the conventional textbooks that the students really liked. These textbooks communicated an organizational world that was *clockwork*. In this story, people know what the organization is about, and they are engaged in purposeful behaviour. People are basically happy in their work, people do not get into anxiety states, and skilled management can overcome any problems. This is the world communicated in the textbooks, in the pronouncements of organizational leaders through their strategies and business plans.

- The second story was that of an organization that was like a *snakepit*. Here everything is felt to be 'falling apart', and members feel that they must create their own little secure spaces. People feel they do not know what is going on and are anxious, stressed, frustrated and miserable. In the snakepit, management problems are felt to be basically insoluble.

Then he asked his students which of these descriptions most resembled their own organization. The majority of them said that the 'snakepit' was a closer depiction of their organization than the clockwork. Schwartz then concluded that what his students really needed to know – from his *Understanding Organizations* module – was how to understand and deal with the snakepit given its pervasiveness. From the students' point of view, however, they wanted to stick with the 'clockwork' view of organizational life – they preferred to think of the organization as communicated through textbooks and strategy documents rather than confront the rough and ready world of experience.

He suggests that the reason for this is that if they can identify with the clockwork depiction of organizations because it represents an ideal to which they can aim, if they can believe that they work for a 'perfect' organization, they are 'perfect' themselves. This takes us into interesting waters that we shall discuss further when we explore the challenges of the psychoanalytic perspective.

## Critical management studies: critical theory enters organization and management theory

In the late 1980s, core ideas from critical theory began to be related to organization theory. The reason for this was that a number of radical European academics began to question the ways management theory avoids asking fundamental questions about the nature of organizations, management and leadership.

The first text in English to deal with the emerging discipline was *Critical Management Studies* edited by Mats Alvesson and Hugh Willmott and published in 1992. In their introduction, they point to the way that conventional presentations portray the discipline of management as a rational, 'scientific' activity with an emphasis on organizational effectiveness and efficiency. Management is 'considered to be a **socially valuable technical function**, normally acting in the general interest of workers, employers, customers, and citizens alike' (p. 1). Similarly, 'managers' are presented as 'carriers of rationality and initiative (e.g., in many versions of strategic management and corporate culture), while other actors appear as objects of managerial action' (p. 1). Alvesson and Willmott suggest, however, that from a critical theory perspective, the impact of management is too powerful 'in its effects upon the lives of employees, consumers and citizens to be guided by a narrow, instrumental form of rationality' (p. 1). In this book, they take two major themes. The first is the critical exploration of the nature of management. The second is the exploration of aspects of management and organization in order to show how theory and practice can be advanced by the 'emancipatory impulse of Critical Theory'.

Alvesson and Willmott then collaborated in the development of *Making Sense of Management: A Critical Introduction* published in 1996 in which they developed their understanding of critical theory and management. Of particular interest is their treatment of organization theory, which they see as 'the most fundamental and pervasive of the management specialisms' (p. 111). They suggest that organizing underpins all the other management specialisms such as marketing, strategic management, accounting, human resource management and so on. They also claim the importance of organization theory in the context of critical management theory as it has the strongest implications for the other specialisms. They suggest that the key purpose of a critical theory perspective in the study of organizations is to stimulate and contribute to dialogues and conversations that challenge and remove the sorts of practices that prevent autonomy and responsibility – the emancipatory interest. Since these texts were written, other authors have developed ideas about the relationship between critical theory and organizations.

At the heart of critical theory, from an organizational perspective, is the proposition that the way we live in organizations discourages fundamental thinking about the very nature of organization. We 'take it for granted' that the forms of organization in which we live are superior to other forms of organization. Because we take these basic issues of such things as leadership, management, the nature of organization and so on as 'common sense', we do not set up deep challenges of exploring the consequences of our ways of being in organizations. In a sense, we are like very sophisticated machines acting out our organizational lives in very clever ways but without really engaging our ability to think deeply and to act creatively to develop radically, reflexive, different ways of being in organizations.

The term *reflexivity*, when used in management and organization theory, is done so to suggest an idea of *shared* deep thought and action between members of the organization. The development of a true understanding of organizational actions and processes such as 'leadership' needs to be a shared understanding – not the leader in his or her ivory tower thinking through what it is to be a 'leader' or the person (with the board) 'responsible' for the organization's strategy; rather, it is a process in which all the members of the organization are truly involved. The aim of reflexive thought is that members can develop a living and therefore constantly changing understanding of their actions and processes. This also involves the belief that no aspect of organizations can be understood unless it is related to its historical context and to the social structure in which it is placed (Connerton, 1976). In this sense, critical theory pushes us to explore and develop organizational theory in the context of the society in which organizations are located.

## Critical theory develops new understanding of 'the scientific approach'

For some writers, a key concern of critical theory lies in its attack on the ways modern societies have come to use 'science' as the fundamental way we understand the world. They use the term 'scientism' to capture the ways the philosophies and methodologies (ontologies and epistemologies) of natural science are used to underpin the investigation of *all* aspects of human behaviour and thought, including philosophy and the social sciences. As we discussed in Chapter 2, a key underpinning claim of natural science is that the 'language of science' is neutral and does not carry with it any values (other than the values of being value free). This issue of claims to value-free knowledge is particularly important, at least within conventional organization theory, when managers and management consultants make claims that their work is 'scientific' and therefore is 'superior' as 'knowledge' to that of others.

The sorts of assumptions that flow from the 'scientific approach' are, for example, that organizations can be 'managed' in a 'scientific' manner. Activities can be controlled through the analysis of data about external markets and internal production of goods and services rather than intuition. Organizational structures can be designed so that their form can fit their function. Managers can develop strategies about the organization's relationship to its external environment and to the running of their organization that are entirely rational and based on 'scientific' understanding. In order for this scientific view to prevail, there need to be people who are specially trained to take this value-free scientific view of the world and who are capable of taking action that ensures that the logic is followed. This assumption legitimizes the appointment of managers and leaders who are paid large salaries and lead privileged lives to conduct their organizations in this manner.

For the critical theorist, however, these assumptions about the 'value-free' nature of science are questionable. Adorno and Horkheimer (1972) argues that the very assertions that science is 'value free' and that it is 'objective' are themselves values behind which other values lie. He suggests that the very purpose of natural science – the domination of nature – is itself irrational and laden with values about our relationship with the natural world. In this sense, scientists have developed highly rational tools and techniques (the 'scientific method') that are used to achieve essentially irrational ends. In the same way, it could be argued that academics and managers have developed elaborate, scientific methodologies for the development of efficient and effective business, although the ends, the purposes, of business (e.g., the maximization of shareholder value) are not rational.

## 'The sciences of the spirit'

This model of natural science is not the only show in town, in Western thought, in terms of reaching the truth. The child psychologist and psychoanalyst Bruno Bettelheim (1983) pointed out that in the German intellectual culture, there were two distinctive and different versions of the nature of science and that both were accepted as equally legitimate in their appropriate fields but had not much in common. There was, on the one hand, the natural sciences; the topic of these sciences (e.g., biology, physics, chemistry, astronomy) was the physical world. The other version of science was the 'sciences of the spirit'. This approach to scientific thought is attractive to critical theorists and is, as we shall show, one of the reasons they were deeply attracted to psychoanalysis as a scientific approach. This approach to science, referred to as *hermeneutics*, is really interested in understanding how people are placed in their history, the development of ideas and values, the understanding of culture. The term *hermeneutic* comes originally from the processes by which scholars interpreted and explained Scriptural texts, the way they tried to enter into the lives, to understand the world of the original authors of the original texts; it is the *science of interpretation*. This approach is not interested in the creation and application of 'natural laws' (a key theme in the natural sciences) but in understanding the individual, group and organization in their uniqueness and then developing understanding of how the unique relates to the more general. The hermeneutic process is designed to uncover the meanings held by members of the organization about themselves and the organization, to develop a new understanding or 'wisdom' about organizational life.

However, we should add a cautionary note. The wisdom gained from hermeneutics will be hard won and maybe even 'has quite a low probability to develop because there are just too many wiseacres around who take it for granted that the profit and excellence of an organization or corporation is the ultimate target, without recognizing the auto-destructiveness these targets are based on' (Sievers, 1994, p. 277). On the other hand, the growth of concepts in recent years such as emotional intelligence and emotional capability suggest that there is hope for reflexive organizations. The development of emotional intelligence relates to the development of ability in self-awareness and the ability to motivate the self and others through this awareness of the self. Emotional capability is concerned with the ability of people at an organizational level to understand the relationship between emotions and change and to understand that emotions are a core aspect of organizational life (Darwin et al., 2002).

## The models of 'natural science' and the 'sciences of the spirit' come together

In some respects, critical theorists are drawn to the hermeneutic tradition, but they also see the quantitative methods of natural science as having a significant place in the development of social science. In a text written collaboratively by members of the Frankfurt Institute for Social Research (1973), they argue that in a world that is increasingly standardized and in which the individual is 'far more powerless than he admits to himself, methods which are standardized' such as surveys and question-naires are 'the suitable means for describing and gaining insight into the situation' (p. 122). They suggest that although 'society' is something that we create through human consciousness, we live in a world 'that to a large extent is dominated by eco-nomic laws over which human beings have little power, it would be an illusion to seek to understand social phenomena in principle as having "meaning"'. In this sense, they make a distinction between those parts of our experience in which exploring 'meaning' is appropriate and those in which fact-finding methods enable us to understand 'reality'. For the critical theorist, however, the notion that 'facts' and 'reality' are 'value free' would be highly problematic; 'facts' and 'reality' are interpreted and understood within a social context. They argue that when a social researcher encounters assertions that come from a 'spiritual' position, then the researcher 'must demand evidence of its truth' through empirical investigation that leads to 'independent and resolute theoretical thinking' (p. 125). There needs to be a unity between the theoretical assumptions that underpin critical theory and the prac-ticalities of research.

Although critical theory has this scepticism of the ways that 'natural science' is practised in the modern world, there is empathy for the underpinning themes and ideas of Enlightenment thought. As we discussed in Chapter 2, the Enlightenment was the period in Western thought when, basically, people began to move from ways of thinking that were based on feudal and religious understandings of the world toward a more urban and 'scientific' way of thinking. This admiration for the Enlightenment is based upon the core value embedded in the Enlightenment of the concepts of rationality and the critique, the idea that we should be constantly scepti-cal and exploring so that we never take the status quo at its face value.

## Critical theory has practical organizational implications

As far as the development of organization theory is concerned, critical theory can be seen as a practical theory in that its key theme of the development of understanding leads, as we shall demonstrate, to important conclusions for organizations.

Habermas has been described as seeking to explore the *optimistic* elements of crit-ical theory. He is interested in discovering the ways people can be released from the oppressions (e.g., the emphasis on consumerism, the ways people are oppressed by working in organizations that cause members stress and anxiety but with little reward beyond the financial) that lie within advanced industrial society. He wants to do this through an appreciation of the value of reason, rationality and the core val-ues of the Enlightenment (Cuff et al., 1998). As we shall see in later sections, one of the core issues that critical theory addresses is that a key aspect of organizational development is toward making organizations more democratic so that the voices of those individuals and groups whose perspectives are customarily silenced are heard. This issue was discussed in Chapter 6. The important consequence of this is so that organizational members can *self-determine* (but not in a self-centred, individualistic manner) the values and direction of their organization (Darwin et al., 2002). This theme is discussed in a later section of the chapter.

## Example: Critical theory as a practical theory

One of the leading writers on critical theory in organizations, Mats Alvesson (2003), writes that although critical theory can appear to be peripheral and esoteric, it does reach into parts of organizations that other approaches do not reach. He suggests a number of challenges to explore in organizations that come from the insights from critical theory. These are some of the issues that he identified, many of which we shall discuss in greater detail as the chapter unfolds:

1. **The dominant language in use:** For example, is there a tendency in the organization for language to be dominated by 'male' ideas? Is the language dominated by metaphors and terms of challenge, confrontation, toughness, lack of emotion and so on?

2. **Distortions in communication:** Are the ways that people speak to each other distorted by the use of words such as *motivation*, *leadership* and *empowerment* that seem to mean a lot but on close inspection mean less than they seem to?

3. **People are fixed in their roles:** Are there ways that members of the organization are rigidly controlled by a culture that places them in specific roles (e.g., 'manager') or gender (e.g., 'women (or men) always behave that way'?)

4. **Power relations:** Are power relations expressed through big differences in status? Is hierarchical position really important in 'placing' people?

5. **A culture that prevents exploration of deep issues:** Are there ways that the culture – especially in myths and stories – seems to put a block on the exploration of deeper issues of the organization?

6. **The organization is ruled by technology:** Is there a predominant belief in the organization that the way for the organization to be truly effective is through its technologies rather than through its members?

7. **Belief that management and leadership are concerned with the technical:** Is there a predominant belief that all organizational problems can be solved through the appropriate technique rather than through human engagement?

8. **Human ethical issues are marginal:** Is there a tendency to observe the ethics of the marketplace rather than the ethics of human communication and respect?

9. **Political correctness:** Is there a tendency in the organization to adopt ethical and moral stances about issues that are based on 'political correctness' so that they cannot be questioned? This is a very interesting challenge for some organizations in the sense that conceptions of 'political correctness' can be used as a power play in order to prevent difficult questions about, for example, performance to be raised.

In the introduction to this chapter, we mentioned that there are two key themes in this chapter – critical theory and psychoanalysis. Within the traditions of critical theory there was an understanding that one of the ways of understanding deeper issues of the relationship between the person and society and organizations was through theories and approaches of psychoanalysis.

## The development of psychoanalysis as a challenging perspective in organization theory

In this section, the challenge is to show how both the theory and processes of psychoanalysis make a genuine contribution to organization theory. Therefore, a little background on the nature of psychoanalysis might be useful.

The key figure in this background is Sigmund Freud, who is introduced below. As he developed his theory of personality, he saw that human beings are a complex mixture of, on the one hand, conscious, rational aspects and, on the other hand, unconscious, irrational, infantile and selfish aspects of the self, and that we can become clever in disguising the latter in the guise of the former. When these unconscious forces become powerful, they lead to distorted communication between people so that the words people say no longer mean what they seem to mean. Habermas (1970) sees psychoanalysis as a 'kind of linguistic analysis pertaining to systematically distorted communication' (p. 206). He also discusses the way that in his writings on cultural theory, Freud moved from considering the individual to broader issues of collective and societal dysfunction.

During the 1930s, with the rise of Nazism, there was a departure of psychoanalysts from Germany and Austria to the United Kingdom and the United States and many other countries. As we shall discuss, psychoanalysts in the United Kingdom and the United States particularly became interested in the application of psychoanalytic thought to organizations.

A key aspect of Freud's work is the way the individual works with the psychoanalyst in order to explore these deep issues. This involves an encounter between the

---

| Biography | **Key figures in psychoanalysis –** **Sigmund Freud (1856–1939)** |
| --- | --- |

Sigmund Freud was born in 1856 in Freiberg in Moravia and died in 1939 in London. He became a medical student in the 1870s and during the 1880s began to become interested in psychoanalysis as a new way of understanding the unconscious mind. He was fascinated by the idea that understanding dreams would enable understanding of the deepest aspects of the personality, and from this he developed his approach to understanding the self. He wrote many books and worked with individuals to develop the science of psychoanalysis. The child psychologist Bruno Bettelheim (1983) wrote:

> The purpose of Freud's lifelong struggle was to help us to understand ourselves, so that we would no longer be propelled, by forces unknown to us, to live lives of discontent, or perhaps outright misery, and to make others miserable, very much to our own detriment (p. 15).

A key aspect of the development of this kind of reflexive thought was the role of the psychoanalyst, the person who helped the person to achieve understanding. Freud and his followers developed the idea of the psychoanalyst as a scientist helping the person to reveal and to interpret the interplay of conscious and unconscious. Freud's work, whatever one feels about it, represents one of the fundamental building blocks to our contemporary understanding of individuals in society.

As his work developed, Freud attracted many followers, some of whom stayed with and developed his original theories, others of whom came to radical disagreement with his position. Some of these individuals will feature in the chapter as it develops.

analyst and the client in which the analyst performs the role of listening and interpretation as the client explores, sometimes through dreams, sometimes through the events of the day, matters of depth and significance in his or her life. Traditionally, these encounters would take place three or four times a week for the 'psychoanalytic hour', maybe over a number of years, although these days there are many approaches to 'brief analysis'. What has this essentially private encounter got to do with organization theory?

One answer to this is to suggest that in many ways contemporary organization theory is dominated by theoretical perspectives drawn from sociology, economics and the political sciences. The contribution of the psychoanalytic approach brings back the individual as lying at the heart of the organization. The psychoanalyst and critical theorist Erich Fromm, in a paper written in 1932, suggests that although Freud's initial interest was to develop understanding of the individual, once the:

> . . . instincts were discovered to be the motive force behind human behavior, and once the unconscious was seen to be the source of man's ideologies and behavior patterns, it was inevitable that analytic authors would make an attempt to move from the problem of the individual to the problem of society, from individual to social psychology. They had to try to use the techniques of psychoanalysis to discover the hidden sources of the obviously irrational patterns in societal life – in religion, custom, politics and education (p. 481).

This means that the often-unconscious forces that motivate members can be understood not as *individual* problems but in the context of the organization and their social environment (Neumann and Hirschhorn, 1999).

Psychoanalysis helps us to understand the nature of 'irrational' behaviour at all levels in organizations. Understanding the irrational enables these behaviours to be seen as a 'normal' element of organizational behaviour that, if not properly understood, creeps up on organizations through the back door (Swarte, 1998). In this way, as we shall see in later sections, psychoanalysis helps us to understand issues about the ways in which individuals and groups relate to their organizations from the boardroom to the factory floor; it helps us to understand some of the core issues of organizational culture, organizational design and leadership.

## Psychoanalysis gives insight into organizations as a 'practical theory'

During the 1940s, there was a clustering of psychoanalysts and other social scientists in London who saw the need to develop approaches to research and clinical practice that would be of value to organizations and society more generally. This grew into the Tavistock Institute of Human Relations, which was founded in London in 1946. It was set up for the specific purpose of actively relating the psychological and social sciences to the needs and concerns of society. In sustaining this endeavour for almost 60 years, it has won international recognition. The objectives of the Tavistock Institute are to study human relations in conditions of well being, conflict or breakdown in the family, the community, the work group and the larger organization, and to

## Ideas and perspectives

# Is psychoanalysis 'scientific'?

Discussion of whether or not psychoanalysis is 'scientific' has been the source of considerable debate and takes us back to some of the debates about 'natural science' and 'hermeneutic knowing' that were discussed earlier in the chapter.

Fromm argues (1970) that the 'most creative and radical achievement of Freud's theory was the founding of a *science* of the irrational' – that is, the 'theory of the unconscious' (p. 12). It is:

> an *empirical* method for the uncovering of the unconscious strivings of a person, masked by ration-alization. . . . It was the great achievement of Freud to have taken up a number of problems so far only dealt with abstractly by philosophy and to transform them into the subject matter of empirical investigation (p. 30).

It is, he wrote in another place, a form of psychology 'which should be classed among the natural sciences' (1980, p.478).

This emphasis on psychoanalysis as a 'natural science' fits with the view that we discussed earlier that the development of understanding of the ways communication becomes distorted and the ways psychological disturbance occurs are best done through rigorous empirical investigation. At the same time, this approach to science is creative with a 'belief in the potency of reason, the belief that human reason and human imagination can penetrate the deceptive surface of the phenomena and arrive at hypotheses that deal with the underlying forces rather than the surface' (Fromm, 1980, p. 11).

Bettelheim took a different view. He argues that to present Freud's work as 'natural science' is misleading. He sees psychoanalysis as coming from the hermeneutic, 'sciences of the spirit', approach. When Bettelheim (1983) worked with severely disturbed children using a psychoanalytic approach, the child needed '*emotional closeness* based on an immediate *sympathetic comprehension* of all aspects of the child's *soul* – of what afflicted it and why. What was needed was . . . *spontaneous sympathy* of our unconscious with that of others, a *feeling response of our soul* to theirs' (p. 5). He argues that when Freud's work was translated into English, it was presented as a form of 'natural science' in order to appeal to the more practical, natural science–orientated Anglo-Saxon audience. Bettelheim argues that the clinical processes favoured by the natural science approach cannot capture the ways that people are actually experiencing the world, the ways that people understand their world.

This view is one that is sympathetic to critical theorists, who believe that understanding the ways that communication becomes distorted need a closer understanding of the emotional aspects of human behaviour.

promote the health and effectiveness of individuals and organizations. Although there are aspects of the consultancy and research undertaken by the Tavistock Institute that are close in spirit to the neo-modernists discussed in Chapter 3 (the learned journal of the Tavistock Institute is called *Human Relations*), its development over the years has been toward the reflexive, critical perspectives discussed in this chapter.

The Tavistock Institute developed these insights to form what came known as a psychodynamic approach to organization theory and consulting. As it developed within the Tavistock Institute, psychodynamic theory is a combination of a number of theories but with a strong emphasis on psychoanalytic ideas – it is, if you will, 'psychoanalysis plus'. This combination of different but related theories enables a deep and multifaceted exploration of organizations. Practitioners claim that psychodynamic theory 'provides social scientific depth by drawing attention to sources of energy and motivational forces being experienced within individuals, small groups, their leaders and the linkages between them' (Neumann and Hirschhorn, 1999, p. 684). As we shall show later in this chapter, this process can include understanding of the ways that organizations can become very difficult places to be – the neurotic organization – and the ways that through understanding these patterns of behaviour, they can develop out of them. However, and this is crucial, the emphasis within the Tavistock tradition is that psychodynamic theory exists in order to be used as a 'practical theory' – as a means of exploring in depth organizational situations with the aim of developing new and improved approaches to them. Some of the ways this is done are discussed later in the chapter.

## The challenge of psychoanalysis to organizations

As far as the critical theorists are concerned, psychoanalysis represents a scientific approach to the development of insight into *the emotional experience of people* within organizations. Psychoanalysis is a way of looking at organizations that proposes that aspects of the 'rational' and taken-for-granted surface realities of organization life are expressions of preoccupations and concerns that lie beneath the level of conscious awareness.

In his influential text *Images of Organizations* (1997), Gareth Morgan points out that Freud believed that there was a struggle within the human being between our instincts for survival, for life, but also that there was within the human spirit a death instinct, an instinct for destruction. These instincts have important implications for organizations. This may be seen as, on the one hand, the desire to achieve and to develop; on the other hand, it can be reflected in the elements of destruction that sometimes pervade organizational life. These destructive, negative aspects can be expressed in many different ways – through the ways people can believe that they have to defend their actions because they think they live in a 'culture of blame', through feelings of persecution, through distorted communications, through profound divisions in leadership and followership, and in other negative behaviours.

These features can lead to what have been termed *neurotic organizations*. These features can become, in times of change and turbulence, quite dominating; they can also be masked by a presentation that seems on the surface to be rational and reasonable.

## The key challenges of psychoanalysis

Two aspects of psychoanalysis that challenge organizations are:

1. **The psychoanalytic method:** This is the process by which members can develop understanding of the individual, group and organization. At its heart, this means the ability to understand, interpret and discuss what is happening to individuals,

# Symptoms of the neurotic organization

The basic idea of the neurotic organization is that organizations can get into a state in which they become, psychologically, unhealthy and dysfunctional. Sometimes they become neurotic because of the nature of their leadership; at other times, key groups and individuals in the organization can develop neurotic tendencies. One of the most important writers on organizations from a psychoanalytic perspective, Manfred F.R. Kets de Vries, has written comprehensively on the ways psychoanalysis can illuminate organizational life. In one of his most significant books, *The Neurotic Organization* (1985), he discusses (with his colleague Danny Miller) the 'neurotic organization'. They suggest that some of the symptoms of this kind of organization include:

- **Commitment to bad decisions:** Members not only take bad decisions but they also stick with them despite all the evidence that the organization is getting into real problems. This is discussed in a later section when we look at the ways that critical theory and psychoanalysis help our understanding of organization culture.

- **Advancement of members who are detached from reality:** This is the way leaders in the organization tend to promote people who present themselves as people with great visions and strategies. They are people who have an idealized sense of the organization (what we referred to as the 'clockwork' view) but who have little grasp of the underlying issues and problems that confront the organization.

- **Magical flight to utopia:** As the members become more neurotic, they start to build between them a fantasy as to what the organization would be like 'if only' it did not have to face such competition, if its finances were better or if the customers were not so difficult. They create a picture of the 'perfect organization'.

- **Discouragement of awkward members who are committed to work:** As the organization becomes neurotic, it discourages people who ask awkward questions, people who want to get on with the organization's core work.

- **Creation of the organizational jungle and an increasing preoccupation with role and hierarchy:** As members become increasingly neurotic, so they develop increasingly complex structures in order to try to manage problems. In order to deal with the feelings of insecurity from which people are suffering, they tend to defend their roles (so that if you ask them to do something unusual, they will say something like, 'It is more than my job is worth', and they tend to become more aware of their position in the hierarchy).

- **Isolation of management and the rupture of communications:** In the neurotic organization, managers, in their desire to protect themselves, will only talk with other managers so that communication with staff becomes distorted and disrupted.

- **The loss of creativity:** As organization members become increasingly defensive and as feelings of 'blame' increase, they become increasingly averse to taking risks.

- **Dominance of control and overcentralization:** As the organization becomes increasingly neurotic, the desire for control increases in order to try to manage the increasing sense of disruption and chaos that people are feeling. More and more decisions have to be referred to 'the centre' for 'permission'.

- **Development of a hostile relationship with the environment:** People in the neurotic organization come to resent the demands of their customers, see all competition as a threat and begin to see their shareholders as the 'enemy' as members of the organization become more isolated and insulated from the outside world.

As you look at these symptoms, do they relate to any organization of which you have knowledge?

groups or an organization. It requires on the part of the person developing the understanding great self-reflection and the ability of people to develop a critical understanding of the implications of their behaviour (Prasad, 2002). Sometimes this can be a consultant working with the organizational members in order to develop this level of understanding. In some organizations, senior managers can develop this level of insight with the aim of managing their organizations with deep understanding of the implications of their style of management. From the perspective of critical theory, the *ideal* would be that this level of insight is not just for an elite but also for the members themselves; all would have access to understanding. This is not unlike the development of emotional intelligence and emotional capability mentioned earlier.

2. **Psychoanalytic theory:** These are the core theories about the nature of the personality and interaction between people. Just one example of the way theory is used is provided by the highly influential critical theorist Marcuse. He took Freud's theory of the 'life instinct' as of crucial importance. This instinct represents the human impulse to 'preserve and enrich life by mastering nature'. Marcuse suggests, however, that we can only begin to experience pleasure when we can overcome the barriers of scarcity of materials that we require to lift us out of subsistence. So, in order to experience pleasure, we need to work – but for us to experience pleasure, we also need to be able to work in ways that we find satisfying and that are integrated into the search for pleasure (Held, 1980). This insight connects with current themes in motivation, especially the work of Mihaly Csikszentmihalyi (2000), who shows how 'serious' work can, if the conditions are right, provide high levels of pleasure and intrinsic, non-financial reward.

These two challenges – method and theory – provide a link into the reasons why the critical theorists were interested in psychoanalytic thought. This theme, the relationship between these two and the ways in which they can be combined to provide rich insight is developed in the next section.

## Psychoanalysis and critical theory in action

In critical theory, psychoanalysis is frequently taken as a social science that enables the emancipation of the person from 'what the person is in the world as it is at present' to 'what the person could be if he/she were able to live in a better world' (Connerton, 1976). There are a number of reasons for this. The psychoanalytic method helps the person to develop a deep understanding of who he or she is and helps develop habits of reflection that enable the person to become more self-aware. The development of insight also enables people to believe that they have more control over their environment. It helps people to lose feelings of powerlessness on the basis that if the person *understands* what is happening to them, they are in a better position to do something about it – self-knowledge is power. Psychoanalysis also helps individuals, groups and organizations to understand neurotic patterns of behaviour and the distortions of communication that come from these patterns. It then helps people learn ways of not getting into the neurotic position in the first place with the result that communications become clearer, less liable to distortion.

Habermas (1973, 1987) illustrates the ways that insight can be developed by taking some key ideas in psychoanalytic theory and shows how these can be used to develop a critical understanding. In what follows we shall first of all look at these key themes and then (in the case study) relate them to an organizational example:

- **Ideological framing:** This is the idea that when we look at ourselves and the world outside, we do so through a particular view of the world that we develop from our personality and through our particular experience of the world. This way of looking at the world can become inflexible. It becomes 'ideological' in the sense that it becomes the only way that we have of seeing the world; there are no alternatives. When this happens, we filter communication and information so that it fits the ideological framework even if the ideology and the information are incompatible. This leads to a distortion of meaning and communication.

- **Unacknowledged conditions:** This is linked to ideological framing. This means that we can completely ignore or not take account of information and communications because we deny its significance. This is a process known as *denial*. When members are in continuing denial, it means that communications become increasingly detached from the reality of members' circumstances as they refuse to acknowledge matters that are uncomfortable to them.

- **Repressions:** At another level, not only do members engage in denial in relation to communications and information, but they also repress, refuse to discuss or refuse to acknowledge deeper emotional states. They present an impression that they are behaving rationally and that emotions are not part of their organizational life. As they do this, however, they are driving their feelings deep underground, and they then become expressed in ways that can be problematic. Repressions can lead to outbursts of anger, bullying, harassment and to disastrous business decisions that seem to be rational on the surface but are driven by negative feelings such as revenge or fear.

- **Power relations are expressed through distorted communications:** In critical theory, notions of power and the abuse of power are very important because power relations (when they are based on notions of one person having power over another) characteristically mean that the 'losers' are robbed of their potential as human beings because they become subservient to 'the winners'. In psychoanalytic terms, when the power relations are not clear, people attempt to exercise power over each other by playing 'language games'. These games are ways that members communicate with each other in destructive ways but that are deeply embedded in the organizational culture. They can be played by, for example, persuading others to feel unsure of what is happening, getting others to feel guilty, manipulating the facts and so on. In all of these indirect methods of exercising power, the communications between people are distorted – nobody is quite telling the truth as they see it.

These underlying features of the development of neurotic patterns that can occur in organizations can be the *causes* of the *symptoms* of the neurotic organization discussed previously.

| **Case study** | **Critical theory and psychoanalysis in action** |
| --- | --- |

As the chapter develops, there will be many examples of the ways that critical theory and psychoanalysis provide a challenge to organizations. This is a brief example of how we can see these theories in action. It is based upon a 'real' example, but the names have been changed. The author of this chapter was working with the organization to help it to improve and develop communications.

The Andreas Corporation is a large business organization with a number of semi-autonomous divisions. One of the divisions, known as BusCo, had been responsible for the delivery of high-grade professional consultancy services to a variety of 'blue-chip' clients. BusCo was relatively small but had a highly knowledgeable staff that worked together very closely. It was unlike the other divisions, which were seen as more 'obedient' to the wishes of the Andreas Head Office. BusCo had been very successful for a number of years and had a clear identity within the corporation – indeed, some of the other divisions were quite jealous of its reputation and the way BusCo tended to disregard the organizational rules and the perceived arrogance of its managing director.

At the beginning of 2004, the frictions between BusCo and the head office began to grow; there were many meetings that became increasingly acrimonious between the chief executive of Andreas and the managing director of BusCo. Toward the end of the year, the managing director left with a generous payoff, and BusCo was absorbed into one of the divisions with the loss of most of the 'blue-chip' clients and the departure of a number of staff.

Although this outcome was presented by the chief executive of Andreas in a highly rational manner, he knew that this was neither his nor his team's finest hour, that the loss of BusCo had damaged the overall business. What was going on? These are some of the issues:

- **Ideological framing:** Both BusCo and Andreas had become trapped in an ideology of who they were. Andreas was the corporate head office, with its particular vision of what represented a 'proper' relationship from the divisions with the head office. BusCo, had an ideological commitment to serving its clients and an ideology of independence from the head office and a disregard for other divisions.

- **Unacknowledged conditions:** The Andreas board was fairly young, and the chief executive and a number of his colleagues had teenage children who were being 'difficult' as they began to express their independence and autonomy. At an unconscious level, this situation in their home lives was also being lived out at work in their relationship with BusCo. This idea – that BusCo was seen as the 'disobedient' child – was an important insight for people at Andreas because it illustrated aspects of their relationship with other divisions.

- **Repressions:** A key issue in both BusCo and Andreas was that no one actually talked about the emotional side to the growing conflict – how they felt about it. So even the most acrimonious of the discussions were essentially an intellectual rehearsal of the issues. Although the raised voices were symptomatic of hurt and anger, those symptoms were never addressed. In this sense, no one ever got to the deeper issues.

- **Power relations expressed through distorted communications:** This was very significant. In Andreas, power is very rarely expressed directly; it prides itself on doing things 'in a civilized way'. Thus, discussions with BusCo were framed around 'revisions' to the business plan, financial targets, processes of 'negotiation', meetings at which the power relations are a hidden presence but rarely overtly expressed. Similarly, in BusCo, there was a constant blurring of the relationship between themselves and the head office. This lack of boundaries meant that there was mutual misunderstanding and a growing suspicion of each other as the two groups continued to play their increasingly elaborated language games with each other.

*(Continued)*

## Case study (Continued)

- **Neurotic symptoms:** As time went by, both 'sides' became increasingly defensive, rumours and wild stories about the situation began to be told and there was 'splitting' of the two sides into 'heroes and villains'; these were all the symptoms of increased stress and anxiety.

From my position of working with them as an organization development consultant, in order to help them improve their communications, the key challenge that I agreed with them was to look at these deeper issues that were affecting their communications. Sometimes when working with individuals or groups over a period of weeks, the deeper issues begin to emerge and be shared. The remaining senior members reflected on what had happened, why it had gone so wrong and how they could perform better. As part of the process of working with them, it was my job to feed back to them these difficult issues, and it was their job to develop understanding and awareness of how they might work more effectively. In many ways, the way I worked with them was that of the organizational psychoanalyst – listening, interpreting and enabling members to see deeper issues. Ultimately, their willingness to undertake this reflexive level of thought led to improved communications and to a much better understanding of the ways unconscious issues can affect the business.

However, awareness is not enough – there is also the need for the person to prepare for action (Habermas, 1987) in the sense of actually *doing* something. From a critical theory perspective, getting the communications right at a senior level in the organization will not be enough. Despite the best efforts of an enlightened senior management, there will still be distortions of communication and the consequent dysfunctions that flow from this if there is a separation between senior management and other levels of the organization. Ideally, in order for it to be truly effective, this kind of approach should be one that is available throughout the organization so that all members have the opportunity to explore and develop new ways of being in the organization. As we shall discuss in the section on organization design, the solutions to the problems of organization from a critical theory perspective are radical.

## The chapter so far

In this chapter we first of all traced the development of critical theory through the Frankfurt school. We saw that critical theory is a way of exploring and understanding society. It takes a view that as the kind of society in which we live has developed, there are built into it many aspects that tend to cause people to lose their sense of who they 'really' are. In addition, the world is one where we have become slaves to consumption, and it is a world where our communications with each other do not really 'come from the heart' but are constantly distorted. Critical theory is optimistic in the sense that it says that if we were able to control these forces, then we would be able to 'become ourselves'.

We then looked at the core ideas that lie behind psychoanalysis. We have seen that although it is a 'science' in its own right, it can also be looked at, with critical theory, as a coherent body of theory that enables us to undertake deep reflection about what is happening to us and ways of developing ourselves and organizations. We then focused in on the ways that, working together, critical theory and psychoanalysis can enable us to explore in deep but practical ways underlying issues in organizations.

In the next sections of this chapter, we shall look at the ways that critical theory and psychoanalysis help us to explore particular aspects of organizational life such as the relationship between individuals, groups and the organization, organization culture, organizational design and leadership.

One of the interesting consequences of the work at BusCo was that this way of reflecting on what is going on in the organization was seen as quite a respectable way of conducting oneself in a busy organization. Although in many ways clinical psychoanalysis is a specialized activity that requires years of training and analysis of the self, there is a tradition within the psychoanalytic movement that insists that it is a method from which all can learn and develop.

## Ideas and perspectives

## Self-analysis as everyday activity

Karen Horney (1885–1952) was a highly influential psychoanalyst. She was born in Germany and moved to the United States in 1932. Although she lived and worked and was deeply respected within the psychoanalytic community, she sought to make the benefits of psychoanalysis available to a wider public – though not as a guru, but as a writer who was able to communicate readily with her readership. From this perspective, one of her most interesting books was *Self-Analysis*, originally published in 1942 but which is still eminently readable and relevant to our own time. In one of the chapters, she writes about 'occasional self-analysis', which is where something important in one's life needs reflection. She writes:

> To analyze oneself occasionally is comparatively easy and sometimes productive of immediate results. Essentially it is what every sincere person does when he tries to account for real motivations behind the way he feels or acts. . . . A man who has ignored his better judgement and given in to his wife or colleagues in an argument could question in his own mind whether he yielded because he was convinced of the comparative insignificance of the subject at stake or because he was afraid of the ensuing fight. I suppose people have always examined themselves in this way. And many people do so who would otherwise reject psychoanalysis entirely.

She suggests that in order to undertake this form of occasional self-analysis:

> It suffices to have some psychological knowledge, and this need not be book knowledge but may be gained from ordinary experience. The only indispensable requirement is a willingness to believe that unconscious factors may be sufficiently powerful to throw the whole personality out of gear. To put it negatively, it is necessary not to be too easily satisfied with ready-at-hand explanations for a disturbance.

It is interesting in this context that Horney is very clear that both those people who say that every disturbance that happens to them is caused by 'the world out there' – and those who say that every disturbance is caused by their own subjective 'inner world' are probably deluded; part of self-reflection is the ability to recognize that which is 'in me' and that which is 'out there' (1994, pp. 138–139).

## Stop and think

As you look around you at friends and colleagues, it is likely that there are people who proceed through life without ever giving even the more tumultuous aspects of their experience a moment's thought. On the other hand, you may know of people who spend vast swathes of their lives in moody introspection. What would you see as the value (if any) of the sort of self-analysis that gets us to look at unconscious aspects of life but that encourages us at the same time to do this in an active sort of way?

Although the development of reflexive ways of thinking is not an easy path to follow, in the following sections, we explore the ways that this approach to organization theory can be applied to different aspects of organizational life.

## The challenges of critical theory and psychoanalysis for understanding the individual, the group and the organization

This section will explore the ways critical theory and psychoanalysis develop an understanding of the individual and the group and their relationship to the organization, and develop an understanding of why these perspectives are significant in the development of organization theory.

As far as the individual in relation to the organization is concerned, the idea that 'work' is a key feature of life is part of, for many of us, our common sense understanding of the world and our place in it. Within critical theory, there is an acceptance of the importance of work as a key aspect of the development of human identity. But for them, the key question is: what kind of work? From their perspective, some sorts of work enable people to be fulfilled – but in their understanding, there is much work that prevents human fulfilment.

The critical theorist and philosopher Charles Taylor suggested in a paper written in 1971 that a number of key aspects enable us to feel that we can have a sense of social identity and fulfilment. In terms of organizational life, the issues that he mentions give us a model of what an 'ideal' organization would look like. The key themes he mentions include the ways in which we create:

1. **Our relationship to the past** and our history so that at the same time, we can remember the past but also 'soar above it'. This means that in order to feel a strong sense of our identity, we need to feel grounded in our organization, that we have a sense of belonging to it and that it belongs to us. At the same time, however, we need to 'soar' above it in the sense that we can look at the organization from a detached perspective so that we are not 'sucked into' it.

2. **Our relationship to the social (and organizational) world** so that we can experience it as free yet interdependent and productive. This means that we are able to work with colleagues in groups and teams in a way that is fulfilling and creative – but are also able to experience freedom and autonomy from them as well.

3. **Our relationship to the environment:** This is the idea that we should be able to feel that the work that we do respects the natural world. This has become a very important theme in some organizations with a growing awareness of the potential for destruction of human activity and the warnings of global warming.

4. **Our awareness of the future and our own finiteness:** This relates to the extent to which we are aware of ourselves, the extent to which we have a notion of the way we can develop within the organization and the extent to which we are aware that the organization in which we work has its limitations. This theme that organizations need to have an awareness of their 'death' is an important one in

psychoanalytic thought because it implies that the organization (or its leaders) does not become arrogant, does not get into a state in which it claims for itself immortality.

5. **'The absolute' human values of freedom integrity and dignity.** In organizational terms, this implies the notion that the organization in which we work has strong ethical values, that we can feel that we 'belong' to an organization that has integrity and respects our integrity.

When you look at these five themes, they are useful to explore the extent to which any organization enables or negates members' sense of identity and enables that sense of identity to be carried into the wider social world.

## Stop and think

Take a look at an organization known to you. To what extent does it:

- Live in the 'constant present' with a ceaseless restlessness or change and transform over time without losing a sense of its past?

- Treat people as individual commodities to be 'processed' in teams whose only purpose is to serve the organization or allow its members autonomy to get on with their work within boundaries that are experienced as 'fair' and legitimate?

- Have little regard for its impact on the environment or regards itself as a custodian of the environment?

- See the future in terms of growth in the interests of the shareholders and senior management or see the future in terms of growth and development for all with a benign impact on society?

- Take a view that notions of freedom, integrity and dignity are meaningless idealisms or that they are important ideas that need to be embedded within organizational life?

There are endless and fascinating debates about the nature of human identity and the ways that our identities interact with organizations. There is, for example, a view that our identity is the outcome of our genetic inheritance and that contemporary organizations are over-civilized and that they need to take into account more our hunter-gatherer genetic history (Nicholson, 1997). In his most recent book, Habermas (2001) suggests that as we begin to understand hereditary factors in our behaviour, they may prove to be restrictive in the choices we can make. Our inherited genetic structures might restrict the extent to which the ideal state of freedom and equality can be achieved. However, as a critical theorist, he suggests that these are issues that we really need to understand and about which we need to develop shared knowledge rather than just take for granted.

Underpinning the critical theorists' conception of the individual, as exemplified by Horkheimer (1972), is an optimistic view that we can achieve autonomy or emancipation from the forces that oppress us. He suggests that the human condition is essentially directed toward purposefulness, spontaneity and rationality so that we can see the relationships between human goals (what we want to be) and the means of achieving these goals. He suggests, however, that the problem is that in contemporary society, the ability to reach this human potential is constrained by the very nature of typical organizational life in our kind of society. From the perspective of the critical theorists, contemporary organizational life is pervaded by its 'rationality'; they would take the perspective suggested by Weber in an essay published in 1920 that 'the more the world of the modern capitalist economy follows its own inevitable laws, the less accessible it is to any imaginable relationship with a religious ethic of brotherliness. The more rational, and thus impersonal, capitalism becomes the more this is the case' (1920b, p. 331). The emphasis on rationality, the 'progress' of the capitalist ethic, the impersonality of organizational life and its lack of connection with each other combine to create an environment in which organization members struggle to 'be themselves'.

It is very important, however, to note that in critical theory, this idea of individual autonomy is completely different from the idea of the 'selfish' individual acting completely on his or her own without regard for others. From the perspective of critical theory, this view of identity with its concentration on the 'self' is a particularly Western view that was encouraged by the growth of capitalist society with its emphasis on individual achievement. In a passage that has resonance at the beginning of the twenty-first century, Horkheimer wrote scathingly, in a paper originally published in 1937, of that kind of individuality that sees the individual as the centre of the world or even to *be* the world. In this sense, he attacks the kind of organization that is driven by personal ambition, in which the atmosphere is entirely competitive, person on person, with 'individual targets' that prevent collaboration with others.

The German critical theorist Ulrich Beck (2006), in his discussion of what he calls 'tragic individualization', has taken up this theme. He argues that the modern condition is one of great uncertainty in the world of work and in an uncontrolled globalized economy. In this situation, the individual is basically on his or her own in attempting to deal with the world. There has been a failure to develop what he calls 'expert systems to manage risks' because these would require high levels of collaboration between organizations and societies. He argues: 'Neither science, nor the politics in power, nor the mass media, nor business, nor the law nor even the military are in a position to define or control risks rationally'. As capitalism develops with its advanced technologies and the better production of markets, the level of risk increases because 'the normal instruments of calculating, anticipating and colonizing the future don't work any more' (p. 31).

## A critique of critical theory

If we bear in mind that one aspect of critical theory is that it attempts a constant questioning of the 'accepted truth', it is appropriate at this stage to mention a critical perspective on critical theory. Feldman (2000) states that there are three main problems connected with the critical approach to the individual and the possibility of emancipation from organizational controls. Essentially, his view is that if we take a radical departure from the advanced business and industrial society that is the characteristic of the Western world, we can run into severe trouble.

The key problem that he identifies is that any attempt to move from the present state of organization to one that fulfils human ambition is risky because, left to themselves, people do not automatically make the right choice nor do they consider others as they develop new solutions. He regards an optimistic picture of human behaviour with considerable scepticism. He also suggests that advanced capitalist society itself is bounded by strong ethical and legal frameworks and that this settled order of things can, in itself, be disrupted by a culture in which the status quo is constantly under criticism.

**Stop and think**

In its vision of organizations and society, there are elements of critical theory that can be seen as idealistic and that take an optimistic view of the nature of humanity. When you look at typical organizations in your society, do you believe that this optimism is warranted?

## Critical theory and psychoanalysis develops challenging perspectives on organization culture

The writers on organization theory Alvesson and Willmott (1996) suggest that for the critical theorist, organization culture has an important part to play in the development of the individual. They suggest that the emphasis on the 'selfish' individual that was mentioned in the previous section is 'much more a function of a particular form of civilization than it is a pure reflection of a woman's or man's essentially problematical psychology' (p. 114). Although these writers do not always agree with the emphasis in psychoanalysis on the individual and what they see as the relative lack of interest in psychoanalysis in culture, they draw heavily upon psychoanalytic terminology in developing their ideas about culture.

Although the early psychoanalysts focused on individual behaviour and the development of the individual personality, the role of culture in that development was of crucial importance. Freud observed that the child passes 'through an immensely long stretch of human cultural development in an almost uncannily abbreviated form' (Freud, 1949, p. 52). He meant that the child learns how to be a member of the family and of the wider society very quickly. Freud also points to the way that as we develop, aspects of the personality become repressed so that 'our highly valued cultural heritage has been acquired at the cost of sexuality and the restriction of sexual motive forces' (p. 72). This means that as children, we become socialized to become 'acceptable human beings', but as we do, many of our basic instincts become repressed, pushed into the unconscious self, so that beneath the safety net of culture, unconscious forces are at work. This idea of the repression into the unconscious of these instincts has important implications for understanding organizational culture.

## A psychoanalytic view of organization culture

In psychoanalytic terms, the organizational culture can be seen as a 'holding environment' for its members. What psychoanalysts mean by this is that the culture is basically a place in which people feel that they are 'safe' to be the kind of person they want to be, within boundaries, in the organization. The idea of the 'holding environment' goes back to images of childhood in which the infant who is loved is held by the parent and protected from the hostility of the external world but also learns that he or she is separate from the loving parent. As we grow older, we enter into many 'holding environments' but none as strong as that of infancy if things have gone well for us at that stage of life. The psychoanalytic writer Lionel Stapley (1996) suggests that organizational culture can be described in a manner that is similar to the human personality. He suggests that:

- **Culture is a process in which the members are interrelated with each other and the holding environment.** An essential part of a culture that is 'safe' is that people feel that they can communicate with each other in a straightforward manner, without the distortions of 'spin' or having to use 'jargon' in order to create confusion. People also feel that they are 'real people,' not just 'machines' – that they can rely on the 'holding environment' to protect them when things go wrong.
- **Culture has features of sameness and continuity that enables members to feel their own worth and a sense of reality as they interact with others.** This means that even if they work in a very exciting work environment that is ambiguous they can understand the 'rules of the game' and that those rules are not suddenly going to change.
- **Organization culture is influenced by both conscious and unconscious features.** This means that in a reflexive organization, one that thinks about how it is working and how the members are feeling about their work, there is an attempt to understand these unconscious features.
- **Organization cultures, across organizations, have features that are similar, yet every organizational culture is unique.** In a reflexive organization, members are able to see how their organization is similar to others but is also 'special' – and value their own uniqueness.
- **Organization cultures are dynamic, ever changing in minor and major ways.** In a 'safe' organizational culture, members are able to work with the ways in which the culture changes so that they can make the changes part of their own experience and lives.

We can see in this description of organizational culture that as a 'holding environment', the culture of the organization is one in which members feel that there are boundaries – they cannot do just as they wish – but that within those boundaries, they experience freedom and autonomy. This culture is different from the corporate culture that we discussed in Chapter 4 that has a strong emphasis on a shared, top-down vision of the organization and the culture. In this case, an overpowering 'holding environment' can increase neurotic forces because a controlling culture causes conflict between the individual's basic needs and his or her everyday experience of control. This means that neurotic behaviours can be seen as the outcome of the *organization* culture rather than the problems of the individual (Alvesson and Willmott, 1996).

## The 'unhealthy' organization culture: when there is conflict

So, what happens when the organization culture becomes 'unhealthy', when it becomes dysfunctional both for the organization and for its members? One way of looking at this is to look at the way we, as individuals, develop from infancy into the adult state. In their earliest years, most infants feel that they are at the centre of a loving world – they feel they are at the centre of the parental universe. As they develop, they realize that they are not the centre of attention; the unconditional love they experienced in infancy is not a universal fact of life. So, most of us (apart from the supremely self-confident or those who were ignored and felt little self-worth) grow up with an understanding that we are only a small part of the universe and that our stay on the earth is temporary. This is what the psychoanalyst Melanie Klein (1975) called the 'depressive position'. Many of us experience this 'depressive position' as a way of understanding our lives as a mixture of 'good' parts and 'bad' parts, and we integrate these two aspects. So, in everyday life in organizations in which we are living in a culture that we experience as meeting our needs, we can be realistic about seeing some aspects of the organization as 'OK' and other aspects as in need of some attention, but at the same time, we just get on with our lives.

However, supposing what we have called the 'holding environment' changes. Perhaps there is a merger in which members feel to be the losers. Perhaps a new manager or leader comes into the organization with a very different style of working; perhaps there is major downsizing or restructuring. In these situations, the normal operation of the depressive position (where it is a 'reality check') moves into overdrive. When it does this, there is a temptation for members to engage in what Klein called 'splitting'. This means that when people are in a state of anxiety, one of the ways they defend themselves against that anxiety is to look at the world in ways that divide people between the 'good' and the 'bad'. Thus, in organizations, members may split 'heroes' and 'villains', 'management' and 'employees', the 'centre' and 'our department' and so on. This splitting can have serious consequences as they split off the 'good aspects of the world' from the 'bad' because when they do this they are in denial about the reality of their situation, they cannot confront the problems that are confronting them. When they do this, they deny the negative aspects of their own behaviour, feelings or understandings of the organization. They do this by constantly blaming others or the situation that they are in for what happens to them. Splitting becomes a core part of the process of communication.

| Biography | **Great figures in psychoanalytic thought: Melanie Klein (1882–1960)** |
|---|---|

Melanie Klein was born in Vienna in 1882. In 1926, she moved to London, where she lived and worked until her death in 1960. She was a pioneer in child psychoanalysis and developed a number of very important and influential theories about the early stages of the life of the infant. Her particular contributions lay in developing understanding of the ways in which the infant establishes his or her identity as separate from the mother and the development of the idea of the 'depressive' position (or melancholy) as part of the human personality. These ideas have profound importance for us as adult members of organizations.

## The unhealthy organization culture: when there is insufficient conflict

We suggested above that this deterioration in the organization culture could be caused by a radical change in the holding environment. Sometimes, however, the holding environment can become, on the surface, comfortable, free of conflict and consensual, a place in which people love to work, but underneath the surface, there are forces at play that make it slip into dysfunction. This can be illustrated by Jerry Harvey's (1974) story and analysis of an incident in his family life. Harvey is a psychologist, a professor of management science at George Washington University in Washington D.C., and is a management consultant.

### Ideas and perspectives

### Going to Abilene: an everyday story of Texas folk

Jerry Harvey went from the University of Washington (where he is professor of management science) with his wife to her parents' house in the small town of Coleman, Texas. It was July and very hot. They were spending a lazy but pleasant Sunday afternoon in and about the house. Then Jerry's father-in-law suggested that they go to Abilene, some 60 miles away, and have dinner in the cafeteria. (This story takes place in the late 1970s – Abilene was a lot less exciting than it is now. If you have ever seen the film *The Last Picture Show*, you will get the idea.) So, although privately Jerry regarded the trip – 120 miles all told – with inner dread, he, his wife and mother-in-law all agreed to it. The journey was horrid, and the quality of the food was basic. Then four hours later they arrived back home. The atmosphere was very quiet with more than a hint of menace. Then Jerry's mother-in-law admitted she had not enjoyed it at all, but that she had felt pressured into going. Jerry then said that *he* only went to satisfy the rest of them. Then Jerry's wife said that she thought that Jerry, her father and her mother really wanted to go, and she just went to please them. Then Jerry's father exploded – he only wanted to go because he thought they were bored in the house and he wanted to please them because his daughter and Jerry visited them only rarely.

Harvey took the story of the trip to Abilene and argued that a fundamental problem for organizations can be the inability to cope with disagreement. This means that members collude to agree to solutions and that this prevents organizations from making high-quality decisions.

### Example: An organization goes to Abilene

Harvey was asked to be a management consultant to a relatively small industrial company that was going through a period of poor profits, low morale and low productivity in a key department – research and development (R & D). As he looked around the company, it came to his attention that the R & D department had invested a large part of its budget in one particular research project. When he interviewed the key members of the board and the research manager, each of them told Jerry that privately they had considerable doubts about the viability of the project. However, they had not shared their doubts with each other; they all thought that the others were so committed to the project that they would resign or at the very least go into a very deep sulk if they felt that they had not the full backing of each other. In this case, what we referred to earlier in the chapter as 'splitting' is found in the way these senior managers see the others as 'good' objects who must not be disappointed and the self as 'bad' because of their feelings of doubt and the sense of guilt associated with not sharing their doubts. In meetings and in communications, there is a shared overt sense of optimism about the project but at a covert level, feelings of guilt and anxiety.

In this situation, the culture of the organization at the surface levels was one of high levels of cooperation, although at its core there seems to have been an unconscious culture with a fear of confrontation in order to bring things to the surface, an underlying feeling of 'passive aggression'. One of the consequences of this was a feeling that to question the status quo meant that the person would be rejected by the 'team'. Because of the fear of rejection, members hesitate to take the risk of confronting others with their view of reality in case they are rejected. The paradox is that they take the very action – non-confrontation – that eventually leads, when things go wrong, to high levels of anger and blaming. This leads inevitably to the very rejection members wished to avoid in the first place.

At the heart of the Abilene paradox, then, is a fear of rejection and the consequent inability to make important and controversial decisions. The outcome of this is that the culture of the organization becomes increasingly one in which it is 'taken for granted' that there are high levels of agreement between members when they are in meetings and formal discussions but there is widespread discontent about the outcomes from these meetings and a general climate of aggression that is expressed in a passive manner. There are, however, ways of escaping from the Abilene paradox and indeed other forms of the dysfunctional culture.

## Understanding the purpose of the organization and embedding it in the culture

One of the ways organization members can avoid getting into the Abilene paradox is through developing awareness amongst organization members of what is called *primary task* and *primary risk*.

The primary task of an organization is a definition of 'what the enterprise is called primarily to do' (Hirschhorn, 1999, p. 8). Understanding the primary task is a complicated but rewarding process. On the one hand, there are bundles of organizational *'realities'* and pressures that members have to face. They have to make sure that customers are satisfied, revenue is generated, key stakeholders are satisfied, employees are paid and so on. On the other hand, there are the ways in which these pressures are *understood* by organizational members. The way we understand external realities and pressures goes through the filter of our interpretation of external reality, the way we may see some particular aspect of 'reality' as, for example, an opportunity or a threat.

When members can reflexively explore these combinations of what Hirschhorn calls 'organizational realities' and the 'fantasies, myths and stories' that they hold about them, they can begin to understand what they *actually* do, their 'primary practices', rather than their *beliefs* about what they do. The primary task of the organization is the outcome of a whole bundle of primary practices.

Connected with the idea of primary task is the idea of primary risk. This is the risk that members feel of 'choosing the wrong primary task, that is a task that ultimately cannot be managed' (Hirschhorn, 1999, p. 9). Connected with this is the idea that organizational members are constantly making choices. As they make one choice, the route taken becomes situated at the front of members' minds, and the path not taken becomes background. The key issue is that after members make a choice, they also need to be aware that there are alternative choices that they *could* make. Hirschhorn suggests that the key issue here, in the reflexive tradition, is that members need to understand clearly the nature of the primary task, including the issues of the choice to be made.

## Example: Making a U-turn

There has long been a tradition in British political life that senior government ministers should never be seen to be changing their minds about a matter of policy. When a change in policy occurs, it is usually handled by junior ministers or by civil servants; for a senior minister to do this represents a loss of face or, worse, a sign of incompetence. In this context, there was a momentous moment on a BBC programme on 22 September 2005, when a minister announced, with pride, that he was performing a 'U-turn' on a major piece of policy. They had evidently done an assessment of the 'primary risk' of the original policy and had decided not to go ahead with it; he had looked at the course of action and realized that it could not be managed and then looked at alternatives.

In order for members to understand the nature of the primary task and the primary risk, members need to develop an understanding of the deeper issues of the ways they are working, the nature of the holding environment that they require in order to work effectively, the consequences of the ways they communicate and other features that enable them to explore the kind of culture that they need in order to work effectively.

### Stop and think

This issue of understanding the 'primary purpose' of an organization can be quite challenging as we try to develop an understanding of the challenges that face it and the ways in which people understand those challenges. You can think about this from your own perspective. If for example, you are a student – undergraduate, postgraduate, doctoral – what is the primary task (and what maybe are the primary risks) of the student group? How does this understanding (or is there a variety of understandings?) become embedded into the culture of the group?

## Critical theory and psychoanalysis present challenging perspectives for organizational design
### Architecture as symbol of organizational design

Look around you at the business, industrial and educational buildings, hospitals and shops in your area, particularly those built in the past 50 or 60 years. If you live in a town or city with a good diversity of architecture, you may notice two main trends.

In a lecture that he delivered in 1981 (but published in 2000), Habermas contrasts these two forms of architecture. His discussion, from a critical theory perspective, links with the issues that were discussed in Chapter 2 in relation to the development of modernism.

Habermas talks of a style of modern architecture that is both organic and rationalist. What he means by this is that the design is one in which the observer experiences the building as a whole. The form of the building arises out of its purpose. When you work in the building, you feel by virtue of the design and scale of the building that you are part of the community. He suggests that this kind of architecture is associated with the notions of order and rationality associated with the Enlightenment.

One of the architects that Habermas took as an exemplar of this form of architecture was Walter Gropius. Figure 8.1 showing Harvard Graduate School captures the essence of the notions of organic 'human' architecture that is also highly rational. The essence of this building lies in its simplicity in architectural design, the way the form of the building is fitted to its function of being a 'place' where academics and students can work effectively. In many respects, the architecture is understated – it does not insist that you 'look at me'; the building is there to serve a purpose rather than being an object for spectacular admiration. The building fits into its environment in an organic manner – notice the carefully tailored lawn in the front of the building. So, the essence of the building lies in its modesty but also in its carefully crafted design.

**Figure 8.1:** Organic architecture: Harvard Graduate School, 1951. (*Source*: © Bettmann/CORBIS.)

**Figure 8.2:** Aggressive capitalism: Canary Wharf, London.
(*Source*: © London Aerial Photo Library/CORBIS.)

Habermas (2000) contrasts this form of architecture with the emergence, particularly from the middle of the twentieth century, with the 'soulless container architecture' that has no relationship with its environment. He points to the development of 'the solitary arrogance of block like office buildings; of monstrous department stores and monumental university buildings and conference centers . . . the destruction of city centers for the sake of the automobile, and so forth' (p. 418).

He wonders whether these 'monstrosities' are the true face of our modern age – or are they 'falsifications', aberrations from the original spirit of modern architecture? He sees powerful forces that lead to what he calls the 'colonization of the lifeworld', a cityscape in which our lives become dominated by the anonymity and uniformity of the physical design of our environment. However, all is not lost; he argues that the 'true' modernist spirit is not lost – that the human ability to be creative and develop new forms *combined* with the idea that buildings need to be functional. He suggests that *this* tradition is one to which we can return if we use our intelligence and understand that design is about creating spaces for human beings to coexist with the world of nature. These are issues that in a different intellectual context also preoccupy postmodernist writers discussed in Chapter 6.

---

### Stop and think

If you look around you – if you live in a city that is undergoing regeneration, if you are working in an organization, if you are studying at university – do you think that the environment around you is creative and human but one in which people can work effectively? Or is the design and architecture still predominantly functional with an emphasis on anonymous efficiency? How does this impact on your life?

---

## Design for people or for strategic competitive advantage?

These debates about the nature of architecture and the city have important implications for the ways organizations are designed. Do we design our organizations so that they are rational, ordered places in which people can work *effectively* and in ways that mean that they can be fulfilled? Or do we design organizations as rational, ordered places in which people can work *efficiently* and in ways that maximize the benefits to the shareholders rather than the interests of the employees? And is there a 'third way' in which people can work in ways that are effective and fulfilling and which meet the legitimate needs of the shareholders?

Within the traditions of critical theory, the key issue in organizational design lies in the development of the democratic self-organization in which members take responsibility for the development of the ways they work. In this context, Habermas (1987) proposes the idea of the 'ideal speech situation'. As our co-author Phil Johnson (2006) suggests, this is a conversation in which members produce rational consensus decisions and agreements based on 'argument and analysis without the resort to coercion, distortion or duplicity' (p. 260). It is a situation in which all participants have an equal chance to bring issues to the discourse and participate in it. In the ideal speech situation the different perspectives and positions expressed by members are open to scrutiny and exploration free from the constraints of differences in the power relations of the members (Johnson and Duberley, 2000). As far as Habermas is concerned, it is only where democratic social relations are established that members can communicate with each other without distortion, and rationally. In the discussion of democratic organizations that follows, it is important to note that the examples that are given are not meant to represent, from a critical theory perspective, *ideal* democratic organizations or situations. They fall within the neo-modernist understanding of democracy discussed in Chapter 3.

## The passion for democratic organization

The spirit of this form of organization in an industrial organization may be found in this excerpt from the 'History' web page of Swann-Morton located in Sheffield, England, one of the world's leading manufacturers of surgical instruments:

---

**Case study**    **Swann-Morton – the leading edge in surgical blades**

### The history of Swann-Morton

Mr W.R. Swann, Mr J.A. Morton and Miss D. Fairweather founded the business in August 1932 to manufacturer and sell razor blades. True to their philosophy, even before they began trading, the founders drew up four statements to guide them in their entry into the capitalist world.

Mr Swann's founding principles

1. Claims of individuals producing in an industry came first, before anything else, and must always remain first. They are the human beings on which everything is built.
2. If the industry cannot pay the rightful reward of labour (while they are producing for profit for the owners) then a new policy is required on the part of the management to make it do so.
3. If the management can't do the job, then a new management is required, as well as a new policy.
4. Individuals in any industry have a perfect right to demand and see that this objective is reached, because they produce the goods.

These four statements, written in Walter R. Swann's handwriting, are displayed at Swann-Morton's head office and remain the principles that guide the business today.

After many years of research and development the emphasis was changed from razor blades to surgical blades. With the market for surgical blades growing considerably by 1957 Swann-Morton was manufacturing over 38 million blades each year. . . . Mindful of the future security of the company, the workforce and its founding principles a trust was formed in the mid-1960s to administer the company within which the employees had a 50% share and the remaining 50% was placed in a charitable trust. It is this unique culture that inspires quality and commitment, and Swann-Morton's staff are very proud to be a part of this.

*Source:* © 2000–2002 Swann-Morton Limited.

---

What this means is that *all* the members of the organization express commitment to democratic principles and practices. The example given above contains some important principles that are significant in the way that they relate to issues in critical theory – although it is doubtful that Walter Swann had read these theorists.

The first of the Swann-Morton principles relates to two issues in critical theory. This principle relates to the essential dignity of, and needs for, respect for the core producers of the goods and services provided by the organization. It relates to the fourth principle, which advocates the rights of any member of the organization to 'demand' that management is undertaking its work effectively. It is built into the structure of relationships that issues are transparent because managers are accountable *to all members of the organization* for the success of their work. In this sense, managers cannot regard themselves as an elite; their task is different from that of the producers, but no more nor no less legitimate.

The remainder of the Swann-Morton principles recognize that although democratic organizations may have owners, there is a need for a balance between their interests and those who work within the organization; there is a sense of justice in the relationship between them. These principles also recognize that organizations can legitimately have a group of people known as managers and that these managers have a role in the development of strategy and policies. However, principles three and four put the work of management into a context in which they are responsible to those who 'produce the goods' as well as the owners. This relates to debates in critical theory that are concerned with the role of managers in contemporary organizations.

This democratic process goes well beyond 'participation' in organizational decision making; rather, it relates to the issue that all aspects of organizational decision making are open to all members of the organization and that the processes themselves are open to question and reconsideration (Alvesson and Willmott, 1996). As we saw in Chapter 3, democratic forms of organization can be found in many countries, but usually in English-speaking countries and in many European countries they are the outcomes of an individual's or group's passionate commitment to this form of organization. As Johnson (2006) points out, this means that, from the perspective of orthodox thought about organizations, democratic organization is usually dismissed as naively idealistic and far removed from the practical demands of everyday organizational life. He suggests that one of the ways that, in these societies, the case for democratic organization is promoted is through the 'business case', a coherent argument that proposes that democratic organization can bring major benefits to the development of the organization. This is a case of aligning the human benefits of democratic organization with business benefits. Alternatively, he argues, democratic organizations should not be assessed in terms of standards they do not share with orthodox business but as organizations with completely different values from theirs. This issue was discussed from a different perspective in Chapter 4.

## Social democracy and the democratic organization

There are, however, some nations in which democratic organizations are part of the social structure. To illustrate this, we briefly look at the idea of democratic organization known as co-determination in Germany and how democratic forms are part of the political and economic structure of Scandinavian countries.

### The example of Germany

The American historian Robert Locke has for some years been interested in what he has seen as the inexorable growth of 'management' in the United States. His basic position has been that the growth of 'new-wave' models of American management discussed in some detail in Chapter 4 is highly problematic because it is at heart the creation of a mystique that enables the elite (those who have become managers) to sustain their grasp on power in organizations. In his exploration of this theme, he undertook studies of different approaches to 'management' in a number of countries. One of his studies was an exploration of the development of democratic processes – known as co-determination – in Germany.

Locke was interested in the development of German society, particularly since the end of World War II. He suggests that in German political thought, there is clear relationship between society and the state, with the latter playing an important part. In a society where there is little state intervention, what Locke refers to as 'civil society', the individual and small groups can be powerful in influencing events and the way society is organized. The consequence, in German political theory, is that if it were left to itself, civil society develops 'contrary interests and passions, beset with numerous factions and parties. Civil society, because of the self-seeking nature of its components, is incapable on its own of organizing a satisfactory human community' (Locke, 1996, p. 56). In this sense, the idea of the 'civil society' is rather like that view of the relationship between the state and the citizen in the United States, where there is great pride in individual and group decision making and where the role of the state (particularly at the federal level) is as small as possible. In the German perspective, however, the means by which a society is developed that protects the vulnerable and marginalized is through the development of a strong state – the state is the mechanism that facilitates freedom for all and protects the citizen from 'the selfish rough and tumble of civil society' (Locke, 1996, p. 57).

Through the development of this notion of the 'strong state' as a means of protecting the interests of all members of society comes the development of the principle of co-determination in German organizations. This is the concept, enshrined in law, of employees' *active* participation in the governance of the firm. The German writer Burkhart Sievers reflects a somewhat more sceptical view of the power of co-determination. He suggests that the key instrument of co-determination, the works council (in which managers and workers have an equal part in decision making), may be 'more tolerated than accepted' because the interests of workers and management are fundamentally different. He also thinks that the main effort of management in relation to co-determination may be 'to avoid conflicts by creating and sustaining an atmosphere by creating an atmosphere of paternalistic benevolence or some kind of mutual gentlemen's agreement' (Sievers, 1994, p. 137). Despite these limitations, the *principle* of co-determination – that worker and manager can have the same interest in the running of their organization – provides a sustaining understanding embedded in the social fabric that state, organization and the individual can work in harmony.

## Case study     Trouble at Volkswagen

The history of Volkswagen illustrates both the advantages and disadvantages of the concept of co-determination. David Gow, a journalist for *The Guardian* Newspaper, reported on 14 July 2005:

> Volkswagen, Europe's biggest car-maker, is in deep crisis and not for the first time. Yesterday it laid out plans to overcome its latest trauma by pledging to increase net earnings by €4 billion within three years with a €10 billion plan for cost savings and performance improvements. But it will require more than budget cuts and better quality cars to repair this company's financial health. VW requires radical surgery.

Gow then mentions revelations of financial corruption in the company that are the symptoms of underlying problems in the company and writes:

> The real scandal is about the close, over-warm links between company executives and supervisory board members, including worker representatives. . . A decade ago VW remained a brave example of the post-war German corporate consensus and social model, where horrendous losses were overcome by moving to a four-day week and saving 30,000 jobs. Today it is a symbol of the failure of the model to adapt to global challenges. It is the epitome of Germany's economic weakness, with a conservative management clinging to past recipes for success and unwilling to embrace change.

He then goes on to write that part of the 'radical surgery' is the need for revision of 'the 50-year-old "co-determination" laws which put "workers" (union bosses) on the board. Change on this scale would signal a genuine new start for VW – and Germany.'

Then, on 16 July a 'letter to the Editor' appeared in the paper, written by Dr George Menz from London. His first paragraph praises co-determination and then takes up Gow's suggestion that the end of co-determination would represent a 'new start'. He writes:

> A start of what exactly? An emulation perhaps of the less-than-stellar track record of management of the motor industry of this country where managers are presumably unimpeded by 'union bosses'? Less ideology and more level-headed analysis would be appreciated, even in your business section.

## The example of Scandinavia

The approach to democratic forms of organization is rather different in the Scandinavian countries and reflects a different social and industrial history. Although there are significant differences between the Scandinavian countries (taken in this case as Denmark, Norway and Sweden), there are a number of common features that give them an interest in the concept of the 'democratic organization'. Haldor Byrkjeflot (2003), an academic at the University of Bergen, Norway, discusses the ways in which there had been a long history – since the 1930s – of the development of social democracy with a profound influence on organizational practices. In relation to management, the Scandinavian countries were seen by many to present a model of good practice with their emphasis on 'compromise and negotiation and with a management philosophy of the democratic participative kind' (p. 33).

The Danish academic Anne Westenholz suggests that in Europe the democratic form of organization has taken strongest hold in the Scandinavian countries. She suggests that industrialization came comparatively late in these countries, and its emergence coincided with the growth of democracy in many Western European countries. One consequence of this was that these countries avoided some of the worst conflicts between management and workers of early industrialization. This has meant that the relationship between management and workers *tended* to be less abrasive than relationships frequently were in countries that industrialized early.

Furthermore, in the Scandinavian countries, management *tended* not to resist unionization so that membership of trade unions in the twentieth century was amongst the highest in the Western world. Thus, Scandinavian *society* invites a high interest and involvement in democratic forms of organizing such that 'in several ways the Scandinavian countries have been unique in their introduction of various forms of industrial democracy' (Westenholz, 2003, p. 43). From the perspective of the critical theorists, this basic interest in Scandinavian countries in democratic processes would be welcomed. Although there is a recognition, at organizational and political levels, that workers and management have different needs and wants from organizations, the notion that these can be dealt with democratically means that there is a reduction in the distortion of communication; people can talk directly with each other and be heard.

| Case study | Democratic ways of working at Volvo |
| --- | --- |

During the 1970s Volvo established in their Kalmar plant in Sweden the construction of cars by the use of autonomous work groups as distinct from the traditional assembly line. The purpose was to give the work of constructing automobiles meaning and significance. In 1990 this developed into a more complete version of empowerment in that the groups had far more responsibility for planning production, personnel issues and quality control and also took a much more active part in the processes of organization development. As a result of improved working conditions 'the economy of the plant' increased dramatically.

In the late 1980s even more dramatic change took place in the plant in Uddeville, Sweden. The emphasis in the changes was to encourage learning and knowledge development. This was achieved through individuals taking responsibility for significant aspects of car building and autonomous groups working in situations where the distinctions between supervisors and employees were merged. Flexibility increased with an increase in individual and group capability.

Why then did the company return, in the early 1990s, to a more traditional form of production with an emphasis on producing cars on a mechanical assembly line and with an increase in the distinction between different levels of the hierarchy? The basic reasons for this are that neither managers nor unions were able to persuade people who were outside the organization of their success; they were not able to gain the commitment of their wider social context. Despite an *ideology* in Swedish organizational and political life that employees could design their own workplace when it came to actual enactment it caused fear for external stakeholders. From the management perspective the fear was that this work process would ultimately 'not deliver the goods' because of loss of control; from the external union perspective the fear was that this process of working could lead to exploitation of the workforce.

*Source:* Based on Westenholz (2003).

Westenholz notes, however, that in recent years, there is a widespread tendency in the Scandinavian countries to use management consultants who carry the American concepts of 'good management' of the sort that were discussed in Chapter 4 as the 'best way' to manage organizations. She seems to suggest that the Scandinavian perspective on the relationship between organizations, its members and society will be diluted by the globalization of these approaches to management. These approaches to management are themselves symptoms of a profound shift in the nature of business organization in the Scandinavian countries. Byrkjeflot (2003) suggests that there is a shift toward looking at shareholder value as a way of thinking about the purpose of organizations. This belief in shareholder value *also* promotes the development of professional managers and consultants. He does suggest, however, that there is still deeply embedded in these societies a distaste for a wholesale movement to shareholder value as the dominating ideology and that there is room for compromise between 'social value' and 'shareholder value'.

## Democracy, rationality and power

| Case study | The Aalborg project |
| --- | --- |

Bent Flyvbjerg, who is professor of planning at the Department of Development and Planning at Aalborg University, Denmark, has written a major study (1998) of the Aalborg project. This project was designed to make substantial improvements to the downtown area through democratic processes so that all the citizens could take part in the development. The basic idea of the project was that it would result in comprehensive improvements; it was designed as a coherent, systematic, rational, democratic plan. The Aalborg project represented the approach to design and organization discussed as modernism in Chapter 2.

In the planning of the project, there was a high emphasis on understanding the project as a system, on planning the project as an ordered sequence of events and a deep faith in the idea that a rational approach will overcome all problems. As time went by, however, it disintegrated into a large number of disjointed subprojects, many of which had unintended consequences, so that in many cases, any pretence of democratic decision making was lost. Institutions in the town that were supposed to represent the public interest were revealed to be deeply embedded in the hidden exercise of power and self-protection.

The desire was to undertake this project as an 'ideal speech act' on a major scale; the outcome was a major distortion of communications. The key determinant of this distortion was the ways that various participants in the project used their power to influence events. One of the key ways power distorted the process was that those who exercised power were able to define what counted as 'knowledge' about the project. The power holders were able to define the way the 'facts' were to be interpreted; they were able to put forward some 'knowledge' and suppress 'knowledge' that did not suit it.

Based on research into the Aalborg project, Flyvbjerg suggested ten propositions that could be used as guidelines for the development of an understanding of the relationship between power, knowledge and rationality. Of these, we have selected and summarized a number that have direct relevance to organizations:

1. **Power defines reality:** Those who hold power are in a position to define what is rational and what is not. Their belief or understanding of what is rational is then worked on by them to achieve the rationalization of their position. As soon as

they have defined what is rational (their rationalization), they can then go on to define the nature of organizational reality.

2. **People prefer rhetoric to rationality:** Communication between members is typically more concerned with rhetoric, eloquence, hidden control, charisma and other devices rather than with rational arguments about the matter in hand.

3. **What happens in public is different from what happens backstage:** The sociologist Erving Goffman, who we discussed in Chapter 7, drew attention to the differences between what happens in the 'front stage' where the public performance takes place and in the 'back stage' where all kinds of mischief can be taking place. In the Aalborg project, it was characteristically the case that in the front stage members would engage in rational discourse; back stage, power and rationalization of the position to be taken dominate.

4. **The greater the power, the less the rationality:** If power defines reality, then it follows that the greater the power, the less need on the part of those who hold power to understand how reality is 'really' constructed. In this sense, the *absence* of rational arguments and factual documentation may be important indicators of power. This is an issue that links back to the discussion of the 'neurotic organization' and is an issue to which we return in the discussion of leadership. Flyvbjerg points out that in a democratic society rational argument is one of the few forms of power the powerless still possess.

5. **Power relations are constantly being produced and reproduced:** Power relations are constantly changing and reforming. In the Aalborg case, the business leaders were more capable of maintaining a dominant position than were politicians and administrators. They worked hard over long periods to ensure their dominance.

6. **When there are situations of confrontation, rationality yields to power:** Flyvbjerg suggests that when members confront each other over difficult issues, the use of power tends to be more effective than any appeal to objectivity, facts or rational argument.

7. **The power of rationality can appear when power relations are stable:** When the power relations between members are stable so that people feel that they can negotiate and establish consensus, then reason and rationality can prevail. This means that the power of rationality is fragile, and to achieve a situation in which it can develop involves long-term strategies that marginalize confrontation and naked power play.

The key issue is that the achievement of democratic institutions (including organizations) is a long-term process, even in 'democratic' societies. To get anywhere near its achievement, members need practical understanding of not only the issues of power but also of the ways in which those who are at the margins can participate fully in decision making. Flyvbjerg sees the rational democratic approach as a means of regulating power and the desire of some to dominate others rather than as something that is easily achievable in its own right. In this sense, the 'ideal speech act' is similar to Weber's ideal type of bureaucracy that we discussed in Chapter 2. It is a model of what 'ideal speech' would look like if all the elements were in place. It is a model that gives a template against which *actual* communications can be reflexively measured.

### Stop and think

In these examples of societies in which social democracy and organizational democracy are in a close relationship with each other, we have seen that there is a continuing commitment to democracy. At the same time, organizational democracy is threatened by such issues as increasing emphasis on shareholder value, arguments about the impact of globalization and the development of 'American' approaches to management, with its emphasis on control and strong management. In the Aalborg case, we also saw the ways power issues can profoundly affect democratic process. Do you see the defeat of the link between social and organizational democracy as being inevitable, or do you think that it can survive and develop?

## A psychodynamic perspective on design – create the boundaries

The key idea that the psychoanalytic perspective brings to design is the need to develop boundaries for the tasks and the processes of organizational life. At the level of the individual member of the organization, the design needs to ensure that individuals in the organization are able to manage the boundary between their inner world – their personal aspirations and needs – and their external roles in the organization (Roberts, 1994). At a group level, the boundaries are there to enable people to be able to work together in interesting and creative ways. At an organizational level, the boundaries are created to enable the organization to understand its own primary task (which we discussed in an earlier section) and how to relate to others. The importance of understanding the boundaries is illustrated in the following case study.

### Case study        Getting the boundaries right – form fits function

In the UK National Health Service, there had been for many years a tradition, in the treatment of people with psychiatric illness, of clear boundaries between care in the community and treatment of patients in the hospital. Teams of staff who worked in community care were very committed to providing the kind of service that enabled people with psychiatric problems to lead normal lives in the community so that they would prevent admission to psychiatric hospitals. They tended to regard the psychiatric hospital as uncaring and oppressive, so that on the occasions that their clients were admitted to hospital, it was seen as a real failure. Additionally, the management of psychiatric care in the community and in the hospital was quite separate. In this sense, in the way that the community centre defined its primary task it also drew a *tight boundary* between itself and other forms of psychiatric care.

As a result of changes in the patterns of care for psychiatric patients, a new structure emerged in which there was an emphasis on the provision of shared responsibility as between the hospital and the community. 'The new boundaries matched and supported the task of providing a comprehensive mental health service. . . . Patients could then be more readily seen as a joint responsibility . . . and rivalry between the hospital and community lessened' (Roberts, 1994, p. 36).

*(Continued)*

**Case study** **(Continued)**

In this example, the boundaries have shifted from being tight and restrictive to a more loose sense of the boundaries. Developing this looser sense of boundaries means that although the tasks become more ambiguous, there is a creative conversation between both the community support and the hospital.

In relation to the development of a reflexive approach to the renegotiation of boundaries, the ideal situation would be that this process of change would have been developed as a consensus agreement in a democratic manner that involved staff and users of the service in an equal relationship.

## Critical theory and psychoanalysis challenge understandings of leadership and management

From the perspective of critical theory, the key issue in exploring leadership and management rests in discussions of the ways that leaders and managers in conventional organizations exercise power and domination over members of the organization. As we have seen in an earlier section and will discuss extensively in Chapter 9, the development of 'professional' managers and leaders enables them to become an elite. This elite (in company with 'business gurus' and cooperative academics from business schools) is then able, so the argument goes, to define the very qualities that enables membership of the elite. Although such issues as maximizing shareholder value, creating a vision, developing strategy and so on can appear to be logical and rational, they can also be seen to be arbitrary, the outcome of particular people in a particular place making judgements based on opinions and beliefs about the nature of organization.

A topic that is discussed in a number of chapters, but particularly in Chapter 4, has been the growth of management as an elite group. Management claim to have a comprehensive understanding of such matters as 'creating the vision', strategy, marketing, organizational design, managing people and so on. They claim that this knowledge gives them an entitlement to determine the very nature and purpose of the organization. In this sense, management achieves the 'right' to exercise power and domination over others – this knowledge they claim to possess gives them power. In addition this elite position leads, from the perspective of the critical theorist, to what Habermas (1970) called 'systematically distorted communications' and that these are deeply embedded in everyday language in organizations. These distortions of communication should not be seen merely as the means by which managers 'oppress' employees. They are also ways that 'managers and leaders' oppress themselves because they also impose controls on managers themselves. Their obligation to 'lead', 'motivate' and 'empower' people in prescribed ways prevents the managers and leaders themselves from realizing their own potential and creativity.

Psychoanalytic writers take an interesting position about leadership. On the one hand, they see it as important. The psychoanalyst Manfred Kets de Vries (2004) argues that although a company can be well placed in its competitive position, without 'strong hands at the helm, environmental advantages melt away and the organization, like a driverless car, runs downhill' (p. 188). This echoes the idea that as members experience greater complexity in their organizations, they need heroic figures who they believe will act with courage and intelligence in order to solve the difficult problems that they encounter.

These issues of heroism and dependency are encouraged by the very nature of the person who aspires to become a leader. At the very heart of leadership lies what psychoanalysts call the *narcissistic impulse*, the ability to have a strong sense of 'who I am', a strong sense of 'my place in the world'. This means that leaders regard their vision as *the* vision that will 'save' the organization. In return, as the vision develops, the organization gives back to the narcissistic leader a sense of identity, a sense of being. A 'solid dose of narcissism. . . offers leaders a foundation for conviction about the rightness of their cause' (Kets de Vries, 2004, p. 188) and provides the driving energy and passion for the development of the organization. However, the problem is that it does not take much for this 'healthy' narcissism to topple into dysfunction and organizational disadvantage; the leader is prone to *hubris*, the arrogance that invites disaster, as the leader moves from the 'solid dose' of narcissism into overdose. In this sense, the leader is akin to the heroic character of Greek tragedy, who as he became increasingly aware of his greatness, the gods could, at a stroke, take it away. In Greek tragedy, this was a warning against the insolent and arrogant seizure of power.

How do we prevent leaders and managers from becoming dominating or overwhelming in their search for control? This takes us back to the key themes of this chapter. Kets de Vries (1993) writes that the balanced leader is one who is able to have human regard for others and also to be able to attend to the primary task of the organization rather than his or her personal agenda. This implies an ability to communicate tasks in a way that does not distort communications and that there is a sense of balance between leaders and followers. At the heart of his argument is that successful leadership consists of an ability 'to combine action with reflection' so leaders can 'have sufficient self-knowledge to recognize the vicissitudes of power and who will not be tempted away when the psychological sirens that accompany power are beckoning' (p. 183). In this way, the myth of the heroic leader or manager can only be broken by reflection and self-knowledge at individual and organizational levels (Bowles, 1997). It also requires understanding that power is an aspect of all human encounters and we need to 'retain some place and hope for democratic decision-making so that all is not reduced to arbitrary power advantages' (Deetz, 1992, p. 36).

## Conclusions

We have shown in this chapter that critical theory and psychoanalysis make important contributions to organization theory, particularly developing amongst organizational members a 'reflexive understanding' of what goes on in their organizations with also clear indications of appropriate action. These contributions may be seen as we link the learning outcomes for the chapter to challenges that face the contemporary organization.

## Concluding grid

| Learning outcomes | Challenges to the contemporary organization |
| --- | --- |
| Explore the development of critical theory as a challenging perspective in organization theory. | Critical theory presents a radical view of the very nature of organizations in that it pushes organizations to think about the ways that members can be genuinely empowered within the development of the democratic organization. To what extent do you think that this radicalism could be an option in the modern business world? |
| Trace the development of psychoanalysis as a challenging perspective in organization theory. | Psychoanalysis challenges organizational members to look at the deep issues that can cause organizations to become dysfunctional. To what extent can this help us to understand organizations as they become ever more complex? |
| Examine the ways that critical theory and psychoanalysis come together to provide reflexive insights into the nature of organizations. | The synthesis of critical theory and psychoanalysis provides organizational members with methodologies that enable them to take a reflexive approach to the issues of power, language and emotion in organizations. To what extent do you think that this reflexive approach helps cope with the stresses and strains of modern organizations? |
| Discuss how critical theory and psychoanalysis challenge understandings of the relationship between the organization and society. Discuss how critical theory and psychoanalysis challenge the individual, the group and the organization. | To what extent does this reflexive approach help our understanding of the relationship between individuals and groups to their organizations and society? |
| Examine how critical theory and psychoanalysis develops challenging perspectives on organization culture. | Psychoanalysis in particular draws attention to the need to explore deeper issues of the culture in order to understand the ways that members need boundaries around which they can perform their primary task. Is this a useful way of understanding 'culture'? |
| Explore how critical theory and psychoanalysis present challenging perspectives for organizational design. | Critical theory in particular helps develop an understanding of the ways that different forms of organization can prevent distortions of communication. How does this approach enable members to work in organizations so that they can both be creative and effective? |
| Discuss how critical theory and psychoanalysis challenge understandings of leadership and management. | Critical theory and psychoanalysis both ask fundamental questions about the nature of leadership and management. How can these enable the reflective manager or leader to explore the very nature of his or her role in a reflexive manner? |

## Annotated further reading

Life in Germany in the formative years of critical theory – the 1930s – may be seen through the semi-autobiographical novels *Mr Norris Changes Trains* (1935) and *Goodbye to Berlin* (1939) by Christopher Isherwood. The latter was made into the film *Cabaret* (1974; directed by Bob Fosse), which is a clever visualization of the collapse of culture in that period.

One of the early themes explored in this chapter is concerned with the notion that in contemporary life, people are separated from their own experience of the world and the world that is communicated to them. One of the best movies to illustrate this theme is *The Truman Show* (1998; directed by Peter Weir). In the movie, Truman Burbank (played by Jim Carey) is the star of the world's most popular TV show – only he does not know this. He thinks he lives in this idyllic small town in the United States in which everybody is friendly (in a rather anonymous way) and the sun always shines. Gradually, he realizes that all is not as it seems, and he begins to experience his own identity as the layers of 'communicated self' begin to be stripped away.

The first text that gained widespread popularity in the United Kingdom that looked at critical theory in the context of organizations is *Critical Management Studies* (edited by Alvesson and Willmott in 1992). This was followed in 1996 by *Making Sense of Management: A Critical Introduction*, which was written by Alvesson and Willmott. What is interesting about both of these books is that they focus on the nature and role of management – they regard organization theory as an aspect of management theory.

There have been a number of texts that look at the application of psychoanalytic approaches to organizations. For an insight into the Tavistock Institute approach, the book of readings edited by Obholzer and Roberts (1994) gives useful perspectives on the use of psychodynamics as a 'useful theory. Stapley (1996) gives a useful discussion of the psychoanalytic approach to culture'. One of the most interesting books on leadership from a psychoanalytic perspective is Kets de Vries (1993). Some of the key issues of power and authority and the nature of leadership can be found in Hirschhorn (1997).

## Discussion questions

1. The critical theorists generally take an optimistic view of humanity and the possibilities for change that will lead to greater possibilities for human autonomy and growth. Do you think this is a realistic understanding of organizational life as you have experienced it?

2. The critical theorists suggest that the contemporary world of organizations is dominated by notions of 'scientific management', by distorted communications between members, by ideas of

selfish competitiveness and by the demands of the consumer. To what extent do you think that this is a fair depiction of contemporary business and industrial organizations?

3. The key advantage of psychoanalysis as a way of understanding the underlying issues of organizations is, it is claimed, that it can give deep understanding of, and more effective approaches to, the development of organizations and their members. The key problem with the approach is that it is very hard work and does not immediately tackle issues of 'the bottom line'. How might psychoanalytic perspectives be implemented in a practical manner within organizations?

4. Is it possible for an organization to have a 'healthy culture'?

5. In the section on the design of organizations, we used modern architecture as a symbol to express the contrast between organizations fit for humans to work in productive and fulfilling ways and organizations that exist purely in order to increase shareholder value. To what extent is this contrast in design an issue of concern in your society?

6. Given the forces of globalization and the apparent dominance of American approaches to scientific management, what are the possibilities for democratic organization in your society?

7. We have explored in this chapter the ideas of critical theory and psychoanalysis as theories that help us to be reflexive – to develop deep understanding of issues in our organization and then engage in processes of change. To what extent has this chapter helped *you* to be reflexive?

## References

Adorno, T. W. and Horkheimer M. (1972) *Dialectic of Enlightenment* New York: The Seabury Press.

Alvesson, M. (2003) 'Critical organization theory', in B. Czarniawska and G. Sevón (eds), *The Northern Lights – Organization Theory in Scandinavia*, Copenhagen: Copenhagen Business School Press.

Alvesson, M. and Willmott, H. (1992) 'Critical theory and management studies: An introduction', in H. Alvesson and H. Willmott (eds), *Critical Management Studies*, London: Sage.

Alvesson, M. and Willmott, H. (1996) *Making Sense of Management: A Critical Introduction*, London: Sage.

Beck, U. (2006) 'Risky business – Interview with Stuart Jeffries', *The Guardian* 11 February.

Bettelheim, B. (1983) *Freud and Man's Soul*, London: Chatto and Windus/The Hogarth Press.

Bowles, M. (1997) 'The myth of management: Direction and failure in contemporary organizations', *Human Relations* 50(7):779–795.

Byrkjeflot, H. (2003) 'Nordic management: From functional socialism to shareholder value?' in B. Czarniawska and G. Sevón (eds), *The Northern Lights – Organization Theory in Scandinavia*, Copenhagen: Copenhagen Business School Press.

Connerton, P. (1976) 'Introduction', in P. Connerton (ed.), *Critical Sociology: Selected Readings*, Harmondsworth: Penguin Books.

Connerton, P. (1980) *The Tragedy of Enlightenment: An Essay on the Frankfurt School*, Cambridge: Cambridge University Press.

Csikszentmihalyi, M. (2000) *Beyond Boredom and Anxiety: Experiencing Flow in Work and Play*, San Francisco: Jossey-Bass.

Cuff, E.C., Sharrock, W.W. and Francis, D.W. (1998) *Perspectives in Sociology*, 4th edn, London: Routledge.

Darwin, J., Johnson, P. and McAuley, J. (2002) *Developing Strategies for Change*, London: Financial Times/Prentice Hall.

Deetz, S. (1992) 'Disciplinary power in the modern corporation', in H. Alvesson and H. Willmott (eds), *Critical Management Studies*. London: Sage.

Flyvbjerg, B. (1998) *Rationality and Power*, Chicago: The University of Chicago Press.

Frankfurt Institute for Social Research (1973) *Aspects of Sociology*, London: Heinemann.

Feldman, S. (2000) 'Management ethics without the past: Rationalism and individualism in critical organization theory', *Business Ethics Quarterly* 10(3):623–643.

Freud, S. (1949) *An Outline of Psycho-Analysis*, London: The Hogarth Press and the Institute of Psycho-analysis.

Fromm, E. (1932) 'The method and function of an analytic social psychology', in A. Arato and E. Gebhardt (eds), (1978) *The Essential Frankfurt School Reader*, Oxford: Basil Blackwell.

Fromm, E. (1970) *The Crisis of Psychoanalysis*, London: Jonathan Cape.

Fromm, E. (1973) *The Anatomy of Human Destructiveness*, New York: Holt, Rinehart and Winston.

Fromm, E. (1980) *Greatness and Limitations of Freud's Thought*, London: Jonathan Cape.

Habermas, J. (1970) 'On systematically distorted communication', *Inquiry* 13:205–218.

Habermas, J. (1973) *Theory and Practice*, Cambridge: Polity Press.

Habermas, J. (1981) 'Modern and postmodern architecture', in K.M. Hays (2000), *Architecture Theory Since 1968*, Cambridge, Mass: The MIT Press.

Habermas, J. (1987) *Knowledge and Human Interests*, Cambridge: Polity Press.

Habermas, J. (2001) *The Future of Human Nature*, Oxford: Blackwell.

Harvey, J.B. (1974) 'The Abilene paradox: The management of agreement', in J.B. Harvey (1988), *The Abilene Paradox and Other Meditations on Management*, San Francisco: Jossey-Bass.

Held, D. (1980) *Introduction to Critical Theory: Horkheimer to Habermas*, London: Hutchinson.

Hirschhorn, L. (1997) *Reworking Authority: Leading and Following in the Post-Modern Organization*, Cambridge, MA: The MIT Press.

Hirschhorn, L. (1999) 'The primary risk', *Human Relations* 52(1):5–25.

Horkheimer, M. (1972) *Critical Theory; Selected Essays*, New York: Herder & Herder.

Horney, K. (1994) *Self-Analysis*, New York: W.W. Norton & Company.

Isherwood, C. (1935) *Mr Norris Changes Trains*, Harmondsworth: Penguin Books.

Isherwood, C. (1939) *Goodbye to Berlin*, Harmondsworth: Penguin Books.

Johnson, P. (2006) 'Whence democracy? A review and critique of the conceptual dimensions and implications of the business case for organizational democracy', *Organization* 13(2):245–274.

Johnson, P. and Duberley, J. (2000) *Understanding Management Research*, London: Sage Publications.

Kets de Vries, M.F.R. and Miller, D. (1985) *The Neurotic Organization: Diagnosing and Changing Counterproductive Styles of Management*, San Francisco: Jossey-Bass.

Kets de Vries, M.F.R. (1993) *Leaders, Fools, and Impostors: Essays on the Psychology of Leadership*, San Francisco: Jossey-Bass.

Kets de Vries, M.F.R. (2004) 'Organizations on the couch: A clinical perspective on organizational dynamics', *European Management Journal* 22(2):183–200.

Klein, M. (1975) 'A contribution to the psychogenesis of manic-depressive states', in *Love, Guilt, and Reparation, and Other Works, 1921–1945*, London: Hogarth Press.

Locke, R.R. (1996) *The Collapse of the American Management Mystique*, Oxford: Oxford University Press.

Lucaćs, G. (1922) 'History and class consciousness', in A. Arato and E. Gebhardt (eds) (1978), *The Essential Frankfurt School Reader*, Oxford: Basil Blackwell.

Marcuse, H. (1964) *One Dimensional Man*, Boston: Beacon.

Marx, K. (1886) 'On the accumulation of capital' in T. Parsons, E. Shills, K.D. Naegele and J.R. Pitts (eds) (1965) *Theories of Society: Foundations of Modern Sociological Theory*, New York: The Free Press.

Morgan, G. (1997) *Images of Organization*, 2nd edn, London: Sage.

Neumann, J.E. and Hirschhorn, L. (1999) 'The challenge of integrating psychodynamic and organizational theory', *Human Relations* 52(6):683–697.

Nicholson, N. (1997) 'Evolutionary psychology: Toward a new view of human nature and organizational society', *Human Relations* 50(9):1053–1078.

Obholzer, A. (1994) 'Authority, power and leadership: Contributions from group relations training', in A. Obholzer and V. Z. Roberts (eds), *The Unconscious at Work: Individual and Organizational Stress in the Human Services*, London: Routledge.

Prasad, A. (2002) 'The contest over meaning: Hermeneutics as an interpretive methodology for understanding texts', *Organizational Research Methods* 5(1):12–33.

Roberts, V.Z. (1994) 'The organization of work: Contributions from open systems theory', in A. Obholzer and V. Z. Roberts (eds), *The Unconscious at Work: Individual and Organizational Stress in the Human Services*, London: Routledge.

Schwartz, H.S. (1990) *Narcissistic Process and Corporate Decay: The Theory of the Organization Ideal*, New York: New York University Press.

Sievers, B. (1994) *Work, Death and Life Itself: Essays on Management and Organization*, Berlin: Walter de Gruyter.

Soyinka, W. (2004) *Climate of Fear: Lecture 3: Rhetoric that Blinds and Binds British Broadcasting Corporation*, Retrieved June 2006, from http://www.bbc.co.uk/radio4/reith2004.

Stapley, L. (1996) *The Personality of the Organization: A Psycho-Dynamic Explanation of Culture and Change*, London: Free Association Books.

Swarte, T. de (1998) 'Psychoanalysis and management: The strange meeting of two concepts', *Journal of Managerial Psychology* 13(7):459–468.

Weber, M. (1920a) 'On Protestantism and capitalism', in T. Parsons, E. Shils, K.D. Naegle and J.R. Pitts (eds), (1965), *Theories of Society: Foundations of Modern Sociological Theory*, New York: The Free Press.

Weber, M. (1920b) 'Protestant sects and the spirit of capitalism', in H.H. Gerth and C. Wright Mills (eds), (1948) *From Max Weber: Essays in Sociology*, London: Routledge and Kegan Paul.

Westenholz, A. (2003). 'Organizational citizens – Unionized wage earners, participative management and beyond', in B. Czarniawska and G. Sevón (eds), *The Northern Lights – Organization Theory in Scandinavia*, Copenhagen: Copenhagen Business School Press.

# Chapter 9

# The evolution of management as reflected through the lens of modernist organization theory

## Introduction

Over the past 100 years or so, management has become a powerful force in most organizations. As we have illustrated throughout this book, much, but by no means all, of organization theory has been developed so as to describe, explain and predict the functioning of those complex social phenomena we classify as organizations so as to notionally 'improve' their effectiveness and efficiency. The explicit aim of this mainstream theory has usually been to meet the presumed needs and concerns of managers through conferring the power of control based upon more rigorous analysis than would otherwise be the case. Hence, much of organization theory has itself been influenced by a particular image of management that has been taken for granted, especially by some forms of modernist organization theory. In this chapter, we turn this relationship on its head and look at what organization theory makes of the development of management as an identifiable social group and function within organizations, and consider some of the challenges to management that derive from particular currents within modernist organization theory.

## Learning outcomes

- Provide an historical account of the origins and evolution of managers as an identifiable organizational group and of management as a separate, hierarchical function within organizational divisions of labour.

- Describe the managerialist thesis and identify different theoretical interpretations of this organizational development.

- Outline the subsequent development of 'new managerialism' and its key characteristics.

- Analyse the diffusion of new managerialism in the workplace and relate recent developments to the impact of new-wave organization theory.

- Investigate the theoretical underpinnings of the economic case for organizational democracy as a potential challenge to managerialism.

## Structure of the chapter

- This chapter begins with an historical account of how and why management developed in the first place. It then moves onto consider what is called the managerialist thesis and how different interpretations of the significance of the development of management, as a specific function and social group, have impacted upon both how we understand management and how what is called new managerialism has recently developed. The diffusion of new managerialism in the workplace, the form it has taken and its effects upon employees and managers are also related to the rise of new-wave management. The chapter concludes with one contemporary theoretical challenge to managerialism – the economic case for organizational democracy. The theoretical rationale and content of this challenge is then explored as well as how it might founder because of institutional pressures that exist in contemporary organizations.

## Conceptualizing management

The close interweaving of management and organization theory is illustrated by how some management theorists actually conceptualize management. For instance, the claim that 'management as an activity has always existed to make people's desires manifest through organized effort' (Wren, 1994, p. 10) is a commonplace and recurring theme in much traditional management writing. It is a definition that conveniently puts management at centre stage in enabling all forms of organization. At first sight, this idea might seem harmless and self-evident because surely all organizations have, and therefore must require, management. But such a claim implies that management is some natural and necessary part of human life that is pivotal to our creative interplay with our often hostile natural environments. Therefore, it implies that we should accept the status quo because a key assumption we are being asked to accept here is that without management, the efficiency and effectiveness of our organized efforts would be threatened. Of course, such notions are highly debatable, and much depends here upon what we mean by management in the first place. For example, Wren defines management as:

> . . . the activity that performs certain functions in order to obtain the effective acquisition, allocation and utilization of human efforts and physical resources in order to accomplish some goal (p. 9).

Here Wren locates management in the primordial requirement for people to work together in order to satisfy their needs, a process that leads to a division of labour when they realized that some people were better at certain tasks than others. So, for instance, some people might plan what needs to be done, where and when, others might acquire the necessary resources, others actually use those resources to do whatever needs to be done and so on. But divisions of labour need organizing so as to accomplish group objectives, and for Wren, this organizational imperative leads to the development of a 'hierarchy of authority and power . . . management' (p. 10).

This theoretical view that management and hierarchy, are essential features 'of all types of cooperative endeavours' (p. 10) can be rather misleading for two reasons. Firstly, one must note the tendency for '[h]egemonic social orders [to] present themselves as historical necessity not as historical accident' (Scarbrough, 1998, p. 698). In other words, the powerful tend to make sure that a version of their own history is disseminated that justifies their powerful position as an inevitable response to the demands of the situation, and therefore their authority is best for all and hence cannot be rationally challenged. If management is something that is inevitable and necessary, how could we, for instance, even consider alternative ways of organizing not based upon a hierarchy of power and authority? Secondly, an account such as Wren's tends to ignore significant historical evidence regarding the development of management as a separate function within organizational divisions of labour and the evolution of managers as an identifiable social group, which presents a somewhat different picture as it theoretically positions the development of management in an array of specific social and historical conditions and processes. This alternative theoretical view is important because it enables us to question the assumption that management, as a hierarchy of authority and power, is indeed a technically necessary feature of all cooperative human endeavours. Moreover, once one questions the prevailing view that management is a necessity and in some sense a 'natural' feature of organizing, the possibility of alternative ways of organizing that are not reliant upon managerial hierarchies become intelligible and hence possible, a possibility we shall explore later in this chapter.

## The historical origins and development of management

A carefully researched historical account of the development of management is presented by the famous historian Sidney Pollard in his seminal work *The Genesis of Modern Management* (1965). Pollard locates the origins of management in Britain firmly within the world-shaking social, economic, and technological changes associated with the Industrial Revolution, which began during the eighteenth century. To locate the origins of management in what has been called the world's 'first industrial nation' (Mathias, 1969) may seem, as Pollard himself notes (1965, p. 6), somewhat contrary because surely such huge projects, such as the building of the pyramids or the Great Wall of China, not to mention military operations and mechantile endeavours, all precede the British Industrial Revolution and must have involved some prototype of management practice because they all required a vast number of people to subordinate their will to the organizational objectives and directions of others. However, Pollard also outlines the combination of factors that confronted entrepreneurs and managers during the Industrial Revolution, which were fundamentally different to anything that had gone before.

> Like the generals of old, they had to control numerous men (sic), but without powers of compulsion: indeed the absence of legal enforcement of unfree work was not only one of the marked characteristics of the new capitalism, but one of its most seminal ideas, underlying its ultimate power to create a more civilized society. Again, unlike the builders of pyramids, they had not only to show absolute results in terms of certain products of their efforts, but relate them to costs, and sell them competitively. While they used capital, like the merchants, yet they had to combine it with labour, transform it first, not merely into saleable commodities, but also into instruments of production embodying the latest achievements of a changing technology (Pollard, 1965, pp. 6–7).

Of course, the above description applies as much to those entrepreneurs who managed their own capital as it does to those who managed capital, and other resources, on behalf of owners. So what explains the organizational differentiation and rise of managers as a distinct social and functional entity during, and after, this period? For Pollard and others (e.g., Clawson, 1980; Marglin, 1974; Thompson, 1968) any theoretical explanation of these developments must begin with the establishment of the *factory system* during the late eighteenth and early nineteenth centuries.

## Example: The world's first factory?

With building started by Richard Arkwright in 1771, Cromford Mill in Derbyshire, England, became the world's first successful water-powered cotton spinning mill and possibly the world's first factory. Technologically, cotton was the most advanced industry of the British Industrial Revolution. Arkwright is seen to be one of the 'founding fathers' of the factory system, and Cromford Mill became the model for hundreds of factories throughout Britain and all over the world. The remote site was chosen because it had a reliable water supply to power its innovative machinery and because it was a good distance from the traditional, largely cottage-based, cotton industry located in Lancashire, where the newly invented cotton machinery was the target for threats and organized attacks by Luddites who saw the new technology as a direct threat to their livelihoods. Indeed, Cromford Mill's high fortress-like walls were built for protection against such dangers (Figure 9.1).

**Figure 9.1:** Cromford Mill in the 1830s. (*Source: The Mirror*, October 22nd 1836, Vol. 28, p. 257.)

Before the development of factories such as Cromford Mill, production in Britain was often a family-based activity undertaken by workers in their own homes. This 'cottage industry' entailed a variety of employment relationships. For instance, with regard to wool and cotton weaving, Thompson (1968, pp. 298–299) notes how these relationships varied from that of the independent producer who owned a loom and who sold finished products directly to customers on the open market; to self-employed part-time and full-time weavers who, whilst still owning the means of production, produced cloth on a 'putting-out', or subcontractual, basis for a single master or merchant who often provided the necessary raw materials and who then either sold on the cloth or turned it into various finished products. According to Thompson, these pre-industrial systems of production were effectively destroyed by the development of the factory system, which took production out of the home and concentrated large numbers of workers in premises owned by entrepreneurs. A crucial outcome of this transition was the transformation of independent producers, who sold the *results* of their work, into employees who sold their *capacity* to work to employers. As we shall illustrate, this was a long and complex process but, initially, it is important to consider why this transition began in the first place.

## Technological change and the factory system

One possible answer to this question lies in the technological developments that were occurring during this period. Domestic production was by its very nature geographically dispersed and, at the time, entailed the use of technologies that could be powered by the producer's own physical effort. However, as this *technological determinist* theoretical explanation goes, the increasing use of water power (and later steam power) demanded the concentration of workers into specific geographical locations close to the power source (e.g., workshops with water wheels powered by mill races or dammed streams). Until the advent of steam power, early factories, such as Arkwright's Cromford Mill, were often in fairly remote rural locations. This was because of the geophysical demands of water power and for protection from enraged domestic workers who were either being put out of work or were experiencing a drastic fall in their standards of living because their products could not compete with those being produced in the factories. Their anger might also have been fuelled by the emergence of a desire amongst some employers to replace skilled workers with unskilled workers in the new factories – a process called deskilling (see the Ideas and perspectives box below). However, once steam power had been developed as a viable industrial technology – the first example being in 1785 at a cotton mill in Papplewick, Nottinghamshire – power became more mobile and enabled the development of factories closer to the developing markets and population centres on the river plains of Britain.

However, Marglin (1974) challenges the received wisdom that it was such technological imperatives that led to the rise of the factory system. Indeed, his argument is that the factory system's success had little to do with the technological superiority of large-scale machinery. Moreover, it is evident that waterpower had been used throughout Europe for centuries for particular tasks such as milling corn. In other words, the technological know-how had, to a degree, long been available but had not been developed and used on the scale that the early Industrial Revolution, in Britain, encouraged.

---

### Ideas and perspectives

## The origins of deskilling?

### Andrew Ure: Philosophy of manufacturers (1835)

In his analysis of the developments in the textile industry, Ure observed that:

'It is in fact the constant aim and tendency of every improvement in machinery to supersede human labour altogether, or to diminish its cost by substituting the industry of women and children for that of men; or that of ordinary labourers, for trained artisans' (p. 23).

'The grand project therefore of the modern manufacturer is, through the union of capital and science, to reduce the task of his work-people to the exercise of vigilance and dexterity – faculties . . . speedily brought to perfection in the young' (p. 21).

Basically, for Marglin, it was the failure of the domestic system, in its various forms, to control work and productivity that was the main problem for the entre-preneur. It was this problem for which the factory provided a viable solution. As Smelser (1959) had earlier noted, the domestic system allowed workers a great deal of autonomy regarding the speed, intensity and duration of their working day. Often domestic workers would work only as much as they needed to in order to meet their own requirements and then they would engage in more enjoyable 'leisure' pursuits (see the Stop and think box below). Moreover, pilferage and embezzlement were a constant concern, particularly with the putting-out system. Smelser documents some of the fears expressed by entrepreneurs who could:

> . . . never tell within a fortnight or three weeks when every web sent out to the neighbouring villages will be returned . . . [and] risk[ed] . . . the work being taken out of the loom to be sold or pawned by the dishonest weaver (p. 142).

### Stop and think

As Smelser indicates, there was from the perspective of the merchant–entrepreneur a problem with controlling the level of output of cottage industry workers, something that possibly lay in workers' attitudes towards work. Some idea of what these attitudes may have been like before the Industrial Revolution is illustrated by Kumar's (1984) claim that:

> Industrial peoples harbour profound prejudices and illusions about non-industrial peoples, one especially potent one being that they are all bowed down by a lifetime of unremitting toil . . . [However] . . . [t]he ancient Romans . . . so piled up festival days that it is estimated that in the middle of the fourth century AD Roman citizens had 175 days a year off. For the European Middle Ages, contemporary evidence suggests that agricultural workers spent nearly a third of the year in leisure, while Paris craftsmen, for instance, worked for only about 194 days in the year – that is, nearly half the year was leisure time' (p. 4).

- What does Kumar's view tell you about the attitudes toward work that pre-industrial cottage workers may have had?
- What problems might this have posed for British entrepreneurs during the early part of the Industrial Revolution, particularly if the size of the market for their products was increasing with urbanization and population growth?
- What potential solutions could the factory system provide to such problems?
- Did the factory system see an end to pre-industrial work attitudes? As Pollard observes using contemporary historical sources:

> St Monday' and feast days, common traditions in domestic industry, were persistent problems. The weavers were used to 'play frequently all day on Monday, and the greater part of Tuesday and work very late on Thursday night, and frequently all night on Friday.

Spinners, even as late as 1800, would be missing from the factories on Mondays and Tuesdays, and 'when they did return they would sometimes work desperately, night and day, to clear off their tavern score and get more money to spend on dissipation, as a hostile critic observed' (p. 182).

- What does Pollard's example tell you about the organizational relationships between employers and employees at the time? Would these relationships be tolerated today by employers?

Clearly, the physical layout and attributes of the factory enhanced the possibility of surveillance and probably would have been seen as a viable means of allaying some of the entrepreneur's fears described by Smelser. Hence, for Marglin, the emergence of the factory system 'owed as much to the desire for closer coordination, discipline and control of the labour force as to the pressures of technology' (1974, p. 180). By substituting entrepreneurial control for workers' control of production processes, the factory system allowed the reduction of costs without being technologically superior. Yet it is also evident that the disciplined working habits entrepreneurs desired in their workforces were difficult to establish, and irregular attendance at work and other pre-industrial customs persisted. Nevertheless, the factory did allow the entrepreneur 'an essential role in the production process, as integrator of the separate efforts of his workers into a marketable product' (Marglin, 1974, p. 34). Thus, through the establishment of the factory system, a new division of labour that might meet the perceived control needs of the entrepreneur became possible even if it was not always realized because of the resistance of workers to attempts at disciplining them.

Some support for Marglin's thesis may be found in Pollard's work where he notes how, for some time, the technology used in the new factories was no different from that used in the older domestic system, 'making adjustment easier and postponing . . . the development of modern management techniques' (1965, p. 8). Here, however, Pollard also shows (p. 43) that many of the new factories also continued to subcontract work both outside and inside the factory. In the latter case, the contract was usually with older skilled workers, who actually employed other operatives, and supervised their work within the factory, with those hierarchical relations often being determined, in part, by either family connections or by craft traditions. What is important about this observation of Pollard is that it implies that direct control over the pace and direction of work often lay with subcontractors and skilled workers, 'who embodied the traditional knowledge and skills of the craft' (Braverman, 1974, p. 59), rather than with the entrepreneur. This evident survival of subcontracting, in various forms, seems to be something that goes against Marglin's view that the primary reason for the development of the factory system was to allow entrepreneurs to exert *direct* control over operatives. Indeed, as Pollard notes, with some irony, the continuation of the subcontract was in effect more 'a method of evading management' and reducing the entrepreneur's 'direct supervisory duties' (p. 38).

According to Pollard, it is evident that the increasing size of British factories during the 19th century, because of market demands and competitive pressures for efficiency (p. 12), further taxed the already limited ability of the entrepreneur to directly control employees though exercising power by 'personally, intervening in the labour process too often to exhort workers . . . and generally acting as despots, benevolent or otherwise' (Edwards, 1979, pp. 18–19). Although most found a solution in internal and external subcontracting, others sought a solution in employing managers. However, the latter solution was a slow and sporadic process. Indeed, as Clawson (1980, p. 8) observes with specific regard to the United States, until the end of the nineteenth century, there was virtually 'no significant category of non-workers who existed to manage and direct the details of work'. In the case of British industry, Littler (1982, p. 69) suggests that during the nineteenth century, it exhibited a range of modes of control, which, despite their differences, did not usually entail the employment of professional managers. However, Littler also argues that by the 1880s, there was, from the employer's side, increasing hostility toward the various forms of internal subcontract that were being used in many factories on the part of employers. He identifies three causes (p. 78):

1. employers' concerns about their own ignorance regarding, and lack of control over, the contractor's activities

2. declining profit margins exacerbated by an economic depression further increased employers' concerns about the cost and efficiency of contracting

3. contracting was tied to traditional working methods that were being superseded by the rapid technological change that was happening.

In response to such problems, employers, despite their long-standing doubts about the integrity and ability of professional managers to discharge their fiduciary responsibilities to them effectively (see Pollard, 1965, pp. 22–24), increasingly began to abolish internal contracting and create organizational hierarchies with managers who would be directly accountable to them.

A significant influence upon the development of such organizational hierarchies, especially in the United States, was the evolution of scientific management and its popularization by Taylor. In particular, scientific management provided the opportunity for employers to escape from the subcontracting systems that were increasingly falling into disrepute. Moreover, it intensified and extended the deskilling processes already underway in some industries (e.g., textiles – see Ure's 1835 observations in the previous example) for some time, to other industries. In doing so, scientific management simultaneously legitimated the transfer of control over work processes from skilled workers and subcontractors to management in a manner that considerably extended and legitimated the latter's role and function through, in effect, bureaucratizing those work processes. Here it is important to note that employers had previously attempted to assert control over certain aspects of work through various regulations and disciplinary procedures, governing attendance, aspects of employee behaviour and so on. An example of such rules is illustrated in the box opposite.

However, as Doray (1988, p. 28) observes, in comparison with what was to come with scientific management, rules such as those illustrated above usually asserted

# Example: Early factory rules

In 1823, at a factory in Tyldesley, near Manchester, the following rules and fines applied to spinners who worked in a temperature of between 80°F and 84°F:

|  | s. | d. |
|---|---|---|
| Any spinner found with his window open | 1 | 0 |
| Any spinner found dirty at his work | 1. | 0 |
| Any spinner found washing himself | 1 | 0 |
| Any spinner found leaving his oil can out of its place | 1 | 0 |
| Any spinner putting his gas out too soon | 1 | 0 |
| Any spinner spinning with gaslight too long in the morning | 2 | 0 |
| Any spinner being sick and cannot find another spinner to give satisfaction must pay for steam per day | 6 | 0 |
| Any spinner heard whistling | 1 | 0 |

The above is merely a selection of the full list of 19 rules and fines used at Tyldesley. It adds:

> At Tyldesley they work fourteen hours per day, including a nominal hour for dinner; the door is locked in working hours, except half an hour at tea time; the workpeople are not allowed to send for water to drink, in the hot factory; and even rain water is locked up, by the master's order, otherwise they would be even happy to drink that.

The source of the above rules is a pamphlet published in August, 1823 entitled *Political Register* (reproduced in Hammond and Hammond, 1917:32–33).

general control over unspecified work-related activities rather than articulating detailed specifications over what those activities should be and how they should be undertaken. Moreover, according to Pollard (1965, pp. 193–197), many rules and fines related to what was considered by employers to be immoral behaviour inside and outside of work – fighting, swearing, whistling, being drunk, 'night rambling' and so on – were the focus of some employers' moral censure and opprobrium. As Pollard also notes, such drives to raise the respectability and moral education of employees 'was not undertaken for their own sakes, but primarily, or even exclusively, as an aspect of building up a new factory discipline' (p. 197). However, this function and focus of rules in the factory was to drastically change with the development of scientific management and the subsequent bureaucratization of work.

## The chapter so far

Historical evidence suggests that management as a separate function, done by an identifiable hierarchical group in organizations, emerged during the later stages of the Industrial Revolution. Hence, we must be very cautious about claims that present this social phenomenon as an inevitable and necessary aspect of all organizations. Nevertheless, the ideological usefulness and significance of such a theoretical stance is only too evident.

## The impact of scientific management

The work of F.W. Taylor (1856–1915) was a significant influence in the development of management during a pivotal period – the gradual transition from owner-managed and controlled enterprises to corporations controlled by salaried professional managers. Taylor's work in the United States also systematized and popularized developments that had been ongoing for some time, developments such as the deskilling of operatives, which had already been hinted at in the United Kingdom as early as 1835 by Andrew Ure (see the earlier Ideas and perspectives box) in his analysis of what he called modern manufacturing.

Taylor (1947/1911) commences his analysis by castigating early managers because of what he saw as their utter incompetence. He thought that management was far from 'scientific' and was instead based upon 'rule of thumb' schemes and practices that failed to appropriately control and discipline shop floor employees. This and the resultant inefficiency occurred primarily because management did not possess a basic understanding of what employees did in undertaking their work. According to Taylor, this lack of knowledge about what work processes on the shop floor entailed left management unable to effectively control employee behaviour. Indeed, such ignorance left shop floor activities under the control of operatives in whose interests it was to 'systematically soldier' – to restrict their output because of their justifiable fears of ratecutting and redundancy if they were more productive. For Taylor, such inefficiencies were further compounded by operatives' employment of inefficient working practices and by what he called 'natural soldiering', which he thought occurred because of the propensity for laziness inherent in human nature.

Important to Taylor's solution to these perceived problems was the usurpation and replacement of the knowledge previously possessed by the skilled operative through the removal of 'conception' from the 'execution' of tasks (see Taylor, 1947, p. 36). That is the conceiving of how tasks should be done – the approach and methods to be used in completing a task must be removed from the control of the operative and become the prerogative and monopoly of management. The latter, having identified the 'one best way' through its rational 'scientific' analysis of operatives' tasks, had to then translate such knowledge into 'rules, laws and formulae' and ensure that operatives followed those protocols and procedures in the completion of their tasks, which were then considered to be 'fixed'. For Braverman (1974), this process entailed breaking down operatives' complex skilled tasks into simplified constituent units, thereby creating a micro division of labour that made the effort expended by the then deskilled operative more directly observable and measurable by managers. This information could be used to increase efficiency by allowing operatives' expenditure of effort to be directly controlled, it was thought, through the administration of cash incentives by managers. Here it is important to note how Taylor's utilitarian philosophical stance assumed that people would not forgo leisure time and work harder unless they could be convinced that it was only by working harder that they would receive more money. Hence the basic formulae were 'more effort = more pay' and 'less effort = less pay' based upon some understanding of what a 'normal' amount of effort was for a 'normal' worker together with the ability to measure the effort actually expended at work. It was then the duty of management to select employees with the 'right' psychological and physiological characteristics demanded by the tasks it had designed for them to do.

Thus planning, designing, coordinating, reintegrating and controlling production processes, based upon a micro division of labour, now became the responsibility of management, with operatives working according to the detailed rules and instructions of the (now) more knowledgeable 'scientific' manager. According to Littler (1982), by bureaucratizing labour processes in this fashion, scientific management thereby attacked the control over work exercised by individual operatives, as well as the control of subcontractors, and replaced it with that of managerial hierarchies. However, it also created opportunities for management as a function in that it constituted 'a science of the management of other people's work' (Braverman, 1974, p. 37): management now had acquired a clear hierarchical purpose that it had not possessed before. The subsequent bureaucratization of labour processes, through the development of a range of different but related initiatives that included Bedaux Systems and fordism, was sporadic (Littler, 1982, pp. 174–185). For instance, although bureaucratization has had a world-wide impact, it became established in the United States between 1900 and 1920 during a period of expansion. But in the United Kingdom, it became established between 1920 and the 1930s during a severe economic depression (Littler, 1982, p. 185).

Meanwhile, in the USSR, Lenin introduced scientific management not long after the 1917 revolution as a means of rapidly industrializing with a largely agrarian workforce that lacked industrial skills. As Thompson observes (1983, pp. 60–61), Lenin thought that Taylorism was a significant scientific achievement that allowed the identification of the correct methods of work and improved productivity and efficiency, which thereby would free workers to participate in the governance of a socialist society. However:

> ... the exclusion of critical evaluation of social relations of production in the factory ... fed ... the decline of [soviet] factory committees, the erosion of workers' control and their replacement by one-man management [sic]' (pp. 61).

It is interesting to note that Lenin faced a similar problem to that which confronted Henry Ford in the United States – a lack of skilled industrial workers. Ford's solution to this problem was to Taylorize jobs and introduce single-purpose machine tools in car manufacturing. Before this, car manufacturing had been on a much smaller scale and had been undertaken by workers who used a technology that demanded their deployment of a vast array of manual skills that took years to develop. However, single-purpose machine tools, or 'farmer machines' as Ford liked to call them, had only one way of operating, which could be easily learned by an operative – the worker did not have to be skilled, he or she just had to be quick. Anyone could use these machines, even the vast number of immigrants from Europe and migrants from the southern United States who were arriving at the time in the northern United States and who lacked industrial skills because they primarily came from agrarian backgrounds. However, these employees could still work at their own pace until Ford developed the assembly line at the River Rouge Ford plant in Detroit. After that, control of the pace and intensity of work was primarily invested in the technology in use, rather than in payment systems as in the case of Taylorism.

So, it would seem that scientific management in an array of guises was an important force behind the spread of management, as a separate organizational function undertaken by a specific social group, not just in capitalist countries but also in nominally socialist countries throughout Eastern Europe. Not only was scientific management widely adopted in the Soviet Union (see also Traub, 1978), it is evident other ostensibly socialist countries were similarly affected by its diffusion (see Haraszti, 1977). Indeed, by the end of the 1930s, most major European countries were already experiencing the application of some form of scientific management (see Fridenson, 1978). Similarly, Kamata's account (1984) of his experiences as an assembly line worker at Toyota would suggest that even Japanese organizations have not been immune to its influence.

The new tasks acquired by management subsequently evolved into various management specialisms (e.g., operations management, personnel management, finance, accounting, marketing and so on) with what Hales (1993, p. 7) describes as 'an increasingly elaborate division of labour with each individual management position contributing a part of the total process', which, of course, itself now had to be managed. However, this evolution of management as a separate grouping of supervisory and technical employees, with its own hierarchies and divisions of labour, was also influenced by other social and economic changes, which were also impacting upon the organization of the workplace during the early part of the twentieth century, some of which were at least ideologically significant in that they provided a moral justification for management.

## Biography — James Burnham (1905–1987)

The son of English immigrants, Burnham was born in 1905 in Chicago. He was a popular political theorist and activist who is best known for his book *The Managerial Revolution* (1941), which heavily influenced George Orwell's book *Nineteen Eighty Four*. Before starting an academic career at New York University, where he taught philosophy, he was educated at Princeton University and Balliol College, Oxford. During the late 1930s, he became an activist on the Trotskyist Left and helped found the Socialist Workers' Party (SWP) in the United States. However, with the beginning of World War II in Europe and the Soviet invasion of Finland, Burnham contended that the Soviet Union was not worthy of support as it was not and never would be a socialist country. This disagreement resulted in him leaving the SWP and his eventual breaking with the socialist movement altogether as he developed his thesis that a new managerialist class was seizing power worldwide and was fundamentally changing capitalism. Indeed, much of Burnham's subsequent work outlined a strategy for the defeat of Stalinism and was prepared for the Office of Strategic Services and later for the CIA. For much of his subsequent career, he continued this work as well as analysed the development of managerialism and attacked liberalism as he adopted an increasingly conservative political stance. Although he fell into some disrepute for his refusal to denounce Senator McCarthy in the 1950s, he received the Presidential Medal for Freedom from President Reagan in 1983, four years before his death.

## The chapter so far

The evolution of management as a separate function, discharged by a discernible organizational grouping, may be seen as being implicated in two gradual, interrelated processes that emerged during the Industrial Revolution and gathered pace during the late nineteenth and early twentieth centuries under the tutelage of scientific management. The first entails the devolution to managers of various responsibilities and functions formally the exclusive prerogative of the owner–entrepreneur. Aided by theoretical developments such as scientific management and its variants, the second entails the expropriation by managers of responsibilities and functions formerly undertaken by employees.

## The managerial revolution and the origins of managerialism

Drawing upon the earlier work of Berle and Means (1932), Burnham announced the arrival of the 'managerial revolution' in 1941 and what might be called the *managerialist thesis* was born. Berle and Means had suggested that there was an increasing divorce between those who owned businesses and those who controlled them – that control had been effectively transferred into the hands of professional, salaried managers. This theory was based upon the proposition that with the rise of the joint stock company, there had been a diffusion of share ownership and a concentration of capital into larger and more complex units. With ownership being dispersed amongst an ever-increasing number of small shareholders, it became more and more difficult for those owners to exert influence upon how their capital was managed on a day-to-day basis. Moreover, with increasing size and complexity, as Bendix (1956) put it:

> It becomes necessary for the owner-manager to delegate to subordinates responsibility for many functions, which he has performed personally in the past (p. 226).

So here, the rise of managerialism is associated with a functional solution to the problem of coordinating work organizations. Not only was the owner–manager ostensibly relegated to the status of an historical curiosity, but the sheer size and complexity of businesses necessitated the employment of non-owning professional managers who, in effect, now exercised power and control because of merit, something that lay in their specialist professional and technical knowledge, rather than because of any direct ownership rights. The importance of these apparent changes was not lost upon management writers, one of whom later declared: 'We no longer talk of "capital" and "labour" we talk of "management" and "labour"' (Drucker, 1955, p. 13). Not only was the manager now 'the dynamic, life-giving element in every business' (p. 13), but management 'will remain a basic and dominant institution perhaps as long as Western Civilization itself survives' (p. 1).

A key aspect of the managerialist thesis was that because this new elite came from a different social and economic grouping from that of shareholders since they did not own capital, their interests and motives were also different. However, there are *two variants* of this notion. For instance, Burnham (1941) first articulated a theory called 'sectionalist managerialism' when he voiced his fear that these managers might constitute a new dominant, or ruling, class that exercised power in their own interests through their control of 'the instruments of production' (p. 64). In this, managers were faced with a 'triple problem':

> (1) To reduce capitalists . . . to impotence; (2) to curb the masses in such a way as to lead them to accept managerial rule. . . .; (3) to compete amongst themselves for first prizes . . . To solve the first two parts of this problem (the third part is never wholly solved) means the destruction of the major institutions and ideologies of capitalist society and the substitution for them of the major institutions and ideologies of managerial society (p. 175).

In contrast, other commentators (e.g., Kaysen, 1957; Sutton et al., 1956) echoed Berle and Means' (1932) 'non sectional managerialism', which argued that the controllers of corporations would 'develop into a purely neutral technocracy balancing a variety of claims by various groups and assigning to each a portion of the income stream on the basis of public policy rather than private cupidity' (p. 356). In other words, these professional, technically competent managers were unlikely to operate with greed and avarice but were somehow more aware of their wider social responsibilities than their self-interested owner–entrepreneur forerunners. According to this theory, not only had managers accepted this ethic of social responsibility, but it was also functional to good management because they now had to run their organizations in a manner that satisfied and balanced a range of competing interests articulated by various stakeholder groups, without whose support their organization's survival would be endangered (e.g., shareholders, customers, employees, trade unions, the local community). This would have to be done in a nonsectional, socially responsible manner, rather than either to serve the shareholder's interest by trying to ensure profit maximization or to serve managers' own perceived interests by, in Burnham's terminology (1941), maximizing their own 'first prizes'.

A key set of mutually supportive theoretical assumptions at play here in this non-sectionalist perspective is *pluralist*:

1. that power in society was now so dispersed no one stakeholder group could persistently dominate affairs because its power was effectively *countervailed* or balanced by the power of others (see Dahl, 1961)
2. that the behaviour of any stakeholder group was constrained by mutual dependency upon other stakeholders
3. that their differences of interest were not so great that they could not be accommodated and harmonised through negotiation and compromise.

By being able to facilitate these processes of negotiation, management now played a pivotal organizational role through acting as a kind of neutral referee to ensure the 'continuity of the organization . . . while . . . keeping the interests of general public paramount' (Sutton et al., 1956, p. 36). In a similar manner, Kaysen (1957, p. 314) claims that the necessary exercise of moral leadership, professional authority and technical competence by management, was in the general public interest. Likewise, Bell (1974) claims that managers were able 'to judge societies' needs in a more conscious fashion . . . on the basis of some explicit public interest' (p. 284). Moreover, this had resulted in the rise of what Kaysen called 'the soulful corporation'. In other words, capitalist enterprise had been tamed, if not yet destroyed, from within by the evolution of salaried professional managers who somehow knew and protected the public good. Moreover, it is important to note that human relations theory (as we saw in Chapter 3) provided an apparently more humanistic discursive repertoire for managers that, perhaps unlike scientific management, lent support to this apparent duty of care.

**Stop and think**

- What factors might prevent managers from operating in the socially responsible manner suggested by Berle and Means and by Kaysen?
- Why might it be important for managers to at least appear to operate in the 'public interest'?

Writing in the late 1960s, Galbraith (1969) has a rather different view of the implications of an ostensible separation of ownership from control and the rise of the professional salaried manager. He suggests that this divorce had not so much resulted in Burnham's managerial revolution but rather in the development of what he termed a 'technostructure' or 'technical bureaucracy'. Power, he argued, had passed from organized capital to an organized intelligence that 'extended from the leadership of the modern industrial enterprise down to just short of the labour force' (p. 69). This technostructure was composed of not just managers, but also of 'technical, planning and other specialized staffs' (p. 69) who were the guiding intelligence of a corporation. However, far from being a nonsectional neutral grouping whose ethic was one of service to the public good and whilst balancing and satisfying the competing demands of various stakeholders, Galbraith argued that this elite exercised power to forestall the attempts of those stakeholders to influence their decision making and simultaneously acted to perpetuate and increase their own power, status and rewards.

From the stance of any sectionalist managerial theory, managers therefore do not act in the public interest; rather, they act, formally and informally, in their own interests. According to economists who adopt a sectionalist managerialist perspective (e.g., Marris, 1964), managers are therefore motivated in their decision making to enhance their own occupational and organizational status and thereby secure enhanced salaries and perquisites. This is primarily achieved by attempting to ensure the growth of their departments and organizations, thereby increasing their domains of responsibility and authority, whilst merely earning sufficient profit and paying sufficient dividend to keep shareholders happy, rather than attempting to maximize profits.

## Stop and think

What does Table 9.1 suggest about whether or not contemporary senior managers behave in a sectionalist or nonsectionalist manner?

**Table 9.1** Pay and profits: Long run performance of FTSE 100 companies (2002 prices)

| % change from 1978–1979 and 2002–2003 | | Highest paid director/CEO | |
|---|---|---|---|
| Net profit (%) | Director/CEO pay (%) | 1978–1979 | 2002–2003 |
| AB Foods 98.6 | 337.2 | 133,588 | 584,000 |
| AVIVA −244.3 | 1,161.4 | 193,435 | 2,440,000 |
| BA −75.6 | 494.1 | 93,080 | 553,000 |
| BAE −729.7 | 288.5 | 110,687 | 430,000 |
| Barclays 145.7 | 684.4 | 234,439 | 1,839,000 |
| BG Group 18.3 | 298.8 | 272,843 | 1,088,000 |
| BP 303.6 | 637.7 | 403,832 | 2,979,000 |
| BAT 37.8 | 248.2 | 300,927 | 1,048,000 |
| BOC 118.8 | 416.9 | 224237 | 1,159,000 |
| Boots 107.7 | 366.6 | 160,305 | 748,000 |
| Cadbury Schweppes 786.3 | 616.4 | 200,721 | 1,438,000 |
| Glaxo 2,302.8 | 1,142.1 | 189,836 | 2,358,000 |

*(Continued)*

| Stop and think | (Continued) |
|---|---|

| % change from 1978–1979 and 2002–2003 | | Highest paid director/CEO | |
|---|---|---|---|
| Net profit (%) | Director/CEO pay (%) | 1978–1979 | 2002–2003 |
| GUS 6.6 | 1,092.0 | 100,668 | 1,200,000 |
| Hanson 374.9 | 266.1 | 137,405 | 503,000 |
| ICI –83.8 | 144.7 | 398,809 | 976,000 |
| Marks and Spencer –37.5 | 1,098.5 | 171,710 | 2,058,000 |
| Pearson –384.1 | 258.7 | 222,500 | 798,000 |
| Prudential 158.0 | 669.3 | 125,954 | 969,000 |
| Rexam –191.4 | 433.7 | 211,189 | 1,127,000 |
| Sainsbury 353.7 | 883.6 | 108,779 | 1,070,000 |
| Scottish and Newcastle 81.3 | 633.4 | 83,588 | 613,000 |
| **Totals: 118.9** | **536.9** | **4,078,530** | **25,978,000** |

All calculations are in 2002 prices, using retail price index (RPI) for adjustment.

*Source:* Annual Report and Accounts, Monks Partnership, published in *The Observer*, 12 December 2004, p. 10.

For other theorists, managers may well be self-interested, but they are not always aware of this, and even if they are, they do not and cannot have the cognitive capacity to optimize their perceived interests by rationally pursing them during their organizational decision making. For example, according to Simon (1957) in order for human beings to be objectively rational when making a decision, they first must have knowledge of all possible consequences of all options in any decision-making situation, and second, they must have a consistent set of goals and preferences by which they might evaluate the outcomes of any decision-making option. For Simon people do not, and cannot, have such perfect knowledge of perfect judgement. Therefore, 'administrative man [sic]':

> . . . cannot reach any high degree of rationality. The number of alternatives he must explore is too great, the information he would need to evaluate them so vast that even an approximation to objective rationality is hard to conceive' (p. 79).

Based upon such limited information and limited understanding, management decision-making processes were therefore conceived in terms of 'muddling through' (Lindblom, 1959), which entailed the deployment of 'bounded rationality' based upon imperfect knowledge and judgement (Simon, 1957). Hence, management decision making is construed as attempts to find 'good enough' solutions that 'satisfice' a range of conflicting interests and goals that derive from the coalition of interests in the organization and try to ensure that minimum acceptable requirements are met (e.g., Cyert and March, 1963).

Of course, if one takes Galbraith's or Burnham's sectionalist view of managers as a self-interested elite, then the moral legitimacy of managers as a social grouping and management as a function become somewhat precarious. Therefore, it tends to be views like that of Kaysen, which construe managers as inherently morally superior agents who use their technical knowledge and skill to balance a range of stakeholder interests in pursuit of the greater good for not only their own organizations but also for society, that seem to have become the predominant managerialist rhetoric and imagery. This has also entailed notions such as bounded rationality becoming relatively muted in much recent discourse because it must undermine the possibility of meritocracy being the keystone of organizational hierarchies. As we shall illustrate later, the presentation of a meritocratic image of the manager is pivotal in legitimizing the power and control exercised by this relatively small group over the activities of the majority in the workplace. Moreover, it has also ideologically legitimized the relatively recent rise of the professional manager to the apex of the authority structures of public sector organizations in many Western liberal democracies.

---

**The chapter so far**

In the last section, we presented two opposing theoretical views of the managerial revolution. One argues that managers constitute a new self-serving ruling group in organizations and society, who pursue their own perceived interests. The alternative views management as guardians of the public interest who have to balance the competing claims of various stakeholder groups. Such competing theories lead us to conceptualize management and its role in organizations very differently and are pivotal in influencing how organization theorists perceive their relationship to management, no matter how tacitly this happens.

---

## Redefining managerialism

In all societies, people are involved in the complex and demanding business of organizing their everyday lives. . . . This management of routines is something we all contribute to and are knowledgeable about – it is 'second nature'. But, in modern societies, the responsibility for the management of everyday tasks, routines, and identities increasingly has become the preserve and monopoly of experts, including managers, who are trained and employed to shape, organize and regulate so many aspects of our lives . . . Government, education, health, consumption, the arts, leisure and, of course, work have all become objects of management knowledge and control (Alvesson and Willmott, 1996, p. 9).

It is worth emphasizing that the twentieth century saw a remarkable transformation in the fortune and social standing of management in the UK and elsewhere. Towards the end of the nineteenth century managers were still a relatively small group of low status employees who were portrayed in the popular British literature of the time as 'oleaginous, untrustworthy creatures, whose services polite society shunned, or at best treated with disdain' (Scarbrough and Burrell, 1996, p. 175). Today, in contrast, even critical commentators talk of the 'managerialization of the world' (Alvesson and Deetz, 2000, p. 209) in which managers and management are usually publicly exalted in dominant contemporary discourses. Such public celebration is illustrated by the following quotation:

Efficient management is a key to the [national] revival. . . . And the management ethos must run right through our national life – private and public companies, civil service, nationalized industries, local government, the National Health Service – Michael Heseltine, British Secretary of State for the Environment, 1980 (quoted in Pollitt, 1993, p. 3).

Managerialism has been broadly redefined in a number of different ways. However, most emphasize the development and articulation of an almost unquestioned faith in the capacity of management to act as a progressive force in society and its institutions. In many respects, Burnham's ideological problem, noted earlier, seems to have been resolved. Pollitt (1993), for instance, emphasizes this ideological dimension when he characterizes managerialism as:

. . . a set of beliefs and practices, at the core of which burns the seldom-tested assumption that better management will prove an effective solvent for a wide range of economic and social ills' (p. 1).

---

## Example: Managerialism in action?

**Intelligence chiefs appoint businessman to bring management expertise**

A senior business figure has been appointed to the top ranks of MI6 in the first major revamp of the organization in modern times.

After the criticisms made by Lord Butler of Brockwell, the former Cabinet Secretary, in his report last year on the faulty intelligence behind the decision to go to war with Iraq, the organization has made two senior appointments aimed at providing tougher oversight of all the service's agent-running operations. The businessman, a senior management expert in the private sector, will provide management expertise . . . [as a] . . . new non-executive director. . . . Several key Iraq agents inside Iraq who supplied information to their MI6 controllers about Saddam Hussein's weapons programme were later shown to be unreliable and lacking in credibility. . . . [The businessman who] . . . cannot be identified . . . will sit on MI6's board of directors.

*Source: The Times,* 12 January 2005, p. 6.

---

As Pollitt goes on to note, management here is now construed as a separate hierarchical organizational function that plays a pivotal role in ensuring social progress through planning, coordinating, implementing and measuring the necessary improvements in productivity. Success in these matters primarily relies upon the superior knowledge, qualities and professionalism of the manager. Hence, management becomes seen as essential to pursuing this common good and, as a necessary condition for performing this duty, 'managers must be granted reasonable "room to manoeuvre" (i.e., the "right to manage")' (Pollitt, 1993, p. 3). Clearly, and almost by default, the sectionalist theoretical view of managers, reported earlier in this chapter, is downplayed in favour of a nonsectionalist managerialist stance that associates managers with operating in the public interest.

So, central to managerialism is the acceptance of the idea that not only do managers work for the greater good of all, but they also seek to do this as efficiently as is possible by maximizing desirable outputs while minimizing the expenditure of scarce resources. As Pollitt (1993, p. 131) observes, 'managerialists conceive of management itself as the guardian of the overall purposes of the organization'. A result is that much of mainstream organization theory exclusively assumes the presumed perspective of the manager and seeks to satisfy their presumed needs. Indeed, as Collins (1997) has recently noted, in mainstream organization theory, the maintenance of hierarchy and managerial prerogative are taken to be natural, *economically* necessary, organizational characteristics. In essence, management has become so normalized and hence is so unquestioned that perhaps Burnham's (1941, p. 64) 'ideological problem' for managers seems to have been resolved.

In a similar manner, Kranz and Gilmore (1990) emphasize how at the heart of managerialism, there lurks a technocratic, almost magical, faith in the ability of managers to use the specialized tools or techniques that have been developed to help them manage, to resolve the problems are that taken to assail contemporary organizations and society at large. However, how managers can resolve these problems has recently altered under the impact of new-wave organization theory. As we saw in Chapter 4, for new-wave theorists, when bureaucracy is seen to fail, its replacement by cultural forms of management control paves the way for new forms of organizational governance. Closely associated with such ideas is the notion that the role of managers must change to one of 'charismatic' (Champy, 1995, p. 77) or 'transformational' leader (Bass, 1999) who 're-enchants' (Kanter, 1989b, p. 281) and 'empowers' (Blanchard et al., 1995) employees with 'visions of business' (Champy, 1995, p. 17) so that they 'fall in love' with the company (Harris, 1996) and thereby ensure 'corporate discipline, cooperation and teamwork' (Kanter, 1989b, p. 10) amongst their 'cultural fellow travellers to ensure success' (Deal and Kennedy, 1988, p. 141). Here two somewhat different processes are being described and, of course, prescribed. These are that managers must now undertake both leadership and management functions. But these two aspects of a manager's job are not perceived as equals: leadership is presented as much more special and significant and has become regarded with an almost mystical awe.

## The chapter so far

In the previous sections, we have shown how management and leadership are now lauded by society. Professional managers, especially visionary leaders, are now assumed to be necessary within organizations for ensuring efficiency and effectiveness. Accompanying this status are all kinds of material and symbolic rewards. Simultaneously, new wave organization theory has been supportive of these developments with its emphasis upon cultural control. However managerialism seems to also have a very mixed impact upon many managers, as we shall explore in the next sections.

## Leadership and managerialism

In this contemporary theoretical discourse, leadership is construed in terms of articulating, promulgating and inculcating in others an organizational vision and mission often driven by some form of strategic analysis of the 'big picture' that confronts the 'business' (Dubrin, 2001; Kotter, 1990). In essence, leaders are presented as strategic visionaries who courageously anticipate and initiate changes through communicating and sharing their visions and enthusing their subordinates: 'Leadership' we are told 'creates new patterns of action and new belief systems' (Barker, 1997, p. 349).

Management, on the other hand, is being recast and construed as being much more mundane, if not virtually banal. Management is apparently now about interpreting the leaders' vision and practically implementing it through various organizational processes whilst maintaining and enhancing employees' productivity. According to this new-wave discourse, although leadership is the primary focus of senior managers – *all* individual managers are expected, to some degree, to undertake aspects of both leadership and management in performing their organizational roles. As Dubrin (2001) starkly puts it, 'Without being led as well as managed, organizations face the threat of extinction' (p. 4).

Pattinson (1997) describes how the ascription of a special leadership status to managers often entails the deployment of quasi-religious metaphors whereby senior managers are somehow endowed with mystical capacity and of being akin to latter-day prophets. Here the connotation is that the denizens of the executive suites are blessed by 'having power from above' (p. 69) because they can see things that others cannot – charismatic figures who have a mission to pursue unquestionable goals and inspire other organizational members to confess their past and faithfully change their (mistaken) ways. Therein lies those members' redemption. Indeed, this ascription of special status may go so far as to liken the leader to 'a savior like essence in a world that constantly needs saving' (Rost, cited in Barker, 1997, p. 348). Such a view of management sets the (senior) manager at the centre stage of organizations as a crucial influence upon organizational culture and performance. To do this, they must become 'transformational,' 'charismatic' leaders – messianic visionaries in the sense that they personally can invoke and energetically disseminate to 'followers' a compelling image of an idealized future state for their organizations that, through stimulating emotional attachment to and trust in the leader, inspires followers to become highly committed to the leader's vision and prepared to make drastic personal sacrifices on its behalf. Engendered cultural conformity, based upon socialization through processes of identification described in Chapter 4, seems to be being alluded to here.

Tourish and Pinnington (2002), in their critical analysis, distil such transformational leadership into the five core points illustrated in Table 9.2.

**Table 9.2** Five core points of transformational leadership

- **Charismatic leadership** (which may be a socially engineered construct in the minds of followers, rather than representing innate qualities on the part of the leader).

- **A compelling vision** (one of a transcendent character, which imbues the individual's relationship to the organization with a new and higher purpose, beyond that of self interest).

- **Intellectual stimulation** (generally, in the direction of transforming the followers' goals, so that they are subsumed into a new, collectivist objective on the part of the whole organization).

- **Individual consideration** (or a feeling that the followers' interests are being attended to and perhaps that they are in some way important to the charismatic leader).

- **Promotion of a common culture** (a given way of thinking, doing and behaving, which is likely to minimize the overt expression of dissent, other than within carefully patrolled boundaries).

*Source:* Tourish and Pinnington (2002, p. 156).

Tourish and Pinnington (2002) go on to explore the similarities between transformational leadership and the characteristics of leadership in organizations generally defined as cults. The evident parallels they identify illustrate how transformational leadership, because communication is strictly a one-way, top-down process, may be to the detriment of the possibility of internal dissent. The possibility of internal dissent, they argue, is a vital ingredient for effective organizational decision making because it entails critique of the status quo. In doing so, they also note how the transformational leadership theory has taken on increasing religious overtones in which the senior manager becomes exalted with revelatory powers as he or she speaks the 'corporate gospel' to which employees must listen and having experienced 'conversion' live with 'devotion' and zeal – not challenge. This grandiose reengineering of (senior) managers as messianic figures lends force to the observation of Williams et al. (1995), who point toward the almost mystical status management has developed, 'where an earlier age believed in miracles, our own believes in management' (p. 9). The authoritarian implications are only too obvious – if one does not publicly conform with enthusiasm to the leader's wishes, regardless of their substance, you may be, to continue the religious analogy, branded as a heretic or even an apostate and possibly expelled from the organization for such wilful and sinful behaviour!

Naturally, one of the main beneficiaries of this imagery, which portrayed managers as making such a pivotal contribution to our organizations, were senior managers themselves – not just in terms of reinforcing management prerogative (management's right to manage) but also in terms of enabling a rising social status with related financial benefits. Indeed, Alvesson and Svengingsson (2003) suggest that the attribution to managers of visionary and strategic powers seems more connected to managers ideologically advancing their own significance and status rather than being a description of what they actually do, or indeed could do, in practice. However, recent financial scandals such as Enron's, increasing income disparities (see the Ideas and perspectives box on page 404) within organizations and the evidence of 'corporate cannibalism' through downsizing and raiding (see Korten, 1995) may well have served to undermine public confidence in the probity of senior managers when discharging both their fiduciary responsibilities to shareholders and their social responsibilities to other stakeholders. Nevertheless, despite these criticisms, one thing is also evident from the statements of various commentators, whether they are politicians, consultants or academics: management and managers today have indeed acquired a high social status and legitimacy, which would have been inconceivable a century ago; whether it is always deserved is a different matter.

One development this public acclamation appears to have encouraged, and is reciprocally encouraged by, has been the recent spread of various management ideas and practices into areas where it previously seems to have had relatively little presence. Two key processes are identified by Scarbrough (1998). The first entails diffusion of management techniques, values and ideas between institutions through the colonization of an increasing range of non-business, publicly funded, organizational settings by practices that seem to derive from the private commercial sector. The second entails diffusion within organizations and the assimilation (or reappropriation?) of formerly management functions and practices by employees.

## Fat cats' pay is the result of greed, not competition

Why are high wages showered upon some while others toil long hours at essential work for very little? Whatever else Labour has done, it has not erased from national consciousness the dismal Thatcher maxim: There is No Alternative.

'It's the market' is the cry, assuming Adam Smith's divine invisible hand has immutable laws to explain what looks irrational to the naked eye. It is just too painful to think there is no good reason why the weary care assistant earns £1 for every £100 her chief executive gets?

Here comes new research to puncture the useful excuses top managers use to hide their blushes over sky-rocketing salaries. Nick Isles's *Life at the Top: The Labour Market for FTSE-250 Chief Executives*, published by The Work Foundation, quietly pulverizes conventional reasons for over-paying managers.

The median salary of FTSE-100 top bananas has grown by 92% in the last 10 years to £579,000, while inflation rose only by 25%. But it was the recent bear market that tore away the fig leaf from executive pay and got Patricia Hewitt at the DTI protesting. In 2001, when the value of top companies fell by 16%, top executives gave themselves a 12% increase in pay, with bonuses up by 34%. . . . Shareholder protests lead to naming and shaming once a year at AGMs, but chairmen seem to regard the annual public humiliation a price well worth paying for their booty, pretending they must pay top dollar for top talent in a global market.

Nick Isles makes elegant mincemeat of business's three excuses. First there is risk: true the shelf-life of top CEOs is not long, but average male job tenure is only five-and-a-half years. While CEOs walk straight into other highly paid directorships, three million men ejected from jobs in mid-life never find another.

Take 'visionary leadership': Isles quotes voluminous research to show CEOs are clever and talented but rarely exceptional. Despite the rhetoric of visionary leaders, for every Branson there are 100 bureaucrats; stewards not risk-takers. Most prefer deal-making and mergers to boost short-term share price to the hard grind of managing their companies. There is no shortage of able people to do the job. . . .

But 'the market' is their best excuse: here Isles lands his biggest blow. There is little global market in British managers. People don't want ours and we don't often recruit from abroad: 86% of FTSE CEOs come from the UK, another 6% from the EU (many from Ireland) and 8% from the US and the rest of the world . . . some two thirds of FTSE CEOs were home grown from within their own companies. . . .

When all other arguments fail, apologists fall back on a blasé view that CEO pay is such an infinitesimal part of the company's outgoings that it hardly matters. But it does. Isles accumulates research showing how dysfunctional it is. Managers set an example in their psychological contract with their staff: large pay differentials demotivate and demoralize. When differentials between top and bottom exceed 14:1, morale slides.

*Source*: Toynbee, P. (2003) *The Guardian*, 24 December 2003.

## Diffusion between institutions: the case of the UK public sector

The economic and political circumstances of the past 20 or so years have been instrumental in promoting dramatic changes in how UK public sector organizations are organized. Underpinned by nonsectionalist managerialist theories, the policy of various governments appears to be based upon the view that many areas of the public sector were in need of greater efficiency and rationalization. On the one hand, the UK public sector was condemned as spendthrift and unaccountable because it seemed to have grown in size and cost without any evident gain in productivity or efficiency. On the other hand, there was a lack of will, or economic resources, on the part of successive governments to fund this sector in the face of ever-increasing demands for resources (Cutler and Waine, 1994).

Significant in the diagnosis and attempted remedial treatment of this problem was the contestable assumption that the self-evidently superior private sector provided an objective 'outsider's view' on improving public sector organizations (Pollitt, 1993, p. 7). Simultaneously, those groups that were taken to block greater public sector productivity and efficiency, whether they were trade unions, various public sector professions, politicians or bureaucrats, were all systematically vilified (p. 8). Since the late 1970s, this privileging of how the private sector operated and its discursive corollary, the vilification of many of those involved in delivering public sector services, have been to varying degrees influential upon its reorganization in a number of OECD countries. Here the greatest emphasis has been evident in countries such as Sweden, the United States, Australia, New Zealand and the United Kingdom (see Hood, 1991; Hood et al., 1999). Redolent with new-wave imagery, commentators put forward the case for disciplining ineffective and wasteful bureaucracy through culture management, and in some cases through the privatization of state enterprises. In essence, government had to be 're-invented' by changing 'staid bureaucracies into innovative, flexible, responsive organizations' (Osbourne and Gaebler, 1992, p. xxii) 'that were responsive to their customers, offering choices of non-standardized services; that lead by persuasion and incentives rather than commands; that give their employees a sense of meaning and control, even ownership . . . institutions that empower citizens rather than simply serving them' (p. 15). For instance, in the United Kingdom, the above analysis led to the emergence of what is called new public management, sometimes also referred to as new managerialism.

## New public management

As we have already implied (see also Chapter 2), new public management is broadly defined as an ideology that involves the application of ideas, values and practices that are assumed to derive from private sector commercial management to the management of public sector organizations (e.g., Deem, 1998; Hood, 1999; Newman, 1998; Reed and Anthony, 1993). Hence, its emergence in the United Kingdom entailed an increasing stress upon discipline and parsimony in resource use. A key dimension of this development was the introduction of a 'culture of competition' (Painter, 1992) into the public sector as a remedial device to ensure efficiency (Hood, 1991, 1995). Here the 'contract' between service providers and purchasers, as a means of bringing competitive market mechanisms and customer choice to bear upon the public sector, became a key aspect of government policy. Indeed, a large-scale contracting-out of services to the private sector and the development of quasi-autonomous in-house contracting teams was evident during the 1980s and 1990s through processes such as market testing and compulsory competitive tendering (CCT). This led to the suggestion that there was movement toward a 'contract culture' in which 'the notion of contracts will become central to our organizations and to our ways of working with each other' (Dutfield, 1992, p. 32) through the creation of 'semi-independent business units' (Vincent-Jones, 1994, p. 17) with the subsequent danger of a loss of common purpose (Shaw et al., 1994).

Although moderated by subsequent government policies, such as best value, there remains today a managerialist focus upon the use of specific output measures as a means of enabling surveillance, accountability and the informing of 'customer' choice in the delivery of services. This is articulated through the benchmarking of service provision so as to establish performance indicators and quality assurance criteria as means of performance management (see Speller, 2001). An important consequence has been the construction of various league tables (e.g., schools, universities, hospitals) to enable comparison and thereby empower 'informed' customer choice.

Clarke and Newman (1995, 1997; Newman, 1998) have described this ongoing restructuring of the public sector as entailing an explicit attack upon the tradition of 'bureau-professionalism' with its replacement by a regime embedded in what they called 'new managerialism'. According to Newman (1998), bureau professionalism embodied the coupling of the exercise of professional expertise with the bureaucratic administration of public services through use of hierarchies and rules to coordinate resources. Bureaucracy provided the organizational context in which various public sector professionals – doctors, teachers, lecturers, social workers and so on – exercised their judgement. For Newman, the resultant combination of administrative rationality and professional expertise protected the exercise of professional judgement in the delivery of a range of public services. Indeed, those who were in those administrative roles usually had been socialized into the dominant values of the particular public sector field, or profession, in which they were working.

Successive British governments during the 1990s saw these professions as embodying characteristics that had to be removed in the pursuit of efficiency. As Foster and Wilding (2000) subsequently observed:

> [T]hey saw the professions as a powerful vested interest, effectively accountable to no one – politicians, managers or consumers. They were inefficient, the inevitable result of their insulation from the bracing competitive stimulus of market forces. . . . They were ineffective in achieving society's aims for particular services. . . . Professions were seen as very much secondary to management as an instrument of effective social policy (p. 146).

However, with the development of new managerialism, the public sector manager is now more likely to allude to the more general values of 'management' and embrace a 'hands-on' approach. As we have already noted, a further difference is that new managerialism deploys the new-wave theoretical assumptions we investigated in Chapter 4. Despite using a different idiom, Newman and Clarke (1995) illustrate the insinuation of new-wave management theory into the public sector where they indicate how new managerialism also construes:

. . . bureaucratic control systems as unwieldy, counterproductive and repressive of the 'enterprizing spirit' of all employees. Its notion of the route to competitive success is to loosen formal systems of control . . . and stress instead the value of motivating people to produce 'quality' and strive for 'excellence' themselves. Managers become leaders rather than controllers, providing visions and inspirations which generate a collective or corporate commitment to 'being the best' (p. 15).

So, it is evident that through the lens of this theoretical stance, good public sector management becomes redefined in terms of a concerted attempt at altering organizations in four key respects, which are summarized below.

1. **Cost effectiveness and economic efficiency:** There has been a shift from a commitment to 'professional' standards as the benchmark for decision making to an emphasis upon efficiency, which stresses the economic aspect of managing organizations in terms of cost effectiveness and a search for competitive advantage over other service providers. Here the stress may be upon continuous improvement and organizational learning so as to enhance any efficiency savings and secure competitive edge.

2. **Customer sovereignty ethos:** With this new managerial discourse, patients, clients, students, pupils and so on, for whom services are provided in accordance with government policy and professional judgement, are redefined as customers with sovereign rights. As Du Gay has observed (1996, 2000), this enterprise-excellence discourse creates an ethos that places the customer at the moral centre of organizational decision making. What is counted as good management and good employee performance is that which is orientated to servicing the market by subordinating all organizational members to the apparent needs, desires and preferences of individual customers.

3. **Culture management:** Closely related to trying to establish this ethos of customer sovereignty are explicit attempts at managing the values of employees through the selective use of an array of management techniques, including total quality management (TQM), human resources management, business process reengineering (BPR) and so on.

4. **Managing the individual 'employee relations':** There is an increasing emphasis upon managing individual relations with employees rather than collective relations through negotiations with trade unions. A result has been to try and marginalize trade unions and to focus management control upon the individual through monitoring and rewarding individual job performance, through deploying various performance indicators and appraisal, rather than remuneration being based upon a collectively negotiated rate of pay 'for the job' with annual increments based upon experience or length of service.

Despite the anti-bureaucratic rhetoric, the managerialization of the public sector has by no means necessarily engendered a move away from bureaucracy per se. Rather, what sometimes seems to have happened is that a new form of bureaucracy has developed that has undermined the autonomy of public sector professions, regarding what they do and how they do things, and made those professionals more directly accountable to managers for the performance of those tasks (see the Example).

## Example: Managerialism and bureaucratization – The McUniversity

For instance, as Parker and Jary (1995) discuss with regard to UK universities, this reorganization has resulted in universities, despite the overt and regular use of new-wave terminology, becoming increasingly rationalized and bureaucratic through the imposition of sophisticated systems of corporate surveillance and control to ensure accountability, quality assurance and efficiency. Indeed, it would seem that professional academic staff are subject to both bureaucratic and normative control, although more of the former than the latter. Parker and Jary go on to note three key outcomes of this process, which they dub 'McDonaldization':

1. An increase in the power, organizational status and numbers of managers who have become legitimated as key decision makers who attempt to control academics and have replaced administrators who originally were there to support, not control, academics in their work.

2. The language of universities is managerialized by terms such as *line manager*, *customers*, *markets* and *products* replacing academic terminology of *collegiality*, *students* and *courses*.

3. A diminishing in the autonomy of professional academics, whose work is increasingly controlled through standardization, and in some cases, casualization, who in response might develop an increasingly instrumental attitude toward their work – something indirectly supported by more recent research in universities regarding work intensification and emotional labour (Ogbonna and Harris, 2004).

So although the development and diffusion of managerialism in the public sector may have been a complex, varied and sporadic process, which does not necessarily entail the demise of bureaucratic governance despite much of the official rhetoric. One thing is evident: it has impacted upon the social status, number and role of those who formally manage public sector organizations. Indeed, as Gordon (1996, p. 34) observed in US corporations, UK public sector organizations, in some cases, may have gained what he calls a 'bureaucratic burden' of unnecessary managerial staff to the extent that they are now 'fat and mean'.

However, a somewhat different picture emerges when we turn to the other process of management diffusion identified by Scarbrough (1998). This is a process of diffusion downward to the shop floor within commercial enterprises in which, perhaps, new-wave management's anti-bureaucratic credentials are more evident in practice than seems to be always the case in the public sector.

## Diffusion within organizations: the infiltration of the rank and file

As noted earlier, Scarbrough (1998) also points to another form of diffusion that might be associated with the spread of managerialism since the late 1980s. For Scarbrough, this second process entails the diffusion of management away from hierarchical roles by ceding control over certain work processes, and technical aspects of the management function, to 'empowered' rank-and-file employees. Obviously, this process has significant implications for lower level managers, whose primary responsibility is for the control and direction of labour, as a distinct occupational group and function in some organizations. This is for two reasons. Firstly, such diffusion downward serves to blur the division of managerial and other forms of labour (e.g., manual) based upon a divorce of conception of how tasks were to be done from their actual execution, first crystallized by scientific management in its various guises. Secondly, such a restructuring of work might constitute a threat to, in particular, middle and junior managers who seemed to be becoming the victims of the accompanying delayering and redundancy as aspects of their work are cascaded downward, as some bureaucracies are dismantled, as hierarchies are flattened and as career structures are attenuated, if not destroyed (see Heckscher, 1995; Inkson and Coe, 1993; Thomas and Dunkerley, 1999; Worrall et al., 2000). As one new-wave theorist put it in the early 1990s, 'middle managers as we have known them, are cooked geese' (Peters, 1992, p. 758) because he thought that they were beginning to be managed out of existence. Likewise, in his new-wave contribution, Morgan (1988) discusses coping with the 'middleless' organization in which visionary senior managers are exhorted to use 'helicopter management' where 'you hover like a helicopter on the scene. If something goes wrong then you can come down and resolve it, but essentially you operate at a distance and let the operation go' (p. 87). We might call this the pine tree effect (Figure 9.2).

Of course, the extent to which managerial posts have actually been removed by delayering and downsizing has been disputed as a 'myth', particularly in the United States (see Gordon, 1996). Although individual managers may be made redundant, the numbers of managerial posts, this argument claims, remain the same with new managers taking them over. Alternatively, when particular posts do disappear through delayering, the post holder is merely redeployed into new managerial roles created by the restructuring. Therefore, the effects of this form of diffusion, in terms of reducing the number of managers, is to a degree contestable. Indeed, it is evident that such diffusion is resisted and reconfigured, by those managers most affected, through various tactics so as to ensure that the implementation of change is congenial to their own parochial self-interests, thereby preserving key aspects of their roles and ensuring their continuing employment (Denham et al., 1997); nevertheless, their roles do change (Wilkinson et al., 1997). Hence, it would also seem that the organizational roles of those surviving middle and junior managers have been reconfigured under the impact of the new wave's anti-bureaucratic trajectory. Indeed, as one recent British survey found, some 65% of the managers sampled had been directly affected by these processes (Worrall et al., 2000).

With reference to organizational changes that began in the late 1980s, Scarbrough (1998) notes how important in the restructuring of work and management practice have been an array of interrelated innovations such as BPR, lean production and TQM. Albeit in different ways, all these developments have ostensibly encouraged the displacement of centrally controlled, multilayered hierarchies and the diffusion of some

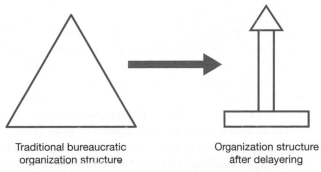

Traditional bureaucratic
organization structure

Organization structure
after delayering

**Figure 9.2:** The effects of delayering upon organizational hierarchies.

managerial practices downward throughout organizations as necessary components of closely related change strategies.

For instance, TQM advocates (e.g., Dean and Evans, 1994) emphasize the necessity of privileging the needs of the internal and external customers in a search for continuous improvement whilst involving all employees in a quest for perfect quality. By placing the responsibility for quality and customer satisfaction onto those who actually produce the product or deliver the service, TQM requires the empowerment of employees, so as to release their creative energies and discretion through their participation in team-based quality circles and the like. This is necessary so as to enable the employee to be involved in the maintenance of production standards; deal with unforeseen customer requirements; and autonomously resolve unpredictable service or product failures on the spot when they arise. But it also entails the displacement of line managers in favour of new forms of surveillance and control usually located in employee commitment and cultural management (Wilkinson, 1992). Likewise, advocates (e.g., Womack et al., 1990) of lean production claim that it results in the redeployment of some management functions to self-managing multiskilled teams of employees who are capable of looking after the details of production themselves and who can deploy that improved task knowledge to pursue continuous improvement.

These themes of employee involvement, empowerment and self-management are also maintained by the advocates of BPR. According to Hammer and Champy (1993), BPR aims to remove any slack and waste in any system of production through its redesign. Key aspects of BPR include instilling a customer focus amongst employees and flattening hierarchies with multiskilled and empowered employees working in process teams, rather than functional departments. In this, management style had to change from supervision to one resembling coaching in which middle management offers coordination and guidance to groups of employees whilst senior managers, we are told, must become inspirational leaders.

One thing is evident about all these innovations – they all deploy new-wave theoretical assumptions to undermine what are construed as the (now inappropriate) command and control structures of bureaucratic modes of organization. Although it is important to be sceptical about much of the anti-bureaucratic hyperbole and the language of employee participation and empowerment deployed by their aficionados, it is evident that at the heart of these systems of production is the often unrealized desire to reorganize work processes so that employees manage production matters themselves in a responsibly autonomous fashion, whilst reconfiguring the role of many of those lower level managers who remain, to one that focuses upon the support, guidance and coordination of self-managing teams.

For instance, following on from our analysis in Chapter 4, it is evident that new-wave theory is implicitly and explicitly allied to various predictions about and prescriptions for fundamental changes in managerial work that undermine the traditional raison d'être of the managerial role and replace it with a 'new breed of managers' (Clarke, 1993). Here a recurrent anti-bureaucratic theme (e.g., Champy, 1995; Kanter, 1989a; Mintzberg, 1998; Morgan, 1988; Peters, 1992; White, 1994) is the need to radically reorganize the role of managers: from the hierarchically ordered calculation, articulation and enforcement of rules through vertical reporting relationships that enable authoritative command and control of subordinates' work performance; to 'learning leadership' (Senge, 1990) in the form of horizontal communication and dialogue (Isaacs, 1993) through roles such as mentor (Garvey and Alred, 2001), co-learner (Marquardt, 1996) and entrepreneur (Halal, 1994). This change is deemed necessary because knowledge in organizations is thought to be no longer hierarchically ordered through task continuity. In other words, because of increasingly volatile markets, hypercompetition and the deployment of non-routine technologies, managers are thought to be losing a clear technical grasp of the complexities of increasingly uncertain and unpredictable work operations. Therefore, employees cannot be commanded in conventional bureaucratic ways. Instead, employees' traditional grudging, and often passive, compliance must be replaced by their 'active', 'responsible' and 'collaborative' deployment of their specialized and discontinuous task knowledge, something it would appear, can only be empowered, guided and facilitated, rather than directly controlled, by their managers (Drucker, 1993; Mueller and Dyerson, 1999).

As noted in Chapter 5, such postbureaucratic restructuring, if it is put into practice, also might spell the end of stable career structures, at least within single organizations, for many middle managers (Heckscher, 1995). Instead, the nomadic existence of the 'portfolio worker', who sells their skills on the market to various customers for relatively short periods of time, could well be the fate of many (Handy, 1998). Moreover, for the organizational survivors of delayering, the experience of increasing job insecurity might lead these managers to redefine their relationship with the organization through undermining their loyalty and commitment to the organizations they happen to be members of at the time and replacing this with cynical personal ambition (Collinson and Collinson, 1997). Simultaneously, the damage done to the psychological contract that survivors have with the organization results in a reduction in feelings of trust, motivation and morale (Worrall et al., 2000). Such responses might be exacerbated because they often also experience increasing task overload with a reduction in task clarity. These changes happen because their spans of control widen, both in terms of numbers of subordinates and in the variety of tasks they have to manage, whilst often having to cope with subordinates' inability, or reluctance, to take on the cascaded managerial functions (Worrall et al., 2000).

Nevertheless, it is important to be cautious here because much of the change implied by the rhetoric of these new-wave management practices may be quite limited. Firstly, the evidence suggests that managerial hierarchies operate to preserve authority relations and severely limit the delegation of power to employees (De Cock and Hipkin, 1997). Employee tasks often remain highly circumscribed, and although employees might be delegated some limited managerial responsibilities, they often lack the necessary power to undertake them (Wilkinson, 1998). Moreover, Hales (2002) has noted how organizational restructuring often creates 'changes within the basic bureaucratic model rather than paradigm shifts to radically new organizational forms' (p. 51). The result is that although organizations might become what Hales calls 'bureaucratic-lite' there is little change in what managers are expected to do or in what they actually do. Secondly, the changes that occur are often accompanied by an extension in managerial control – only the way in which that control is enacted might change, for instance, to forms of peer pressure and electronic surveillance (see Barker, 1999; Sewell, 1998) as well as to various forms of normative control that attempt to restructure attitudes to ensure that the notionally 'empowered' employee uses that power responsibly (see Simons, 1995). Thirdly, aspects of scientific management, in terms of a separation of conception and execution and how technology is used to de-skill employees, do persist (Knights and Willmott, 2000), and organization restructuring often entails 'an intensification of, not a departure from, bureaucratic control' (Hales, 2002, p. 55).

However, despite this complex picture, it is also evident to Scarbrough (1998) that one effect of this diffusion downward has been the infiltration of the rank-and-file organization membership by managerialism. He argues that:

> . . . As managerial practices are diffused through the technologies of surveillance and accountability, management itself is steadily naturalized as an integral part of organizational life. The hierarchical connotations of management are steadily flattened into superficially democratic forms. The cumulative effect of such technological and organizational changes is to drive managerial practices and accountability deep into every level of organizational activity). . . . These changes make it much easier (and cheaper) to eliminate middle management and control the productive part of the organization through versions of self-management based on worker empowerment, technological surveillance, and the unrelenting pressure of the market (pp. 703–706).

Nevertheless, managerialism has been recently theoretically challenged, predominantly but by no means exclusively, in the United States, by the emergence of arguments for organizational democracy that have also developed out of, yet have drastically changed, new-wave management. These arguments entail a direct attack upon the economic efficiency of hierarchical modes of organizational governance and present workplace democratization as a pragmatic remedial device to counter the symptoms of what is construed as employee alienation and simultaneously ameliorate the organizational problems associated with destabilized capitalism. Below we outline the origins and nature of this particular case for organizational democracy and, through comparison with orthodox new-wave management, uncover the underlying rationale that justifies its democratic prescriptions for the workplace.

## The chapter so far

From the previous sections, it would seem that managerialism, although it is still being reconfigured to a degree under the theoretical aegis of new-wave management, now reigns supreme. It seems to have won the ideological high ground in the sense that management hierarchies are usually taken to be natural, economically necessary, features of organizational landscapes: Just as certain layers of management, as an identifiable organizational grouping with particular functions in regard to employees, are being eroded, managerialism seems to be ideologically colonizing new organizational territories.

## Organizational democracy and a case against managerialism

The ideologues of capitalism and the market economy tell us that there can be no alternative to. . . . capitalism. . . . The cheerleaders for US . . . capitalism with their mantra 'there is no alternative' can be countered with a well-formulated perspective that replaces managerial hierarchy with workplace democracy as the organizing principle of production . . . Systematic change towards workplace democracy has a further secret weapon. It can increase the productivity of capital without alienating it at all (Melman, 2001, pp. 390–392).

As we have seen, managerialism in its various guises is intimately linked to hierarchical forms of organizational governance in which sovereign managers routinely try to enforce their will upon other employees through the media of different kinds of formal and informal control. A result is that within Western liberal democracies, a vast range of public and private sector workplaces are managed by technocratic managerial elites, a situation typically justified on the grounds that such hierarchy is based upon merit and is essential for ensuring both the efficient use of scarce resources and the protection of property rights. In these societies, the result is a sharp divide between the democratic ideals and processes that ostensibly infuse our civic lives and, for most of us, our everyday experience of undemocratic workplaces. Here a significant incongruence arises because the ethical principle 'that those affected by the decisions of a government should have the right to participate in that government' (Dahl, 1970, p. 64) is widely accepted when it applies to state governance, but is tacitly dismissed or ignored when it comes to the governance of our workplaces. It is perhaps somewhat ironic that throughout the twentieth and into the twenty-first century, numerous wars, both hot and cold, have been fought with the avowed aim of securing and extending political democracy but have left workplace governance virtually untouched.

Writing in the mid-1970s, Pateman (1975) observed that this apparent incongruence between state and workplace governance reflected a key feature of liberal democratic theory itself: 'the separation or autonomy of the political and private spheres' (pp. 6–7), which 'provides a barrier against consideration of the question of organizational democracy' (p. 10). As noted earlier in this chapter, the above incongruence is replicated in much of mainstream organization theory in which the maintenance of undemocratic hierarchies and managerial prerogative are assumed to be natural, economically necessary, features of organizational landscapes. Indeed, as argued in Chapter 1, this mainstream organization theory is almost indistinguishable from management theory.

However, such managerialist assumptions that imply managerial hierarchies are self-evidently essential so as to ensure economic efficiency because, it is claimed, all organizations have them, also entail a circular argument that conflates questions of economic efficiency with existence (Hodgson, 1988). This notion that managerial hierarchies are essential to economic efficiency because most organizations have them is something which cannot be empirically validated, nor theoretically justified, without a simultaneous comparative analysis of the economic efficiency of non-hierarchical forms of organizational governance (see also Blaug, 1999; Tam, 1998). So, it is hardly surprising that there are some important exceptions to the dominant managerialist perspective. Ironically, one such heterodox theoretical stance seems to have recently emerged out new-wave theory, or at least shares some of its theoretical characteristics, but which simultaneously articulates some very important theoretical differences that justify the development of what amounts to an anti-managerialist stance.

## The economic efficiency case for organizational democracy: a challenge to managerialism?

A case for organizational democratization and the reform of managerialism has recently (re)-emerged in organization theory (see also Chapter 8). This perspective is unusual because it is explicitly couched in terms of a business imperative – that democratic organizations are economically more efficient than their managerialist counterparts. So, aimed specifically at the individual workplace, this economic case usually takes the form of a call for reforms aimed at engendering various kinds of democratic organizational governance that, it is assumed, will ameliorate the perceived excesses and inefficiencies of undemocratic hierarchies yet pragmatically ensure increased economic efficiency (e.g., Bechtold, 1997; Block, 1993; Bowles and Gintis, 1990, 1993, 1996a, 1996b; Cloke and Goldsmith, 2002; Estes, 1996; Korten, 1995; Melman, 2001; Tam, 1998; Wisman, 1997). In this fashion, mainstream theoretical assumptions and prescriptions about the necessity of hierarchies are challenged. This challenge articulates particular assumptions about both the significance of work to human beings and the nature of the societies in which we now live to justify the prescription that work organizations must be democratized in order to be more economically efficient. Below we shall outline how advocates present the need for such democratization:

1. as a pragmatic remedial device to ameliorate the organizational problems that they associate with the advent of destabilized capitalism
2. as way of countering the symptoms of employee alienation that they see to be directly caused by the undemocratic workplace.

It is with regard to this second argument that we can see an overt divergence with new-wave theory.


## Destabilized capitalism

As we have seen with new-wave management and the development of postbureaucracies in previous chapters, advocates of the economic case for organizational democracy also argue that organizations now confront a new destabilizing environment in which changes in the processes of production, distribution, exchange and consumption have not just dramatically accelerated but those processes have themselves also become increasingly diverse, specialized and temporary. Like new-wave theorists, advocates of the economic case for democracy associate these social, economic, technological and political changes with the necessary demise of bureaucracy and demand a 'massive metamorphosis in the way we work . . . which . . . [is] . . . being held back . . . by the system and institution of management itself' (Cloke and Goldsmith, 2002, p. 7).

As with new-wave theory, the reasoning here circulates around the idea that bureaucracies, if they are to be efficient, must have a hierarchical ordering of knowledge based upon task continuity (Mouzelis, 1975; Offe, 1976), where those members higher up the hierarchy have intimate knowledge of what those lower down the hierarchy must do in order to undertake their tasks efficiently. However, as we saw in Chapter 4, such a formal rationality is only viable in conditions of stability when people have experience of doing tasks and hence those tasks are both predictable and programmable. If such experience is lacking, for instance because of the causes of organizational instability mentioned above, then it becomes very difficult, and indeed inappropriate, to try to bureaucratically programme those tasks through, for instance, the development and imposition of rules, procedures and the like. It follows, therefore, that the employee cannot be commanded in traditional ways.

As we have seen, an important outcome of new-wave analysis of the implications of destabilized capitalism has been a demand for postbureaucratic organizations that require functionally flexible high-performance workforces (Applebaum et al., 2000), capable of exercising discretion so as to cope with a situation of rapid, unpredictable change (Volberda, 1998; Wood, 1999). Hence, organizational changes are necessary to cope with this new situation, but management is still necessary so as to ensure economic efficiency – although the form that management takes, as we have seen earlier in this book, must also change (see Chapters 4 and 5).

The above analysis articulated by new-wave theorists has also been appropriated to justify elements of the economic case for organizational democracy. This argument runs along the following lines:

1. The foundation of management authority has been traditionally located in managers' presumed superior knowledge, experience and expertise, which confer powers of command and control.

2. Because of an increasingly volatile and therefore uncertain globalized environment, a hierarchical ordering of knowledge is no longer evident, or possible, in many organizations; managers no longer know what their subordinates should do.

3. Hence, the traditional basis of managerial prerogative is eroded and the raison d'être of management as both an occupational group and a separate function becomes precarious.

4. Indeed, managers and management are seen by some theorists as dysfunctional, an unnecessary (and increasing) administrative cost that undermines, rather than ensures, economic efficiency.

For instance, Block (1993), Tam (1998), Melman (2001) and Cloke and Goldsmith (2002) all argue that organizations now require employees to collaboratively recognize problems, exercise power and accept responsibility for subsequent actions. However, management as a system can act to prevent this because, according to Block, hierarchies, which operate as patriarchal class systems and accord more value to managing than doing, militate against such collaboration; compliance and repression are built into hierarchies' system of governance. Therefore, Block argues that democracy at work, with its sense of self-rule, justice, and freedom, is the only means of enabling such responsible autonomy, self-management and empowerment. In a similar manner, Melman (2001) argues that workplace democracy, by creating a more conducive social environment, empowers employees to learn, use their discretion, take responsibility for their own actions and eliminate inefficiency by improving information flow.

## The chapter so far

As we have presented it, the economic case for organizational democracy relies upon an analysis that is similar to that proposed by new-wave theorists, but a key difference is how advocates attack, rather than glorify, managerialism. To understand why these attacks happen, we must turn to the second set of assumptions noted above, which more clearly differentiates the economic case for organizational democracy from the new-wave theory.

## Employee alienation as the key problem

In the previous section, we saw how these advocates of organizational democracy argued that democratic organizations are more competitive because they create and access new knowledge that results in innovative work processes, products and services. However, Block (1993), for instance, also claims that 'the reintegration of managing work with the doing of work' (p. 91) integrates what Block claims is best for the 'human spirit' (p. 91) with economic efficiency. He justifies this claim (p. 240) by warning us that organizations with central hierarchical control, in which democratic principles are viewed with contempt, will fail in business because they oppress the human spirit and create a sense of powerlessness. In contrast, workplace democracy increases the control people have over their working environments and thereby fosters personal autonomy and a democratic culture in civic life (see also Bowles and Gintis, 1996a, p. 64; Pateman, 1975). In a similar vein, Cloke and Goldsmith (2002, p. 95) assert that hierarchy and bureaucracy 'force human relationships to conform to patterns that run counter to their natural directions and for this reason generate resistance'. But now we can 'shape our workplaces and organizations to serve human needs, realize our values and increase our happiness' (p. 96).

By drawing upon Maslow (1943) and McGregor (1960), advocates of the economic case for organizational democracy argue that as soon as lower order needs are satisfied, higher order needs such as self-actualization become prepotent and democratic participation is a necessary part of their pursuit. Here the underlying model of the employee in the economic case for organizational democracy is one of *alienation* rather than the underlying model of *anomie* that underpins the analyses of new-wave management.

In Chapter 4, we considered how *anomie* was used by new-wave theory to create a particular analysis of the problems thought to be currently facing organizations. Here it is important to point out that the concepts of *anomie* and alienation are based upon a fundamental divergence with regard to their philosophical assumptions about human nature that each presupposes to be correct. It is worth reiterating that according to Lukes (1978, pp. 141–145), from the philosophical stance articulated by *anomie*, human beings are assumed to be irrational because they are composed of bundles of hedonistic desires and aggressive instincts that need to be regulated, tamed, repressed, manipulated and given direction for the sake of social order. If they were not, society and its institutions would be in a constant state of disorder and conflict as these dangerous desires and instincts would be let loose upon the world. In contrast, at the heart of the philosophical orientation articulated by alienation there is the assumption that human beings are inherently rational and good and are naturally prepared to work in harmony and cooperation with one another to achieve agreed objectives – when given the opportunity. But for these propensities to be expressed in everyday behaviour requires what is construed as a rational and good society, a society free from external constraint. So, according to the economic case for organizational democracy, it is precisely organizational democracy that can only provide such freedom. Indeed, management hierarchies based upon external authority prevent the development and expression of this essential human potential and hence are the root cause of a whole host of problems.

So, although from the theoretical stance created by *anomie*'s philosophical assumptions about people, coercion, external authority and restraint are desirable in organizations because they are necessary for ensuring social order and individual happiness. In contrast, from the point of view of alienation's philosophical assumptions, any form of coercion, hierarchy and the like are offences against reason and attacks upon human freedom.

Hence, the application of the concept of alienation to the problems that might assail organizations around, for instance, employee motivation, leads to an analysis couched in terms of overcontrol, whilst the application of the concept of *anomie* leads to the opposite – an analysis framed in terms of a lack of control, moral or otherwise. The differences in these underlying philosophical models and their theoretical expression, together with their implications for resolving the organizational problems they constitute through the lens provided by their assumptions, and how they then analyse those problems, are illustrated in Table 9.3. For more on *anomie*, see Chapter 4.

So, in the economic case, ameliorating and ultimately resolving the problems associated with alienation will not only be beneficial to the employee but will also result in greater productivity because of the higher levels of morale, job satisfaction and organizational commitment they yield. For instance, Bowles and Gintis (1993, pp. 92–94) point to three economic efficiency gains promised by the democratic firm in comparison with its undemocratic counterpart.

1. Integration by political process creates a 'participation effect' that has important motivational implications as it reduces the alienation of workers caused through their exclusion from decision making and ownership of the products of their labour.
2. Relative to hierarchical information and control systems, workers are more efficient and effective at monitoring each others' task performance and would have a direct interest in the effort levels of fellow workers.
3. Opportunity cost savings made by removing hierarchical work monitoring systems may be redistributed to increased wages and thereby create a 'wage incentive effect'.

In the economic case for democracy, management is sometimes presented as a barrier to adaptation that requires elimination (e.g., Melman, 2001, p. 313). Indeed, some proponents of the economic case talk about 'the end of management' (Cloke and Goldsmith, 2002). Others (e.g., Bowles and Gintis, 1993, 1996a, 1996b; Wisman, 1997) are more cautious and call for the slimming down of managerial hierarchies rather than their removal.

## The chapter so far

Orthodox new-wave management usually seeks to ameliorate the problems caused by *anomie* and the demise of bureaucracy by instituting a panoply of normative, or cultural, forms of control. In contrast, the economic case presumes that the demise of bureaucracy creates opportunities for developing a new democratic organizational form that will counter alienation, managerial incompetence and excess yet herald a new age of freedom, social justice and greater economic efficiency (see the Example on page 419).

**Table 9.3** Ideas and perspectives: alienation and *anomie* compared

| Concept | Alienation | *Anomie* |
|---|---|---|
| Definitions | Blauner (1964) identifies four key aspects of alienation that impact upon employees:<br>• **Powerlessness:** The employee's inability to exert control over work processes<br>• **Meaninglessness:** The employee's lack of sense of purpose in production processes<br>• **Self-estrangement:** The employee's failure to become involved in work as a mode of self-expression<br>• **Isolation:** The lack of a sense of belonging | *Anomie* is a condition of moral lawlessness and conflict in which people are outside moral and therefore cultural control; a breakdown in the traditional cultural structure of society and a lack of social cohesion; exacerbated by economic, political and technological change |
| Theoretical origins | Rousseau (1983/1762), Marx (1971/1844), and McGregor (1960) | Hobbes (1962/1651), Durkheim (1933/1893), and Mayo (1940) |
| Philosophical assumptions | According to Rousseau, people in their natural state are noble savages who are egalitarian, kindly and altruistic, but the development of society and its institutions results in inequalities that corrupt and distort these natural propensities and are a prime cause of social ills and moral depravity. Human redemption is only possible by the (re)establishment of the individual's moral worth, freedom and dignity through the sovereignty of the people. | According to Hobbes but for the controls provided by society and its institutions, the human being's inherent propensities of aggression, egotism and greed would be let loose and cause a 'war of all against all'. People therefore have to be controlled and regulated in order to maintain social order – part of which entails absolute rulers persuading everyone that it is reasonable to entrust power to them. |
| Theoretical expressions in organization theory | McGregor's theory Y<br>• Employees may appear to be recalcitrant, but this is not because of an inherent dislike of work itself but rather because of their experience of how work is usually organized, particularly in bureaucratic hierarchies.<br>• Most employees are capable of responsibly exercising imagination, creativity and self-direction in the pursuit of objectives to which they are committed; such capacities are usually under-utilized.<br>• The most significant motivators are intrinsic to work itself and relate to the satisfaction of higher order needs. | McGregor's theory X<br>• People have an inherent dislike of work and will avoid it if they can.<br>• Because of this inherent indolence, employees must be coerced to gain their compliance to the demands of work.<br>• Rather than desiring autonomy and responsibility at work, most employees have to be directed by hierarchical superiors who know best.<br>• For Mayo, *anomie* causes a situation of perilous instability in which the employees' pathological instincts are let loose and threaten management's legitimate exercise of sovereignty. |
| Key problem in organizations | Overcontrol of employees by managers | Undercontrol of employees or the use of inappropriate controls by managers |
| Remedial prescriptions | Various job redesign strategies to make work more intrinsically satisfying, or as in the economic case for organizational democracy, the democratization of work organizations. | Design of various formal controls to improve the surveillance and discipline of employees. However, because bureaucratic controls may no longer be appropriate, there is a need for this to be done through the development of moral regulation through cultural or normative controls. |

## Example: Are democratic organizations more economically efficient?

Ben-Ner, Tzu-Shian and Jones (1996) conducted a comparative review of empirical evidence generated by research undertaken in an array of 16 organizational forms. These organizations were differentiated in terms of the extent and types of participation, which varied from conventional undemocratic hierarchies in which employees had no participation in either economic returns or in control of the enterprise, through to worker-owned and democratically controlled cooperatives. Their most significant finding was that when organizational arrangements entail both participation in economic returns *and* participation in control of the enterprise, productivity is enhanced. Moreover, this effect seemed strongest in cooperatives when workers have dominant control and receive the majority of the economic returns.

Nevertheless, with regard to the comparative literature generally, and including their own findings, Ben-Ner et al. (1996, p. 241) urge caution in interpreting such results because most studies suffer from severe methodological problems in that it is very difficult to isolate the effects of variables such as ownership and democratic control upon economic efficiency from other things that might simultaneously affect economic efficiency.

### Stop and think

How could you measure variations in economic efficiency?

- What other variables, either inside or outside the organization, besides worker ownership and democracy, might also influence the degree of economic efficiency?
- Could one ever be sure if worker ownership and democracy has actually caused the apparent economic gains rather than some other organizational variable?
- Conversely, could one ever be sure that managerial hierarchies enhanced economic efficiency?

A key question that bedevils this case for organizational democracy is how can the governance of the democratic workplace be meaningfully determined by all its members whilst ensuring that they operate efficiently? On these matters, Wisman (1997; see also Bowles and Gintis, 1990, 1993, 1996a and b) expresses a preference for representative democracy because he sees it as more efficient than if workers were to vote on every decision because, he argues that such direct participatory democracy would be impractical because it would be too clumsy and time consuming. However, Wisman (1997) is relatively optimistic about the future of managers. He foresees some delayering and a shift in role to one in which managers are democratically answerable to workers who 'would seek out the best managers and fire (or not re-elect) those who perform poorly' (p. 1402). In contrast, Tam (1998) broadens democratic accountability to 'the community of stakeholders who make the company concerned a viable operation' (p. 175). However, he too argues that members of this community do not need to be directly involved in every decision; rather, many decisions should be delegated to members the community trusts. However, Melman (2001) argues that capital also needs to be democratized by employee ownership. Employees can accumulate power and capital by setting up organizations with their own money and thereby wield real decision-making power (see also Cloke and Goldsmith, 2002, p. 187). As Bowles and Gintis (1990, 1993) point out, the advent of employee ownership would end the separation of ownership and control that has plagued contemporary capitalism.

**The chapter so far**

The form of organizational democracy usually – representative democracy – envisioned imports the political practices significant in the civic experience of advocates. This prescription entails a meritocratic hierarchy to ensure economic efficiency, albeit ultimately controlled by a democratic political apparatus in which all members exercise their sovereignty by electing other members to represent them. Thus, for most advocates, the demand for economic efficiency means that the distinction between managers and the managed cannot be realistically eliminated and hence they opt for managers being democratically accountable to the workforce. By implication, alternative forms of democracy, such as direct participative democracy, are simultaneously rejected as unwieldy and impractical and hence inefficient.

However, as Pateman (1975), Deetz (1992) and Cheney (1999) all argue, surely the implementation of organizational democracy must entail consideration of the empowerment of members through their *direct* participation, political education and the development of what Bernstein (1982) has called a *democratic consciousness*. This raises a key paradox: How the economic case for organizational democracy presents and pursues organizational democracy as an efficiency enhancing organizational innovation may mean that the representative form of democracy prescribed could undermine the desired ends. By excluding many members from direct influence over significant areas of decision making in the name of efficiency, the result may be a democratic form that perpetuates or develops imbalances of power in organizations (Stohl and Cheney, 2001) and creates a tendency for oligarchy (see the Ideas and perspectives box below) in which power falls into the hands of a few members, to corrupt and displace democracy (see Rothschild-Whitt and Lindenfield, 1982).

**Ideas and perspectives**

## Robert Michels

In his 1915 book *Political Parties: A Sociological Study of the Emergence of Leadership, the Psychology of Power, and the Oligarchical Tendencies of Organization* (republished in 1959), Michels argues that organizations that were originally democratically organized eventually degenerated into oligarchies. Given when this work was written, Michels' work shows a remarkable foresight regarding what was to subsequently happen in, for instance, the USSR. Working in the early 1900s, his analysis mainly concerned the trade union and socialist movements of his time and recorded how these organizations had become increasingly oligarchical. These oligarchies occurred where a small, self-serving, self-perpetuating, group of members who had originally achieved positions of power and responsibility through the democratic structure came to dominate all aspects of organizational life. In particular, Michels used the example of socialist parties to illustrate how even in organizations that espouse and enshrine equality and democracy, at all levels, their political activities were undermined by characteristics he considered inherent to organizing. In this work, Michels tries to explain why this 'iron law of oligarchy' operates through explaining why power tends to fall into the hands of an emerging elite. According to Michels, oligarchies arise in democratic organizations for the reasons listed below:

1. As democratic organizations grow in size and complexity, it becomes increasingly difficult for all members to get together every time a decision has to be made. As a result, Michels argues, because the membership is unable to take any action through direct democracy, a system of delegation has to be implemented in

which a few are chosen to represent and carry out the will of the rank and file. Consequently, a small elected group of representatives is given the responsibility of making decisions. This group are often chosen to lead the organization because of their administrative competencies and ability to deal with public relations. The result is a division of labour in the organization and with it a division of power.

2. Michels argued that eventually the people in this leading group would become enthralled by their elite position and become increasingly inclined toward making decisions that preserve their power and authority rather than represent the interests of the membership of the organization. This happens despite these leaders' having originally come from the same social class as rank-and-file members. Often this process is morally justified by those in positions of responsibility and power by their emergent belief that they are indispensable because they are more knowledgeable than those they are supposed to serve. Simultaneously, their organizational roles remove them and eventually isolate them from the everyday experiences of the rank and file, who become socially distant.

3. There is a tendency for apathy and indifference amongst rank-and-file members to grow as the organization increases in size and complexity. In part, apathy naturally occurs because attempting to maintain influence over organizational affairs is time consuming, but it is exacerbated by an increasing sense of a lack of influence over organizational affairs. The resultant lack of participation in organizational affairs by the rank and file and their increasing sense of impotence and alienation further serve to concentrate power in the leadership's hands by default.

4. Over time, the leadership's desire to preserve power and status becomes a goal in itself and comes to dominate all its decision-making. The result is the emergence of an increasingly conservative stance so that conflict with powers outside the (political) organization is avoided so as to protect the elite's organizational position. Internally, the elite begins to control communication and information within the organization so as to protect its intellectual superiority; control who is promoted or demoted; and assign workloads and deploy various sanctions with regard to the membership, including restricting democratic rights. Thereby, the elite operates to preserve the status quo and defend its own positions and interests. However, simultaneously, how the elite operates undermines the efficiency and effectiveness of the organization with regard to its original founding goals as it is corrupted into an oligarchy.

In effect, for Michels, organizations originally designed to bring power to the people seem to have the opposite effect as they concentrate power in the hands of their leadership.

## Stop and think

- In what ways might Michels' analysis undermine the economic efficiency case for organizational democracy?
- Given Michels' analysis, how might democratic organizations, whether they are businesses, political parties, or trade unions, avoid the oligarchical processes identified by Michels nearly a century ago?

## Conclusions

In this chapter, we have traced the remarkable and dramatic development of management over more or less 200 years from its traumatic birth pangs during the British Industrial Revolution; through its adolescent development and growth under the territorially aggressive tutelage of scientific management; through its adult divorce from the owners of capital; to its 'maturity' as a dominant moral, social and organizational influence in its guise as 'new' managerialism for the past 20 years or so; through to recent demands for its compulsory retirement, or at least semi-retirement, by some organization theorists. During this period, the transformation in the material and symbolic fortunes of some, but by no means all, managers – as well as the recent diffusion of management into new organizational arenas – are testament to these incredible changes. Simultaneously, management has spread beyond the workplace to a vast spectrum of social, economic and political issues, which are now (re)configured as problems that might be resolved through more effective management thereby further enhancing managerial roles, power and prestige.

Within the workplace, as Reed and Watson (1999) have recently noted, managerialism has become a dominant organizational discourse with management acquiring the status of a universal practice and with managers as specialists in control and the locus of organizational knowledge and wisdom. One question that arises here is why has this glorification of hierarchy happened at the expense of alternative ways of organizing? This is a question rarely asked by mainstream organization theory, which tends to uncritically assume that the status quo is in some sense necessary, natural and inevitable. It seems that managers have developed, survived and prospered because there is no alternative, so organization theory must be geared to dealing with management's preoccupations, whatever those concerns might be.

For instance, Williamson (1985) puts forward the hypothesis that because capitalist economic institutions have the main purpose of economizing transaction costs, more efficient forms of organization will eventually supplant the less efficient. Hence, organizational forms have to demonstrate their 'relative fitness' by passing the survival test of the market's hidden hand through a 'weak-form' (p. 23) of natural selection. Hence, managerialism and the hierarchical relations it spawns are ubiquitous because they are economically more efficient, and nonhierarchical organizational forms are of 'ephemeral duration' (Williamson, 1980, p. 35) precisely because they are less economically efficient. However, as Papendreou (1994, p. 253) warns, an outcome of Williamson's economic efficiency hypothesis is a stark determinism: things are as they are because they are for the best in economic terms. Of course, we can challenge Williamson's economic determinism by showing how power relations, conflicts of interest and habit may be the key cause of the evolution, establishment and diffusion of hierarchies and managerialism, rather than the hidden hand of the market selecting the most efficient and exterminating the inefficient.

As we shall further discuss in Chapter 10, this is precisely what institution theorists (e.g., Di Maggio and Powell, 1983; Meyer and Rowan, 1977; Scott and Meyer, 1983) attempt to show. Institution theorists argue that instead of seeking to maximize economic efficiency, organizations are socially impelled to adopt the practices and procedures regarding the organization of work that predominate in wider society – that is in their external 'institutional environments'. To put it bluntly, those who manage organizations adopt the practices that a 'good' organization is supposed to undertake. But at the heart of this process is myth making: powerful, taken-for-granted, but socially constructed beliefs support certain organizational practices and conventions at certain times as being the most appropriate, regardless of whether or not these practices have any immediately evident efficacy or efficiency. By default, alternative modes of organizing become proscribed or just unthinkable. Organizations must conform to these dominant injunctions about how to organize if they are to 'receive support and legitimacy from the environment' (Scott and Meyer, 1983, p. 140). In other words, organizing in the ways others have organized, something that is called *isomorphism* (i.e., taking or adopting the same form or shape), 'gains the legitimacy and resources needed to survive' (Meyer and Rowan, 1977, p. 352). Conversely, to deviate from these mythical but powerful socially accepted practices might threaten the perceived competency of organizational decision makers and thereby undermine their legitimacy. What is important here is that significant organizational players *believe* that those practices are effective and ensure economic efficiency; whether they actually are or not is a different matter.

Hence, these essentially social and ideological processes, according to institution theorists, explain why certain managerial practices are embraced, or indeed discarded, in rapid succession by organizations. Of course, it might also might explain the continuing institutionalization and diffusion of managerialism itself. Conforming to managerialist nostrums demonstrates, ideologically, a commitment to 'progress', 'rationality' and economic efficiency, and therefore secures legitimacy – at least for the time being! So as we noted earlier, perhaps Burnham's ideological problem of accepting managerial rule has been resolved because managerial prerogative is itself so rarely challenged, either by organizational theorists or in the everyday organizational practice of organizational members. It seems that many people can neither see, nor imagine, any alternative.

## Concluding grid

| Learning outcomes | Challenges to contemporary organizations |
|---|---|
| Provide an historical account of the origins and evolution of managers as an identifiable organizational group and of management as a separate, hierarchical function within organizational divisions of labour. | Because management as a function and as an identifiable organizational group has a relatively short history, does the current tendency to delayer organizations signify the possibility of managing without managers, or is it just an expression of a changing role for managers who are left? |
| Describe the managerialist thesis and identify different theoretical interpretations of this organizational development. | Which of the managerialist theses (the sectionalist and nonsectionalist) are the most accurate description of managers in contemporary organizations? |
| Outline the subsequent development of 'new managerialism' and its key characteristics. | Does new managerialism signify a significant break with the past in terms of how managerial roles are developing, or is it merely rhetoric, largely irrelevant to what managers actually do in practice? |
| Analyse the diffusion of new managerialism in the workplace and relate recent developments to the impact of new-wave organization theory. | Is new managerialism in its various forms a benefit to most stakeholders in organizations in both public and private sector organizations, or is it actually damaging to those organizational interests? |
| Investigate the theoretical underpinnings of the economic case for organizational democracy as a potential challenge to managerialism. | Is organizational democracy an economically efficient alternative to managerialism, or is it doomed to failure in economic terms, in terms of an inevitable degeneration into oligarchy, or both? |

## Annotated further reading

A key source for delving into the development of management in the United Kingdom remains Pollard's (1965) carefully researched historical analysis. For a more recent but equally informed historical account of management in the United States, see Locke (1996). Scarbrough's (1998) work in which he puts forward the two forms of diffusion hypothesis was followed in this chapter. Clarke and Newman (1997) and more recently Kirkpatrick et al. (2005) present insightful critical analyses of the political forces behind, and the nature of new managerialism and its impact upon, public sector management and professionals in the United Kingdom. Tourish and Pinnington (2002) give a devastating critique of transformational leadership with an incisive outline of the dangers it poses. Although Melman (2001) provides a vigorous analysis of an array of evidence to show how workplace democratization increases economic efficiency, further economic evidence is provided by the edited collection of Pagano and Rowthorn (1996). Meanwhile, Parker (2002) provides an accessible and highly entertaining analysis of managerialism as a form of global ideology in which he opens up the possibility of alternative ways of organizing as well as a providing a very useful coverage of anti-management cultural movements and organization theory that question the need for managers and management.

## Discussion questions

1. Discuss the extent to which delayering signifies the end of the middle manager.
2. Critically evaluate the relevance of sectionalist and nonsectionalist theses to understanding the behaviour of contemporary managers.
3. What is new managerialism in the public sector, and why does it matter?
4. What are the similarities between transformational leadership and the leadership of cults? What are the implications of your analysis for business organizations?
5. To what extent is the economics case for organizational democracy using the wrong values to promote and evaluate democratic organizations?

## References

Alvesson, M. and Willmott, H.C. (1996) *Making Sense of Management: A Critical Introduction*, London: Sage.

Alvesson, M. and Deetz, S. (2000) *Doing Critical Management Research*, London: Sage.

Alvesson, M. and Sveningsson, S. (2003) 'Good visions, bad micro-management and ugly ambiguity: Contradictions of (non)leadership in a knowledge intensive organization', *Organization Studies* 24(6):961–988.

Applebaum, E., Bailey, T., Berg, P. and Kalleberg, A.L. (2000) *Manufacturing Advantage: Why High-Performance Work Systems Pay off*, Ithaca, NY: ILR Press.

Barker, R. (1997) 'How can we train leaders if we don't know what leadership is?' *Human Relations* 50:343–362.

Barker, J.R. (1999) *The Discipline of Teamwork: Participation and Concertive Control*, London: Sage.

Bass, B. (1995) 'From transactional to transformational leadership: Learning to share the vision', *Organizational Dynamics* 18:19–31.

Bechtold, B.L. (1997) 'Toward a participative organizational culture: Evolution or revolution', *Empowerment in Organizations* (5)14–15.

Bell, D. (1974) *The Coming Post-Industrial Society*, London: Heinemann.

Bendix, R. (1956) *Work and Authority in Industry: Ideologies of Management in the Course of Industrialization*, New York: John Wiley.

Ben-Ner, A., Tzu-Shian, H. and Jones, D.C. (1996) 'The productivity effects of employee participation in control and in economic returns: A review of empirical evidence', in U. Pagano and R. Rowthorn (eds), *Democracy and Efficiency in the Economic Enterprise*, London: Routledge.

Berle, A., and Means, G.C. (1932) *The Modern Corporation and Private Property*, New York: Macmillan.

Bernstein, P. (1982) 'Necessary elements for effective worker participation', in F. Lindenfield and J. Rothschild-Witt (eds), *Workplace Democracy and Social Change*, Boston: Porter Sargent.

Blanchard, K., Carlos, J.P. and Randolph, A. (1995) *Empowerment Takes More Than a Minute*, CA: Wharton.

Blaug, R. (1999) 'The tyranny of the visible: Problems in the evaluation of anti-institutional radicalism', *Organization* 6(1):33–56.

Block, P. (1993) *Stewardship: Choosing Service over Self-Interest*, San Francisco: Berrett-Koehler.

Bowles, S. and Gintis, H. (1990) 'Contested exchange: New microfoundations for the political economy of capitalism', *Politics and Society* 18:165–222.

Bowles, S. and Gintis, H. (1993) 'A political and economic case for the democratic enterprise', *Economics and Philosophy* 9:75–100.

Bowles, S. and Gintis, H. (1996a) 'Is the demand for workplace democracy redundant in a liberal economy?' in U. Pagano and R. Rowthorn (eds), *Democracy and Efficiency in the Economic Enterprise*, London: Routledge.

Bowles, S. and Gintis, H. (1996b) 'The distribution of wealth and the viability of the democratic firm', in U. Pagano and R. Rowthorn (eds), *Democracy and Efficiency in the Economic Enterprise*, London: Routledge.

Braverman, H. (1974) *Labor and Monopoly Capital: The Degradation of Work in the Twentieth Century*, New York: Monthly Review Press.

Burnham, J. (1941) *The Managerial Revolution*, Bloomington, IN: Indiana University Press.

Champy, J. (1995) *Reengineering Management*, London: Harper Collins.

Cheney, G. (1999) *Values at Work: Employee Participation Meets Market Pressure at Mondragon*, Ithaca, NY: Cornell University Press.

Clawson, D. (1980) *Bureaucracy and the Labour Process: The transformation of US Industry, 1860–1920*, New York: Monthly Review Press.

Clarke, K. (1993) 'Survival skills for a new breed', *Management Today*, December.

Clarke, J. and Newman, J. (1997) *The Managerial State*, London: Sage.

Cloke, K. and Goldsmith, J. (2002) *The End of Management and the Rise of Organizational Democracy*, San Francisco: Jossey-Bass.

Collins, D. (1997) 'The ethical superiority and inevitability of participatory management as an organizational system', *Organization Science* 8(5):489–507.

Collinson, D. and Collinson, M. (1997) 'Delayering managers: Time–space surveillance and its gendered effects', *Organization* 4(3):357–407.

Cutler, T. and Waine, B. (1994) *Managing the Welfare State*, Oxford: Berg.

Cyert, R.M. and March, J.G. (1963) *A Behavioral Theory of the Firm*, Englewood Cliffs, NJ: Prentice-Hall.

Dahl, R.A. (1961) *Who Governs? Democracy and Power in an American City*, New Haven and London: Yale University Press.

Dahl, R.A. (1970) *After the Revolution*, New Haven, CT: Yale University Press.

Dahl, R.A. (1985) *Preface to the Theory of Economic Democracy*, Berkeley, CA: University of California Press.

Deal, T. and Kennedy, A. (1988) *Corporate Culture*, London: Penguin.

Dean, J.W. and Evans, J.R. (1994) *Total Quality: Management, Organization and Strategy*, St Paul, MN: West.

De Cock, C. and Hipkin, I. (1997) 'TQM and BPR: Beyond the myth', *Journal of Management Studies* 34(5):659–675.

Deem, R. (1988) 'New managerialism in higher education – The management of performances and cultures in universities', *International Studies in the Sociology of Education* 8(1).

Deetz, S.A. (1992) *Democracy in the Age of Corporate Colonization: Developments in Communication and the Politics of Everyday Life*, Albany, NY: State University of New York Press.

Denham, N., Ackers, P. and Travers, C. (1997) 'Doing yourself out of a job? How middle managers cope with empowerment', *Employee Relations* 19(2):147–159.

DiMaggio, P. and Powell, W. (1983) 'The iron cage revisited: Institutional isomorphism and collective rationality', *American Sociological Review* 48:147–160.

Doray, B. (1988) *A Rational Madness: From Taylorism to Fordism*, London: Free Association Books.

Drucker, P. (1955) *The Practice of Management*, London: Heinemann.

Drucker, P. (1993) *Post-Capitalist Society*, New York: Harper and Row.

Dubrin, A. (2001) *Leadership. Research Findings, Practice and Skills*, Boston: Houghton Mifflin.

Du Gay, P. (1996) *Consumption and Identity at Work*, London: Sage.

Du Gay, P. (2000) *In Praise of Bureaucracy*, London: Sage.

Durkheim, E. (1933/1893) *The Division of Labour in Society*, New York: The Free Press.

Dutfield, M. (1992) *The Effective Management of Contract*, Birmingham, United Kingdom: PEPAR.

Edwards, R. (1979) *Contested Terrain: The Transformation of the Workplace in the Twentieth Century*, New York: Basic Books.

Estes, R. (1996) *Tyranny of the Bottom Line: Why Corporations Make Good People Do Bad Things*, San Francisco: Berrettt-Koehler.

Foster, P. and Wilding, P. (2000) 'Wither welfare professionalism', *Social Policy and Administration* 34(2):143–159.

Fridenson, P. (1978) *Corporate Policy, Rationalization and the Labour Force: French Experiences in International Comparison, 1900 – 1929*, London: Nuffield Paper.

Galbraith, J.K. (1969) *The New Industrial State*, Harmondsworth: Penguin.

Garvey, B. and Alred, G. (2001) 'Mentoring and the tolerance of complexity', *Futures* 33:519–530.

Gordon, D.M. (1996) *Fat and Mean: The Corporate Squeeze of Working Americans and the Myth of Managerial Downsizing*, New York: The Free Press.

Halal, W.E. (1994) 'From hierarchy to enterprise: Internal markets are the new foundation of management', *Academy of Management Executive* 8(4):69–83.

Hales, C. (1993) *Managing Through Organization*, London: Routledge.

Hales, C. (2002) 'Bureaucracy-lite and continuities in managerial work', *British Journal of Management* 13(1):51–66.

Hammer, M. and Champy, J. (1994) *Re-engineering the Corporation*, London: Harper Business.

Hammond, J.L. and Hammond, B. (1917) *The Town Labourer (1760–1832)*, London: Longmans, Green and Co.

Handy, C. (1998) *The Hungry Spirit*, London: Arrow.

Haraszti, M. (1977) *A Worker in a Workers' State*, Harmondsworth: Penguin.

Harris, J. (1996) *Getting Employees To Fall in Love with Your Company*, New York: Amacon.

Heckscher, C. (1995) *White Collar Blues: Management Loyalties in an Age of Restructuring*, New York: Basic Books.

Hobbes, T. (1962/1651) *Leviathan*, Cambridge: Cambridge University Press.

Hodgson, G.M. (1988) *Economics and Institutions*, Cambridge: Polity.

Hood, C. (1991) 'A public management for all seasons', *Public Administration* 69(1):3–19.

Hood, C. (1999) 'The "new public management" in the 1980s: Variations on a theme', *Accounting Organizations and Society* 20(2/3):93–109.

Hood, C., Scott, C., James, O., Jones, G. and Travers, T. (1999) *Regulation inside government: Waste-watchers, quality police and sleaze busters*, Oxford: Oxford University Press.

Inkson, T. and Coe, T. (1993) *Are career ladders disappearing?* London: Institute of Management.

Isaacs, W.N. (1993) 'Taking flight: Dialogue, collective thinking and organizational learning', *Organizational Dynamics* 22(2):24–39.

Kanter, R.M. (1989a) 'The new managerial work', *Harvard Business Review* Nov/Dec:85–92.

Kanter, R.M. (1989b) *When Giants Learn Dance: Mastering the Challenges of Strategy, Management and Careers in the 1990s*, London: Unwin Hyman.

Kaysen, C. (1957) 'The social significance of the modern corporation', *American Economic Review* 47(2):301–320.

Knights, D. and Willmott, H. (eds) (2000) *The Reengineering Revolution*, London: Sage.

Korten, D.C. (1995) *When Corporations Ruled the World*, San Francisco: Berrett-Koehler.

Kotter, J. (1990) *Force for Change: How Leadership Differs from Management*, New York: The Free Press.

Kranz, J. and Gilmore, T.N. (1990) 'The splitting of leadership and management as a social defence', *Human Relations* 43(2):183–204.

Kumar, K. (1984) 'The social culture of work: Work, employment and unemployment as ways of life', in K. Thompson (ed.), *Work, Employment and Unemployment: Perspectives on Work and Society*, Buckingham: Open University Press.

Lindblom, C.E. (1959) 'The science of "muddling through"'. *Public Administration Review* Summer:79–88.

Littler, C.R. (1982) *The Development of the Labour Process in Capitalist Societies*, London: Heinemann Education Books.

Locke, R. (1996) *The Collapse of American Management Mystique*, Oxford: Oxford University Press.

Lukes, S. (1978) 'Alienation and anomie', in P. Laslett and W.G. Runciman (eds), *Philosophy Politics and Society*, Oxford: Blackwell.

Marglin, S.A. (1974) 'What do bosses do?' *Review of Radical Political Economics* 692:60–112.

Marquardt, M.J. (1996) *Building the Learning Organization: A Systems Approach to Quantum Improvement and Global Success*, New York: McGraw-Hill.

Marris, R. (1964) *The Economic Theory of 'Managerial' Capitalism*, London: Macmillan.

Marx, K. (1971/1844) *Economic and Philosophical Manuscripts*, London: Lawrence and Wishart.

Maslow, A. (1943) 'A theory of motivation', *Psychological Review* 1:370–396.

Mathias, P. (1969) *The First Industrial Nation*, London: Methuen.

Mayo, E. (1940) *The Human Problems of an Industrial Civilization*, Boston: Harvard Business School.

McGregor, D. (1960) *The Human Side of the Enterprise*, New York: Harper and Row.

Melman, S. (2001) *After Capitalism: From Managerialism to Workplace Democracy*, New York: Alfred A. Knopf.

Meyer, J.W. and Rowan, B. (1977) 'Institutionalized organizations: Formal structure as myth and ceremony', *American Journal of Sociology* 83:340–363.

Michels, R. (1959/1915) *Political Parties: A Sociological Study of the Emergence of Leadership, the Psychology of Power, and the Oligarchical Tendencies of Organization*, New York: Dover.

Mintzberg, H. (1998) 'Covert leadership: Notes on managing professionals', *Harvard Business Review* 76(5):140–147.

Mouzelis, N. (1975) *Organization and Bureaucracy*, London: Routledge and Kegan Paul.

Morgan, G. (1988) *Riding The Waves of Change: Developing Managerial Competencies for a Turbulent World*, San Francisco: Jossey-Bass.

Mueller, F. and Dyerson, R. (1999) 'Expert humans or expert organizations', *Organization Studies* 20(2):225–256.

Newman, J. (1998) 'Managerialism and social welfare', in G. Hughes and G. Lewis (eds), *Unsettling Welfare: The Reconstruction of Social Policy*, London: Routledge.

Newman, J. and Clarke, J. (1995) 'Going about our business? The managerialization of the public service', in J. Clarke, A. Cochrane, and E. Laughlin (eds), *Managing Social Policy*, London: Sage:

Ogbonna, E. and Harris, L. (2004) 'Work intensification and emotional labour among UK university academics: An exploratory study', *Organization Studies* 25(7):1185–1203.

Offe, C. (1976) *Industry and Inequality*, London: Edward Arnold.

Osbourne, D. and Gaebler, T. (1992) *Re-inventing government*, Reading, MA: Addison-Wesley.

Pagano, U. and Rowthorn, R. (eds) (1996) *Democracy and Efficiency in the Economic Enterprise*, London: Routledge.

Painter, J. (1992) 'Culture of competition', *Public Policy and Administration* 7(1):58–68.

Papandreou, A.G. (1994) *Externality and Institutions*, Oxford: Clarendon.

Parker, M. (2002) *Against Management*, Cambridge: Polity.

Parker, M. and Jary, D. (1995) 'The McUniversity: Organization, management and academic subjectivity', *Organization* 2(2):319–338.

Pateman, C. (1975) 'Part 1. A contribution to the political theory of organizational democracy', *Administration and Society* 7(1):5–26.

Pattinson (1997) *The Faith of Managers*, London: Cassell.

Peters, T. (1992) *Liberation Management: Necessary Disorganization for the Nanosecond Nineties*, London: Macmillan.

Pollard, S. (1965) *The Genesis of Modern Management: A Study of the Industrial Revolution in Great Britain*, London: Edward Arnold.

Pollitt, C. (1993) *Managerialism and the Public Services: The Anglo-American Experience*, Oxford: Basil Blackwell.

Reed, M. and Anthony, P. (1993) 'Between a ideological rock and an organizational hard place', in T. Clarke and C. Pitelis (eds), *The Political Economy of Privatisation*, London: Routledge.

Reed, M. and Watson, S. (1999) *New Managerialism and the Management of Higher Education*, Presentation at the Association of Business Schools Research Conference, University of Manchester Institute of Science and Technology.

Rousseau, J-J. (1983/1762) *On the Social Contract and Discourses*, Indianapolis: Hackett Publishing.

Rothschild-Whitt, J. and Lindenfield, F. (1982) 'Reshaping work: Prospects and problems of workplace democracy', in F. Lindenfield and J. Rothschild-Witt (eds), *Workplace Democracy and Social Change*, Boston: Porter Sargent.

Scarbrough, H. (1998) 'The unmaking of management? Change and continuity in British management in the 1990s', *Human Relations* 51(6):691–716.

Scarbrough, H. and Burrell, G. (1996) 'The Axeman Cometh: the Changing Roles and Knowledges of Middle Managers', in S.R. Clegg and G. Palmer (eds), *The Politics of Management Knowledge*, Sage: London.

Scott, W.R. and Meyer, J.W. (1983) 'The organization of societal sectors', in J.W. Meyer and W.R. Scott (eds), *Organization Environments: Ritual and Rationality*, London: Sage.

Senge, P.M. (1990) *The Fifth Discipline: The Art and Practice of the Learning Organization*, London: Century.

Sewell, G. (1998) 'The discipline of teams: The control of team based industrial work through electronic and peer surveillance', *Administrative Science Quarterly* 43:406–469.

Shaw, K., Fenwick, J. and Foreman, A. (1994) 'Compulsory competitive tendering for local government services: The experience of local authorities in the north east, 1988–92', *Public Administration* 72(2):201–217.

Simon, H.A. (1957) *Administrative Behaviour*, 2nd edn, New York: Macmillan.

Simons, R. (1995) 'Control in the age of empowerment', *Harvard Business Review* 73(1/2):80–88.

Smelser, N.J. (1959) *Social Change in the Industrial Revolution*, London: Routledge.

Speller, S. (2001) 'The best value initiative', in G. Johnson and K. Scholes (eds), *Exploring Public Sector Strategy*, London: Prentice-Hall.

Stohl, C. and Cheney, G. (2001) 'Participatory processes/paradoxical practices: Communication and the dilemmas of organizational democracy', *Management Communication Quarterly* 14(3):349–407.

Sutton, F.X., Harris, E., Kaysen, C. and Tobin, J. (1956) *The American Business Creed*, Boston: Harvard University Press.

Tam, H. (1998) *Communitarianism: A New Agenda for Politics and Citizenship*, London: Macmillan.

Taylor, F.W. (1947/1911) *The Principles of Scientific Management*, New York: Harper and Row.

Thomas R, and Dunkerley, D. (1999) 'Careering downwards – Middle managers' experiences in the downsized organization', *British Journal of Management* 10(2):157–170.

Thompson, E.P. (1968) *The Making of the English Working Class*, Harmondsworth: Penguin.

Thompson, P. (1983) *The Nature of Work: An Introduction to Debates on the Labour Process*, London: Macmillan Press.

Tourish, D. and Pinnington, A. (2002) 'Transformational leadership, corporate cultism and the spirituality paradigm: An unholy trinity in the workplace?' *Human Relations* 55(2):147–172.

Traub, R. (1978) 'Lenin and Taylor: The fate of scientific management in the early Soviet Union', *Telos* 37:82–92.

Ure, A. (1835) *The Philosophy of Manufactures: Or an Exposition of the Scientific, Moral and Commercial Economy of the Factory System of Great Britain*, London: Charles Knight, reprinted 1967 by August M. Kelley, New York.

Vincent-Jones, P. (1994) 'The limits of near-contractual governance: Local authority internal trading under CCT', *Journal of Law and Society* 21(2):214–237.

Volberda, H. (1998) *Building the Flexible Firm: How to Remain Competitive*, Oxford: Oxford University Press.

White, B.J. (1994) 'Developing leaders for the high-performance workplace', *Human Resource Management* 33(1):161–168.

Wilkinson, A. (1992) 'The other side of quality: Soft issues and the human resource dimension', *Total Quality Management* 3(3):323–329.

Wilkinson, A. (1998) 'Empowerment: Theory and practice', *Personnel Review* 27(1):40–56.

Wilkinson, A., Godfrey, G. and Marchington, M. (1997) 'Bouquets brickbats and blinkers: Quality management and employee involvement in practice', *Organization Studies* 18(5):799–820.

Williams, J., Adcroft, A. and Willis, R. (1995) 'Management practice or structural factors: The case of America versus Japan in the car industry', *Economic and Industrial Democracy* 16:9–37.

Williamson, O.E. (1980) 'The organization of work: A comparative institutional assessment', *Journal of Economic Behaviour and Organization* 1(1):5–38.

Williamson, O.E. (1985) *The Economic Institutions of Capitalism*, London: The Free Press, Collier Macmillan.

Wisman, J. D. (1997) 'The ignored question of workplace democracy in political discourse', *International Journal of Social Economics* 24(12):1388–1403.

Womack, J., Jones, D. and Roos, D. (1990) *The Machine that Changed the World*, New York: Macmillan.

Wood, S. (1999) 'Human resource management and performance', *International Journal of Management Reviews* 1:367–413.

Worrall, L., Cooper C. and Campbell, F. (2000) 'The new reality for UK managers: Perpetual change and organizational instability', *Work, Employment and Society* 14(4):647–668.

Wren, D. (1994) *The Evolution of Management Thought*, New York: John Wiley.

# Chapter 10

# Perspectives and challenges

## Introduction

In this, our concluding chapter, we aim to draw together the diverse perspectives discussed in the preceding chapters by thinking about how each provides a different lens through which to study organizations. We will do this by examining one short case study from each of the perspectives and briefly considering the different aspects of the case that each highlights. We will also outline some recurrent debates in organization theory, for example the concept of paradigm and its role in organization theory and the debate concerning the practical use of organization theory seen in discussions of mode 1 and mode 2 science. Finally, we will take a brief look at current trends and make some tentative projections regarding the future of organization theory. We finish this chapter with seven questions that we believe students of organization theory should think about in trying to assess how they would like organization theory to develop in the future.

## Learning outcomes

- Briefly recap the core issues from each of the chapters.
- Examine commentators' views on the state of the field.
- Review the debate concerning paradigm commensurability and incommensurability.
- Consider the debate concerning the practical utility of organization theory.
- Outline possible future trends and directions for organization theory.

## Structure of the chapter

- This chapter begins with an overview of the different perspectives discussed in each chapter of the book and applies each perspective briefly to a case study of a UK scientific establishment. Whilst this is only brief, it is intended to illustrate the different kinds of issues which would be illuminated from alternative perspectives. The chapter then moves on to discuss the role of paradigms in organization theory and the continuing relevance of the paradigm debate. The next section addresses an issue that has (re)emerged recently – the practical utility of social sciences and organization theory. In particular we address the differences between mode 1 and mode 2 science and consider the implications for organization theory. We then move on to consider some emerging and important areas of study in organization theory before finishing by posing what we see as fundamental questions for organization theorists to consider in the development of this field.

## Case study — The British Geological Survey

The British Geological Survey (BGS) is a public sector organization responsible for advising the UK government on all aspects of geoscience as well as providing impartial geological advice to industry, academia and the public. Founded in 1835, it is the world's longest established national geological survey and the United Kingdom's premier centre for earth science information and expertise. The BGS is part of the Natural Environment Research Council (NERC), which is the UK's leading body for basic, strategic and applied research and monitoring in the environmental sciences. The BGS employs almost 800 permanent staff. The scientific staff of nearly 500 encompasses a wide range of skills covering all aspects of the earth sciences. The BGS is organized through a matrix structure. The work programme is grouped into three programme directorates, geology & resources, environment & hazards, and information, which are responsible for the management and delivery of the operational science programmes (coherent packages of related projects). The resources (staff, facilities and infrastructure) necessary for this work programme to be carried out are managed by a fourth directorate, geoscientific skills & facilities. Essential cross-directorate support is also provided by the business development & strategy directorate and the administration & operations support directorate. The BGS has its headquarters at Keyworth, just outside Nottingham, and there is a large regional office at Edinburgh, as well as offices at Wallingford, Exeter, London and Cardiff.

The annual budget of the BGS is in the region of £37 million, about half of which comes from the UK government's science budget, with the remainder coming from commissioned research from the public and private sectors. In recent years, the BGS, like all government-funded research institutes, has undergone a huge amount of change. There has been an increasing emphasis placed on commercial activity and because government funding has been reduced, the BGS has had to develop new ways of working with private sector organizations, including acting as consultants and doing contract research projects. This has involved, to some extent, changes in structure, culture and strategy in the organization.

*Source:* Adapted from the BGS website (http//www.bgs.ac.uk) and Cohen et al. (1999).

## Comparing the different perspectives

In the introduction to this book, we outlined the rationale for our approach. Throughout the chapters, it is clear that we have drawn boundaries around particular aspects of organization theory. The diverse and dynamic nature of the field makes it impossible to do justice to every writer, and although we have tried to be comprehensive, the book to some extent reflects our interests and preoccupations. We hope that these match those of our readers. Chapter 1 begins by outlining the role of organizations in society and the importance of organizations and organizing to our everyday lives. We also spend some time defining what we mean by the term *theory* and explain how we see theory as underpinning all of our activities, not just an academic exercise that is unrelated to practice. We finish Chapter 1 by outlining the ontological and epistemological assumptions that underpin the various perspectives to be addressed in the book. Although matters of ontology and epistemology are rarely popular with students, it is important, if we are to compare these different approaches, that we understand the assumptions made in each concerning the nature of reality and how we can make judgements about that reality. To briefly review each perspective, we provide a short case study on the previous page, which we will then analyse from each view point.

## A modernist perspective

In Chapter 2 we examine the fundamentals of modernist organization theory. This involves consideration of organizations as systems and a view that organizations can be managed in an efficient manner. An important feature of modernist organization theory is interest in bureaucracy and its location in wider society. The chapter examines a fierce debate as to whether bureaucracy, with its impersonality and amoral approach, represents a force for evil or a force for order – bringing harmony out of chaos. This perspective highlights the systemic nature of the organization. The BGS might be examined in terms of its inputs, outputs and transformational processes and in terms of how efficiently it operates. There would be an assumption that the organization could be designed rationally to meet the needs of its various constituents. From this perspective, emphasis is placed on the formal organization and on the development of appropriate systems for planning, decision making and control. Thus, analyses would concentrate on issues such as organizational design. There may be some consideration of how an organization could use modernist techniques such as business process reengineering (BPR) to develop a more effective and efficient approach toward undertaking its primary tasks.

## A neomodernist perspective

In Chapter 3, we address neomodernist organization theory, in particular focusing on human relations and the emergence of democratic organizations. Although modernism continued through the twentieth century and remains a powerful force in organizational theory and practice, a newer form of modernism began to emerge in the first half of the past century that has had a significant influence on organization theory. Neomodernism recognizes the importance of the human side of organizations. People and their needs are put at the centre and, with the recognition that the values and beliefs of people both shape and are shaped by their experience of organizational life, comes an interest in areas such as organizational culture, leadership and management. The chapter discusses two traditions in neomodernism in detail. The human relations approach focuses on how to develop leadership and management with a human face in order to create the 'best' environment for people. In contrast, approaches that stress the 'democratic organization' emphasize concepts of empowerment of all members of the organization. From a neomodernist perspective, analyses of BGS would include consideration of issues such as levels of communication and understanding between the various groups in the organization. One interesting area, for example, might be to examine the efficacy of communication between administrators and scientists. Attention might also be given to levels of participation in decision making, morale and commitment. Another potential focus for study would be the link between organizational culture and the psychological contract that scientists have with their employing organizations. This would be particularly interesting given the reduced level of government funding and the increased pressure upon scientists to engage in commercial activity. Attention may also be given to the management of culture and the development of BGS as a learning organization through processes such as organizational development.

## A new-wave perspective

Chapter 4 deals with an enduring issue of interest in organizational theory, control, particularly the forms of control used in 'new-wave management'. Three different kinds of formal control are examined: bureaucratic, output based and cultural, and then attention is paid to the ways that new-wave management emphasizes cultural forms of control exerted by management over organization members. The chapter then traces possible reasons for this development. Two different explanations of this apparent development are presented. One adopts an argument akin to contingency theory – that new-wave management was a necessary response to increasing levels of uncertainty in the environment faced by many organizations. The second traces the theoretical origins of new-wave management back to Durkheim's concept of *anomie* and explains its emergence in terms of ideological and rhetorical shifts in management discourse and how it challenges the humanistic guise of new wave management. Studies from this perspective would focus on the different approaches toward control used in BGS. Accountability has been a central drive in the government's approach toward managing public sector research laboratories. As a result, there is a great deal of focus on output-based controls and bureaucratic rules. In addition, organizations such as BGS have been called upon to develop an increasingly commercial culture, and analyses from this perspective might examine managerial attempts to manage culture and spread commercial values throughout the organization and the extent to which there has been a shift from bureaucratic to cultural forms of control.

## A postmodern perspective

Chapter 5 begins our section on postmodernism. In that chapter, we consider the concept of postmodernism as an 'epoch', a period of time after modernism. This chapter outlines the ways that postmodernism has been expressed as a new historical era in which the modernist notion of form fitting function is rejected in favour of disunity, contradiction and play. Concepts such as the post-industrial society, the information society and post-fordism are explored in order to make sense of what is argued to be a transition toward a more uncertain and dynamic environment that emphasizes technology, consumerism and more flexible organizational forms. We examine the different forms of organization that theorists have suggested belong in this new postmodern world and examine various critiques of these conceptualizations. From this perspective, an analysis of BGS might include consideration of the ways the organization has developed partnerships with other organizations in the delivery of its services. Attention would be given to the design of jobs and the organizational structure to assess the extent to which the organization is flexible. As shown in the case study, BGS has a matrix structure. Studies might examine the extent to which this maps onto the postbureaucratic model or whether there is a move toward a network form of organization for BGS. We may also see consideration of how the use of information technology has changed the way in which people work, perhaps allowing scientists to work more easily at a distance from their offices. The concept of knowledge work and knowledge workers will also be important in analysing how the organization manages these highly skilled employees.

In Chapter 6, we deal with postmodernism as a philosophy. Although the term *postmodernism* is applied again here, this is a fundamentally different approach to that seen in Chapter 5. This approach provides us with a new theoretical position from which to try to make sense of the world around us and offers a fundamental challenge to traditional modernist forms of organization theory. The postmodern perspective rejects the metanarratives or grand theories that modernist approaches seek to develop. Hence, there is no attempt to develop or discern universal laws of organizational functioning. Instead, the core elements of the postmodern position include rejection of the enlightenment belief in progress through knowledge; a recognition of the constitutive power of language, shaping what we can see and express; an understanding of the subjective nature of the world, such that all claims to knowledge are seen as contingent and temporary; and finally, a commitment to enable those previously silenced in traditional organization theory to find a voice. A postmodern philosophical perspective on the organization poses many possible challenges. Firstly, we would expect consideration of the discourses at play in the organization. For example, it may be possible to highlight competing discourses such as those of scientific excellence, public service and commercialization. The role these discourses play in the organization would include consideration of how people think and speak about their work – obviously, this would mean paying attention to the language that people use. However, we would not be seeking to develop theories of how scientific organizations in general should be managed; rather, the aim would be to develop context specific insights – 'petits recits'.

## A reflective perspective

We return to sense and meaning making in Chapter 7. Two schools of thought, symbolic interactionism and phenomenology, that have underpinned the development of knowledge concerning how individuals make sense of their worlds and imbue it with meaning are addressed. These perspectives shed light on the ways individuals and groups construct their organizational identities and the ways these identities become enmeshed in the organizational culture. The chapter examines the enduring significance of these approaches, showing that they can help organizational members to develop deep understanding of, and to reflect on, their circumstances. Studies from this perspective might include trying to understand how scientists make sense of science and commercialism. In particular, emphasis might be placed on how they perceive of themselves as professionals and the tensions experienced between being on the one hand a professional who is oriented toward his or her profession and on the other hand an organizational member. Another interesting issue for study would be the ways that different people present themselves in BGS – whether they present themselves as managers, scientists or administrators – and the roles they perform.

## A critical theory and psychoanalytic perspective

Next, Chapter 8 examines critical theory and psychoanalysis. The chapter traces the history of critical theory and its emergence in management and organizational studies in the1980s. We examine how the radical view of the ways organizations should operate provided by critical theory enables us to reflect on issues that both theorists and practitioners should consider in order to make organizations fulfilling places in which to work. The chapter then moves on to examine the link between critical theory and psychoanalysis, showing how early critical theorists saw psychoanalysis as an approach that would enable insight into and exploration of deep issues in institutions and society. In this chapter, we show how psychoanalysis helps us to consider the ways that unconscious aspects of behaviour can impact upon organizational design and functioning. A critical perspective on BGS would examine the ways that leaders, managers and members of the scientific community exercise power over other members of the organization. Furthermore, there would be an exploration of the ways in which all workers could be genuinely empowered. There might, for example, be an examination of the use of short-term contract workers and technicians and how they are often invisible in accounts of how science progresses. The commercialization of science would be the subject of critical enquiry. In addition, from a psychoanalytic perspective, there may be examination of neurotic aspects of the organization and deep issues that can cause problems. For example, this may shed light on the role of the heroic scientific leader. In some laboratories, this person is held up uncritically as a role model for scientists to follow, which from a psychoanalytic perspective, may encourage dependency.

## A managerialist perspective

Finally, Chapter 9 deals with the evolution of management, developing a theoretical understanding of managers themselves as a significant, identifiable organizational group. This is often ignored in texts on organization theory but provides important insight into the functioning of organizations. The chapter begins with an historical account of how and why management developed. The managerialist thesis is then examined in depth to show how different interpretations of the significance of the development of management, as a specific function and social group, have impacted upon both how we understand management and managerialism. The chapter concludes by examining organizational democracy as a contemporary theoretical challenge to managerialism. BGS, like other public sector laboratories, has undergone significant changes in recent years – many of which come under the heading 'new public sector management'. The government has increasingly put faith in management to ensure that scientific establishments are contributing to national wealth. Studies from this perspective might examine the evolution of management within BGS and perhaps critically evaluate the impact of increased managerialism on scientific productivity.

### The chapter so far

Up to this point, we have briefly reviewed the different perspectives that are contained in the preceding chapters. We have shown how each of these perspectives would place emphasis on different aspects of the case study organization in order to highlight the diversity of approaches that are available in organization theory.

## The paradigm debate

Our aim so far has been to demonstrate how each approach provides a slightly different focus on organizations. It should be noted, though, that there are elements of overlap. For example, both critical theory and postmodernism point to marginalized groups within society. Similarly, both modernism and postmodernism as an epoch focus on organizational structures, albeit from different standpoints. We also hope that it is clear that these chapters do not provide a neat, linear account of the development of the field or suggest that one approach has achieved dominance. Rather, these different approaches have developed at different times, and each remains in some form in current thinking about organizational theory. Thus, although postmodernism received a good deal of attention in the 1990s, there remained a healthy modernist tradition, and critical theory has recently also made something of a comeback. It is our position that each of the approaches poses challenges for understanding organizations and that inevitably, there are areas of conflict, continuity and overlaps between the various perspectives.

Perhaps one reason for such high levels of diversity is that the field of organization theory is still relatively young in the social sciences. Some commentators see it as still unstructured because there are no universally agreed upon tools and methods as seen in some of the natural sciences. Writers such as Stanford professor Jeffrey

Pfeffer (1983) bemoan this lack of standardization. He compares the state of the field to a 'weedpatch' rather than a 'well tended garden' (p. 1) and questions whether the level of diversity in the field prevents a sense of progress. Similarly, James March (1996) argues that as the field has grown, it has:

> . . . continually been threatened with becoming not so much a new integrated semidiscipline as a set of independent, self congratulatory cultures of comprehension. . . . in the name of technical purity and claims of universality energized subfields have tended to seal themselves off, each seemingly eager to close further the minds of the already converted, without opening the minds of others (p. 280).

In other words, these writers are concerned that the organization theorists from different perspectives do not effectively communicate with each other or share ideas. Instead, subgroups are developing that have increasingly narrow specialisms.

This is obviously an area of debate. Some writers argue that consensus over both what was studied and how it was studied did exist in the past. For example, Mike Reed (1996) points to some unity of approach between the 1950s and 1970s, and Lex Donaldson (1985) argues that contingency theory, discussed in Chapter 3, is a central theme that provided organization theory with a scientific basis around which theorists should work. Others, such as Gibson Burrell (2003), question this consensus, seeing it as illusory. He comments that the field of organization theory has always been diverse, and although developments in the 1980s may have perhaps added to the diversity, dating back to Weber, there has been considerable diversity between both the subject areas and the methods of different groups of theorists (see, for example, Chapters 2 to 4). Indeed, Burrell uses Weber's work to highlight this diversity, showing how it could be seen on the one hand as modernist and on the other as critical (see Chapter 2 for more discussion).

Working with Gareth Morgan, Burrell produced a framework to help map the territory of organizational theory. They use Kuhn's concept of paradigm to explain the often unspoken assumptions made by particular groups of writers on organizational theory (Burrell and Morgan, 1979). A paradigm can be defined as a particular way of seeing the world. It is similar to a frame or a lens through which organizations are viewed, which directs attention to the appropriate aspects of organization to study and how they should be studied. In an interview with American academic Albert Mills, Morgan explained paradigms further as:

> . . . different realities within the world of social science. Different social scientists are living in these different realities and they've made different assumptions about the world. There is a self contained nature to the theorising that goes on according to the paradigm you're in (http://aurora.icaap.org/archive/morgan.html).

Burrell and Morgan apply Kuhn's notion of paradigm in a very broad sense and agree with Kuhn that paradigms are 'incommensurable'. In other words, they are mutually exclusive. Although Burrell and Morgan argue that more than one paradigm can exist at any point in time, each is incompatible with each of the others, so if we adopt one paradigm to understand organizations, we cannot use another at the same time.

Central to Burrell and Morgan's thesis is the idea that organizational theory can be understood in terms of a matrix of four paradigms whose two axes are based upon different assumptions about the nature of social science and the nature of society. They argue that all social scientific theory will inevitably make implicit or explicit assumptions along these dimensions – if the theory in question does not, then it is not proper social science!

The horizontal axis concerns organizational theorists' assumptions about the nature of the social world and how it might be best investigated. This dimension is split between subjectivist and objectivist approaches. An objectivist view assumes that we can get an objective picture of reality. The focus is on observable behaviour and there is an assumption that it is possible to develop laws of behaviour that explain why people behave the way they do in organizations. On the other hand, the subjectivist perspective focuses much more on how people make sense of their situation, recognizing that there is no objective means for judging reality. These are mutually exclusive or incommensurable, so by accepting one set of assumptions, the social scientist denies the alternative.

In a similar manner, the assumptions about the nature of society provide the vertical axis of the matrix. Burrell and Morgan, again, see this as two mutually exclusive extremes: the sociology of regulation versus the sociology of radical change. The former assumes that society and its institutions are characterized by underlying equilibrium, consensus and cohesiveness without fundamental differences of interest between different groups in society. Analysis is directed toward preserving the status quo. When conflict happens, it is viewed as a temporary irregularity that is necessary for adaptation to changed circumstances. In contrast, the sociology of radical change assumes that society is riddled with fundamental conflicts, domination, exploitation and deprivation. It is therefore concerned with change and freeing people from a society that stunts human development. By accepting the assumptions that underpin the sociology of regulation, those assumptions that constitute the sociology of radical change are denied, and vice versa.

The two dimensions are combined to produce the four paradigms illustrated in Figure 10.1.

It is impossible to map the perspectives covered in the preceding chapters neatly onto this model. Because each perspective includes a number of slightly different theoretical approaches, some fit into more than one category. For example, different approaches discussed in the chapter on critical theory and psychoanalysis can be seen in both of the two upper quadrants. We prefer to illustrate the differences between the perspectives by using Table 1.1 (see later) because this shows that although each perspective has some unique characteristics, there are also areas of overlap. However, perhaps it is no surprise that a good deal of the work discussed in this text would fall broadly into the functionalist category. Functionalism was the most dominant of the paradigms during the early development of organization theory. The increase in attention given to interpretive approaches and critical theory means, though, that each of the four paradigms can still be seen in organization theory today. For an example of a study using all four of the paradigms, see the Ideas and perspectives box on page 441.

Throughout their work, Burrell and Morgan (1979) are adamant that the four paradigms are mutually exclusive, that it is impossible to operate in two paradigms and share information across them. This is because:

> . . . they offer different ways of seeing. A synthesis is not possible, since in their
> pure forms they are contradictory. . . . They are alternatives, in the sense that one
> can operate in different paradigms sequentially over time, but mutually exclusive,

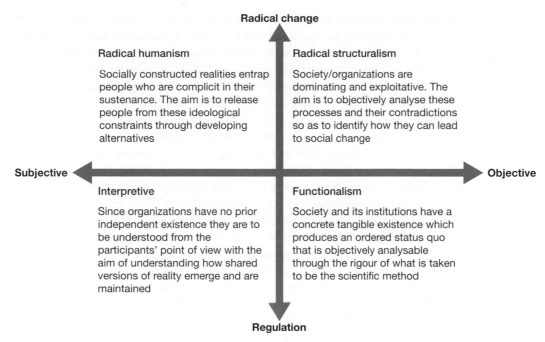

**Figure 10.1:** Burrell and Morgan's four paradigms. (*Source:* Johnson and Duberley (2000), Burrell and Morgan (1979).)

in the sense that one cannot operate in more than one paradigm at any given point in time, since in accepting the assumptions of one, we defy the assumptions of all the others (p. 25).

Indeed, as Hassard shows in the Ideas and perspectives box below, the issue of incommensurability pervades not just research methods but also the choice of topics

## Ideas and perspectives

## Using four paradigms to study firefighters

John Hassard (1991) attempted to do a study of the British Fire Service using all of the different paradigms. He shows how using the four paradigms in one research setting gives totally different perspectives in a study of work behaviour. Each account was based upon a theory and methodology consistent with a particular paradigm. Thus, the functionalist account used psychometric techniques to provide a factual account of the firefighters' orientation toward work. In contrast, the interpretive account attempted to assess people's meaning systems and focused on how firefighters created informal rules for interacting with each other and undertaking their tasks. The radical humanist study analysed the training practices on courses designed to prepare firefighters for promotion to first-line supervision. The research examined how senior training officers were able to select training materials that reinforced the logic of the existing authority structure. From a radical structuralist perspective, a labour process study of firefighting was undertaken. This looked at the history of the fire service and analysed the strategic relations between capital and labour, especially with regard to the development of the employment contract. The research highlights crisis points and describes the role of state agencies in seeking to mediate contradictory forces and restore equilibrium.

and the perception of problems. Instead of aiming for homogeneity in the field and the development of standardized tools and techniques, Burrell and Morgan argue that each paradigm should be valued in its own right and developed separately so that the weaker, emergent paradigms, such as radical humanism, are not eroded and incorporated into the dominant structural functional approach.

Much debate has ensued concerning whether paradigms are incommensurable or not. On one side are those (e.g., Jackson and Carter, 1991, 1993) who defend incommensurability and advocate the shutting off of paradigms from each other as means of survival for the less established paradigms. In opposition, writers such as Reed (1985, 1992) propose a pluralistic view of organization theory development. Furthermore, Scott (1998) makes the point that very different relationships exist between different perspectives in organization theory. New approaches emerge, and rather than replacing the old, they may complement each other, conflict or perhaps partially overlap. Thus, the notion of paradigm incommensurability has been challenged and could perhaps be argued to be too simplistic.

Thus, the paradigm debate has yet to be resolved. Paradigms still seem to attract considerable attention in organization theory, although recently Westwood and Clegg (2003), reviewing the debate, argue there have never been paradigms in organization studies because the field is too young for them to have developed. Instead, they argue that each of these are just perspectives. For some, the debate itself may seem to be academic navel gazing; however, it seems important that organization theorists know where they stand with regard to the two axes put forward by Burrell and Morgan. Current trends in organization theory toward postmodernism have raised the issue of paradigms again and in particular have provoked debate concerning relativity as we discuss in Chapter 6. In the next section, we move on to consider a related issue – the practical utility of organization theory.

## The practical utility of organization theory

A key issue that we introduced in Chapter 1 is: who is organization theory for? Is it for academics, managers, people working in organizations, consultants? Recently, this debate has been couched in terms of what Gibbons et al. (1994) call the transition from mode 1 to mode 2 forms of knowledge production. They argue that a new way of producing knowledge is emerging that affects not only what knowledge is produced but also how it is produced, the context in which it is pursued, the way it is organized and how it is managed. Mode 1 refers to the more traditional practice of science: pure, 'blue skies' research that focuses on developing and testing theories about the social world. In contrast, mode 2 focuses on application. New knowledge is not just developed in universities by academics but also by practitioners in industry or by practitioners and academics working together. Gibbons et al. (1994) examine the change in terms of five key dimensions: context, discipline base, social organization, accountability and quality control (Table 10.1). They maintain that mode 2 has not replaced mode 1 but is emerging alongside it.

Gibbons et al. (1994) insist that their framework is value free – that they do not claim that mode 2 is inherently better than mode 1 or vice versa; rather, they must be

**Table 10.1** Two modes of knowledge production

|  | Mode 1 | Mode 2 |
|---|---|---|
| Context | Research is undertaken that follows the norms of academic practice and pure research. It is driven by the interests of the academic community. | Research is use driven but constrained by resources (especially time). Knowledge is produced in diverse teams and is more applied. |
| Discipline base | Knowledge is developed within single disciplines, each of which has particular ways of working. Those who are developing theories are separate from those who might be applying them in organizations. | Knowledge is transdisciplinary. People from very different perspectives work together, and there is much more emphasis on the application of new theories about organizations. |
| Social organization | There is little joint work between academics, government bodies and industrial organizations. | People work together on projects that are of practical use to organizations. Teams of academics and industrialists work together to solve current problems and in doing so, develop knowledge. |
| Accountability | Writers of organization theory are accountable to and judged by their peers, so other academics judge the value of organization theories. | Writers of organization theory are accountable to lots of different people, including other academics, those who work in organizations, and society in general. |
| Quality control | The social scientist is seen as the expert. Quality control is based upon the idea of doing excellent science. | Quality is judged on a broad range of criteria, including intellectual merit, cost effectiveness and economic and social relevance. |

*Source:* Adapted from Gibbons et al. (1994).

seen as fundamentally different, with their own particular sets of ideas, social norms and values. There does seem to be an assumption, though, that social sciences are moving more and more in the direction of mode 2 and that organizational theory will therefore increasingly be developed with more concern for the needs of industry. It could be argued that the emergence of the mode 2 approach as the preferred model is a result of the political and economic situation we currently face. From a Marxist perspective, the sort of science that is predominant at any one time is determined by the influence that economic factors exercise on the development of science. It has also been suggested that in capitalist countries, the relative decline of interest in basic science is a manifestation of the economic cycle such that science policy is governed by short-term tactical or anti-inflationary objectives.

One implication for organization theory is that there is more pressure to meet the needs of industry and to focus on the practical application of ideas. Gibbons et al. and others (Turpin and Deville, 1995; Ziman, 1994) also argue that knowledge production is now transdisciplinary. This means that mode 2 is problem oriented and involves the integration of different theoretical perspectives. As Table 10.1 indicates, the social organization of research will, as a result, become more complex and dynamic. From this perspective, the provider (e.g., scientist, academic, professional) is no longer seen as the expert, imparting his or her knowledge to a largely uninformed public. Instead, there is a much more participative approach toward developing knowledge and solving problems. The people who live and work in the organizations under study have some say in what is studied and how it is studied. However, there may be difficulties managing relationships between different people involved in research, particularly when professional, scientific, organizational, institutional and national borders are transcended.

Social responsibility is also fundamental to mode 2 knowledge production. Gibbons et al. (1994) suggest that whereas the quality of new theories and knowledge in mode 1 is typically assessed by other academics, mode 2 takes a different approach. Consistent with the principle of applicability, knowledge is increasingly judged according to its practical value. In other words, does this knowledge help the organization to function better? Does it solve current problems being faced?

In summary, the characteristics of mode 2 knowledge production include:

- **Increasing diversity in the location of research activities** with a greater range of organizations involved in research (e.g., universities, research institutes, hospitals, firms, industry associations).

- **Increasing focus on interdisciplinary and, more particularly, transdisciplinary research**, with teams of researchers coming together to work on a common problem that cannot be tackled adequately within a single disciplinary framework (e.g., environmental or health problems).

- **Increasing focus on problems rather than techniques** with solutions being sought from a range of disciplinary tools and techniques and valued for their contribution to the solution rather than for their methodological sophistication.

- **Increasing blurring of organizational borders and greater emphasis on collaborative work and communication** with a more flexible team approach in which teams form around problems and then break up and move on to form different teams around different problems.

- **Changes in modes of communication**, including some increase in commercial grounding of intellectual property, less emphasis on publication in refereed journals and more on informal communication through networks of researchers.

### Stop and think

What are the implications for you as a student of a move from mode 1 to mode 2 forms of knowledge production? Consider:

- What will you learn?
- How will you learn?
- How will you be assessed?

The mode 1 and mode 2 debate has not been completely uncritical. Some authors have criticized the assumption that we are definitely moving toward mode 2. It is also open to question whether mode 2 offers anything dramatically different. There has always been a stream of organization theory concerned with meeting the presumed needs of management – most explicitly neomodernism, discussed in Chapter 3. However, it does seem that there has been a shift with regard to research funding that means that both natural and social scientists are having to take on the needs of 'users' more than was previously the case. Of course, an interesting issue for organization theorists is to think about who their users are. Is it the shareholders of organizations who want to see the best possible return from their investment? Is it managers seeking to make their organizations more effective? Or is it employees seeking to lead fulfilling lives within organizations? In some senses, it could be argued that a move to mode 2 forms of knowledge production, if happening, could support the democratization of organization theory, with all sorts of people being involved in research, not just academics. American academics Marta Calas and Linda Smircich (2003) see the potential to help make organizations better places to live and work – to offer more democratic organizations, as discussed in Chapter 9. They point out that there are a wide range of critical perspectives available in organizational theory but also comment that, to date, critical organization theory has had little impact upon the design and functioning of organizations (p. 598). Although they do not use the terms *mode 1* and *mode 2*, they do suggest that organizational theorists replace the idea of experts (some of us) with co-researchers (all of us) so we open up organization studies to deal with the problems and issues that people around the world face.

On the other hand, a move toward mode 2 could be seen as a cynical way of justifying the increasing commercialization of research and cutbacks in government funding for research. This could signal a move toward a consulting model for organization theory in which academics are driven purely by the needs of commercial organizations. Thus, we return to the fundamental question posed in Chapter 1: what is organization theory for? As Burrell (2003, p. 527) questions, is it about knowledge for management, knowledge by management or knowledge of management? This is a question that will continue to challenge organization theory as it further develops. In the next section, we take a brief look at how organization theory seems to be developing at present and consider some of the themes that currently seem to be important in the field.

## The chapter so far

The previous two sections have addressed two important current debates in organization theory. The first relates to the existence of paradigms as particular ways of understanding organizations and the disagreement that exists between different authors as to whether the different paradigms are so incompatible that to adopt one means all others must be dropped. The second relates to the extent to which organization theory as a social science is becoming more oriented to the practical needs of organizations.

## Current trends

To examine current trends, we undertook a brief review of articles published in a selection of top-ranking US and UK organization and management journals over the past five years. The following provides a flavour of the areas that seem to be receiving considerable or growing levels of attention. There remains a huge degree of diversity in both the areas covered and the methods used. Some subject areas endure and seem to provide a sense of continuity. Others are emerging, and as Scott (1998) suggests, sometimes overlapping or complementing existing perspectives. The most popular areas of theory that were covered included change management, critical management studies, globalization and cross-cultural management, discourse analysis, institutional theory, knowledge management, new organizational forms, in particular, network forms of organization. New subject areas emerging seem to be areas such as co-evolutionary theory and aesthetics. This was clearly a very broad sweep, and it is impossible to do justice to all areas, so in the next section, we pick a few of these to look at in a little more depth and discuss possible future directions and challenges for organization theory.

## Globalization

A term that is used continually in the literature and is said to pose major challenges for organization and organization theory is *globalization*. We touched on this briefly in Chapter 5 on postmodernism as an epoch. In recent years, there has been huge debate over the nature and extent of globalization and its implications for organization. However, the term *globalization* is not without ambiguity, often used interchangeably with internationalization. John Child (2005) argues that it is used in so many ways that there is a danger that it loses any real meaning. He suggests that the term came to prominence in the mid-1980s as a way of encapsulating a variety of changes, including the growth of world trade and direct investment, the global integration of currency and capital markets, the spread of value-added chains, the widespread application of new information technologies and the dissemination of 'best practice' management concepts (p. 29). Similarly, Peter Dicken (2003) explains how strong globalization involves ties between countries becoming stronger 'deep integration', organized primarily within the production networks of transnational corporations (pp. 10–12) as opposed to shallow integration through arm's-length trading.

Some writers argue for a 'strong' globalization thesis, which suggests that there has been a rapid and recent process of economic globalization: a truly global economy is claimed to have emerged or be in the process of emerging in which distinct national economies become less and less relevant. A new kind of organization is emerging – the transnational corporation. Transnational corporations are the prime economic actors in the global economy. These organizations do not have allegiance to any particular country and locate themselves wherever they are able to secure global advantage. Child (2002) argues that these transnational organizations adopt a universalistic approach, lacking sensitivity to particular nations or regions as special contexts. Driving this universalism are economic and technological forces, which suggests that there will be an increasing convergence between modes of organization as countries develop similar economic and political systems. The strong globalization thesis can be described as low

Ideas and perspectives

## Globalization and the wealth of transnational organizations

1. Of the 100 largest economies in the world, 51 are corporations; only 49 are countries. Wal-Mart – the number 12 corporation – is bigger than 161 countries, including Israel, Poland, and Greece. Mitsubishi is larger than the fourth most populous nation on earth: Indonesia. General Motors is bigger than Denmark. Ford is bigger than South Africa. Toyota is bigger than Norway.

2. The Top 200 corporations' combined sales are bigger than the combined economies of all countries minus the biggest nine; that is they surpass the combined economies of 182 countries. At latest count, the world has 191 countries. If you subtract the GDP of the big nine economies: the United States, Japan, Germany, France, Italy, the United Kingdom, Brazil, Canada, and China, the combined GDPs of the other 182 countries is $6.9 trillion. The combined sales of the Top 200 corporations is $7.1 trillion.

3. The Top 200 have almost twice the economic clout of the poorest four-fifths of humanity. The world's economic income and wealth remain highly concentrated among the rich. Indeed, according to the United Nations, some 85% of the world's GDP is controlled by the richest fifth of humanity; only 15% is controlled by the poorest four-fifths. Hence, the poorer 4.5 billion people in the world account for only $3.9 trillion dollars of economic activity; this is only a little over half the combined revenues of the Top 200's $7.1 trillion.

*Source:* From Anderson and Cavanagh (2000) *Top 200 The Rise of Global Corporate Power*
http://www.globalpolicy.org/socecon/tncs/top200.htm

context because there is a strong presupposition of eventual convergence and the impact of national distinctiveness is minimized (Rees and Edwards, 2006).

Technological change is often seen as an important contributory factor underlying globalization. Following a contingency theory type argument, it is suggested that whatever the national setting, the adoption of a given technology will have the same consequences for the design of organization and for the way that social relations at work are structured. In other words, technologies are seen as determining structures and behaviours independent of the local context. Similarly, underpinning the globalization thesis are assumptions concerning psychological and political universalism – an assumption that human beings share common needs and motivational structures and the notion that countries are converging on the model of society found in much of Western Europe and North America.

In summary, the strong globalization thesis includes:

- National and regional economies are becoming dominated by new global systems of economic coordination and control in which competition and strategic choices are organized at the global level.

- National and international firms are becoming subordinated to transnational firms that differ significantly from them and are accountable only to global capital markets.

- The ability of the nation states to regulate economic activities is rapidly declining, and global markets increasingly dominate national economic policies.

- National economic policies, forms of economic organization and managerial practices are converging to the most efficient ones as a result of global competition (Rees and Edwards, 2006, p. 10).

There are a number of critics of the strong globalization thesis. Key critics such as Hirst and Thompson (1999) for example, argue that globalization is nothing new. They, along with others, point to a number of problematic issues:

1. There have been other periods in history that have seen a large amount of international trade.
2. There is not a huge shift of capital mobility from the advanced to the developing world.
3. Trade, investment and financial flows are concentrated in the 'triad' of Europe, Japan and North America.
4. Completely transnational firms are pretty rare. Most companies are based nationally and maintain strong roots in their country of origin whilst trading multinationally.
5. Domestic trade is still of massive importance and should not be underestimated.
6. Insufficient attention is paid to the impact of national culture.
7. Insufficient consideration is given to the importance of managerial decision making with regard to control, which means that decisions are not always rational.
8. Although some of the actions of multinational corporations may lead to common processes across countries, these organizations will seek to take advantage of national differences in order to compete and therefore may actively reproduce nationally distinct patterns.

There are also other important criticisms of globalization with regard to its uneven impact, the levels of environmental degradation and the widening gap between rich and poor companies that seem to accompany the movement of capital around the world. (See the case study below and also the case studies in Chapter 5.)

## Case study     Guatemala: supermarket giants crush farmers

Mario Chinchilla, his face shaded by a battered straw hat, worriedly surveyed his field of sickly tomatoes. His hands and jeans were caked with dirt, but no amount of labour would ever turn his puny crop into the plump, unblemished produce the country's main supermarket chain displays in its big stores. For a time, the farmer's cooperative he heads managed to sell vegetables to the chain, part owned by the giant Dutch multinational, Ahold, which counts Stop & Shop among its assets. But the co-op's members lacked the expertise, as well as the money to invest in the modern greenhouses, drip irrigation and pest control that would have helped them meet supermarket specifications. Squatting next to his field, Mr. Chinchilla's rugged face was a portrait of defeat. 'They wanted consistent supply without ups and downs', he said, scratching the soil with a stick. 'We didn't have the capacity to do it.'

Across Latin America, supermarket chains partly or wholly owned by global corporate goliaths like Ahold, Wal-Mart and Carrefour have revolutionized food distribution in the short span of a decade and have now begun to transform food growing, too. The megastores are popular with customers for their lower prices, choice and convenience. But their sudden appearance has brought unanticipated and daunting challenges to millions of struggling, small farmers.

The stark danger is that increasing numbers of them will go bust and join streams of desperate migrants to America and the urban slums of their own countries. Their declining fortunes, economists and agronomists fear, could worsen inequality in a region where the gap between rich and poor already yawns cavernously and the concentration of land in the hands of an elite has historically fuelled cycles of rebellion and violent repression. 'It's like being on a train with a glass on a table and it's about to fall off and break,' said Prof. Thomas Reardon, an agricultural economist at Michigan State University. 'Everyone sees the glass on the table – but do they see it shaking? Do they see the edge? The edge is the structural changes in the market.'

*Source:* Dugger, C.W. *New York Times*, 28 December 2004.

### Stop and think

- What are the benefits of transnational corporations to consumers, workers and society?
- What are the possible disadvantages of them?

As with most areas of organization theory, the globalization thesis is the subject of debate. However, it is difficult to deny that we are witnessing a huge increase in interest in the nature and operation of multinational corporations. There has also been a surge in academic interest in the operation of organizations in different national contexts. In particular, China, with its recent rapid development, has been an area of interest to many authors. In Chapter 5, we discussed the movement of lower skilled jobs to areas of the world where labour is cheaper. Other interesting trends, such as the move toward off-shoring skilled jobs as well as lower skilled work to countries in the developing world, mean that this will continue to be an important area for research and theorizing about organizations. We are also starting to see some interesting critical examinations of the impact of global trade, from both critical theory and postmodern perspectives.

One particularly interesting angle has been postcolonial theory. This has involved examination of how much organization theory, as a fundamentally Western discipline, makes ethnocentric assumptions about human nature, organization and society. Writers from this perspective examine the ways that different groups develop a generalized image of others. In particular, Said (1978) shows how, for Europeans, what he terms *Orient* (the Middle East and most of Asia) is the Other, the contrasting image, idea, or personality to the West. Western depictions of 'the Orient', and in particular for Said, Arab people, have developed as a result of the previous relationship between the West and former colonies and are highly selective, if not distorted. Other writers from a similar perspective include Spivak (1996), who shows how citizens in developing nations are imbued with qualities, beliefs and aspirations by policymakers and writers in the West. Postcolonial theory, as applied to organization theory, like some postmodern approaches illuminates 'the Other' in organizations and provides an alternative perspective for understanding how organization theory has developed.

It could also contribute to organization theory by analysing how concepts and categories such as race, ethnicity and religious beliefs are used in organizations to deal with practical problems and to mediate conflicts (Styhre, 2002). An example in the case below shows how it has been applied to consider different conceptualizations of Japanese workers by Swedish employees.

| Case study | The adoption of Japanese practises in Sweden |

Based upon interviews with Swedish managers, employees and consultants concerning the adoption of *kaizen* in Sweden, Styhre (2002) shows how Swedish workers constructed a generalized image of the Japanese that strongly deviated from the generalized image of the Swede. The construction has both positive and negative elements. Interviewees suggested that Japanese manufacturing industry deserved respect. However, they also viewed Japanese workers as very different from themselves, as shown in the quotes below:

'We are not going to stand in front of the factory gates every morning and sing the company song and do gymnastics.'
'In Japan they are not exactly individualists.'
'They love campaigns in their *kaizen* work, for instance what we might regard as being childish and ridiculous.'

The interesting point is that the Swedish interviewees constructed an image of Japanese workers that assumed there were more differences than similarities between themselves and their Japanese counterparts.

Thus, the issue of globalization has been brought into organization theory from a variety of perspectives. One interesting approach comes from institutional theory and neoinstitutional theory, which, although developed some years ago, seems to be enjoying a revival, as we discuss below.

## Institutional and neoinstitutional theory

Linked to globalization, there has been an increase in interest in institutionalism and neoinstitutionalism. Neoinstitutional theory focuses at a macro level, concerning itself with concepts such as organizational fields, social institutions and societal sectors. An organizational field can be thought of as a group of organizations that constitute a recognized area of institutional life – for example, suppliers, consumers, competitors and regulatory agencies (DiMaggio and Powell, 1983).

Much of early institutional theory was concerned with developing an alternative to functional and rational explanations of organizational form. An early statement of institutional theory can be found in Meyer and Rowan's (1977) seminal article, which drew attention to the ways organizational structure is shaped by what they call *institutional rules*. These rules provide taken-for-granted templates that define the appropriate ways to manage organizations and to structure relations. They are part of the institutional environment that varies across different cultures, different sectors and different fields. Although they furnish models of how organizations should operate, they are not necessarily based upon a clear link to organizational performance. Rather, they can be seen as 'rationalized myths' (Mckinley and Mone, 2003). In other words, they appear rational but have little concrete evidence to back them up. An example that is often given for this is the way that accountancy firms tend to be organized as partnerships.

In their original framework, Meyer and Rowan (1977) argue that conformity to institutional rules is rewarded with increased legitimacy – that is, organizations that follow the rules are seen as reliable and accountable. An interesting example of this relates to organizational downsizing, which was particularly popular in the 1990s. Mckinley et al. (1995) have shown how downsizing has become institutionalized as a management response to perceived organizational difficulties despite a lack of evidence that downsizing increases profitability. They discuss how the language of downsizing, using terms such as *lean* and *flexible*, naturalizes the process and makes it seem like an external rational phenomena rather than a management decision. Similarly, a 1997 study in the United States by Cascio et al. showed that downsizings had negligible impact on firm profitability relative to the size of the layoffs and that there was no evidence that downsizing firms were generally and significantly able to improve profits. And yet organizations around the world copy each other, and downsizing is seen as a rational response to difficult situations.

A few years later, DiMaggio and Powell extended the work of Meyer and Rowan by focusing on what they called 'institutional isomorphism' in organizational fields. This refers to the tendency of organizations to become more similar over time. Thus, the fundamental question underlying DiMaggio and Powell's neoinstitutionalist theory was why are organizations so similar? Their answer involved three distinct processes:

1. **Coercive isomorphism:** This results 'from both formal and informal pressures exerted on organizations by other organizations upon which they are dependent and by cultural expectations in the society within which the organization functions' (DiMaggio and Powell, 1995, p. 7). This includes external pressures from government, regulatory bodies and other agencies to adopt particular systems or structures. It can also stem from contractual obligations with other organizations or people.

2. **Mimetic isomorphism:** The tendency to copy other organizations in the field. Innovations and working practices that are seen to enhance legitimacy are attractive and are likely to be copied, especially in times of uncertainty during which the likely level of success of adopting different systems or processes is difficult to assess.

3. **Normative isomorphism:** The ways that organizations strive to become professionalized and legitimized and therefore adopt professional standards. These norms or standards are usually conveyed through the education and training of professionals and certification processes. For an example, see Table 10.2 (over leaf).

They also highlight specific conditions that are likely to lead to strong institutional isomorphism.

1. When resource dependence is high, coercive isomorphism is likely to be higher.
2. When there is technological uncertainty, mimetic isomorphism is likely to be higher.
3. When there is goal ambiguity, mimetic isomorphism is likely to be higher.

**Table 10.2** Contrasting types of isomorphism

|  | Mimetic | Coercive | Normative |
| --- | --- | --- | --- |
| Reason to adopt | Uncertainty | Dependence | Duty, obligation |
| Carrier | Innovation, visibility | Political law, rules, sanctions | Professionalism, including certification, accreditation |
| Social basis | Culturally supported | Legal | Moral |
| Example | Reengineering, benchmarking | Pollution controls, school regulations | Accounting standards, consultant training |

*Source:* Adapted from *Organization Theory and Design*, 8th edition by Daft. 2004 Reprinted with permission of South-Western, a division of Thomson Learning (www.thomsonrights.com, fax 800 730 2215.)

Neoinstitutional theory is not without drawbacks, however. For example, Mckinley and Mone (2003) note an ambivalent position on the issue of rationality. They comment that early neoinstitutional theorists suggest that the motives for conforming were concerned with gaining legitimacy and reducing uncertainty rather than any rational analysis of a link to financial performance. However, they do also suggest that legitimacy was necessary for organizational survival and therefore they could be argued to be rational. Donaldson (1985) also criticizes neoinstitutional theory for what he sees as loose conceptualization and ambiguous constructs.

There is also a concern that the emphasis on stability in DiMaggio and Powell's early paper (1983) resulted in a lack of attention to issues of power and the informal organization that were central to the 'old institutionalism' of writers such as Phillip Selznick. More recently, there have been attempts to examine both continuity and change in neoinstitutionalism (Greenwood and Hinings 1996; DiMaggio and Powell 1991; Scott, 1995). Thus, emerging neoinstitutionalism is incorporating both macro and micro perspectives and giving increased importance to the micro-political processes inherent in institutional change. This desire to incorporate both micro and macro processes in organizational analysis has also resulted in calls to consider institutionalism in the examination of discourse, which we now briefly move on to.

## Discourse

Although discourse has been covered in some depth in Chapter 6, we return to it briefly here to note its increased significance in organization theory in the past ten years. It seems that what has been termed the *linguistic turn* continues to have a huge impact on the field. There have been special issues of *Organization*, *Journal of Management Studies* and the *Academy of Management Review* in the past three years focusing on discourse and organizations. Phillips and Hardy (2002) provide a useful framework for categorizing the various approaches toward discourse analysis prevalent in organizational theory. Their model, like so many in this field, is based

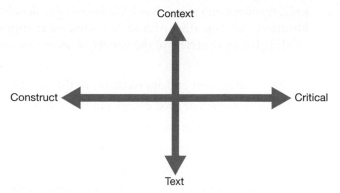

**Figure 10.2:** Different approaches to discourse in organization theory. (*Source:* Phillips and Hardy (2002).)

upon a $2 \times 2$ matrix (Figure 10.2). The horizontal axis differentiates between constructivist and critical approaches. Constructivist approaches suggest that discourses construct organizational reality by shaping the ways issues can be talked about, how individuals conduct themselves in relation to a particular issue, and the knowledge that is constructed about an issue (Hardy, 2004, p. 416); see Chapter 6 for more discussion of this. The critical view is more concerned with how discourse embodies structures of power and ideology, following the work of Foucault, which was discussed in Chapter 6. Phillips and Hardy also differentiate discourse analysis according to whether there is a focus on text or context – in other words, whether they provide a micro analysis of text or whether the broader social context is included in analysis.

Hardy (2004) suggests that future work should focus not just on the individual quadrants but also on the interfaces between them – in other words, that future considerations of discourse within organization theory should consider both the micro and the macro levels of analysis and also the relationship between power, discourse and text. Clearly, this means that organization theorists will need to develop and use multiple methods of inquiry to study organization and organizing. Phillips et al. (2004) also point out that to date, discourse analysis has failed to connect to broader issues of interest to organization theorists. As mentioned earlier, they particularly see possible future links with institutional theory and neoinstitutional theory. Hence, there are calls to consider multiple levels of analysis in order to develop more comprehensive theories of organization. Before we move on to discuss this and other challenges facing organization theory, we first turn to another area that is currently emerging in the literature – organizational aesthetics.

## The aesthetics of organizing

Aesthetics is a relatively new area of organization theory. It is basically concerned with knowledge that we gain from our sensory experiences – for example how a particular smell, such as that of a hospital, can evoke strong feelings in us. It deals with how we understand, perceive and experience things with adjectives such as *beautiful*, *ugly*, *revolting* and so on. Aesthetic knowledge depends upon sensing and feeling, on intuition and empathy. Although a somewhat slippery concept, Dale and Burrell (2002) give an overview of the variety of usages of the term as follows:

- the measurement and appreciation of the beautiful
- the appreciation of good design and that which provides good form (e.g., cosmetics)
- the ability to make harmonious appealing whole from disparate elements
- the ability to perceive contrasts between contiguous elements (e.g., colour)
- the appreciation of the sensuous – that which appeals to all the senses
- the appreciation of that which requires the higher cultivated senses
- that which requires perceptiveness
- that which requires time to appreciate and is beyond the immediacy of the moment
- that which concerns itself with phenomenological appearance and not substance
- the ability to draw all the above elements into one piece of artistic creation.

One aspect of organizational aesthetics relates to viewing organizations as arenas for creative performance. There is a long tradition of using artistic forms as a metaphor for organizations. Perhaps the most well known is organization as theatre used by writers such as Irving Goffman, who we introduced in Chapter 7, and more recently Ian Mangham. This uses the theatrical metaphor of the stage, actors and audiences to observe and analyse the intricacies of social interaction. Everyone is at once actor and audience in relation to others. Expectations that apply in each situation constitute a social script that actors use to guide their performance. Following this interest in management as a performing art, there has also been discussion in the popular management press about lessons from management to be found, for example, in the works of Shakespeare (Burnham et al., 2001).

Another stream of writing focuses on how an understanding of aesthetics can help us gain a better insight into organizations. Rafael Ramirez (2005) examines why aesthetically appealing forms are favoured over those that are purely efficient – why, as he puts it, 'it is working beautifully' captures the essence of proper managerial action. He argues that form and our appreciation of it is central to organizations. Thus it is essential to be attentive to the symbols used in experiencing organization. In a similar vein, Gagliardi (1992, 1996) argues that organizations are full of artefacts that people perceive through their senses. He examined organizations in terms of their premises, furnishings, office equipment and public relations materials. His argument is that a lot of effort had been put into making these attractive; that the meeting rooms, chairs and sofas had been designed in order to make the corporation look attractive. He surmised that these objects were used to try to show the aesthetic appeal of cooperation, both within the organization and with external stakeholders.

Others focus on aspects of organizations that are fundamentally aesthetic. For example, Martin (2002) examined the sensory experience of old people's homes such as smell, sound and so on and how they contribute to a (lack of) feeling of dignity.

In a slightly different vein, Nissley et al. (2002) concentrated on sound. They examined corporate songs as a means of gaining understanding of the organizational culture of a major American home appliance manufacturer. They link aesthetics to organizational experience by considering the extent to which organizational songs either act as an expression of organizational memory or seek to create organizational memories for people within the organization.

Another slant on researching organizational aesthetics has come from writers who have tried to apply organizational theory to the study of organizations in cultural industries – that is, industries in which products are primarily defined in terms of their symbolic or aesthetic value. One stream of research on aesthetics considers how artistic and cultural organizations are organized and managed. Examples include the work of French organizational theorist Eve Chiapello (1998), who examined the operation of orchestras and publishing houses, and Guillet de Monthoux (2004) who has studied organizations such as opera groups and ballet companies. Here there is much consideration of the relationship between management and art. In particular, Chiapello makes the point that managers in these organizations see themselves as artists, and art is co-opted for commercial purposes.

A different approach comes from those who use aesthetic methods to research organizations. One example is art therapy. Although quite rare in organization theory, writers such as Barry (1996, 1997) use drawings and other art forms to explore issues within organizations. Art therapy is a form of psychotherapy that uses the process of making art as a part of the therapeutic process. Essential components of art therapy include selecting and using art materials, creating a visual or tactile image, and thinking about and making meaning of the process of making art and the image itself. The idea is that these mental processes and physical actions create opportunities for individuals to become aware of inconsistencies in thinking and feeling and to clarify and make sense of their feelings and beliefs and the events in their lives. Similarly, Brearley (2001, 2002) uses poems, songs and images to capture the feeling of the transition in organizational life, encouraging people to use these different forms to articulate what transition meant for them.

A particularly important approach has been the use of photographs in organizational research. There has been a growing interest in the ways that photographs can help gain insight into people's behaviour within organizations. In some instances, this has involved using photographs as visual recordings of things such as buildings (Kersten and Gilardi, 2003). Other studies have used photographs to gain insight into organizational processes. For example, Alferoff and Knights (2003) used photographs taken within a call centre to show how managers tried to manage the aesthetic dimension of the work environment in such a way as to manipulate the behaviour of employees. These show, for instance, colourful mobiles hung from the ceilings to remind employees how they should deal with clients and their target levels of performance. Warren (2002) used a slightly different approach to try to gain an understanding of what it means to work in an organization. Rather than taking photographs of the research setting herself, she provided a sample of the employees with disposable cameras and asked them to photograph aspects of their working environment that expressed how they felt about their job and the company. This provided a powerful insight into their working lives.

**Stop and think**

Examine Figure 10.3 and think about how it could be interpreted. Can you draw any conclusions about the organization and what it might be like to work there from this picture? What other pictures or information would you like?

**Figure 10.3:** The office. (*Source:* Photodisc/Punch Stock.)

Whether organizational aesthetics is just the latest in a long line of fads or whether it offers anything new and dramatically different in organizational theory has yet to be determined. Organizational aesthetics seems to have developed out of traditions covered previously in this book – for example, the interest in performance from symbolic interactionism and the interest in language, art and alternative modes of expression in postmodernism. It promises the chance to give insight into aspects of organization previously not considered in organization theory. Thus, it holds interest for theorists who see it as a new way to enable them to develop new understandings of organizational processes and people's sense making about organizations. For practitioners, it can also be attractive because it provides a means to explore the tacit knowledge that guides much of organizational behaviour (Taylor and Hansen, 2005). As well as being seen as a new management tool – for example, building on the work of writers on corporate identity and design, writers such as Dickinson et al. (2000) argue that a strong corporate 'personality' is a competitive advantage or differential that the most successful companies use as part of their overall strategy. These 'beautiful companies' use excellence in corporate expression such as visual design, written communications and the ergonomics of the workplace to create competitive advantage with regard to acquiring and keeping customers and employees, motivating the workforce and positively influencing the public and stakeholders.

Before we move on to our concluding section, we want to return one more time to the subject of culture. This has been raised in a variety of different chapters in the book. We have returned to the issue time and time again because it is an area that has received a huge amount of attention in the literature on organizational theory, and we thought it would be interesting to contrast the alternative approaches.

## One final look at organizational culture

In Chapter 7, we explored the interpretavist approach to organization culture. We looked at this from the perspective that jokes, stories and myths are symbols that give meaning to organizational experience. As we have seen, interpretavists look at culture as highly complex. By contrast, modernists and neomodernists (discussed in Chapter 2 and Chapter 3) have a different understanding. They assert, in their different ways and with different emphases, that the components of organizational culture can be understood as a 'system' or 'cultural web'. If we look, for example, at the work of the writers on strategy, Johnson and Scholes (1999), they claim that the 'cultural web' of an organization can be analysed and understood in a concrete, definite way. This is very different from the interpretavist approach. However, when we look at the ingredients of the cultural web, we find that in order to understand the culture, there needs to be an analysis of organizational stories, rituals, structures, control systems, power structures and symbols. These issues are similar to those of the interpretavists. The key difference (apart from the greater depth of analysis that the interpretavist would give) is that of purpose. For the modernist and neomodernist, the purpose is to advance the development of organizational goals and values as defined by the leaders and senior managers of the organization. For the interpretavist, the approach is more to enable the development of reflection amongst all members of the organization.

Traditionally, these two perspectives have been thought to be irreconcilable, but Hatch (1993) argues that developing theories of organizational culture can 'be represented equally well (or equally poorly) within either perspective, but that bridging them creates a more satisfying picture than either offers on its own' (p. 684). She developed this idea of bridging between these different perspectives on organization culture through the idea of 'interplay' (Schultz and Hatch, 1996) between them. Hatch suggests that both these approaches to organization culture have their differences, but they also share some common features and she concludes that it can be very useful to take whatever position is most appropriate in the development of an understanding of organizational culture.

In addition to the interpretavist and neomodernist perspectives in this book we have also considered postmodern and psychoanalytic perspectives on organizational culture. In Chapter 6 on postmodernism, culture is seen as fluid and dynamic, and its fragmented nature is emphasized. Culture here is sometimes thought of as a web, but it is a very different kind of web from that put forward by Johnson and Scholes. From a postmodern perspective, individuals are seen as nodes on a web, connected to some, but not all, of the other members of an organization by shared concerns. The pattern of the web changes as different issues become salient. Hence, attention is directed to the multiple cultures that exist and their fragmented and dynamic nature. In Chapter 8, from a psychoanalytic perspective, culture is analysed as a symbol of deeper aspects of organizational life or as a response to anxieties. Here organizational culture can be seen as a 'holding environment' for its members. What psychoanalysts mean by this is that the

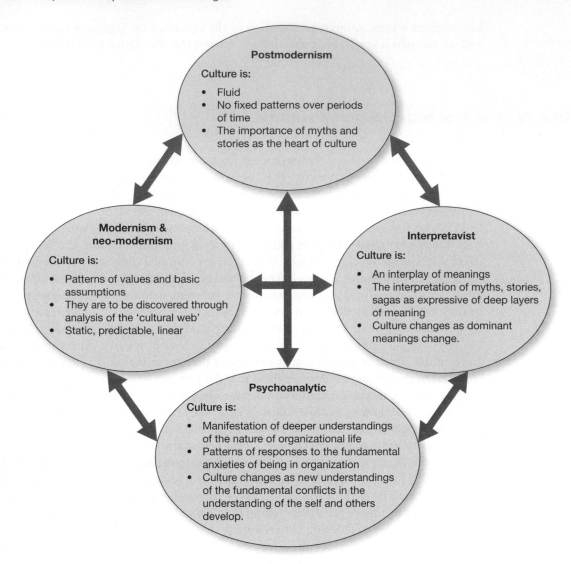

**Figure 10.4:** The interplay between different approaches to culture. (*Source:* Based on Schultz and Hatch, 1996.)

culture is basically a place in which people feel that they are 'safe' to be the kind of person they want to be, within boundaries, in the organization. In Chapter 8, we discuss the implications of this holding environment and what can happen when things go wrong.

The similarities and differences between the perspectives on organization culture that are considered in this text are summarized in Figure 10.4.

This model is an acknowledgement that whatever their limitations, the postmodern, the modernist, the interpretavist and the psychoanalytic perspectives within organization theory all have something interesting to say about organizational culture and, indirectly, the relationship between organizational culture and goals. Insights from each perspective can provide opportunities for both connections and contrast. In common with Schultz and Hatch, we argue that in the study of organization culture, it is preferable to take a 'both/and' position rather than one that suggests that the 'best way' to understand culture is 'either/or' modernist, interpretavist, postmodern or psychoanalytic.

# Conclusions

It seems then that there are many new ideas and issues arising in organizational theory and that rather than supplanting existing perspectives, they can sit alongside them, complement them, compete with them or perhaps integrate with them. Much to the chagrin of writers such as Pfeffer and March, mentioned earlier, the field seems to be expanding and increasing in diversity and complexity rather than becoming more homogeneous.

Why are there so many organization theories? Organizations are highly complex entities with many problems to be solved and with many issues that can be addressed from a variety of different perspectives and at different levels of analysis. Haridimos Tsoukas (2003) argues that organization theory has become more complex because 'real life complexity has been let in' (p. 609). He argues that organizational theory should become even more complex, that it should not just focus on formal organizations but should be studying the process of *organization*. This would free theorists to look at different forms of organization and the processes underlying them and also to gain better understanding of networks that operate across the boundaries of formal organizations. The emphasis then becomes the study of coordination between actors at a variety of different levels. He suggests that organization theory can move forward by focusing on patterns of coordination between actors at a variety of levels – for example, coordination among individuals, governments, corporations and nongovernmental organizations in all permutations (Tsoukas, 2003, p. 611).

Clearly, some writers will worry that this will mean further fragmentation of the field in which a search for new theories dominates research. Too many new theories at too fast a pace could create a situation in which the community is unable to evaluate them properly or integrate them into a coherent programme of research (Knudsen, 2003, p. 265). Others call for greater widening of the field: Burrell (2003) calls for 'neo-disciplinarity', which he argues is about widening the field of our interest to learn from others. In particular, he points to geography, accounting and cultural studies (p. 533) in which interesting studies of human behaviour within and around organizations are taking place.

In conclusion, the field of organization theory seems more diverse than ever. Below we pose a number of questions that we think organizational theorists should reflect upon in developing their work.

1. An important issue for organization theory concerns the relationship between theory and practice. Are we seeing a shift toward mode 2 knowledge production, and if so, what are the implications of this for organization theory? What is meant by practice anyway? Who are the customers of organization theory? Are they managers, employees, society in general or other academics? Linked to this, what should the relationship be between researchers and theoreticians and those who live and work in organizations? Is it desirable to move toward a model in which those who are being studied become co-researchers, able to influence the development of organization theory? In developing organization theory, should concern be given to how theories relate to the needs of various stakeholders?

2. Many organizational theorists discuss the desirability of multilevel analyses that include looking at micro processes as well as macro contextual factors. The question arises, though, what would these look like? And do we want more complex theories, or should we be aiming for simplicity?

3. As discussed earlier in the chapter, the paradigm debate is still going on in organization theory. Therefore, the extent to which paradigms can coexist remains a challenge to consider. Perhaps the field should now move beyond the insular approach suggested by the paradigm incommensurability theses? If so, how? And how can newly emerging perspectives be given the space to grow? Or should the field look to develop standard approaches toward studying organizations and limit diversity in order to develop further?

4. Critical approaches to organization theory have recently increased in popularity in organization theory. This raises an important issue: how can organization theory become and remain an arena in which those typically marginalized in organizations or who lack voice become visible and in which power asymmetries are removed and democratic agendas pursued?

5. There have been a number of calls to develop organization theory into a more transdisciplinary subject so that theorists and students can benefit from knowledge held in other disciplines. How should organization theorists engage in transdisciplinary research – or as Burrell calls, it 'neo-disciplinary' research – that brings in ideas from other disciplines?

6. Given that we live in an increasingly global economy, is it desirable to develop global organizational theories, or are these merely ethnocentric perspectives that assume the superiority of Western organizational forms? How should organization theorists develop more contextually sensitive organizational theories?

7. Finally, students of organization theory might consider whether the high level of diversity in organization theory is really based upon academics trying to make names for themselves rather than genuinely novel theoretical developments. Furthermore, if this is the case, how can organization theory avoid the cycle of fads and fashions upon which academic careers are built?

Although these questions have no right or wrong answers, we think that they provide interesting areas of debate for organization theory of the future and that by considering them, students of organization theory can reflect upon how they wish their field to develop. As we discussed in Chapter 1, organizations have a massive impact upon the lives of everyone. From schools, through to employing organizations, colleges, clubs, hospitals, residential homes, public transport, banks, retailers and so on, we cannot avoid organizations. How we seek to understand them and develop theories about them that both describe and inform practice remains a major challenge to both students and academics. In this book, we have attempted to provide a map of some of the existing theory of organizations. We look forward to seeing the different ways organization theory will develop in the future.

## Concluding grid

| Learning outcomes | Challenges to organization theory |
|---|---|
| Examine commentators' views on the state of the field. | Is the field of organization theory too diverse and fragmented, or should diversity be preserved in order to enable new approaches to thrive? What are the dangers of overspecialization and fragmentation? |

Review the debate concerning paradigm commensurability and incommensurability.

The paradigm incommensurability debate has been going on for nearly 30 years, but there remains disagreement. Is it possible to operate within only one paradigm at a time, or is it possible to use more than one paradigm simultaneously?

Consider the debate concerning the practical utility of organization theory.

Mode 2 approaches toward knowledge production are heralded by some as a major change to the development of theory. Is a new mode of knowledge production emerging? To what extent does this differ? Is this a good thing? How can organization theory meet the needs of various stakeholders?

Outline possible future trends and directions for organization theory.

Do trends such as organizational aesthetics and globalization pose new opportunities for organizational theorizing? Why do new trends arise in organization theory?

## Annotated further reading

A good overview of current debates in organization theory is provided in the *Oxford Handbook of Organization Theory* edited by Tsoukas and Knudsen (2003). Another interesting collection is provided by Westwood and Clegg (2003). Although a little older, Clegg et al. (1996) is also very comprehensive.

With regard to the mode 1 and mode 2 debate, it is worth looking at Gibbons et al. (1994) as well as Nowotny et al. (2001). For a discussion of the implications of this for management and organizational research, see Tranfield and Starkey (1998). For discussion of paradigms, see Burrell and Morgan (1979) and contrast this with Hassard (1991) and Reed (1985). Finally, Scott (2001) provides an excellent overview of institutional theory.

## Discussion questions

1. Design a study of worker motivation from each of the following perspectives: functionalist, radical humanist, radical structuralist and interpretavist.
2. What are the implications for organization theory of a shift to mode 2 approaches toward knowledge development? Do you think this is a good thing?
3. Think about the aesthetics of the university in which you are studying. To what extent have lecture theatres been designed to produce particular forms of behaviour?
4. Drawing on examples from this book, how would you answer the question: what is organization theory for?
5. Having read this book, to what extent do you now agree with Lewin's famous statement that there is nothing as practical as a good theory?

# References

Alferoff, C. and Knights, D. (2003) 'We're all partying here: Target and games, or targets as games in call center management', in A. Carr and P. Hancock (eds), *Art and Aesthetics at work*, Basingstoke: Palgrave, pp. 70–92.

Anderson, S. and Cavanagh, J. (2000) *Top 200: The Rise of Global Corporate Power*, Retrieved June 2006, from http://www.globalpolicy.org/socecon/tncs/top200.htm.

Barry, D. (1996) 'Artful inquiry: A symbolic constructivist approach to social science research', *Qualitative Inquiry* 2(4):411–438.

Barry, D. (1997) 'Telling changes from narrative family therapy to organizational change and development', *Journal of Organizational Change Management* 10(1):30–46.

Brearley, L. (2001) 'Foot in the air: An exploration of the experience of transition in organizational life', in C. Boucher and R. Holian (eds), *Emerging Forms of Representing Qualitative Data*, Melbourne: RMIT Press.

Brearley, L. (2002) *Beyond Univocal Authority: An Exploration of Creative Voices in Academic Research*, Melbourne: Common Ground.

Burnham, J., Augustine, N. and Adelman, K. (2001) *Shakespeare in Charge: The Bard's Guide to Learning and Succeeding on the Business Stage*, New York: Hyperion.

Burrell, G. (2003) 'The future of organizational theory: Prospects and limitations', in H. Tsoukas and C. Knudsen (eds), *The Oxford Handbook of Organization Theory: Meta-Theoretical Perspectives*, Oxford: Oxford University Press, pp. 525–535.

Burrell, G. and Morgan, G. (1979) *Sociological Paradigms and Organizational Analysis*, Ashgate.

Calas, M., and Smircich, L. (2003) 'At home from Mars to Somalia: Recounting organization studies', in H. Tsoukas and C. Knudsen (eds), *The Oxford Handbook of Organization Theory: Meta-Theoretical Perspectives*, Oxford: Oxford University Press, pp. 596–606.

Cascio, W.F., Young, C.E., and Morris, J.R. (1997) 'Financial consequences of employment-change decisions in major U.S. corporations', *Academy of Management Journal.* 40:1175–1189.

Chiapello, E. (1998) *Artistes versus Managers*, Paris: Métailié.

Child, J. (2002) 'The International crisis of confidence in corporations', *Academy of management Executive*, 16(3):145–147.

Child, J. (2005) *Organization: Contemporary Principles and Practice*, Oxford: Blackwell.

Clegg, S., Hardy, C. and Nord, W. (eds) (1996) *Handbook of Organization Studies*, London: Sage.

Cohen, L., Duberley, J. and McAuley, J. (1999) 'Fuelling innovation or monitoring productivity – The management of research scientists', *Organization* 6(3):473–497.

Daft, R. (2004) *Organization Theory and Design*, Cincinnati: South-Western.

Dale, K. and Burrell, G. (2002) 'An-aesthetics and architecture', *Tamara* 2(1):77–90.

de Monthoux, P. Guillet (2004) *The Art Firm: Aesthetic Management and Metaphysical Marketing*, Palo Alto, CA: Stanford University Press.

Dicken, P. (2003) *Global Shift: Reshaping the Global Economic Map in the 21st century*, 4th edn, New York: Guildford.

Dickinson, P., Leonard, R. and Svensen, N. (2000) *Beautiful Corporations*, London: Financial Times Prentice Hall.

DiMaggio, P. and Powell, W. (1983) 'The iron cage revisited: Institutional isomorphism and collective rationality in organizational fields', *American Sociological Review* 48:147–160.

DiMaggio, P. and Powell, W. (1991) *The New Institutionalism in Organizational Analysis*, Chicago: University of Chicago Press.

DiMaggio, P. and Powell, W. (1995) *The New Institutionalism in Organizational Analysis*, 2nd edn, Chicago: University of Chicago Press.

Donaldson, L. (1985) *In Defence of Organization Theory: A Reply to the Critics*, Cambridge: Cambridge University Press.

Gibbons, M., Limoges, C., Nowotny, H., Schwartzman, S., Scott, P. and Trow, M. (1994) *The New Production of Knowledge: The Dynamics of Science and Research in Contemporary Societies*, London: Sage.

Greenwood, R. and Hinings, C. (1996) 'Understanding radical organizational change: Bringing together the old and the new institutionalism', *Academy of Management Review* 21(4):1022–1054.

Gagliardi, P. (1992) *Symbols and Artefacts: View from the Corporate Land*, New York: de Gruyter.

Gagliardi, P. (1996) 'Exploring the aesthetic side of organizational life', in S. Clegg and W. Nord (eds), *Handbook of Organization Studies*, London: Sage.

Hardy, C. (2004) 'Scaling up and bearing down in discourse analysis: Questions regarding textual agencies and their context', *Organization* 11(3):415–425.

Hassard, J. (1991) 'Multiple paradigms and organizational analysis: A case study', *Organization Studies* 12(2):275–299.

Hatch, M.J. (1993) 'The Dynamics of Organizational Culture', *The Academy of Management Review* 18(4):657–693.

Hirst, P. and Thompson, G. (1999). *Globalization in Question: The International Economy and the Possibilities of Governance*, Cambridge, UK: Polity Press.

Jackson, N. and Carter, P. (1991) 'In defence of paradigm incommensurability', *Organization Studies* 12(1):109–127.

Jackson, N. and Carter, P. (1993) '"Paradigm wars": A response to Hugh Willmott', *Organization Studies* 14(5):721–725.

Johnson, P. and Duberley, J. (2000) *Understanding Management Research: An Introduction to Epistemology*, London: Sage, p. 80.

Johnson, G. and Scholes, K. (1999) *Exploring Corporate Strategy*, London: Pearson.

Kersten, A. and Gilardi, R. (2003) 'The barren landscape: Reading US corporate architecture', in A. Carr and P. Hancock (eds), *Art and Aesthetics at Work*, Basingstoke: Palgrave, pp. 138–154.

Knudsen, C. (2003) 'Pluralism, scientific progress and the structure of organization theory', in H. Tsoukas and C. Knudsen (eds), *The Oxford Handbook of Organization Theory: Meta-Theoretical Perspectives*, Oxford: Oxford University Press, pp. 262–288.

March, J.G. (1996) 'Continuity and change in theories of organizational action', *Administrative Science Quarterly* 41:278–287.

Martin, P. (2002) 'Sensations, bodies and the "spirit of the place": Aesthetics in residential organizations for the elderly', *Human Relations* 55(7):861–885.

Mckinley, W., Sanchez, C. and Schick, A.G. (1995) 'Organizational Downsizing: Constraining, Cloning, Learning', *Academy of Management Executive* 9:32–42.

Mckinley, W. and Mone, M. (2003) 'Micro and macro perspectives in organization theory: A tale of incommensurability', in H. Tsoukas and C. Knudsen (eds), *The Oxford Handbook of Organization Theory: Meta-Theoretical Perspectives*, Oxford: Oxford University Press, pp. 345–372.

Meyer, J. and Rowan, B. (1977) 'Institutionalised organizations: Formal structure as myth and ceremony', *American Journal of Sociology* 83:41–62.

Nissley, N., Taylor, S. and Butler, O. (2002) 'The power of organizational song: An organizational discourse and aesthetic expression for organizational culture', *Tamara* 2(1):47–62.

Nowotny, H., Scott, P. and Gibbons, M. (2001) *Re-thinking Science: Knowledge and the Public in an Age of Uncertainty*, Cambridge: Polity Press.

Pfeffer, J. (1983) 'Barriers to the advance of organizational science: Paradigm development as a dependent variable', *Academy of Management Review* 18:599–620.

Phillips, N. and Hardy, C. (2002) *Understanding Discourse Analysis*, Thousand Oaks, CA: Sage.

Phillips, N., Lawrence, T. and Hardy, C. (2004) 'Discourse and institutions', *Academy of Management Review* 29(4):635–652.

Ramirez, R. (2005) 'The aesthetics of cooperation', *European Management Review* 2(1):28–35.

Rees, C. and Edwards, T. (2006) 'Globalization and international management', in T. Edwards and C. Rees (eds), *International Human Resource Management*, Harlow: Pearson.

Reed, M. (1985) *Redirections in Organizational Analysis*, London: Tavistock.

Reed, M. (1992) *The Sociology of Organizations: Themes, Perspectives and Prospects,* Hemel Hempstead: Harvester Wheatsheaf.

Reed, M. (1996) 'Organizational theorizing: A historically contested terrain', in S.R. Clegg, C. Hardy, and W. Nord (eds), *Handbook of Organization Studies*, London: Sage, pp. 31–56.

Said, E. (1978) *Orientalism*, Stockholm: Manpocket.

Scott, W.R. (1995) *Institutions and Organizations*, Thousand Oaks, CA: Sage.

Scott, W.R. (1998) *Organizations: Rational Natural and Open Systems*, 4th edn, Englewood Cliffs, NJ: Prentice Hall.

Scott, W.R. (2001) *Institutions and Organizations*, 2nd edn, Thousand Oaks: Sage.

Schultz M. and Hatch M.J. (1996) 'Living with multiple paradigms: The case of paradigm interplay in organizational culture studies', *Academy of Management Review* 21(2):529–557.

Spivak, G.C. (1996) in D. Landry and G. Maclean (eds), *The Spivak Reader – Selected Works of Gayatri Chakraviety Spivak*, London: Routledge.

Styhre, A. (2002) 'Constructing the image of the Other: A post colonial critique of the adaption of Japanese human resource management practices', *Management Decision* 40(3): 257–266.

Taylor, S. and Hansen, H. (2005) 'Finding form: Looking at the field of organizational aesthetics', *Journal of Management Studies* 42(6):1211–1231.

Tranfield, D. and Starkey, K. (1998) 'The nature, social organization and promotion of management research: Towards policy', *British Journal of Management* 9:341–353.

Tsoukas, H. (2003) 'New times, fresh challenges: Reflections on the past and future of organization theory', in H. Tsoukas and C. Knudsen (eds), *The Oxford Handbook of Organization Theory: Meta-Theoretical Perspectives*, Oxford: Oxford University Press, pp. 607–622.

Tsoukas, H. and Knudsen, C. (eds) (2003) *The Oxford Handbook of Organization Theory: Meta-Theoretical Perspectives*, Oxford: Oxford University Press.

Turpin, T. and Deville, S. (1995) 'Occupational roles and expectations of research scientists and research managers in scientific research institutes', *R&D Management* 25(2):141–157.

Warren, S. (2002) 'Show me how it feels to work here: Using photography to research organizational aesthetics', *Ephemera* 2(3):224–245.

Westwood, R. and Clegg, S. (2003) 'The discourse of organization studies: Dissensus politics, and paradigms', *Debating Organization: Point-Counterpoint in Organization Studies*, London: Blackwell, pp. 1–42.

Ziman, J. (1994) *Prometheus Bound: Science in a Dynamic Steady State*, Cambridge: Cambridge University Press.

# Index